STATES IS FOUNDED ON AGRICULTURE

P9-CQZ-298

Live stock represent about one-third of the value of all farm products. They play an essential part in maintaining the fertility of the soil. Also they consume crops which humans could not consume, and by turning these crops into meat they make them valuable. Successful agriculture is largely dependent on live stock and the growing of live stock is in turn dependent on successful marketing of the meat animals. Because nearly all industries depend on agriculture, the prosperity of the entire nation is inseparably linked with the marketing of meat and other animal products through the packing industry.

J. Ogden Armour

KEY TO NUMBERS

1. Cattle
2. Swine
3. Sheep
4. Corn
5. Wheat, oats, rye, barley
6. Oranges and lemons
7. Apples, pears and peaches
8. Cotton
9. Rice
10. Tobacco
11. Sweet potatoes
12. Sugar Cane
13. Turkeys
14. Poultry
15. Celery
16. Dairy
17. Grapes
18. Sugar Beets
19. Fish
20. Oysters
21. Peanuts
22. Honey
23. Irish Potatoes
24. Grape Fruit and limes
25. Olives

ALSO BY MOLLY O'NEILL

Mostly True: A Memoir of Family, Food, and Baseball

New York Cookbook: From Pelham Bay to Park Avenue,
Firehouses to Four-Star Restaurants

Famous Dishes

FROM EVERY STATE

FUN FOOD

Want something different?

48 new JELL-O ENTREES RELISHES SALADS DESSERTS

ONE BIG TABLE

A
PORTRAIT
OF
AMERICAN
COOKING

BIG

TABLE

600 RECIPES FROM THE NATION'S BEST
HOME COOKS, FARMERS, FISHERMEN, PIT-MASTERS, AND CHEFS

MOLLY O'NEILL

Simon & Schuster
New York London Toronto Sydney

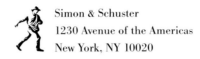

Simon & Schuster
1230 Avenue of the Americas
New York, NY 10020

Copyright © 2010 by Molly O'Neill

All rights reserved, including the right to reproduce this book or portions thereof in any
form whatsoever. For information address Simon & Schuster Subsidiary Rights Department,
1230 Avenue of the Americas, New York, NY 10020

First Simon & Schuster hardcover edition November 2010

SIMON & SCHUSTER and colophon are registered trademarks of Simon & Schuster, Inc.

For information about special discounts for bulk purchases, please contact
Simon & Schuster Special Sales at 1-866-506-1949 or business@simonandschuster.com.

The Simon & Schuster Speakers Bureau can bring authors to your live event.
For more information or to book an event contact the Simon & Schuster Speakers Bureau
at 1-866-248-3049 or visit our website at www.simonspeakers.com.

Designed by Joel Avirom and Jason Snyder
Images edited by Rebecca Busselle

Permissions and acknowledgments appear on page 862.

Manufactured in the United States of America

1   3   5   7   9   10   8   6   4   2

Library of Congress Cataloging-in-Publication Data

O'Neill, Molly.
One big table : A portrait of American cooking : 600 recipes from the nation's best home
cooks, farmers, fishermen, pit-masters, and chefs / by Molly O'Neill.
p. cm.
1. Cooking—United States. I. Title.
TX907.2.O54 2010
641.50973—dc22   2010028841

ISBN 978-0-7432-3270-8
ISBN 987-1-4516-0977-6 (ebook)

For Rebecca Busselle, photographer, writer, cook, colleague,
fellow traveler, and friend, with gratitude as large as the America
we discovered, mile by mile, dish by dish, story by story.

"BAD DINNERS GO HAND IN HAND WITH TOTAL DEPRAVITY,

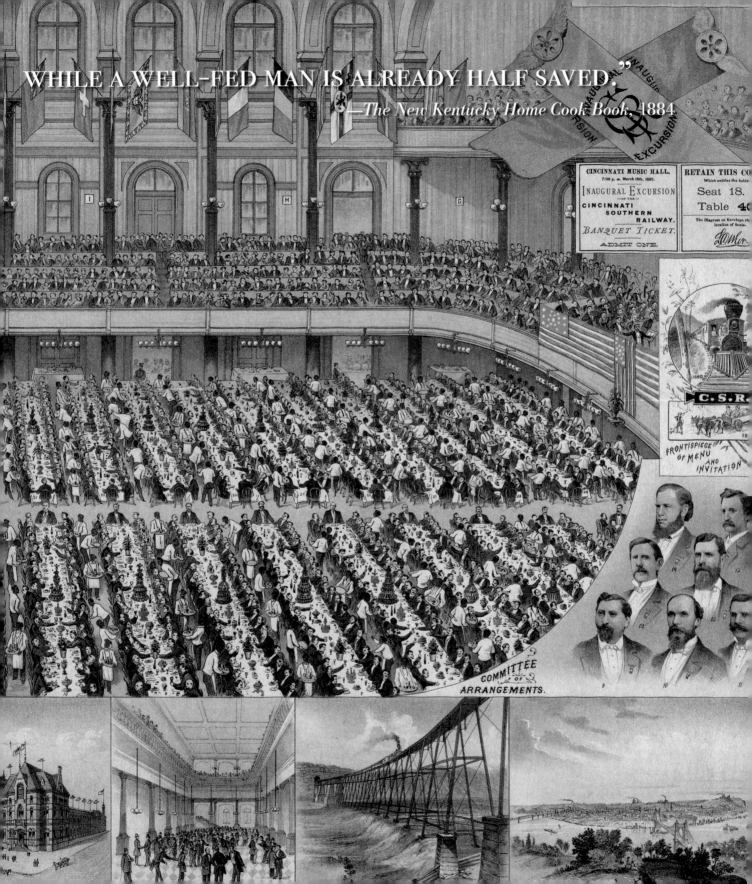

WHILE A WELL-FED MAN IS ALREADY HALF SAVED."

—*The New Kentucky Home Cook Book, 1884*

D GROCERY CO.
ERS STORE
COME

QUALITY MEATS

NEW LARGE
POTATOES
6 LB 23

NEW
POTATOES
6 LB
23

ORANGES
1¢

APPLES
DELICIOUS
4 LB 25

UNION
LEADER
For PIPE OR CIGARETTE

RICE KRISPIES RICE KRISPIES RICE KRISPIES RICE KRISPIES RICE KRISPIES RICE KRISPIES RICE KRISPIES CE PIES

BETTER LOAF FLOUR

BETTER LOAF FLOUR

DRINK
Pepsi·Cola 5¢
AMERICAS BIGGEST NICKEL'S WORTH

PROUDLY
7UP
IT LIKES YOU

BEECH·NUT
CHEWING TOBACCO
Quality made & famous

Chew
Copenhagen
It's a pleasure

CONTENTS

INTRODUCTION

HOMETOWN APPETITES

For many years I lived in a Hell's Kitchen loft, and from its windows I could see a patch of the Hudson River. I liked knowing that the water was there, keeping the place that I'd chosen to live, New York City, safely apart from Ohio, the place I'd left behind. But for about fifteen years, I forgot to look out the window. I was a restaurant critic and I was eating, drinking, inhaling the city, writing books and stories, living the life that I'd imagined when I was growing up in Columbus.

But in the mid-1990s, I began to stare at the river. Work was great, life was good, but there I was, staring at its far shore in the direction I'd come from. I did not imagine any connection between my reveries and my sudden mania for transforming my terrace into a small farm. To my mind, the container garden was an early expression of locavorism. After the garden, a dog moved in with the boyfriend. And as far as I was concerned, these creatures and cultivars accounted for my otherwise inexplicable enthusiasm to follow the river north to find a weekend house.

I had no trouble explaining to myself the difference between my city and country cooking. My Manhattan kitchen was not all that different from the restaurants where I'd worked: I imagined a dish, I ordered the ingredients—*et voilà*!: Centerfold Cuisine. But there was no such cornucopia ninety miles up the river from Manhattan. The availability, not imagination, determined dinner. The best produce that the local farms had to offer was sold in the city; what was left required long, slow, homey cooking to coax out its flavor.

Nevertheless, at Manhattan's restaurants, at dinner parties and charity events, my colleagues and other members of the food cognoscenti began to talk about the end of American home cooking. The argument was that the more people spend on their kitchen range, the less likely they are to cook on the thing and that the fastest-growing department in grocery stores was the prepared foods. One survey found that an increasing number of Americans tuned in to the Food Network on their kitchen TVs so they'd have someone cooking. In New York City, dinner had long meant eating out, or getting take-out, which was no longer my experience. But I refused to believe that this philosophy had crossed the Hudson and infiltrated the mainland.

To reassure myself, I called each of my five brothers in Ohio. Our conversations were less than comforting.

"How many times a week do you cook dinner at home?" I asked.

"How are you defining cooking?" one answered warily.

I was soon reading reports that somewhere between supersizing and the current romance of farmers' markets, Americans had stopped cooking. The possibility that the results might be true gave me a sense of urgency about finding true American cooking.

My weekends upstate began to stretch to four days. I cooked more, ate out less, spent days lurking on food sites chatting with people about what they cooked and why. A wall of my study was soon covered with historic maps of the United States: the Armour Company's Food Source Map ("The Greatness of the United

States is founded on Agriculture"), the hog-shaped Porcineograph, and Miguel Covarrubias's Map of Good Eating were soon joined by contemporary examples like Gary Nabhan's Regional Map of North America's Place-Based Food Traditions, the National Golden Arches Locator, and Kentfield's America Eats Organic Coast to Coast. I spent a year reading American food writing and constructing maps of my own—what was grown, what was eaten, when, why, and by whom.

I've never known a food-obsessed person who did not have someone in a cotton apron—a grandmother or mother, an uncle, a father, a neighbor, a teacher—standing behind them who could turn an ordinary meal into an extraordinary one and make the world seem larger, full of heart, and bursting with possibility. But these American cooks had been forgotten over the past several decades as "cooking" morphed into "cuisine." I wanted to find them and cook with them and get a taste of their America. I had no idea that I'd also find a part of myself.

In 2001, I packed my maps and divided the country into roughly twenty-five geographic patches. I traveled to a particular spot for a few weeks or months, and then returned home to write and cook. I was aided and abetted in my search by motley crews of local food obsessives. Comprised of food cart owners and retired food editors, local dining clubs, slow food consortiums, gourmet societies and cooking contest winners, grocers, bloggers, farmers who grow the high quality ingredients that lure fine cooks and people who live to eat, these advance teams guided me into corners of the nation where cooking is still something that pulls people together.

Some communities come together around long-established feasts—Maine's beanhole dinner and clambake; the St. Pius Barbecued Mutton day in Kentucky; New Mexico's horno tamales; the fish boils of Door County, Wisconsin. Others converge for what the writer Jonathan Gold describes as Folkloric Food: fried chicken, hamburgers, hot dogs, and French fries, clam chowder, boiled lobster, corn on the cob, and macaroni and cheese, which are as much about cultural identity as they are about dinner. Still others converge for occasions—family reunions, weddings, bar mitzvahs, coming-of-age ceremonies in New Mexico, the Blessing of the Fleet in Provincetown, Indian Diwali feasts, and Iranian No-Rooz. And then there are the smaller tables that bring families and friends together. I found melting-pot moments and incidents of "unmeltable" pots, but the nation I discovered was more like one big table.

Almost as soon as I decamped from one place at this table to another, I knew that the reports of the demise of home cooking were greatly overstated. I found a preponderance of grocery stores, markets, and farmstands with stocks of uncooked food—irrefutable evidence that most homes still contain working kitchens—and observed many people preparing dinner.

The more miles I logged, the clearer it became that "Americans don't cook" is an updated version of an old slur. From the birth of the nation until quite recently, Europeans and those Americans who measure culture in relationship to European society claimed that Americans can't cook. The assertion may have been reality-based in the nation's early days—rare is the culture that mints a refined cuisine before it clears the wilderness and establishes communities—but in more than 300,000 miles, I found that my fellow citizens can and do cook. Some cook badly, some cook well, all cook to say who they are and where they come from.

Recipes are family stories, tales of particular places and personal histories. They bear witness to the land and waterways, to technology and invention, to immigration, migration, ambition, disappointment, triumph, and most of all, change.

After stalking the country's best cooks by region, I spent several years in the home kitchens of recent immigrants. And then I had the good fortune to spend a year creating potluck dinners across the United States that raised money for 232 local food banks and brought me recipes and covered dishes to consider for this book. Hundreds of additional recipes arrived from magazines, newsletters, and Internet postings, from friends and friends of friends, from people I'd met, and people who'd heard about my quest. My tower of recipes began to resemble Pisa's.

When cooks were conflicted about which of their recipes to offer to this project, I often said: "Which recipe embodies your life and times and your own personal America? If you could leave one recipe to your family, which one would it be?"

In the end, it was the endless highway that showed me the most about American cooking. Between the tasty tidbits and the occasional stomach-turner, I experienced the narcotic rumble of the road, the fear (and frequent reality) of getting lost, the fatigue and tedium. Then, turning a corner, I would meet someone in a kitchen, or digging a pit on a beach, or stoking the coals in an oil-drum smoker. American cooks are wacky, idiosyncratic, and heartfelt. They refuse to bow to time constraints, overwork, and media pressure, refuse to eat like everybody else, insist on making their dinner—and often their lives—with their own hands.

Americans don't *have* to cook anymore. Those who choose to cook are throwbacks, the last living cowboys, Huck Finns, would-be Julias, embracing America's unbridled individuality. Many are capable of creating deliciousness. Most cook from the heart as well as from a distinctly American yearning, something I could feel, but couldn't describe until thousands of miles of highway helped me identify it in myself: hometown appetite.

"We all have hometown appetites," wrote the cookbook author Clementine Paddleford in 1960, "every other person is a bundle of longing for the simplicities of good taste once enjoyed on the farm or in the hometown [he or she] left behind." This book is a journey through hundreds of the "hometowns" that fuel the American appetite, recipe by recipe, bite by bite.

Over the past decade, I collected more than 10,000 recipes, tested about one-third of them, and narrowed the final collection down to around 600. In the winnowing process, there were many duplicates. Generally they were recipes that had first appeared in old cookbooks or cooking pamphlets issued by food manufacturers, became "standards," and were then passed from one generation to the next. When their origins were lost, these dishes were ascribed to the person who passed the recipe along. The provenance was not meant to be misleading—for instance, a man who finally passes along his great-great-grandmother's recipe for dumplings has no idea that the same formula appears in the original edition of *The Settlement Cookbook*. He has a desire to hold on to a piece of his family's past, to connect an heirloom recipe to a person rather than the cookbook she must have used.

I endeavored to research the recipes included here, and when it seemed appropriate, to credit the original "inspiration," but it is impossible to ensure the provenance of every recipe. If you should find a familiar recipe, I would love to hear your stories about it. Please send them to comment@onebigtable.com.

Because grocery stores are stocking an increasing array of ingredients that were once difficult to obtain and because online and mail-order sources shift constantly, an up-to-date list of mail-order sources for specialty cookware and ingredients can be found at www.onebigtable.com.

CHAPTER 1

NIBBLES, NOSHES, AND TASTY LITTLE PLATES

THE AMERICAN APPETITE

GRAND PORTAGE, MINNESOTA

To define the moment of a cuisine's birth is an attempt to describe the spirit of a people, the ineffable appetite that is held in common, undiminished by time. Americans want a single point of origin, but history refuses to cooperate.

Scholars as well as school-children long considered New England the Eden of our national cuisine. The yearly recreation of Plimoth Plantation's first harvest meal is an ode to this myth. Each traditional Thanksgiving dish became evidence that the American cuisine sprang from an exchange between New England's corn-eating, chowder-making, bird-hunting Wampanoag Indians and the Puritan settlers who tried to "civilize" the same ingredients by cooking them British style.

This feather-and-shoe-buckle theory survived until the 1960s, when scholars began to question the Massachusetts colony's claim. After all, more than a century before the *Mayflower* landed, Spanish explorers were cooking in St. Augustine, Florida.

Their 1503 encampment was short-lived, and a French group landed nearby—and, some say, celebrated the first Thanksgiving—in June of 1564. Within a year, religious zealots from Spain sacked this settlement and, according to other historians, created the earliest Thanksgiving on September 8, 1565. Still other scholars claim that Jamestown was the birthplace of American cuisine.

Karl Koster is an amateur historian and historic reenactor who is obsessed with cooking historically correct American meals. He has little patience with the Big Bang theory of New World cuisine and says that there was no single First Feast.

"Wherever water met land, people converged. They came from different places, they cooked for survival, they ate a lot of nasty things, and most of the time they only had two things in common: purpose and hope. They all believed that the best was yet to come. They approached everything they did as the beginning of a great new world. That's America. I feel it every time I go back to 1607 for a weekend."

Since he was a teenager, Mr. Koster has spent most weekends making sense of the present by repeating (or reinventing) the past. He is a historic reenactor. His ability to absorb research and channel the spirit of other times is uncanny. In 1997, he became one of the rare reenactors given the chance to turn pro when he was offered a position as a park ranger at the Grand Portage National Monument on the north shore of Lake Superior. In the mid-eighteenth century, Grand Portage was the inland headquarters of the North West Company, and trappers for British-licensed, Scottish-owned fur companies, French Canadians, and the indigenous Anishinaabeg clan of the Ojibwe nation created a major gateway into the interior of North America. Wearing period clothing, Mr. Koster builds birch-bark canoes, skins beaver tails, and grills moose snout for visitors.

"There are all levels of reenactors," he says modestly. "You have the guys who want to dress up, play Civil War, and guzzle beer. Then you have the families that want to go back to a Colonial-era farm and learn history together. And then you have a few like me who spend their lives researching and creating museum-quality reenactments. I've always been more or less a nerd."

His single-mindedness has not always been easy. Once at a local 7-Eleven he slipped into an eighteenth-century cadence at the checkout counter. The cashier looked scared. A tollbooth attendant had a similar reaction when Koster had to drive to a pre-Colonial-era reenactment in his costume.

Mr. Koster doesn't mind the stares. "It's gotta be jarring to see somebody dressed up in a billowy linen shirt, drop-front hemp britches, and a wide woven sash, with a big tuque on his head, driving an old, beat-up Buick Century," he said. But he is not without support. His wife, he says, "understands the difficulty of moving from one historical reality to another. She's never questioned my passion." Her parents made historically correct period garments and worked the reenactment circuit.

Mr. Koster spent several decades finding his personal spot in the nation's past—"I'm 1763 to 1821, the British period of the Great Lakes fur trade"—and he has built hundreds of lean-tos, sod huts, and log cabins; worn animal skins, knickers, and trousers; acted out just about every pre–Civil War era of American history; and cooked his way back to the foundation of the nation's cuisine: the ingredients that were on hand.

"When they talk about the origins of American cooking, everybody goes on about who was here and who came here. But when you start to cook, the first question is 'What?' not 'Who?'

"What was here?" he asks. And then he answers: "Fish and game. And as soon as they cleared a patch of land, there was corn, beans, and squash. No matter where they came from or where they landed, the continental United States gave them corn, beans, and squash. Indigenous people called these 'the three sisters.' You might have caught fish, you might have hunted yourself some nice venison or wild boar, but the next thing in the pot was corn, beans, and squash.

"Back when I started, we just took an old-looking pot, dumped some cans of Dinty Moore stew in it, and called it history. Then the research got better. Heck, I spent years experimenting with green wood grills, mud ovens, cooking on hot rocks near the fire, hanging food from wooden tripods over the fire, and working with three-legged pots," he says, adding, "When you read a journal entry about eating bear meat dipped in boiling maple syrup, well, you just gotta have that and you gotta get it right, so you go back and you read as much as you can find."

Some find it difficult to understand what the shape and thickness of, say, a 250-year-old pot reveal about why we eat what we eat today, but as he adjusts the forked sticks of the rotisserie where he's roasting a moose snout in the fire pit at Grand Portage, Mr. Koster is eager to explain. "In my experience, the righter the pot, the righter the utensils, the righter the ingredients, the better your chances of connecting with what the pot or the rotisserie or the clay oven or the food meant to people. The closer you get to what they thought and felt and dreamed when they stirred or tended a cook fire," he says. "When you connect at that level, you can feel their hunger, feel what it has in common with your own understanding that you are the continuation of a grand dream that often takes the form of a meal."

"Life is a banquet and most poor suckers are starving!"

—Rosalind Russell as
Mame Dennis in *Auntie Mame*

Maggi Smith Hall's Minorcan Fromajardis

ST. AUGUSTINE, FLORIDA

Maggi Smith Hall's family has lived in St. Augustine for four generations and is happiest when working to preserve the city's Old-World churches, stores, homes, and history. She relates tales of the Spanish explorers who landed here in the early 1500s, carrying the cattle that would become longhorns, and the missionaries who would attempt to create New Spain in the American Southwest. It was the Spanish, says Mrs. Hall, a former high school teacher, who created the vibrant Florida port, but it was the Minorcans—people brought from Greece, Italy, and the island of Minorca in 1768 and indentured to nearby indigo plantations—who turned St. Augustine into a pan-Mediterranean settlement. Their dishes were united by at least one ingredient: the tiny, hot datil peppers that are still grown in window boxes and kitchen gardens in St. Augustine today. Mrs. Hall was so captivated by the pepper that she created a community cookbook, researching and collecting recipes from the descendants of the original settlers. These Minorcan fromajardis (fried cheese tarts) were traditionally handed out to singers serenading the old neighborhoods on a spring night each year to celebrate the anniversary of the Minorcans' arrival in Florida. The "Fromajardis Serenade" still continues in St. Augustine the week after Easter. Today, says Mrs. Hall, the zesty little tarts are given most often to those who agree to stop singing.

FOR THE DOUGH

3 cups unbleached all-purpose flour

1 tablespoon baking powder

1 tablespoon sugar

1 teaspoon kosher salt

Pinch of freshly grated nutmeg

1 cup vegetable shortening

½ cup water

FOR THE FILLING

8 ounces sharp cheddar cheese, shredded (about 2 cups)

2 tablespoons unbleached all-purpose flour

4 large eggs, lightly beaten

½ teaspoon kosher salt

⅛ teaspoon Datil Pepper Sauce (recipe follows)

Pinch of freshly grated nutmeg

4 tablespoons (½ stick) unsalted butter, melted

1. Place the oven racks in the bottom and top positions and preheat the oven to 425°F. Line two baking sheets with parchment paper.

2. To make the dough: In a large bowl, whisk together the flour, baking powder, sugar, salt, and nutmeg. Cut in the shortening with two knives or a dough blender. Add the water and stir until the dough comes together into a ball. Cover and set aside.

3. To make the filling: In a medium bowl, toss the cheese with the flour. Stir in the eggs, salt, hot sauce, and nutmeg.

4. To assemble the pastries: Roll out the dough on a lightly floured work surface until it is ⅛-inch thick. Using a 3-inch biscuit cutter, cut the dough into 24 circles. Place a well-rounded teaspoon of the filling on one side of each circle, then fold the dough over the filling to make a half-moon shape. Pinch the edges of the dough together to seal. Reroll leftover dough to make more pastries with any remaining filling.

5. Brush the pastries with melted butter. Cut two 1-inch slashes in the tops to make a cross. Place on the prepared baking sheets.

6. Bake one baking sheet at a time on the bottom rack about 10 minutes, until lightly browned. The cheese will puff up through the crosses. Transfer the baking sheet to the top rack and bake for 2 to 3 minutes more, until well browned and crisp. Repeat with the second baking sheet. Serve warm or at room temperature.

MAKES 24 PASTRIES, SERVES 8 TO 12

Datil Pepper Sauce

It's easy to double or triple this recipe and adjust the spiciness to individual tastes. The sauce also makes a wonderful companion to grilled fish, poultry, and meat.

½ cup olive oil

4 large tomatoes, cored and chopped

2 medium-size sweet onions such as Vidalia or Maui, finely chopped

2 whole datil chiles, stemmed

1 cup water

2 teaspoons minced fresh oregano

1 teaspoon kosher salt

1 teaspoon freshly ground black pepper

In a medium saucepan, heat the oil over medium heat. Add the tomatoes, onions, and chiles and cook, stirring occasionally, about 6 minutes, until the vegetables are soft. Stir in the water, oregano, salt, and pepper. Bring to a simmer and cook over low heat, stirring occasionally, about 2 hours, until thick. Store covered in the refrigerator.

MAKES ABOUT 2 CUPS

GRAB, GOBBLE, AND GO

AMERICANS HAVE ALWAYS EATEN ON THE RUN. AS EARLY as 1677, two French monks visiting New York described the habit: "So intent are they on their business that they do not stop to dine like gentle folk elsewhere. From the multitudinous vendors of clams and corn, oysters and yams, they snatch up what they wish, much as they march." In Frances Trollope's 1830 *Domestic Manners of the Americans*, she summarized the American dining style as "Grab, gobble and go." Not much has changed. Today snack foods, soft drinks, and alcohol account for 30 percent of the calories consumed in this country, and handheld nibbles, like many of the recipes that follow, remain the top choice for social eating.

Norma Naranjo's Tamales

Highway 84 runs from Santa Fe to Colorado. About forty minutes north of Santa Fe, the highway cuts a paved path through Ohkay Owingeh, a Native American reservation, and the roadside becomes dense with fast-food outlets, outposts of national grocery chains, Walmart, and billboards for Ohkay Casino. Hutch and Norma Naranjo's sprawling midcentury home is set about fifty yards back from the road, a shrine to the tug-of-war between new ways and traditional ones. In the backyard Mr. Naranjo built two hornos (beehive-shaped adobe ovens). Inside the house, a handmade wreath of dried chiles hangs on one wall and a string of made-for-tourists ceramic peppers on another. A naïve painting of St. Francis hangs not far from a cluster of the dream catchers that the couple and their two grown children fashion from string, feathers, and yarn, just as their Pueblo ancestors did.

"We go to church one Sunday and dance the traditional dances the next," said Mrs. Naranjo. A retired social worker, she gives cooking classes and does a little catering. But she spends most of her mornings working the two-acre minifarm where she grows vegetables from seeds that have been passed from one Pueblo generation to another for at least a thousand years. "The history of our people is in those seeds," she says. In the evenings, when her husband builds hornos on the terraces of hotels and McMansions, Mrs. Naranjo visits the elderly women in Ohkay Owingeh, who remember life and cooking when it was closer to the land, and collects their recipes and food stories. "Our history lives in our hands as well," she says.

Mrs. Naranjo moves with the efficiency of a modern professional as she smooths cornmeal paste on damp cornhusks. Tiny white kernels from several ears of heirloom corn, and diced green chiles and squash, along with a thick, bloodred chile sauce and shredded fresh cheese, are lined up in small stainless-steel bowls at the head of her tamale assembly line. She notes that tamales were stuffed with rabbit, venison, pork—whatever people had. Vegetable tamales were a fine way to make use of the gardens' overflowing crops.

She swathes the dough, sprinkles filling, folds, ties, and places the tamale bundles on a rack set over water in a big enameled pot. From time to time, she glances out the window to the backyard, where her husband is feeding small, dry sticks into his new four-by-four horno. Her smaller tamales are, she says, her only concession to modernity: "People love the little ones as snacks, and Hutch and I love them in these green chile stews we make in the horno."

FOR THE HUSKS AND TAMALE DOUGH

One 8-ounce package dried corn husks, approximately 48 individual husks

3 cups masa harina (preferably Maseca brand)

6 tablespoons (¾ stick) unsalted butter, softened

¼ vegetable oil or fresh lard

¾ teaspoon kosher salt

1½ teaspoons baking powder

About 1½ cups warm water

FOR THE FILLING

1 teaspoon vegetable oil

3 cups diced peeled calabaza, zucchini, or summer squash, in ½-inch pieces

1 cup Red Chile Sauce (recipe follows)

2 cups fresh chico corn kernels or other small, sweet corn kernels

4 to 6 roasted green chiles (canned or fresh), seeded and thinly sliced into 2-inch-long strips

2 cups shredded mozzarella or other fresh mild cheese

1. To prepare the husks: Separate the bundle into individual husks, place them in a pot of warm water over medium-low heat, and simmer for 5 to 10 minutes, until soft. Remove from the heat, place a plate on top of the husks to keep them under water, and soak for 1 hour.

2. Meanwhile, prepare the dough by placing the masa harina in a large bowl. Knead in the butter. Add the vegetable oil. Add the salt and baking powder and knead to combine thoroughly. Add the water, ½ cup at a time, stirring or kneading after each addition, until the dough is slightly pliant and rather pasty. Cover and set aside.

3. To prepare the filling: Warm the vegetable oil in a cast-iron skillet over medium-high heat. Add the squash and cook 1 to 2 minutes, shaking the pan so that each side of the squash toasts slightly. Transfer to a bowl.

4. To assemble the tamales: Pat the cornhusks dry and cut into 4-inch squares. Cut some of the husks into thin strips for tying the tamales (cut at least 40 strips). Spread 1 tablespoon of the dough in the center of a husk square to create a 2 ½-inch square. Brush a little chile sauce over the dough, sprinkle on a little squash, and then a little corn. Lay a piece of green chile on the middle of the filling and sprinkle with cheese.

5. As if covering a small package with wrapping paper, fold the sides of the husk toward the center, then the ends. Tie the bundle with a husk strip. When the tamales have been assembled, place upright on a steaming rack over boiling water. Cover and cook for 20 minutes. Serve as an appetizer or with a green chile sauce.

MAKES ABOUT 36 SMALL TAMALES

Red Chile Sauce

Mrs. Naranjo says, "A lot of these traditional dishes are being modernized. You see chefs putting spices and things in their red chile. My grandmother only used salt. I only use salt. This sauce can also be used to make red meat chile or chile filling for tamales, or to give thickness and smoky fire to other soups and stews."

15 large dried New Mexico red chiles

Boiling water

2 teaspoons vegetable oil, butter, or meat fat such as lard or suet

2 teaspoons masa harina, corn flour, or unbleached all-purpose flour

1 to 2 teaspoons kosher salt

1. Preheat the oven to 350°F. Place a baking sheet in the oven until hot. Put on rubber gloves and remove the stems and seeds from the chiles. Pull the baking sheet out of the oven and use tongs to arrange the chiles on it in a single layer. Slide back in the oven and roast until the chiles are fragrant, about 5 minutes.

2. Remove from oven and use tongs to transfer the chiles to a heatproof bowl. Add enough boiling water to cover the chiles and allow to sit until cool, 30 to 40 minutes. Transfer the peppers and 3 cups of the soaking liquid to a food processor or blender. Reserve the remaining liquid. Blend or process the chiles until smooth.

3. Warm the oil over medium heat. Whisk in the masa harina. Reduce the heat to low and slowly add the pureed chiles, whisking constantly. Slowly whisk in salt to taste. Add additional water, if necessary, to get a thick but pourable consistency. This sauce will keep in a tightly covered glass jar up to 2 weeks in the refrigerator. It can also be frozen.

MAKES ABOUT 4 CUPS

JOHN NEWMAN'S "BETTER THAN FAMOUS" ABLESKIVERS—*Stuffed Danish Pancakes*

John Newman is 41 years old, and he began cooking from Charles Schulz's *Peanuts Cook Book* when he was in grade school. His mother was less than enthusiastic about his constant presence in the kitchen: "Gender roles are generally not bent much in Mormon households," he says. But in addition to mastering the art of Peanuts cooking, Mr. Newman absorbed some of the recipes that his family brought from Denmark in the mid-1800s when they followed the Mormon founder Brigham Young to Utah. His great-grandmother, Rebecca Hales, was a captain in the Daughters of the Utah Pioneer and was famous for her ableskivers. The small, round batter cakes are cooked in distinctive iron pans with cupcake-shaped depressions and are usually filled with fruit. His great-grandmother made her ableskivers with gooseberry jam, plain sugar, or a traditional apple filling. Mr. Newman has pushed the recipe into a more savory direction, adding sausage or blue cheese and serving the puffs as appetizers or brunch, with tart currant jam on the side.

2 cups all-purpose flour

2 tablespoons baking powder

½ teaspoon kosher salt

6 large eggs, separated

2 cups buttermilk

4 tablespoons (½ stick) unsalted butter, melted

1 pound firm blue cheese, cut into 48 small pieces

1. In a large bowl, whisk together the flour, baking powder, and salt. In a medium bowl, whisk the egg yolks until smooth, then whisk in the buttermilk until well blended. In another large bowl, whip the egg whites with an electric mixer until stiff peaks form.

2. Stir the buttermilk mixture into the flour mixture just until blended. Do not overmix. Fold the egg whites into the batter until almost no white streaks remain.

3. Heat an ableskiver pan over medium heat. Lightly brush the inside of each well of the pan with the melted butter. Working in batches, spoon 1 rounded tablespoon of batter into each well, drop a piece of blue cheese in the batter, and top with a little more batter. Cook for 2 to 3 minutes, until the top of the batter becomes very bubbly. Flip the ableskivers using a metal skewer, and cook for 2 to 3 minutes more, until browned.

4. Using the metal skewer, transfer the ableskivers to a paper-towel-lined plate to drain briefly. Repeat with the remaining batter, brushing the pan with butter between each batch. Serve warm.

SERVES 6 TO 8

NOTE: Ableskiver pans are available in most cookware shops.

CHARLIE SHACKLETON'S NAKED PIZZA

WOODSTOCK, VERMONT

Born in Ireland and educated in British boarding schools, Charles Shackleton came from a family of adventurers. His forebears dared the harsh and uncharted Antarctic; Mr. Shackleton, along with his wife, Miranda Thomas, dared the uncharted territory of a handmade life. Situated in a sprawling former woolen mill, his furniture workshop and her pottery studio have become shrines for artists, craftspeople, gardeners, and passionate home cooks, and have helped revive a desolate New England mill town. "We like to make things with our hands and to connect people with each other and to the land," says Mr. Shackleton. The couple are in their early fifties, have two grown children, two young Jack Russell terriers, twenty employees, and the reputation for giving some of the best parties in the Green Mountains. Their home, an 1814 stone and clapboard cottage perched on a hillside 1,000 feet above the Ottaquechee River, has no foundation, and despite the hay bales stuffed under the structure, fierce drafts blow up through the floorboards. From October until April, life, dinner, and parties revolve around the wood-fired oven that shares the massive chimney with the red brick fireplace.

"I grew up next to the fireplace in a drafty old Irish country house, so this house feels like home," says Mr. Shackleton. "We're about being present and living well, not nostalgia. But sometimes you just need a fix of the past. I can get a little obsessive. Once I spent months trying to make the perfect crumpet—traveling to a mill, trying to find the right flour, the right pan, the right technique. I even sponsored a contest just to see other people make them. Crumpets are a stovetop operation. I moved on to bread, and I figured out pretty quickly that the bread bakes best in the wood oven. Pizza followed naturally.

"Every week or so, I make the dough, the naked pizza, and we put out bowls of roasted peppers, tomato sauce, cheese, herbs, chicken, sausage, wafers of ham, black olives, sautéed vegetables. People, lots of people, show up and make their own pies. When we cook together and put the food on the pottery that Miranda makes and set it out on a table I've built, people understand why we do what we do and why we

care about the things we care about. The next thing you know, they've pushed all the furniture out of the way and turned the house into a disco, out-of-town guests, our friends, the kids who apprentice with us, town elders, and members of the local homemakers' club. Ordinary pizza might not have the same power.

"I started with a recipe from Alice Waters and added some more brown grains. My father was a miller, you know, and there are a few wonderful artisanal grain growers and millers in Vermont. If I didn't have a wood oven that I can fire up to 700 degrees in ten minutes, I probably wouldn't make pizza. But I do know someone who gets a wonderful smoky, crisp crust by grilling his pizza. He pats out the dough, lays it on a hot grill without the toppings. He cooks it on one side, flips it, adds the toppings, covers the grill and cooks it until it is all lovely and bubbly."

2 tablespoons active dry yeast

1½ cups lukewarm water

3¼ cups unbleached all-purpose flour, plus more for kneading

1½ cups stone-ground rye flour

¼ cups Irish wholemeal flour (or stone-ground whole-wheat flour)

1 tablespoon fine sea salt

2 cups water

¾ cup high quality olive oil

Miranda Thomas's Modest Red Sauce (recipe follows)

Toppings (such as roasted peppers, sautéed vegetables, cooked Italian sausages and chicken, wafers of ham, black olives, cheese, and herbs)

1. Dissolve the yeast in the lukewarm water in a large bowl. Stir in 1½ cups of the unbleached flour, ¾ cup of the rye flour, and the wholemeal flour, and let sit in a warm place until the mixture is bubbly, about 30 minutes.

2. In another bowl, combine the remaining flours with the salt. Stir this mixture, 2 cups water, and the olive oil into the yeast mixture. Lightly flour a work surface and knead the dough until it is satiny and no longer sticky, about 5 minutes. Place in a large, clean bowl, cover with a clean kitchen towel, and allow to rise in the refrigerator overnight.

3. Two hours before serving, remove the dough from the refrigerator and allow to come to room temperature. Punch it down and divide the dough into six equal pieces. Pat each into a ball and let sit on a tray at room temperature, covered with a towel, for another hour. While the dough is rising, set the oven rack in the lowest position and preheat oven to its highest heat (450°–500°F).

4. Lightly flour the work surface and use a rolling pin to roll each ball into a thin, 10-inch circle. Transfer to a baking sheet. Apply a thin layer of sauce or olive oil along with other desired toppings, and bake until the dough is golden and crisp and the toppings are cooked through, 5 to 15 minutes depending on the oven's heat. Serve each pizza as soon as it is done.

MAKES SIX 10-INCH PIZZAS

Miranda Thomas's Modest Red Sauce

Miranda Thomas says, "When I was in art school back in England, there was a boy from France who made pots with me, and he taught me to make this sauce. He used fresh tomatoes, blanched them and skinned and seeded them, but that was only because we couldn't get high quality canned crushed tomatoes. It is important to get the measurements right, especially the pepper, and to cook the sauce very slowly to get a mellow, slightly sweet taste. Charlie and I use this sauce on the pizzas we serve to big groups. We usually put the toppings out for people to choose and serve a big salad as well."

¼ cup high quality olive oil

1 medium yellow onion, minced

Kosher salt

2 garlic cloves, smashed

One 28-ounce can crushed plum tomatoes and juice

1 tablespoon dried oregano

1 tablespoon dried basil or 2 tablespoons chopped fresh basil

20 turns of black pepper from a grinder

1. Warm the olive oil in a large saucepan over medium heat. Add the onion, season with a pinch of salt, reduce the heat to low and cook, stirring occasionally, for 5 minutes. Add the garlic and cook, stirring, until the onion is translucent, 5 to 10 minutes more.

2. Add the tomatoes, oregano, basil, and black pepper. Reduce the heat to the very lowest setting, partially cover the pot, and simmer for 30 to 45 minutes, stirring occasionally, until the sauce is thick. Add salt to taste. The sauce will keep up to 1 week in a tightly-covered glass or plastic container in the refrigerator.

MAKES ABOUT 3½ CUPS, ENOUGH FOR EIGHT 10-INCH PIZZAS OR A POUND OF PASTA

MAILE NGUYEN'S BANH XEO
Vietnamese Shrimp Pancake

BILOXI, MISSISSIPPI

Maile Nguyen is 36 years old, the daughter of a shrimper, and the wife and sister of shrimpers. Her earliest memory is how her mother, a Vietnamese refugee and a widow, smelled when she returned home after working fourteen hours in a fish-processing house. After they moved to Biloxi as a result of bad weather and low harvests the family lived cheek by jowl in refugee housing. Before anyone in the family learned English, shopping for food was scary. In the grocery stores, basil and mint was sold dried, not in the bunches found year-round today; there was only one variety of rice; and finding fish sauce, the ketchup of Vietnamese cooking, was impossible. But even in bad years, there was shrimp enough to eke by. Today in Biloxi, there is a Buddhist temple, the major holidays are celebrated in a big way, some of the markets rival those of Saigon, and Mrs. Nguyen has the luxury of staying at home to raise her children and look after her mother. For the family's two biggest holidays—Tet, the Vietnamese lunar New Year, and the Fourth of July—she makes this traditional Vietnamese pancake. Her husband calls them "Vietnamese tacos," her mother calls them "thank God somebody else is cooking them," and people in their neighborhood call them delicious.

FOR THE SAUCE

¼ cup water

2 tablespoons Vietnamese fish sauce (nuoc mam), plus additional to taste

4½ teaspoons fresh lime juice

2 teaspoons sugar

1 teaspoon Vietnamese chili paste, or 1 small red chile, stemmed, seeded, and finely chopped

1 garlic clove, minced

FOR THE PANCAKES

2 cups fresh mint leaves

2 cups fresh Thai basil leaves, lightly packed

2 cups fresh cilantro leaves, lightly packed

2 cups bean sprouts

2 cups rice flour

1 cup water

1 cup unsweetened coconut milk

1 teaspoon ground turmeric

¼ teaspoon kosher salt

¼ cup vegetable oil, plus more as needed

4 ounces white mushrooms, thinly sliced (optional)

½ pound ground pork

1 pound medium shrimp (21 to 25 per pound), peeled and deveined

4 scallions, green and white parts, thinly sliced

1. To make the sauce: In a small bowl, stir together water, 2 tablespoons fish sauce, lime juice, sugar, chili paste, and garlic. Season with additional fish sauce to taste, and cover.

2. To make the pancakes: Arrange the mint, basil, cilantro, and bean sprouts on a serving platter and refrigerate. In a large bowl, whisk together the rice flour, water, coconut milk, turmeric, and salt.

3. In a large nonstick skillet, heat 1 tablespoon of the oil over high heat. Add the mushrooms (if using) and cook for 4 to 6 minutes, until lightly browned. Add the pork and cook, stirring frequently, for 3 to 4 minutes, until any lumps are broken up and the meat is no longer pink. Stir in the shrimp and scallions and cook about 3 minutes, until the shrimp are pink. Transfer the mixture to a bowl.

4. In an 8-inch nonstick skillet, heat 2 teaspoons oil over medium-high heat. Add ¼ cup of the batter and tilt the pan to coat the bottom and sides. Reduce the heat to medium and cook about 2 minutes, until the pancake begins to brown on the bottom and is crisp at the edges. (If needed, add 1 to 2 teaspoons more oil around the edges to keep the pancake crisp.)

5. Mound about ½ cup of the shrimp mixture on one half of the pancake, then fold the pancake over the filling to make a half-moon shape. Slide the pancake out of the pan. Repeat with the remaining oil, batter, and filling. Serve with the fresh herbs, bean sprouts, and sauce.

SERVES 4

CAVIAR IN AMERICA

WHEN WHITE SETTLERS ARRIVED ON the North American continent, no fish were more abundant than the sturgeon that lived in the lakes, streams, and rivers from New England to the Great Lakes, the Mississippi River, and the Pacific Northwest. By the nineteenth century, the United States produced 90 percent of the world's caviar. Maine's Kennebec River was second only to the Hudson River in sturgeon production, and no one, particularly no member of Downeast clans like the Brownes of Harpswell, Maine, who'd worked the local waters since before Maine was a state, could "fawthum" (as they say) that the giant sturgeon would ever disappear. But in 1949, Rod Browne (above) caught the last great sturgeon that anyone remembers, a 145-pound female, nine and a half feet long. Sturgeon fisheries in the Caspian Sea took over the caviar trade, but concern about that area eventually led to international limits on importation, and by the 1980s scientists were experimenting with alternative ways to grow domestic sturgeon and harvest their caviar. Today, Tennessee, North Carolina, Kentucky, Ohio, Arkansas, California, Washington, and Alaska are producing caviar from different varieties of sturgeon, most of them farm-raised.

ROD BROWNE MITCHELL'S CLAM PANCAKE

PORTLAND, MAINE

Rod Browne Mitchell, the nephew and namesake of the man who caught the last Kennebec River sturgeon, is still in the family business. His Browne Trading Company in Portland, Maine, is one of the nation's premier caviar suppliers. He samples pounds of the world's best each year. The flavor of the fish eggs always takes him back to early mornings at his grandfather's fishing camp on Quahog Bay and the smell of his grandmother's clam pancakes. Downeast families sold the finest fish, and ate what remained. That was the thrifty and proper thing to do. The sturgeon are gone, but there are still lots of clams. These pancakes are exclusive to the Browne family: "The regular clam cake was not popular in our house; maybe that is why my grandmother tried pancake batter," he says. As children, they wanted a sweet batter and drowned the pancakes in maple syrup. This savory version makes a fine first course or finger food.

1 cup milk

¼ cup heavy cream

¼ cup water

1 large egg, lightly beaten

1½ cups all-purpose flour

1 tablespoon baking powder

2 teaspoons sugar

1½ teaspoons kosher salt

Vegetable oil, for the griddle

2 dozen littleneck clams, steamed, removed from the shell, and left whole

1. In a medium bowl, combine the milk, cream, water, and egg. In a large bowl, whisk together the flour, baking powder, sugar, and salt. Make a well in the center of the dry ingredients, add the milk mixture, and stir until combined.

2. Heat a griddle or large nonstick skillet over medium heat and lightly brush with oil. Working in batches, spoon 1-tablespoon portions of batter onto the griddle, spaced 1 inch apart, and cook for 1 to 2 minutes, until small holes appear. Place 1 clam on the top of each pancake, flip, and cook for 1 to 2 minutes more, until lightly browned. Transfer the pancakes to a serving plate and repeat with the remaining batter and clams, brushing the griddle with oil between each batch. Serve.

MAKES 24 PANCAKES; SERVES 8 TO 12

Nuns clamming on Long Island, 1957.

BOBBY BRIDGES'S CLAM CLOUDS

WILLIS WHARF, VIRGINIA

The Eastern Shore of Virginia, which stretches from the Eastern Shore of Maryland to the mouth of the Chesapeake Bay, has been a prosperous fishing ground for oysters, crabs, and clams for centuries. There, clam fritters are ubiquitous, and the competition to make the finest flat, fluffy fritter has gone on for generations. Right now, nobody makes them better than Bobby Bridges, a 58-year-old waterman and house painter.

Mr. Bridges moved to the Eastern Shore after high school, married a local girl and never left. From the start, he made a greaseless clam fritter. He says that his recipe has been in his wife Debbie's family since the nineteenth century.

"It's not that hard. You want to use real fresh chowder clams, grind them with a Universal food chopper, not a food processor, and get them real dry before you put them in the batter, and you want to make sure to make the fritters bigger than your hamburger bun. Nothing worse than a bigger roll and you have to lift up the top to see what's in it. A clam fritter got to hang out of the roll. That's the way I like it. I want to see it, not hide it."

1 pound freshly shucked chowder clams, with their juices

½ white onion, minced

Vegetable oil or lard, for frying

2 large eggs

¼ teaspoon fine sea salt

Pinch of freshly ground black pepper

Pinch of cayenne pepper (optional)

¼ cup baking mix (preferably Bisquick)

4 hamburger buns, for serving (optional)

Mustard, mayonnaise (preferably Duke's brand), and lettuce leaves, for serving (optional)

1. Pour clams and juice into a hand-cranked food grinder and coarsely grind into a fine-mesh strainer set over a bowl. Lift and turn the clams gently, pressing down lightly with spatula so they're as well drained as possible. The clam juice can be used for chowder or frozen up to six months.

2. Pass the onion through the food grinder into a fine-mesh strainer over another bowl. Discard the onion juice.

3. Line two baking sheets with paper towels. Working in batches, spoon the clams on to the first baking sheet. Blot as dry as possible.

4. Place a large, deep cast-iron skillet over medium heat. Add enough vegetable oil to reach halfway up the sides.

5. Meanwhile, in a mixing bowl, beat the eggs until frothy. Season lightly with the salt, black pepper, and a few grains of cayenne, if desired. Stir in the baking mix, then the onions. Working quickly, fold in the clams.

6. When the oil is hot, drop 3 tablespoons of the batter for each fritter into the oil and gently flatten with a heatproof rubber spatula to a circle 5 to 6 inches in diameter. Fry for 7 minutes on each side.

7. When fritters are golden and cooked through, drain on paper towels and blot well. If desired, serve on soft white hamburger rolls, with mustard, mayonnaise, and lettuce.

MAKES 4 FRITTERS

MIKE DiMUCCIO'S
RHODE ISLAND FRIED CALAMARI

Master plumber and amateur chef Mike DiMuccio is part of a cooking club comprised of fifteen of his food-obsessed friends who meet in his basement to bottle their own wine. As the club grew, its operations spread to the first floor of his commercial building, so he installed a professional kitchen, where the club members now compete with each other. His fried squid with hot pepper sauce is a product of his own Italian background, but also reflects some of the Portuguese influence of his hometown. He feels that the local Kenyon's Grist Mill white or yellow cornmeal is best for breading, but whatever you choose, the single most important factor is to bread the squid very lightly so that the flavor comes through. It doesn't hurt to grow your own peppers and pickle them, either.

4 cups whole milk

1 pound squid, cleaned, tentacles removed and reserved, bodies cut into ½-inch rings

8 tablespoons (1 stick) unsalted butter

4 garlic cloves, minced

1 cup drained sliced pickled peppers such as Italian Banana or Portuguese Hot

1 teaspoon onion powder

Vegetable oil, for frying

Kosher salt and freshly ground black pepper

1 cup unbleached all-purpose flour

1. In a large bowl, combine the milk and squid, cover, and let soak in the refrigerator for 12 to 24 hours.

2. About 1 hour before frying, drain the squid and spread in an even layer on a baking sheet to dry.

3. While the squid dries, in a large skillet, melt the butter over medium heat. Add the garlic and cook about 30 seconds, until aromatic. Stir in the peppers and onion powder and cook until the peppers are tender, 2 to 4 minutes. Keep warm.

4. In a Dutch oven, heat 2 inches of oil until a deep-frying thermometer reads 365°F to 375°F, or a pinch of flour sizzles in the oil. Season the squid with salt and pepper and lightly coat with flour, shaking off the excess. Carefully add one-third of the squid to the hot oil and cook for 45 seconds to 1 ½ minutes, until light golden brown and tender. Transfer the squid to a paper-towel-lined baking sheet to drain. Return the oil to 375°F and repeat with the remaining squid in two more batches.

5. Add the squid to the skillet, toss with the butter mixture, and serve.

SERVES 4

Jody Williams's
Nobel Laureate Crab Cakes

FREDERICKSBURG, VIRGINIA

Jody Williams, cofounder of the Internet campaign to ban land mines, and Nobel Peace laureate, has traveled the globe advocating for social justice. *Forbes* magazine named her one of its most powerful women in the world, but the few days a year that she is at home and cooking with her husband, Steve Goose, are her happiest. The couple loves to meld Asian ingredients—like the panko bread crumbs and lime juice in this crab cake recipe—with her family's traditional Sicilian cooking. Cooking one's way to peace is just as good as any other path. "At the end of the day, people commune over food," she says. "Cooking and eating brings people together and is the building block of community." (Her avocado sauce recipe makes a fine dip for chips, as well.)

FOR THE SAUCE

1 avocado, halved, pitted, and flesh scooped out

¼ cup half-and-half

2 tablespoons fresh lime juice

2 teaspoons finely chopped jalapeño chile

Kosher salt and freshly ground black pepper

FOR THE CRAB CAKES

8 ounces lump crabmeat, picked over for shells and cartilage

¼ cup half-and-half

2 tablespoons finely chopped onion

1 tablespoon fresh lime juice

1 large egg, lightly beaten

2 garlic cloves, minced

1½ teaspoons Worcestershire sauce

1 teaspoon celery seed

¼ teaspoon freshly ground black pepper

4 dashes hot sauce

½ cup panko bread crumbs, plus more for coating the cakes

1 tablespoon extra virgin olive oil

1 tablespoon unsalted butter

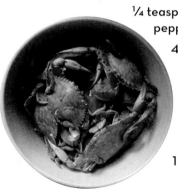

1. To make the sauce: In a blender or food processor, process the avocado, half-and-half, lime juice, and jalapeño about 30 seconds, until smooth. Transfer the sauce to a small bowl and season with salt and pepper to taste. Cover and refrigerate until needed.

2. To make the crab cakes: In a medium bowl, mix together the crabmeat, half-and-half, onion, lime juice, egg, garlic, Worcestershire sauce, celery seed, pepper, and hot sauce. Cover and refrigerate for at least 1 hour.

3. Stir the panko into the chilled crab mixture and shape into eight patties about 1 inch thick. Lightly coat the outside of the patties with panko.

4. In a large nonstick skillet, heat the oil and butter over medium heat. When the butter is sizzling, add the crab cakes and cook for 6 to 8 minutes, gently turning over once, until golden brown on both sides. Transfer the crab cakes to a serving platter or individual plates and serve with the sauce.

SERVES 4

CHAN'S PINE-CURED SALMON

Gravlax, a Scandinavian dish, is cured with salt and sugar and lightly flavored with mustard powder and black pepper. But in the Pacific Northwest, where wild salmon are still plentiful, other herbs and wild greens that evoke the untamed flavor of the northern woods are used. In this recipe, pine needles add a citrus bite that cuts the rich, gamey flavor of the wild fish. (With the exception of yew, which can be toxic, most pine, spruce, fir, and juniper needles are edible in moderate quantities. Check a reliable field guide for any counter-indications.) Channing Ockley, a medical technologist whose forebears emigrated from Scotland to help build the salmon industry in the early nineteenth century, sometimes uses maple syrup in place of the sugar to pack the salmon. It adds a subtle smoky flavor to the cured fish.

½ cup sugar

6 tablespoons kosher salt

Two 1-pound center-cut salmon fillets

1½ cups pine needles, rinsed well and coarsely chopped

2 teaspoons white peppercorns, crushed

1. In a small bowl, combine the sugar and salt. Pat the salmon dry with a paper towel. Sprinkle 2 tablespoons of the mixture evenly over the flesh side of each fillet. Sprinkle the bottom of a glass baking dish with ¼ cup of the mixture.

2. Chop the pine needles and peppercorns together to make a coarse mash. Scatter 1 tablespoon of this mixture on top of the sugar mixture in the baking dish.

3. Lay one of the salmon pieces skin side down in the glass dish. Spread one-half of the remaining pine needle mixture on the exposed flesh side of the fish, then sprinkle with 3 tablespoons more sugar mixture. Place the second salmon piece flesh side down on top of the first piece. Sprinkle with the remaining 3 tablespoons of the sugar mixture and the remaining pine needle mixture.

4. Cover the salmon loosely with aluminum foil. Weight the salmon with a cutting board or a small platter and refrigerate for 5 hours to allow the salt to leech out as much liquid as possible.

5. Drain the liquid in the dish, turn the fish over, keeping the "sandwich" together, and reapply the weight. Refrigerate for at least 48 hours more.

6. Before serving, wipe off the pine needles with a paper towel. Slice the salmon paper thin on a bias and serve.

SERVES 12

BILL TAYLOR'S OLYMPIA OYSTERS WITH SOY MIGNONETTE

SHELTON, WASHINGTON

Bill Taylor's great-grandfather began cultivating shellfish over a century ago, and today the family continues to grow some of the nation's best oysters and mussels in the bays and inlets of Puget Sound. Like most inveterate oyster lovers, Mr. Taylor believes that a great oyster needs no embellishment. This sauce, inspired by the Japanese watermen who help tend the family's acres, is almost enough to change his mind.

⅔ cup citrus-seasoned soy sauce

⅓ cup finely chopped daikon

2 tablespoons grated fresh ginger

2 dozen oysters (preferably small ones like Kumamoto), on the half shell

In a small bowl, stir together the soy sauce, daikon, and ginger. Top each oyster with 1 teaspoon of the soy sauce mixture and serve on a bed of crushed ice.

SERVES 6 TO 8

OYSTERS

THE CONTINENTAL UNITED STATES HAS NEARLY 5,000 MILES OF COASTLINE, AND SOME of the richest oyster patches in the world are created where the shores dip into estuaries or break into inlets and the ocean meets fresh water. American waters hold more than 200 known varieties of oysters, and their flavors range from sweet to briny, plump to lean, creamy to coppery. Their sizes range from the teeny Olympia variety of the Pacific Northwest to the big, gnarly-shelled Blue Points from Long Island, New York.

If you begin in northern New England and follow the American coastline, the first oysters you'll eat will be clean and briny, thanks to the cold northeast waters. South along the Atlantic seaboard and around the Gulf of Mexico, oysters grow increasingly fatty and their flavor milder. On the Pacific Coast, the mollusks gain more mineral tones.

OYSTERS ROCKEFELLER-STYLE

For nearly half a century, Antoine Alciatore, the classically trained chef and founder of Antoine's restaurant in New Orleans, had watched *le tout le monde* thrill to his haute escargots. But by 1899, appetite for the dish began to wane. Casting about for a solution, Antoine's son Jules created a dish of oysters baked with parsley and added local spinach and bacon. He christened it Huitres en Coquille à la Rockefeller. And an American classic was born. Soon, fine restaurants nationwide had their own version of "Oysters Rockefeller"; the dish remains a menu staple today. The Alciatore family has never shared the original recipe. This version is adapted from the recipe for Oysters Rockefeller included in *The Revised Edition of the Up-to-Date Cook Book* compiled under the auspices of the Ladies Aid Sewing Society of New Orleans, and first published in 1915.

8 tablespoons (1 stick) unsalted butter, softened

¾ cup minced fresh parsley

2 scallions, green and white parts, minced

¼ teaspoon cayenne pepper

Pinch of kosher salt

2 dozen oysters, on the half shell

4 slices bacon, each cut into 6 squares

1 packed cup stemmed, washed, and finely shredded fresh spinach

⅓ cup fresh bread crumbs

1. Preheat the broiler.

2. In a medium bowl, combine the butter, parsley, scallions, cayenne, and salt.

3. Place the oysters on a baking sheet or broiler pan and cover each with a generous teaspoon of the butter mixture and a square of bacon.

4. Divide the spinach evenly among the oysters and pack it on. Top each with equal amounts.

5. Broil the oysters about 5 minutes, until the bread crumbs are lightly browned and the mixture is bubbly. Serve immediately.

SERVES 12

Sue Wespy Ceravolo's
Wood-Fired Spicy Oysters

NEW ORLEANS, LOUISIANA

Sue Wespy Ceravolo, former garde-manger at the Ritz-Carlton in New Orleans, says: "I remember seeing it around in the 1990s and it's been spreading like kudzu ever since. In order to get a strong, wood-smoked oyster, you need to shuck the oysters and place them in melted butter so they can soak up the flavor, and heat the shells over a screaming hot fire. Then you place the oyster and its juice back in the shell and top it with the butter. It doesn't get overcooked in the couple minutes it takes to melt the butter and let the flavors marry."

2 dozen large oysters

FOR THE COMPOUND BUTTER

½ pound (2 sticks) unsalted butter, softened

2 anchovy fillets, rinsed, patted dry, and minced (to equal 1½ teaspoons)

4 to 6 garlic cloves, minced (to equal 2 tablespoons)

1 small shallot, minced (to equal 1 tablespoon)

3 drops sriracha sauce, or more to taste

¼ teaspoon minced fresh chili or red pepper flakes

⅛ teaspoon freshly ground white pepper

2 tablespoons fresh lemon juice

1 tablespoon minced flat-leaf parsley

FOR THE TOPPING

1 tablespoon unsalted butter

½ cup fine dry bread crumbs

2 tablespoons grated Parmesan cheese

1. Prepare a charcoal grill or preheat the oven to 500°F. Place a fine-mesh strainer over a pint container. Open the oysters, and place the meat in the strainer to allow the juices to drain. Refrigerate both. Thoroughly scrub the shells.

2. To make the compound butter: Combine the butter, anchovies, and the reserved oyster juice in a food processor and pulse. Add the garlic, shallot, sriracha sauce, chili, white pepper, and lemon juice and pulse. Transfer to a bowl and fold in the parsley. Transfer one-quarter to a container, cover, and refrigerate. Place remaining three-quarters of the compound butter in a warm place to melt.

3. To make the topping: Melt the butter in a cast-iron skillet over medium heat. When hot, add the bread crumbs and toast lightly, stirring constantly, about 3 minutes. Transfer to a bowl. When cool, stir in the cheese.

4. When the compound butter is melted, add oysters and stir gently to coat them. Place scrubbed shells on a grill rack over the fire or on a baking sheet in the oven until very hot. Carefully spoon an oyster and a little of the melted butter into each shell. Place about 1 teaspoon of topping on each oyster. Top with a chunk of cold compound butter and an additional sprinkling of topping, and cook until the oysters begin to plump. Serve immediately.

SERVES 4 TO 6

Vincent Vellotti's Barbecued Clams

Vincent Vellotti had bright blue eyes, a cherubic face, and a cleft chin, and stood not a bit over five feet six inches tall. But to his grandchildren, whom he roused before dawn to take fishing or practice baseball, he was larger than life. A child during the Great Depression, Grandpa Vellotti supported his family by selling toothbrushes and pocket combs door to door and by fishing for dinner in the Norwalk, Connecticut, harbor. Eventually, he became one of the best-known and most successful real estate brokers around. He also founded the local Little League, and his dedication to young players earned him a place in the Little League Baseball Hall of Fame. Next to witnessing a 10-year-old's grand slam, he was most enthusiastic about digging clams. The late patriarch's clam preparation—which his grandson has taken up a notch by adding garlic and hot pepper sauce—is served whenever his descendants gather.

4 tablespoons (½ stick) unsalted butter

1 shallot, finely chopped

3 garlic cloves, minced

2 teaspoons hot sauce

Kosher salt and freshly ground black pepper

Fresh lemon juice

1½ dozen littleneck clams, soaked in cold water for 30 minutes and drained

2 tablespoons minced fresh parsley

1. Prepare a charcoal grill or heat a grill pan on high heat.

2. In a small saucepan, melt the butter over medium heat. Add the shallot and garlic and cook for 2 to 4 minutes, until just beginning to brown. Remove from the heat, stir in the hot sauce, and season with salt, pepper, and lemon juice to taste.

3. Drain the clams and place them on the grill, spaced evenly apart, arranged neatly. Grill about 8 minutes, until the clams open slightly, then use tongs to open them completely.

4. Spoon about 1 teaspoon of the sauce onto each clam and grill for 1 to 2 minutes more. Transfer the clams to a serving platter, sprinkle with parsley, and serve.

SERVES 4 TO 6

Tony and Julie Hook's Gourmet Fried Cheese

MINERAL POINT, WISCONSIN

Florida is oranges. Texas is beef. Maine is lobster. And in the 1920s, some marketer decided that Wisconsin should be cheese. The state had no history of cheese making, and no more dairy cows than Vermont or New York. It did, however, have a surplus of milk. By 1945, through a combination of savvy public relations and strategic agricultural investment, the state had 1,500 cheese factories that produced 515 million pounds of cheese a year. There were giant wheels and bricks of compressed dairy product called Swiss, Mozzarella, Provolone, Gorgonzola, Camembert, Brie, Muenster, Limburger, Cheddar, Gouda, and Edam. Most were orange, but that didn't matter. There was lots and lots of it. In 1964, the world's largest cheese, a fourteen-and-a-half-foot-diameter cheddar that weighed seventeen tons, was shipped to the World's Fair in New York. By then, most of the state's cheese factories were owned by large companies like Kraft or Borden, not small farmers.

But about ten years ago, artisanal cheeses began appearing in the land of Big Cheese. Cheese makers like Tony Hook, whose factory in Mineral Point produced 1.5 million pounds of commercial-grade cheese a year, and his wife, Julie, switched to making fine farmstead cheeses and selling them at farmers' markets. Mr. Hook, who made industrial cheese for thirty-nine years before "learning to make real special cheese," won praises for his double-cream blue cheese and Stilton-inspired Tilston Point. In a state where fried cheese curds are ubiquitous, he and his wife realized they'd better invent a snack using their super-rich, quick-to-melt cheeses. This recipe is their answer.

The Hooks, who don giant cheese-wedge hats as quickly as any other Wisconsin sports fan, find these gourmet curds difficult to resist.

1 cup unbleached all-purpose flour

4 large eggs

2 cups fresh bread crumbs

1 tablespoon minced fresh thyme

2 teaspoons cornstarch

1 teaspoon sweet paprika

Freshly ground white pepper

1 pound sharp cheddar cheese (preferably Hook's Three Year Sharp Cheddar), cut into 2-inch chunks

¼ cup vegetable oil, for frying

Kosher salt

1. Place the flour in a shallow bowl. In another shallow bowl, whisk the eggs together. In a third shallow bowl, combine the bread crumbs, thyme, cornstarch, paprika, and ½ teaspoon white pepper.

2. Working with a few cheese chunks at a time, dip in the flour, shaking to remove any excess so the cheese chunks are only lightly coated. Dip the chunks in egg, then lightly coat with the bread crumb mixture. Place the breaded chunks on a large plate. Repeat until all of the chunks are breaded, then freeze for 30 minutes.

3. In a large skillet, heat the oil until a deep-frying thermometer reads 365°F to 375°F or a pinch of flour bubbles and sizzles in the oil. Using tongs, carefully add the frozen chunks and fry about 3 minutes, until crisp and golden brown on all sides, turning as needed. Season with salt and pepper to taste, and serve immediately.

SERVES 6 TO 8

BILL McINTYRE'S MARINATED FETA

For several decades, Bill McIntyre has driven trucks and stalked roadside ethnic food across the United States. His tractor-trailers are often carrying huge deliveries of snack food—Pop Tarts, Cheerios, or potato chips—but his appetite runs more toward Indian, Mexican, Vietnamese, Syrian, Somali, and Caribbean restaurants off the beaten track. One particular weakness has remained constant. The guy cannot say no to a good Greek meal. He was converted (literally) years ago by a Greek friend when he spent a short stint in England. Returning home, Mr. McIntyre joined St. Michael's Greek Orthodox Church. He's been an active member for twenty-five years and looks forward to church suppers even more than to a no-name Greek diner by the side of the road. At home, he and his wife, Gail, replicate dishes like this marinated feta. It makes a wonderful appetizer or party fare with toasted pita. The success of the dish depends on using only high quality kalamata olives and creamy Bulgarian feta. "Once you taste it, you won't buy any other kind," says Mr. McIntyre. "We drive thirty miles to Louisville where there's an ethnic market that sells it."

1 pound Bulgarian feta cheese, cut into
½-inch cubes

2 cups seeded and coarsely chopped roasted
red bell peppers

1 cup kalamata olives, pitted

1 medium red onion, finely chopped

½ cup olive oil

1 tablespoon balsamic vinegar

2 garlic cloves, minced

2 teaspoons minced fresh thyme

Kosher salt and freshly ground black pepper

Fresh lemon juice

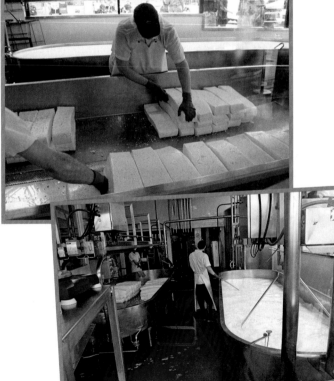

1. In a medium bowl, combine the feta, red peppers, olives, onion, oil, vinegar, garlic, and thyme. Cover and refrigerate for 12 to 24 hours.

2. Season with salt, pepper, and lemon juice to taste, and serve.

SERVES 6 TO 8

*Beecher's Cheese,
Seattle, Washington.*

Catherine Lorenze Fahrner's
Swiss Fondue

Locals think of Eleanor Mailloux as the mayor of Helvetia, West Virginia. The town, founded just after the Civil War by a group of Swiss and German Americans from Brooklyn, New York, hasn't changed much, and for at least the last half century, Mrs. Mailloux has been a tireless proponent of local preservation. When Helvetia's general store and post office floundered, she opened The Hutte Restaurant to safeguard the building. In 1969, she began talking to local families to gather recipes, many of which are the ones that the settlers from Switzerland brought with them when they came to Helvetia a century ago. Says Mrs. Mailloux, "Some of them are 'secret' and have been guarded by the families as fiercely as if they had been stored in a Swiss bank." Her own family's treasure is her grandmother's fondue. Mrs. Mailloux uses locally made cheese, and of course advises others to do the same. The original earthenware Swiss fondue pot was called a caquelon, but the dish is easily made in an enameled pan (one purchased in Helvetia is sure to give the best results). Made over a small burner at the table, fondue is a great party food. If served with a green salad, it's a lovely meal.

1 garlic clove

⅔ cup white wine

6 ounces Gruyère cheese, shredded (about 1½ cups)

6 ounces Emmentaler cheese, shredded (about 1½ cups)

¼ cup Kirsch or other cherry-flavored brandy

2 teaspoons cornstarch

½ teaspoon freshly grated nutmeg

1 loaf rustic bread, cut into 1-inch cubes

1. Rub the interior of a traditional fondue pot or enameled pan with the garlic clove, set the fondue pot over a spirit heater or set the pan over hot water to make a double boiler.

2. Add the wine to the pot and heat until warm. Stir in the Gruyère and Emmentaler and heat until melted. Add the Kirsch, cornstarch, and nutmeg and cook, stirring constantly, about 5 minutes, until the mixture comes to a simmer.

3. To serve, if using a traditional fondue pot, set it and the spirit heater on the table. If using an enameled pot, set the pot on the table on a hot plate. Keep the fondue at a simmer, stirring occasionally. Use a fondue fork (or any long-handled fork) to spear the bread cubes and dip them into the simmering cheese.

SERVES 2 TO 4

Georgie's Little Caramelized Onion and Feta Tarts

VENICE, CALIFORNIA

Australian-born cinematographer and producer Georgie Smith hopes to be known for her television projects such as *Noble Women*, *The Rhymatist*, and *No Right Turn*, but she already has Plan B in place. The small tarts that she offers with drinks or with a salad make a light meal achieve the impossible: they have a deep, earthy flavor but are light enough to fly. "My onion tart has evolved into something that caused a worldly guest to say not long ago, 'If you do nothing else in your life, that tart would be an extraordinary legacy.'"

1 tablespoon olive oil

1 large onion, finely chopped

1 large red onion, finely chopped

1 tablespoon honey

4 garlic cloves, minced

8 ounces feta cheese, crumbled (about 2 cups)

½ cup chopped fresh parsley

¼ cup chopped fresh basil

1 large egg

One 9- x 9½-inch sheet frozen puff pastry, thawed, or homemade puff pastry

2 ounces Parmesan cheese, grated (about ½ cup)

2 cups baby arugula

1 teaspoon highest-quality balsamic vinegar

Freshly ground black pepper

1. In a large skillet, heat the oil over medium heat. Add the onions and cook, stirring occasionally, about 4 minutes, until soft. Stir in the honey and cook for 4 to 6 minutes more, until the onions are golden brown. Stir in the garlic and cook about 1 minute, until aromatic. Transfer the onions to a medium bowl and cool to room temperature.

2. While the caramelized onions cool, place an oven rack in the center position and preheat the oven to 425°F.

3. Stir the feta, parsley, basil, and egg into the onions.

4. Cut the pastry sheet into six 3- x 4¾-inch rectangles and transfer to a parchment paper–lined baking sheet. Bake for 6 to 8 minutes, until light golden brown. Sprinkle the Parmesan evenly over the tarts and bake about 5 minutes more, until the cheese is melted.

5. Spoon the onion-feta mixture on top of the Parmesan and bake for 10 to 15 minutes more, until the pastry is golden brown.

6. Remove from the oven and transfer the tarts to a platter or individual serving plates. Arrange the arugula evenly on top. Drizzle with the vinegar, sprinkle with pepper, and serve.

SERVES 6

THE ORIGINAL DEVILED EGG

KANSAS CITY, MISSOURI

How deviled food got its name seems straightforward enough. Before refrigeration, food preservation relied for centuries on a number of techniques including hot spices. The word "devil" was in use by 1800 to refer to foods made hot by mustard, cayenne peppers, or vinegar. Deviled foods—particularly eggs—are on the wane in Europe, but in America, after the introduction of mass-produced mayonnaise and mustard, they became essential to picnics and big summer parties. Even the antifat, anticholesterol movement of the late twentieth century failed to extinguish the American soft spot for deviled eggs. To celebrate this, the Southern Foodways Alliance held a Deviled Eggs Contest in 2004. Entries ranged from the simple (from finalist Robert Croft of Kansas City, Missouri, with just "mayonnaise, sweet pickle relish, a tad of dry mustard, perhaps a little black pepper, and the salt adjusted depending on the saltiness of the mayonnaise") to the exotic (Madras curry and shad roe) to the quirky (jalapeños and salsa).

Regardless of the variations, modern deviled eggs have one common ingredient: a surfeit of jarred mayonnaise. However, the earliest American recipes for deviled eggs, like this one adapted from *Common Sense in the Household: A Manual of Practical Housewifery* (1882), do not use mayonnaise at all.

6 large eggs, hard boiled, cooled, peeled, and halved lengthwise

1 tablespoon unsalted butter, melted

1 teaspoon white vinegar

¼ teaspoon mustard powder

⅛ teaspoon cayenne pepper

¼ teaspoon kosher salt

¼ teaspoon freshly ground black pepper

¼ teaspoon sugar

1 bunch watercress, washed, tough stems discarded and leaves roughly chopped, for garnish

1. Gently remove the egg yolks from the whites and place them in a small bowl. Add the butter and mix to a paste. Stir in a dash of the vinegar, the mustard powder, and the cayenne.

2. Spoon or pipe the egg yolk mixture into the egg white halves.

3. In a medium bowl, mix the remaining vinegar with the salt, black pepper, and sugar. Add the watercress and toss until coated with the vinegar mixture. Arrange the watercress on a serving platter and nestle the deviled eggs onto the greens. Serve.

SERVES 6

Elisabetta Lecce Baiamonte's Devilish Eggs

Elisabetta Lecce arrived in New Orleans in 1916 when she was 18. She wanted to be an American without forgetting her Sicilian heritage, and the kitchen turned out to be the easiest place to meld both worlds into an easy alliance. Her Devilish Eggs, served on a nest of chopped radicchio and lettuce, are a good example, and her granddaughter, Elizabeth Williams, believes she began making the dish in the 1940s. When Ms. Williams entered them in the Deviled Eggs Invitational held by the Southern Foodways Alliance, people were horrified that they did not contain mayonnaise. She says they insisted that these "just don't taste like deviled eggs." Mayonnaise easily spoils in the hot New Orleans summer, and Ms. Williams says her grandmother "simply craved these flavors." More open-minded souls will find them a delicious accompaniment to cocktails.

12 large eggs, hard boiled, cooled, peeled, and halved lengthwise

3 anchovy fillets, drained

3 tablespoons minced black olives

2 garlic cloves, minced

½ teaspoon grated lemon zest

½ cup extra virgin olive oil

Tabasco sauce

Kosher salt and freshly ground black pepper

Shredded lettuce and radicchio, for garnish

Smoked paprika, for garnish

2 tablespoons minced fresh basil or parsley, for garnish

1. Gently remove the egg yolks from the whites and place them in a small bowl. Add the anchovies and mash. Stir in the olives, garlic, and lemon zest. Stirring constantly, gradually add the olive oil and stir until the mixture is thick. Season with hot sauce, salt, and pepper to taste.

2. Spoon or pipe the egg yolk mixture into the egg white halves. Arrange the lettuce on a platter and nestle the deviled eggs onto the greens. Sprinkle with paprika and basil and serve.

SERVES 12

29

Nibbles, Noshes, and Tasty Little Plates

NONNIE ROBINSON'S PECAN CRISPIES

After elementary school teacher Nonnie Robinson retired, she became a professional storyteller—stories about "people I have known or wish I had known," she says. Pecans appear with surprising regularity. Ms. Robinson remembers running into the road to collect the nuts after their shells had been cracked by passing automobiles, and shelling them on her porch. Perhaps, half a century from now, another generation will remember the pecan crispies that Ms. Robinson gives as gifts. The sweet, glazed nuts have a hot little kick and are pretty darned addictive.

Nonstick cooking spray

3 large egg whites

2 pounds pecan halves

2 teaspoons garlic salt

¼ teaspoon cayenne pepper

1. Place an oven rack in the center position and preheat the oven to 275°F. Lightly coat a large baking sheet with cooking spray.

2. In a large bowl, whip the egg whites with an electric mixer until stiff peaks form. Gently fold the pecans into the egg whites. Spread in a single layer on the prepared baking sheet.

3. In a small bowl, combine the garlic salt and cayenne. Sprinkle the mixture evenly over the pecans and toss to coat. Spread the pecans in a single layer again and bake for 30 to 40 minutes, until crisp, dry, and crunchy, turning with a spatula halfway through baking. (Don't let the pecans get dark brown.)

4. Transfer the baking sheet to a wire rack and let the nuts cool about 10 minutes. Break apart the clumps of nuts, then turn the nuts with a spatula every 10 minutes or so to make sure they don't stick together as they cool. Serve.

MAKES ABOUT 8 CUPS

NOTE: The pecans can be stored in an airtight container at room temperature up to two weeks.

TODD PORTER'S GINGER AND GARLIC ROASTED PEANUTS

Todd Porter grew up on a cattle ranch in Elgin, Oregon, and says that when you know quality in one thing, like beef, understanding the difference between good and ordinary ingredients becomes a way of life. Mr. Porter's current area of discernment studies is peanuts. His tutor is his girlfriend, Diane Cu, who was 2 years old when Saigon fell and her parents escaped to Los Angeles. Mr. Porter explains, "Peanuts are the most common and familiar nut in America, but to the Vietnamese, crushed peanuts signal luxury, and they are treated accordingly." In this snack, as a nod to the West he uses the whole nut, which he pan-roasts with Vietnamese seasoning. The recipe can be varied to suit individual tastes, he says, adding: "Once you roast your own, you'll never pop open another can of peanuts again."

2 tablespoons peanut or grapeseed oil

2 tablespoons soy sauce

6 garlic cloves, minced

1 tablespoon grated fresh ginger

1½ teaspoons fish sauce

1½ teaspoons sugar

1 pound shelled raw peanuts

Kosher salt and freshly ground black pepper

1. Place an oven rack in the center position and preheat the oven to 325°F. Line a baking sheet with parchment paper.

2. In a medium bowl, combine the oil, soy sauce, garlic, ginger, fish sauce, and sugar.

3. Spread the nuts in a single layer on the prepared baking sheet and bake for 15 minutes, until aromatic and beginning to brown.

4. Stir the peanuts into the marinade, then pour the mixture back onto the baking sheet. Bake for 10 to 15 minutes more, until the peanuts are light golden brown. (Take them out just before you think they are perfect, because they will continue to cook after being removed from the oven.)

5. Let the peanuts cool, then season with salt and pepper to taste. Serve.

———

MAKES ABOUT 4 CUPS

NOTE: The peanuts can be stored in an airtight container at room temperature up to two weeks.

UNITED STATES OF NUTS

AT TEMPERANCE TEALLEYS AND REVEREND WILLIAM WORTHINGTON'S three-day wedding feast in Stonington, Connecticut, in 1726, platters of oyster and fish, roast fowl and venison, pig and potatoes, and puddings were followed by trays of nutmeats and a molasses brittle made with the indigenous hickory nut. Black walnuts, pecans, and butternuts are also native, but the most popular nuts in the country today are transplants like almonds and pistachios, which, along with more than 80 percent of the nation's edible nuts, are grown in California. Virtually all of the nation's hazelnuts are from Oregon, macadamias come from Hawaii, and Georgia and Texas duel over pecans. Georgia remains the dominant force in peanuts, although peanuts are no strangers to Alabama, Florida, Mississippi, and South Carolina.

MR. PEANUT

Greetings from Mr. Peanut

JAVIER H. FREYRE'S SPANISH-STYLE ALMONDS

LOS ANGELES, CALIFORNIA

When he was a little boy in Spain, Javier Freyre and his grandfather—"a classic vermouth gentleman who always wore a Borsalino hat and carried a walking cane"—shared a ritual: They nibbled fried almonds before lunch or tapas. It became a lifelong habit, and Mr. Freyre has been passing it along to his friends since moving to Los Angeles twenty years ago. It took a little effort to find true Spanish pimentón (paprika)—sweeter, brighter, and smokier than Hungarian varieties—and high quality olive oil. But his favorite Spanish ingredients are not as challenging to find in the United States these days. His friends often have meals made up of little plates as opposed to one large main course.

12 ounces blanched Marcona almonds

¼ cup extra virgin olive oil

Sea salt

Smoked paprika (preferably La Vera de San Juan)

1. In a large saucepan, place the almonds in a single layer, then pour the oil over them. Set the saucepan over medium heat and cook, stirring frequently, about 10 minutes, until the nuts darken slightly. (The oil should be hot but never smoky, no more than 180°F.)

2. Immediately transfer the nuts with a slotted spoon to a plate, season with salt to taste, and cool to room temperature. Season the nuts with smoked paprika and serve.

MAKES ABOUT 3 CUPS

NOTE: The almonds can be stored in an airtight container at room temperature up to two weeks.

One Big Table

A CROSS-COUNTRY TOUR OF MINI SANDWICHES

IN AMERICA, THE SANDWICH HAS ALWAYS HAD A DOUBLE LIFE. EARLY IN OUR NATIONHOOD, it was little more than leftovers layered between two slabs of bread, and they were also a way to use lesser cuts of meat.

By the Civil War, the sandwich had taken its place in polite society. Cookbooks encouraged the use of thinly sliced bread, petit rolls, or even day-old sponge cake, and recommended genteel fillings that could be eaten without a lot of fuss. In taverns and pubs, hefty, meat-laden sandwiches were still the norm.

The British called these portable meals "American sandwiches," although the name had little to do with the ingredients. Americans bestowed the name "club" on any multitiered sandwich. Creators or geography became names: The Hot Brown was a toasted sandwich first made at Brown's Hotel in Louisville, Kentucky. Others, like the Hot Dago—Italian Parmesan cheese, ground meat, and bread crumbs—employed an ethnic slur. Still others showcase regional specialties: The Reuben presents the corned beef of New York City's Lower East Side Jewish delis but adds "uptown" (non-kosher) cheese, sauerkraut, and creamy dressing; the lobster roll is a simple homage to Maine's famed crustacean; and the muffuletta is an embarrassment of salumeria riches attesting to New Orleans's old and well-established Italian roots.

The early twentieth-century mass production of bread pushed national sandwich consumption up to about 200 per person per year, and that number has remained steady, even as Americans reinterpret sandwiches and serve them as party fare. Cucumber sandwiches with an Indian twist might add spice to a ladies' luncheon, while arepas (a South American corncake) can be used to reinvent grilled cheese.

Roopa Unnikrishnan's Cucumber Pudina Sandwiches

Roopa Unnikrishnan, a former Rhodes scholar and a senior vice president of a pharmaceutical company in New York, was born in southern India and cooks to bridge both worlds. Before the birth of her twins, cooking and "home arts" were the furthest things from her mind. But, she says, "When kids come along, you want to give them tradition, you want to give them a taste-memory and association to their native foods, so I started cooking more." In order to include her parents in India in the daily life of her family, Ms. Unnikrishnan began cataloging her kitchen experiments online. On warm Indian evenings she used to have cucumber pudina sandwiches, which were likely a take on the colonial idea of "afternoon tea." Today she often tucks them into her children's lunch boxes or serves them as a party appetizer.

FOR THE PUDINA PASTE

1 packed cup fresh mint leaves

½ packed cup fresh cilantro leaves

¼ cup fresh lemon juice

¼ cup unsweetened grated coconut

1 teaspoon sesame seeds

1 jalapeño chile, stemmed

½ teaspoon grated fresh ginger

FOR THE SANDWICHES

4 tablespoons (½ stick) unsalted butter, softened

12 thin slices good quality white sandwich bread

5 small Kirby cucumbers, peeled, halved lengthwise, seeded, and thinly sliced

Kosher salt and freshly ground black pepper

1. To make the pudina paste: In a food processor, process all of the ingredients into a slightly coarse paste.

2. To make the sandwiches: Spread 1 teaspoon butter on each slice of bread. Spread a thin layer of the pudina paste on top of the butter on 6 of the slices, then arrange 4 to 6 cucumber slices on top. Sprinkle the cucumbers with salt and pepper. Place the remaining slices of bread on top, buttered side down, to make 6 sandwiches.

3. Trim the crusts, cut each sandwich into four triangles, and serve.

SERVES 6 TO 8

NOTE: The paste can be refrigerated in an airtight container up to one week.

TINY MAINE LOBSTER ROLLS À LA WATERMAN'S

Four miles outside the fishing village of South Thomaston, Maine, a tree-lined road meanders toward a tiny peninsula where a weathered, gray-shingled beach shack crouches beside the cold blue surf. The shack, like the road, bears the family name and is located at the edge of a twenty-five-acre plot that has been in the Waterman family for more than 200 years. The land is dotted with eleven homes where members of the clan still live. And shaded by an awning, visitors and locals flock to the shack for the quintessential "taste of Maine summer." The signature roll recipe, handed down through the generations, is as unembellished as a Downeaster's speech: mayonnaise, absolutely fresh lobster, and a buttered soft roll, preferably a hot dog roll. Clam and lobster shacks like this one are plentiful along Maine's coast, but only the Waterman's lobster roll has been celebrated as an American Classic by the James Beard Foundation.

One 1¼-pound soft-shell lobster, steamed
   and cooled

2 to 3 tablespoons mayonnaise

Kosher salt and freshly ground black pepper

4 tablespoons (½ stick) unsalted butter, softened

16 small (2-ounce) buns or rolls, split (or 2 half
   slices of white bread, crust removed)

1. Pick all the meat from the lobster and place in a large bowl, discarding the shells. Stir the mayonnaise into the lobster, 1 tablespoon at a time, until it holds together in a loose "salad." Season with salt and pepper to taste.

2. Butter both sides of each bun. Divide the lobster mixture evenly on the bottoms of the buns and cover with the tops.

3. Heat a griddle or large nonstick skillet over medium heat. Place the sandwiches on the griddle and cook, pressing lightly on the buns, about 2 minutes on each side, until the buns begin to crisp. Serve.

SERVES 8

DANIELA SALES'S BOSNIAN ĆEVAPI

"Asking for a ćevapi recipe in Bosnia is a little bit like asking for a pasta sauce recipe in Italy," says Daniela Sales, a 31-year-old herbalist who came to America with her family from Bosnia and Herzegovina as war refugees in the early 1990s. Every city and town and almost every family has its own variation on the theme. Just as American kids play in the yard during barbecues, she and her friends and cousins used to play in ćevapi aroma–filled air at family gatherings. After the war, forty to sixty Bosnians settled in St. Louis. Today, the city has one of the largest Bosnian populations in the nation, and its annual street festival is where Ms. Sales takes her 5-year-old son to sample different versions of ćevapi.

¾ pound 85% lean ground beef

¾ pound ground lamb

1 small onion, finely chopped

4 garlic cloves, minced

1 tablespoon minced fresh parsley

½ teaspoon kosher salt

¼ teaspoon freshly ground black pepper

¼ teaspoon chili powder

¼ cup sparkling mineral water (preferably Perrier)

Vegetable oil, as needed

Scallions, green parts only, thinly sliced, for garnish

Sour cream, for garnish

1. In a large bowl, mix together the beef and lamb. Add the onion, garlic, parsley, salt, pepper, and chili powder and knead well until combined. Add the water, cover, and refrigerate for 2 to 3 hours.

2. Shape the meat mixture into 18 oblong patties about 2 inches long and ½ inch thick.

3. Heat a grill or grill pan over medium-high heat and lightly brush with oil. Cook the patties for 8 to 10 minutes, until well browned on both sides and cooked through. Sprinkle with the scallions and serve with sour cream.

MAKES 18 PATTIES; SERVES 6

SUSMITA SHARMA'S SHAMI SLIDERS

From the time she was in grade school, Susmita Sharma has been a secret foodie. Raised in a strictly vegetarian Hindu home in Pune and New Delhi, India, Ms. Sharma first tasted meat kebabs at a friend's home. The 10-year-old was thrilled by the idea of the forbidden food, even though she expected her mother to disapprove. Instead, her mother—an English teacher who pushed her children to experience new things—told her daughter that if she liked kebabs, she should eat kebabs.

Traveling the world to pursue her education (Ms. Sharma is a molecular biologist), she sampled dozens of different cuisines before settling in Seattle fifteen years ago. As precise a cook as she is a scientist, Ms. Sharma, now 37 years old, cooks her life. Here she has combined brioche with shami (lamb) kebabs to create an appetizer that is more American slider than the secret favorite of a little Hindu girl in India.

FOR THE LAMB KEBABS

½ pound ground lamb

½ cup finely chopped onion

½ cup plus 1 tablespoon water

⅓ cup red lentils (*masoor dal*)

3 garlic cloves, minced

1 teaspoon grated fresh ginger

1 teaspoon kosher salt

One 1-inch piece cinnamon stick, finely chopped or ground in a spice mill

¼ teaspoon cayenne pepper

¼ teaspoon ground cumin

¼ teaspoon ground coriander

⅛ teaspoon freshly ground black pepper

Pinch of ground cloves

All-purpose flour, as needed

1 large egg

1 cup slivered almonds, finely chopped

2 tablespoons vegetable oil

FOR THE SAUCE

1 cup yogurt cheese (lebni or kefir cheese)

1 small shallot, minced

2 tablespoons fresh lemon juice

2 tablespoons minced fresh cilantro

2 teaspoons minced fresh mint

Kosher salt

FOR THE SANDWICHES

1 loaf brioche, cut into ½-inch-thick slices and toasted

4 cups baby salad greens

1 teaspoon olive oil

Pinch of kosher salt

1. Place the oven racks in the bottom and top positions and preheat the oven to 200°F.

2. To make the lamb kebabs: In a large skillet, combine the lamb, onion, ½ cup water, the lentils, garlic, ginger, salt, cinnamon, cayenne, cumin, coriander, black pepper, and cloves. Bring to a simmer, cover, and cook about 20 minutes, until the lamb and lentils are cooked through. Uncover and cook for 3 to 5 minutes more, until any excess water is evaporated.

3. Transfer the meat mixture to a food processor and process into a paste. It should be thick enough to shape into balls. If the mixture is too wet, add a few tablespoons of flour.

4. Using a spoon or ice-cream scoop, portion the mixture into 1-inch balls, then flatten into patties approximately 1½ inches in diameter.

5. In a small bowl, beat together the egg and the remaining 1 tablespoon water. Place the almonds in a shallow bowl. Dip the kebabs in the egg, then roll in the almonds to coat.

6. Heat 1 tablespoon of the oil in a large nonstick skillet over medium heat. Add 8 kebabs and cook about 4 minutes, until well browned on both sides. Transfer the patties to a baking sheet and keep warm in the oven until ready to serve. Wipe out the skillet and repeat with the remaining 1 tablespoon oil and kebabs.

7. To make the sauce: In a small bowl, stir together the yogurt cheese, shallot, lemon juice, cilantro, and mint. Season with salt to taste, cover, and refrigerate.

8. To make the sandwiches: Using a 2-inch biscuit cutter, cut the toasted brioche into circles. Place the brioche rounds on a wire rack set over a baking sheet and keep warm in the oven until needed.

9. Toss the greens with the olive oil and salt. Top each brioche round with a generous teaspoon of the yogurt sauce then place a lamb kebab. Dollop a small amount of the yogurt sauce on top of each kebab, then top with the greens, and serve.

SERVES 4 TO 6

NOTES: Both the meat paste and the sauce can be stored in an airtight container in the refrigerator up to one day. Let the meat paste come to room temperature before forming the kebabs.

THE EVER-ADAPTABLE DOG

MARK REITMAN BEGAN SERVING HOT DOGS AT HIS dad's pharmacy in Chicago fifty-four years ago. It must have been a seminal experience for the 8-year-old, because after a twenty-five-year career as a school guidance counselor, he retired, bought a cart, and peddled Chicago-style hot dogs on weekends at the Prime Outlets mall in Pleasant Prairie, Wisconsin. After people asked him about starting and franchising a hot dog business, he established Hot Dog University, a two-day course that covers all aspects of the hot dog cart business. He taught a handful of students once a month, including both book work and "field work" peddling dogs.

Mr. Reitman sees hot dogs as the quintessential American food. Historians would agree. We eat just over 20 billion of them a year. Often called the original fun food, they are inseparable from ballparks, picnics, boardwalks, barbecues, and big-city sidewalks coast to coast. Mr. Reitman divides these dogs into three categories: the Chicago dog—always pure beef with a natural casing, served on a steamed poppy seed bun with yellow mustard, neon-green pickle relish, chopped onions, two tomato wedges, a kosher dill pickle spear, two sport peppers, and a dash of celery salt; the Southern dog—a mixture of beef and pork served on a bun with coleslaw, chili, onions, and ketchup; and the New York dog—all beef or a mixture of pork and beef, held in "dirty water" (hot water laced with the spices leached from the dogs) and dressed with red onion sauce, sauerkraut, brown mustard, and chopped onions. He cautions, "Always dress the dog, not the bun."

Regional variations abound. There is the Seattle Dog (cream cheese, onions, and mustard) and the L.A. Mexican cart dog, served with salsa and Queso Blanco. One of Mr. Reitman's friends, Jim Pittinger, owner of Biker Jim's Hotdogs, spreads cream cheese on his pheasant dogs with a caulk gun, then tops them with chopped jalapeños. "When I ask people if they want cream cheese on their dogs, they usually say no right off. Then I ask them if they like cheeseburgers and usually they say yes. So I point out that a hot dog is nothing more than a 'linkburger' and that the flavors are much the same, so why not give it a try."

DOUG DUCAP'S MINI FALAFEL DOGS

CHARLESTON, SOUTH CAROLINA

In late 2004, New Jersey–born Doug DuCap, his wife Tabetha Dunn, and their spaniel, Penny the Wonderdog, took to the road in a vintage thirty-four-foot motor home. Three years later, the former Fortune 100 company manager, New York cabbie, literary journal editor, barista in northern Spain, and tobacco harvester, "and a lot more," showed up tending bar on James Island, South Carolina. There he conjured a chili that won the Taste of the South cooking competition sponsored by Piggly Wiggly grocery stores. His secret ingredient is boiled peanuts.

Corn dogs—skewered wieners covered in cornmeal batter, then deep fried—are another southern "delicacy" that Mr. DuCap considers wrongly maligned by folks up north. Never content to leave well enough alone, he developed a healthy alternative, creating the falafel dog: a ground lamb kebab coated with falafel batter and lightly pan-fried. Mr. DuCap makes them bite-size, and serves them as appetizers with his date yogurt and hazelnut dipping sauces on the side.

FOR THE FALAFEL BATTER

½ cup water, plus more as needed

½ teaspoon baking soda

1 cup dried chickpeas, soaked in cold water overnight or in boiling water for 3 hours

6 scallions, green and white parts, finely chopped

⅓ cup minced fresh parsley

¼ cup chickpea flour

6 garlic cloves, minced

1½ teaspoons ground coriander

1 teaspoon ground cumin

½ teaspoon kosher salt

2 large eggs, lightly beaten

FOR THE SAUSAGES

1 pound lean ground lamb

2 small inner celery stalks with leaves, minced

6 garlic cloves, minced

2 tablespoons chopped dried apricots

2 tablespoons minced fresh parsley

2 tablespoons minced fresh cilantro

4 teaspoons whole cumin seeds, lightly toasted

2 teaspoons fresh lemon juice

1 teaspoon kosher salt

1 teaspoon freshly ground black pepper

½ teaspoon ground cinnamon

½ teaspoon cayenne pepper

32 short bamboo skewers or long bamboo skewers cut into thirty-two 4-inch lengths and soaked in water for about 1 hour

Vegetable oil, for frying

Spiced Date-Coriander Yogurt or Hazelnut-Cashew Tarator (recipes follow), for serving

1. To make the falafel batter: In a small bowl, mix together ½ cup water and the baking soda. Drain the chickpeas well, transfer to a food processor, and process it about 30 seconds, until grainy. Add the baking soda water, scallions, parsley, chickpea flour, garlic, coriander, cumin, salt, and eggs and process until smooth. Blend in more water as needed until the batter reaches the consistency of mustard. Refrigerate the batter.

2. To make the sausages: Mix together the lamb, celery, garlic, apricots, parsley, cilantro, cumin, lemon juice, salt, black pepper, cinnamon, and cayenne until well combined. Scoop out 32 rounded tablespoons of the mixture and roll them gently between your palms to form cigar shapes about 2 ½ inches long. Insert a skewer into each sausage.

3. Heat a grill pan over high heat and grill the sausages about 3 minutes, until just cooked through. Transfer the sausages to a baking sheet and let cool slightly.

4. Use a deep fryer or pour enough oil into a Dutch oven to come ½ inch up the sides. Heat the oil to 360°F. Line a plate with several layers of paper towels.

5. Dip each sausage into the batter and use a butter knife to spread it evenly over the sausage. Gently lay the skewers into the oil a few at a time. Cook about 4 minutes, until well browned, turning with tongs as needed. Transfer to a paper-towel-lined plate to drain briefly, and repeat with the remaining skewers.

6. Serve with one of the dipping sauces.

MAKES 32 SAUSAGES, SERVES 8 TO 10

NOTE: The falafel batter can be used to make traditional falafel patties by omitting the water (add the baking soda with the other ingredients) and processing to a thick paste. Form the mixture into 2-inch-wide patties about ½ inch thick, and panfry until golden brown on both sides. Serve them on ciabatta bread, dressed with mint leaves, olive oil, and fresh lemon juice and topped with thinly sliced cucumbers, peppery sprouts, and Hazelnut-Cashew Tarator; serve alongside assorted olives, sliced plum tomatoes, and goat cheese.

Spiced Date-Coriander Yogurt

This recipe can be doubled. It also makes a wonderful companion for spicy grilled meat.

¾ cup plain yogurt

⅓ cup chopped pitted dates

1 teaspoon ground coriander

⅛ teaspoon cayenne pepper

Pinch of kosher salt

Pinch of freshly ground multicolor pepper (pink, green, white) or freshly ground white pepper

In a food processor, process all of the ingredients about 30 seconds, until smooth. Cover and refrigerate.

MAKES ABOUT 1 CUP

Hazelnut-Cashew Tarator

This recipe can be doubled, and is delicious with grilled chicken as well.

¾ cup very finely ground blanched hazelnuts

¼ cup very finely ground cashews

1 tablespoon extra virgin olive oil

1 garlic clove, minced

½ teaspoon dried thyme, crushed

2 tablespoons fresh lemon juice

2 tablespoons water

Kosher salt

In a mortar and pestle or food processor, grind the hazelnuts, cashews, oil, garlic, and thyme into a fine paste. Transfer the mixture to a small bowl and gradually stir in the lemon juice and water until emulsified. Season with salt to taste. Cover and refrigerate.

MAKES ABOUT 1 CUP

THE SURMAS' PIEROGI

For the past twenty-five years, Anna Surma, her husband, John, and their friends have gathered to make traditional Polish cuisine. The secret to the delicious results is a combination of dogged practice and the liberal use of their "secret ingredient"—shots of Polish vodka for the cook. "We have a collective knowledge here that keeps the old recipes alive," said Mrs. Surma, an architect. She and her husband are the acknowledged pierogi experts. He began rolling the dumpling dough twenty-five years ago when his ailing mother, a Polish émigrée, longed for the food of her youth. She had a gift for motivating "stuffers." Pierogi are a group activity and can be made ahead and frozen, though Mr. Surma prefers to boil his dumplings on the spot. It's best for the dough, which he refers to as a person, as in: "Hold him up to the light and you can see through him."

FOR THE FILLING

2½ pounds Yukon gold potatoes, peeled and cut into 2-inch chunks

6 tablespoons (¾ stick) unsalted butter, softened

1 medium onion, finely chopped

2 pounds soft farmer's cheese

Kosher salt and freshly ground black pepper

FOR THE DOUGH

3 cups unbleached all-purpose flour, plus more as needed

2 large whole eggs plus 1 large egg, separated

2 tablespoons milk

Pinch of kosher salt

FOR SERVING

4 tablespoons (½ stick) unsalted butter, plus more as needed

1 medium onion, finely chopped

1. To make the filling: In a large saucepan, cover the potatoes with water. Bring to a simmer and cook for 15 to 20 minutes, until tender.

2. While the potatoes are cooking, melt 1 tablespoon of the butter in a medium skillet over medium heat. Add the onion and cook for 4 minutes, stirring occasionally, until soft.

3. Drain the potatoes and mash them with the remaining 5 tablespoons butter. Stir the onion into the mashed potatoes. Stir in the cheese until well mixed. Season with salt and pepper to taste. (The trick is to overly salt the filling slightly since some of the salt will leach out into the boiling water.)

4. To make the dough: Mound the flour in the middle of a large cutting board or other dry work surface. Create a well in the middle and add the whole eggs, egg yolk, milk, and salt. Knead the ingredients together, adding water as needed, about 10 minutes, until a soft, slightly sticky dough forms.

5. Line a baking sheet with parchment paper and lightly flour the paper. Divide the dough into six equal pieces. Cover the dough with a kitchen towel. Using a heavy wooden rolling pin and working with one piece of dough at a time, roll the dough on a lightly floured work surface until it is very thin. (You should be able to see light coming through it.) Using a 3-inch biscuit cutter, cut the dough into rounds. Discard any scraps. Place the dough rounds on the prepared baking sheet in a single layer; as you fill the sheet, cover with another piece of parchment paper; lightly flour the paper before adding another layer of dough rounds. Cover the rounds with a kitchen towel and repeat with the remaining dough.

6. Line another baking sheet with parchment paper and lightly beat the egg white just enough to mix it.

7. To shape the pierogi, working with one dough round at a time, lightly brush outside edge with the egg white. Cup the round in your hand, spoon about 1 tablespoon of filling into the center, fold to make a half moon and pinch the dough around the filling to create a tight seal. As each of the pierogi is finished, place it on the second baking sheet. Cover the finished pierogi with a kitchen towel. Repeat with the remaining dough and filling.

8. To cook the pierogi, bring a large pot of salted water to a boil. Add one-third of the pierogi and cook about 4 minutes, until tender. Using a large wire skimmer, transfer the pierogi to a large colander to drain. Return the water to a boil and repeat with the remaining pierogi in two batches.

Nibbles, Noshes, and Tasty Little Plates

9. For serving: While the pierogi are boiling, melt the butter in a large skillet over medium heat. Add the onion and cook about 8 minutes, stirring occasionally, until golden brown.

10. Add the drained pierogi to the onion and cook for 4 to 6 minutes, turning them over gently, until light golden brown. Add additional butter if the pan seems dry. Serve hot.

MAKES ABOUT 4 DOZEN PIEROGIS

MONA'S IRON RANGE PASTIES

The business cards on the kitchen counter in her suburban home in Minnesota's Iron Range read "Mona Abel, Food Goddess, Former Go-Go Dancer." Next to the cards are her self-published books, displayed with their price tags ($25). Ms. Abel, who is a product of what is locally referred to as a "mixed marriage" (her mother is English; her father, Finnish), is a staunch Anglophile and is famous for her pasties. The savory turnovers were brought to northern Minnesota by Cornish miners, and Ms. Able has made sure that neither local church suppers nor the regular meetings of her Red Bra Society (for women who do not have to learn how to have fun) lack them. At the former, she serves tea from Harrods; at the latter, everyone gets a jigger of ice-cold vodka on the side.

FOR THE DOUGH

4 cups unbleached all-purpose flour, plus more as needed

1 tablespoon kosher salt

8 ounces lard, cut into small pieces

1 cup cold water, plus more as needed

Water, for sealing

FOR THE FILLING

2 medium Yukon gold potatoes, peeled and cut into ½-inch pieces

½ pound top round steak, cut into ½-inch pieces

1 medium onion, finely chopped

1 small rutabaga, peeled and shredded

6 tablespoons (¾ stick) unsalted butter, cut into ½-inch pieces

1 teaspoon kosher salt

½ teaspoon freshly ground black pepper

1. Place an oven rack in the center position and preheat the oven to 425°F. Line two baking sheets with parchment paper.

2. To make the dough: In a large bowl, whisk together the flour and salt. Cut the lard into the flour until the dough forms balls the size of peas. Gradually add the water, stirring until the dough comes together and is slightly sticky. Divide the dough into six balls and cover with a kitchen towel.

3. To make the filling: In a large bowl, toss the potatoes, steak, onion, rutabaga, butter, salt, and pepper together.

4. To assemble the pasties: On a floured work surface, roll each dough ball into a 10-inch circle. Lightly brush the edges of the dough with water. Place a generous cup of the filling on one side of each circle, then fold the dough over the filling to make a half-moon shape. Press the edges together to seal, then crimp or flute the edges. Transfer the pasties to the prepared baking sheets.

5. Bake the pasties for 30 minutes. Reduce the temperature to 400°F and bake for 25 to 30 minutes more, until golden brown. Serve warm or at room temperature.

SERVES 6

Ilhan Omar's Somali Sambusa

COLUMBIA HEIGHTS, MINNESOTA

Every year at Ramadan, Ilhan Omar makes more than 100 sambusas, fried pockets filled with beef and onion that Muslims eat at sundown to break their daylong fast. Ms. Omar's family fled Somalia after the civil war in the 1990s, and making sambusas reminds her of the miracle of her escape. Now a wife, mother, and nutrition educator, she found a sambusa shortcut that she can live with: Instead of making the dough from scratch, she uses store-bought Chinese egg roll wrappers. "And you know what?" says Ms. Omar. "They taste better!"

Vegetable oil

1 medium onion, finely chopped

½ pound 85% lean ground beef

2 tablespoons dried parsley

1 teaspoon curry powder, plus more to taste

1 garlic clove, minced

1 teaspoon kosher salt

½ teaspoon freshly ground black pepper

1 package egg roll wrappers

Water, for sealing

1. In a large skillet, heat 1 tablespoon oil over medium heat. Add the onion and cook about 4 minutes, stirring occasionally, until soft. Stir in the beef, parsley, curry powder, garlic, salt, and pepper, and cook about 5 minutes, stirring to break up lumps, until the meat is no longer pink. Taste and add more curry powder if you want. Transfer the meat mixture to a medium bowl and cool to room temperature. Wipe out the skillet.

2. Line a baking sheet with parchment paper. Cut each egg roll wrapper in half diagonally. Working with one triangle at a time, lightly brush the edges of the wrapper with water. Fold the long side of the triangle in half, pinching the edge to seal and form a little cup.

3. Place a generous tablespoon of the meat mixture into the cup, then pull the open flap of the wrapper over the cup, pressing to seal. As each sambusa is finished, place it on the baking sheet. When the sheet is full, cover the sambusas with another piece of parchment paper and continue layering with finished sambusas.

4. Line a platter with several layers of paper towels. In the skillet, heat about 1 inch of oil until a deep-frying thermometer reads 365°F to 375°F, or a pinch of flour bubbles and sizzles in the oil. Add half of the sambusas to the oil and cook for 2 to 4 minutes, turning once, until golden brown on both sides. Using tongs or a skimmer, transfer the sambusas to the paper-towel-lined platter to drain briefly. Repeat with the remaining sambusas. Serve.

SERVES 4 TO 6

Nibbles, Noshes, and Tasty Little Plates

Louise Etoch's Lamb-Stuffed Grape Leaves

When Louise Brown married Mike Etoch, she had to learn to cook Lebanese food. Fortunately, her mother-in-law lived two blocks away and was a sympathetic cook; Adele Hesni Etoch had learned the family recipes the same way when she was a young bride. Before her mother-in-law died, Louise had mastered kibbe, stuffed squash, grape leaves, tabbouleh, and roasted leg of lamb—not bad for a Scotch-Irish girl from Fayetteville. She makes these dishes for family celebrations. These days, she even picks grape leaves in the fall to make this wonderful dish.

1 pound ground lamb

⅔ cup long grain rice, rinsed

½ cup fresh lemon juice

1 tablespoon finely chopped fresh mint

½ teaspoon kosher salt

¼ teaspoon freshly ground black pepper

Pinch of ground cinnamon

One 16-ounce jar grape leaves in brine, well rinsed and stemmed

1 lemon, thinly sliced

2 tablespoons olive oil

1½ cups homemade chicken broth or low-sodium store-bought chicken broth

Yogurt cheese, for garnish

1. In a large bowl, combine the lamb, rice, 3 tablespoons of the lemon juice, the mint, salt, pepper, and cinnamon until the mixture is blended but still loose.

2. Lay out one grape leaf on the work surface, vein side up. Shape a generous tablespoon of meat mixture into a 1½-inch-long cylinder and place on the lower third of the leaf. Roll once, fold in both sides, and continue rolling upward to close. Place seam side down in a large saucepan.

3. Repeat with the remaining grape leaves and meat mixture to make three layers, arranging the rolls in each layer neatly and alternating the direction of each layer.

4. Lay a few grape leaves on the top of the last layer, pressing them flat. Arrange the lemon slices over the top. Drizzle with the olive oil, then pour the remaining lemon juice and the chicken broth evenly over everything. Top with a plate that fits down inside the pan and sits securely on the rolls.

5. Bring to a simmer over medium heat, then reduce the heat to low, cover, and cook for 40 minutes. Serve at room temperature with the yogurt cheese.

———

MAKES ABOUT 3 DOZEN PIECES

Sai Vang's Hmong Egg Rolls

An ethnic Hmong who escaped the Khmer Rouge and immigrated to Minneapolis from Laos in the 1990s, Sai Vang rents a plot of land near St. Paul, Minnesota, and grows traditional vegetables so that her children can have a taste of "home." Her children have offered to buy her modern tools, but Mrs. Vang works her plot with a simple hoe, rake, and shovel. Now that her children are grown, she shares the wealth from her land, selling the vegetables at a farmers' market. She also delivers part of her harvest to her former husband, his second wife, and their children. Once family, forever family. Her light and crispy egg rolls are coveted throughout her extended clan. She adapted the Vietnamese foods she knew in her homeland with the Chinese and Thai flavors she's discovered in St. Paul's immigrant communities. For the Hmong New Year, she triples the recipe and organizes an assembly line of relatives in the kitchen to roll them all.

FOR THE EGG ROLLS

Vegetable oil

2½ pounds lean ground pork

1 large red onion, halved and thinly sliced

2 cups minced fresh cilantro

2 bunches scallions, finely chopped

1 cup minced fresh parsley

¼ cup fish sauce

1 tablespoon oyster sauce

½ teaspoon kosher salt

½ teaspoon freshly ground black pepper

6 large eggs, lightly beaten

8 ounces very thin cellophane noodles (also known as bean thread noodles or mung bean noodles), cooked according to the package directions and cooled to room temperature

3 packages square egg roll wrappers

2 large egg yolks, lightly beaten

FOR THE SPICY SAUCE

½ cup reserved vegetable mixture

¼ cup warm water

2 tablespoons fish sauce

6 small Thai chiles, stemmed, seeded, and finely chopped

Sugar

FOR THE SWEET AND SOUR SAUCE

¼ cup warm water

¼ cup fish sauce

3 tablespoons fresh lime juice

3 tablespoons sugar

2 tablespoons crushed peanuts

2 small Thai chiles, stemmed, seeded, and finely chopped

1. To make the egg rolls: In a large skillet, heat 2 tablespoons oil over medium heat. Add the pork and cook about 5 minutes, stirring to break up lumps, until the meat is no longer pink. Transfer the pork to a bowl and cool to room temperature.

2. In a very large bowl, combine the onion, cilantro, scallion, parsley, fish sauce, oyster sauce, salt, and pepper. Reserve about ½ cup of this mixture for the remaining sauce. Add the pork, eggs, and noodles to the vegetable mixture and mix until combined.

3. To make the spicy sauce: Combine the reserved vegetable mixture with the water, fish sauce, chiles, and sugar to taste.

4. To make the sweet and sour sauce: Combine the water, fish sauce, lime juice, sugar, peanuts, and chiles.

5. Line a baking sheet with parchment paper. Working with one egg roll wrapper at a time, place a wrapper on a work surface with one corner facing you. Place a generous 2 tablespoons of the filling in the center of the skin. Roll the skin over once, enveloping the filling, then fold in the sides. Lightly brush the exposed edges of the wrapper with egg yolk and continue to roll into a cigar shape, pressing to seal the edges. Repeat with remaining wrappers and filling. As each egg roll is finished, place it on the baking sheet. When the sheet is full, cover the egg rolls with another piece of parchment paper and continue layering the finished egg rolls.

6. Line another baking sheet or a platter with several layers of paper towels. In a Dutch oven, heat 2 inches of oil until a deep-frying thermometer reads 350°F. Slide 8 of the egg rolls into the oil and cook for 2 to 4 minutes, turning occasionally with tongs, until golden brown on all sides. Using tongs, transfer the egg rolls to the paper towels to drain. Repeat with the remaining egg rolls in batches and serve with the two dipping sauces.

MAKES ABOUT 3½ DOZEN EGG ROLLS

KIMEE BALMILERO'S KALUA PORK LUMPIA

A Filipina raised in Kaneohe, Hawaii, Kimee Balmilero appeared in the original Broadway cast of *Mamma Mia!* before starting a line of jewelry. She lives in Los Angeles and often uses her father's traditional kalua pork recipe. Many Hawaiians serve the pork in tacos, alongside lomi salmon, or in a lumpia, a Filipino-style egg roll, long and thin like a cigar. She loves kalua pork lumpia best of all—perhaps because the slender rolls unite her Filipino and Hawaiian heritage, perhaps because they are "portable and delicious, which is good for beach trips in Hawaii."

Vegetable oil

1 pound Kalua Pork (page 491), shredded

½ small head green cabbage, shredded (about 2 cups)

Kosher salt and freshly ground black pepper

30 lumpia wrappers

Water, for sealing

1. In a wok or large skillet, heat 1 tablespoon oil over low heat. Add the pork and cabbage and cook about 4 minutes, stirring occasionally, until the cabbage is tender but still has a little crunch. Transfer the mixture to a medium bowl, season with salt and pepper to taste, and cool slightly. Wipe out the wok with a paper towel.

2. Line a baking sheet with parchment paper. Working with one lumpia wrapper at a time, place one on a work surface with a corner facing you. Place a generous 3 tablespoons of the filling in the center of the wrapper. Roll the wrapper over the filling once, then fold in the sides. Lightly brush the exposed edges of the wrapper with water and continue to roll into a cigar, pressing to seal the edges. Repeat with remaining wrappers and filling. As each lumpia is finished, place it on the baking sheet. Keep the lumpia covered with plastic wrap as you work.

3. Line another baking sheet or platter with several layers of paper towels. In the wok, heat ½ inch of oil until a deep-frying thermometer reads 350°F. Slide 10 of the lumpia into the oil and cook for 2 to 4 minutes, turning occasionally with tongs, until golden brown all over. Using tongs, transfer the lumpia to the paper-towel-lined baking sheet to drain briefly. Repeat with the remaining lumpia in two batches, and serve.

MAKES 30 LUMPIA

Nibbles, Noshes, and Tasty Little Plates

Rinaldo Campana's
St. Louis Toasted Ravioli

ST. LOUIS, MISSOURI

When she was a child, every Sunday after church, Donna Drake-Dunninger trooped over to her paternal grandparents' home. The old folks lived on The Hill, the community in St. Louis where Italian immigrants began to settle in the 1890s. Her grandfather Rinaldo Campana was born in Switzerland, and "he made sure to tell you he was born in the Italian part of Switzerland," says Ms. Drake-Dunninger. "He'd owned a restaurant and cooked at the University Club for years, but he spent Sunday making chicken cacciatore and old-fashioned polenta and the St. Louis specialty, fried ravioli, for us." A tradition that she continues, not on Sunday, but whenever she is giving a big party.

1 large egg

1 cup fresh bread crumbs

¼ cup olive oil

1 pound homemade ravioli, thawed if frozen

1 cup homemade tomato sauce, warmed

2 ounces Asiago cheese, grated (about ½ cup)

1. In a shallow bowl, lightly beat the egg. In a second shallow bowl, place the bread crumbs. Line a platter with several layers of paper towels.

2. In a large skillet, heat the oil over medium-high heat. One at a time, dip the ravioli in the egg, then the bread crumbs. Carefully add the ravioli to the oil in batches and cook for 4 to 6 minutes, turning once with tongs, until golden brown and puffy on both sides. Using tongs or a skimmer, transfer the ravioli to the platter to drain briefly.

3. Dip the cooked ravioli in tomato sauce to coat, dip in the cheese, and place on a serving platter. Serve hot.

SERVES 4 TO 6

"Noncooks think it's silly to invest two hours' work in two minutes' enjoyment; but if cooking is evanescent, well, so is the ballet."
—Julia Child

SHEM'S MARINATED BERKELEY CHIPS

Most food historians agree that potato chips were invented in 1853 by George Crum, a part–Native American, part–African American former wilderness guide who was the chef at the Moon Lake Lodge Resort in Saratoga Springs, New York. According to legend, Mr. Crum was "of irascible nature" and responded to a customer's request for crisper fried potatoes with shaved, deep-fried slices. Others credit his sister, Kate Wicks, with slicing a potato so thin that it could be fried crisp. Later William Tappendon, of Cleveland, Ohio, traveled by horse and carriage to deliver chips that he made in his home kitchen.

The mechanical potato peeler, the airtight bag, and the continuous fryer made short work of the small-batch chips in the 1920s. And for the next thirty years, innovations in commercial production provided enough "product" to turn potato chips into the nation's favorite snack. Every year American consumers spend $6 billion on potato chips, and the average American eats sixteen pounds of them a year.

The artisanal chip was reborn in the 1980s, when potato chip fanatics restored dignity to the snack, putting kettles in their garages and using local potatoes. The most successful of these tend to be regional: Cape Cod Potato Chips, Hawaiian Kettle Style Potato Chips, and Route 11 Potato Chips from Mt. Jackson, Virginia, are so good, the only way to improve on the theme is to make your own. That is precisely what Michael Shemchuck, a fine arts painter, does. Served hot, these marinated chips take the idea of deep-fried potato slices to a whole new level. Serve them in brown paper bags at Super Bowl parties or barbecues.

4 large russet potatoes, peeled and sliced about ¹⁄₁₆-inch thick

½ cup kalamata olives, pitted and coarsely chopped

⅓ cup olive oil

4 garlic cloves, minced

2 teaspoons minced fresh rosemary

½ teaspoon grated lemon zest

½ teaspoon kosher salt

¼ teaspoon freshly ground black pepper

1. In a large bowl, toss the potatoes, olives, oil, garlic, rosemary, lemon zest, salt, and pepper together. Cover and let marinate for 30 minutes to 12 hours, stirring occasionally.

2. Place an oven rack in the center position and preheat the oven to 400°F.

3. Place the potato mixture on a baking sheet and distribute in a single layer. Bake about 30 minutes turning once or twice, until crisp. Serve hot.

———

SERVES 4 TO 6

Nibbles, Noshes, and Tasty Little Plates

ELLA'S BETTER THAN ONION SOUP MIX DIP

SHELLEY, IDAHO

Today, rather than finding uses for new convenience products, home cooks try to use old-fashioned, homegrown ingredients to echo—and elevate—icons of the convenience food age. This sour cream dip with caramelized onions and frizzled leeks is a case in point.

Ella McIntyre, a graphic artist, gardener, and cook in Idaho, competed with three other "football widows" to improve on the formula of onion soup mix dip. She was committed to using only ingredients from her garden. The deeply caramelized onions she'd prepared and stored in her refrigerator gave the dip a wonderfully sweet flavor, but, she says, "there was something missing. It didn't really come together until I added a little beef bouillon. A dash of tamari was almost as good."

4 medium yellow onions, peeled and minced by hand

1 garlic clove, peeled

1 tablespoon unsalted butter

Salt and freshly ground pepper to taste

½ teaspoon crushed celery seeds

2 teaspoons beef bouillon powder or crushed bouillon cube

½ teaspoon honey

4 leeks, white parts only, sliced in thin rounds, rinsed well, and dried

½ teaspoon tamari sauce

One 16-ounce container sour cream

1. Place the onions, garlic, and butter in a large skillet over medium-low heat. Season lightly with salt and pepper and cook, stirring frequently, until deep gold, 10 to 15 minutes. Watch carefully to avoid burning. When the onions are soft, add the celery seed, bouillon, honey, and leeks and cook, stirring frequently, until the leeks are soft, about 10 minutes.

2. Transfer the mixture to a mixing bowl, stir in the tamari sauce, and allow to cool. Add the sour cream, taste, and adjust seasoning with additional salt and pepper if desired.

MAKES 3 TO 4 CUPS, ENOUGH FOR 3 POUNDS OF CHIPS

CREAM CHEESE: NOT A PHILADELPHIA STORY

THE 1872 INVENTION OF THE SILVER-WRAPPED BRICKS OF SOFT, FRESH CHEESE— creamier than French Neufchâtel and thicker than Italian mascarpone, its two closest antecedents—was a very American collision of accident, luck, the entrepreneurial spirit, and technology. The story began in the late 1860s on the western fringe of the Catskill Mountains. During the Civil War, bark from the area's hemlock trees had been used to supply leather tanneries, and when the war ended, the region needed new industry. The hilly, rocky soil was good dairy land, but refrigeration was not advanced enough to preserve large quantities of milk for shipment to New York City. Cheese makers in New Jersey had had better luck with a fresh creamy cheese. Legend holds that William A. Lawrence of South Edmeston, New York, overheard the idea and ran with it: He made a rich, spreadable fresh cheese and packaged it in foil. At that time, Philadelphia was a high-society grazing ground and a gourmet mecca so Mr. Lawrence named his cheese "Philadelphia Cream Cheese." It was, however, New York's Eastern European community who embraced the invention—cream cheese could be spread on bagels and used to make the strudels and cheesecakes they missed from home. It could also be piped through a pastry bag to create canapés and made a terrific base for spiced cheese spreads. Kraft purchased the company in 1928, and its modest factory continued to employ 67 of South Edmeston's 206 residents until it was closed by Kraft in 2005.

JUST ADD SOUR CREAM

Like many technical innovations in American food, dehydrated soup was pioneered by the military, then packaged and marketed to the public as early as 1930. But sales were disappointing, and companies like Lipton quickly discovered that home cooks weren't praying to be liberated from the soup pot. Then in 1952, when an anonymous homemaker in Los Angeles stirred dried onion soup mix into sour cream to create a party dip, this unintended and innovative use of a convenience food quickly became the rage, and sales skyrocketed.

The timing was perfect: The suburban lifestyle was taking hold, the cocktail party was replacing the urban barroom, making passable, munchable food as essential as ice cubes. And one night just, at about the time that American women were getting restless at home and beginning to think about a more sweeping liberation, this housewife dared to do something that no one else had done and ended up creating a sensation. Her name was never established, but had she been born forty years later, she might have been crowned the queen of cuisine.

Hearing rumors of the homemade creation, food technologists at Lipton scrambled to establish the precise ratio of mix to sour cream—one packet of soup mix to a pint of sour cream—and printed it on the box. Half a century later, sales of the dried soup—a mixture of dehydrated onion, beef bouillon, onion powder, and, depending on which food-product deconstructionist you talk to, perhaps crushed celery seeds and sugar—are brisk. The Thomas J. Lipton Company estimates that Americans consume a quarter-million packets of its Recipe Secrets Onion Soup Mix daily. Sales are highest during football season—from mid-November to January.

Ourania Kallas's Yia Yia's Weekend Tzatziki Dip

Every year at Christmas, The Cabinet convenes at 85-year-old Ourania Kallas's home. Consisting of Mrs. Kallas—called Yia Yia, the Greek term for grandmother—and seven of her grandchildren, The Cabinet drafts the menus for the Poconos ski weekend that Mrs. Kallas hosts for her three daughters and their families. Once the menus are roughly drawn, it is up to The Cabinet's president and secretary to fine-tune the recipes. They have had Mexican Night, Mediterranean Night, All-Appetizer Night, and Hearty Man Night (all stews). If, after three years of tweaking, a dish is deemed worthy enough, it makes it into The Book, a volume of family recipes that Mrs. Kallas distributes to family members.

Mrs. Kallas also holds an annual cooking class each Christmas season where she teaches the recipes to her grandchildren. Mastering tzatziki is the first step. The yogurt dip is an everyday condiment to be eaten with everything from traditional souvlaki to burgers, potato chips, and baked potatoes. It is also delicious as a dip for vegetables, crackers, or warm pita.

2 cups plain whole milk yogurt, drained for 8 to 24 hours, or 1 cup Greek- or Bulgarian-style "strained" yogurt (which do not require additional draining)

1 medium cucumber, peeled, seeded, and chopped

1 tablespoon extra virgin olive oil

1 tablespoon distilled white vinegar

1 tablespoon minced fresh dill

1 teaspoon minced fresh mint

1 garlic clove, minced

Kosher salt

In a small bowl, stir together the yogurt, cucumber, oil, vinegar, dill, mint, and garlic. Season with salt to taste. Cover and refrigerate about 30 minutes, until the flavors have blended. Serve.

———

MAKES ABOUT 2 CUPS

CELERY

CELERY WAS NOT NATIVE TO MICHIGAN, BUT IN THE LATE
nineteenth century, the vegetable reached a pinnacle of perfection in
the black, loamy, mucky floodplains outside of Kalamazoo. George Taylor
brought the seeds from his native Scotland and planted his first crop in
1856, and ten years later, thanks largely to a flood of Dutch immigrants, the
region was producing pale, tender stalks. Unlike the nearly bitter Pascal
variety grown in California, Kalamazoo celery was a more subtly flavored
variety called Golden Hue.

"It is no genteel light work or child's play to grow celery," wrote Frank Little in 1886 in his book on the
subject. Celery likes mucky soil about three feet deep, the water table merely two feet below the surface, and
for the earliest of three annual crops, the tiny seeds had to be planted in covered seedbeds, then transplanted
by hand into the fields outside. Each row of celery had to be banked with substantial wooden "bleaching
boards" that protected the stalks from the sun, suppressing some of the
plant's naturally bitter taste and keeping the stalks white and tender. Growers
harvested each bunch by hand. Whole families worked the celery flats in wide
wooden shoes designed to keep them from stumbling as they slogged. So
did the draft horses that pulled plows through the hundreds of acres of fields
along the banks of Portage Creek.

As celery crops expanded, farmers imported manure from the Chicago
stockyards to replenish the soil. The growers marketed their celery so widely that the words
"Kalamazoo" and "celery" were, said one historian, as "indelibly associated as Boston and baked beans."
The town was called "Celery City," and the vegetable was not just a member of the chorus of traditional
aromatics used in soups, stuffings, and stews, but became the indispensable crunch in stylish chicken and
shrimp salads, the star of its own cream soup, and, when stuffed or set out for dipping, an A-list party food.
Celery also became the main ingredient in hundreds of patent medicines that were "ever-soothing," had
aphrodisiac abilities, and promised to boost a person's "exhausted nature."

Ironically, man's exhaustion of nature contributed to the demise of Celery City. The construction of paper
mills began lowering the water table in the 1920s, and failure to rotate crops led to a celery blight in the
1930s. Celery production moved back to California. The
Dutch farmers planted flowers, and enterprising real estate
developers built houses and shopping centers. In the 1950s,
"Celery City" was renamed "Mall City." The landscape
is still scored by the ditches dug by celery planters. The
celery flats are now a historical district and thanks to its
interpretive center (locally called the Celery Museum), the
area remains a treasure trove for home gardeners and
small growers who want to grow extraordinary celery.

DOROTHY STEEN'S AWARD-WINNING PIMENTO CHEESE DIP

VICKSBURG, MISSISSIPPI

During the 1950s, dips featuring sour cream, processed cheese, or cream cheese became the secret cocktail party weapon for hostesses across America. Regional variations quickly appeared. In Southern culture, pimento cheese is a passion, generating intensely held opinions about base ingredients, flavorings, mixing methods, and consistency. Dorothy Steen is the self-proclaimed pimento cheese chef for the Women's Auxiliary of the Salvation Army in Vicksburg, Mississippi. She has made at least 180 gallons in the past twenty years, and her recipe took honorable mention in the Pimento Cheese Invitational sponsored by the Southern Foodways Alliance in 2003. Mrs. Steen judges her success in other ways. At local benefits, she said, "Ladies vie to be first in line to purchase any leftover pimento cheese. They even call ahead to wheedle a jar."

1 pound sharp cheddar cheese, shredded

One 4-ounce jar pimentos, drained and chopped

¼ cup mayonnaise

1 tablespoon lemon pepper

1 tablespoon fresh lemon juice

2½ teaspoons Worcestershire sauce

¼ teaspoon kosher salt

⅛ teaspoon freshly ground black pepper

⅛ teaspoon hot sauce

In a food processor, process all of the ingredients about 15 seconds, until combined, but still slightly chunky. Transfer to a serving bowl, cover, and refrigerate about 2 hours, until the cheese has set and the flavors have blended. Serve.

MAKES ABOUT 3 CUPS

THE NEW, IMPROVED DIP-ABLE CARROT

MOST OF THE WORLD'S GREAT CUISINES HAVE BEEN A RESULT OF CLIMATE AND history, culture and economy colliding with genius in the kitchen. In addition to these factors, American cuisine has industrial innovation. Take "baby carrots."

Far from the slender infants their name suggests, the stubby little fixtures on crudité plates sprang from the mind, not the land, of Mike Yurosek, a carrot grower in Newhall, California. For decades, he was sick and tired of seeing up to 70 percent of his carrots labeled "culls"—carrots that were too large, too small, or otherwise shy of the Bugs Bunny ideal—and being sold cheap to processing plants.

"It was such a waste," said Mr. Yurosek, who described himself as an "out of the carrot patch thinker." Inspiration struck in 1999. "I knew that all my culls were going to plants that cut them up, so why couldn't I cut them into something people wanted fresh? A perfect carrot stick."

Farideh Khoury's Muhammara

Farideh Khoury keeps a recipe book for her son, Nabin, and daughter, Dina. Written by hand, each recipe is faithful to the ingredients and methods she learned in her home, Damascus. Although her children make Syrian dishes at home for Mrs. Khoury's four grandchildren, they "Americanize" them. "They put a twist on everything so that it is more Arabic American," she said.

Mrs. Khoury and her husband, Elie, arrived in Michigan in 1965, in a wave of immigration that now gives Michigan the second-highest concentration of Arab Americans in the country.

For this beloved walnut dip, Mrs. Khoury substitutes cayenne pepper for the milder, darker-hued Syrian spice. A founder of her community's American-Syrian-Arab Cultural Association, Mrs. Khoury says muhammara is popular at all gatherings, but she particularly likes muhammara when she is dieting: "I eat it with celery," she says.

2 large red bell peppers, stemmed, seeded, and coarsely chopped

1 small onion, coarsely chopped

1 cup walnuts, chopped, plus more for garnish

2 tablespoons pomegranate molasses

1 teaspoon ground cumin

½ teaspoon Aleppo or cayenne pepper

Kosher salt

Plain fresh bread crumbs, as needed

Extra virgin olive oil, as needed

1. In a food processor, process the bell peppers, onion, walnuts, molasses, cumin, Aleppo pepper, and ½ teaspoon salt together about 20 seconds, until combined but still slightly chunky. If the mixture is too loose, add bread crumbs; if the mixture is too thick, add oil.

2. Season with salt to taste and transfer to a serving bowl. Sprinkle with chopped walnuts, drizzle with oil, and serve.

MAKES ABOUT 2 CUPS

He devised a system that cuts carrots into two-inch sections, then pumps them into a cement-mixer-size mechanical peeler, where they are sculpted and polished into perfectly shaped bite-size cigars. The invention legally is a "baby-cut carrot." "Baby [cut] carrots" (or "minis," as they are called in the trade) have nearly doubled American carrot consumption. In the 1960s, Americans ate about six pounds of carrots a year; today they eat almost eleven.

In Bakersfield, California, where 20 million pounds (virtually all of the nation's beta-carotene cigars) are grown and carved, growers worked to breed the bitterness and woodiness from their crops. Ironically, they ended up breeding larger carrots. Prior to the mini revolution, the ideal carrot was six to seven inches long. Today it is eight inches or, as they say in the trade, a "three-cut" that can make three two-inch minis.

Mr. Yurosek lived to see his idea revolutionize carrots in America. The change made him as proud as it made him rich. "When you've done something you're proud of and it's been acknowledged—that's a dream come true," said the 82-year-old carrot man shortly before his death in 2004.

Mirza Gasemi's Persian Eggplant Dip

Beth Hassid's family, a close-knit clan of Italian, Russian, and Jewish descent, lived in western Massachusetts for three generations before her parents moved to Southern California to open a clothing store in Los Angeles in the late 1960s. Accustomed as she was to huge family gatherings, she was lonely at first. But that changed in 1976 when she married George, whose family owned a rug store near her parents' boutique, and became part of the city's rapidly growing, close-knit Persian community. During the early rumblings of the Islamic revolution in 1978, Iranians began arriving in Los Angeles. A million Iranians now live in the city that is increasingly, and affectionately, called "Tehran Angeles." Mrs. Hassid has fully adopted her husband's Persian-Jewish culture and the cooking that she learned from her mother-in-law. This eggplant dip, which she makes for light lunches, late-night snacks, and parties, is based on traditional methods, but streamlined to suit the pace of modern American life.

8 to 10 small eggplants

6 tablespoons olive oil

5 garlic cloves, minced

3 medium tomatoes, peeled, seeded, and cut into ½-inch pieces

1 teaspoon ground turmeric

½ teaspoon ground cumin

½ teaspoon kosher salt

¼ teaspoon freshly ground black pepper

4 or 5 large eggs, lightly beaten

Saffron threads, for garnish

1. Place an oven rack in the center position and preheat the oven to 350°F.

2. Arrange the eggplants on a large baking sheet and bake about 1 hour, until the skins crack. Cool to room temperature, then remove the stem and skin. Cut the eggplant flesh into ½-inch pieces.

3. In a large skillet, heat 5 tablespoons of the oil and the garlic over medium-low heat about 2 minutes, until sizzling and aromatic. Add the eggplant, increase the heat to medium-high, and cook about 4 minutes. Stir in the tomatoes, turmeric, cumin, salt, and pepper and cook for 3 to 6 minutes, until the pan is dry. Remove from the heat.

4. In a large nonstick skillet, heat the remaining tablespoon oil over medium-low heat. Add the eggs and cook, stirring constantly, about 1 minute, until almost set. Stir in the eggplant-tomato mixture and cook about 2 minutes more, until the eggs are cooked through. Sprinkle with the saffron and serve.

SERVES 6 TO 8

AFAF SHAHEEN'S HUMMUS

Eli Shaheen didn't marry his wife Afaf, for her hummus, but after fifty-seven years of marriage, he is proud to tell you that no one makes it better. For this reason, Mr. Shaheen tends to spend as much time holding forth on the proper hummus as he does selling clothing at Shaheen's, his family's department store in downtown Louisville. His great-grandfather was part of a wave of Lebanese Syrian immigrants who arrived in the area in the first decades of the twentieth century. Today, Louisville's official city government documents are still printed in both Arabic and English, and the town is home to nearly 4,000 Lebanese and Arab Americans. And, thanks in no small part to Mr. Shaheen's tireless efforts to detail his Lebanese-born wife's recipes to anyone who walks into his store, it is also home to some of the most sophisticated Lebanese cooking in the nation.

One 15.5-ounce can chickpeas, drained, with
    ¼ cup liquid reserved

1 garlic clove, minced

Kosher salt

1½ tablespoons tahini

1½ tablespoons extra virgin olive oil, plus more
    for garnish

2 tablespoons fresh lemon juice

1. In a food processor, process the chickpeas and reserved liquid for 30 seconds, until smooth.

2. On a cutting board, mash the garlic with ¼ teaspoon salt using the flat side of a knife. Scrape into a small bowl and stir in the tahini and oil. Transfer the mixture to the food processor and process about 30 seconds. Add the lemon juice and process until nearly the consistency of sour cream. Season with salt to taste.

3. Transfer to a serving bowl, cover, and refrigerate. Drizzle with more oil before serving.

MAKES ABOUT 2 CUPS

Nibbles, Noshes, and Tasty Little Plates

The Piping and Marching Society of Lower Chalmers Street Shrimp Dip

The Piping and Marching Society of Lower Chalmers Street is a dinner club comprised of professional men in Charleston's "high society" that was, according to several members, founded for the purpose of copious beer drinking under the guise of intellectual pursuit. The club meets monthly at the home of a member who is chosen to give a paper and talk on any subject outside his area of expertise. Past discussions have included the history of the hot dog and Charlestonians' drinking habits. The club's annual winter rout is the one time of year when family members and the public interact with the society. Members clad in black tie and kilts and bearing torches lead a procession down the two-block length of Chalmers Street. Before this, however, the marchers and their guests gather in the Pink House (so called for its building material) to partake of a buffet heavy in Low Country dishes like barbecue, shrimp, and grits, and most of all, shrimp paste. Dr. Jane Tyler, the wife of a member, credits her mother-in-law, Floride McDermid Worthington, with the recipe for this beloved dip that is great on crackers and also delicious stirred into fish stews or buttered grits.

1½ pounds small shrimp, preferably creek shrimp

2 celery stalks, strings removed, finely chopped

8 tablespoons (1 stick) unsalted butter, softened

1 cup mayonnaise, plus more as needed

Fresh lemon juice

Hot sauce

Kosher salt

1. In a large pot, bring 4 quarts water to a boil over medium-high heat. Stir in the shrimp and cook until the water just begins to boil again. Immediately drain the shrimp and rinse under cold water until cool.

2. Peel and devein the shrimp, then chop them into pea-size pieces. In a medium bowl, combine the shrimp, celery, butter, and mayonnaise. Add more mayonnaise as needed to get a spreadable consistency. Season with lemon juice, hot sauce, and salt to taste.

3. Transfer the mixture to a serving dish, cover, and refrigerate for 8 to 12 hours. Serve.

MAKES ABOUT 3 CUPS

MOLLY'S BE-STILL-MY-HEART CHOPPED CHICKEN LIVER

MONTCLAIR, NEW JERSEY

Sally Hechinger says: "I grew up in Washington, D.C. Every holiday, Grandmother Molly would arrive from New York at our door with one small suitcase and one large suitcase. The small bag contained a few simple clothes and toiletries. The larger bag was reserved for plastic containers of her delicious chopped liver. When her mother arrived, my mother said 'Hello,' gave her a quick kiss, and cracked open the big suitcase. It was like opening a vault full of gold bricks. Within moments, my siblings and I were slathering this yummy stuff on rye bread. Grandma had arrived. I serve it once a year—at Christmas, which is a little odd, seeing that I am Jewish—and rest well, knowing that my cholesterol quota has been filled."

1 pound fresh chicken livers, cleaned

Kosher salt and freshly ground black pepper

½ cup rendered chicken fat, plus more as needed

1 large onion, finely chopped

4 large eggs, hard boiled, cooled, and peeled

1. Pat the chicken livers dry and season with salt and pepper. In a large skillet, melt 6 tablespoons of the chicken fat over medium-high heat. Add half of the chicken livers and cook for 4 to 5 minutes, until browned on both sides. Transfer them to a plate. Return the skillet to medium-high heat and cook the remaining chicken livers.

2. Pour off the fat in the skillet and wipe out with a paper towel. Add the remaining 2 tablespoons chicken fat to the skillet and heat over medium heat. Add the onion and cook about 4 minutes, stirring occasionally, until soft. Transfer the onion to a large bowl.

3. In a food processor, pulse the eggs until finely chopped. (Do not overprocess.) Transfer them to the bowl with the onion. Working in two batches, pulse the livers in the food processor until finely chopped. Transfer them to the bowl with the eggs and stir to combine. Add more chicken fat until the mixture is loose and muddy. Season with salt and pepper to taste. Cover and refrigerate for 8 to 24 hours, until set. Serve.

SERVES 6 TO 8

Nibbles, Noshes, and Tasty Little Plates

ILA DOUGLAS'S CORTON PÂTÉ

"I was born in Sunburst and I lived there most of my life," says Ila Douglas. "My grandfather moved south from Canada into eastern Montana when he was a young man, around 1830. My mother told me stories about prairie life. It was backbreaking and unending work, clearing the land of rocks in order to plant, herding buffalo, and driving cattle. The winters were brutally cold. Now I live with my daughter in Portland, Oregon, where the weather is milder, but it is not as easy to get good, fatty pork or leaf lard. No matter how tough it was, the family gathered at Christmas and there was corton, a pork pâté that you spread on fresh bread. We always had it after midnight Mass."

3 pounds pork belly or pork butt, rind discarded and cut into 1-inch chunks

1 large onion, coarsely chopped

Kosher salt

6 whole black peppercorns

2 whole cloves

1 bay leaf

½ teaspoon dried thyme

1 pound leaf lard, cut into 1-inch chunks

½ teaspoon ground cloves

½ teaspoon freshly grated nutmeg

½ teaspoon ground cinnamon

Freshly ground black pepper

¼ teaspoon ground allspice

1. In a Dutch oven, cover the pork with cold water. Add half of the onion, 1 tablespoon salt, the peppercorns, whole cloves, bay leaf, and thyme and bring to a simmer over medium heat. Reduce the heat to low, cover, and cook for 3 hours, until the pork is tender. Remove from the heat and cool to room temperature in the broth.

2. Meanwhile, in a large skillet, cook the lard over medium heat until the fat is rendered and the cracklings are golden brown. With a slotted spoon transfer the cracklings to a large bowl. Pour off and reserve all but two tablespoons of the fat from the skillet.

3. Return the skillet to medium heat, add the remaining onion, and cook about 4 minutes, stirring occasionally, until the onion is soft. Transfer the onion to the bowl with the cracklings.

4. Transfer the pork to the bowl with the cracklings. Pour the broth through a fine-mesh strainer and reserve. Add the ground cloves, nutmeg, cinnamon, ½ teaspoon pepper, and the allspice to the pork and stir until the ingredients are combined. Using a traditional hand-cranked meat grinder or a food processor, grind or pulse the pork mixture.

5. Add the reserved pork fat and pork broth as needed until the mixture is a spreadable consistency. Season with salt and pepper to taste. Transfer the pâté to a crock or a bowl, pour ¼ inch of the reserved pork fat over top, and refrigerate for 3 days before serving.

SERVES 20

One Big Table

Jam Sanitchat's Satay

Jam Sanitchat, who grew up in a suburb of Bangkok, Thailand, was waitressing one summer before attending graduate school when she fell in love with cooking. "I was giving dinner parties to say goodbye to people. I couldn't stop cooking. I realized that earning a Ph.D. was something that I felt I should do, but that all I wanted to do was cook." Within weeks she met Mark Barnes, and together they imagined the life they wanted to live. They opened Thai Fresh, a grocery store with a nineteen-seat restaurant.

Although Indonesian in origin, satay is a ubiquitous street food in Thailand. Chicken is the most common satay served in the United States, says Ms. Sanitchat, but the dish can be made from pork, beef, tofu, or seafood. "You can use less expensive cuts of meat because the marinade will tenderize as it flavors it." She serves hers with an unusual peanut sauce and cooling cucumber relish.

¼ cup unsweetened coconut milk, plus more for basting

2 tablespoons finely chopped cilantro root, or about 1 inch of the stems closest to the root end, minced

2 tablespoons vegetable oil

2 teaspoons sugar

1½ teaspoons fish sauce such as Vietnamese nuoc mam

½ teaspoon curry powder

½ teaspoon ground turmeric

1 teaspoon minced fresh ginger

1 teaspoon minced fresh galangal

½ stalk lemongrass, green leaves removed, white part finely minced

¼ teaspoon minced fresh Thai chili

1½ pounds tenders, chicken, beef, pork, or firm tofu, cut into ½-inch-thick, 2- to 3-inch-long strips

12 short bamboo skewers or longer bamboo skewers cut into twelve 4-inch lengths, soaked in water for 1 hour

Peanut Sauce for Satay (recipe follows)

Jam Sanitchat's Quick Thai Pickle (page 78)

1. To make the marinade, combine the coconut milk, cilantro, oil, sugar, fish sauce, curry powder, turmeric, ginger, galangal, lemongrass, and chili in a medium bowl and allow mixture to sit for 1 hour at room temperature. Add the meat, stir to coat it well, cover, and refrigerate for 3 to 18 hours.

2. Thread marinated meat lengthwise onto a well-soaked bamboo skewer. Blot excess marinade with a paper towel, place on a platter, cover, and refrigerate.

3. Prepare charcoal grill or preheat broiler. Grill the skewers for 2 minutes, basting with coconut milk. Turn, baste again, and cook for 2 minutes more. Serve with peanut sauce and the cucumber relish.

—

SERVES 4 TO 6

Peanut Sauce for Satay

This sauce should be slightly sweet, followed by a touch of tartness and saltiness—adjust the seasoning with tamarind juice and salt to your taste. It can be refrigerated in an airtight container up to four days.

3 tablespoons vegetable oil

2 tablespoons Thai red curry paste

½ teaspoon ground coriander

½ teaspoon ground cumin

2 cups unsweetened coconut milk

¾ cup coarsely ground roasted salted peanuts

2 tablespoons sugar

2 tablespoons tamarind juice or lime juice, plus more to taste

Kosher salt

1. In a medium saucepan, heat the oil over medium heat. Add the curry paste and cook about 1 minute, until aromatic. Stir in the coriander and cumin and cook about 30 seconds. Add the coconut milk, peanuts, and sugar, and simmer for about 3 minutes, stirring occasionally, until thick.

2. Stir in the tamarind juice and ½ teaspoon salt, transfer to a bowl, and cool to room temperature.

MAKES ABOUT 2½ CUPS

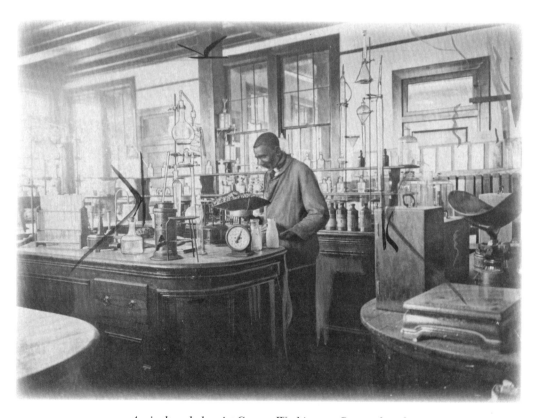

Agricultural chemist George Washington Carver found 300 uses for peanuts in his Tuskegee Institute laboratory, 1923.

SIGNIFICANT EVENTS IN POPCORN

POPCORN IS AMERICA. THE NOTION OF HEATING HARD KERNEL CORN over an open fire until the kernel's internal steam forced the corn to POP! was a gift of the Amerindians. It has inspired technology, been closely linked to baseball, been cause for patriotism and served as the profit center for movie theaters. Even before the invention of Cracker Jack, popcorn inspired cooks. Savory popcorn—dusted with Cajun spices, salt and pepper, finely grated hard cheese, olive oil, or herb or spice butters—makes fine snacking with beer, cocktails, or even wine.

1 C.E. Native Americans in what is now Arizona pop corn in a hole dug in the hot desert sand.

1621 Myth holds that Native Americans introduced colonists to popcorn beer and popcorn soup. But evidence is lacking.

1760s to 1770s Colonists served popcorn as breakfast cereal, with sugar or molasses and milk. The Philadelphia Dutch standardize kettle corn by adding a touch of syrup, molasses, or honey to the corn popping in big iron kettles.

1830 An enclosed popcorn popper is invented, replacing kettle cooking.

1840 Popcorn sold publicly by boy vendors at public gatherings and train stations. In Boston, popcorn balls are a popular street snack, sold by the wagonload.

1885 The first popcorn machine is invented by Charles Cretors, who owns a Chicago sweet shop. By 1890 he put his steam-based machine onto wheeled carts, which became urban fixtures.

1896 Cracker Jack is invented and sold widely at baseball games and expositions. The song "Take Me Out to the Ball Game," written in 1908 with the lyric "Buy me some peanuts and Cracker Jack," solidifies the treat as an American food icon.

1914 Jolly Time, America's first branded popcorn, is sold.

1919 At the age of 12, Orville Redenbacher grows his own popping corn in Brazil, Indiana. He eventually produces a hybrid that becomes the best-selling popcorn in the country.

1959 America welcomed the introduction of Jiffy Pop popping corn, sold in a disposable pan that could be used indoors or out.

Early 1980s Microwave popcorn is introduced.

Diane Cu's Nem Nuong
Skewered Vietnamese Meatballs

Diane Cu was a toddler when Saigon fell in 1975. Along with her parents and an uncle, she was among the 120,000 Vietnamese refugees who fled to the United States. Church groups helped relocate families, and hers found its way to Los Angeles and the largest Vietnamese expatriate community in the country. Through the upheaval, nem nuong was constant. The ground pork dish is an economical way to feed a family; it can be eaten with rice noodles, steamed rice, or Vietnamese rice and wheat baguettes. The pork paste can also be molded onto bamboo skewers and grilled, as Ms. Cu does for the parties and family gatherings she hosts in her backyard. The grilled skewered meat can also be served on a tangle of Southeast Asian herbs—perilla, cilantro, and Thai basil—to make a sit-down first course or light summer meal.

1 pound ground pork

¼ pound fatback, finely chopped (optional)

1 small shallot, finely chopped

1 tablespoon fish sauce

1 garlic clove, minced

1 teaspoon sugar

½ teaspoon kosher salt

½ teaspoon freshly ground black pepper

6 long bamboo skewers, soaked in water for 1 hour

1. In a large bowl, combine the pork, fatback, if using, shallot, fish sauce, garlic, sugar, salt, and pepper. Cover and refrigerate for 30 minutes to 12 hours.

2. Heat a grill to medium heat.

3. Using a spoon or ice-cream scoop, portion the meat mixture into 1-inch balls. With your hands, roll into smooth meatballs and thread onto the skewers, leaving ¼ inch between each.

4. Grill the meatballs about 4 minutes, turning several times, until cooked through. Serve.

SERVES 4

KATHY FARLEY'S GRILLED FIGS

Kathy Farley grew up with a vegetable garden, but now, an interior designer with no space to garden, she prowls local farmers' markets. When figs are in season and dinner involves firing up the grill, she likes to use local cheese to make her grilled figs for company. They are a thing of beauty and a wonderful way to start a meaty meal—or a vegetable feast.

1 pint raspberries

2 tablespoons balsamic vinegar

1 tablespoon sugar

8 ripe figs, halved

1 tablespoon olive oil

½ pound Teleme or Bellwether Crescenza cheese

1. In a small saucepan, cook the raspberries over medium heat about 8 minutes, until broken down. Press the raspberries into a bowl through a fine-mesh strainer to remove the seeds. Return the puree to the saucepan and stir in the vinegar and sugar. Simmer about 6 minutes, until thick.

2. Heat a grill to medium heat.

3. Lightly brush the cut sides of the figs with oil. Place the figs cut side down on the grill and cook for 2 to 3 minutes, until lightly browned.

4. Transfer the figs, cut side up, to a serving platter or individual plates and place about 1 tablespoon of the cheese on top of each fig half. Drizzle the raspberry sauce over the top and serve.

SERVES 8

Nibbles, Noshes, and Tasty Little Plates

CHAPTER 2

PICKLES, SALSAS, AND OTHER CONDIMENTS, SAVORY AND SWEET

RETURN OF THE RELISH TRAY

An oval or oblong tray of metal or glass with compartments for fresh vegetables, pickles, and other condiments, the relish tray has been a fixture on the American table. Full of raw vegetable crudités, radishes, scallions, and sweet peppers, it provided a way to brag about one's garden. The small wells filled with dilly beans and several varieties of cucumber pickles—as well as those made from watermelon, pearl onions, beets, and even quail eggs—bespoke a knowledgeable, talented, and thrifty cook. The cavities filled with exotic chutneys, fruit preserves, spiced dips, or "catsups" made from tomatoes or nuts were emblematic of travels, worldliness, and, of course, immigrant help in the kitchen.

Relishes might be nibbled before the first course to take the edge off an appetite, or used as a counterpoint—be it crisp and cool, sweet, spicy, sharp or salty—to various courses. A good rule of thumb: The more abundant and imaginative the relish offerings, the more important the occasion.

The creation of relish trays peaked between the late nineteenth and early twentieth centuries. Not long after, Grandma's relish tray was attic bound, to be unpacked only for holiday meals. Perhaps the ornate trays eclipsed their contents. Perhaps relish offerings became less toothsome as more of them were made outside the home. Or maybe the relish custom was collateral damage to the rise of the cocktail party.

The current return of the relish tray is likewise related to cultural shifts. There is less stand-around-with-a-cocktail time and more hang-out-at-the-table time these days. Gardening has returned with a vengeance, and homemade pickles and preserves are badges of honor. Condiments also add a note of exotica to an otherwise ho-hum meal.

Jicama, Japanese daikon, and varietal radishes have joined the carrots and celery, and if the celery is stuffed today, it is most likely with goat cheese rather than cream cheese. Olives are no longer merely green or black. They may be Arancino from Italy, Amfissa from Greece, Araban du Var from France. Salsa and Asian chile dips occupy the former catsup compartment; sweet peppers are more likely to be roasted and served in olive oil; pickles are as likely to be from East Asia as they are from Grandma's recipe box.

DOROTHY KALINS'S
BREAD AND BUTTER PICKLES

EASTHAMPTON, NEW YORK

It is not possible to overstate the importance of pickles in America. The Spanish pickle merchant and explorer Amerigo Vespucci stocked the ships of Columbus's voyage with scurvy-fighting pickles, and when the crews lived to plant the flag in the New World, the pickle man lent his name to the continent. For many, pickle-making has remained the best sort of patriotism. Dorothy Kalins, the founder of *Saveur* magazine, and her husband, Roger Sherman, a documentary filmmaker, fell in love with the pickles that they bought from a farmstand near their summer house at the eastern tip of Long Island. In fact, their appetite for pickles—on sandwiches, served with roasted meat like duck or turkey—soon outstripped the local supply, and they had to make their own. "I knew that I wanted crispness, so I wanted a refrigerator pickle, not a canned pickle. I was afraid that the water bath would turn them limp. Limp is the enemy. We wanted a classic American bread-and-butter pickle, nothing innovative, nothing fancy, no overpowering seasonings. This recipe emerged after trying a bunch of batches. For perfect crispness, slice the cucumbers at least ⅓ inch thick; thinner slices go limp. I like to use small onions so that you see a whole slice in the jar. Stored in the refrigerator, they stay perfectly crisp for eight or nine months."

60 Kirby cucumbers, well scrubbed but unpeeled

½ cup kosher salt, plus more if necessary

8 small white onions, thinly sliced

2 quarts cider vinegar

7 cups sugar

1 tablespoon plus 1 teaspoon yellow mustard seeds

2 tablespoons ground turmeric

Eight 1-quart canning jars and lids, washed, sterilized, and standing in scalding-hot water

1. Cut the cucumbers into slices ⅓ to ½ inch thick and form a neat layer in the bottom of a very large nonreactive pot. Season lightly with salt. Add another layer of cucumbers, cover with a thin layer of onions, and sprinkle lightly with salt. Continue cutting and layering the cucumbers, onions, and salt until all ingredients are used up. Place the pot in the refrigerator overnight.

2. In the morning, drain the cucumbers and discard the liquid. Working in batches as necessary, place cucumbers in a colander to drain further.

3. Rinse the pot and add the vinegar, sugar, mustard seeds, and turmeric. Place over low heat and cook until the sugar is dissolved, about 5 minutes. Return the cucumbers to the pot, cover, and bring to a boil over medium-low heat. Simmer until cucumbers are no longer bright green but are still crisp, about 20 minutes.

4. Transfer the pickles to the sterilized jars, filling them with the pickling liquid to within ½ inch of the rim, and refrigerate. When cool, wipe the rims and put the lids on the jars.

MAKES 8 QUARTS PICKLES

Two Sisters' Green Tomato Pickles

Growing up in southern Virginia, Andrea Meyer admired her grandmother's basement shelves of beautiful and colorful jars of vegetables. But they never found stringing beans and snapping the ends much fun, so she swore she would never can. But after teaching in Saipan, Colombia, and Saudi Arabia, the mother of three "rambunctious boys" returned to Virginia and reconsidered her position on not stocking the larder. "My sister, Angela, is really the Canning Queen," she said, "but the more we grow our own food, the more I understand and appreciate farmers, especially how their lives can revolve around harvesting. As the cold temperatures creep in, I find myself pulled into the garden, collecting what is left of our summer herbs and vegetables, and then back into the kitchen as we preserve what we grew." Green tomato pickles are especially delicious with wafers of ham or other rich meat. They are not bad with fried chicken, either. Making pickle brine was once guesswork because the density of commercial salt varied. To ensure a brine with a salt concentration sufficient for winter preservation, early picklers followed the rule of enough salt to float an egg, but the resulting pickles were often so salty that they had to be soaked in water for days before eating.

71

Pickles, Salsas, and Other Condiments

FOR THE PICKLES

36 garlic cloves, peeled

24 jalapeño or serrano chiles, stemmed, halved, and seeded

¾ cup chopped fresh dill

¼ cup olive oil

1 tablespoon pickling spice

1 tablespoon powdered alum (optional)

Twelve 1-pint or six 1-quart canning jars and lids, washed, sterilized, and standing by in scalding-hot water

5 pounds green tomatoes, cored and quartered

FOR THE BRINE

3 quarts water

2 quarts distilled white vinegar

¾ cup pickling salt

1. To make the pickles: Evenly divide the garlic, chiles, dill, oil, pickling spice, and alum (if using) among the jars. Pack each jar tightly with tomatoes.

2. To make the brine: In a large saucepan, bring the water, vinegar, and salt to a boil over high heat. Reduce the heat to medium and simmer for 15 minutes.

3. Fill the jars with the hot brine up to ½ inch below the rim. Run a knife down and around each jar to release air bubbles. Wipe the rims and seal the jars. Cool to room temperature and refrigerate for two weeks before serving. The pickles will keep for one year in the refrigerator.

MAKES 12 PINTS OR 6 QUARTS PICKLES

"On a hot day in Virginia, I know nothing more comforting than a fine spiced pickle, brought up trout-like from the sparkling depths of the aromatic jar below the stairs of Aunt Sally's cellar."

—Thomas Jefferson

Maw Maw's Chow-Chow

Kim McVicker and her husband, Bryan, are partial to healthy, adventuresome cooking, and, oddly, few recipes satisfy their tastes as succinctly as her grandmother's recipe for chow-chow, a traditional American pickled relish. Sometimes spelled "chowchow," some linked its name to nineteenth-century Chinese railway workers, for whom the term described a condiment of orange peel and ginger in heavy syrup. Others claim chow-chow comes from the French *chou*, or cauliflower, which is often a primary ingredient. In Pennsylvania, a sweeter version prevails, but further south, Cajun-ish versions like Ms. McVicker's are used like hot sauce.

"My grandmother never had a food processor, so making chow-chow was an all-day, all-hands-on-deck type of thing," says Ms. McVicker. She remembers an uncle slicing onions with a piece of bread in his mouth to keep the tears from flowing. She first ate chow-chow on red beans and rice, influenced by their Cajun/Creole neighbors. "I loved it! It was always on the table at my grandmother's house. I really like it on hot dogs and black-eyed peas. I gave a jar once to my sister-in-law's mother, who is from the Midwest and had never had it before. She said her jar was gone in a week. She and her husband ate it on scrambled eggs for breakfast."

5 pounds green to pink (unripe) tomatoes, cored and finely chopped

2 medium heads green cabbage, cored and finely chopped

10 medium onions, finely chopped

6 green bell peppers, stemmed, seeded, and finely chopped

4 red bell peppers, stemmed, seeded, and finely chopped

2 to 4 jalapeño chiles (optional), stemmed, seeded, and finely chopped

⅓ cup kosher salt

6 cups cider vinegar

3 cups sugar

1½ teaspoons ground turmeric

1½ teaspoons ground allspice

1½ teaspoons ground cinnamon

1½ teaspoons celery seeds

Fourteen 1-pint canning jars and lids, washed, sterilized, and standing by in scalding-hot water

1. Toss the tomatoes, cabbage, onions, bell peppers, and chiles (if using) with the salt in a large nonreactive container, cover, and refrigerate for 8 to 12 hours.

2. Transfer the vegetables to a large nonreactive pot and stir in the vinegar, sugar, turmeric, allspice, cinnamon, and celery seeds. Bring to a simmer and cook, stirring occasionally, for 20 minutes.

3. Pack the mixture into the prepared jars. Run a knife down and around each jar to release air bubbles. Wipe the rims and seal the jars. Process in boiling water for 10 minutes. Let the jars cool on the counter without touching before storing.

MAKES 14 PINTS CHOW-CHOW

Dave Umphress's Piccalilli

Having plowed up every inch of the yard surrounding his home in Woodbury, New Jersey, to plant vegetables, mail carrier Dave Umphress produces so much bounty that his kitchen becomes all but a food processing station in the late summer and early fall. In the front he grows eggplant and peppers, since they add color "in a more traditional landscape sort of way." On his mail route, he encourages gardeners to plant more vegetables among their flowers and shrubs. Each fall he looks forward to making old-fashioned piccalilli from the peppers and green tomatoes that keep coming until a hard frost. He adds jalapeño chiles for heat, a hedge against the winter ahead.

2 pounds green tomatoes, cored, and coarsely chopped

6 tablespoons kosher salt

3 cups sugar

2 cups cider vinegar

¼ cup yellow mustard seeds

1 teaspoon whole cloves

1 teaspoon celery seeds

1 teaspoon freshly ground black pepper

1 teaspoon mustard powder

1 teaspoon ground cinnamon

1 teaspoon ground allspice

2 large red bell peppers, stemmed, seeded, and coarsely chopped

1 large onion, coarsely chopped

2 jalapeño chiles, stemmed and finely chopped

Six 1-pint canning jars and lids, washed, sterilized, and standing by in scalding-hot water

1. In a large nonreactive bowl, mix the tomatoes and salt until combined. Cover and refrigerate for 8 to 12 hours. Drain the tomatoes.

2. In a large nonreactive saucepan, bring the sugar, vinegar, mustard seeds, cloves, celery seeds, pepper, mustard powder, cinnamon, and allspice to a boil and cook about 2 minutes, until the sugar has dissolved. Stir in the tomatoes, bell peppers, onion, and jalapeños. Bring to a simmer and cook, stirring occasionally, for 30 minutes.

3. Following the instructions from the USDA (see page 74), pack the mixture into the prepared jars. Run a knife down and around each jar to release air bubbles. Wipe the rims and seal the jars. Cool to room temperature. The relish will keep refrigerated for one year.

MAKES 6 PINTS PICCALILLI

Pickles, Salsas, and Other Condiments

KACHUMBARI *Kenyan Coleslaw*

Anna Otieno's father, like Barack Obama's, left Kenya to pursue educational opportunities. He married the daughter of a white midwestern couple who hosted him while he was in school. Anna's parents settled in Minneapolis because her dad felt the city's large population of Somalis and East Africans needed black doctors. Her extended family now includes Christian, Jewish, and Muslim relatives all over the world. President Obama's inauguration was an emotional day for her because, as she says, her "family's differences became shared similarities . . . my family's differences were finally celebrated as the American story." Many Americans and Africans prepared celebration meals in honor of the historic inauguration, including kachumbari to accompany chicken or roast meats—perhaps lamb in the United States or goat in Kenya.

4 medium-size ripe tomatoes, cored and coarsely chopped

1 medium onion, finely chopped

1 jalapeño chile, stemmed, seeded, and finely chopped

¼ cup fresh lime juice

2 tablespoons extra virgin olive oil

2 tablespoons chopped fresh cilantro

Kosher salt and freshly ground black pepper

In a medium bowl, mix together all of the ingredients until combined. Season with salt and pepper to taste, and serve.

SERVES 4 TO 6

WELL PRESERVED

THE BACTERIUM *CLOSTRIDIUM BOTULINUM*, WHICH IS PRESENT IN the form of spores on the surfaces of most fresh food, can cause botulism, a deadly form of food poisoning in canned food. The bacteria grows in anaerobic environments (such as vacuum-sealed jars or cans) and is not destroyed by washing or blanching. Highly acidic foods and high heat—240 to 250 degrees over a long period of time—are the safest way to protect against these toxins.

In general, ingredients that are typically lower in acidity—red meats, seafood, poultry, milk, and all fresh vegetables except for most tomatoes—are preserved in vinegar, lemon juice, or citric acid and are processed at high heats. Fruits, pickles, sauerkraut, fruit jams, jellies, marmalades, and fruit butters are generally acidic enough to pose no risk. However, to ensure canned food safety, refer to the most current edition of the USDA's *Complete Guide to Home Canning,* currently posted at http://foodsafety.psu.edu/canningguide.html. It is also useful to consult books. *Well-Preserved* by Eugenia Bone (New York: Clarkson Potter, 2009) is a very good source.

One Big Table

BALL JARS

NOTHING REVOLUTIONIZED THE SAFETY AND EASE OF HOME food preservation as much as the Mason jar. Replacing more primitive sealing with wax, in 1859, John L. Mason, a 26-year-old New York City metalworker, patented a self-sealing zinc lid to fit glass preserving jars. He quickly sold his patent, but his name remained. Produced in several sizes, from cup to half-gallon, a boiling water bath makes sterile jars reliable storage by creating a vacuum seal.

The Ball brothers began their company in 1880 in Buffalo, New York, with a borrowed $200 to produce paint, varnish, and kerosene containers. By 1884 they were manufacturing home canning jars, a business they later moved to Muncie, Indiana, to take advantage of natural gas, critical to the glass-making process. The company printed the first *Ball Blue Book*, giving canning techniques and recipes, in 1909.

Antique canning jars have an avid following among collectors, who value them for shape, markings, closure, and color, chasing down rare examples of amber, dark green, cobalt blue, and milk glass jars. In 2001, one deep cobalt fruit jar sold for $29,000.

Pickles, Salsas, and Other Condiments

Sweet and Sour Zucchini Relish

YAKIMA, WASHINGTON

An avid gardener, Paulette Brown began taking a master gardener's class in 1980, the year the Mount St. Helens volcano erupted 150 miles away and covered her Yakima, Washington, garden in ash. Now, using cow manure, leaves, and compost, she organically grows only two zucchini plants a year because they are so prolific. Sometimes she gets as many as thirty or forty squash per plant. "If a zucchini wants to produce," she says with a laugh, "you can't stop it." The zucchinis start out small but "if the water and sun are right, they can grow twelve, sixteen, or eighteen inches long." One year she had a twenty-four-inch-long zucchini that was five inches in diameter. She dressed it up—adding buttons for eyes and grape leaves for ears—and gave it to a neighbor with a note that said "Help, I've been kicked out of my garden!" She makes twenty-five to thirty large loaves of zucchini bread each year and puts her relish in pint-size jars to give to dinner guests. The relish is a perfect topping for sandwiches and hamburgers and works well as a side dish with pork.

5 pounds zucchini, halved lengthwise, seeded, and shredded

4 medium onions, finely chopped

2 red bell peppers, stemmed, seeded, and finely chopped

1 green bell pepper, stemmed, seeded, and finely chopped

5 tablespoons kosher salt

5 cups sugar

2½ cups distilled white vinegar

2 teaspoons celery seeds

2 teaspoons yellow mustard seeds

½ teaspoon freshly ground black pepper

Eight 1-pint canning jars and lids, washed, sterilized, and standing by in scalding-hot water

1. In a large colander set over a bowl, toss the zucchini, onions, and bell peppers with the salt. Cover and let sit at room temperature for 8 to 12 hours.

2. Drain and rinse the vegetables and transfer to a large nonreactive pot. Stir in the sugar, vinegar, celery and mustard seeds, and black pepper. Bring to a simmer and cook for 30 minutes, stirring occasionally.

3. Divide the mixture evenly among the jars. Run a knife down and around each jar to release air bubbles. Wipe the rims and seal the jars. Process in boiling water for 10 minutes. Cool the jars on the counter without touching them and store for two weeks before serving, to give the flavors a chance to ripen.

MAKES 8 PINTS

Sister Marie Antonia's Zucchini Relish

When Sister Marie Antonia, a member of the Religious Sisters of Mercy since 1943, retired from her teaching work in Belize, Nicaragua, and Providence, Rhode Island, she continued the routines she developed over a lifetime of service to the poor. For decades she chopped and minced the squash and peppers that teemed in the convent gardens to make this relish, which, she said, converted devout zucchini haters into fans. Its high vinegar content is a natural preservative, and the good sister simply packs the relish into sterile jars. She may have special protection, but to be safe, process the jarred relish according to the USDA standards (page 74).

77

12 cups finely chopped zucchini

4 cups finely chopped onion

2 red bell peppers, stemmed, seeded, and finely chopped

5 tablespoons pickling or kosher salt

6 cups sugar

2 teaspoons turmeric

2 teaspoons cornstarch

2 teaspoons celery seed

2 to 4 cups apple cider vinegar

1. Mix together the chopped zucchini, onion, and bell peppers in a large bowl and sprinkle with salt. Cover and refrigerate overnight.

2. The next day, transfer the vegetables to a fine strainer, working in batches if necessary, and run them under cold water for a few minutes. Squeeze the vegetables dry in clean kitchen towels until they clump together and then transfer them to a large pot.

3. Add the sugar, turmeric, cornstarch, celery seed, and 2½ cups vinegar to the vegetables and stir until well combined. Bring the vegetables to a rapid boil, reduce the heat, and simmer, uncovered, for 30 to 45 minutes, until the vegetables are soft and transparent. Halfway through the cooking time, taste and add more vinegar if necessary to get the sweet and sour balance you prefer.

MAKES 6 TO 8 PINTS

Pickles, Salsas, and Other Condiments

Jam Sanitchat's Quick Thai Pickle

With traditional dills, sours, and bread-and-butter pickles so firmly identified with mass production, home cooks are increasingly drawing from arriving cultures to create alluring pickles. Ms. Sanitchat serves this quick Thai pickle with her satay (page 63). It also makes a wonderful counterpoint to grilled meat, crackers, rich pâté, or fried nibbles.

¼ cup water

3 tablespoons distilled white vinegar

3 tablespoons sugar

1 small pickling (Kirby) cucumber, halved lengthwise and thinly sliced

4 shallots, thinly sliced

1 serrano chile, stemmed and thinly sliced

1 tablespoon chopped fresh cilantro

Pinch of kosher salt

In a medium bowl, combine all of the ingredients. Let sit for 20 minutes before serving.

—

MAKES ABOUT 1½ CUPS

One Big Table

COMMERCIAL PICKLES

A MILESTONE IN THE TRANSFER OF PICKLES FROM GRANDMA'S KITCHEN to the industrial processing plant occurred in 1893 at the World's Fair in Chicago. To promote its "57 Varieties," the Heinz Company gave away lapel pins—a green, wrinkly, curved pickle—to lure people to their booth. It worked. Rare now is the refrigerator door that lacks at least one jar of commercially made pickles. Pickles have become de rigueur on hamburgers, and commercial pickle juice—a well-balanced brine of vinegar, salt, and spices—has been used as a medicinal drink, energy tonic, and hangover cure. Or maybe all three. When the Philadelphia Eagles beat the Dallas Cowboys on a ferociously hot September day, Philadelphia defensive end Hugh Douglas said, "I may start drinking pickle juice when I'm just sitting home chilling."

Marya and Otis Baron's Dilly Beans with Thai Chiles

PORTLAND, MAINE

Marya and Otis Baron live in Portland, Maine, in an 1837 house that Mr. Baron, a custom woodworker, is restoring. Mr. Baron learned canning from his mother on Cape Cod, who "always had a garden of some sort. She always made traditional New England dilly beans." Mr. Baron has revamped traditional recipes that call for the dill—which gives dilly beans their name—to remain in the mixture throughout the process, preferring to strain it out after heating the brine and adding dill seeds to the jars.

The Barons like to serve the beans with steamed lobster—and just about anything else.

FOR THE BRINE

5 cups cider vinegar

5 cups water

¼ cup plus 3 tablespoons pickling salt

1 large bunch fresh dill, tied with string

FOR THE PICKLES

24 dried Thai chiles, crushed, or ¼ teaspoon red pepper flakes

12 garlic cloves, thinly sliced

¼ cup yellow mustard seeds

2 tablespoons dill seeds

2 tablespoons whole black peppercorns

Twelve 1-pint canning jars and lids, washed, sterilized, and standing by in scalding-hot water

4 pounds fresh green beans, yellow wax beans, or a mix, ends trimmed to fit in 1-pint jars

1. To make the brine: In a large nonreactive saucepan, bring the vinegar, water, salt, and dill to a boil over high heat. Reduce the heat to medium and simmer for 15 minutes. Remove and discard the dill.

2. To make the pickles: Evenly divide the chiles, garlic, mustard and dill seeds, and peppercorns among the jars. Pack each jar tightly with beans, then fill with brine up to ½ inch below the rim.

3. Run a knife down and around each jar to release air bubbles. Wipe the rims and seal the jars. Process in boiling water for 10 minutes. Cool the jars on the counter and store for 1 month before serving to give the flavors a chance to ripen.

———

MAKES 12 PINTS

Pickles, Salsas, and Other Condiments

SHALA'S TORSHI-E LITTEH
Persian Giardiniera

Shala Nostrat learned to pickle after the 1979 Iranian revolution. Unable to return home and missing her family, she used books and her memory to re-create traditional dishes such as litteh, one of many Persian pickles. The pickles were part of the celebration of the winter solstice, when the season's harvest is picked and enjoyed or preserved for the cold months. When one of Ms. Nostrat's twin sons was 8 years old, he proved his talent for identifying subtle flavors. Tasting litteh for the first time, he immediately recognized the marjoram, cilantro, and golpar—a bitterish Persian spice—that define the Iranian condiment.

Ms. Nostrat will not cook with eggplant that has not had a chance to live outdoors and ripen in the sun. She desperately misses the four-season climate of Iran and at the first signal of a cold spell or rain will cook something warming.

In Iran, litteh is stored for many years; after a decade, the preserve is used in folkloric home cures.

1 quart distilled white vinegar, plus more
　　as needed

2 large eggplants, finely chopped

1 large bunch celery with leaves, finely chopped

2 cups finely chopped fresh parsley

2 cups finely chopped fresh cilantro

2 jalapeño chiles, stemmed and finely chopped

12 garlic cloves, peeled

3 medium carrots, peeled and grated

1½ teaspoons dried tarragon

1½ teaspoons dried marjoram

1½ teaspoons golpar (optional)

1½ teaspoons kosher salt

1 teaspoon freshly ground black pepper

1 teaspoon ground turmeric

1 teaspoon ground cumin

1 teaspoon black caraway seeds

1 teaspoon ground coriander (optional)

Six 1-pint canning jars and lids, washed, sterilized,
　　and standing by in scalding-hot water

1. In a large nonreactive pot, bring the vinegar and eggplant to a simmer. Cook about 10 minutes, until the eggplant is soft. Transfer to a large bowl and cool completely.

2. Stir the remaining ingredients into the eggplant until combined. Divide the mixture evenly among the jars. Add more vinegar to each jar as needed to cover the vegetables completely. Wipe the rims and seal the jars. Refrigerate for at least two weeks before serving. The pickles will keep for one year in the refrigerator.

MAKES 6 PINTS

Manisha Pandit's Lime Pickle

LOUISVILLE, COLORADO

Manisha Pandit and Divyesh Patel were friends in the same Bombay computer company before they married, started their own technology business, and traveled through twenty-seven of the United States looking for adventure and customers. They liked the sun in Louisville, Colorado—it shines 300 days a year—and so they settled there in 2005 with their daughter. Ms. Pandit made sun pickles for the first time when she ran out of the nimboo pickles that her sister in Bombay supplied. She couldn't get nimboo citrus, a thin-skinned fruit that is about the size of a key lime, but found that small American varieties such as Key or Bearss Limes, as well as small lemons, can make admirable pickles. An excellent nibble that dances in the mouth, the spicy lime brightens up anything dull. Their daughter likes to sprinkle the pickle juice on a cheese and lettuce sandwich.

1 teaspoon methi (fenugreek) seeds

1 teaspoon yellow mustard seeds

¼ teaspoon asafetida

10 small limes, scrubbed and dried well

8 lemons, scrubbed, dried well, and quartered

20 to 30 green Thai chiles, stemmed and halved

4-inch piece fresh ginger, peeled and cut into 1-inch matchsticks

½ cup sugar

½ cup kosher salt

¼ cup fresh lemon juice

2 teaspoons ground turmeric

One 2-quart canning jar and lid, washed, sterilized, and standing by in scalding-hot water

1. In a small skillet, toast the methi seeds, mustard seeds, and asafetida for 4 to 5 minutes, until the methi seeds are a light reddish brown. Let the spices cool to room temperature, then grind to a powder with a mortar and pestle or spice grinder.

2. Pack all of the ingredients in the jar, cover tightly, and shake well. Set the jar in the sun for 4 hours a day for about 4 weeks, until the juices have thickened and the peels are soft, shaking the jar each day.

3. Let the jar sit in a cool, dark place for 4 to 5 days, then transfer into smaller jars and refrigerate. The pickles will keep for 1 year in the refrigerator.

MAKES 4 PINTS

NOTE: You must have a window that gets at least four hours of bright sun every day; the jar must get very warm for this pickle to cook.

Pickles, Salsas, and Other Condiments

Meryam's Preserved Lemons

ASTORIA, NEW YORK

In Astoria, Queens, a three-block-long stretch of bakeries, shops, and cafes known as Little Morocco makes architect Meryam Ouzzano feel at home. She moved to the United States to finish her professional training and to establish the sort of independent life that is not easily accomplished by women in Morocco. About 85,000 Moroccan expatriates now live in the United States. "It feels exactly like Morocco," Meryam says. "The food, the smells, the products are the same. The tables set up outside are the same. Even the noise is the same." The greatest single difference between cooking in the United States and cooking in Morocco, she notes, is scale. In Astoria, she cooks for one, a phenomenon that astounds her mother, who counts on family and friends dropping by at mealtime and cannot imagine cooking for fewer than a dozen.

One Big Table

5 to 10 small, unblemished lemons, scrubbed

Sea salt

One 1-quart wide-mouth canning jar and lid, washed, sterilized, and standing by in scalding-hot water

Fresh lemon juice, as needed

1. Cut the protruding tip from the stem end of the lemons. Make one lengthwise cut through each lemon, but leave the two halves attached at the stem end. Make a second cut perpendicular to the first, leaving the quarters attached.

2. Stuff the lemons generously with salt, then pack them tightly into the jar, pressing down so they release some juice. Cover the jar and store at room temperature in a dark closet or cabinet. After 3 days, check to make sure the lemons are covered with their juice. If the lemons on top are not covered, add lemon juice as needed. Let the lemons cure for 1 month before using, then refrigerate. The lemons will keep for about 6 months in the refrigerator.

3. To serve, remove the lemons from the jar with tongs and rinse to remove the excess salt.

———

MAKES 5 TO 10 PRESERVED LEMONS

EL TONAYENSE TACO TRUCKS
TOMATILLO SALSA

Salsa is the refining point for the simple, fresh tacos sold by Benjamin Santana from his four trucks in San Francisco's Mission District. Mr. Santana and his wife, Marisela, consider their two salsas, red and green, their secret weapons and the tacos' *razón de ser*. Mrs. Santana, working alone, makes fifteen gallons of salsa twice daily. This version, she says, while not the secret recipe, is a version that she likes nearly as well with chips or with El Tonayense's Chicken Burrito (page 367).

1 pound tomatillos, husks removed and rinsed in hot water

2 serrano chiles, stemmed

1 medium white onion, peeled and quartered

½ cup water

2 garlic cloves, peeled

Kosher salt

½ cup chopped fresh cilantro

1 tablespoon fresh lime juice

Freshly ground black pepper

1. In a blender or food processor, process the tomatillos, chiles, onion, water, garlic, and ½ teaspoon salt together until mostly smooth.

2. Transfer the mixture to a large skillet, bring to a simmer, and cook for 10 to 15 minutes, stirring occasionally, until thick and the flavors have blended.

3. Transfer to a serving bowl and cool to room temperature. Stir in the cilantro and lime juice. Season with salt and pepper to taste, and serve.

MAKE ABOUT 2 CUPS

THE SALSA GAMES

From the cutting of the rosca de reyes (Three Kings cake) in January to the tamale-making party at Christmas, Martha Ojeda-Aguilar Bayer's family—between her twelve siblings, their spouses and children, and the grandchildren, there are seventy-nine of them—have a full calendar of birthday parties, anniversaries, graduations, and holidays, plus the Saturday cooking and knitting club and Wednesday lunches. For Sunday dinner they congregate at the home of Reynalda Aguilar de Ojeda, the clan's matriarch. It can get crowded—and loud—with folks from San Diego and Tijuana in the kitchen to prepare traditional dishes. Salsa is a constant source of contention; everyone claims there is only one true version: his or hers. It has surpassed ketchup in condiment sales in the United States, but most Americans know it only as the dance partner for a tortilla chip. This, says the Mexican-born Ms. Bayer, seems strangely limiting. Salsa is a many-splendored thing with many uses. "It brings the flavor of my roots to all my dishes. I wouldn't consider myself a true Mexican if I didn't have homemade hot sauce in the refrigerator." Everyone has a signature salsa—her own variations include salsa cruda (raw), salsa cocida (boiled), and salsa asada (roasted). Her brother-in-law Juan makes the chile de molcajete using a traditional lava stone mortar and pestle. One sister, Rosa, makes the salsa borracha (drunken salsa), while another, Mercedes, makes the hot salsa in the blender. "It's the easiest to make, and everyone knows that Mercedes is lazy!" Martha declares, and then adds, "Or maybe she is just more practical than the rest of us."

Grandmother Ojeda's Toasted Pasilla Chile and Sunflower Seed Salsa

SAN DIEGO, CALIFORNIA

"My family has two words to describe sauce," said Martha Ojeda-Aguilar Bayer. "*Salsa* is the one we use to give other foods an extra flavor when cooking, and in general, it's not very spicy. *Chile* is the one we use as a condiment. We like this very hot and add it to almost everything on our plate. My father's mother taught my mother how to make this salsa, and it's one our entire family agrees upon. The nuts give body to soups or sauces, but its toasty, nutty flavor is also delicious on roasted meat and tacos."

2 dried pasilla chiles, seeds removed

¼ cup raw shelled unsalted sunflower seeds

1 dried finger chile or chile de árbol

3 garlic cloves, peeled

3 medium tomatoes, quartered

2 tablespoons olive oil

¼ cup chopped fresh cilantro

Kosher salt

1. In a dry cast-iron skillet, toast the pasilla chiles and sunflower seeds over medium heat about 4 minutes, until aromatic. Transfer the pasilla chiles and sunflower seeds to the food processor.

2. Add the finger chile and garlic to the skillet and toast over medium heat for 2 to 4 minutes, until soft. Transfer the finger chile and garlic to the food processor.

3. Drizzle the tomatoes with the oil, add to the pan, and cook over medium heat about 10 minutes, stirring occasionally, until tender. Transfer the tomatoes to the food processor. Process about 30 seconds, until smooth.

4. Transfer the salsa to a bowl, stir in the cilantro, and season with salt to taste. Cool to room temperature, and serve.

———

MAKES ABOUT 3 CUPS

Pickles, Salsas, and Other Condiments

Martha Ojeda-Aguilar Bayer's Salsa de Tomatillo and Pineapple

SAN DIEGO, CALIFORNIA

This raw salsa is picada—finely chopped so that the individual ingredients explode in the mouth, says Martha Ojeda-Aguilar Bayer. She shares her family's tastes and habits in salsa, using salsa de chile colorado (dried red peppers) for beef and pork tamales or stews, and salsa verde (green salsa that is usually made with serrano or jalapeño peppers and tomatillo) for seafood and sometimes for pork ribs. The Ojeda-Aguilar family does not, however, make fruity salsa, but Martha has a taste for hot salsas made from plums, mangoes, or pineapple. She finds this tart, hot, and refreshing salsa a perfect counterpoint to a hot, sunny day at the market. It is delicious with chips and makes a wonderful condiment for any grilled fish.

½ fresh pineapple, peeled, cored, and chopped

1 pound tomatillos, husks removed, rinsed in hot water, and chopped

2 jalapeño chiles, seeded, veins removed, and finely chopped

1 small red onion, finely chopped

2 tablespoons minced fresh mint

1 tablespoon olive oil

1 tablespoon fresh lemon juice

Kosher salt

In a medium bowl, stir together the pineapple, tomatillos, jalapeños, onion, mint, oil, and lemon juice. Season with salt to taste. Cover and refrigerate for at least 1 hour. Serve.

MAKES ABOUT 3 CUPS

Mercedes Ojeda Hernandez's Hot Salsa

SAN DIEGO, CALIFORNIA

"Why would anyone go through all that work with a molcajete if they have a blender?" asks Mercedes Ojeda Hernandez. "The molcajete has mythical status in my family, but that is about tradition, not taste. We all keep some variation of this chili in our refrigerator and use it on everything. I add more jalapeño to make a spicier sauce. A molcajete makes better decoration than it does a kitchen appliance."

1 cup water

2 large tomatoes, chopped

4 jalapeño chiles, stemmed and chopped

2 garlic cloves, peeled

¼ cup minced fresh cilantro

Kosher salt and freshly ground black pepper

1. In a medium saucepan, bring the water, tomatoes, chiles, and garlic to a simmer. Cook over low heat for 6 to 8 minutes, until tender. Drain the vegetables, reserving the water.

2. Transfer the vegetables to a blender, add the cilantro, and process about 1 minute, until smooth, adding the reserved water as needed to thin. Transfer the salsa to a bowl, season with salt and pepper to taste, and cool to room temperature. Serve.

MAKES ABOUT 2 CUPS

El Chile de Juan Siordia

Juan Siorda, an Ojeda-Aguilar Bayer in-law, grew up on a farm in Mexico and is the family's designated molcajete guy. The large lava mortar and pestle is traditionally used to make salsa and makes everything taste better, he says. "There is something about this rock that gives salsa a unique flavor. It also tastes better when made in large amounts and with my secret ingredient, beer." This salsa is as excellent with meat, chicken, and fish as it is with tortilla chips.

6 ripe plum tomatoes

3 tomatillos, husks removed

3 güerito chiles or yellow Fresno chiles

2 jalapeño chiles

1 serrano chile

2 garlic cloves, peeled

1 dried small red chile

¼ teaspoon finely chopped habanero chile

Mexican lager beer, such as Tecate or Corona, as needed

Kosher salt

1. Preheat the oven to 450°F.

2. Arrange the tomatoes, tomatillos, güeritos, jalapeños, serrano chile, and garlic in a single layer on a baking sheet and roast for 15 to 20 minutes, until soft. Cool the vegetables to room temperature.

3. In a molcajete, grind the güeritos, jalapeños, serrano, garlic, dried red chile, and habanero to a fine paste. Add the tomatoes and tomatillos and grind until thick, adding beer as needed to loosen. The salsa should be thick and slightly chunky.

4. Transfer the salsa to a bowl, and season with salt to taste. Serve.

MAKES ABOUT 3 CUPS

Rosa Ojeda Lyons Drunken Salsa

SAN DIEGO, CALIFORNIA

"My sister Rose found the perfect balance of beer and lime in this fresh fiery salsa," said Martha Ojeda-Aguilar Bayer. It is delicious on chips, grilled meat, tacos, and fish.

8 ripe, firm plum tomatoes, seeded and coarsely chopped

3 serrano or 2 jalapeño chiles, stemmed, seeded, and finely chopped

5 or 6 scallions, green and white parts, or 1 white onion, finely chopped

½ cup minced fresh cilantro, plus more for garnish

¼ cup fresh lime juice

Splash of beer (optional)

Kosher salt and freshly ground black pepper

1. In a medium bowl, stir together the tomatoes, chiles, scallions, cilantro, and lime juice. Add beer as needed to loosen. Season with salt and pepper to taste. Cover and let sit at room temperature about 1 hour, until the flavors have blended.

2. Sprinkle with more cilantro and serve.

MAKES ABOUT 3 CUPS

CHAPTER 3

STEAMING BOWLS: SOUPS, CHOWDERS, AND OTHER CONSOLATIONS

PHO, BIGGER, BETTER, BOUNTIFUL PHO

Kim Nguyen was born in Hanoi, grew up in Saigon, and now lives in Columbus, Ohio. She can tell the story of her life through her experiences with cooking and eating pho, the noodle soup that is considered the national dish of Vietnam. "The first time [a] man tells me that pho was invented in Hanoi, I am sure that he is not well in his head from the war. I was born in Hanoi. In Hanoi, pho is brown water with one piece of meat that you do not dare to eat because maybe, well, you do not know." She says of the Communists, "They do not like good cooking, good time, or good news." And she did not like their pho.

"My parents had eight children, I am in the middle, and my father was a soldier. He thought that if we could get to the south, we could get to America. I was very scared because in school, the Communists told us that Saigon is poor and that everyone starves. We get to Saigon and it is sunny and warm. So much food!"

And so many more ingredients in the pho: "Beef tripe, meatballs! Rice noodles. Bean sprouts, cilantro, Thai basil, hoisin sauce, sometimes shrimp! You could never tell what you would find. They sell pho on the streets; my grandmother makes pho with everything she can buy." Her father decided to leave Vietnam and rented a boat that could fit only half the family, so only the eldest and youngest children went with him.

Mrs. Nguyen was 8 years old. She was one of the middle children who remained in Saigon with their grandmother. Months passed with no news from her father and the others, and her grandmother assumed the worst. Then a decade later, a long-delayed letter arrived in Saigon. "They are in America!" Several years later, when she was 23 years old, Mrs. Nguyen and the rest of the family were reunited with the others in Ohio.

She remembers her first days in America: "My brothers took me to Kroger's, and all I could do was stand and stare. More food than my whole country in one grocery store."

Mrs. Nguyen studied English and met a Vietnamese man whom she soon married. Like the hundreds of thousands of immigrants who preceded her, she learned to cook the food that she had left behind, but in America, her efforts in the kitchen were both an homage to her homeland and a celebration of freedom from want.

From all parts of the world, soups that were subsistence fare in the old country could be made bigger and more complex in the new one, thanks to the bounty of America. Minestrone went from an end-of-the-week soup that was often built from odds and ends to a company meal, thickened with up to three kinds of meat and garnished with a cascade of Parmesan cheese. Greek egg soup acquired meatballs, spinach, lemon, and sometimes orzo. Chinese hot and sour soup became thicker and more dense with meat and exotic mushrooms, Mexican chicken and lime soup gained a mountain of fried corn tortillas and all but turned into a taco salad. The fresh tomato soups made in England and central Europe were enriched with cream.

Some of the bigger and better versions of foreign soups were a result of recipes from various regions converging in America. Borscht may have originated in the Ukraine, but the soup met and married so many other Eastern European cousins in the United States that by the early twentieth century, the beet soup was simply attributed to the Jews (et voilà, the Jewish resorts in the Catskill Mountains north of New York City became known as the Borscht Belt).

When Mrs. Nguyen first made pho with her daughters one Sunday, it was, she says, "to remind them of where we came from. Now when I ask what they want, the answer is always pho, pho, pho." This pho is a far more elaborate affair than the version first mentioned in an American cookbook. In 1936, *Recipes of All Nations* noted: "Pho is the name of an Annamese soup held in high esteem. It is made with beef, a veal bone, onions, a bay leaf, salt and pepper, and a small teaspoon of nuoc-man [sic], a typically Annamese condiment which is used in practically all their dishes. It is made from a kind of brine exuding from decaying fish."

When Mrs. Ngyuen and her husband took their daughters back to Vietnam several years ago, "They hated the pho, even in Saigon. They said it wasn't good, it wasn't pretty, it wasn't filling.

"When I was leaving on the airplane I looked down at my country, it was so green and beautiful, and I knew I was leaving behind everything. That I would not be Vietnamese anymore. The morning after I arrived back in the States, it snowed. I had never seen snow. My mother made pho, the best of my life. I knew right away that it was better to be Vietnamese when you are American."

> "*There is nothing like soup. It is by nature eccentric; no two are ever alike, unless of course you get your soup from cans.*"
> —Laurie Colwin, *Home Cooking*, 1988

Mrs. Nguyen's America the Bountiful Pho

This recipe calls for saw-leaf herb, which is also called long coriander. It is similar in taste to cilantro and can be found in Asian markets.

FOR THE BROTH

3 pounds beef marrow or knuckle bones

Two 3-inch pieces fresh ginger, cut in half lengthwise

2 large yellow onions, unpeeled

2 pounds beef short ribs

1 pound boneless beef chuck

¼ cup fish sauce, such as Vietnamese nuoc mam

3 tablespoons sugar

10 whole star anise, lightly toasted in a dry skillet

6 unpeeled garlic cloves, lightly toasted in a dry skillet

1 cinnamon stick

1 tablespoon coarse sea salt

FOR THE GARNISH AND NOODLES

½ pound boneless beef sirloin

1 pound dried rice sticks, ¹⁄₁₆-inch wide

Vietnamese Meatballs (recipe follows), optional

1 large yellow onion, sliced paper thin

3 scallions, green and white parts, cut into thin rings

1 bunch fresh cilantro, with stems, chopped

1 pound mung bean sprouts

1 bunch basil (preferably Thai basil), separated into sprigs

10 sprigs fresh mint

12 saw-leaf herb leaves (optional)

6 Thai bird chiles or 1 serrano chile, cut into thin rings

1 lime, cut into 6 thin wedges

1. To make the broth: At least 1 day before you plan to serve the pho, preheat the oven to 400°F. Place the bones in a roasting pan and roast, turning frequently, until fragrant and nicely browned, about 20 minutes.

2. While the bones are roasting, set a bowl of cold water by the stove. Use the flat side of a knife to slightly flatten the ginger pieces. Turn a burner on high. One at a time, place the ginger pieces on a cooking fork and hold over the heat, turning frequently to char the skin. When nicely charred, plunge the ginger in cold water. When cool enough to handle, remove the skin and place the ginger in a soup pot.

3. Repeat the charring and peeling process with the onions.

4. When the bones are done, transfer them to the soup pot. Add 1 or 2 cups cold water to the roasting pan and scrape up the bits. Pour the drippings into the soup pot. Add the short ribs, chuck, fish sauce, and sugar. Add enough water to cover everything by at least 2 inches, and set the pot over medium heat. Bring to a boil and immediately reduce the heat to the lowest possible level. Skim frequently to remove impurities that rise to the surface.

5. Wrap the star anise, garlic, and cinnamon in cheesecloth and tie with a long piece of kitchen string. Tie the loose end to the pot handle and the wrapped spices after 1 hour. Remove the spices after 4 hours, but do not discard them.

6. Simmer for 12 hours in all, skimming as needed. Never allow the liquid to boil. Add cold water as necessary to cover the bones by at least 2 inches at all times. In the final hour of cooking, return the wrapped spices to the pot and add the salt.

7. Set a fine-mesh strainer over a tall storage container. Ladle the broth through the strainer. Carefully transfer the short ribs and chuck to a plate until cool enough to handle. Discard the remaining solids.

8. Remove the bones, membranes, and fat from the short ribs and discard. Remove the gristle from the chuck. Shred all the meat into bite-size pieces with a fork and return to the broth. Cover and refrigerate overnight.

9. About 45 minutes before serving, skim the layer of fat from the broth and transfer the broth to a large saucepan over low heat.

10. Place the sirloin in the freezer for 30 minutes. Meanwhile, place the noodles in a large bowl, cover with hot water, and soak for 15 minutes. Drain the noodles in a colander and run cold water over them. If using the meatballs, at least 20 minutes before serving, add them to the broth or warm them separately in a little broth to serve on the side. Warm six large, deep bowls. Arrange the remaining garnishes in serving bowls on the table.

11. For the garnish: with a very sharp knife, slice the sirloin across the grain into wafer-thin slices. Bring a large pot of water to a boil. Plunge the noodles into the boiling water for 1 minute, then drain. Divide noodles into the six bowls. Ladle the broth and cooked meats over the noodles, top with the raw sirloin and serve. Guests can customize their pho by adding garnishes at the table.

———

SERVES 6 WITH ENOUGH BROTH AND COOKED MEAT FOR ANOTHER MEAL

Vietnamese Meatballs

These meatballs are traditionally braised in Vietnamese caramel sauce and eaten between slices of bread or spread like pâté. For this soup, they are browned in a skillet but finish cooking in the broth.

1 pound ground chuck

2 tablespoons fish sauce, such as Vietnamese nuoc mam

1 tablespoon soy sauce

2 tablespoons sugar

1 teaspoon freshly ground black pepper

½ teaspoon kosher salt

3 garlic cloves, minced

2 shallots, minced

Vegetable oil, for panfrying

1. Line a baking sheet with waxed paper. Using a fork, combine the ground chuck, fish sauce, soy sauce, sugar, pepper, salt, garlic, and shallots in a large bowl. Shape the mixture into 2-inch balls and place on the baking sheet. Cover with plastic wrap and refrigerate for at least 1 hour.

2. Warm several tablespoons of oil in a large heavy skillet over medium-high heat. Working in batches, add the meatballs, taking care not to crowd the pan. Fry, turning carefully to brown on all sides, and transfer them to an unlined baking sheet. If making ahead, cover them with plastic wrap, and refrigerate until needed.

MAKES ABOUT 20 MEATBALLS

Olga Napolilii's Borscht

Until it was sold to the United States in 1867, Alaska was part of the Russian empire, and the onion-shaped domes of Orthodox churches still rise against the sky. Through Russians, Russian descendants, and "Creoles" (children of mixed Russian and Native American marriages), Russian dishes have long since become part of Alaskan cooking. When she first arrived to supervise an exchange program for gifted high school students, Olga Napolilii quickly found that borscht, the meaty cabbage and beet soup of Russia, became her lingua franca. "Every Russian and Ukrainian family cherishes their borscht," she says. People in Alaska relish the hearty soup and want to know the secret of making the best. Some add navy beans, some like it sweeter, some more tart, some add beef, some use water, some add kielbasa at the end. Ms. Napolilii, who settled in Fairbanks, where she now teaches school, promises that no matter what recipe is used, borscht is always better on the second day.

½ pound slab bacon or pancetta

2 quarts homemade beef broth or low-sodium store-bought beef broth

1 medium onion, finely chopped

2 bay leaves

3 medium Yukon gold potatoes, scrubbed and cut into ½-inch pieces

½ small head green cabbage, cored and shredded

2 medium tomatoes, cored and coarsely chopped

1 tablespoon sugar

1 tablespoon distilled white vinegar

1 tablespoon olive oil

2 medium carrots, cut into 2-inch matchsticks

1 medium beet, peeled and shredded

2 garlic cloves, minced

Kosher salt and freshly ground black pepper

½ cup sour cream, for garnish

¼ cup chopped fresh parsley, chives, or dill, for garnish

1. In a Dutch oven, cover the bacon with water by 2 inches, bring to a simmer, and cook for 20 minutes. Remove the bacon and pour out the water.

2. Return the bacon to the pot with the beef broth, onion, and bay leaves. Bring to a simmer, cover, and cook about 2 hours, until tender.

3. Transfer the bacon to a carving board to cool slightly; separate the meat from the fat and skin. Discard fat and skin and finely chop the meat.

4. Strain the broth and discard the solids. Clean the pot and return the broth to the pot. Add the potatoes and cabbage, bring to a simmer, and cook for 15 minutes. Stir in the tomatoes, sugar, and vinegar, and cook for 2 minutes.

5. Meanwhile, in a medium skillet, heat the oil over medium-low heat. Add the carrots and beet and cook about 10 minutes, until soft. Stir in the garlic and cook about 1 minute, until aromatic.

6. Stir the carrot mixture and reserved bacon into the broth. Cook about 5 minutes, until the flavors have blended. Season with salt and pepper to taste. To serve, ladle into bowls and garnish with the sour cream and herbs.

SERVES 6

Sharon Martinelli's Italian Beef and Barley Soup

Sharon Martinelli has been recording her family's favorite recipes in a three-ring binder for decades. They are part of her inheritance. She got this recipe, a variation on a classic Eastern European soup, from a friend of a friend. She serves it as a main course, accompanied by bread and salad. It is so good that it can be intimidating. "To my family, I am the best cook in the world," she says. "My son brought a girlfriend home for dinner not long ago and she kept saying 'I don't know if I can compete with you as a cook.'"

One 1-pound bottom or top round steak, trimmed and cut into ³⁄₄-inch pieces

Kosher salt and freshly ground black pepper

2 tablespoons olive oil

6 cups homemade beef broth or low-sodium store-bought beef broth

One 14.5-ounce can diced tomatoes

½ pound green beans, trimmed and cut into 2-inch lengths

8 ounces white mushrooms, thinly sliced (optional)

1 large onion, finely chopped

1 celery stalk, finely chopped

4 garlic cloves, thinly sliced

½ cup fresh or frozen peas or corn (optional)

½ cup pearl barley

3 carrots, peeled and cut into ½-inch pieces

½ cup grated pecorino Romano cheese (about 2 ounces), for garnish

1. Pat the beef dry and season with salt and pepper. In a Dutch oven, heat the olive oil over medium-high heat. Add the beef and cook for 6 to 8 minutes, until well browned on all sides.

2. Pour off the excess fat from the pot and stir in the broth, tomatoes with their juice, green beans, mushrooms (if using), half of the onion, celery, garlic, peas (if using), and barley. Bring to a simmer and cook about 1 hour.

3. Stir in the remaining onion and the carrots and cook about 35 to 45 minutes more, until the carrots are soft and the meat is tender. Season with salt and pepper to taste.

4. To serve, ladle into bowls and sprinkle with the cheese.

SERVES 6 TO 8

AUNT TATI'S BAKED BEEF VEGETABLE SOUP

"My great-grandmother's family immigrated to Texas from Germany around the turn of the century," says Becca Vlasta, a pediatrician. "They didn't like the heat, so they moved north near the town now called Tabor, in South Dakota. They didn't like the cold there, plus life in general was harder. They lived in a mud hut, and when the snow got too heavy, the ceiling would fall down in little clumps. When I was little, my grandmother told me that if you live in a mud hut you better cook in a covered pot. Her sister, Tati, kept this soup in a big covered pot buried in the coals of her cook fire. It acted as both furnace and dinner. Aunt Tati died when I was 6 years old; she was over 90 years old. She looked about 110 to me, but I thought she was really cool because she baked her soup in my grandmother's fireplace in Sioux Falls. Everybody was afraid that she'd burn the house down, but she never did. We always had this soup and the soft, buttery cheese bread she made when we visited. I'm fortunate to have a wood oven on my terrace, so I make Tati's vegetable soup in a ten-gallon cast-iron pot on Saturday, and we eat it for lunch after church on Sunday in the winter. When I don't have spaetzle, I serve the soup with big, rustic croutons that I make by taking bite-size hunks of stale bread, tossing them with olive oil, and letting them dry out in the oven while the soup bakes."

Lard was traditionally used for cooking this soup, but Dr. Vlasta uses olive oil.

*A prize-winning vegetable arrangement displayed on
Astroturf at the Butler County Fair in Ohio.*

96

One Big Table

1 pound beef chuck-eye roast, trimmed and cut into ¾-inch chunks

2 teaspoons coarse kosher salt

½ teaspoon freshly ground black pepper

1 tablespoon olive oil or vegetable oil

1 small chicken, cut into quarters

1 cup high quality canned crushed tomatoes

2 medium yellow onions, finely chopped

½ cup parched corn, dried hominy, or frozen corn kernels

1 red bell pepper, coarsely chopped

4 celery stalks, coarsely chopped

4 carrots, coarsely chopped

1 parsnip, peeled and coarsely chopped

1 cup fresh or frozen lima beans

1 cup brown lentils

1 cup yellow split peas

1 cup green split peas

1 smoked ham hock

10 cups homemade chicken broth or low-sodium store-bought chicken broth, plus more as needed

1 cup dried spaetzle or short, thick pasta (such as rotini or gemelli)

Red pepper flakes to taste

Toasted croutons, for garnish (optional)

1. Preheat the oven to 250°F. Pat the beef dry and season it lightly with salt and black pepper. In a Dutch oven, heat the oil over medium-high heat. Add the beef and cook for 6 to 8 minutes, until well browned on all sides. With a slotted spoon, transfer the beef to a large bowl.

2. Season the chicken lightly with salt and black pepper. Brown it on both sides in the Dutch oven, about 6 to 8 minutes. Use the slotted spoon to transfer it to the bowl with the beef.

3. Reduce the heat to low, add the crushed tomatoes, and cook, stirring frequently. Add the onions, corn, bell pepper, celery, carrots, parsnip, and lima beans, and stir to combine. Add the lentils and the split peas. Return the beef and the chicken to the pot, and add the ham hock, chicken broth, and enough water to cover the ingredients by 1 inch. Season with half of the remaining salt and black pepper.

4. Cover the pot tightly and place in the oven for 1 hour. Do not allow the broth to boil or the meat will toughen.

5. Reduce the heat to 225°F and bake for 4 hours. Add additional broth or water to keep the ingredients covered by 1 inch.

6. Stir in the spaetzle, add red pepper flakes to taste, and adjust the seasoning with salt and pepper. Cover and return the soup to the oven. When it returns to a simmer—about 10 minutes—turn off the heat and leave the pot in the warm oven overnight.

7. Warm the soup on the stovetop prior to serving in large bowls, garnished with toasted croutons, if desired.

———

SERVES 8 TO 12 AS A MAIN COURSE

Homa Movafaghi's Ashe Reshteh
Persian Noodle Soup

MCLEAN, VIRGINIA

Homa Movafaghi grew up in Mashhad, Iran, and moved to the United States thirty years ago. During the workweek, she is a public school administrator. In the evenings and on weekends, she assumes her favorite role, that of tutor, and focuses on her favorite subject, teaching Farsi to Americans and third-generation Iranian Americans. She organizes poetry nights in which all verse is recited in Farsi. She feels that cooking is as powerful a cultural ambassador as language, and makes this soup for the picnic that is traditionally held the thirteenth day after the Persian New Year, Sizdah Bedar, in the early spring. The soup is finished when it is not too watery and not too thick. You should be able to see all of the ingredients.

10 cups water

6 ½ cups homemade beef broth or low-sodium store-bought beef broth

¼ cup dried red kidney beans, soaked in cold water overnight or in boiling water for 3 hours and drained

¼ cup dried navy beans, soaked in cold water overnight or in boiling water for 3 hours and drained

6 tablespoons olive oil

3 medium onions, finely chopped

12 garlic cloves, minced

One 15-ounce can chickpeas, drained and rinsed

½ pound spinach, stemmed and coarsely chopped

1 bunch scallions, green and white parts, coarsely chopped

1 cup coarsely chopped fresh parsley

1 cup coarsely chopped fresh cilantro

1 cup coarsely chopped fresh dill

2 teaspoons ground turmeric

Kosher salt and freshly ground black pepper

2 tablespoons dried mint

4 ounces *reshteh* (Persian wheat noodles) or cappellini, broken into 3 pieces

1 cup sour cream or *kashk* (See Note)

2 tablespoons fresh lemon juice

½ teaspoon ground saffron mixed with 2 tablespoons hot water

1. In a Dutch oven, combine the water, broth, and kidney beans. Bring to a simmer and cook for 30 to 45 minutes, until just beginning to become tender.

2. Stir in the navy beans and simmer for 45 minutes to 1 hour, until all the beans are tender.

3. In a large skillet, heat 3 tablespoons of the oil over medium heat. Add the onions and cook for 8 to 10 minutes, until the onions begin to brown. Stir in the garlic and cook about 1 minute, until aromatic. Add half the onion mixture to the soup and set aside the remaining onion mixture for garnish.

4. Stir the chickpeas, spinach, scallions, parsley, cilantro, dill, turmeric, 1 teaspoon salt, and ¼ teaspoon pepper into the soup. Bring to a simmer, partially covered, and cook over low heat for 2 to 3 hours, until the soup thickens.

5. Meanwhile, in a small saucepan, heat the remaining 3 tablespoons oil over medium heat. Add the mint and cook about 10 seconds. Remove from the heat.

6. Stir the noodles into the soup and cook for 5 to 10 minutes, until tender.

7. In a small bowl, whisk together the sour cream, lemon juice, and ½ teaspoon salt. Stir all but

2 tablespoons of the sour cream mixture into the soup, then stir in the mint oil.

8. To serve, ladle into bowls, sprinkle with the reserved onion mixture, and drizzle with the remaining sour cream mixture and saffron water.

———

SERVES 6

NOTE: When Ms. Movafaghi first moved to the United States, it was difficult to find kashk, the special whey that is traditionally used to make this soup, so she got in the habit of using sour cream. Kashk is far more available today.

Persia, Cossacks at lunch, circa 1900.

Mavis Lowe's West Indian Pumpkin Soup

When Mavis Lowe was 12 years old, living on the island of Grenada, her mother had a stroke. She remembers that her mother told Lizzie, the woman who helped around the house, "'Show this child everything you can do in the kitchen.' So, everything I cook is West Indian that I learned from Lizzie, rather than my mother, including this pumpkin soup."

Mrs. Lowe married at age 19 and bore five children. She moved to the United States in 1942 and worked as a nurse for twenty-five years before retiring in Orlando. Her pumpkin soup is popular with everyone, especially her four living children. "It is a West Indian recipe," she says. "Most people make it in the islands."

She married her current husband, James Lowe, who is of Chinese descent and grew up in Jamaica, ten years ago. Nowadays, Mrs. Lowe only reaches for her pots when someone asks her to make one of her traditional soups. "My husband does most of the cooking," she laughs, "which is fine by me. He's a very, very nice man, and he loves to make his Chinese food. I'm a very lucky woman."

This pumpkin soup can be made without plantains, yams, and dumplings, but with them it becomes a main course. Tannia root is native to the Americas and West Indies. Also known as malangá in Cuba and yautia in Puerto Rico, it belongs to the same family as taro.

½ pound pig tails

12 or 13 cups water

1½ pounds pumpkin, peeled, seeded, and cut into large chunks

2¼ cups all-purpose flour (optional)

Kosher salt

2 green plantains, peeled and thinly sliced (optional)

2 sweet potatoes, peeled and cut into 1-inch pieces (optional)

1 small onion, finely chopped

2 scallions, green and white parts, chopped

2 garlic cloves, minced

2 tannias, peeled and cut into 1-inch chunks

1 red chile, stemmed, seeded, and finely chopped

1 sprig fresh thyme

Freshly ground black pepper

1. In a Dutch oven, cover the pig tails with 12 cups of the water. Bring to a simmer and cook about 2 hours, until tender.

2. Stir in the pumpkin and cook about 40 minutes, until the pumpkin is soft. Using a slotted spoon, transfer the pumpkin to a food processor and process until smooth. Return the pumpkin puree to the pot.

3. If making dumplings, in a medium bowl, combine the flour and 1 teaspoon salt. Stir in the remaining 1 cup water until a dough forms. Portion and form into 12 small balls.

4. Stir the plantains and yams (if using), the onion, scallions, garlic, tannias, chile, and thyme into the soup and bring to a simmer over high heat. Add the dumplings, one at a time. Reduce the heat to medium-low and cook for 10 to 15 minutes, until the vegetables are soft and the dumplings are cooked through.

5. Discard the pig tails and the thyme sprig. Season with salt and pepper to taste, and serve.

SERVES 6 TO 8

Pamela Gurock's Gruenkern Soup
Green Wheat Kernel Soup

When it comes to ritual, Pamela Gurock is fervently pan-denominational. She's borrowed from the pagan winter solstice festival to create her Christmas celebration, from secular history to mount a Pilgrim pageant for Thanksgiving, and from a Druid's reverence for nature to observe Sukkoth, the Jewish harvest festival in the late fall. She has celebrated Sukkoth in a lean-to of woven vines, grapes, and leaves on a terrace thirty stories above Park Avenue, on a low-lying table under a pup tent in the garden of a tenement, and in a sturdy caterer's tent on a patio in a New York City suburb. This stout, steamy soup is so insulating and satisfying, it could be dinner itself.

3 quarts water

1 pound gruenkern (green wheat kernels), rinsed and soaked overnight

4 pounds beef short ribs

2 meaty beef shin bones

2 medium onions, coarsely chopped

3 medium carrots, peeled and coarsely chopped

Kosher salt and freshly ground black pepper

1. In a large Dutch oven, combine the water, gruenkern, short ribs, bones, onion, and carrots with 2 teaspoons salt and ½ teaspoon pepper. Bring the mixture to a simmer over medium heat, skimming off the foam as it rises. Reduce the heat to medium-low and cook about 2 hours, until the wheat is soft and the meat is tender and falling off the bones.

2. Transfer the short ribs and beef bones to a carving board to cool slightly, then separate the meat from the bones. Discard the fat and gristle, cut the meat into ½-inch pieces, and return it to the soup. Scoop out any marrow and return it to the pot. Discard the bones.

3. Skim any fat off the surface of the soup. Season with salt and pepper to taste, and serve.

SERVES 8 TO 10

FREE TRADE · DEMOCRACY · CLEVELAND SOUP 1893 · "LEST WE FORGET" · STRIKES = LOCK-OUTS = NO WORK. · LEON BARRITT

Barbara Tropp's Chinese Chicken Broth

SAN FRANCISCO, CALIFORNIA

The late Barbara Tropp, an anthropologist who spent years studying Asian cultures before opening her restaurants, was admired by serious Chinese food fanatics—and feared by pretenders. She credited this soup with much of her success.

One Big Table

3 to 3½ pounds chicken necks and backs, cut into 2-inch pieces

4 quarts water

One 1-inch piece fresh ginger, peeled, cut into 4 coins, and smashed

1 large scallion, cut into 3-inch lengths and smashed

4 whole Sichuan peppercorns (optional)

1. In a large Dutch oven, combine the chicken bones and water. Bring to a simmer over low heat, skimming off the foam as it rises, and cook for 15 minutes. Add the ginger, scallion, and peppercorns (if using), and simmer for 3 to 4 hours, without stirring, until the liquid is reduced by half. Make sure liquid never boils.

2. Remove the pot from the heat and let sit for 30 minutes.

3. Line a fine-mesh strainer or colander with a triple layer of damp cheesecloth and set it over a tall container. Gently ladle the broth into the strainer, being careful not to include any sediment from the pot. Refrigerate the broth until needed. Skim any fat from the broth before using. The broth may be frozen up to two months.

MAKES ABOUT 8 CUPS

1538 Arbor Day Picnic.

FAITH KRAMER'S HOT AND SOUR SOUP

The first time Faith Kramer tasted Sichuan-style hot and sour soup, she had a cold. "A friend came over with take-out from a place in San Francisco," she says. "One whiff and my sinuses cleared. One taste and I knew it was not just medicine for my cold but my soul." A good hot and sour soup should be spicy and tangy, with a rich, full-bodied taste and lots of texture from mushrooms and vegetables, she says. Now married, Ms. Kramer is rearing two sons, cooking constantly, and blogging about it all.

3 tablespoons soy sauce

3 tablespoons shaoxing wine (Chinese rice wine) or dry sherry

2 tablespoons water

2 tablespoons cornstarch

Freshly ground black pepper

6 ounces boneless, skinless chicken thighs, trimmed and cut into 1½- by ¼-inch strips

¼ cup dried lily buds

¼ cup dried wood ear mushrooms

6 medium dried shiitake mushrooms

Boiling water

1-ounce bundle cellophane (bean thread) noodles

6 cups chicken broth, homemade, or low-sodium store-bought chicken broth

One 1-inch piece fresh ginger, peeled

1 carrot, cut into 1½- by ¼-inch strips

½ small head bok choy, white stalks only, trimmed and cut into 1½- by ½-inch strips

8 ounces firm tofu, cut into ¼-inch cubes

⅓ cup rice vinegar, plus more to taste

1 tablespoon Asian sesame oil

Sugar to taste

Chili oil (optional)

2 tablespoons chopped fresh cilantro, for garnish

2 scallions, green and white parts, thinly sliced, for garnish

1. In a medium bowl, whisk together 1 tablespoon each of the soy sauce, wine, water, cornstarch, and ⅛ teaspoon pepper. Add chicken, and mix until combined. Set aside.

2. In a medium bowl, combine the lily buds, wood ears, and shiitakes and cover with boiling water. Let sit about 15 minutes, until soft. In a small bowl, cover the noodles with cold water and let sit about 15 minutes, until soft.

3. Drain the mushrooms. Halve the lily buds crosswise. Remove and discard any hard bits from the wood ears. Rinse the shiitakes to remove any grit from their gills. Thinly slice the mushrooms. Drain the noodles and cut them into 2- to 3-inch lengths.

4. In a Dutch oven, combine the chicken broth and ginger. Bring to a simmer and cook for 15 minutes. Discard the ginger. Stir in the lily buds, wood ears, shiitakes, noodles, carrot, and bok choy. Return to a simmer, stir in the chicken and marinade, cover, and cook for 2 to 3 minutes.

5. Gently stir in the tofu, the remaining 2 tablespoons soy sauce, 2 tablespoons wine, and ¼ teaspoon pepper. In a small bowl, mix together the remaining 1 tablespoon cornstarch and 1 tablespoon water. Add to the soup and cook, stirring constantly, until soup has thickened.

6. Stir in the vinegar and sesame oil, remove the soup from the heat, season with sugar, vinegar, pepper, and chili oil (if using) to taste. Ladle into bowls and garnish with the cilantro and scallions.

SERVES 6

Marianne Faso's Chicken Noodle Soup

ERIE, PENNSYLVANIA

When Miss Gillis, a proper, young Pennsylvania Dutch lady, married Mr. Faso, a Sicilian, they "talked about food, argued about food, obsessed about food, even glorified it," says Miss Gillis's granddaughter, food writer Melanie Barnard. Ms. Barnard has spent much of her life finding culinary bridges, like this classic Pennsylvania Dutch noodle soup enlivened with basil and grated cheese. "My Pennsylvania Dutch grandma, Cecelia Shepard Gillis, made the egg noodles from scratch, and my Sicilian nonna [grandmother] Stephanie Faso grew a lot of herbs. They never made this soup together; the coalition is from my mother, Marianne Faso, who cooked constantly." To keep the chicken succulent, Ms. Barnard poaches it for only an hour—less than one would to make a full-bodied chicken broth—and then adds high quality commercial broth to boost the flavor. Homemade fresh or frozen stock could certainly be substituted for the store-bought stock in the recipe. The result, which she sometimes serves with Pennsylvania Dutch biscuits and other times with Italian bread or bread sticks, is clear evidence of the power of a "melting pot."

FOR THE BROTH

10 cups water

One 3½- to 4-pound chicken with neck, cut into 8 pieces and trimmed

1 onion, quartered

1 carrot, cut into 1-inch pieces

1 celery stalk, cut into 1-inch pieces

½ small fennel bulb, cored and cut into 1-inch pieces

¼ cup chopped fresh parsley stems

1 tablespoon chopped fresh oregano

1 tablespoon chopped fresh thyme

2 teaspoons kosher salt

1 bay leaf

3 black peppercorns

FOR THE SOUP

1 quart low-sodium store-bought chicken broth

2 carrots, thinly sliced

½ cup fresh or thawed frozen peas

12 ounces Fresh Egg Noodles (recipe follows) or 8 ounces store-bought very thin dried egg noodles

¼ cup grated Parmesan cheese (about 1 ounce), plus more for garnish

2 tablespoons chopped fresh basil

Kosher salt and freshly ground black pepper

1. To make the broth: In a large Dutch oven, cover chicken and all of the vegetables and seasonings with water and bring to a simmer over low heat. Skim off the foam as it rises, and cook for 45 minutes to 1 hour, until the chicken is firm and an instant-read thermometer reads 175°F in the thighs and drumsticks and 165°F in the breasts.

2. Transfer the chicken to a carving board until cool enough to handle. Remove the skin from the chicken and the meat from the bones and shred the meat into bite-size pieces. Strain the broth through a fine-mesh strainer and return it to the Dutch oven. Skim any fat from the broth.

3. To make the soup: Add the store-bought broth to the pot and bring to a simmer. Add the carrots and cook for 2 minutes. Add the peas and noodles and cook for 3 to 4 minutes more, until the noodles are tender. Stir in the chicken and cook about 1 minute, until heated through. Remove from the heat and stir in the cheese and basil. Season with salt and pepper to taste.

4. To serve, ladle the soup into bowls and garnish with more cheese.

———

SERVES 6

Fresh Egg Noodles

1½ cups unbleached all-purpose flour

2 large eggs

2 teaspoons olive oil

2 teaspoons water, plus more as needed

2 tablespoons chopped fresh oregano

2 tablespoons grated Parmesan cheese

½ teaspoon kosher salt

1. Combine all the ingredients in a food processor and process about 1 minute, until a ball of dough forms. If the dough does not come together, add water, 1 teaspoon at a time, until it does. Transfer the dough to a lightly floured counter and knead by hand about 3 minutes until smooth. Shape into a ball, cover, and let rest for 10 minutes.

2. Lightly flour a rimmed baking sheet. If using a pasta machine, follow the directions for making noodles about ⅛ inch thick and ½ inch wide. Cut the noodles into 2-inch lengths. If rolling the dough by hand, lightly flour your work surface. Roll the dough until ⅛ inch thick, then cut it into ½ by 2 inches. Spread the noodles out on the baking sheet to dry for at least 15 minutes or up to 2 hours before using.

———

MAKES ABOUT 12 OUNCES

Joseph Bruchac's
Wild Rice and Turkey Soup

Joseph Bruchac, a writer and storyteller, lives with his wife, Carol, in the same house in the Adirondacks where he was raised by his maternal grandmother. His grandfather Jesse Bowman was an Abenaki Indian and his grandmother Maryann Dunham came from a Mayflower family. Mr. Bruchac's stories draw on the majestic New York mountains and his Abenaki forebears. His grandmother, who taught him to cook, passed away when he was 16, but not before making him self-sufficient. He continues to garden, forage, and seek out indigenous meat like buffalo and moose.

This rice soup is a special occasion dish. Wild rice, an aquatic grass that grows in the Great Lakes region, was considered sacred. Mr. Bruchac tells the story of Nanabozho, a Native American hero who went out in his canoe looking for something good to eat: "The grasses brushed alongside his canoe and spoke to him, whispering, 'We're good to eat.' Nanabozho responded, 'That's too easy, I've got to keep going, I have to find something good.' He found and ate a plant that made him ill. When he was well enough to start the return journey, his boat brushed by the same grasses and again they said, 'We're good to eat.' He listened and cooked the grains, which he ate and enjoyed."

According to native mythology, those grasses were the first wild rice eaten by man. "From then on," says Mr. Bruchac, "people have found wild rice and accepted it as a great blessing. Nanabozho's story is so typical of humanity: we don't see the obvious in front of us; we take things for granted."

2 quarts water

Three ¾-pound turkey drumsticks

1 medium onion, finely chopped

4 ounces white mushrooms, coarsely chopped

1 green bell pepper, stemmed, seeded, and coarsely chopped

1 teaspoon dried thyme

2 medium Yukon gold potatoes, peeled and cut into ½-inch pieces

2 carrots, coarsely chopped

½ cup winter squash, coarsely chopped and peeled

1 cup cooked wild rice

Kosher salt and freshly ground black pepper

1. In a large Dutch oven, bring the water, turkey, onion, mushrooms, bell pepper, and thyme to a simmer over high heat. Reduce the heat to medium-low and cook about 1½ hours, until the meat is tender and falling off the bone.

2. Transfer the drumsticks to a plate and cool slightly. Remove the skin and bones and shred the meat into bite-size pieces.

3. Stir the potatoes, carrots, and squash into the soup. Bring to a simmer and cook about 30 minutes, until the vegetables are tender. Stir in the reserved turkey and wild rice, and simmer for 5 to 10 minutes more. Season with salt and pepper to taste, and serve.

SERVES 4 TO 6

ROSALIE HARPOLE'S WEDDING SOUP

Rosalie Harpole learned how to make this soup by watching her mother prepare it for the weddings that she catered. Her paternal and maternal grandparents were children when they relocated from Rome and Sicily, respectively, and settled in Missouri and Louisiana. Rosalie's father was a butcher, famed for his sausages and spiedini, and her mother was admired for her Sicilian cooking, so they were often prevailed upon to prepare weddings. The celebrations were usually for 300 to 400 people and began with a ten a.m. mass and breakfast. This soup was always featured, along with tomato and olive sandwiches, cheese, fruit, and clusters of grapes at the midday meal. At seven p.m., the big party began, with a live band, dancing, pasta and meatballs, chicken and fancy red sauce, homemade Italian breads, salad, and, of course, spiedini. After her mother's death, Rosalie compiled and self-published her mother's recipes in a book called *Rosalie Serving Italian*.

Steaming Bowls: Soups, Chowders, and Other Consolations

One 3- to 4-pound whole chicken

5 quarts water

3 celery stalks with leaves, halved crosswise

2 medium carrots, halved crosswise

1 medium onion, halved

3 fresh parsley sprigs

Kosher salt and freshly ground black pepper

1 pound 85% lean ground beef

¼ cup plain bread crumbs

1 garlic clove, minced

2 tablespoons chopped fresh parsley

2 large eggs

1 head escarole, coarsely chopped

8 ounces *acini di pepe* pasta

1 ounce Parmesan cheese, grated (about ½ cup; optional)

1. In a large Dutch oven, combine the chicken, water, celery, carrots, onion, parsley sprigs, 1 tablespoon salt, and ½ teaspoon pepper. Bring to a simmer over low heat, skimming off the foam as it rises, and cook for 45 minutes to 1 hour, until the chicken is firm and a meat thermometer reads 175°F in the thighs and drumsticks and 165°F in the breasts.

2. Transfer the chicken to a carving board and let cool. Strain the broth through a fine-mesh strainer and return it to the Dutch oven. Skim any fat from the broth. Remove the meat and shred or cut into bite-size pieces.

3. In a medium bowl, mix together the beef, bread crumbs, garlic, parsley, eggs, 1 teaspoon salt, and ⅛ teaspoon pepper. Using wet hands, form the mixture into teaspoon-size balls, about 1 inch in diameter.

4. Bring the broth to a simmer, drop in the meatballs, one at a time, and cook for 5 to 10 minutes, until cooked through.

5. Return the chicken to the broth, stir in the escarole and pasta, and cook for about 10 minutes, until the pasta is tender. Season with salt and pepper to taste.

6. To serve, ladle into bowls, garnish with pepper and cheese (if using), and serve.

SERVES 8 TO 10

Almond-Flour "Matzo" Balls

BOULDER, COLORADO

Elana Amsterdam was not about to abandon her family's matzo ball tradition when she was diagnosed with celiac disease. Unable to tolerate gluten, a protein in wheat, rye, and barley, she came up with this version twelve years ago, using her family recipe and the memory of making matzo balls with her bubbe. Blanched almond flour is essential. Unblanched flour will result in "miserable failures," she warns.

4 large eggs

Kosher salt

¼ teaspoon freshly ground black pepper

2 cups blanched almond flour, preferably Honeyville, sifted

6 cups homemade chicken broth

1. In a medium bowl, combine the eggs, 1 teaspoon salt, and the pepper. Whisk about 2 minutes, until frothy. Stir in the almond flour until well combined. Cover and refrigerate at least 2 hours and up to 1 day.

2. In a Dutch oven, bring 3 quarts water and 1 teaspoon salt to a boil. Drop the batter by the tablespoonful into the water. Reduce the heat to low, cover, and simmer for 15 to 20 minutes, until cooked through.

3. Meanwhile, bring the broth to a simmer in a large saucepan. Using a slotted spoon, transfer the balls to the broth and simmer for 5 minutes, uncovered, before serving.

SERVES 6

POSTMODERN MATZO BALLS

MATZO BALLS, ALSO CALLED KNAIDLACH, ARE A Jewish Eastern European dumpling traditionally eaten during Passover, generally eaten far more often, and obsessed about more often still. Like most things they love, Americans have tinkered with and personalized them. This goes way back—in the Golden Age of Hollywood, the commissary at Metro-Goldwyn-Mayer served broiled matzo balls in dark broth—and people not bound by tradition have added vodka, basil, garlic powder, shiitake mushrooms, green chiles, ground chicken, dill, or scallions. Some claim club soda or seltzer as a secret ingredient, others say that only the water on New York City's Lower East Side will do. Some substitute vegetable oil for the traditional chicken fat in the recipe, but even traditionalists respect a matzo ball that caters to dietary needs, such as the gluten-free version on this page. Some even allow that regional variations should be viewed with compassion, and perhaps even tasted—at least once. Matzo balls can be small or large, fluffy or dense, depending on the maker's preference. The dumplings can be made well in advance and frozen, then thawed overnight in the refrigerator and reheated gently in chicken broth.

RAYNA GREEN'S BARBECUED MATZO BALLS

When Rayna Green's grandmother bought matzo balls from a deli in Dallas, she got an idea. Like many things Texan, these dumplings were big, closer to the size of a baseball than a golf ball, and they seemed to want the grill, not the soup pot. "Texans do love to barbecue," says Dr. Green, who is the director of the American Indian Program at the Smithsonian Institution's National Museum of American History in Washington, D.C. Her grandmother, whose family had been part of the great wave of German immigration to Texas shortly after 1900, split the big things, slathered them with sauce, and put them over a fire. A new cultural hybrid was born. Dr. Green's mother and her father, a Cherokee from Oklahoma, pushed the boundaries even further when they served the barbecued balls with ribs, instead of in soup. "It's good," says Dr. Green, "but I've gone back to the traditional soup."

FOR THE MATZO BALLS

4 large eggs

¼ cup seltzer or tap water

¼ cup schmaltz (chicken fat), melted and cooled

1 teaspoon kosher salt

Pinch of freshly ground black pepper

1 cup matzo meal

FOR THE SAUCE

⅓ cup beer or water

3 tablespoons crushed dried ancho chiles

2 teaspoons red wine vinegar

1 teaspoon tomato paste

½ teaspoon kosher salt

¼ teaspoon freshly ground black pepper

FOR THE SOUP (OPTIONAL)

6 cups homemade chicken broth

1. To make the matzo balls: In a medium bowl, using a fork, beat the eggs until combined. Stir in the water, schmaltz, salt, and pepper. Mix in the matzo meal until combined. Cover and refrigerate for 30 minutes to 1 hour.

2. In a Dutch oven, bring 3 quarts water and 1 teaspoon salt to a boil. Using wet hands, form 2 tablespoons of the dough into balls about 1½ inches in diameter. Drop the balls, one at a time, into the boiling water. Reduce the heat to low, cover, and simmer for 25 to 30 minutes, until cooked through.

3. Using a slotted spoon, transfer the matzo balls to a large bowl and set aside to cool.

4. To make the sauce: In a medium bowl, combine all the ingredients.

5. If grilling the matzo balls, heat a grill to high. Lightly oil the grate. Cut each matzo ball in half. Grill the halves, cut side down, for 4 to 6 minutes, until heated through and well browned. Carefully transfer them to a serving platter, brush with the sauce, and serve.

6. If serving in soup, bring the broth to a simmer, add the matzo balls, and simmer uncovered for 5 minutes before serving.

———

SERVES 6

Steaming Bowls: Soups, Chowders, and Other Consolations

Mrs. Hassid's Gundi
Persian Meatball Soup

BEVERLY HILLS, CALIFORNIA

When Javaher Hassid was growing up in Kashan, Iran, she learned to cook from her mother, and many of those lessons survived the family's exodus to the United States in 1979. After settling in Southern California, she married, had five children, and, like generations of Farsi women before her, produced an extravagant Shabbat, the traditional Jewish Sabbath meal, every Friday night. America, says Mrs. Hassid, who is now 80 years old and lives with her oldest son and his family, has been good for gundi. "We used to grind the chickpeas by hand, and now we buy it ground into flour at the Persian market," she says. She serves the meatballs in chicken soup along with lots of fresh herbs and rice.

½ pound ground veal, turkey, or chicken

½ cup finely ground chickpea flour

1 garlic clove, minced

¾ teaspoon ground cardamom

¼ teaspoon ground turmeric

Kosher salt and freshly ground black pepper

1 quart homemade chicken broth or low-sodium store-bought chicken broth

1. In a medium bowl, mix the meat, chickpea flour, garlic, cardamom, turmeric, ½ teaspoon salt, and ¼ teaspoon pepper together until well blended. Cover and refrigerate for 2 hours.

2. In a medium saucepan, bring the broth to a simmer. Meanwhile, using wet hands, form 1 tablespoon of the meat into balls about 1½ inches in diameter. Drop the meatballs, one at a time, into the broth. Cover, reduce the heat, and gently simmer for 15 to 20 minutes, until the meatballs are cooked through. Season with salt and pepper to taste, and serve.

SERVES 4

One Big Table

Simca Horowitz's Tortilla-Lime Soup

BOSTON, MASSACHUSETTS

Simca Horowitz spent time in Guatemala when she was a graduate student studying food and agricultural policy. Cooking quickly became the common language: "It creates connections and transcends language barriers," she says. Nearly a decade later, this soulful Guatemalan iteration of the familiar Mexican tortilla soup remains the dish that her family and friends request most often. Store-bought or frozen broth can be used, but nothing beats a rich, homemade Jewish chicken soup.

Ten 6-inch corn tortillas, cut into ½-inch strips

1 quart water

9 garlic cloves, peeled and smashed

2 tablespoons olive oil

1 medium red onion, finely chopped

4 cups high quality canned, crushed tomatoes

3 cups homemade chicken broth or low-sodium store-bought chicken broth

2 medium chipotle chiles in adobo sauce, minced

1 teaspoon ground cumin

6 tablespoons fresh lime juice

¼ cup chopped fresh cilantro, plus more for garnish

Kosher salt and freshly ground black pepper

1 ripe avocado, pitted, peeled, and cut into ½-inch cubes, for garnish

2 ounces Cheddar cheese, shredded (about ½ cup), for garnish

1. Place oven rack in the center position and heat the oven to 425°F.

2. Spread the tortilla strips out on a rimmed baking sheet and bake about 15 minutes, until lightly browned and crisp, tossing them halfway through.

3. In a medium saucepan, bring the water and garlic to a simmer and cook for 5 to 10 minutes, until cloves are soft. Transfer the garlic and water to a blender or food processor and process until smooth.

4. In a Dutch oven, heat the oil over medium heat. Add the onion and cook about 4 minutes, until soft. Add half of the tomatoes and cook about 10 minutes, until soft. Stir in the garlic puree, the remaining tomatoes, chicken broth, chiles, and cumin. Bring to a simmer and cook about 15 minutes, until all the tomatoes are soft. Add the lime juice and cilantro, and season with salt and pepper to taste.

5. To serve, divide the tortillas among four bowls, ladle the soup over the top, and garnish with avocado, cheese, and additional cilantro.

SERVES 4

Steaming Bowls: Soups, Chowders, and Other Consolations

Dan Ansotegui's Basque Garlic Soup for Gringos

BOISE, IDAHO

Dan Ansotegui is a mover and shaker in the Basque community in Boise, Idaho. Both his grandfathers immigrated to the United States to herd sheep in the Idaho mountains; his father began herding when he was 13 years old. Dan learned traditional cooking, music, and dancing at home, and now teaches in the Basque studies program at Boise State University. He also plays the button accordion and the txistu, a recorder-like whistle, and is a member of the Basque rock band Amuuma Says No. A former restaurateur, he is one of the best Basque cooks around. People still remember his restaurant and this soup. Mr. Ansotegui's family ate the soup, traditionally made from stale bread, after dancing at the local sheepherders' balls. When he was planning the menu for his restaurant, he worried that people outside the Basque community, particularly tourists, might be turned off by a soup made from stale bread. His solution—using croutons instead—was dubbed "Basque Garlic Soup for Gringos" and became a local legend. The garlic level can be calibrated to taste.

FOR THE CROUTONS

6 ounces day-old French bread, cut into 1-inch cubes (about 3 cups)

2 tablespoons extra virgin olive oil

1 tablespoon paprika

1 tablespoon garlic powder

Kosher salt

FOR THE SOUP

¼ cup extra virgin olive oil

6 garlic cloves, thinly sliced

1 tablespoon red pepper flakes

2 tablespoons chopped fresh parsley

3 quarts homemade chicken broth or low-sodium store-bought chicken broth

Kosher salt

½ cup grated Manchego or Petit Basque cheese (about 2 ounces), optional

1. To make the croutons: Place an oven rack in the center position and preheat the oven to 425°F. In a medium bowl, toss the bread with the oil, paprika, garlic powder, and 1 teaspoon salt until evenly coated. Transfer the bread to a baking sheet and bake for 10 to 15 minutes, stirring a couple times during baking, until golden brown. Cool to room temperature.

2. To make the soup: In a Dutch oven, heat the oil over medium-low heat. Add the garlic and cook, stirring constantly, for 2 to 4 minutes. When the garlic begins to brown, stir in the pepper flakes and cook for 1 minute, until aromatic. Add the parsley and stir until coated with the oil. Add the broth. Bring to a simmer and cook about 10 minutes. Season with salt to taste.

3. To serve, ladle into bowls and sprinkle with the croutons and cheese, if using.

SERVES 6 TO 8

HAL & MAL'S VEGETABLE SOUP

H al White, half of Hal & Mal's Restaurant & Brewery, has been making soup "forever, or at least longer than I can remember." He's developed close to 200 recipes, and makes at least a gallon and a half of soup every morning. He has the pot on the stove by 9:00 or 9:30 a.m. and it simmers until the lunch crowd comes in. Some days he just knows the restaurant will sell "beaucoups" (pronounced *boo-coos*) soup. The vegetable soup is famous. Arguments have erupted between the customer who ordered the last bowl and the one who wishes he had. The soup is an ode to Mr. White's forebears: "My granddaddy had a big garden," he says. It is testimony to being wise with a nickel. The chablis he uses "is my favorite wine for this soup. Clean and acidic. I guess I could use sauvignon blanc, but you can't beat chablis for cheap." His vegetable soup also owes a debt to a bartending friend. "He made this great Bloody Mary mix. He taught me that nothing beats Coke for balancing the acidity of tomatoes."

8 tablespoons (1 stick) unsalted butter

2 celery stalks, finely chopped

1 medium onion, finely chopped

4 medium tomatoes, cored and chopped

½ small head green cabbage, cored and chopped

2 large Yukon gold potatoes, scrubbed and cut into ½-inch pieces

5 ounces white mushrooms, thinly sliced

6 cups homemade chicken broth or low-sodium store-bought chicken broth

3 cups vegetable juice, such as V8

1 cup dry white wine, such as chablis

½ cup Coca-Cola

1½ teaspoons Worcestershire sauce

1½ teaspoons seasoned salt, preferably Lawry's

1 teaspoon red pepper flakes

½ teaspoon ground allspice

½ teaspoon sweet paprika

½ teaspoon dried basil

¼ teaspoon dried oregano

¼ teaspoon dried dill

2 bay leaves

2 tablespoons chopped fresh parsley

Kosher salt and freshly ground black pepper

1. In a large Dutch oven, melt the butter over medium heat. Add the celery and onion and cook for 6 to 8 minutes, until they are soft.

2. Stir in the remaining ingredients and bring to a simmer over high heat. Reduce the heat to medium-low and cook for 30 to 45 minutes, until the potatoes are cooked through.

3. Season with salt and pepper to taste, and serve.

SERVES 6 TO 8

Kavanah Ramsier's Tidewater Peanut Soup

Kavanah Ramsier was only three months old when her family left Africa so that her father could study at The College of William & Mary in Williamsburg, Virginia. They lived in a townhouse with a view of the James River. On Sunday afternoons, they rode their bikes down to the riverbank and took the Jamestown–Scotland Ferry over to the town of Surrey. After pedaling around town all day, the family often went to the Surrey House, a restaurant and county inn known for its Tidewater-style peanut soup. The soup, far creamier than the African versions her mother and aunts made, was served with hot, salty ham biscuits. Ms. Ramsier, who directs a youth program dedicated to inner city gardening, says, "In my typical indecisive fashion, I was unable to settle on a favorite, so I combined elements of each: the creaminess of the Southern version with the tomato of the African version."

4 tablespoons (½ stick) unsalted butter

1 large onion, finely chopped

3 garlic cloves, peeled and smashed

3 tablespoons all-purpose flour

8 cups homemade chicken broth or low-sodium store-bought chicken broth

2 cups unsalted natural peanut butter

1 cup heavy cream or whole milk

⅓ cup tomato paste

½ teaspoon cayenne pepper

½ teaspoon ground coriander

Kosher salt and freshly ground black pepper

2 scallions, green and white parts, thinly sliced, for garnish

2 tablespoons chopped roasted peanuts, for garnish

1. In a Dutch oven, melt the butter over medium heat. Add the onion and garlic and cook about 4 minutes, until the onion is soft. Stir in the flour and cook for 2 minutes. Stir in the broth and bring to a simmer, then whisk in the peanut butter, cream, tomato paste, cayenne, coriander, 1 teaspoon salt, and ¼ teaspoon pepper.

2. Return to a simmer and cook, stirring occasionally, for 1 to 2 hours, until thickened. Season with salt and pepper to taste.

3. To serve, ladle into bowls and garnish with the scallions and peanuts.

SERVES 6

John Coykendal's Filibuster Bean Soup

KNOXVILLE, TENNESSEE

A good way to ensure the perpetuation of a tradition is to argue over its origins. This helps explain the century-long run of white bean soup on the menu of the Senate Dining Room—since at least 1903. Some claim that Idaho Senator Fred Dubois requested a bean soup, and out of respect for his home state, mashed potatoes were added to the bean, ham hock, and onion combination. Some claim that Senator Knute Nelson requested the soup. The recipes for both versions are on the United States Senate's Web site.

John Coykendal is a master gardener at Blackberry Farm in Walland, Tennessee. He has been walking through the mountains of east Tennessee, collecting all-but-forgotten beans from hardscrabble farms, as well as the family stories that explain where each bean came from and what it is good for. He was not aware of the Senate's soup squabble thirty years ago when he began experimenting with several dozen varieties of shucky beans. But he had dried a lot of beans, loving ham hock broth and wanting to add more layers of flavor. His top choice for soup is a dried butter bean. But crowder, lady, and zipper cream peas are nothing to be scoffed at, nor is a fine black bean, navy bean, or great Northern. Cooking times vary, but the fresher the beans, the less water and time they require. Any bean needs time to "gurgle and listen and get over itself," says Mr. Coykendal, and this, he adds, explains the name of his soup.

FOR THE BROTH

1 tablespoon bacon fat or vegetable oil

1 onion, cut into large chunks

2 carrots, cut into large chunks

1 ham hock

1 bay leaf

2 whole cloves

2 sprigs fresh thyme

4 black peppercorns

FOR THE SOUP

2 quarts water

Sea salt

3 cups fresh shelled beans, preferably butter beans, crowder peas, lady peas, or zipper cream peas

4 slices bacon, cut into ½-inch pieces

2 yellow onions, cut into ½-inch dice

2 carrots, cut into ½-inch dice

2 celery stalks, cut into ½-inch dice

3 garlic cloves, minced

Freshly ground black pepper

¼ teaspoon mustard powder

¼ teaspoon ground coriander

4 plum tomatoes, peeled and seeded

1 cup heavy cream

Cider vinegar

½ bunch flat-leaf parsley

Coarsely ground black pepper

2 cups well-toasted croutons

1. To make the broth: Warm the bacon fat in a soup pot over medium heat. Add the onion and cook, stirring frequently, until the onion begins to caramelize, about 7 minutes. Add the carrots and cook until they begin to brown. Add the ham hock, bay leaf, cloves, thyme, peppercorns, and 2 quarts cold water and reduce the heat to low. Simmer, without boiling, for 3 hours. Strain the broth through a fine-mesh strainer, discard the solids, and refrigerate the broth overnight.

2. To make the soup: Bring 2 quarts water and 1 tablespoon sea salt to a rapid boil in a large pot. Add the beans and cook 5 minutes. Drain and cool the beans in a colander under cold running water.

3. Cook the bacon in a soup pot over medium heat about 10 minutes, until it becomes brown and crisp. Using a slotted spoon, transfer it to paper towels to drain. Discard half the bacon fat. Add the onions, carrots, celery, and garlic to the remaining bacon fat, season lightly with salt and pepper, and cook, stirring frequently, about 5 minutes. Add the beans, broth, and additional water if necessary to cover the beans. Stir in the mustard and coriander. Crush the tomatoes by hand and stir in. Simmer for 2 hours, adding more water as necessary to keep the beans covered.

4. When the beans are tender, cover the pot, remove from the heat, and allow to sit at least 2 hours at room temperature or up to 24 hours in the refrigerator. Warm before serving. Stir in the cream and more water if necessary. If too thick, add additional water. Add vinegar, salt, and pepper to taste. Add half the parsley. Serve with the remaining parsley, and croutons.

SERVES 8 TO 12

ANGELINA AVELLAR'S PORTUGUESE KALE SOUP

PROVINCETOWN, MASSACHUSETTS

Angelina Jacinta Soares Avellar was born in the Azores into a family of fishermen, who, like many Portuguese families in the mid to late nineteenth century, followed the fish to the tip of Cape Cod. The fishing was extraordinary, and when the sandy soil was enriched with fish bones, it was just fine for vegetables, particularly sturdy greens that could take a family through the winter. Her husband's skills on the water were as respected as Mrs. Avellar's were in the kitchen. They prospered and eventually bought Avellar's Wharf, a big house, a hunk of land large enough to support pigs and a garden. They also rented summer cottages to writers such as Eugene O'Neill and Wilbur Daniel Steele. Mrs. Avellar says that her granddaughter Tillie Steele can't make a pot of soup without sharing it, and given their fabulous garden, a day without a fresh pot of soup is rare.

This recipe appeared in the *Provincetown Portuguese Cookbook*, a local fund-raising publication, and is a classic meld of the Yankee and Portuguese kitchens. Some people add carrots or tomatoes to this soup, a practice that Mrs. Avellar frowns upon, says her granddaughter. And while some people add a ham bone for extra flavor, Ms. Steele has remained faithful to salt pork.

10 cups water

2 large bunches kale (ribs removed), coarsely chopped

2 ounces salt pork

1 ham bone (optional)

2 large onions, coarsely chopped

1 pound linguiça sausage, chopped

1 pound chouriço sausage, chopped

3 medium red potatoes, scrubbed and cut into ½-inch pieces

One 29-ounce can cannellini or red kidney beans, drained and rinsed

Kosher salt and freshly ground black pepper

1. In a Dutch oven, combine the water, kale, salt pork, ham bone (if using), onions, linguiça, and chourico. Bring to a simmer and cook about 15 minutes, until the kale is tender.

2. Stir in the potatoes and beans and simmer about 20 minutes more, until the potatoes are tender. Discard the ham bone (if using). Season with salt and pepper to taste, and serve.

SERVES 8

POLK FAMILY BLACK-EYED PEA AND MUSTARD GREENS SOUP

Georgia Downer Polk's grandfather was a farmer during the Depression. Desperate not to lose his farm, he asked the local grocery owners what to plant that would be profitable. They suggested that if he grew black-eyed peas and dried them, the crop could be sold all winter long. Following their advice, he was able to use the money from this one crop to pay the taxes on his farm.

Around New Year's, most grocery stores in the South carry fresh black-eyed peas because it is traditional to eat them for good luck. When Ms. Polk makes this soup at other times of the year, she uses frozen peas. The recipe came from Ms. Polk's sister-in-law, Kerry Polk, a singer-songwriter living in Austin. Georgia Polk has also used collards in place of the mustard greens and a spicier sausage in place of the more traditional smoked sausage. She usually begins the soup on the morning of New Year's Day, simmers it all day, and has it ready for the party that gathers to watch football games. She serves this soup with cornbread.

4 tablespoons (½ stick) unsalted butter

1 large onion, finely chopped

2 celery stalks, finely chopped

½ cup finely chopped red bell pepper

12 medium garlic cloves, peeled and smashed

1 pound kielbasa or andouille sausage, cut into ¼-inch pieces

1 bay leaf

1 sprig fresh thyme

Kosher salt and freshly ground black pepper

10 cups homemade chicken broth or low sodium store-bought, plus more as needed

1 pound fresh or frozen black-eyed peas

1 large bunch mustard greens (ribs removed), coarsely chopped

One 14.5-ounce can whole tomatoes, drained and chopped

2 scallions, green and white parts, coarsely chopped

¼ cup chopped fresh parsley

Hot sauce

1. In a Dutch oven, melt the butter over medium heat. Add the onion, celery, bell pepper, and garlic and cook for 4 to 6 minutes, until the vegetables are soft. Stir in the sausage, bay leaf, and thyme, and cook for 5 minutes more. Season with salt and pepper to taste, transfer to a medium bowl, and set aside.

2. Bring the broth and black-eyed peas to a simmer in the Dutch oven. Stir in the mustard greens, tomatoes, scallions, and parsley, return to a simmer, and cook for 30 minutes.

3. Stir in the reserved vegetable mixture and simmer about 1 hour more, until the soup is slightly thickened and the vegetables are soft, adding more broth as needed (the soup should be brothy). Discard the bay leaf and thyme sprig. Season with salt, pepper, and hot sauce to taste.

SERVES 6

Leila Abu-Saba's Egyptian Red Lentil Soup

Leila Abu-Saba's father is a first-generation Lebanese Christian who came to the United States to study at Virginia Tech; her mother is a Southerner and the daughter of a Methodist minister. "My parents were progressive, cosmopolitan people," says Ms. Abu-Saba, who studies environmental issues and policy. "I inherited a little of their talent for trading worldviews and recipes." She first tasted this soup in the home of an Egyptian Muslim during Ramadan, the month-long Islamic observance dedicated to purification through prayer and self-sacrifice; observant celebrants also fast from sunrise to sunset. The evening meal often includes humble but satisfying soups like this one.

2 tablespoons plus 1 teaspoon olive oil

1 large onion, finely chopped

7 cups homemade vegetable or chicken broth or low sodium store-bought vegetable or chicken broth, plus more as needed

1¾ cups red lentils

1 teaspoon cumin seeds

½ teaspoon ground turmeric

⅓ cup chopped fresh cilantro

3 tablespoons fresh lemon juice

Kosher salt and freshly ground black pepper

2 tablespoons extra virgin olive oil, for garnish

Toasted pita bread wedges, for serving

Lemon wedges, for serving

1. In a Dutch oven, heat 2 tablespoons of the olive oil over medium heat. Add the onion and cook about 4 minutes, until soft. Stir in the broth and lentils, bring to a simmer, and cook about 30 minutes, until the lentils dissolve, adding more broth as needed.

2. Meanwhile, in a small skillet, heat the remaining 1 teaspoon olive oil over medium heat. Add the cumin seeds and turmeric and cook about 1 minute, until aromatic.

3. Before serving, stir the spices, cilantro, and lemon juice into the soup. Season with salt and pepper to taste. Ladle into bowls, drizzle with extra virgin olive oil, and serve with the pita and lemon wedges.

SERVES 6 TO 8

Steaming Bowls: Soups, Chowders, and Other Consolations

TED WILLIAMS'S FENWAY CHOWDER

In the world according to the late Ted Williams, there was no reason to bother hitting a ball, casting a fishing line, or cooking a meal if you didn't do it right. Life is full of things you can't control, he said in an interview in his home kitchen in 1999. The winners pay attention to the sliver of effort they can control: their timing at the plate, the arc of their bats, and the heat of their skillets. For the high-strung perpetual perfectionist, cooking became a singular solace. "The only thing I remember as a young player coming close to comfort was a good meal."

Growing up in San Diego, California, with a mother who marched with the Salvation Army, a brother who rebelled, and a father who eventually marched away from the family, Williams ate eggs. "My mother wasn't much of cook. I'd make eggs for myself—it was the Depression and eggs were cheap and plentiful, you see."

Although he cooked for thousands of players and friends over half a century, Williams was never able to give his guests a sense of complete trust along with a great meal. He said that it started back in spring training in 1927, when he cooked for Wade Hoyt.

"Now, this guy's been around longer and been to better places to eat than you and I, but I know that the little public market over in Winter Haven has the best steak, I mean beautiful, the best you can get. So I go over there and get some beauties. And I come home and I make a little fire in the grill and I rub those babies good with salt and pepper and garlic and I make a beautiful salad. And I keep him waiting. I brown those steaks up good; gee, I did a great job. They were terrific steaks. I see he's getting hungry.

"I take 'em off the heat, let 'em sit, and he's getting real eager. Finally, I serve the meat and by that time, I'm telling you, he's hungry; he darned near demolished the thing. And I say to him, 'You like alligator?' and he gets sorta pale."

The next day in the clubhouse, Williams heard Hoyt describing the flavor of alligator. "Tasted pretty good, but I wouldn't want to make a steady diet of it."

Williams continued to appall dinner guests. He couldn't help it. He got a kick out of big, tough athletes, politicians, and movie stars paling at his table. But Williams also understood the conservative tastes of most ballplayers. He ate a lot of Mexican food growing up. He was partial to fiery peppers, hot and sour chili sauces, and garlic in quantities that would make Dracula wince. Even so, he admitted, "as a young man, I thought you couldn't beat a good steak or chop."

"I regret that I haven't eaten platypus or sturgeon," he said. "Shark's pretty good, and I love octopus and any kind of sushi. But I coulda been more adventuresome." He added, "I don't cook a variety of foods. But what I cook is excellent."

He is partial to fish, a taste born in the years he played for the Boston Red Sox. For fifty years he fished around the globe. Every fish, he said, like every pitch, is different. Recipes can't replace the feel for a thing, the instinct to meet either ingredient or ball with the certainty of a home run. "Except for my chowder, a thing that a recipe can come close to approximating, a thing of beauty." As the aroma of the fish and seafood simmering gently on his stove reached him, he smiled. "Chowder," he said, "is my number one lingering desire."

3 tablespoons rendered pork fat or olive oil

½ cup finely chopped red onion

1 large shallot, finely chopped

¼ cup finely chopped red bell pepper

¼ cup finely chopped green bell pepper

2 teaspoons Lawry's Seasoned Salt

2 teaspoons Old Bay Seasoning

2 teaspoons dried thyme

1½ teaspoons dried garlic flakes

One 4-ounce skinless grouper fillet, cut into
   ½-inch cubes

One 4-ounce skinless red snapper fillet, cut into
   ½-inch cubes

¼ pound bay scallops

½ cup chopped shucked clams

4 cups whole milk

2 cups half-and-half

¼ cup dry sherry

¼ cup clam juice

¾ pound mussels, scrubbed and beards removed

½ cup chopped shucked oysters with their juice

2 small white potatoes, peeled and cut into
   ¼-inch pieces

½ cup fresh or thawed frozen corn kernels

2 teaspoons fresh lemon juice

½ cup heavy cream

Kosher salt and freshly ground black pepper

1. In a large Dutch oven, heat the fat over medium heat. Add the onion, shallot, and bell peppers and cook about 4 minutes, until soft. Stir in the seasoned salt, Old Bay, thyme, and garlic flakes and cook about 1 minute, until aromatic. Add the grouper, snapper, scallops, and clams, and cook for 3 minutes.

2. Stir in the milk, half-and-half, sherry, and clam juice, and bring to a simmer.

3. Stir in the mussels, oysters, potatoes, and corn, and simmer very gently for 5 to 8 minutes, until the mussels open and the potatoes are tender. (If desired, remove the mussels, discard the shells, and return the meat to the chowder.)

4. Stir in the lemon juice and cream. Season with salt and pepper to taste, and serve.

———

SERVES 10

1957 — Hot September For Ted

VISPAL'S CRAB DUMPLING AND RICE VERMICELLI SOUP

Vispal Khunn's grandmother used dumplings to make this soup, but his cousins, who live in California, began using local crabmeat and Mr. Khunn, a cabinet maker who grows Asian herbs for the local market, believes that the change is "proof that the old way is not every time the best way."

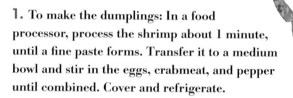

FOR THE DUMPLINGS

¼ pound medium shrimp (20 to 25 per pound), peeled and deveined

5 large eggs, lightly beaten

½ pound lump crabmeat, picked over

¼ teaspoon freshly ground black pepper

FOR THE SOUP

¼ cup vegetable oil

4 shallots, halved and thinly sliced

4 garlic cloves, minced

4 scallions, green and white parts, thinly sliced

2 tablespoons tomato paste

1 teaspoon Asian chili paste

4 plum tomatoes, cored and quartered

5½ cups homemade chicken broth or low-sodium store-bought chicken broth

¼ cup fish sauce

1 teaspoon sugar

Freshly ground black pepper

FOR SERVING

8 ounces thin rice vermicelli, cooked according to package directions

4 large Bibb lettuce leaves, shredded

2 cups bean sprouts

½ cup chopped fresh mint

½ cup chopped fresh cilantro

Lemon wedges

4 Thai chiles, stemmed and thinly sliced

1. To make the dumplings: In a food processor, process the shrimp about 1 minute, until a fine paste forms. Transfer it to a medium bowl and stir in the eggs, crabmeat, and pepper until combined. Cover and refrigerate.

2. To make the soup: In a Dutch oven, heat the oil over medium heat. Add the shallots, garlic, and scallions, and cook, stirring constantly, about 2 minutes. Stir in the tomato paste and chili paste, then add the tomatoes and cook for 1 minute more. Add the broth, fish sauce, and sugar, and bring to a simmer.

3. Spoon the shrimp mixture into the broth, cover, and cook about 5 minutes, until the seafood is slightly firm and floats. Season with pepper to taste.

4. To serve: Divide the noodles among four soup bowls and top each with some lettuce, bean sprouts, and additional scallions. Ladle the soup and dumplings over the top and garnish with the mint and cilantro. Serve with the lemon wedges and chiles.

SERVES 4

ALIX SHULMAN'S SPRING BEACH SOUP

In 1982, when Alix Kates Shulman was 50, she began spending her summers on Long Island, off the coast of Maine. Accessible only by the Casco Bay ferry or private boat, the island is isolated and remote. Her closest neighbor is a twenty-minute walk away. Her goal was solitude, with time to think, write, and explore, and the experience became the subject of her book, *Drinking the Rain*.

A friend built her a cabin of pine boards in the board-and-batten style. It has no electricity or plumbing. "The technology in the kitchen is circa 1910," she explains. "There is a hand pump in the kitchen connected to the rainwater cistern, and a hand-powered grater, juicer, mixer, strainer, and chopper, along with a propane stove and small propane refrigerator."

She forages for wild edibles for her food, and the low dunes become her salad bar, where she gathers lamb's quarters, strawberry goosefoot, sea rocket, dock, and chicory. On the rocks she finds a seaweed garden replete with sea lettuce, kelp, laver, and Irish moss. The waters provide mussels, crabs, lobster, and periwinkles, while the fields offer apple trees and edible fungi.

Many of the plants that she finds were cultivated and eaten in the nineteenth century. The seeds of curly dock come from the flower stalk that grows in the fall. "They are one of the most nutritious plant foods in the world," she says. "I always put a couple of tablespoons in my cornbread or muffins. They don't provide a lot of flavor, but give the baked goods a nice crunch." The seeds of sea rocket have a flavor reminiscent of horseradish and have no substitute. Beach peas are "like ordinary garden peas, but teeny little pods . . . they dry as the season progresses." She cautions that cooks should not gather greens from roadsides, where the plants could be laced with chemicals.

3 tablespoons olive oil

1 medium onion, finely chopped

3 garlic cloves, minced

1 tablespoon sea rocket seeds, chopped (optional)

1½ pounds assorted greens (lamb's quarters, dandelions, curly dock), coarsely chopped

8 cups mussel or fish broth

24 littleneck clams, steamed, meats picked, broth reserved

1 cup beach peas or small English peas

Kosher salt and freshly ground black pepper

½ cup lightly packed whole mustard flowers

¼ cup chopped arame seaweed

1. In a Dutch oven, heat the olive oil over medium-high heat. Add the onion and cook about 4 minutes, until soft. Stir in the garlic and sea rocket seeds (if using), and cook about 1 minute, until aromatic. Stir in the greens, one handful at a time, and cook about 3 minutes, until slightly wilted.

2. Add the mussel broth and the reserved clam broth. Bring to a simmer, and cook about 5 minutes, until the flavors have blended. Stir in the beach peas and cook for 3 to 5 minutes, until they float to the surface. Stir in the reserved clams. Season with salt and pepper to taste, garnish with mustard flowers and arame, and serve.

SERVES 4 TO 6

LUKE PYENSON'S ASPARAGUS SOUP

Whether cooking or playing drums in a jazz ensemble, Luke Pyenson likes to improvise. An 18-year-old freshman at Tufts University, he starts with a particular ingredient, then riffs on it by adding spices. This soup began after school one day when he sautéed asparagus with onions. He decided to turn it into soup, and asked his mom what to add. She suggested chicken stock. The cardamom and nigella seeds give the soup its exotic zip.

Mr. Pyenson came of age watching cooking shows on PBS and the Food Network, and credits television and his parents for his passion for cooking. *Iron Chef* taught him about ingenuity under pressure, "putting stuff together and hoping it tastes good."

He explores the ethnic restaurants and markets in the Boston area. This soup's flavoring comes from his meals at Indian restaurants, his current obsession. He had just bought the nigella seeds, and their flavor reminded him of peppermint. "I know asparagus and mint are good together, so I made the connection," he said.

3 tablespoons olive oil

2 pounds asparagus, ends snapped off, stalks cut into 1-inch pieces

1 small onion, halved and thinly sliced

2 garlic cloves, thinly sliced

1½ teaspoons ground cardamom

Kosher salt and freshly ground black pepper

4 cups homemade chicken broth or low-sodium store-bought chicken broth

Nigella seeds, for garnish

Truffle oil, for garnish (optional)

1. In a large Dutch oven, heat the olive oil over medium-high heat. Add the asparagus and onion and cook for 4 to 6 minutes, until soft. Stir in the garlic, cardamom, ½ teaspoon salt, and ¼ teaspoon pepper and cook about 1 minute, until aromatic. Add the broth, bring to a simmer, and cook about 10 minutes.

2. Working in two batches, process the soup in a blender or food processor until almost smooth. Return the soup to a clean saucepan and season with salt and pepper to taste. Warm over low heat until hot.

3. To serve, ladle into bowls, sprinkle with the nigella seeds, and drizzle with the truffle oil (if using).

SERVES 6 TO 8

One Big Table

VÉRONIQUE NGUYEN'S COLD AND FROTHY FRESH PEA SOUP

"My father was born near Hanoi, but his parents moved to Brittany when he was very young, and his first memory was pea soup with mint," said Véronique Nguyen. "One of his cousins had married a Frenchwoman and she made that soup. He assumed that pea soup was a French birthright and my father determined to marry a Frenchwoman as well—et voilà, my mother. Although she recalls their courtship differently, she does make a wonderful pea soup, and I have many memories of picking peas in our garden. My sister and I put the peas in a colander and washed them with the garden hose and my mother used the shells to make broth. When I visited Vietnam, I fell in love with the mint and basil combination and use them both in this soup. I use more vegetable broth and less cream, and I got the idea of frothing it from a chef's blog. My mother loves my version. My father prefers my mother's soup."

FOR THE VEGETABLE BROTH

1 pound celery, chopped

2 leeks, white and light green parts only, rinsed well, coarsely chopped

4 cups English pea pods, or snow peas (if you are using frozen peas for the soup)

1 cup coarsely chopped baby fennel

1 baby carrot

3 white peppercorns

8 sprigs flat-leaf parsley

4 sprigs fresh chervil

11-inch section lemongrass, finely chopped (optional)

3 tablespoons olive oil

FOR THE SOUP

3 cups fresh or thawed frozen peas

½ cup heavy cream

Sea salt

Fresh minced mint, sliced thinly for garnish (optional)

Fresh Thai basil, sliced thinly

1 teaspoon lemon zest, for garnish (optional)

1. To make the vegetable broth: Place all the vegetables in a pot, cover with the olive oil, and allow to sit for about an hour. Cover with 1 gallon cold water, place over low heat, bring to a bare simmer, and cook for 90 minutes.

3. Strain through a fine-mesh strainer into a storage container. Cool the broth to room temperature, then refrigerate. When it is completely chilled, spoon out the olive oil, then cover the broth and refrigerate for 4 hours or up to 3 days.

4. To make the soup: Measure 2 cups of the vegetable broth. Working in small batches, combine the peas and broth in a blender to make a very smooth puree. Strain through a fine-mesh strainer into a saucepan, pressing on the solids to extract as much liquid as possible. Stir in half of the cream. Warm the soup slowly over medium-high heat, whisking until it reaches 130°F on an instant-read thermometer. Do not boil the soup. Cook for 3 to 5 minutes more, stirring frequently and adjusting the heat as necessary to maintain a constant temperature of 130°F. Transfer to a clean storage container and chill overnight.

5. Before serving, stir in the remaining cream and adjust the seasoning with sea salt. Use an immersion blender to froth the soup. Pour into bowls, and serve; sprinkle with mint, basil, and lemon zest, if desired.

SERVES 4 TO 6

Joan Churchill's Cold Avocado Soup

Growing up in a 1908 Dutch colonial farmhouse on forty acres of avocado and pixie tangerine orchards in Ojai, California, Joan Churchill thought that everybody had bumper crops of avocados. Now a documentary filmmaker, she and her husband, an orchardist, divide their time between Venice, California, and the house and orchards she inherited in Ojai. She got this recipe from her friend Suellen Miller, and though she has embellished it, she prizes it for the four avocados the recipe requires, as well as its flavor. The lemon juice helps keep the avocado from browning and adds a zesty, summery flavor. A smoky note from the chipotle chile works well, "but if you let the soup sit for a while, it'll get hotter and hotter, so be careful," she warns.

4 ripe Hass avocados, halved, pitted (reserve the pits), and peeled

3 cups buttermilk

1 cup dry white wine

½ cup homemade chicken or vegetable broth or low sodium store-bought chicken or vegetable broth, plus more as needed

3 tablespoons fresh lemon juice

2 tablespoons chopped fresh cilantro

2 scallions, green and white parts, chopped

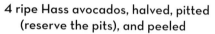

1 medium chipotle chile in adobo sauce, minced (preferably La Costeña brand)

½ teaspoon chili powder, plus more for garnish

Kosher salt and freshly ground black pepper

1 lemon, thinly sliced, for garnish

Cilantro leaves, for garnish

1. In a large bowl, with a potato masher, mash the avocados until only small chunks remain. Stir in the buttermilk and wine until incorporated.

2. In a blender or food processor, process the broth, lemon juice, cilantro, scallions, chipotle, and chili powder until smooth. Stir into the avocado mixture until combined. If too thick, add a little broth as needed. Season with salt and pepper to taste. Cover and refrigerate about 2 hours, until chilled.

3. Ladle into bowls and garnish with the lemon slices, cilantro leaves, and a sprinkle of chili powder.

SERVES 8

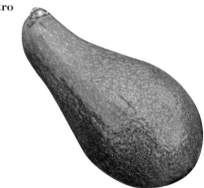

126

One Big Table

LINDA HILLEL'S CHILLED FAVA BEAN SOUP WITH MINT AND LEMON OIL

OAKLAND, CALIFORNIA

Linda Hillel's parents are Baghdadi Jews, and fava beans were no stranger at the family's table. Growing up in Tokyo, she ate them as deep-fried, salty snacks. But it wasn't until she and her husband tasted a soup called maccu when vacationing in Sicily that she understood the glory of fava beans, which is why she tends a sizable patch of them in her garden. Canned or dried beans can be used to make this robust peasant soup, but Mrs. Hillel, a former cooking teacher, believes that nothing compares to the fresh beans. "I wait until the moment when there are enough beans of similar size, rush out and pick them, then rush back and make my fresh fava version of maccu," she says.

5 pounds fresh fava beans, shelled

3 tablespoons extra virgin olive oil

2 teaspoons grated lemon zest

1 medium onion, chopped

Kosher salt and fresh ground black pepper

3 garlic cloves, minced

¼ cup chopped fresh mint leaves, plus more small leaves for garnish

3 tablespoons crème fraîche or Greek-style yogurt, for garnish

1. In a medium saucepan with a steamer insert, bring 4 cups water to a boil. Put the beans in the insert, cover, and steam for 6 to 8 minutes, until tender. Remove the insert from the pot and rinse the beans under cold running water to stop the cooking. Drain, transfer the beans to a medium bowl, cover, and refrigerate for 1 hour. Pour the cooking liquid in a separate container and refrigerate until cold.

2. Peel the chilled fava beans by pinching the skins and squeezing to pop out the beans. Transfer to a blender or food processor.

3. In a small bowl, combine the oil and lemon zest. Heat 1 tablespoon of the lemon oil in a large skillet over medium heat. Add the onion, ½ teaspoon salt, and ¼ teaspoon pepper and cook about 4 minutes, until soft. Stir in the garlic and cook about 1 minute, until aromatic.

4. Scrape the onions and garlic into the blender with the beans. Add 1 cup of the reserved cooking liquid and the chopped mint. Pulse until the beans are finely chopped. Scrape down the bowl. With the blender running, add more of the reserved fava liquid until the soup reaches the desired consistency. The soup should be thick; depending on the maturity of the fava beans, you will need 2 to 3 cups of the reserved liquid.

5. Transfer the soup to a storage container. Stir in the remaining lemon oil and season with salt and pepper to taste. Cover and refrigerate about 2 hours, until chilled.

6. Whisk the crème fraîche until smooth. To serve, ladle the soup into bowls, drizzle with the crème fraîche, and garnish with mint leaves.

SERVES 4 TO 6

Steaming Bowls: Soups, Chowders, and Other Consolations

A LEGEND IN A CAN

JOHN T. DORRANCE, A NEPHEW OF THE COFOUNDER OF THE JOSEPH A. CAMPBELL Preserve Company, went to work for his uncle's company in 1897. He had earned a doctorate in chemistry at the University of Göttingen in Germany and soon invented a process that condensed half the water from soup, making cans of it cheaper to ship. Within five years, the company was selling 15 million cans of soup a year.

No variety has sold more than Dr. Dorrance's first invention, Campbell's Tomato Soup. Along with the company's cream of mushroom, the soup eventually became the goo in an overwhelming number of casseroles. In a series of paintings and silk screens, Andy Warhol (who said that he drank Campbell's tomato soup every day for lunch) turned the can with its familiar red and white label into a pop icon. But the soup had loftier beginnings. Fannie Farmer said that Dr. Dorrance made soup with "English thoroughness and French art," and in fact, the good doctor honed his soup-making abilities with the masters.

"Three months out of every year I became anything from a vegetable parer to assistant cook in some of the most famous kitchens in the world. The Café de Paris in Paris and Paillard's were my training fields, the Waldorf in New York City another. From these famous chefs I learned all that I know of the delicate flavoring of soups, and the fact that they made me an honorary member of the Société de Secours Mutuels et de Retraite [sic] des Cuisiniers de Paris is one of my proudest achievements." Dorrance succeeded his father as president of the company in 1910, became the sole owner, renamed the company Campbell Soup, and left an estate of $128 million when he died in 1930. One of Mr. Warhol's soup can images sold for $11.8 million in 2006.

Rita Nader Heikenfeld's Approximately Campbell's Tomato Soup

Rita Nader Heikenfeld received her first request for a clone of a famous recipe about ten years ago, when she started her column, "Rita's Kitchen," in a community newspaper in Ohio. A reader wanted to make Skyline Chili, made famous by a Cincinnati restaurant, and between readers' suggestions and her own experimenting, Mrs. Heikenfeld mastered the art of duplicating restaurant dishes and convenience products, such as canned soup, in her home kitchen.

It is an unlikely specialty for Mrs. Heikenfeld, the daughter of a large Lebanese family of serious cooks, who for the past thirty-six years has chopped wood, raised chickens, and grown vegetables along with her husband and three sons. Nevertheless, Mrs. Heikenfeld has obliged her readers with home-kitchen recipes for everything from Famous Amos Chocolate Chip Cookies and York Peppermint Patties to Emeril's Cajun spice blend.

Although she does not eat packaged or convenience foods, she understands the American connection to canned tomato soup. "Canned tomato soup hasn't changed over the years," she says. "A granddaughter can imagine her mother and grandmother opening a can and eating the same bowl of soup. It's a comfortable part of our history, knowing that so many generations used the same soup."

4 tablespoons (½ stick) unsalted butter

6 tablespoons all-purpose flour

½ teaspoon onion powder

1 quart vegetable juice such as V8

1 teaspoon tomato paste

1 teaspoon celery salt, plus more to taste

1 teaspoon sugar, plus more to taste (optional)

Freshly ground black pepper

1. In a medium saucepan, melt the butter over medium-low heat. Stir in the flour and onion powder and cook about 1 minute, until bubbly but not brown.

2. Whisk in vegetable juice, tomato paste, and celery salt. Bring to a simmer and cook 5 to 10 minutes, stirring occasionally, until slightly thickened.

3. Season with celery salt, sugar (if using), and pepper to taste, and serve.

SERVES 4

All the rich tomato goodness is in Campbell's Tomato Soup!

Isabel Caudillo's Fideo
Vermicelli Soup with Chard

SAN FRANCISCO, CALIFORNIA

People love Isabel Caudillo's roasted meats, soups, and tacos. On Saturday and Sunday at the Noe Valley Market, the lines at her food stand are long and deep. On other days, she caters weddings and office parties. She has not worked fewer than seventy hours a week since she arrived in San Francisco ten years ago. Why would she? Her five sons have "lots of stuff"; she has her own business, business cards, even a Web site. Someday she will have her own restaurant, but for now she is living the American dream.

"My husband, Juan Carlos, came to San Francisco to paint houses and make money for us. He sent little presents home to our five sons—music, tennis shoes, jeans, things that the kids really liked and could not get in Mexico City. Juan Carlos wanted to make money and come home, but I thought, why are we here and he is sending this stuff? Why not be there where the kids can have stuff all the time? Juan Carlos did not like that idea. He wanted to come back to Mexico City, but Mexico is not a good place right now. There are robberies and no opportunities for our kids, and we all came to San Francisco. I made a little restaurant in my house, a secret one, not official. I loved it, and people came to eat. After two years, I wanted to be legal in cooking. And so I went to La Cocina, where they let you work in a licensed kitchen and help people get permits. My business is called El Buen Comer, which means 'Eating Well.' I am very happy. I like using California olive oil, but the chicharrón are better in Mexico. I miss the herbs that my friend grows and powders to make mole verde. Fideo is the most common soup in my country. You can make it without chicken broth, just use water if you have no money. It depends on your family, how you like to serve fideo. I make it with spinach and serve it with lime. Some Mexican people add cheese, avocado, or shredded chicken. I know one man who must have banana in his fideo."

FOR THE BROTH

4 pounds chicken legs, thighs, and wings

1 bay leaf

1 onion, cut in half

½ teaspoon cumin seeds

1 teaspoon black peppercorns

Dash of chili sauce (optional)

FOR THE FIDEO

½ pound roma tomatoes, cored

2 garlic cloves

½ cup chopped onion

4 to 8 cups chicken broth or water, plus more if necessary

½ teaspoon salt, plus more to taste

¼ to ½ cup olive oil

One 10-ounce package fideo (vermicelli)

1 small garlic clove, minced

2 cups spinach or chard, washed, dried, and cut into thin julienne

Mexican limes, chopped avocado, shredded chicken, cilantro, chili sauce (optional) for garnish

1. To make the broth: Put all the ingredients in a large pot. Cover with cold water and cook slowly for 2 hours. Reserve the broth and the chicken, discard the onion. When the chicken is cool enough to handle, discard the skin, shred the meat, and set it aside to add as a garnish or use for another dish.

2. To make the fideo: Place the tomatoes, garlic, and onion in a blender and cover with cold broth or water. Blend on high speed until totally liquid. Strain the mixture through a fine-mesh strainer placed over a pot. With a wooden spoon or rubber scraper, press the vegetables against the strainer to remove as much liquid as possible. Discard the solids and set the juice aside.

3. Place the olive oil in a large pot over medium heat. When it is hot, add the noodles and stir constantly until they are golden. Be careful not to burn them. If they turn too brown, they will make an acrid soup. When the noodles are done, add the strained tomato juice and enough broth just to cover the noodles, and simmer until they are tender but not too soft.

4. While the noodles are cooking, warm the remaining olive oil in a pan with the minced garlic clove. When the garlic is golden, add the julienned greens, toss them quickly to wilt, remove from heat, and set aside. Add the greens to the noodles, stir, season with salt, black pepper, and chili sauce. Serve immediately with the garnishes of your choice.

MAKES 8 SERVINGS

KATE'S COMPOST SOCIAL SOUP

In 2001, Kate McDermott met Jon Rowley, the man who would become her mulch-mate (and husband) on GardenWeb.com's soil, compost, and mulch forum. So it made sense when the couple announced that for their nuptials they would create an altar at a compost station at the Interbay P-Patch Community Garden. It even made sense when they said they would make a wedding compost. "We'd both been married before, so we were recycling ourselves," says Ms. McDermott, a pianist and gardener. "We were taking all the life experience that most people discard and turning it into something bountiful and full of life."

Many guests had difficulty divining exactly what constituted wedding-worthy garbage. Bill Rice, a food writer for the *Chicago Tribune*, made a luminous mosaic from his leftovers, with recipe attached ("one skin of Wisconsin natural smoked trout, cut up . . ."). Julia Child sent a single perfect banana peel, gift wrapped.

The wedding menu included this rib-sticking soup that they typically serve for lunch after Saturday morning work sessions in the garden.

½ pound dried great Northern white beans, soaked in cold water overnight or in boiling water for 3 hours, then drained

3 tablespoons olive oil

5 garlic cloves, peeled and smashed

2 tablespoons chopped fresh rosemary

2 medium beefsteak tomatoes, cored and halved

Kosher salt

1 cup butternut squash, peeled and coarsely chopped

2 plum tomatoes, peeled and coarsely chopped

2 carrots, peeled and coarsely chopped

2 quarts homemade chicken or vegetable broth or low-sodium store-bought broth

1 bunch black kale (ribs removed), coarsely chopped

8 ounces tubetti or ditali pasta

Freshly ground black pepper

2 tablespoons extra virgin olive oil

2 tablespoons chopped fresh parsley

1. In a Dutch oven, cover the beans with water by 2 inches. Bring to a simmer and cook for 1 to 1½ hours, until tender. Drain the beans and return to the pot.

2. In a small saucepan, heat 2 tablespoons of the olive oil over medium heat. Add the garlic and rosemary and cook until aromatic, about 1 minute. Stir in the halved tomatoes and ½ teaspoon salt, bring to a simmer, and cook about 20 minutes, until soft.

3. Process the cooked tomatoes in a blender or food processor until smooth. Strain the puree through a fine-mesh strainer into the soup pot.

4. Place an oven rack in the center position and preheat to oven to 400°F.

5. In a large baking dish, toss the remaining 1 tablespoon olive oil with the squash, plum tomatoes, and carrots. Roast about 20 minutes, until the edges are golden brown. Add to the beans.

6. Bring the broth to a simmer and add the kale one handful at a time. Stir in the pasta and cook for 6 to 10 minutes, until the pasta and kale are tender. Drain and reserve the broth. Add the pasta and kale to the beans and stir. Add as much broth as needed to get desired consistency. Season with salt and pepper to taste.

7. To serve, ladle into bowls, drizzle with extra virgin olive oil, and sprinkle with the parsley.

SERVES 6 TO 8

Steaming Bowls: Soups, Chowders, and Other Consolations

Thornton Dial, 2005.

Valeria Ponte's White Minestrone

The daughter of an Italian father and Colombian mother, Valeria Ponte grew up in Venezuela and came to the United States on her own as a young woman. She is an artist, gardener, and mother of two, and her heritage gives her an enviable culinary repertoire. From her Italian nonna, she has an unusual recipe for white minestrone, a hearty soup of vegetables, beans, and pasta that omits the usual tomatoes. Its thick, creamy texture comes from pureeing a quarter of the soup and mixing it back in. A big pot of the minestrone was always in the family's fridge when Ms. Ponte was growing up. "My mom did whatever she could to make sure we ate our vegetables. This soup usually did the trick."

One Big Table

4 medium russet potatoes, peeled and cut into ½-inch chunks

3 small zucchini, coarsely chopped

3 carrots, coarsely chopped

2 large leeks, white parts only, coarsely chopped

2 celery stalks, strings removed, coarsely chopped

1 head green cabbage, quartered, cored, and coarsely chopped

1 small butternut squash, peeled, seeded, and cut into ½-inch chunks

1 medium head cauliflower, cored and cut into 1-inch florets

1 bunch broccoli, stems removed, cut into 1-inch florets

8 ounces dried red kidney, pinto, or cannellini beans, soaked in cold water overnight or in boiling water for 3 hours, then drained

8 ounces small pasta, such as ditali or small shells

3 tablespoons olive oil

1 teaspoon freshly grated nutmeg

1 bay leaf

Kosher salt and freshly ground black pepper

1 cup grated Parmesan cheese (about 4 ounces)

¼ cup chopped fresh parsley

1. In a large stock pot, combine the potatoes, zucchini, carrots, leeks, celery, cabbage, squash, cauliflower, broccoli, beans, pasta, oil, nutmeg, bay leaf, 1 tablespoon salt, and ½ teaspoon pepper. Cover with water by 1 inch. Bring to a simmer, partially cover, and cook about 1 hour, until the beans and vegetables are tender.

2. Remove and discard the bay leaf. Working in batches, process about one-quarter of the soup in a blender or food processor until completely smooth. Stir the puree into the soup and reheat if necessary. Season with salt and pepper to taste.

3. To serve, ladle into bowls and sprinkle with the cheese and parsley.

SERVES 12

Fayrene Sherritt's
Hungarian Mushroom Soup

As a kid in Fairbanks, Fayrene Sherritt wore one scarf over her head to protect her sinuses and another over her mouth and nose to prevent "frostbite of the lungs." "It was 60 to 70 degrees below zero," she says "and all our groceries were shipped, barged, or trucked in. The day after we married forty-four years ago, my husband and I moved from Fairbanks, where we grew up, to Anchorage. I wanted out of Alaska, it was too cold. In Anchorage, the temp got down to only minus 15 degrees; the rest of the time, it was above zero, it was like the tropics.

"Things have changed in Alaska. Now with global warming it gets to 40 to 55 below, and Anchorage has everything that is available in New York except Red Lobster and Olive Garden. Get out of Anchorage and you're back to Alaska. We live on the peninsula where gold was discovered in 1888. The town of Hope started in 1894; there's only 130 to 150 people who live here year-round. I first made this soup as barter for Tito's Discovery Café here in Hope. I got the recipe from my daughter-in-law. It called for fresh milk, but we are eighty-eight miles away from the nearest grocery, so I tried it with canned. It's much better, creamier. We have a lot of wild mushrooms. You never know what you are going to get.

"People always ask for the recipe. I am on the library board. So I typed it up and made it available for five dollars, which goes to the library. I also write 'Hope Happenings' for the local paper, *The Turnagain Times*, and I volunteer. I'm busy. It's been a wonderful life."

6 tablespoons (¾ stick) unsalted butter

1 pound white mushrooms, coarsely chopped

2 medium onions, finely chopped

6 tablespoons all-purpose flour

3 cups water

2 cups homemade chicken broth or low-sodium store-bought chicken broth

2 cups whole milk or 1 cup evaporated milk plus 1 cup water

1 tablespoon chopped fresh dill or ¾ teaspoon dried

1 tablespoon tamari sauce

2 teaspoons paprika, preferably smoked bittersweet

Kosher salt and freshly ground black pepper

½ cup sour cream

¼ cup chopped fresh parsley

2 teaspoons fresh lemon juice

1. In a Dutch oven, melt the butter over medium heat. Add the mushrooms and onions and cook for 8 to 10 minutes, until the vegetables are soft. Sprinkle in the flour and cook, stirring, about 1 minute, until incorporated.

2. Slowly whisk in the water, broth, milk, dill, tamari, paprika, ½ teaspoon salt, and ¼ teaspoon pepper. Bring to a simmer and cook for 15 to 20 minutes, stirring occasionally, until thickened.

3. In a small bowl, mix the sour cream with ¼ cup of the soup, then stir the mixture into the soup, along with the parsley and lemon juice. Season with salt and pepper to taste, and serve.

SERVES 6

135

Steaming Bowls: Soups, Chowders, and Other Consolations

John Cope's Dried Corn Chowder

Martin Cope dried his first batch of corn kernels in 1900 in Rheems, Pennsylvania, using a traditional Pennsylvania Dutch technique. Corn is harvested when its sugars are at their highest. The corn goes into the air-drier right after picking, before the sugars turn to starch. The drying removes moisture and caramelizes the natural sugars in the corn, creating a toasty, nutty, sweet flavor that many people find addictive. Not even fresh corn can deliver the same intensity of flavor or creamy texture. Plus, it's available all year long. The corn is sold in specialty food markets and on the Internet. Martin Cope's grandson, John, uses this family recipe for his own harvest feast.

FOR THE CORN BROTH

12 corn cobs, kernels removed and reserved

1 tablespoon unsalted butter

1 onion, chopped

1 garlic clove, peeled and chopped

12 sprigs fresh thyme

½ teaspoon kosher salt

4 black peppercorns

2 quarts water

FOR THE SOUP

6 slices bacon, coarsely chopped

2 medium onions, finely chopped

2 tablespoons all-purpose flour

2 cups cooked dried corn

2 cups reserved corn kernels (use the rest for another dish)

2 medium Yukon gold potatoes, peeled and cut into ½-inch pieces

2 cups corn broth

2 cups whole milk

Kosher salt and freshly ground black pepper

¼ cup chopped fresh parsley

1. To make the broth: Preheat the oven to 350°F. Slather the corncobs with the butter and roast on a baking sheet for 30 minutes, turning occasionally.

2. Remove from oven and place the cobs in a large soup pot with the onion, garlic, thyme, salt and peppercorns. Add the water, cover, and simmer for 1½ hours.

3. Strain though a fine-mesh strainer into a storage container. Discard the solids and place the broth in the refrigerator. Skim the fat before using.

4. To make the soup: Cook the bacon in a large saucepan over medium-low heat about 10 minutes, stirring occasionally, until crisp. Using a slotted spoon, transfer it to paper towels to drain. Remove half of the bacon fat and set aside for another use. Add the onion to the remaining fat in the pot and cook over medium heat, stirring often, until soft, about 4 minutes. Stir in the flour to make a smooth paste.

5. Add the cooked and fresh corn, potatoes, broth, and milk. Bring to a simmer and cook for 15 to 20 minutes, until the potatoes are tender. Season with salt and pepper to taste, and stir in the parsley. Serve in warm bowls, sprinkled with the bacon.

SERVES 4 TO 6

Steaming Bowls: Soups, Chowders, and Other Consolations

Cecil Lapeyrouse's
Corn Maque Choux Soup

CHAUVIN, LOUISIANA

In southern Louisiana, decades are remembered by their hurricanes—1950s: Audrey; 1960s: Betsy and Camille; 1970s: Edith, Carmen, and Bob; 1980s: Juan, Bonnie, and Gilbert; 1990s: Andrew, Frances, and Georges; 2000s: Katrina, Rita, and Gustav. Each storm surge rips communities apart and scars the landscape forever. But the Cecil Lapeyrouse Grocery Store, built in 1914 on Bayou Petit Caillou within a few miles of the Gulf of Mexico, is still standing. Cecil Lapeyrouse's grandfather Gustave, who was in the oyster business, opened it to serve the people in the area. Gustave's son Chester ran it, and now Chester's son Cecil is the proprietor. The shelves are stocked with groceries, tackle, tools, and galvanized aluminum boats. Fishermen purchase bait, ice, and fuel.

Louisiana men pride themselves on their cooking, but Mr. Lapeyrouse is nonchalant about his abilities. "I like to cook, yeah. Gumbos, jambalayas, pasta." A specialty of all southern Louisiana cooks is corn maque choux, a corn and tomato dish that is sometimes enhanced with fresh Gulf shrimp. Many believe corn maque choux may have evolved from Spain's caldo, a corn and cabbage dish. Others maintain that "maque" meant "corn" in the native Natchez language. "Choux" are cabbages in French. Regardless of origin, corn maque choux is a tasty side dish, casserole, or soup. The only difference among the three options is the amount of liquid added. Mixed with cornbread it makes a delicious dressing, too.

One Big Table

1 pound salt pork, diced

8 tender, well-developed ears fresh corn

½ cup vegetable oil

1 cup diced onions

3 cups Gulf shrimp (optional, 70 to 90 per pound), peeled and deveined

One 14.5-ounce can chopped tomatoes, drained

One 8-ounce can tomato sauce

1 quart homemade chicken broth or low-sodium store-bought chicken broth

Kosher salt and freshly ground black pepper to taste

1 nest dried vermicelli or heavy handful fine noodles

1. Bring a large saucepan of water to a boil. Add the pork and cook for 5 minutes to remove the salt. Drain and pat dry.

2. Shuck the corn. Cut lengthwise down the cob with a sharp knife to remove the kernels. Scrape each cob with the back of the knife to remove all the "milk" (juice) and pulp remaining on the cob. The richness of this dish will depend on how much milk and pulp can be scraped from the cobs.

3. In a large heavy-bottomed pot, heat the oil over medium-high heat. Add the onions and salt pork and cook for 5 to 10 minutes, stirring occasionally, until the onions are wilted. Add the corn, corn milk, and pulp and cook for 3 minutes, stirring often. Add 1 cup of the shrimp, if using. Stir in the tomatoes and tomato sauce. Cook for 5 to 7 minutes, until the mixture has thickened.

4. Add the broth and bring to a rolling boil. Reduce to a simmer and cook 30 minutes. Season to taste using salt and pepper.

5. Add the remaining shrimp, if using, and the vermicelli and cook for 12 minutes more or until noodles are cooked.

SERVES 6 TO 8

Steaming Bowls: Soups, Chowders, and Other Consolations

CAROLYN YOUNG'S CHESTNUT BISQUE

RIDGEFIELD, WASHINGTON

After retiring from teaching in Southern California, Carolyn and Ray Young moved to the northern end of the Willamette Valley in Washington State. Today they have a chestnut orchard called Allen Creek Farm and do all the work, including weeding, fertilizing, harvesting, processing, and marketing. Ms. Young runs the sweeper, while Mr. Young runs the harvester.

They grow Colossals, a Japanese-European hybrid, without insecticides, fungicides, or fumigation. The chestnuts turn brown in late September and are harvested through October. It takes three people to run the processing line, and friends help out or they hire an extra hand. During National Chestnut Week in mid-October, up to 500 people attend an open house at the orchard, some traveling from as far away as the East Coast. Hosting gives the Youngs the opportunity to educate "two generations of Americans who have never known chestnuts."

They have met with chestnut growers in Slovenia, Croatia, Italy, and Australia. One of their favorite trips was to Tuscany, where they learned to make chestnut flour. Ms. Young is allergic to wheat and uses the chestnut flour in combination with other nonwheat flours to make gluten-free baked goods and pancakes.

Chestnuts are low in calories and fat compared to other nuts. Their water content is high, about 50 percent, and they keep best under refrigeration. But most produce managers display them with other nuts, where they often dry out or show signs of mold within a few days.

Ms. Young says this recipe came from another source, but she has tweaked it enough over the years until she feels safe calling it her own. She likes to serve the soup with chestnut honey cornbread.

1 tablespoon unsalted butter

1 small onion, finely chopped

1 carrot, finely chopped

1 celery stalk, finely chopped

1 pound fresh chestnuts, peeled

3 cups homemade chicken broth or low-sodium store-bought chicken broth

¼ cup apple juice

¼ cup chopped fresh parsley

½ teaspoon dried tarragon

Pinch of freshly grated nutmeg

Kosher salt and freshly ground black pepper

Plain yogurt or sour cream, for garnish (optional)

1. In a large saucepan, melt the butter over medium heat. Add the onion, carrot, and celery, and cook about 4 minutes, stirring occasionally, until soft. Stir in the chestnuts and cook about 5 minutes more, until they begin to soften.

2. Stir in the broth, apple juice, parsley, tarragon, nutmeg, ¼ teaspoon salt, and a pinch of pepper and bring to a simmer over high heat. Reduce the heat to medium-low and cook for 15 to 20 minutes, until the chestnuts are tender.

3. Working in two batches, process the soup in a blender or food processor until smooth. Return the soup to the saucepan and warm over low heat. Season with salt and pepper to taste.

4. Ladle into bowls and garnish with the yogurt.

SERVES 4

IN PURSUIT OF THE SMOOTH

FOOD MILL   Before mechanical food mills, mashing food was arduous work. Cooks used the backs of spoons to force soft-cooked food through drum- or cone-shaped fine-mesh strainers, until Jean Mantelet invented a pan-shaped strainer with a hand-cranked blade. It was patented on August 8, 1933. After Walter Ringer, a manufacturer in Minneapolis, bought the patent, his company, Foley Manufacturing, produced and marketed the machine allowing the home cook to turn out pureed soups without breaking a sweat.

ELECTRIC BLENDER   With electricity, kitchen tasks changed forever. In 1910, L. H. Hamilton, Chester Beach, and Fred Osius started the Hamilton Beach Manufacturing Company to develop kitchen appliances. In 1922, Stephen Poplawski put a spinning blade at the bottom of a container to chop, grind, and puree food, according to Mary Bellus, an expert on inventions for About.com. He sold the blenders to drugstores so they could make Horlick's malted milkshakes.

In 1935, Mr. Osius improved upon Mr. Poplawski's design and sold it to Fred Waring, who introduced it as the Miracle Mixer at the National Restaurant Show in Chicago. It cost $29.75. Mr. Waring renamed his company the Waring Corporation and the mixer the Waring Blender. According to Ms. Bellus, Mr. Waring sold the mixer to hotels and restaurants, to upscale department stores such as Bloomingdale's, and finally to bars. "This mixer is going to revolutionize American drinks," he told a reporter.

340 RECIPES for the new Waring Blendor

Four years before the one millionth Waring blender was sold in 1954, the immersion blender—also called a stick, wand, or hand blender or a Bermixer (after professional models made by Dito-Electrolux)—was invented in Switzerland by Roger Perrinjaquet. He called the new appliance, a handy and powerful wand that blends the soup right in the pot, a *bamix*, a portmanteau of the French *bat* (beat) and the English word mix. European professional kitchens adopted them in the 1960s, and they were adapted for home use in the United States in the 1980s.

WANTED!
500 BAKERS FOR THE U.S. ARMY
(ALSO 100 COOKS)

If you can bake bread Uncle Sam wants you—if you can't bake bread Uncle Sam will teach you how in a Government School.

A BAKERY COMPANY CONSISTS OF 61 MEN
so that you and your "pals" can join the same unit and bake and break bread together.

ENLIST FOR THE WAR - BAKERS PAY $33 TO $45 PER MONTH
AGES 18 TO 45   COOKS PAY $38 PER MONTH

WITH CLOTHING, FOOD, QUARTERS AND MEDICAL ATTENTION.

Recruiting Office: Cor. 39th St. and 6th Ave. (South East Corner)

Bread:
AN UNREFINED HISTORY

The history of the United States can be told as an endless striving for better bread. Before fields of amber grains were sown on the continental United States, arriving colonists in Virginia and Massachusetts disembarked from their ships clutching chunks of hard brown bread. There was no wheat to be found, so the settlers planted stores of grains they'd brought with them. But their crops failed. When the settlers were starving, the indigenous people introduced them to corn, the ancient survival grain of Mesoamerica. The Europeans viewed maize as animal fodder; they thought it was revolting. But they started to cook with it, beginning with native fry cake, which they called hoe bread or hoecake.

In America, bread baking began at the open fire, became an industry, and is now the star of an artisanal movement.

The Indians munched corn on the cob, popped the kernels, used them to make mush and puddings, and pounded them into flour. They taught colonists to make a corn batter which, when cooked on

Hoecake . . . Ash Cake . . . Journey Cake . . . Johnnycake . . . Corn Dodgers

a rock griddle or wooden board, became the flat bread known as johnnycake or journey cake for its rock-hard texture and inability to spoil. By the mid-eighteenth century, settlers cooked cornmeal hoecakes on paddles over open fires—and according to one Pennsylvania legend, on the blades of weeding hoes—and baked them in brick ovens cut into the mass of their walk-in fireplaces. The most rudimentary mixture of cornmeal, water, and a little pork fat made a bread called corn pone, corn dodgers, or skillet bread; this was a staple of slaves and poor rural white folks in the South. A loftier bread favored by the upper classes was made by adding eggs, buttermilk, salt, butter, and leavening such as baking powder or soda. In the North, more shortening plus sugar created "Yankee cornbread." Today, cornbread tends to be crumbly yet moist. Cooks often change the texture by combining cornmeal with other flours and sometimes fresh corn kernels. Often savory seasonings such as chiles or herbs are added, as in Jamie Pagana's Rich & Herby Cornbread (see next page). When baked in an oiled, preheated cast-iron skillet, cornbread develops a crisp, nutty crust that makes a lovely contrast to the moist interior.

CORN PONE OPINIONS

CORN PONE WAS SO ALIGNED WITH THE RURAL POOR that the term is used interchangeably with hayseed, yokel, or hick. In an essay found in his papers and published in 1923, after his death, Mark Twain quotes a childhood friend on "corn-pone philosophy." The society of his friend was "very dear to me because I was forbidden by my mother to partake of it. He was a gay and impudent and satirical and delightful young black man— a slave—who daily preached sermons from the top of his master's woodpile, with me for sole audience." According to the orator, a man cannot afford views that might interfere with his bread and butter. "If he would prosper, he must train with the majority; in matters of large moment, like politics and religion, he must think and feel with the bulk of his neighbors, or suffer damage to his social standing and his business prosperities. He must restrict himself to corn-pone opinions—at least on the surface."

Jamie Pagana's Rich & Herby Cornbread

NORTHAMPTON, MASSACHUSETTS

While Jamie Pagana was studying photography at Hampshire College in Amherst, Massachusetts, she was bitten by the bread bug when she visited friends who worked at the Hungry Ghost Bakery in nearby Northampton. Pathologically shy, she says that she is happiest behind a camera or in the night kitchen, minding the oven and baking cookies, tarts, scones, muffins, and this fabulously rich cornbread. At the bakery, a citadel of slow sourdough risen bread, her quick bread is an anomaly. It is also a departure from the lean sustenance breads of an earlier America. It is simple to make and a soul-satisfying companion to hearty soups and stews.

4 cups whole-wheat pastry flour, plus more if necessary

4 cups finely milled cornmeal

1 cup sugar

4 tablespoons baking powder

Kosher salt

2–4 tablespoons chopped fresh rosemary leaves

4 tablespoons (½ stick) butter, melted

2 cups buttermilk

4 large eggs, lightly beaten

2 cups corn kernels, fresh or frozen, thawed and drained

1 cup shredded sharp Cheddar cheese (about 4 ounces)

1. Generously grease a 9- x 13-inch baking pan or 13-inch cast-iron skillet with 2 tablespoons of the butter. Place the pan on an oven rack in the center position. Preheat the oven to 350°F.

2. Meanwhile, combine the whole-wheat flour, corn flour, sugar, baking powder, 2 teaspoons salt, and the rosemary in a large bowl. Combine the melted butter with the buttermilk and eggs in a separate bowl.

3. Form a well in the center of the dry ingredients. Add the wet ingredients, and, using a rubber spatula and a few strokes, combine the two. Fold in the corn kernels and half the cheese.

4. Remove the preheated baking pan from the oven. Pour the batter into the pan and sprinkle the remaining cheese over the batter. Bake until firm, 30 to 35 minutes.

———

SERVES 8 TO 12

The Apache Reaper, *Edward Curtis, c. 1906.*

In 1830, producing 100 bushels of wheat required about 250 to 300 labor hours by hand, using broadcast sowing, a walking plow, scythes to cut, and flails to thresh kernels from the chaff. Sixty years later, after the patent of the McCormick reaper and the introduction of John Deere's steel plow, practical threshing machines, horse-drawn straddle-row cultivators, and grain elevators and silos, 100 bushels of wheat could be produced in forty to fifty labor hours. This increase in efficiency coincided with the mass immigration of Mennonites fleeing mandatory Russian military service; members of the same religious sect fleeing Prussia had turned Russia into the breadbasket of the world. They brought their knowledge of farming and their trunks full of hearty Turkey Red wheat—first developed in the Fertile Crescent—to Nebraska, Kansas, the Dakotas, and the central Canadian plains, and planted an American wheat revolution.

Amber Waves of Grain

Traditionally grain had been stone-ground, but during the Industrial Revolution a process was developed to roller-mill wheat, crushing the germ (but removing the nutrients and flavor) and extending its shelf life past one day, thus making "refined" white flour—once used only by the wealthy—affordable to the larger population. Today, as an emphasis on whole grains returns, small stone grinders are being revived and large food producers such as ConAgra are installing gigantic stone mills.

In 1909, the Alsop Process Company of St. Louis filed a patent for a process that used chlorine to bleach flour.

Naturally present wild yeast has been used to leaven bread and make ale since at least 5000 B.C.—but the yeast cells that would make commercial yeast possible weren't isolated until the middle of the nineteenth century. Before then, bakers made their own leaveners from ingredients such

Technology

as hops and the water left from boiling or soaking potatoes, then saved a portion of each bread batch as a starter for the next one.

Wagon trains setting off from Independence, Missouri, on the Oregon Trail expected to cross the country in six months. Some families walked a cow or two and perhaps had some hens tucked into the wagon, but bread was their mainstay. Guides suggested packing 200 pounds of flour and half a bushel of cornmeal for each adult. To transport their starter most efficiently, some women soaked bedsheets in it, dried, folded, and packed the sheets, then reconstituted the starter on the trail by moistening the sheets with water. Pioneers often pampered bread starter in the warmest part of the wagon, and when winter weather came, took the precious substance into their beds. The "overlanders" baked bread in folding tin reflector ovens or heavy cast-iron Dutch ovens with three legs and a lid over fires of scrounged fuel—from buffalo chips to dried weeds. For quick bread, they mixed dough in empty flour sacks, inserted a long stick, and, compacting the dough around it, stuck the "bread pop" in the ground beside the campfire to roast.

Because biological yeast was unreliable, most bakers supplemented their sourdough starter with saleratus, an alkali bicarbonate of soda that replaced the colonial-era pearl ash or potash (potassium carbonate) derived from leaching wood or plant ashes. By 1850, baking powder—combining sodium bicarbonate with cream of tartar—replaced saleratus, making a greater range of baked goods, such as scones, biscuits, and fruit and nut breads, all quick and easy to prepare.

The introduction of baking powder brought about a sea change in cake and bread making. Spurred on by the new quick-rising formula, layer cakes, sponges, Swiss rolls, and soda bread were developed. Baking powder, moisture, and heat, when combined, liberate carbon dioxide gas to raise the dough or batter.

In 1876 Charles and Maximilian Fleischmann introduced commercially produced yeast at the Philadelphia Centennial Exposition, luring many of the 10 million visitors to their Viennese bread concession by circulating the scent of baking bread through the exhibition hall.

Thirty-three horse team harvester, cutting, threshing, and sacking wheat, 1908.

Before the invention of chemical leavening agents such as baking soda and baking powder, bakers who wanted air in their bread and didn't have the time for yeast rising beat the daylights out of stiff dough. The dough was leavened by the continual folding of air between its layers, administered by thwacking it with a skillet or mallet—or, as legend has it, a granny with her musket. Beaten biscuits, made of flour, milk, and lard and pricked on top with a fork before baking, were the pride of the South. They are the rich, dense cousins of crackers.

Beaten to a Puff

Because of the hard work required to produce it, the beaten biscuit soon became a status symbol, a chore for the plantation cook. Recipes called for using a tree stump as a work surface, and giving 200 wallops with a flat ax blade for everyday biscuits, and 500 to make them smooth enough for company. In the late nineteenth century, a Missouri manufacturer produced the biscuit brake, a worktable with a hand-cranked double roller like a toothed washing wringer that eased the burden of biscuit beating. With the invention of baking powder and the marketing of commercial yeast, the labor-intensive biscuits fell out of favor—though the memory of their distinctive flavor and texture persists. Linton Hopkins, the chef-owner of Restaurant Eugene in Atlanta, developed a food processor method for beaten biscuits that satisfies the urge for the heavy, old-fashioned bread.

FROM OPEN FIRE TO CLOSED STOVE

IN 1869, CATHERINE BEECHER WROTE, "WE CAN not but regret, for the sake of bread, that our old steady brick ovens have been almost universally superseded by those of ranges and cooking stoves, which are infinite in their caprices, and forbid all general rules." Nevertheless, when women could get rid of their old brick beehive ovens, they eagerly did so.

Early oven, Jamestown, 1620.

148

Bread wrappers offer a double bonus: the baker can advertise on the wrapper, and bread wrapped by machine is handled less by bakery employees. The first wrapping machine appeared in 1911; it used a wax seal to close the ends of the paper. Three years later, a new machine folded waxed paper around the loaf and sealed it by means of a heating plate. This process was not perfected until 1930, but because the cost of the new equipment raised the price of bread, many bakers did not install bread wrappers until the Depression ended.

It's a Wrap: The Best Thing After Sliced Bread

The automated bread slicer was invented by Otto Frederick Rohwedder of Davenport, Iowa, in 1912. It was first used commercially by the Chillicothe Baking Company in Missouri, whose Kleen Maid Sliced Bread was released on July 7, 1928. The bread was advertised as "the greatest forward step in the baking industry since bread was wrapped."

Sliced bread may be one of civilization's greatest achievements, but it goes stale much faster than uncut loaves, and bakers were slow to offer it. Wrapping machines were improved, and later, preservatives were added to keep bread fresh.

Bread slicer, St. Louis, 1930.

One Big Table

Great Depression bread lines, New York City.

By the early twentieth century, only one in four households still baked bread at home. The number continued to slide by 1930, when Wonder Bread marketed sliced bread nationwide.

Wonder Bread defines factory bread. This originally unsliced bread was first baked by the

Commercial Bread

Taggart Baking Company of Indianapolis around 1920. Taggart was acquired by Continental Baking Company in 1925, which sold sliced Wonder Bread in 1930 and promoted it extensively throughout the decade. Wonder Bread was produced at a full-scale bakery at the New York World's Fair in 1939–40 and was the sponsor of popular radio programs. During the 1940s, the federal government became concerned with the nutritional deficiency of white bread and temporarily mandated that it be "enriched" with B vitamins, iron, folate, and calcium to curb pellagra and beriberi. Continental also found a way to create a loaf so soft that it could be squeezed into a fist-sized ball, and "enriched" Wonder Bread was advertised on children's radio and television programs such as *Hopalong Cassidy* and *Howdy Doody* beginning in 1941. In the 1950s, the company introduced the slogan "Wonder Bread Builds Strong Bodies 8 Ways" for the product. During a backlash against overly refined foods in the 1960s, Wonder Bread became a prime target for criticism.

Watch 'em grow!

WONDER BREAD

GROWTH and WEIGHT RECORDER

INSTRUCTIONS: For ease in checking on child's growth, chart should be permanently attached with tacks or tape to door moulding or wall, 2 feet from floor. Place child with back to chart and mark off height. Next to this, write child's weight and the date.

HEIGHT	WEIGHT AND DATE HERE

6'
11"
10"
9"
8"
7"
6"
5"
4"
3"
2"
1"
5'
11"

WONDER BREAD

In an effort to fight wartime shortages, the sale of sliced bread was banned briefly in 1943.

LEFT: *Learning to make good bread, Bethune-Cookman College* (GORDON PARKS, 1943).

BELOW: *Marine Corps, USN School of Baking c. 1917.*

Years of flattened lunch box sandwiches helped fuel a small market backlash against the whitest of all white breads. By the 1950s, many consumers longed for a more authentic packaged bread, a niche soon filled by Pepperidge Farm, a company started by Margaret Rudkin, a Connecticut housewife. When Mrs. Rudkin, who wanted chemical-free bread for her allergic son, used quality ingredients to produce thinly sliced bread, the desire for tea sandwich elegance and the trend toward dieting were joined.

Sylvester Graham and Whole-Grain Bread

Bread emerged from the dark ages of bleaches, bromides, and hydrogenated fats just as approximately 1 million young people established counterculture homesteads in the late 1960s and early 1970s. Espousing the "simple life" of self-sufficiency—vegetable gardens, farm-raised meats, foraged greens, wood heat, and bread made of unprocessed whole-grain flour—"whole earth" proponents who had been raised on fluffy white bread formed co-ops and bought oats, millet, amaranth, wheat bran, brown rice, and seeds. They baked dense, barely edible New Age loaves. But once they learned to bake healthy bread, they longed for tasty bread.

To this yearning mass came the *Tassajara Bread Book* by Edward Espe Brown, head cook for a California Zen meditation retreat. An unpretentious paperback with a gentle philosophy and clear instructions and line drawings for the neophyte, it inspired the counterculture to fire up the wood stove, suburbanites to preheat the electric ovens, and everyone to roll up their sleeves and knead dough. People who had barely heard of whole-grain bread became baking fanatics. By the mid-1970s, homemade bread was once again the staff of life for many.

Some home bread bakers cherish the sourdough starter they've had since the 1970s; they swear by their favorite bread flour; they scour their houses and apartments for a spot near a radiator—or air conditioner—to rise or retard a

The Rise of Artisanal Breads

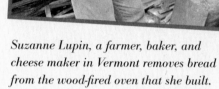

sponge; they find kneading dough, coaxing the rough mass into elastic life, close to spiritual; they mist the oven with a plant sprayer, or drop ice cubes into a hot pan to make steam for a crusty baguette. They are passionate, ecstatic, gaga about bread baking. Some build elaborate outdoor ovens, as normal people have done for centuries.

Suzanne Lupin, a farmer, baker, and cheese maker in Vermont removes bread from the wood-fired oven that she built.

Many cooks, unable to buy good bread, bake bread of necessity. But they resent the sweat and mess of kneading and the time it takes to proof dough. They do not want to devote an entire day to baking. They want tasty bread, made with prime ingredients and little fuss.

In 1894, African American inventor, cook, and restaurateur Joseph Lee of Boston patented his dough-kneading machine; almost a century later, the bread machine, a Japanese-made refinement, caught on in America. Fully automated to add ingredients at the proper time, mix and knead the dough, and proof, raise, and bake the loaves, it rejuvenated home baking for many cooks.

Other time-stressed home bakers pounced on the recipe for no-knead bread originally developed by Jim Lahey of Manhattan's Sullivan Street Bakery that food writer Mark Bittman shared in *The New York Times* in 2006. Bakers who tried the recipe filled blogs and chat rooms with their comments. The bread's authentic rustic look, full-bodied taste, and easy preparation triggered another mini revolution.

HUNGRY GHOST BREAD

IVY ALMOST COVERS THE WINDOWS OF THIS HISTORIC BRICK BAKERY IN NORTHAMPTON, Massachusetts. It threatens the sign, a drawing of a hand that grips a gnarled loaf of bread and the name: Hungry Ghost Bread. The front yard is a patch of wheat. Inside, Jonathan Stevens and Cheryl Maffei, partners in business and life, take the most basic of ingredients—water, flour, salt, wild yeast sourdough starter—to make complex, crusty artisan breads with Old World depth and character. They bake in a massive two-chambered oven—one for the apple and softwood fire, one for bread—with an iron door that looks forged by Vulcan himself. The oven fills the room, a chest-height stone hearth enlivened by kindergarten-painted tiles below, the rounded terra-cotta oven, charred like a loaf of bread, above.

To make French bâtards or anadama, breads of rye or spelt, fougasse with olives and semolina, they need flour, and for flour, they need wheat. They bought the highest quality organic flour, but to counteract

rising wheat prices and the long distance from mill to bakery, they began a project to grow local wheat. Starting with their own front yard and four local farmers who put eight acres into cultivation, they then gave 100 customers wheat berries to plant and harvest on their own small plots. The differences in soil types, microclimates, and wheat varieties provide a fascinating laboratory for their Little Red Hen's Wheat Patch Project. Some customers returned a single small bag of wheat, but some brought large sacks. Ms. Maffei and Mr. Stevens ground it in a hand-cranked mill and made flatbreads and crackers. In 2009, they went to France, with 160 bakers from thirteen countries to learn from paysan-boulangers (peasant bakers) who have bucked corporations and the industrialized European grain system to grow, mill, and process heritage wheat. Inspired by the bakers' commitment to their craft, Hungry Ghost wants to follow their example by acquiring land for growing grain, storage barns, and a gristmill to produce flour for other local bakers.

The Hungry Ghost bakers also feel a special kinship with the Northern New Mexico Organic Wheat Project, a cooperative formed by a group of mainly Native American and Latino farmers who want to stay on their land rather than take jobs in Albuquerque or Santa Fe. Banding together, they grow wheat to produce and market Nativo brand premium organic flour to dozens of markets in northern New Mexico. To organizer Willem Malten, who ran Santa Fe's upscale Cloud Cliff Bakery, the goal is to restore genetic diversity to New Mexico, which boasted more than 250 wheat varieties in the 1880s. But for the growers in one of the poorest counties in America, the goal is to increase their meager profit margin. They still grapple with the problem of transporting grain vast distances for processing, and increasingly, they struggle against persistent drought.

THE ARTISAN'S ARTISAN

MARK FURSTENBERG BECAME A BAKER WHEN HE WAS WORKING AT A BOYS' CAMP and the head cook became ill. He was 19 years old and taught himself to make rolls and simple yeasted bread. He baked and cooked as a college job, then went to work in President Kennedy's War on Poverty. He intended to spend his life in public service, but ended up working as the personnel director for the Boston Police Department and as a journalist for the *Washington Post* and ABC News. But he never stopped baking bread. He became a professional baker when he opened Marvelous Market, which became an instant hit in Washington, D.C. His next restaurant, Breadline, across from the White House, has long lines every day at noon. He is the artisanal bakers' baker, and in his humble opinion, home bakers cannot compete with the pros. In his own words:

As I watch the dough, I think about the tremendous advantage professional bakers have over home bakers. We have better flour, more accurate scales (bakers weigh everything), filtered water, a starter (levain) that is perfect all the time, more efficient mixers, and better temperature controls. Most important, we make bread every day and learn a little each time.

I opened my first bakery twelve years ago; I was 52 years old. It was an audacious thing to do—because I didn't know how to make bread. I thought that because I had been a home baker since boyhood, I could make bread professionally. I didn't know that one has nothing to do with the other. And even when the bakery opened—even, a few months later, when we became a retail fad in Washington—I still didn't know how to make bread.

I went to France to see bread made there and to work a little in bakeries. I worked for a few days at Acme in Berkeley, California, one of the "daddies" of the new traditional American bakeries. I visited other bakeries. And then in 1995, I was invited to start a bread instruction program at Greystone, the California branch of the Culinary Institute of America in Napa Valley. I am always embarrassed to acknowledge that only then, five years after I had opened my first bakery, I really began to learn how to make bread.

Toast

A merica adores toast, the alchemy of bread dry-heated until its surface caramelizes into a sweet, crunchy gold crust. Throughout history, toast has had one major problem: it burns—easily. And the search to develop a gizmo that would produce perfectly browned toast indoors, without the aid of a flame or hearthstone, gripped the imagination of many an engineer and tinkerer.

The invention of the electric toaster is credited to Albert Marsh, who in 1905 patented a nickel and chromium alloy that could be shaped into an element capable of heating bread to 310°F without burning down the house. The first electric toasters were a marvel of exposed coiled wires on a ceramic base. From then on they became objects of beauty and ingenuity: some could flip toast, some carried toast in metal baskets, one used a conveyor belt to move the toast. But none could automatically prevent burning.

In 1926, Charles P. Strite patented his pop-up toaster, the Toastmaster. A few years later, along came sliced bread, making the toasting process a snap, and the perfect marriage was born. Innovations continued: wide slots accommodating bagel halves, toaster ovens, sleek and stylish toasters, glass toasters, even Pop Art toasters that burn designs onto bread.

The Wrong Way to Disconnect a Toaster (ANN ROSENER, 1942).

CHAPTER 4

CONSPICUOUS CONSUMPTION OF CELLULOSE: SALADS

LOS ANGELES, CALIFORNIA

Salad is all about opposites: Healthful or sinful. Simple or complex. Thrifty or luxurious. Spontaneous or studied. You love it or you hate it. But if you are American, in salad you trust.

The definition of salad has shifted, and its social meaning has steadily morphed throughout the nation's history, but it has usually embodied the aspirations of each era. A bowl of raw, leafy things united by some sort of dressing has symbolized by turns health, wealth, virtue, privilege, glamour, necessity.

Megan Bomba, Sara Carnochan, and Kathleen Redmond, the young proprietors of Heart Beet Gardening in Los Angeles, have discovered that the upscale meaning of homegrown, organic heirloom greens is at odds with their dream of urban gardens.

"We're all about easing hunger, increasing healthy eating, and making edible gardens available to everyone," said Ms. Carnochan. When they

started their business two years ago, they had been cruising Watts and Eagle Rock, figuring out the cost of turning rubble-ridden vacant lots into food-for-all and wondering how they'd ever afford the veggie oil–powered truck that could help rein in their greenhouse emissions. Then their cell phones began singing with requests for edible gardens in L.A.'s pricey neighborhoods. Contracts to build and maintain kitchen gardens in Santa Monica, Brentwood, Bel-Air, and Hollywood Hills promised to deliver the cash they needed to fund their sustainable organic-vegetables-for-all vision.

While many urban gardeners scrounge any possible patch for sustenance, Heart Beet's clients' directions to replace the front lawns with vegetables puzzled them. But the shifting of the location of a household's "micro farm" was also exciting. "Just think of how much food could be grown if we replaced lawns with gardens," says Ms. Redmond, "what a positive effect that could have on

OPPOSITE: *Mexican ambassador teaches daughter art of making salads, Wasington D.C., 1939.*

seeming, well, common. But as salad consumption grew, maintaining regional distinctions became more and more challenging. Cookbooks created for and sponsored by salad dressing manufacturers inspired creativity in the home kitchen, resulting in a flurry of carved and stuffed tomatoes, avocados, and peppers. Gelatin companies followed suit and intricate congealed salads proliferated.

By the 1920s, caesar salad, Cobb salad, and green goddess dressing were created for Hollywood stars. Food writers fiercely debated the precise origins of the dishes; cooks closely guarded their recipes. But this patina began to fade midcentury. By the 1980s, when Ms. Bomba, Ms. Redmond, and Ms. Carnochan were born and began to toddle around the lush lawns of Westside Los Angeles, society was taking salad for granted. Even before fast-food establishments featured meal-size plastic tankards of lettuce, salad's image was languishing. And it was going to take more than the sum total of health, creativity, and celebrity to coax mixed greens from their generic fog.

people's lives. Not to mention decreasing the ecological imprint of our city."

As early as the Colonial era, salad signaled privilege. After all, only the wealthy owned the land it takes to cultivate vegetables, and only they could afford "exotic" olive oil to dress them. The image of a green leafy salad as a food of the well-fortuned few continued throughout the nineteenth century as chefs in restaurants favored by *le tout monde* served dainty creations of vegetables and greens as accompaniments to cold lobster, chicken, or crab in that most elegant of French sauces, mayonnaise.

In the early twentieth century, the mass production of mayonnaise, along with refrigerated railroad cars to ship greens to markets north of Florida and east of California, threatened salad's exclusively seasonal nature. But even before then, health gurus like John Harvey Kellogg had begun to champion raw roughage. So even as it became increasingly accessible, salad was saved from

Once again, the distinction came from restaurants, specifically Chez Panisse in Berkeley, where the talent for creating extraordinary salads was matched only by Alice Waters's insistence on knowing the origin, botanical category, culinary history, and growing conditions of each leaf.

In their school cafeteria, Ms. Bomba, Ms. Redmond, and Ms. Carnochan learned that "organic" is better than "conventional," "local" is better than "from far away," and "carbon footprint" is every bit as worrisome as "calories" and "carbs." By the time they were fourteen, the three friends knew their arugula, radicchio, mâche, and mizuna. It was the dawning of the Age of Arugula, and these young idealists were at the forefront of a clean-eating, clear-eyed generation determined to change the world by living "green."

Returning to Los Angeles after college, they saw themselves as liberationists and formed their gardening service as well as a compost co-op and a seed-saving program. "By building and maintaining vegetable gardens for our clients, we give households independence from the commercial food system," said Ms. Bomba, who is now studying for her doctorate in food and environmental policy.

As their installations began to bear fruit, they felt it was the first step in making the world a better place. They tended each client's ripening patch and left notes of advice and joyful birth announcements: "The rocket is ready! Pick it for salad tonight!"

"The heirloom tomatoes are perfect! Pick them for dinner!"

"The baby red leaf and romaine will go to seed! Use it quick!"

But returning two days later to water and weed, they were stunned to find rocket rusting, fat tomatoes rotting on the ground, and the baby lettuces bolted and bitter. When zucchini, summer squash, melons, sweet peppers, and eggplant began joining the lettuce and herbs in the compost pile, the proprietors of Heart Beet had their first lesson in the difference between "life" and "lifestyle." One person's dinner, they realized, is another person's status symbol: heirloom organic vegetable patches as front lawn.

In a flash, the three idealists saw that they are part of a cultural ecosystem in which conspicuous cellulose was inevitable. They couldn't change the social history of salad—or its destiny—but they could create a Community Supported Agricultural initiative for people who *would* eat their vegetables. All they had to do was give fair warning to those for whom eating is somewhat beside the point.

"The lemon cucumbers are ready! Pick them for dinner! If you aren't able, we'll come by and pick them for market tomorrow!"

Sara Carnochan's Herb Salad Cream

LOS ANGELES, CALIFORNIA

Ms. Carnochan takes a one-size-fits-all approach to this creamy, fragrant dressing, which works for lettuces as well as chopped vegetables, pasta, rice, and other grains. "I tried a bunch of different stuff and came up with this. You can use yogurt if you are scared of the crème fraîche and heavy cream," she says. Some of the earliest salad dressings in the American colonies were "creams," which the Dutch used in slaw and the British used on lettuce, cucumbers, and tomatoes.

1 teaspoon minced fresh ginger

1 garlic clove

Fine sea salt

2 tablespoons heavy cream or milk

¼ cup crème fraîche or Greek-style yogurt

2 tablespoons rice vinegar or Champagne vinegar

Dash of hot sauce (preferably a green variety)

1 cup olive oil

½ cup cucumber, peeled, seeded, and diced

¼ cup minced fresh flat-leaf parsley leaves

¼ cup fresh basil leaves, torn into small pieces

1 tablespoon minced fresh mint leaves

¼ cup fresh lemon balm, chopped (or ¼ teaspoon grated lemon zest)

2 tablespoons minced fresh chives

1. Combine the garlic, ginger, ½ teaspoon salt, and 1 tablespoon of the cream in a blender and pulse to make a smooth paste. Add the crème fraîche and vinegar a little at a time, pureeing between each addition. Add the hot sauce and, with the blender still running, slowly drizzle in the olive oil. Add the cucumber and pulse a few times. If the cream is too thick for your liking, add more cream (or milk) to thin it.

2. Scrape into a bowl and stir in the parsley, basil, mint, lemon balm, and chives. Taste and adjust seasoning with additional salt and hot sauce, if desired.

MAKES 2 CUPS

Kelly's Green Goddess Dressing

Growing up in a Minneapolis suburb, Kelly Rich always felt her taste was "inherently different." She'd been adopted from Korea as an infant and came of age in the Midwest. Her mother was a flawless midcentury cook whose offerings were based not so much on her Swedish background as on Campbell's soup. "Her casseroles had no recognizable vegetables," says Ms. Rich. "I loved them; I just loved them in a different way from everybody else." The first member of her family to live outside the Midwest, she moved to Amherst, Massachusetts, to attend college and was immediately smitten with the farmers' markets and fresh produce. When she went home for a visit, she made her mother's green goddess dressing and served it with heaps of tender fresh vegetables, barely blanched and chilled. The experiment was a success. After she returned to Massachusetts, her aunt called from Minneapolis for instructions in blanching.

½ cup mayonnaise

½ cup plain whole milk yogurt

3 anchovy fillets, minced (optional)

1 scallion, green and white parts, finely chopped

3 tablespoons chopped fresh parsley

3 tablespoons chopped fresh chives

2 tablespoons chopped fresh tarragon

1 teaspoon tarragon vinegar or white wine vinegar

Kosher salt and freshly ground black pepper

Place all the ingredients in a blender or a food processor and pulse until smooth. Adjust the seasoning with salt and pepper to taste. Transfer to a serving bowl, cover, and refrigerate about 30 minutes, until the flavors blend. Serve as a salad dressing or dip.

MAKES ABOUT 1½ CUPS

The New CALENDAR of SALADS

365 ANSWERS to the DAILY QUESTION "WHAT SHALL WE HAVE for SALAD?"

Revised and Prepared by ELIZABETH O. HILLER

PUBLISHED AND COPYRIGHTED P. F. VOLLAND COMPANY NEW YORK CHICAGO TORONTO

Debby Morse's Ranch Dressing

Debby Morse doesn't remember her first encounter with ranch dressing, but she never forgot her response. "I swooned," she said. "Smack me with a lettuce leaf, those are the flavors I want in my mouth." Her mother was a Navy wife and entertained a lot, and kept bottled salad dressing, but from the time Ms. Morse was on her own and "a young hippie cook," she has made her own. Her herbs are fresh, her olive oil and vinegar local: Her salad dressings are beyond reproach. Ranch dressing is her sole exception. "I love the taste of ranch the same way people can crave Doritos," she says, adding, "You have to use dried herbs so it tastes a little junky. Fresh herbs don't cut it."

½ cup buttermilk, plus more as needed

½ cup sour cream

½ cup plain whole milk yogurt

1 teaspoon dried oregano

1 teaspoon dried dill weed

¼ teaspoon garlic powder

Kosher salt and freshly ground black pepper

In a medium bowl, whisk together the buttermilk, sour cream, yogurt, oregano, dill, and garlic powder until combined. Season with salt and pepper to taste. If necessary, add more buttermilk to adjust the consistency. Cover and refrigerate about 30 minutes, until the flavors blend. Serve with lettuce or vegetable salads.

MAKES ABOUT 1½ CUPS

DEBBIE CHRISTENSEN'S
FENNEL FROND–YOGURT DRESSING

When she was an executive with Starbucks, Debbie Christensen traveled the world collecting recipes, food memories—and a lot of cooking equipment. When she left the company and settled in East Honolulu, her kitchen was so small that every piece of equipment needed multiple purposes. This mind-set also affected her recipes. She uses this yogurt-fennel dressing on greens, on salads of local exotic fruit, on cauliflower, broccoli, or potatoes, and even on fish.

¼ cup chopped fresh parsley

¼ cup chopped fennel fronds

2 tablespoons fresh lemon juice

1 tablespoon extra virgin olive oil

1 cup plain Greek-style yogurt

Kosher salt and freshly ground black pepper

In a food processor, process the parsley, fennel fronds, lemon juice, and oil together until a paste forms. Add the yogurt and process until smooth. Season with salt and pepper to taste. Transfer to a serving bowl, cover, and refrigerate about 30 minutes until the flavors blend.

MAKES ABOUT 1¾ CUPS

Rogue Creamery's
Best Blue Cheese Dressing Ever

When David Gremmel and Cary Bryant decided to open a wine shop, they began exploring artisanal cheeses to offer their customers. Along the way, they met Ignacio "Ig" Vella, the son of Thomas Vella, a premier American cheese maker, and fell in love with making blue cheese. When the master of mold decided to retire, he asked them to carry on. Within three years, the couple's Rogue River Blue earned the title "Best Blue in the World" at the World Cheese Awards in London, England.

The cheese makers say they have tried a lot of blue cheese dressings in their lives, but have never had one better than this version made by their friend Erica Bishop. "She figured out how to bring out the pear and honey tones in the blue cheese while still preserving the cheese's savory, almost cured bacon-like finish."

1 cup mayonnaise

3 garlic cloves, minced

¼ cup chopped fresh parsley

½ cup sour cream

1 tablespoon fresh lemon juice

½ teaspoon Worcestershire sauce

1 tablespoon red wine vinegar

2 ounces Oregon blue cheese, crumbled
   (about ½ cup)

Kosher salt and freshly ground black pepper

In a medium bowl, whisk together the mayonnaise, garlic, parsley, sour cream, lemon juice, Worcestershire, vinegar, and blue cheese until combined. Season with salt and pepper to taste. Cover and refrigerate about 30 minutes, until the flavors blend.

MAKES ABOUT 1½ CUPS

BALSAMICO VINAIGRETTE

Twenty-five years ago, when he was the chef of Chez Panisse in Berkeley, Paul Bertolli fell for aged balsamico. Hoping to produce the thick aged elixir at home, he traveled to Modena, Italy, to study with a master. He soon found that the time and care required to make extraordinary balsamic vinegar made it impossible for him to produce it commercially. That did not stop him from turning an old garage into an aging room, buying barrels and grapes, and forming a balsamico club with friends and neighbors. In the fall, they purchase grapes, mash them, boil down the juice to make a thick syrup, and then begin aging the vinegar in ever-smaller barrels. The highest quality aceto balsamico is closer to a condiment than a normal vinegar and needs no herbs or spices to make its flavor shine. He makes this simple vinaigrette at Oliveto, his restaurant in Oakland. It is delicious on peppery greens such as arugula, with a wonderful Parmesan cheese and good croutons.

1 medium shallot, finely chopped

2½ tablespoons aged balsamic vinegar

Kosher salt and freshly ground black pepper

2½ tablespoons extra virgin olive oil

In a large bowl, whisk together the shallot, vinegar, ½ teaspoon salt, and ¼ teaspoon pepper. Whisk in the oil until combined. Season with salt and pepper to taste.

—

MAKES ABOUT ½ CUP

Paul's Garlic Croutons

1 loaf crusty peasant bread, preferably day-old Pugliese-style, cut into 1½-inch-thick slices

1 large garlic clove, peeled and halved

About ½ cup extra virgin olive oil, plus more if necessary

Toast or grill the bread until it is dark brown and crisp. Lightly rub each piece with the garlic, brush with the oil, and serve.

—

MAKES 12 TO 16 SERVINGS

NOTE: The croutons can be broken into smaller pieces, if desired, to serve with salad.

Nan McEvoy's Walnut-Sherry Vinaigrette

In 1996, Nan McEvoy retired as chair of the board of the *San Francisco Chronicle*, the newspaper her grandfather had cofounded. She went looking for a house in the country, but she fell hard for a 550-acre former dairy farm and decided to plant 100 olive trees. Today she has 18,000 trees and produces award-winning organic olive oil; her annual harvest party is one of the hottest tickets around. The combination of olive and walnut oils in her vinaigrette creates a fruity flavor with a nutty finish that is delicious on peppery late-season greens as well as with endive, watercress, peppers, and shaved winter vegetables.

¼ cup sherry vinegar

2 teaspoons finely chopped shallot

½ teaspoon kosher salt, plus more to taste

½ teaspoon Dijon mustard

¼ teaspoon freshly ground black pepper, plus more to taste

½ cup extra virgin olive oil

¼ cup walnut oil

Whisk together the vinegar, shallot, salt, mustard, and pepper in a small bowl. Keep whisking while slowly drizzling in first the olive oil and then the walnut oil. Whisk until combined. Season with salt and pepper to taste.

MAKES ABOUT 1 CUP, OR 8 SERVINGS

168

One Big Table

WILD THINGS

DESCENDED FROM PIRATES AND DIPLOMATS OF THE JAMESTOWN COLONY, SUNNY Savage was born to back-to-the-land parents and grew up in the middle of Minnesota's Smoky Hills State Forest without running water or electricity. Today, traveling in an RV fitted with bamboo flooring and white net curtains, she and her young son follow the spring and eat from the land.

Spring first touches the United States in areas at 35 degrees latitude and southward—the bottom third of California, and Arizona, New Mexico, Texas, Oklahoma, Arkansas, Louisiana, most of the South below Kentucky and Virginia, and across the Gulf Coast to Florida. The first edible plants to appear are wild mustards, common mallow, and chickweed, which are available year-round in areas with a mild climate like the Pacific Northwest, followed by dandelions, violets, oxalis, and pokeweed, then nettles, lamb's quarter, and purslane. Ms. Savage loves making meal-size salads from tender dandelion greens and burdock root with a vinaigrette of mustard, soy sauce, and honey.

Wild Mustard: This huge family—including garlic mustard, rock mustard, and field mustard—is available all over the continental United States. Crush the leaves for mustard's distinctive smell. You can eat the roots, seeds, leaves, and yellow flowers, which look similar to broccoli flowers. They can be used to flavor vinegar. People with ulcers or gastrointestinal sensitivity should avoid wild mustard.

Common Mallow: Originally from Eurasia and very mild in flavor, this huge family includes hibiscus and hollyhocks and is found on every continent except Antarctica. The widespread weed is grossly underutilized. It doesn't have much flavor, and, like okra, is mucilaginous when cooked. The leaves and fruit should be eaten when young. You can eat it raw, steam it in miso soup, stir-fry it, or add it to casseroles.

Dandelion: A perennial whose name means "tooth of the lion" in French, it has a characteristic toothed jagged leaf that's easy to identify, especially with its single yellow flower on a long, thin stem. The flavor of the leaves is similar to endive, with a bitter quality that is improved by cooking in fat, especially olive oil. Eaten raw in the spring, it is especially tender. A mild diuretic and loaded with potassium, it is often made into a tonic.

Violet: Readily available east of the Mississippi River, it has a heart-shaped leaf; the most common variety has a blue flower. It has a mild flavor; the leaves and flowers are edible, but not the roots. It is high in vitamin C and trace minerals. It grows in shady areas or partial shade. Wild violets should not be confused with the houseplant known as African violet, which is not edible.

Wood Sorrel (Oxalis): It grows in sun or shade and 70 percent of Easterners have it in their backyards. It is often confused with clover because of its heart-shaped leaf. The wood sorrel leaf has three heart-shaped leaflets; in the Pacific Northwest, there is a variety with leaves the size of your palm. The leaf, stem, flower, and seedpod are all edible. With a lemony taste akin to French sorrel and loaded with vitamin C, it can be cooked in soups, blended in drinks, and eaten raw in salads or as a trail nibble. People with kidney stones should avoid large quantities since the body metabolizes vitamin C to produce oxalic acid.

A general rule: Eat all young greens raw when they first emerge and are very tender. Sorrel is tender year-round. All others should be lightly cooked as they age to counter any bitterness. Ms. Savage points out that many books show how to identify wild plants, but just a smattering teach how to cook them.

BLOODROOT'S SESAME AND SOY DRESSING

In 1977, Selma Miriam, Noel Furie, and Betsey Beaven opened a feminist vegetarian restaurant and bookstore, Bloodroot, in Bridgeport, Connecticut, and created a community. "Feminism is not a part-time attitude for us," Ms. Miriam has written, "but how we live all day, every day." The restaurant also serves seasonal foods and dishes created by people from all over the world. A chalkboard lists choices, and patrons order and receive their food from a counter that opens into the kitchen. Ms. Miriam compares the person staffing the counter to an orchestra conductor, who must give orders to the kitchen staff so they appear on time and together. Describing qualifications for the role, she said, "Bossy women are good at it." Ms. Miriam is grateful for her "rich home life" and sees it as inseparable from her equally rich work life. "It's all one thing," she said. The restaurant staff and regular customers are her friends, with the latter often supplying services in trade for food. When asked what she sees herself doing in the future, Ms. Miriam says, "More of the same."

This recipe has remained a constant. The collective serves it on a mixture of raw cabbage, shredded carrots, and daikon, and on sliced tofu. It is lovely on peppery greens and chopped vegetable salads, too.

1 cup grapeseed or vegetable oil

¼ cup toasted sesame oil

¼ cup tamari sauce

2 tablespoons fresh lemon juice

2 tablespoons rice vinegar

In a medium bowl, whisk all of the ingredients together until combined.

MAKES 1¾ CUPS

Chris Burrill's Meyer Lemon Vinaigrette

At home in Santa Monica, Chris Burrill makes documentary films. Whenever she visits friends and family in Ojai, the scent of rare varieties of lemons and limes have inspired her, and she has created a few recipes such as this mellow Meyer lemon vinaigrette. Because of its thin skin, dark pulp, and mild acidity, the Meyer lemon is presumed to be a cross between a lemon and an orange. It has a more complex flavor than most lemons, with hints of lime and mandarin orange. This dressing is delicious on salads, particularly those containing cold meat or fish, and is also tasty on steamed asparagus, poached leeks, and grilled summer vegetables. Covered and refrigerated, it will keep up to two weeks, but it is best to add the fresh tarragon just before serving. In its place Chris has also used chervil, basil, and parsley.

8 tablespoons of Meyer lemon juice
    (approximately 3 Meyer lemons)

½ teaspoon lime juice

1 teaspoon lemon juice

½ teaspoon soy sauce

1 teaspoon grainy mustard

¼ teaspoon salt, plus more to taste

Black pepper to taste

1 cup olive oil

1 tablespoon chopped tarragon leaves

Put the lemon and lime juices, soy, mustard, and salt and pepper in a bowl and whisk to combine. Whisking constantly, add the olive oil in a slow, steady stream. Taste, and adjust seasoning with more salt or black pepper. Stir in the tarragon just before serving.

MAKES 2 CUPS

JOHNNY APPLESEED

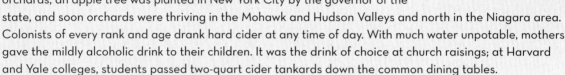

JOHN CHAPMAN, THE FOLK HERO KNOWN AS JOHNNY
Appleseed, wandered west from Massachusetts in the beginning of the
nineteenth century to plant tree nurseries throughout Pennsylvania,
Ohio, and Indiana, distributing seeds of a national treasure: the apple.
From colonial days on, apples were valuable for eating, but their juice
was even more valuable. By 1629, Virginia and Massachusetts had
orchards, an apple tree was planted in New York City by the governor of the
state, and soon orchards were thriving in the Mohawk and Hudson Valleys and north in the Niagara area.
Colonists of every rank and age drank hard cider at any time of day. With much water unpotable, mothers
gave the mildly alcoholic drink to their children. It was the drink of choice at church raisings; at Harvard
and Yale colleges, students passed two-quart cider tankards down the common dining tables.

When hard cider was fermented a second time by naturally present bacteria, the result was cider
vinegar, which cost three times as much and outranked the beverage for medicinal and health benefits.
It was used during the Civil War to speed wound healing, and doctors who promote natural healing still
recommend unpasteurized cider vinegar as a home remedy to soothe insect bites and sunburns; some
believe it aids digestion and eases arthritis.

Mr. Diggs's Fine Dressing

ROSLYN, SOUTH DAKOTA

Lawrence J. Diggs believes so deeply in the sour power of vinegar that he calls himself Vinegar Man. This energetic African American is the leading scholar on the subject and the president of Vinegar Connoisseurs International. He founded and curates the International Vinegar Museum. While he was a paramedic in San Francisco, the Peace Corps tapped him to help set up an emergency medical unit in Burkina Faso. He learned that many people were malnourished due to a nutrient-poor, unvaried diet. As he experimented with ingredients to make tasty, healthful sauces for rice and beans, he quickly understood the need for an acidic counterpoint. Usually, that meant vinegar.

If Vinegar Man were to recommend just one kitchen vinegar, it would be rice vinegar, a staple in Japan. He calls it a blank canvas for infusion. Tarragon, herbes de Provence, and dried garlic are among his favorite aromatics. He suggests putting vinegar in mason jars with plastic tops and controlling the infusions' intensity by how long they steep.

Smoky oysters give this dressing a not-quite-identifiable salty, smoky hint. It is delicious on sturdy lettuces and chopped greens, on hearty salads like bean salad, or as a dip or sauce for vegetables. Mr. Diggs also uses it to dress hot or cold rice. Smoked salt or smoked black pepper can be used in this recipe, if desired.

One 3.75-ounce can fancy smoked oysters in oil

3 tablespoons rice vinegar

Kosher salt and freshly ground black pepper

In a blender, process the oysters, their oil, and the vinegar until smooth and creamy. Season with salt and pepper to taste.

MAKES ABOUT ¾ CUP

Amy's Kilt Lettuce

MARYVILLE, TENNESSEE

Everyone in Maryville, Tennessee, recognizes Amy Campbell. She wears overalls and big sunglasses, and has an exuberant laugh and gracious Southern ways. A portrait painter, she taught design for many years at Maryville College and managed the Maryville Farm Market. She learned to make "kilt salad" from her grandmother, who used family-grown greens and served it as a light supper with cornbread. It is the Appalachian version of a warm salad, known in some places as "killed" salad, and in Eastern Kentucky and other regions as "wilted salad."

8 slices bacon, cut into ½-inch pieces

2 pounds dark green, loose-leaf lettuce, turnip greens, young dandelion greens, young pokeweed, or early chickweed, cut into 1-inch pieces

Kosher salt and freshly ground black pepper

Vinegar, in a shaker-top bottle

1. Line a plate with paper towels. In a large Dutch oven, cook the bacon over medium-low heat for about 15 minutes, stirring occasionally, until brown and crisp. Using a slotted spoon, transfer the bacon to the plate.

2. Add the greens to the fat and toss until fully coated and bright green, 2 to 4 minutes. Season with salt and pepper to taste.

3. Transfer the greens to a serving platter, sprinkle with the bacon, and serve, passing the vinegar separately.

SERVES 4

Haley Watkins's Warm Spinach Salad with Fig-Balsamic Glaze

Fig preserves are a staple of Haley Watkins's kitchen: her grandfather had a "sad little fig bush," but her uncle's produces copious fruit. She created this warm salad for Thanksgiving, but likes it as an evening meal when she's home alone in the company of her cats and a good television show.

Ms. Watkins says, "This recipe is a great way to incorporate a salad or some greens into your Thanksgiving menu. The warm greens are homey and appealing, and the fig-balsamic dressing is autumnal and perfect with traditional Thanksgiving flavors. Fig preserves might be one of my favorite things in the world; they're as sweet as candy, and they might be the best thing ever invented to spread on a biscuit. The chunks of fig in the preserves add texture, and with a splash of balsamic the dressing isn't cloyingly sweet. The fried shallots add texture and a nice sweet-and-salty component." (See the recipe for fig preserves, page 788.)

Vegetable oil, for frying

3 large shallots, thinly sliced

Kosher salt and freshly ground black pepper

¼ cup fig preserves

2 tablespoons balsamic vinegar

2 teaspoons low-sodium soy sauce

8 cups lightly packed baby spinach

1. Line a plate with paper towels. In medium skillet, add enough oil to measure 1 inch deep. Heat over medium-high heat. Add the shallots and cook for 3 to 5 minutes, stirring occasionally, until golden brown, adjusting the heat as needed so they do not burn. Using a slotted spoon, transfer the shallots to the plate. Season with salt and pepper to taste.

2. Pour off all but 3 tablespoons of the oil and return the skillet to low heat. Whisk in the fig preserves, vinegar, and soy sauce until combined. Stir the spinach, one handful at a time, and cook until it is slightly wilted. Season with salt and pepper to taste. Transfer to a serving platter, sprinkle with the shallots, and serve.

SERVES 4

Chipotle Caesar Salad with Tequila-Cured Salmon

The American taste for salad is proportioned like a classic vinaigrette. Mix one part sensual appeal with three parts social and creative aspiration, add a liberal sprinkling of health concerns, and salad becomes an American institution. Even weighted with cheesy, creamy, gooey dressings, salad feels virtuous. Perhaps more than any other dish, salad represents the peculiar American attitude that dietary virtue is high class. Consider Caesar salad.

Mythology—and the occasional food historian—date the origin of Caesar salad to 1903, when an Italian cook in Chicago, Giacomo Junia, made a salad of cos (romaine) lettuce and named it after that great Roman, Julius Caesar. However, most historians credit Caesar Cardini, who kept a restaurant across the California border in Tijuana (to avoid Prohibition) that was *the* nightspot for starlets and tycoons.

More mythology lays the salad's fame on the bony shoulders of Wallis Warfield Simpson, the divorced woman for whom King Edward VIII abdicated his throne. Allegedly, she became intimate with both the king, and the salad, in Tijuana, and then she popularized Caesar salad in Europe

There is much argument on the role of anchovies. Many say they are indispensable; Julia Child believed they had no place in the salad.

The Dutchess of Windsor

One of my early remembrances of restaurant life was going to Tijuana in 1925 or 1926 with my parents, who were wildly excited that they should finally lunch at Caesar's restaurant. Of course they ordered the salad. Caesar himself rolled the big cart up to the table, tossed the romaine in a great wooden bowl, and I wish I could say I remembered his every move, but I don't . . . I can see him break two eggs over that romaine and roll them in, the greens going all creamy as the eggs flowed over them . . . And garlic-flavored croutons, and grated Parmesan cheese? It was a sensation of a salad from coast to coast, and there were even rumblings of its success in Europe.

In the 1990s, Caesar Cardini's daughter, Rose, insisted that her father never used anchovies, but she allowed that her uncle Alex, who was her father's partner, may have used them in his version.

Since its invention, the salad has become more of a concept than a precise recipe. Topped with chicken, lobster, or shrimp, the salad has become a showcase of a chef's creativity. This version, from chef Dave Jones of the Log Haven restaurant in Salt Lake City, Utah, is one of the greats. To reduce the risk of salmonella, use organic eggs or lightly coddle the yolks prior to using them.

FOR THE SALMON

1 cup kosher salt

1 cup sugar

2 jalapeño chiles, minced

Grated zest of 3 limes (save the limes for juice for the dressing)

½ cup chopped cilantro

2 dried guajillo chiles, toasted, seeded, and crumbled

1 small side very fresh wild sockeye salmon (about 1¼ pounds), skin on, pin bones removed

¼ cup tequila

FOR THE DRESSING

⅓ cup fresh lime juice

4 large egg yolks

2 cups extra virgin olive oil

3 chipotle chiles in adobo, drained and pureed

4 garlic cloves, minced

2 tablespoons minced shallot

4 to 6 white anchovy fillets, drained and pureed

1 jalapeño chile, minced

1 tablespoon minced cilantro

½ teaspoon ground cumin

Pinch of cayenne pepper

3 tablespoons grated Parmesan cheese

Fine sea salt

Freshly ground black pepper, preferably smoked pepper

FOR THE SALAD

2 heads romaine, separated into individual leaves, rinsed, and patted dry

Guacamole (recipe follows)

2 cups Paul's Garlic Croutons (page 167)

4 heirloom tomatoes, quartered and lightly salted (best choices include Hawaiian Pineapple, Hillbilly, Caspian Pink, Green Zebra, Black Krim, and Brandywine)

Parmesan cheese, shaved into wafers, for garnish (optional)

2 cups toasted or pan-fried corn tortilla strips (optional)

1 cup bite-size bits queso fresco, cut or crumbled

Pico de gallo, for garnish (optional)

1. To make the salmon: 2 to 3 days before serving, thoroughly mix together the salt, sugar, jalapeños, lime zest, cilantro, and guajillos. Spread one-third on the bottom of a glass baking dish just large enough to hold the salmon. Place the fish skin side down in the dish and spread with the remaining cure. Sprinkle the tequila evenly over the salmon. Cover with plastic wrap, then place a slightly smaller baking dish on top and add some weights to ensure even curing (5 pounds is enough). Refrigerate the salmon for 2 to 3 days, depending on the thickness.

2. Once the salmon has cured, remove from the pan and scrape off the cure ingredients. Rinse under cold water and pat dry with paper towels. If not using immediately, wrap in plastic wrap and refrigerate. The salmon will keep for about five days in the refrigerator.

3. To make the dressing: In a glass or plastic bowl, whisk together the lime juice and egg yolks. Drizzle in the oil, whisking continuously, until the yolks have absorbed all of the olive oil and the base has been emulsified. Stir in the chipotles, garlic, shallot, anchovy puree, jalapeño, cilantro, cumin, cayenne, and Parmesan. Stir in salt and pepper to taste. Transfer to a covered storage container and refrigerate. (You can also make the dressing in a food processor or a blender: Combine the lime juice and egg yolks. With the machine running, slowly drizzle in the oil and process until an emulsion forms. Add the remaining ingredients and blend until combined. Season with salt and pepper.) This makes about 2¾ cups of dressing; it will keep for about 1 week in the refrigerator.

4. To assemble the salad: Cut the salmon on an angle into very thin slices—cutting down to, but not through, the skin. Arrange the romaine leaves on four dinner plates and top with salmon slices. Drizzle the dressing over the leaves. Garnish with dollops of guacamole, croutons, tomato wedges, and, if desired, shaved Parmesan, tortilla strips, queso fresco, and pico de gallo.

SERVES 4

Guacamole

2 ripe Hass avocados, pitted and peeled

1 tablespoon fresh lemon juice

1½ teaspoons fresh lime juice

3 tablespoons pico de gallo

Kosher salt and cayenne pepper

Mash the avocados with the lemon and lime juices. Stir in the pico de gallo and season to taste with salt and cayenne. Use immediately.

MAKES ABOUT 2 CUPS

Drew Kime's Iceberg Wedges with Blue Cheese and Bacon

The first time he ordered a "wedge salad" in a California restaurant, Drew Kime, a former U.S. Marine, was eager to try something new. When it arrived, he burst out laughing. The "wedge" turned out to be the trendy name for the salads his mother, a no-frills "baked chicken, baked potato, vanilla ice cream" cook, served when he was growing up. Mr. Kime's version relies on homemade bacon bits. "It's just a matter of grinding and frying the bacon," he said. "Unless you've got a large, heavy-duty grinder, it's a lot easier if you slice it into small chunks and freeze it first for an hour or so. Once it's frozen, feed it through your grinder. It will look like long strands of meat, but it's actually lots of little bits that are slightly stuck to each other. Once they hit the frying pan they'll separate without any special effort."

The advantage of iceberg lettuce is not only its longevity—it keeps for days—but also its crispness and handsome presentation.

1 medium head iceberg lettuce, cored and quartered

2 medium-size ripe tomatoes, cored and quartered

1 medium cucumber, peeled, halved lengthwise, seeded, and thinly sliced

1 medium red bell pepper, stemmed, seeded, and cut into ¼-inch strips

8 slices bacon, cooked, drained, and crumbled

1 cup Paul's Garlic Croutons (page 167)

1 recipe Rogue Creamery's Best Blue Cheese Dressing Ever (page 166)

1 ounce blue cheese, crumbled (about ¼ cup), for garnish

Divide the iceberg quarters among four plates. Top evenly with the tomatoes, cucumber, bell pepper, bacon, croutons, and dressing. Sprinkle with the blue cheese and serve.

———

SERVES 4

179

Conspicuous Consumption of Cellulose: Salads

Matthew Ronconi's
Better Than Chef Salad

SALT LAKE CITY, UTAH

Like many culinary classics, the meal-size green salad composed of several meats and cheeses, hard-cooked eggs, various vegetables, and "French" dressing comes with many myths about its origins. Before the name "chef's salad" was given to the specific salad that we know today, it implied a dish made from the ingredients that were on hand; there are also stories about diners hijacking the salad a chef had made for himself. The earliest printed mentions appeared in New York City in the 1930s, when chef Louis Diat created a meal-size salad with anchovies, smoked tongue, and watercress. With the presumption that it was "light" and "dietetic," the salad rode the slick of fame from fine dining to ho-hum; somewhere along the way, "chef's" became "chef" and the salad devolved into a bale of iceberg lettuce topped with strips of yellow and white cheese, hard-boiled eggs, deli ham, and turkey roll. But in the past decade, the chef salad has made a comeback in combinations like this one, in which sliced lamb is combined with a raw artichoke salad, potatoes, and shaved Parmesan cheese. This salad is inspired by leftover meat and potatoes, but is more than worth making from scratch.

FOR THE POTATOES

2½ pounds small red potatoes, scrubbed and quartered

1 tablespoon olive oil

1 tablespoon chopped fresh rosemary

Kosher salt and freshly ground black pepper

FOR THE LAMB

Six 6-ounce slices boneless lamb loin, trimmed

Kosher salt and freshly ground black pepper

2 teaspoons olive oil

FOR THE SALAD

2 pounds fresh fava beans, shelled

2 teaspoons olive oil

Kosher salt and coarsely ground black pepper

½ cup Meyer Lemon Vinaigrette (page 171)

12 cups tart greens such as arugula or watercress

2 cups Raw Artichoke Salad (page 205)

2 cups Paul's Garlic Croutons (page 167)

1 cup pitted Kalamata or oil-cured olives

1 teaspoon chopped fresh parsley

2 ounces Parmesan cheese, shaved (1½ to 2 cups)

1. To make the potatoes: Preheat the oven to 425°F. In a roasting pan, toss the potatoes with the olive oil, 2 teaspoons of the rosemary, ½ teaspoon salt, and ¼ teaspoon pepper. Roast for 30 to 40 minutes, stirring occasionally, until golden brown and tender.

2. Cool to room temperature. Toss with the remaining rosemary. Season with salt and pepper to taste.

3. To make the lamb: Pat the lamb dry with paper towels and season on both sides with salt and pepper. In a large nonstick skillet, heat the oil over medium-high heat. Cook the lamb about 4 minutes per side, until browned on both sides and an instant-read thermometer registers 125°F (for medium).

4. Transfer the lamb to a carving board and let rest for 5 minutes. Thinly slice the lamb across the grain and season with salt and pepper to taste.

5. To make the salad: Bring 1 quart water to a boil in a medium saucepan and add 1 tablespoon salt. Add the fava beans and cook until tender, 4 to 8 minutes. Drain in a colander and rinse under cold running water until the beans are cool. Pinching the skins, squeeze the beans out into a bowl. Toss with the olive oil and season with ½ teaspoon salt and ½ teaspoon coarsely ground black pepper.

6. Place the vinaigrette in the bottom of a large bowl, add the greens, and toss. Add the potatoes, artichoke salad, fava beans, croutons, and olives, and toss again. Divide the salad among six plates and top with the sliced lamb. Sprinkle with the chopped parsley and scatter the Parmesan over the top. Serve.

SERVES 6

Salt Lake City, circa 1908.

Rob Lam's
Shaking Beef Cobb Salad

Cobb salad's undisputed Los Angeles origin comes with a tale of midnight refrigerator scrounging followed by enthusiasm from a Hollywood promoter. That it all happened in the Brown Derby restaurant—famous for its novelty hat-shape architecture and its celebrity clientele and caricatures—made the salad seem even sexier. One night circa 1936, Brown Derby owner Bob Cobb diced up leftover avocado, tomato, eggs, chicken, bacon, and Roquefort cheese, arranged them in a striped pattern in a flat salad bowl, and topped it all with French dressing. His promoter pal Sid Grauman, of Chinese Theater fame, who may have witnessed the birth—or not—quickly trumpeted the salad's delights. Movie stars flocked to try it, and Jack Warner often sent his chauffeur to pick up a carton. Although the landmark Brown Derby closed in 1985 and was demolished in 1994 after earthquake damage, Cobb salad has sold more than 4 million servings in Brown Derby–licensed restaurants from Tokyo to Las Vegas.

Rob Lam, the son of a Vietnamese refugee, grew up in Orange County, California's Little Saigon. The Cobb salad that he serves at his San Francisco restaurant, Butterfly, reflects his East-meets-West background. His addition of "shaking beef" exemplifies, he says, "the shift from dainty side dish to something grown men order for dinner."

607 BROWN DERBY RESTAURANT, LOS ANGELES, CALIFORNIA

FOR THE BEEF

2 tablespoons minced garlic

2 tablespoons minced ginger

1 tablespoon thinly sliced scallion

1 teaspoon oyster sauce

Pinch of freshly ground black pepper

1 pound beef tenderloin, trimmed and cut into ½-inch cubes

Vegetable oil, for sautéing

FOR THE SALAD

6 slices bacon, cut into ½-inch pieces

6 large eggs

12 cups mixed baby greens or mesclun mix

Shallot-Thyme Balsamic Vinaigrette (recipe follows)

6 ounces thinly sliced prosciutto

6 ounces Maytag blue cheese, crumbled (about 1½ cups)

½ pint cherry or grape tomatoes

½ medium English cucumber, thinly sliced

2 Hass avocados, pitted, peeled, and sliced

1. To make the beef: Combine the garlic, ginger, scallion, oyster sauce, and pepper in a medium bowl. Add the beef and mix well to coat the meat. Cover and refrigerate to marinate beef for 1 hour.

2. Heat a wok or large skillet over medium-high heat. When hot, pour in 1 to 2 tablespoons oil and heat until shimmering but not smoking. Add the beef, working in batches if necessary so it is not crowded, and stir-fry until the beef is cooked to medium-rare, 4 to 5 minutes.

3. Transfer the beef to a baking sheet. Line two plates with several layers of paper towels.

4. To make the salad: Cook the bacon in a large skillet over medium-low heat about 15 minutes, stirring occasionally, until brown and crisp. Using a slotted spoon, transfer the pieces to a plate. Discard the fat.

5. Poach the eggs until the white is barely firm and the yolk is still liquid, 2 to 3 minutes. Remove from the water with a slotted spoon and gently place on a plate to drain.

6. In a large bowl, toss the greens with dressing to taste. Divide the greens among serving plates or shallow bowls and arrange slices of prosciutto on top. Scatter the blue cheese, tomatoes, cucumber, and bacon across the greens. Add slices of avocado, and finish with the beef and a poached egg.

SERVES 5 TO 6

Shallot-Thyme Balsamic Vinaigrette

1 medium shallot, coarsely chopped

1½ teaspoons fresh thyme leaves

¼ cup balsamic vinegar

1 cup olive oil

Kosher salt and freshly ground black pepper

Combine the shallot, thyme, and vinegar in a blender and blend until smooth. With the blender running, slowly add the oil until an emulsion forms. Season with salt and pepper to taste.

MAKES 1¼ CUPS

ALICE WATERS'S GOAT CHEESE SALAD

BERKELEY, CALIFORNIA

A farmers' market is a delightful counterpoint to modern life, a little patch of green in an asphalt city, an oasis of sight and touch and smell in a climate-controlled, vaccuum-sealed world. Having been eclipsed by the glamour of the supermarket some fifty years ago, farmers' markets are flourishing again. This resurgence began in places like Ferry Plaza in San Francisco, where, every Saturday morning, one of the richest and liveliest markets in America is held.

Here truck farmers can sell their produce directly to the public, and there is something infinitely satisfying about meandering through it, taking in the smell of fresh-cut basil and mint, along with the aroma of diesel fuel and the sound of traffic from the highway nearby. Direct contact is the lure of the farmers' market—direct contact with the growers, with the produce, and, if one is lucky, with one's appetite.

This leads to a certain kind of improvisational cooking—simple and straightforward—characteristic of the cooks who minted California cuisine and who can be counted on to be at Ferry Plaza on Saturday mornings: to pinch the peaches and sniff the apricots and talk, as people do when their senses are engaged, with respect (and not a little awe) for the bounty of the Bay area, where mesclun is always in season and produce is nearly always pretty. Forty years ago, when she opened Chez Panisse, Alice Waters could not find the mélange of peppery lettuces that she'd fallen for for Salade Niçoise. There were no farmers' markets, and she scoured ethnic markets in the Bay Area in vain. The only solution was to bring the seeds back from France and plant them in her backyard. She never imagined that the simple salads she fashioned with her home-grown greens and little discs of delicate goat cheese that a friend made for her would capture the American imagination and become the poster child for eating close to the earth and in accord with the seasons.

"You never know when you begin. Later you start to see how one thing that attracted you was connected to something else, and in hindsight a sort of logic emerges that makes you think you knew what you were doing. But forty years ago, I couldn't have imagined that I'd one day have to bring seeds from my garden in north Berkeley back to France. But I do. And I have to constantly revisit every ingredient we use. Last year's artisanal cheese is next year's mass-produced one; the same is true of olive oil. There is no place to hide in a simple dish like this. Each ingredient has to be flawless."

½ cup extra virgin olive oil

4 sprigs fresh thyme

1 bay leaf, crumbled

4 ounces soft mild goat cheese, sliced into four ½-inch rounds

½ cup fine dry bread crumbs

2 tablespoons balsamic vinegar

Kosher salt and freshly ground black pepper

5 cups lightly packed fresh greens (arugula, lamb's lettuce, small oak leaf and red leaf lettuces, and chervil)

1. In a small shallow dish, combine ¼ cup of the olive oil, the thyme, and bay leaf. Add the cheese, coating well with oil, cover, and refrigerate for 2 to 12 hours.

2. Place an oven rack in the center position and preheat the oven to 450°F. Grease a small baking dish with some of the oil from the goat cheese marinade.

3. Dip the goat cheese in the bread crumbs to coat on all sides. Place the breaded cheese in the prepared baking dish and bake about 5 minutes, until the cheese is lightly bubbling and golden brown.

4. Meanwhile, in a large bowl, whisk together the remaining ¼ cup oil and the vinegar. Season with salt and pepper to taste. Add the greens and toss to coat with the vinaigrette. Divide among four plates. Place a goat cheese round on the center of each salad, and serve.

SERVES 4

BUILD YOUR OWN

AMONG THE MANY CULTURAL CHANGES OF THE 1970S, THE SALAD BAR HIT AMERICA full force. Before then, restaurant diners ordered from menus and waited for their salads to be served to them on a plate. There were salad buffets in hotel dining rooms as early as 1939; one Hawaiian restaurant dates its self-serve salad station to 1959, the year that Hawaii became a state. That same decade, The Cliffs in Springfield, Illinois, noted a "salad bar buffet" in its Yellow Pages listing. But build-your-own salads became trendy in the early 1970s, when a Chicago singles' bar and restaurant called R. J. Grunts offered a salad bar. The genius of freeing diners from their chairs to roam a restaurant in search of personalized fixings or to help themselves at a single all-you-can-eat price revolutionized mass-market dining. The Ohio-based Rax restaurant chain understood the benefit of promoting its "endless salad bar" as fast food and catering to customers' culinary creativity. Choices vary from one salad bar to another, but tomatoes generally top the popularity list, with sprouts—bean and Brussels—near the bottom. Regional preferences can dictate other choices: from artichoke hearts, chickpeas, pickled peppers, and Swiss and cottage cheese, to bacon bits, turkey strips, croutons, chow mein noodles and pasta, and Jell-O. And then come the dressings, from creamy Italian to raspberry vinaigrette to "lo-cal."

Salad bars spread into supermarkets and became good business, as weight determined price and ever-heavier (and more profitable) offerings graced the bar. "Special event" salad bars at parties and in restaurants touted Mexican, Greek, and Asian ingredients, and as salad bars became fixtures of the American dining landscape, restaurants got smart about outfitting their buffets with small plates and making the most expensive items (such as crab legs or shrimp) more difficult to reach.

Sicoutris Family's Greek Salad

Corinna Sicoutris, 38, cooks as her grandmother taught her—by taste and sight. Once a month she puts aside responsibilities as an acute-care nurse practitioner working with a surgical critical care service to travel from Philadelphia to join her family as they celebrate a birthday or holiday. Spread from New Jersey to metro D.C., in this extended family the primary event planners and food preparers are the grandchildren, who only allow their mother, aunts, and grandmother to advise. Still, although the younger generation has assumed the physical labor, and Ms. Sicoutris likes to bring new tastes to the table, they all keep the Greek traditions much in mind. Aunt Demetria buys one-pound blocks of feta cheese from a D.C. Greek grocery to distribute at family events, while Ms. Sicoutris scoops out Kalamata olives from barrels in a "phenomenal" Philly store. Add tomatoes, onions, and cucumbers into an enormous bowl, and pass the horiatiki—Greek salad—family style.

4 medium ripe tomatoes, cored and cut into 1-inch wedges

1 English cucumber, halved lengthwise and sliced ½-inch thick

1 medium red onion, halved and sliced ½ inch thick

8 ounces feta cheese, crumbled (about 2 cups)

1 cup pitted kalamata olives

¼ cup chopped fresh basil

1 teaspoon grated lemon zest

½ cup extra virgin olive oil

¼ cup fresh lemon juice

Kosher salt and freshly ground black pepper

In a large bowl, gently toss the tomatoes, cucumber, onion, cheese, olives, basil, and lemon zest together. Drizzle with oil and lemon juice and toss to coat. Season with salt and pepper to taste, and serve.

———

SERVES 6

SICOUTRIS FAMILY'S GREEK ORZO SALAD

The base of their orzo salad is horiatiki, the traditional Greek salad. Ms. Sicoutris adds plenty of lemon zest because it should "taste like summer . . . fresh, tangy, and light."

Kosher salt

1 pound orzo

½ cup olive oil

Freshly ground black pepper

1 pint grape tomatoes

1 English hothouse cucumber, quartered lengthwise and sliced

⅓ cup chopped fresh basil

1 cup pitted kalamata olives

1 pound Greek feta cheese, crumbled

Grated zest of 3 lemons

2 tablespoons fresh lemon juice, plus more as needed

1. Bring a large saucepan of salted water to a boil. Cook the orzo until al dente. Drain well, rinse with cold water, and drain again. Spread out on a baking sheet to cool, then mix with a little of the olive oil and season with salt and pepper.

2. Transfer the orzo to a large bowl. Add the tomatoes, cucumber, basil, olives, feta, and lemon zest. Add black pepper to taste. Toss to mix.

3. Drizzle with the remaining olive oil, then add the lemon juice. The salad should be very tangy. Toss well and serve immediately, or cover and refrigerate to allow the flavors to blend. Toss again before serving.

SERVES 6 TO 8

Conspicuous Consumption of Cellulose: Salads

Nova Kim and Les Hook's Wild Spring Salad

Although she was born in Oklahoma Osage territory, Nova Kim didn't learn the art of foraging for wild edibles from her Osage forebears, but from books. "An entire generation has lost its connection to the earth," she argues. "This is just as true for Native Americans as anyone else." But her partner in life and work, Leslie Hooks, learned early on to scrounge free things to survive. Growing up mountain poor with eight brothers and sisters, Mr. Hooks could hunt and fish for dinner by age 11, and he learned from his father how to locate fiddleheads, watercress, and wild leeks with the accuracy of a GPS system. Today Ms. Kim and Mr. Hooks are celebrated for having brought 150 varieties of mushrooms to the Vermont culinary trade. They still supply a few restaurants, but spend most of their time teaching wild plant use and sustainability to college students and the public.

Kosher salt

24 fresh fiddlehead ferns, trimmed

2 cups lightly packed wild watercress, stemmed and coarsely chopped

2 cups lightly packed tender wild oxeye daisy greens, stemmed and coarsely chopped

1 cup bright yellow wild daylily tubers with tender shoots, trimmed

2 tablespoons extra virgin olive oil

1 tablespoon red wine vinegar or raspberry vinegar

Freshly ground black pepper

½ cup wild red raspberries

1. In a large pot, bring 2 quarts water and 1 tablespoon salt to a boil. Fill a medium bowl with ice and water to make an ice bath.

2. Add the fiddleheads to the boiling water and cook for 3 to 5 minutes, until tender. Using a slotted spoon, transfer them to the ice bath and let cool, then drain well and transfer to a large bowl.

3. Add the watercress, daisy greens, daylily tubers and shoots, oil, and vinegar to the fiddleheads, and toss gently to combine. Season with salt and pepper to taste. Sprinkle the raspberries over the top, and serve.

SERVES 6

Paula Ives's Raw Asparagus Salad with Loquat Dressing

ST. PETERSBURG, FLORIDA

When Paula Ives was growing up in Indiana, her mother kept a garden with tomatoes and the usual vegetables, but a neighbor grew one that, back then, was exotic: asparagus. It was the beginning of a love affair. Now Ms. Ives lives in Florida, where she grows fruit trees by collecting local seeds or pits that she finds in vacant lots and foreclosed houses. She trades seedlings with her neighbors, one of whom has a loquat tree loaded with fruit, many more than he and the wild parrots that squawk around the tree can eat. So Ms. Ives picks a few pounds and pairs them with new asparagus.

8 to 10 ripe loquats, peeled and seeded

½ cup olive oil

¼ cup rice vinegar

½ teaspoon ground coriander

½ teaspoon ground marjoram

½ teaspoon mustard powder

⅛ teaspoon sugar

2 bunches pencil-thin asparagus, trimmed and cut on the bias into 1-inch pieces

Kosher salt and freshly ground black pepper

In a blender, process the loquats, oil, vinegar, coriander, marjoram, mustard, and sugar together until smooth and creamy. Transfer the dressing to a medium bowl, and stir in the asparagus until evenly coated. Season with salt and pepper to taste, and serve.

SERVES 4 TO 6

AGGIE NEHMZOW'S TOMATOES

IN HER YARD NEAR O'HARE AIRPORT, AGGIE NEHMZOW, THE WOMAN EVERYONE CALLS the Tomato Lady, tends 125 varieties of organic heirloom tomatoes. Growing up in Summit, Illinois, the grandchild of Croatian immigrants, Ms. Nehmzow learned to garden by osmosis: Everyone in the neighborhood had gardens and chickens, she said, "and one neighbor had a goat." Her Croatian grandparents made their own wine, roasted lamb on a spit, and cooked with as many tomatoes as their Neapolitan neighbors. She's always been serious about her tomatoes, and so, after her husband of forty years passed away in 2004, no one was surprised that Ms. Nehmzow decided to plant tomatoes, rather than a tree or flowers, in his memory. She has many sources for seeds, from a pipe fitter in Illinois who has 3,000 varieties to a pen pal in Russia who "has a whole stack of seeds from the old Soviet Union." She is "on the hunt" for two varieties from China, would be thrilled to get seeds from the tomatoes Nelson Mandela grew during his incarceration, and participates in the Svalbard Global Seed Vault, the Norwegian storage facility that saves seed samples in order to offset the extinction of rare breeds. When invited to dinner she is likely to bring not a covered dish but a basket of tomatoes. Some of her favorite varieties include Japanese Black Trifele, Gold Medal, Black Krim, and Green Moldovan. She drizzles them with extra virgin olive oil and sprinkles them with freshly grated Asiago cheese.

Elizabeth Williams's Three-Generation Olive Salad

NEW ORLEANS, LOUISIANA

Elizabeth Williams calls this "Three-Generation Olive Salad" because both she and her mother have tweaked her grandmother Elisabetta Lecce Baiamonte's traditional Italian olive salad to make it their own. While she uses it most often as a dressing for a muffaletta sandwich, Ms. Williams likes it best on an antipasto platter, served on an artichoke leaf as an appetizer, or in a tossed green salad. The best part of her variation, she says, is that it is forgiving in terms of amounts. But using the best olives is nonnegotiable. "The better the olives, the better the salad."

1 anchovy fillet

Extra virgin olive oil

2 cups coarsely chopped pitted black olives

3 cups coarsely chopped pimento-stuffed green olives

One 9-ounce package frozen quartered baby artichokes, thawed, drained, and coarsely chopped

1½ cups coarsely chopped cauliflower (optional)

3 celery stalks, coarsely chopped

3 carrots, peeled and coarsely chopped

1 lemon, halved and very thinly sliced

¼ cup capers, drained and coarsely chopped

¼ cup chopped fresh oregano or 1 tablespoon dried

4 garlic cloves, minced

Freshly ground black pepper

Fresh lemon juice

In a large bowl, mash the anchovy and 1 tablespoon oil with a fork, until a smooth paste forms. Stir in the black and green olives, artichokes, cauliflower, if using, the celery, carrots, lemon, capers, oregano, and garlic until combined. Season with pepper and lemon juice to taste. Add enough olive oil to just barely cover the mixture. Cover and let sit about 30 minutes, until the flavors have blended.

MAKES ABOUT 8 CUPS

KALYN'S GREEN BEAN SALAD
WITH GREEK OLIVES AND FETA CHEESE

SALT LAKE CITY, UTAH

Kalyn Denny grew up in Salt Lake City, where she taught elementary school for thirty years. For ten of those years, she spent her summer vacations cooking on (and sometimes even driving) houseboats on Lake Powell. Those summers gradually took a toll on her waistline, and a few years ago she began to invent lean dishes; while visiting her family in Chicago, she made this salad. "We were going to have a picnic at the Chicago Botanic Garden later in the day, and I started poking around in the refrigerator—I like to use what is on hand—and this is what I came up with. It's become a family favorite." One of the secrets is the roasted tomato–basil vinaigrette, which follows the principles of a low-glycemic diet but has a rich, concentrated flavor.

Lake Powell boat area, Arizona

FOR THE DRESSING

¾ cup Slow-Roasted Tomatoes (recipe follows) or one 14.5-ounce can fire-roasted tomatoes, drained

¼ cup white balsamic vinegar or white wine vinegar

¼ cup chopped fresh basil

2 tablespoons water

1 garlic clove, minced

½ cup extra virgin olive oil

Kosher salt and freshly ground black pepper

FOR THE SALAD

1 pound green beans, trimmed and cut into 2-inch pieces

1 medium red onion, halved and thinly sliced

½ cup pitted kalamata olives, halved

6 ounces feta cheese, crumbled (about 1½ cups)

1. To make the dressing: In a blender, process the tomatoes, vinegar, basil, water, and garlic together until smooth. Transfer the dressing to a medium bowl and whisk in the olive oil until combined. If necessary, add the water to adjust the consistency. Season with salt and pepper to taste.

2. To make the salad: Fill a medium bowl with ice and water to make an ice bath. In a large saucepan with a steamer insert, steam the green beans about 5 minutes, until just crisp-tender. Using a slotted spoon, transfer the green beans to the ice bath and let cool. Drain well and transfer to a medium bowl.

3. Stir the dressing, onion, and olives into the green beans. Cover and refrigerate about 4 hours, until completely chilled. Sprinkle with the cheese, and serve.

⸻

SERVES 4 TO 6

Slow-Roasted Tomatoes

2 tablespoons olive oil, plus more for the pan

2 tablespoons dried basil

1 tablespoon ground fennel

1 tablespoon dried oregano

1 tablespoon dried marjoram

20 plum tomatoes, cored and halved lengthwise

1. Place an oven rack in the center position and preheat the oven to 250°F. Grease a large rimmed baking sheet with olive oil.

2. In a large bowl, mix together the oil, basil, fennel, oregano, and marjoram. Add the tomatoes and toss until well coated. Arrange the tomatoes cut side down on the baking sheet. Bake for 8 to 9 hours, until the skins puff up and tomatoes have reduced in size by at least half. Store covered in the refrigerator.

⸻

MAKES ABOUT 3 CUPS

SUZUKI STEINBERGER'S AVOCADO SALAD

ROCKLAND, MAINE

At Suzuki's Sushi Bar in Rockland, Maine, the chefs are all women. Without stoves, ovens, or a deep-fat fryer, the cooking happens on three electric induction burners topped with pots of boiling water and a homemade steaming system of wooden and glass boxes. Fish are likely to come from the Gulf of Maine, and chef-owner Keiko Suzuki Steinberger usually has surf clams, sweet shrimp, scallops, grey sole, line-caught mackerel, and local oysters. This refined avocado salad with seaweed is as elegant as a sliver of sashimi.

FOR THE DRESSING

2 tablespoons dry sake

2 tablespoons water

5 tablespoons sweet white miso

1 tablespoon sugar

1 large egg yolk

Soy sauce

FOR THE SALAD

2 ripe Hass avocados, halved, pitted, and sliced ½ inch thick

½ cucumber, halved lengthwise, seeded, and thinly sliced

¼ cup dried wakame, reconstituted in warm water

¼ cup sesame seeds, toasted and crushed

1. To make the dressing: In a large saucepan, bring 1 quart water to a bare simmer over medium-low heat. Fill a large bowl with ice and water to make an ice bath.

2. Meanwhile, in a small bowl, mix together the sake and water. In a medium heatproof bowl (preferably metal), whisk together the miso, sugar, and egg yolk until smooth and the sugar has completely dissolved. Slowly whisk in the sake mixture until combined. Season with soy sauce to taste.

3. Place the bowl with the dressing on top of the saucepan and cook over barely simmering water, whisking constantly, for 6 to 8 minutes, until thickened. Place the bowl in the ice bath and let sit, whisking occasionally, until cool.

4. To make the salad: Divide the avocados, cucumber, and wakame among four shallow serving bowls. Drizzle 2 tablespoons dressing over each pile, sprinkle with the sesame seeds, and serve.

SERVES 4

Conspicuous Consumption of Cellulose: Salads

Paula's Corn Salad

When Paula Hennig first moved to Alabama from Pennsylvania, where her Mennonite dairy-farming grandparents also lived, "it was culture shock." Her mom made bread and baked cakes, sending her sisters and her to school with whole-wheat bread sandwiches, while "everyone else had white bread." They had a family garden on their forty acres of land, and her dad went into hydroponic farming. For a short time she and her sister operated a northern Italian restaurant, making everything from scratch. Ms. Hennig called it a "new experience for people in town who expected red sauce."

Now living in Dothan, which proclaims itself the "peanut capital of the world," Ms. Hennig came up with this recipe in honor of the corn that she, her mother, and her sisters froze every year. The annual process took a whole Saturday, and the kids dreaded it. She remembers thinking, "'I'm never going to freeze corn,' but somehow you turn into your parents and start to see the logic." She first made this salad as a side dish with grilled chicken thighs, and it was so good that whenever they had corn, her husband, an airline pilot, said, "Make that again."

Kosher salt

5 ears corn, husks and silks removed

1 medium tomato, cored and coarsely chopped

2 ounces feta cheese, crumbled (about ½ cup)

½ cup finely chopped red onion

3 tablespoons cider vinegar

3 tablespoons extra virgin olive oil

Freshly ground black pepper

½ cup shredded fresh basil

1. In a large pot, bring 10 cups water and 1 tablespoon salt to a boil. Fill a large bowl with ice and water to make an ice bath. Cook the corn for 2 minutes. Using tongs, transfer the corn to the ice bath and let cool, then drain well. Cut the kernels from the cobs and transfer to a medium bowl, discarding the cobs.

2. Add the tomato, feta, onion, vinegar, oil, ½ teaspoon salt, and ¼ teaspoon pepper to the corn, and toss to combine. Check the seasoning and adjust with salt and pepper to taste. Before serving, add the basil and toss to combine.

SERVES 4

One Big Table

194

Alex Vlack's
Summer Corn and Crab Salad

A lex Vlack's parents divorced when he was a toddler, and at age 5 he moved with his mother to California. He spent vacations and some holidays in New York with his father, a restaurant-obsessed "amateur gourmet" who took the 7-year-old Alex to the legendary French restaurant Lutèce. Back on the West Coast, his mother and grandmother endlessly discussed, sampled, and ate tomatoes during their annual season. Mr. Vlack now demonstrates his own reverence for tomatoes by pairing them with his two other loves, height-of-summer corn and crab, for a salad he likens to "a lobster or crab roll without the mustard or mayo." He cuts thick tomato slices and uses them as an edible plate with the salad on top.

Conspicuous Consumption of Cellulose: Salads

Kosher salt

2 ears corn, husks and silks removed

1 pound jumbo lump crabmeat, picked over for shells and cartilage

2 cups chopped fresh cilantro

1 mango, peeled, pitted, and cut into ½-inch pieces

2 teaspoons extra virgin olive oil

Freshly ground black pepper

2 large ripe heirloom tomatoes, cored and sliced ½ inch thick

1 ripe Hass avocado, halved, pitted, peeled, and sliced ½ inch thick

1. In a large pot, bring 10 cups water and 1 tablespoon salt to a boil. Fill a large bowl with ice and water to make an ice bath. Cook the corn for 2 minutes. Using tongs, transfer the corn to the ice bath and let cool, then drain well. Cut the kernels from the cobs and transfer to a medium bowl, discarding the cobs.

2. Add the crabmeat, cilantro, mango, and oil to the corn and stir gently to combine. Season with salt and pepper to taste.

3. Arrange the tomato slices on a serving platter. Place 2 or 3 avocado slices on each slice. Top with a mound of salad, and serve.

SERVES 4

Katherine Dieckmann's
Beet and Corn Salad

Writing screenplays, directing films, teaching screenwriting in the Film Division at Columbia University's Graduate School of the Arts, raising two children: Each of these occupations alone could be a career. Katherine Dieckmann juggles all these things and insists that the family sit down to a homemade dinner together four nights a week. Having grown up in Ithaca, home of both the Moosewood Restaurant and the Cabbagetown Café, she loves vegetarian cooking as much as she loves bacon. Vegetables are her forte, and she approaches them as she does any ingredient, without measuring utensils or a timer. This salad is different every time she makes it, but it is a favorite at the girls' night suppers that Katherine and her artist and writer friends share in Rensselaerville, a village in upstate New York where she spends the weekends.

FOR THE SALAD

3 medium beets, scrubbed and trimmed

1 tablespoon kosher salt

4 ears corn, husks and silks removed

1½ cups chopped red cabbage

¼ cup chopped fresh dill or cilantro

1 medium red onion, minced

FOR THE DRESSING

2 tablespoons balsamic vinegar

1 teaspoon Dijon mustard

6 tablespoons extra virgin olive oil

Kosher salt and freshly ground black pepper

1. Fill a large bowl with ice and water to make an ice bath. In a medium saucepan, bring the beets and 2 quarts water to a simmer until tender, 40 minutes to 1 hour. Using tongs, transfer the beets to the ice bath. When cool enough to handle, peel under running water and cut into medium dice. Transfer to a large bowl.

2. In a large pot, bring 10 cups water and 1 tablespoon salt to a boil. Cook the corn for 2 minutes. Using tongs, transfer the corn to the ice bath and let cool, then drain well. Cut the kernels from the cobs and transfer to the bowl with the beets, discarding the cobs. Add cabbage, dill or cilantro, and onion. Toss lightly.

3. To make the dressing: Whisk together the vinegar and mustard in a small bowl. Keep whisking while slowly drizzling in the olive oil. Whisk until combined. Season with salt and pepper to taste.

4. Add dressing to the salad, toss, cover, and refrigerate for at least a couple of hours before serving.

SERVES 6

Cynthia Hodges's Luscious Beet Salad

One of Cynthia Hodges's favorite recipes came to her a decade ago, when her children were babies and she was a member of La Leche League of Ann Arbor, Michigan, and Lenawee County. For the annual fund-raiser, the World Walk for Breastfeeding, the women would hold a mini-walkathon followed by a fabulous potluck. A friend brought beet salad, and Ms. Hodges has been tweaking the recipe and eating the salad ever since. Her version uses fresh herbs, but she says that dried could be used in a pinch. Her son Edward started cooking when he was 5 or 6, "just as soon as he was able to get up to the counter." She thinks the reason he likes to make this recipe has more to do with the chopping than anything else. "He uses a Zyliss chopper. I think he just likes to make a lot of noise."

1 bunch beets (4 large beets, scrubbed and trimmed)

¼ cup shelled raw pumpkin seeds

2 scallions, green and white parts, finely chopped

3 tablespoons extra virgin olive oil

2 tablespoons balsamic vinegar

¾ teaspoon Dijon mustard

¼ teaspoon freshly ground black pepper

1 tablespoon finely chopped fresh basil

¼ pound feta cheese (optional)

1. Remove and reserve the greens from the beets, leaving about ½ inch of the stems intact. Scrub the beets. Place them in a large saucepan filled with water, and bring to a boil over high heat. Lower the heat, and simmer about 1 hour, until the beets are tender. Drain and let cool.

2. Toast the pumpkin seeds in a dry skillet over medium heat until fragrant. Remove the seeds from the skillet.

3. Wash the greens by submerging them in a sink full of cold water, then drain. Pour 1 inch of water into a large skillet, and heat to a simmer over medium heat. Drop the greens into simmering water, and cook about 30 seconds, until tender and juicy. Drain the greens in a colander, and gently run cold water over them to halt the cooking.

4. Peel the beets by cutting off the tops and slipping the skins off with your hands. Slice the beets into thin half-moons, and place them in a large salad bowl. Squeeze any excess water out of the greens, and chop them. Add the greens, pumpkin seeds, and scallions to the beets.

5. Combine the oil, vinegar, mustard, pepper, and basil in a jar with a tight-fitting lid and shake well. Pour the dressing over the salad, and toss gently. Crumble the feta cheese on top, if using. Serve at room temperature or chilled.

SERVES 6

Floyd Cardoz's Watermelon Salad

Floyd Cardoz, executive chef of Tabla in New York City, has received dozens of accolades for his innovative cooking, but, he says, he is just "scratching the surface of Indian American cuisine." With a background in biochemistry and culinary training in India, Switzerland, and the United States, Chef Cardoz understands the currents of cross-cultural experience. In the past decade, along with the wave of well-educated East Asian immigrants who followed high-paying technology jobs to the United States, the demand for artful Indian cooking has boomed. The affluent transplants—and their American-born friends—are not interested in the "gooey, overpowering, spicy, greasy, unidentifiable" renditions of North India's Mughlai cooking traditionally offered in American restaurants, says the chef. He draws from the disparate cooking traditions of the twenty-eight states in his native country but leans on local ingredients. Instead of using imported frozen pomfret for a fish curry, for instance, he might use fresh striped bass or halibut. He embraces New Mexico chiles "for their red sweetness," substituting them for Kashmiri chiles. "I grill more with Indian spices than is normal in India," he said. "If I'm cooking a good piece of meat or fish I wouldn't cook it well done, as in India, but medium rare." His often-mimicked watermelon salad is all about family: His father ate watermelon with salt, and his wife eats it with chaat masala—a popular Indian spice mixture—and this brought him to watermelon with salt, pepper, and lime juice, a perfect example of the balance of sweet, salt, sour, and spice. He added, "And then I like to put in mint since there is always mint in summer. Sometimes I put in ginger or heart of palm to play with texture."

2 limes

1 teaspoon grated fresh ginger

½ teaspoon finely chopped serrano chile

¾ teaspoon chaat masala

½ teaspoon freshly ground black pepper

2 tablespoons extra virgin olive oil

8 generous cups diced seeded watermelon

1 cup lightly packed arugula, torn into pieces

¼ cup sliced hearts of palm

½ cup chopped fresh mint

¼ cup chopped fresh cilantro

Kosher salt

1. Remove the zest from the limes and cut into thin strips. Juice the limes and reserve the juice.

2. In a small bowl, combine the lime zest, lime juice, ginger, chile, chaat masala, pepper, and oil. In a large bowl, gently toss together the watermelon, hearts of palm, arugula, mint, and cilantro.

3. Slowly pour the dressing over the watermelon mixture, season with salt, and combine gently. Serve.

SERVES 8

Russell "Fat Man" Fields, Harlem, New York.

Girl Scouts in Mrs. Herbert Hoover's garden.

COLESLAW

WHETHER HEAPED ON A PLATE NEXT TO FRIED FISH OR PRESSED INTO A PLASTIC CUP TO accompany take-out sandwiches, coleslaw is beloved or reviled, a preference often determined at the school cafeteria. A salad without the quick-wilting qualities of lettuce, coleslaw—or just slaw, as it's known in the South—has become an iconic American dish with passionately held regional variations. While there is national consensus that the base of coleslaw is thinly sliced raw cabbage, the additions that give it character differ widely. For some, simple mayonnaise, salt, and pepper make coleslaw. Others embellish it with pineapple, shredded carrots, grated cheese, apples, raisins, or peanuts. The spectrum of dressings is also dramatic, from tangy vinegar-based to creamy, encompassing ingredients from Miracle Whip to crème fraîche, sugar, honey, or maple syrup. Mexican-heritage recipes may include cumin and cilantro, while Asian-influenced recipes often include dried noodles and toasted sesame seeds. While some New Yorkers wouldn't eat a hot dog without sauerkraut—shredded cabbage that becomes sour through fermentation—in other areas, including West Virginia, many top their hot dogs with coleslaw.

Early Dutch settlers brought cabbage seeds from the old country, and soon it was a favorite crop in New York's Hudson Valley. The word "coleslaw" first appeared in *American Cookery*, the earliest extant cookbook in America, written by Amelia Simmons in 1796. Food historians believe it to be a corruption of the Dutch *koolsla*, or "cabbage salad."

DAN HUNTLEY'S RED SLAW

COLUMBIA, SOUTH CAROLINA

Self-proclaimed "barbecue provocateur" Dan Huntley believes that even the best smoked pig is not fully authentic until it snuggles up to some traditional Carolina red slaw. See his recipe for Baby Back Ribs (pages 503–505).

1 large head green cabbage

½ cup packed dark brown sugar

⅓ cup apple cider vinegar

½ cup ketchup

¼ cup tomato-based barbecue sauce (preferably Sweet Baby Ray's, or your favorite)

2 teaspoons kosher salt

2 teaspoons freshly ground black pepper

¼ teaspoon cayenne pepper

1½ teaspoons hot sauce (preferably Tabasco sauce)

Core and quarter the cabbage, then slice quarters into matchsticks by hand or in a food processor, and place in a large bowl. Combine the sugar, vinegar, ketchup, barbecue sauce, salt, black pepper, cayenne, and hot sauce in a small bowl. Pour over the cabbage and mix thoroughly. Cover and chill for 1 hour before serving.

SERVES 8 TO 10

Sharon Capps's Classic Coleslaw

When Livingston and Bonnie Paulk's Florida farm failed in 1917, the couple moved back to Union Springs, Alabama. They planted two pounds of cabbage seed and sold every plant. More than ninety years later, Bonnie Plant Farm, the company they created, is so successful that it supports a remarkable program to give cabbage plants—a million and a half of them in 2009—to third graders to get them interested in gardening, nature, and the outdoors. The students grow giant heads over the summer and take them to school in the fall along with a picture. As part of the program, Bonnie Plant awards a $1,000 scholarship to a student in each state.

As a thirty-five-year employee and now office manager of Bonnie Plant, Sharon Capps has seen a lot of cabbage in her 54 years. Her family and coworkers love her coleslaw. "I'm making it next week for the board of directors using cabbage from our garden plot. We'll serve it with fried catfish, some kind of potatoes, and hush puppies."

1 medium head green cabbage, cored and shredded

1 cup mayonnaise

⅓ cup chopped sweet pickles

¼ cup sugar

¼ cup distilled white vinegar

Kosher salt and freshly ground black pepper

In a large bowl, mix together the cabbage, mayonnaise, pickles, sugar, and vinegar until combined. Season with salt and pepper to taste. Cover and refrigerate for 1 hour before serving.

SERVES 6 TO 8

Cheng Lor's Hmong New Year's Green Papaya Salad

When the Hmong community in St. Paul, Minnesota, gathers to celebrate New Year in early December, the young and eligible play a ball-toss game. Traditional belief holds that the ball will point them to their soul mate. They also eat tuav gaub—spicy green papaya salad. A teenage boy in baggy jeans, Cheng Lor has been making it as an afternoon snack since the age of 8. He pays attention to technique, mixing the salad enough to blend with the seasoning, but not so much that the green papaya loses its crunch. For supper, it's a spicy accompaniment to roast pork, chicken, and grilled fish.

2 tablespoons unsweetened peanut butter

4 cherry tomatoes, finely chopped

1 Thai bird chili, stemmed and finely chopped, plus more as needed

1 garlic clove, minced

1 teaspoon shrimp paste (preferably Twin Chicken brand)

½ teaspoon crab extract

1 small green papaya, peeled, seeded, and shredded

3 tablespoons tamarind soup base mix

4½ teaspoons fish sauce

2 tablespoons sugar

2 tablespoons fresh lime juice

3 Chinese long beans, minced

1 teaspoon monosodium glutamate (preferably Twin Chicken brand, optional)

Kosher salt

In a large bowl, whisk the peanut butter, tomatoes, chile, garlic, shrimp paste, and crab extract together until combined. Stir in the papaya, soup base, fish sauce, sugar, lime juice, beans, and MSG, if using. Cover and let sit for 15 minutes, until the papaya has softened slightly. Season with additional chile and salt to taste, and serve.

SERVES 4

THE TIPTON-MARTIN SUMI SALAD

AUSTIN, TEXAS

Toni Tipton-Martin grew up in the center of Los Angeles, but her family's hillside yard could easily have been mistaken for a farm. "My mother was obsessed," she said. "We had every vegetable you could imagine: California stone fruit, black and red raspberries, a half-dozen types of citrus, apples, and avocados. My mother even tried to cultivate Asian pears. And Friday night dinner was salad, a big chef salad." Her children's favorite, on the other hand, is this cabbage and Ramen noodle salad that was inspired by a recipe that appeared in the *Los Angeles Times*. "Neighbors ask me to bring it to potlucks, even in the dead of winter," said Ms. Tipton-Martin, who founded a nonprofit that teaches at-risk youngsters to take better care of themselves by growing and preparing fresh produce of their own.

Conspicuous Consumption of Cellulose: Salads

FOR THE SALAD

2 (3-ounce) packages Ramen noodles

2 tablespoons oil

¼ cup sliced almonds

¼ cup sesame seeds

8 green onions, thinly sliced

1 head cabbage, finely chopped

FOR THE SUMI DRESSING

¼ cup sugar

1 teaspoon black pepper

1 teaspoon salt

1 cup oil

6 tablespoons rice vinegar

1. For the salad: Break the noodles into 1-inch pieces and place in a large bowl. Reserve the seasoning packet for another use. Heat the oil in a skillet, and sauté the almonds and sesame seeds until lightly browned. Remove from heat and allow to cool.

2. For the Sumi dressing: Combine the sugar, pepper, salt, oil and vinegar in a glass jar and shake well.

3. Add the onions, cabbage, and cooled almonds and sesame seeds to the noodles. Toss with the Sumi dressing, cover, and chill for several hours to allow the flavors to meld.

MAKES 10 TO 12 SERVINGS

Gina Caldrone Tsongas's Fennel Slaw with Orange, Cumin, and Chiles

SCOTTSDALE, ARIZONA

A year after they emigrated from Sicily to Pittsburgh, Gina Caldrone Tsongas's great-grandparents were finally able to have the raw sliced fennel salad that had always been a part of Christmas Eve dinner: "They couldn't buy it, they had to grow it." Her forebears sliced the bulb in wafer-thin, carpaccio-like slices, but when she brought the dish to potlucks and cookouts when she was in college, she cut the fennel like slaw. She added the cumin and chiles after marrying and moving to the Southwest. Today, her grandmother uses this recipe for her Christmas Eve meal. The slaw is terrific with spicy grilled fish or meat.

One Big Table

3 medium fennel bulbs, cored and thinly sliced

¼ cup chopped fennel fronds

3 tablespoons fresh lemon juice

3 tablespoons fresh orange juice

2 tablespoons fennel seeds, lightly crushed

1½ teaspoons extra virgin olive oil

1 teaspoon grated orange zest

1 garlic clove, minced

¾ teaspoon ground cumin

¼ teaspoon red pepper flakes

⅛ teaspoon red chili flakes

Kosher salt and freshly ground black pepper

In a large bowl, mix together the sliced fennel, fennel fronds, lemon and orange juices, fennel seeds, oil, orange zest, garlic, cumin, pepper flakes, and chili flakes until combined. Season with salt and pepper to taste. Cover and let sit at room temperature for 1 hour before serving.

SERVES 6

RAW ARTICHOKE SALAD

Artichoke season peaks in the spring, but there is a second crop in September, in time for the annual Castroville Artichoke Festival. Castroville is the self-proclaimed "artichoke capital of the world," and in fall artichokes are piled high along the streets and cooked in hundreds of guises. Once the leaves have been peeled or trimmed away, the cook is left with the artichoke heart, which looks like the inverted center of a daisy. It is as dense as a winter tuber, but its flavor is as delicate as spring.

2 tablespoons plus 2 teaspoons fresh lemon juice

8 large fresh artichokes

4 teaspoons extra virgin olive oil

Kosher salt and freshly ground black pepper

4 large radicchio leaves

1 ounce Parmesan cheese, thinly shaved

1 scallion, green part only, thinly sliced

1. In a large bowl, combine 2 tablespoons of the lemon juice with 2 quarts cold water. Cut the stem from the artichoke and snap off the tough, dark outer leaves. Cut off the tops of the remaining leaves, leaving about 1 inch. Use a spoon to scoop out the choke from the center of the artichoke. Use a paring knife to trim any remaining dark green bits. Drop into the lemon water. When you have prepped all the artichoke hearts, slice them very thinly and return to the acidulated water.

2. In a medium bowl, whisk together the remaining 2 teaspoons lemon juice and the oil. Season with salt and pepper to taste.

3. Drain the artichoke slices and dry on paper towels. Add the artichoke hearts to the dressing and toss to combine. Season with salt and pepper to taste.

4. To serve, place 1 radicchio leaf on each of four plates. Divide the salad evenly among the plates, arranging it so that it spills out of the radicchio leaves. Sprinkle each salad with the cheese and scallion, and serve.

———

SERVES 4

Stephen's Marinated Root Vegetable Salad

Stephen Smith describes himself as a "recovering architect." After twenty-seven years in the business, he and his wife, Elise, a novelist writing under the name Holly Chamberlin, have discovered a new life within fifty yards of the Portland harbor. He grew up in the Midwest, so his idea of seafood was frozen fish sticks. Today, however, he can watch commercial fishing boats unload the catch across the street from his home, and he's passionate about healthful food, beautifully cooked. After doctors diagnosed him with type 2 diabetes in 2008, he began revising old recipes to bring their nutritional values in line without giving up flavor. When his CSA (Community Supported Agriculture) farm share overloaded him with kohlrabi, carrots, and turnips, he created this root vegetable salad. The dressing is based on one he uses for spicy slaw.

Kosher salt

2 small white turnips, peeled and cut into ¼-inch pieces

1 carrot, peeled and cut into ¼-inch pieces

1 medium kohlrabi, peeled and cut into ¼-inch pieces

½ medium celery root, peeled and cut into ¼-inch pieces

1 teaspoon coriander seeds

1 teaspoon fennel seeds

1 teaspoon cumin seeds

½ cup coarsely chopped red onion

¼ cup coarsely chopped radicchio

2 tablespoons minced fresh tarragon

2 tablespoons minced fresh parsley

2 tablespoons olive oil

2 tablespoons fresh lime juice

1 serrano chile, stemmed, seeded, and thinly sliced

Freshly ground black pepper

Hot sauce

1. Fill a medium bowl with ice and water to make an ice bath. In a Dutch oven, bring 10 cups water and 1 tablespoon salt to a boil.

2. Boil the turnips for 2 to 4 minutes, until crisp-tender. Using a slotted spoon, transfer the turnips to the ice bath and let sit about 2 minutes, until cool. Using the slotted spoon, transfer the turnips to a colander to drain. Repeat this process with the carrot, kohlrabi, and celery root, replenishing the ice as needed.

3. In a small dry skillet, toast the coriander, fennel, and cumin seeds over high heat about 2 minutes, stirring often, until aromatic and slightly darker. Grind to a powder with a mortar and pestle or spice grinder.

4. In a large bowl, mix the blanched vegetables and ground spices with the onion, radicchio, tarragon, parsley, oil, lime juice, and chile. Season with salt, pepper, and hot sauce to taste. Cover and refrigerate, stirring occasionally, for 4 to 12 hours.

5. Before serving, bring the salad to room temperature and season with salt, pepper, and hot sauce to taste.

YIELD 8

Heather Arndt Anderson's
Celeriac Rémoulade

PORTLAND, OREGON

Heather Arndt Anderson, a Portland, Oregon, native recently covered her front lawn and part of her back lawn with cardboard and mulch to kill the grass, then dug it up to plant vegetables. Even with her enormous garden, she still loves finding new vegetables or fruits at the grocery store. "I like to bring it home, cut it open, and smell it, so it tells me what to do with it." She considers celeriac (celery root) unappreciated, "possibly the ugliest vegetable you could ever buy," but one with wonderful flavor. She looks for celeriac with no soft spots or blemishes, although since "this is a vegetable with a face only a mother could love, it will be hard to tell if the skin is unblemished."

Ms. Anderson urges cooks to make their own mayonnaise for this recipe. "If you are going to the trouble of peeling and julienning the celery root, you shouldn't cut corners with the mayonnaise."

FOR THE RÉMOULADE SAUCE

1 large egg yolk, at room temperature

2 teaspoons white wine vinegar or sherry vinegar

1 teaspoon Dijon mustard

Kosher salt and freshly ground black pepper

1 cup olive oil

1 small shallot, finely chopped

2 tablespoons finely chopped cornichons

2 tablespoons drained capers, finely chopped

1 tablespoon chopped fresh tarragon

1 tablespoon chopped fresh parsley

1 teaspoon grated lemon zest

Fresh lemon juice

FOR THE SALAD

1 large celery root, peeled and cut into 2-inch matchsticks

3 inner celery stalks with leaves, thinly sliced

Kosher salt and freshly ground black pepper

1. To make the rémoulade: In a blender, process the egg yolk, vinegar, mustard, ½ teaspoon salt, and ¼ teaspoon pepper until combined. With the blender running, slowly add the oil in a thin stream, until the mixture thickens. When all the oil has been incorporated, transfer the mayonnaise to a small bowl and stir in the shallot, cornichons, capers, tarragon, and parsley. Season with salt, pepper, lemon zest, and lemon juice to taste.

2. To make the salad: In a large bowl, mix the celery root and celery with enough rémoulade to coat. Cover and refrigerate about 4 hours, until chilled. Season with salt and pepper to taste, and serve.

SERVES 4 TO 6

AUNT GLADYS'S BROCCOLI SALAD WITH BACON

When the Edwards clan gathers in Surry, Virginia, they always feel the presence of Aunt Gladys. With the family in the pork business since ferryboat captain Wallace Edwards—called PopPop—founded the company in 1926, a gathering usually includes an Edwards dry-aged country ham. Along with biscuits, potatoes, and vegetables, broccoli salad—made with the Edwards bacon that wins blue ribbons at the Virginia State Fair—holds a place for Aunt Gladys. She passed away more than two decades ago, but introduced a salad so lively and enduring it's almost as though she's there in person.

One Big Table

FOR THE DRESSING

1 cup mayonnaise

½ cup sugar

2 tablespoons cider or distilled white vinegar

FOR THE SALAD

2 medium heads broccoli, cut into ½-inch florets

1 medium head cauliflower, cut into ½-inch florets

10 slices thick-cut bacon, cooked and crumbled

⅔ cup raisins, soaked in hot water for 15 minutes and drained

½ cup finely chopped onion

Kosher salt and freshly ground black pepper

1. To make the dressing: In a large bowl, whisk the mayonnaise, sugar, and vinegar together until combined.

2. To make the salad: Stir all of the ingredients into the bowl with the dressing until combined. Season with salt and pepper to taste. Cover and refrigerate 2 hours before serving.

SERVES 6 TO 8

Erin McCleary's French Lentil, Beet, and Asparagus Salad

On Erin Riley's sixteenth birthday, her culinary world expanded beyond sloppy Joes, spaghetti, and barbecued chicken when she was treated to a dinner at Le Vichyssois, a French restaurant in the Chicago suburb where she grew up. The meal awakened her to the power of flavor and fine craftsmanship, and several years later, cooking became one of the passions she shared with Kyle McCleary, a fellow student at St. Mary's University in Minnesota, who became her husband. He became a professional cook, and she managed marketing for an architectural firm, but inevitably, the search for flavor lead them to buy a sprawling 1880s farmhouse, where they could grow small crops of vegetables and cook. Ms. McCleary's jams have garnered blue ribbons at the state fair cooking contest—and with dishes like this lentil salad, she and her husband are part of a new generation redefining American farmhouse cooking.

FOR THE SALAD

2 medium beets, scrubbed and trimmed

1 tablespoon olive oil

Kosher salt and freshly ground black pepper

1 cup French green lentils, rinsed

1 carrot, peeled and coarsely chopped

½ bunch pencil-thin asparagus, trimmed and cut into 1-inch pieces

2 or 3 wedges Meryam's Preserved Lemons (page 82), rinsed, pulp discarded, rind minced

3 tablespoons roasted, salted shelled pepitas (pumpkin seeds)

FOR THE DRESSING

5 tablespoons extra virgin olive oil

2 tablespoons white wine vinegar

2 teaspoons honey

1 shallot, finely chopped

¼ cup lightly packed fresh mint leaves

Kosher salt and freshly ground black pepper

1. To make the salad: Place the oven rack in the center position and preheat the oven to 400°F.

2. In a small bowl, coat the beets with the oil, 1 teaspoon salt, and ¼ teaspoon pepper. Wrap them in aluminum foil and place in a baking dish. Bake for 40 to 50 minutes, until tender. Cool to room temperature.

3. When the beets are cool, peel them, and cut into ½-inch pieces. Transfer to a large bowl.

4. Meanwhile, in a medium saucepan, bring 2 quarts water, the lentils, carrot, and 1 teaspoon salt to a simmer over medium-high heat. Reduce the heat to medium-low and cook for 25 to 35 minutes, until the lentils are tender. Drain the lentils and carrot in a colander, rinse under cold running water until cool, and drain again. Add to the beets.

5. Fill a medium bowl with ice and water to make an ice bath. In the saucepan, bring 3 cups water and 2 teaspoons salt to a boil. Add the asparagus and cook about 2 minutes, until crisp-tender. Using a slotted spoon, transfer the asparagus to the ice bath and let cool. Drain well and add to the beets and lentils.

6. Stir in the preserved lemons and pepitas.

7. To make the dressing: In a blender, combine the oil, vinegar, honey, shallot, and mint, and process until smooth. Stir the dressing into the salad until combined. Season with salt and pepper to taste. Serve.

SERVES 4 TO 6

JEFF'S SPECIAL THREE-BEAN SALAD

KNOXVILLE, TENNESSEE

Jeff Ross is a gardener and a biker who cooks to relax, he says, "to make sure that everybody loves me—that is very important, you know." For this salad, which was inspired by a version served at Blackberry Farm, he prefers crowder, zipper cream, and lady peas for their great flavor, and shuns store-bought black-eyed peas. The salad is wonderful with fried chicken or barbecue, makes a great potluck offering, and when packed carefully holds up well on the back of a bike.

3 cups fresh shelled peas, preferably crowder, zipper cream, or lady

Kosher salt

4 slices bacon, cut into ½-inch pieces

2 tablespoons cider vinegar

1 large egg yolk

2 garlic cloves, minced

1 teaspoon mustard powder

¼ teaspoon ground coriander

¼ cup grapeseed oil, plus more as needed

Freshly ground black pepper

1 medium red onion, finely chopped

¼ cup chopped fresh parsley

¼ cup chopped fresh chives

¼ teaspoon minced fresh chili pepper

1. In a large saucepan, bring 6 cups water and 1 tablespoon salt to a boil. Fill a large bowl with ice and water to make an ice bath. Line a plate with paper towels.

2. Boil the peas until tender, about 5 minutes, transfer the peas to the ice bath, and let cool. Drain well and set aside.

3. In a medium skillet, cook the bacon over medium-low heat about 15 minutes, stirring occasionally, until brown and crisp. Using a slotted spoon, transfer the bacon to the plate. Strain the bacon fat through a fine-mesh strainer and set aside.

4. Combine the vinegar, egg yolk, garlic, mustard, and coriander, and process in a blender until smooth. With the blender running, slowly add the oil in a thin stream, until the mixture thickens. Blend in the reserved bacon fat. Season with salt and pepper to taste.

5. Stir the dressing, bacon, onion, parsley, chives, and chili pepper into the peas. Season with salt and black pepper to taste. Let sit for 30 minutes before serving.

SERVES 6

LEE SMITH'S POTATO SALAD

Novelist Lee Smith's mother, Virginia Smith, came to the Appalachian Mountains to teach home economics, fell in love with Lee's "handsome daddy, Ernest Smith, and spent the rest of her life trying to civilize him and his whole rowdy clan, without much luck." Lee's mother's kitchen was "the most interesting place on earth, not only because of the food but also because of the stories—she always had company, and they were always talking, talking, talking (and smoking Salem cigarettes and drinking coffee from the big old percolator in the corner). "Even today, my sense of a story is spoken, not written, and often it's my mother's voice that's whispering excitedly in my ear, giving me the real lowdown." Getting the lowdown has led the author to eleven novels, including a *New York Times* bestseller, three collections of short stories, and a loose-leaf binder full of recipes from family and friends.

This parsleyed potato salad recipe came to her thirty-five years ago, from her friend Lillia Johnston, whom Lee calls "the best hostess I have ever known. She plans and cooks ahead so *she* can relax—and she always seems to have a wonderful time at her own parties. I started making her potato salad because I wanted to have as much fun at mine." She loves this recipe because of the horseradish that gives it a special tang and because "every time I have ever fixed this, it gets *entirely* eaten up."

The salad is best if refrigerated overnight. You can use more potatoes if you wish—Lee usually throws in an extra—and the amount of scallions is really up to you.

2 pounds small red potatoes, scrubbed and sliced ¼ inch thick

Kosher salt

1¼ cups sour cream

1¼ cups mayonnaise

1½ teaspoons prepared horseradish

½ teaspoon celery seeds

1 bunch scallions, green and white parts, finely chopped

1 cup minced fresh parsley

Freshly ground black pepper

1. In a large saucepan, bring 6 cups water, the potatoes, and 1 tablespoon salt to a simmer. Cook for 5 to 7 minutes, until the potatoes are just tender. Drain the potatoes, transfer to a rimmed baking sheet, and let cool to room temperature.

2. Meanwhile, in a small bowl, combine the sour cream, mayonnaise, horseradish, and celery seeds. In a second small bowl, combine the scallions and parsley.

3. In a 9 x 13-inch baking dish, arrange one-quarter of the potatoes in a single layer and season with salt and pepper. Spread about ⅔ cup of the sour cream mixture over the potatoes, then sprinkle with about ½ cup of the scallion mixture. Repeat to make four layers.

4. Cover and refrigerate the salad for 8 to 12 hours before serving.

SERVES 6 TO 8

ELI'S FARRO WHEAT TABOULE

AMHERST, MASSACHUSETTS

Eli Rogoso, the founder of the Heritage Wheat Conservancy, spends her winters in Middle East gathering seeds from ancient Fertile Crescent wheat varieties and spends the summer and fall growing those seeds in a small experimental plot at the University of Massachusetts in Amherst. She dreams of the day when hundreds of drought-resistant wheat varieties can nourish the American soil and calls her work "repatriation." The ancient grains, such as the farro that Italians dote upon, can be used to lend a distinct nuttiness to taboule, which is generally made with bulgur wheat.

½ cup farro wheat

Kosher salt

4 cups coarsely chopped fresh parsley

5 large ripe plum tomatoes, cored, seeded, and finely chopped

2 scallions, finely chopped

¼ cup fresh lime juice

Freshly ground black pepper

1. In a medium bowl, combine 2 cups boiling water, farro, and ½ teaspoon salt. Let sit for 15 to 20 minutes, until the farro is tender. Drain, transfer to a large bowl, and set aside to cool to room temperature.

2. Stir the parsley, tomatoes, scallions, lime juice, ½ teaspoon salt, and ½ teaspoon pepper into the bowl with the cooled farro. Season with salt and pepper to taste, and serve.

SERVES 4 TO 6

HELGA VON SCHWEINITZ'S KARTOFFELSALAT
German Potato Salad, Northern Style

Helga von Schweinitz grew up in Herford, Germany, near Hanover. As an adolescent in the years after World War II, "I didn't want to be known as a girl who liked to cook," she remembers. "My friends and I were interested in Shakespeare and existentialism, in ideas, not cooking. We were going to college." And she wanted to see the world. Sponsored by relatives in Milwaukee, she came to the United States to work for a year. But she fell in love with her future husband, an Air Force officer, and the year turned into the rest of her life. But her ties to her homeland remain strong, as does her cooking.

"When I first came to Central Texas in 1975, it was a big surprise how much German Texans had contributed to the cultural life, how much German influence there is here. I don't think many people in Germany are aware of this. The early German settlers in Texas were educated and community-minded; they established schools, symphonies, and libraries." This recipe for a mayonnaise-based potato salad comes from her father. "It's typical of the kartoffelsalat of northern Germany," she says. "Although after the war, oil was precious and ham was scarce, so we'd eat the ham on the side instead of mixed in the salad."

2 tablespoons olive oil

2 tablespoons cider vinegar

1 teaspoon Dijon mustard

Kosher salt and freshly ground black pepper

1½ pounds small red potatoes, scrubbed and sliced ¼-inch thick

¼ pound smoked ham, cut into ½-inch cubes

½ cup finely chopped onion

¼ cup finely chopped dill pickle

2 radishes, trimmed and finely chopped

2 large eggs, hard boiled, peeled, and roughly chopped

¼ to ½ cup mayonnaise

1. In a small bowl, combine the oil, vinegar, mustard, ¼ teaspoon salt, and ¼ teaspoon pepper.

2. In a large saucepan, bring 6 cups water, the potatoes, and 1 tablespoon salt to a simmer. Cook for 5 to 7 minutes, until the potatoes are just tender. Drain the potatoes, transfer to a large bowl, and gently stir in the oil mixture. Let sit for 15 minutes.

3. Gently stir in the ham, onion, pickle, radishes, and eggs until combined. Gently stir in the mayonnaise, 2 tablespoons at a time, until the salad is creamy. Season with salt and pepper to taste. Serve.

SERVES 4

PADMA PRIYA VENKATA'S RUSTIC BREAD SALAD

Priya Venkata left her hometown, Hyderabad, the south-central Indian city with a population of more than 7 million, to earn a master's degree in mechanical engineering at the University of Cincinnati. She had been a "passive cook," she says, watching her mother prepare meals, but during her graduate school years homesickness took her into the kitchen. To the delight of her roommates and friends, she was able to re-create her childhood foods in a small apartment kitchen. Cooking shows on television exposed her to unfamiliar ingredients and cuisines, and she began to expand her knowledge with international recipes.

South Indian cuisine uses rice as a staple, with few or no wheat-based products, but Ms. Venkata now bakes bread every other week. One of the new recipes she tried is the Italian bread salad panzanella. To enhance the dish, she sometimes uses some of her homemade sun-dried tomatoes in place of some of the fresh ones and substitutes her own black peppercorn bread, creating a unique version that is Tuscany via Hyderabad via Cleveland.

Six 1-inch-thick slices French or Italian bread, cut into 1-inch cubes

6 tablespoons extra virgin olive oil

Kosher salt and freshly ground black pepper

2 cups cherry tomatoes, halved

2 ripe Hass avocados, halved, pitted, peeled, and cut into ½-inch pieces

2 large oranges, peel and pith removed, segmented, juice reserved

1 red onion, finely chopped

1 English cucumber, cut into ½-inch pieces

1 or 2 jalapeño chiles, stemmed, seeded, and finely chopped (optional)

½ cup chopped fresh cilantro

4 teaspoons fresh lemon juice

1. Place an oven rack in the center position and preheat the oven to 400°F.

2. On a large rimmed baking sheet, toss the bread with 2 tablespoons of the oil, ½ teaspoon salt, and ¼ teaspoon pepper and spread in an even layer. Bake about 15 minutes, stirring every 5 minutes, until light golden brown. Cool to room temperature.

3. In a large bowl, combine the tomatoes, avocados, oranges, onion, cucumber, chiles, if using, and cilantro. Just before serving, stir in the bread and season with salt, pepper, reserved orange juice, and lemon juice to taste.

SERVES 4 TO 6

One Big Table

Sakowitz's Sky Terrace Shrimp and Avocado Salad

In the mid-nineteenth century, the department store entered American life with the opening of A. T. Stewart's "Marble Palace" in New York City, soon followed by Macy's, B. Altman, Lord & Taylor, and Abraham & Straus. In cities large and small, elegant emporiums soon sold everything from perfume to carpets. Considered a natural environment for ladies of means, many featured restaurants or tearooms where shoppers could nibble salads and small sandwiches while grooming their daughters in the culture of mealtime conversation and feminine behavior. By the 1950s, department stores often featured both a tearoom and a grill where gentlemen could have an after-work drink or a hearty lunch. In many smaller towns, the in-store eatery might have been the nicest place in town to have a meal. In Texas, department store dining reached a fine art; Dallas residents still consider Neiman Marcus the last bastion of fine department store fare.

In 1951, Charles Pack often took his young bride, Mary, to lunch at Sakowitz Bros.'s Sky Terrace restaurant in Houston. They ordered the signature dish: chilled shrimp salad served over half of an avocado. When their daughter, food writer Mary Margaret, visited the Sky Terrace with her mother in the 1960s, she was awed by fragile glasses of iced tea, air-conditioning, and the occasional designer-clad model strolling between the tables. She also remembers ordering the shrimp and avocado salad that she has re-created here.

FOR THE SAUCE

1 cup mayonnaise

¼ cup cooked spinach, well drained and finely chopped

1 large egg, hard boiled, peeled, and coarsely chopped

4 garlic cloves, minced

2 scallions, green and white parts, finely chopped

1 tablespoon Worcestershire sauce

1 tablespoon Dijon or Creole-style mustard

1 tablespoon fresh lemon juice

1 teaspoon anchovy paste

Kosher salt

Hot sauce

FOR THE SALAD

1½ pounds medium shrimp, boiled, peeled, deveined, and chilled

3 celery stalks, finely chopped

2 tablespoons fresh lemon juice

Kosher salt and freshly ground black pepper

1 medium head iceberg lettuce, cored and shredded

3 ripe Hass avocados, halved, pitted, peeled, and sliced ½ inch thick

1. To make the sauce: In a food processor, combine the mayonnaise, spinach, egg, garlic, scallions, Worcestershire, mustard, lemon juice, and anchovy paste, and process until smooth. Season with salt and hot sauce to taste and transfer to a large bowl.

2. To make the salad: Gently stir the shrimp, celery, and lemon juice into the sauce. Season with salt and pepper to taste. Cover and refrigerate for 1 hour.

3. To serve, divide the shredded lettuce evenly among six plates, fan the avocado slices over the lettuce, and top with the shrimp salad.

SERVES 6

ELIZABETH PEARCE'S
SHRIMP SALAD RÉMOULADE

NEW ORLEANS, LOUISIANA

With eight generations of Louisiana family behind her, Elizabeth Pearce "loves New Orleans like a person" because the city supports "people who do unusual or quirky things." One of her unusual contributions was cooking in an 1830s kitchen over an open hearth. When she became a docent at the Hermann-Grima House in the French Quarter, she also became senior curator for the Southern Food and Beverage Museum, known as SoFAB, which celebrates the food and drink of the entire South. Following Hurricane Katrina, she organized the exhibition "Come Hell or High Water: Stories of Eating, Drinking and Surviving in Katrina's Wake" and interviewed some of the 3,000 New Orleans evacuees who were bussed to a Memphis, Tennessee, neighborhood where residents pulled out their barbecue grills, emptied their freezers, and started cooking for them. Elizabeth firmly believes a recipe is only a starting point. New Orleans traditionally presents shrimp salad as whole boiled shrimp on a bed of greens, dressed with rémoulade sauce, but she points out that in this "wonderful sauce," there is "room for variation." She never makes it the same way twice. She says, "The best rémoulade is the one you eat when you

are happy and are dining with loved ones. It's that synergy that makes food memorable. I've been to dinner parties where the food was just okay, but it tasted fantastic because we were having such a good time. Where we are in our hearts and heads affects how food tastes and how we remember it."

1 cup mayonnaise (preferably Hellmann's or Best Foods)

½ cup Creole-style mustard (preferably Zatarain's)

2 dashes of hot sauce (preferably Crystal)

½ to 1 tablespoon fresh lemon juice

2 garlic cloves, minced

1 teaspoon sweet paprika

1 or 2 celery stalks, minced

2 large eggs, hard boiled, peeled, and chopped (optional)

1 pound medium shrimp, peeled, deveined, and boiled until tender

4 cups mixed salad greens or 4 large tomatoes, hollowed out (optional)

Milk (optional)

Chopped scallions, for garnish

1. Combine the mayonnaise, mustard, hot sauce, lemon juice, garlic, and paprika in a medium bowl and stir until blended. Stir in the celery and eggs, if using. Cover and chill for 30 minutes.

2. To serve, toss the shrimp with the sauce and, if you wish, arrange on a bed of greens or in hollowed-out tomatoes. Or thin the sauce with milk and drizzle over shrimp presented on a bed of greens. Garnish with scallions.

SERVES 4

THE MIGHTY TUNA, TAMED

AMERICANS BUY MORE THAN 1 BILLION CANS OF TUNA
each year to make scoops of salad on lettuce, lunch-box
sandwiches, and casseroles. What elevated the fast-moving
fighting fish from fabulous sport to kitchen staple? Canning.
Many cultures, including those from the Mediterranean
and Asia, have eaten fresh tuna for centuries, but until the
beginning of the twentieth century, Americans ate little of
it. In 1903, when the sardine supply failed, Wilbur F. Wood,
supervisor in a California canning plant, needed a new product
to fill his empty sardine cans, and began to experiment with albacore, then plentiful in Pacific waters.
By steaming the fish and removing its natural oils to change the meat from pink to white, he created
a product Americans would buy. When tuna packers launched the Bumble Bee brand, and the Van
Camp Seafood Company called their product Chicken of the Sea, tuna became desirable. World War I
brought high-protein canned tuna to the troops; its affordability during the Great Depression sealed its
popularity. After tuna fishing practices nearly wiped out the populations of dolphins that swim with tuna,
a federal law in the 1970s prohibited the importation of tuna caught
with drag nets. Tuna canning
companies, in compliance
with Federal regulations,
display a "dolphin safe" label
on the can.

While acknowledging
that canned tuna has made
the fish accessible to all,
some claim that the canning
process has made the fish
unpalatable. High-grade tuna
packed in olive oil are being
imported from Italy and Spain,
and increasingly, fresh tuna
is appearing in salads such
as the Niçoise and Balinese
versions that follow.

DOMINIC'S ITALIAN-AMERICAN NIÇOISE SALAD

SAN PEDRO, CALIFORNIA

"I never understood why my mother used the canned tuna. Her house was up on a hill looking out over the harbor and toward some of the best tuna grounds in the world," said Dominic Urbana. "But she bought oil-packed tuna from the grocery store. She made oil-poached fresh tuna and served it with potatoes and beans. My salad just takes that idea a little further and throws in some French attitude. My daughter makes the same thing, but adds ancho chiles to the fennel and black pepper to give a little more bite. This makes a great summer meal."

One 12-ounce tuna steak (1-inch thick)

¾–1½ cups olive oil

1 tablespoon fennel seeds

½ tablespoon black peppercorns

Kosher salt

4 garlic cloves, thinly sliced

1 pound small Yukon gold potatoes, scrubbed

½ pound green beans or wax beans, trimmed

1 garlic clove, minced

2 anchovy fillets, rinsed and finely chopped, plus more for garnish if desired

1 tablespoon fresh lemon juice

Freshly ground black pepper

1 large tomato, seeded and chopped

½ cup chopped fresh parsley

⅓ cup black olives, pitted and sliced

1. Place the tuna steak in a small pan over low heat and pour in ¾ cup olive oil, or enough to barely cover the fish. Set aside the remaining olive oil for the dressing. Wrap the fennel seeds and peppercorns in cheesecloth and add to the oil. Cook over very lowest heat until the tuna is nearly cooked through, 12 to 15 minutes. Carefully turn the steak once. Remove from heat, and remove the tuna from the hot oil.

2. Transfer the tuna to a bowl and coat with the olive oil and sliced garlic. Cover and refrigerate for at least 6 hours or overnight.

3. A half hour before serving the salad, remove the tuna from the refrigerator. Scrape off the garlic and discard. Place the potatoes in a large saucepan and cover with cold, salted water. Bring to a boil, lower the heat, cover, and simmer until tender, about 20 minutes. Drain, cool, and slice.

4. Meanwhile, fill a large bowl with cold water. Bring another large saucepan of salted water to a boil. Add the beans and cook just until they begin to become tender, about 3 minutes. Drain and immediately plunge them into the cold water. When cool, drain them, and if they are large, chop them in half.

5. Place the minced garlic, chopped anchovy, lemon juice, salt, and ground pepper in a bowl and, while whisking steadily, slowly drizzle in the remaining olive oil. Remove 1 tablespoon of the dressing and set aside. Add the potatoes, beans, tomato, parsley, and olives. Toss well, and season to taste with salt and pepper. Divide the vegetables among four plates.

6. Using a sharp knife, slice the tuna on the bias into thin slices. Lay the slices carefully over the vegetables, drizzle with the reserved dressing, garnish with additional anchovy fillet if desired, and serve.

SERVES 4

Kahn's Indonesian Tuna Salad

"I met my husband when he was in Jakarta on leave from the military," said Kahn Pierson. "I didn't like America so much in Pennsylvania or Georgia or Washington State, but Key West, I love. It is a happy place; it makes me want to cook like my mother. After the children are gone and we both retired, we began to spend the winters in Key West. He fishes and I cook like my mother, outdoors, on our deck in the shade. I always made a lot of the spice paste, because I use it in just about everything and so does anybody who tastes it, so you will like to have the leftovers from this recipe. It will keep for a month in the refrigerator if you cover it good. It is a good marinade for just about any fish and is good on chicken, too."

FOR THE SPICE PASTE

⅔ cup vegetable oil

15 shallots, coarsely chopped

15 Thai chiles, stemmed, seeded, and coarsely chopped

5 lemon or lime leaves, thinly sliced, or ½ teaspoon grated lime zest

4 stalks lemongrass, white parts only, finely chopped

4 garlic cloves, minced

2 tablespoons fresh lime juice

1½ teaspoons kosher salt

1 teaspoon shrimp paste

¾ teaspoon freshly ground black pepper

FOR THE TUNA

One 1½-pound tuna steak (1-inch thick)

Kosher salt and freshly ground black pepper

1 tablespoon fresh lime juice

3 tablespoons vegetable oil

1. To make the spice paste: In a food processor, process all of the ingredients together until smooth, or use a mortar and pestle to do the same.

2. To make the tuna: Pat the tuna steak dry with a paper towel, season with salt and pepper, and sprinkle with the lime juice. In a large skillet, heat the oil over high heat. Add the tuna and cook about 10 minutes, turning once, until no longer pink in the center. Transfer the tuna to a plate and let cool to room temperature.

3. Break the tuna in bite-size chunks and transfer to a large bowl. Stir in the spice paste and toss to coat. Cover, and let sit for 30 minutes before serving.

SERVES 6

Thornton Dial, 2005.

BILL BAYLEY'S WEST INDIES CRAB SALAD

THEODORE, ALABAMA

In the 1940s, Bill Bayley worked as a steward for the Alcoa Steamship Company on freighters that sailed the West Indies. He came to appreciate the local method of preparing the fresh-caught seafood that comprised the bulk of the crew's meals. When he left Alcoa in 1947, he opened Bayley's Restaurant in Theodore with his wife, Ethel, and created a crab salad in the ceviche or pickling style. Over time, West Indies Salad, as Mr. Bayley called it, became iconic in the area, finding its way into the Junior League of Mobile's cookbook in 1964. Others have tried to improve upon the dish, using olive oil instead of vegetable oil or flavored vinegar in place of cider. But Bill Bayley Jr. says simplicity is the genius of his father's recipe, which needs no improvement. "They always come back to tell me it's perfect the way it is." Serve on a bed of lettuce, if desired.

1 medium-size sweet onion, finely chopped

1 pound fresh lump or claw crabmeat, picked over for shells and cartilage

Kosher salt and freshly ground black pepper

½ cup vegetable oil

½ cup cider vinegar

½ cup ice water

In a large serving bowl, arrange half of the onion in an even layer. Cover with the crabmeat. Spread the remaining onions over the crab and season with salt and pepper. Pour the oil, vinegar, and ice water over the top. Cover and refrigerate for 12 to 24 hours before serving.

SERVES 4

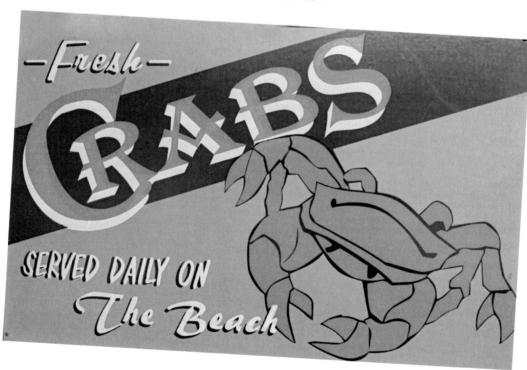

GIA LY QUACH'S VIETNAMESE CHICKEN SALAD

Just before the fall of Saigon in 1975, Vietnamese people began settling in Orange County, California, and today, with more than a quarter million people of Vietnamese descent, "Little Saigon" has the largest concentration of Southeast Asian people in the United States. Gia Ly Quach works in an advertising agency in Los Angeles, and one of the few dishes she's claimed from her homeland is the family's chicken salad, a traditional goi-ga ("goi" is a salad made from leftover meat or fish), which is served with a basket of fresh Vietnamese herbs. These are easily had in Orange County, but still difficult to find in other areas of the country. Ms. Quach suggests some possible substitutions:

You can use lemon mint for la tia to, the perilla leaf (called shiso in Japan), which is omnipresent in Southeast Asia. A combination of peppermint and fresh cilantro can take the place of rau ram, a peppery and minty purple leaf. Ngo om, or rice paddy herb, tastes faintly of miner's lettuce and sorrel. Cilantro can substitute for ngo gai, which is also called saw-leaf or coarse coriander. And in a pinch, vine leaves, lovage leaves, or the Japanese leaf shiso can replace la lot, a mildly acidic and faintly peppery vine leaf that is indispensable to the Vietnamese kitchen.

"If you add a cold goi or two and a couple of different dipping sauces—all of which can be prepared ahead of time—you'll have a light meal with enough variety to appease the pickiest guests," says Ms. Quach. "It's simply a matter of stab and dip, wrap and roll."

One 3½- to 4-pound whole chicken

1 teaspoon white peppercorns

One 1-inch piece fresh ginger, peeled and quartered

Kosher salt

2 large red onions, halved and very thinly sliced

3 tablespoons fresh lime juice (preferably Key lime)

½ cup chopped fresh mint

Freshly ground black pepper

1. In a large pot, bring the 4 quarts water, the chicken, peppercorns, ginger, and 2 teaspoons salt to a simmer over medium-high heat. Reduce the heat to medium-low and cook about 45 minutes, until an instant-read thermometer registers 175°F in the thigh and 165°F in the breast.

2. Transfer the chicken to a plate and cool to room temperature. Strain the broth through a fine-mesh strainer, and reserve for another use. Remove the skin and bones from the chicken, and shred the meat into bite-size pieces.

3. In a large bowl, combine the chicken, onions, lime juice, mint, ½ teaspoon salt, and ½ teaspoon pepper. Season with salt and pepper to taste, and serve.

———

SERVES 4 TO 6

221

Conspicuous Consumption of Cellulose: Salads

Chau Tran Smith's Vietnamese Beef and Watercress Salad

The bucolic estate that Chau Tran Smith called home in her native Vietnam encompassed gardens and century-old fruit trees, all tended by servants. But during the war, the trees on the estate and in the village were considered good cover for Vietcong militants, so the American army cut them down. Later, the mansion was mistakenly bombed, and the family moved into a shack. Ms. Smith escaped the misery when she married an American GI. After the marriage soured, he left her in Independence, Missouri, with two small daughters. She went to work as a seamstress and married Mickey Smith in 1990. The couple bought ten acres in Oak Grove, Missouri, just outside Independence, where they built a five-bedroom home, planted fruit trees and flower and vegetable gardens, and constructed a large pond that they stocked with catfish, bluegills, and frogs.

In Vietnam, Ms. Smith ate beef and watercress salad only on special occasions because watercress didn't grow in the dry southern part of the country where she lived, and was a pricey commodity. Today it flourishes along the edge of her pond, and this salad is a weekly event.

FOR THE MARINADE

4 garlic cloves, minced

1 tablespoon fish sauce

1 teaspoon toasted sesame oil

1 teaspoon sugar

¼ teaspoon freshly ground black pepper

⅛ teaspoon baking soda

One 1-pound, 1-inch-thick sirloin steak, thinly sliced crosswise

FOR THE DRESSING

1 cup peanut oil

⅓ cup fresh lime juice or rice vinegar

4 garlic cloves, minced

1 small onion, halved and thinly sliced

2 teaspoons fish sauce

1½ teaspoons toasted sesame oil

1 teaspoon sugar or honey, plus more to taste

FOR THE SALAD

3 Thai bird chiles

2 bunches watercress, heavy stems trimmed

1 firm ripe tomato, cored, halved, and thinly sliced

2 tablespoons peanut or vegetable oil

8 sprigs fresh cilantro

1 package rice paper rounds (optional)

1. To make the marinade: In a large bowl, combine the garlic, fish sauce, sesame oil, sugar, pepper, and baking soda. Add the beef, and stir to coat. Cover and refrigerate for 1 to 24 hours.

2. To make the dressing: Whisk together all the ingredients in a small bowl.

3. To make the salad: Quarter the chiles lengthwise from the pointed end up to the stem, leaving them attached to the stem, so there are four "petals." Discard the seeds.

4. In a medium bowl, toss the watercress with 2 tablespoons of the dressing. Transfer to a serving platter, and arrange the tomato slices over the watercress.

5. Heat the oil in a large nonstick skillet over high heat. Drain the beef, add to the skillet, and cook for 1 to 2 minutes, stirring frequently, until lightly browned and no longer pink. Arrange the beef over the tomatoes, and lay the cilantro and chiles on the top.

6. If using the rice papers, dip a wrapper in hot water for a few seconds to make it more pliable. Blot it dry on a kitchen towel and roll some salad in it. Pass the remaining dressing separately.

———

SERVES 4

CHAPTER 5

FROM SEA TO SHINING SEA: FISH AND SHELLFISH

LOBSTER TALES

STONINGTON, MAINE

Dick Bridges has big, callused hands that have been thickened by half a century of fishing. They are not the sort of hands you expect to see mincing onions in a church kitchen. But on a recent Saturday evening, Mr. Bridges grasped a flimsy knife, reached for a sack of yellow onions, and launched into a soliloquy about fishing in America and the dish that tells the story: chowder.

Early colonial versions of chowder called for fish to be layered with onions, biscuits, and water in a cauldron; by the mid-nineteenth century, when Ishmael and Queequeg downed steaming bowls of the stuff in *Moby-Dick*, milk, cream, and salt pork had found their way into the pot. But other than those additions, the dish Melville's whalers ate—"chowder for breakfast, and chowder for dinner, and chowder for supper"—changed very little for nearly 200 years.

Down Easters say that the greater the variety of fish in the pot, the "deepah the flavah." Like most sons of sons of Maine fishermen, Mr. Bridges grew up eating fish stews that were as diverse and densely packed as the local waters. Cod, haddock, white hake, halibut, cusk, and dozens of other groundfish—species that live near the ocean bottom—mingled with clams, shrimp, lobster, and mussels under the creamy surface of the stew, cresting with a puddle of yellow butter here, a slick of smoky pork fat there.

In 1985 fishermen landed 7 million pounds of groundfish in Stonington, Maine, alone. Ten years later, those fish disappeared from Penobscot Bay, and for the first time in nearly two centuries, chowder changed. Mr. Bridges was "worried so sick" about the condition of the fisheries that in 2003 he and three others broke the fishermen's traditional code of silence and began sharing their knowledge about feeding and spawning grounds.

Along with their wives, they founded Penobscot East Resource Center. The advocacy group created the nation's first fishermen-funded lobster hatchery and built an alliance among fishermen that would manage the local fisheries. They even learned how to cook. And on evenings like these, when they gather to raise funds and share information about the state of the local waters, these men are often found in the kitchen.

In this town where chowder is the measure of a cook and a way of life, Mr. Bridges is known as the "Chowdah King." To him, building a chowder is more than making dinner. It is a celebration of America's past and a warning about its future. By 2008, there was little to be fished commercially near Stonington except lobster, so lobster floats alone in the local chowder. It pinks the cream, and in the minds of food lovers, perhaps elevates this everyman's dish to luxury status, but when Mr. Bridges looks at a single-species stew, he sees a dangerously impoverished fishery.

"The only stable fishery is a diverse fishery," he tells me, as he begins his preparations for chowder for several dozen people. No place in the world is richer in lobster than the waters around Stonington today, but the population explosion was caused, in part, by the vanishing of the groundfish. "They fed on the young lobsters, the spats, but the large fin fish are also part of an ecosystem that actually protects the lobster." Even with good management, the lobster too could disappear.

"And when they go," he says, grasping one of the crustaceans and twisting off its claws and tail in a single flourish, "the last of America's colonial industries will go with them."

Stonington, Maine, is a cluster of shingled houses, picket fences, widow's walks, and church spires that rises up a hillside from a shallow natural harbor. Unlike the fleets of deeper ports such as New Bedford, Massachusetts, and Portland, Maine, which sail far offshore for days at a time, Stonington's fleets are made up of day boats, small craft that fish close to home. The fishermen went out before dawn and came home in midafternoon—generally clanging a pail of fish—ready to tuck into a bowl of the chowder that their wives had made from the contents of the previous day's bucket. As Ted Hoskins, another supporter of the Resource Center, explains, "They could go to the Little League games, join the school board, volunteer at the fire department."

Before retiring, Mr. Hoskins was a "boat minister" with the Maine Sea Coast Mission, who called on the islands on the far side of Penobscot Bay. When the groundfish began to vanish, he saw the changes in the sea affect life on land. His congregants' problems—depression, drinking, and family trouble—grew. State and federal efforts to protect the fisheries limited a fisherman's catch as well as the number of days he could work. So as the

Ted Ames, 2009.

fishing stock in the bay was depleted, fishermen had to move farther out to sea.

"The math didn't work: It cost more, there were fewer fish, and they were allowed to take less of them," Mr. Hoskins says. "They got second jobs. Their wives went to work. They started selling their boats." Many of the older watermen retired; others went to work for large corporate fishing concerns who could afford the expensive boats needed to fish in deeper waters. This often meant driving hours to meet the boat and staying on it for up to two weeks at sea. "The men were no longer independent, no longer free. They were employees. The women and children were home alone. I was watching an entire way of life slip away."

The fishermen who persevered switched to lobstering, an industry that is closely regulated. Lobstermen are told when and where they can fish, and they must report their whereabouts and provide detailed accounting of their catches. But, says Bridges, "using the technology available today, a guy can learn what I know in a month. You don't have to use a compass, read a map, or remember where the lobsters are. You don't even have to steer a decent course."

■   ■   ■

"Fishermen have always cooked on their boats," Ted Ames tells me as he shrugs out of his slicker. "We just didn't admit it at home." He smiles then, toward the four burly fishermen already crowding around the small electric stove in the church basement.

Aprons wrapped around their flannel shirts, they watch as Mr. Bridges explains the importance of sautéing the lobster meat in butter before adding it to the simmering onions, potatoes, and cream. "It brings out the color and the sweetness." This and a sprinkle of basil are the secrets of his champion chowder. The men nod intently; they could be charting a course past dangerous shoals.

Mr. Ames, who was a commercial fisherman for half a century before retiring last year, has a master's degree in biochemistry and spent the past decade using the memories of retired fishermen to create maps of the spawning and nursery grounds of cod, the areas that must be strictly protected if the

Dick Bridges, 2009.

groundfish are to regenerate. His efforts earned him a MacArthur Foundation grant in 2005.

"The only ones who can restore these fisheries are us, the fishermen who worked them and broke them," he says. Pointing to the success of Maine's closely controlled—and peer-enforced—lobster industry, he adds, "We learned our lesson."

The Penobscot East Resource Center has helped give men like Mr. Bridges and Mr. Ames a voice with lawmakers. They argue that the fisheries are a massive collection of tiny and particular habitats that can be tended only by those who know them. If fishing regulations reflect the knowledge and the needs of the Stonington lobstermen, their smaller day boats will have a fighting chance against the enormous commercial vessels. And so will the fish.

"We can't turn the clock back on technology," Mr. Ames says. "We can only regulate it, the way we regulate the size and speed of vehicles on the highway." He and his group plan to ask federal regulators to allow them to manage the local fisheries and to limit technology. Without a change in the rules, he says, the owner-operated day boats will continue their steady demise and the large fishing crews will be the only ones left. "We are in the final stage of a natural, national resource being converted into a private, corporately owned resource."

But a single predator or a few degrees' rise in the temperature of the water could wipe out all the lobster in any given area. Already the catch is shifting away from Stonington, says Carl Wilson, the lobster biologist for Maine's Department of Marine Resources. If the trend continues, the lobstermen who borrowed heavily to buy high-tech boats—younger men, mostly, who have known only gold-rush times—stand to lose everything.

The implications of this shift on the nation's table are huge. Seafood markets that offer a variety of wild fish now need to import it, so fish reach the market a day later at a much higher price. "In 1975 I got twenty-five cents a pound for groundfish," Mr. Bridges says. "If you can find it you can get $2 to $4 a pound today." Consumers, he noted, pay about three times what the fisherman receives.

After a good hour of impassioned discussion and lobster shucking, the fishermen gather around the reddening lobster in the skillet. Their thick fingers look like the hands of giants arranging a smaller, entirely manageable world.

SEAFOOD WATCH

OVER THE PAST THREE DECADES, FISHERMEN, BIOLOGISTS, AND FINALLY THE PUBLIC have realized that the convergence of pollution, erosion, water diversion, changes in water temperature and salinity, and overfishing have left the nation's wild fisheries dangerously depleted. Many believe that fish farming is the only solution, but the narrow gene pool of a hatchery-based fish population is no match for the genetic diversity of a healthy, wild-spawning one. Federal and state regulations have helped rebuild the nation's fisheries, but the fisheries that have made the most dramatic comeback are those like Maine lobster that are regulated by the local fishermen themselves.

The size and health of particular fisheries shifts constantly, and in an effort to help consumers make informed choices at the fish market, the Monterey Bay Aquarium began issuing "Seafood Watch"—small pocket guides that help consumers avoid endangered species and buy the fish that are most plentiful in a given region. The guides are updated frequently and are available at www.montereybayaquarium.org.

DICK BRIDGES'S LOBSTER CHOWDER

According to Dick Bridges, the Chowder King, the sweetness of evaporated milk is the key to balancing the brine in the chowder and accentuating the sweetness of the lobster meat. Many traditional New Englanders prefer the canned milk to fresh cream, but Bridges tends to combine the two. When he and his fellow fishermen get together to assemble "chowdah" for a hundred, he uses his thirst instead of a clock to gauge cooking times. "One beer, the onion and water and potato are done. Another beer, the base is simmered. A third beer, the lobster is done and so are you."

229

8 tablespoons (1 stick) unsalted butter

1 medium onion, chopped in ½-inch dice

6 cups lobster broth or cold water

3 large russet potatoes, peeled and cut into ½-inch cubes

Kosher salt and freshly ground black pepper

5 pounds steamed and shelled lobster, claws intact, tails cut in large bite-size pieces

Three 12-ounce cans evaporated milk

1 teaspoon dried basil

1 cup milk or cream, if necessary

1. In a Dutch oven over low heat, melt 2 tablespoons of the butter. Add the onion and cook, stirring occasionally, until soft, about 5 minutes. Add the broth, potatoes, ½ teaspoon salt, and ¼ teaspoon pepper and bring to a simmer. Cook about 30 minutes, until the potatoes begin to soften.

2. Meanwhile, in a large skillet over medium-high heat, melt 2 more tablespoons butter. Add about one-third of the lobster and cook about 1 minute. Transfer to a bowl and set aside. Repeat with remaining butter and lobster.

3. Stir the lobster, evaporated milk, and basil into the onion and potato mixture and simmer over medium heat until heated through. Season with salt and pepper to taste. If mixture is too thick, add milk or cream. Serve.

SERVES 12

From Sea to Shining Sea: Fish and Shellfish

COD

WHEN THE FIVE-FOOT-LONG WOODEN CARVING CALLED *THE SACRED COD* **WAS** originally hung in the Massachusetts State House more than two hundred years ago, it was a symbol of the importance of the fish to the state's economy: Fortunes were made on cod in New England. Even today, when older cooks along the country's Eastern coastline recall the everyday dish of their youth, it is nearly always some variation on salt fish, pork fatback, onion, and potato. And rare is the ethnic group that lacks its own particular twist on salt cod, be it stewed, fried in chunks, turned into cakes or croquettes, or creamed with garlic and potatoes in the manner of the French brandade.

But the cod supply, as well as its financial importance, began waning in the mid-1800s, and the advent of flash freezing and refrigeration also changed the salt cod economy. Today cod and its closest family members—Atlantic pollock, cusk (which is sold as scrod), haddock, hake (also sold as whiting)—are far less plentiful and more likely to be eaten fresh. They swim in cold water, close to the bottom of the ocean, and are generally lean, white, flaky, and delicately flavored. They can be sautéed, fried, grilled, poached, braised, baked, or broiled.

ELMER BEAL'S
CORNED HADDOCK IN LEMON CREAM SAUCE

Elmer Beal never wanted anything more than to eat his mother's finnan haddie and to follow his family onto the Maine waters. His great-grandparents were lighthouse keepers; his grandfather and father were fishermen and fish dealers. Dr. Beal, a professor of anthropology at the College of the Atlantic, began working on the family dock at age 14. Somewhere between college, the Peace Corps, and graduate school, he became less enamored with catching fish and more with cooking them.

When Dr. Beal returned home to teach, he found Mt. Desert Island transformed. "There was French on the menus," he says. The old Yankee fare that his mother and her mother and *her* mother had cooked—cod boiled with fatback and potatoes, smoked cod simmered with potatoes and cream—was suddenly difficult to find. He married Allison Martin, a culinary school graduate, and together they opened Burning Tree, a seasonal restaurant that was widely praised for its spare, modern ways of cooking local ingredients.

Shortly after his daughter was born, he was at the fish market when he found himself nostalgic for the pickled mackerel or hake and salted fish and smoked fish. He also noted that customers were asking the fishmonger to "corn" (or lightly salt) their fish. The light coating would be wiped off in several hours. "They weren't preserving the fish. They were gesturing toward a tradition, echoing a taste."

In his restaurant, he salts his fish fillets and makes his favorite dish—haddock, hake, or cod finished with a lemon cream sauce, served with steamed kale and boiled potatoes. The fish is fresh, not salted or smoked; the sauce is cream, not roux-thickened milk. But its resemblance to his mother's finnan haddie is impossible to deny.

Four 6- to 8-ounce haddock fillets, skin on

Kosher salt

2 cups heavy cream

3 tablespoons fresh lemon juice

Freshly ground white pepper

2 tablespoons (¼ stick) unsalted butter

1 tablespoon minced fresh dill

1 tablespoon minced fresh chives

1. Pat the fillets dry with a paper towel, sprinkle with 1 tablespoon salt, cover lightly with plastic wrap, and refrigerate.

2. Bring the cream and the lemon juice to a simmer in a saucepan over medium-low heat and cook, stirring occasionally, until the mixture measures about 1 cup, 7 to 10 minutes. Stir in ¼ teaspoon salt and ⅛ teaspoon white pepper. Season with salt and white pepper to taste, cover, and set aside to keep warm.

3. Thoroughly wipe the salt from the fish with a paper towel. Melt the butter in a large skillet over medium-high heat. When it is melted, raise the heat to high and carefully slide the fish into the pan, skin side down. Cook until the skin is well browned, 3 to 5 minutes. Carefully turn over and cook for 3 to 5 minutes longer, until the fish is starting to flake.

4. Carefully transfer the fillets to plates. Spoon the sauce over them, sprinkle with the dill and chives, and serve.

SERVES 4

K. D. Copeland-Baum's
Braised Laotian Fish

JAMAICA PLAIN, MASSACHUSETTS

Kham Dao Copeland-Baum, a midwife and passionate home cook: "My mother came to this country when she was sixteen years old. Her parents stayed in Laos, so my mother and her brother came alone, and Jewish Family Services helped them. My mother cooked in a fancy restaurant in Back Bay.

"At home she would only cook Laotian food and Thai food, even for breakfast. When we played in the backyard, my friends would sniff-sniff the air and make faces. I hated Laotian food—until I went to Paris for my junior year abroad. Two of my roommates were French. I asked them to teach me to cook. They wanted me to teach them Laotian cooking, so I learned to cook from my mother on the telephone, which she thought was hilarious, since all I'd ever done was beg her to order pizza."

2 tablespoons coconut or vegetable oil

2 shallots, sliced thin

1-inch piece galangal or fresh ginger, peeled and thinly sliced

One 4-inch stalk lemongrass, white part only, minced

2 kaffir lime leaves, center rib removed and sliced thin, or 1 teaspoon grated lime zest

1 Thai chile, stemmed, seeded, and minced

8 to 12 mussels, scrubbed and debearded (or littleneck clams)

2 teaspoons Thai fish sauce

Four 1-inch-thick 6- to 8-ounce cod or other mild white fish fillets

2 tablespoons minced fresh cilantro

2 tablespoons fresh lime juice

2 tablespoons coconut cream (see Note), frozen and cut into small chunks

1 tablespoon unsalted butter, cut into small chunks and chilled

1 tomato, peeled, seeded, and cut into small chunks

2 teaspoons fresh minced chives

1. In a shallow saucepan, heat the oil over high heat until very hot. Add the shallots and stir frequently for 1 minute, until they begin to turn golden brown. Stir in the galangal and cook for 1 minute. Stir in the lemongrass, lime leaves, and chile. Add 1 cup water, the mussels, and the fish sauce, cover, and cook until the mussels are just open. Using tongs, remove them, shaking each to leave as much broth as possible in the pot, and transfer to a bowl to keep warm.

2. Add the fish and add enough water to come halfway up the sides of the pan. Reduce the heat to medium-low, cover, and simmer for 10 to 12 minutes, until the fish flakes easily. Carefully transfer to warm plates.

3. Strain the broth through a fine-mesh strainer into a saucepan and boil over high heat until the liquid is reduced to about 2 cups. Stir in the cilantro and lime juice, then whisk in the coconut cream and butter, a chunk at a time, until the sauce is slightly thickened. Stir in the tomato and season with fish sauce to taste. Arrange the mussels on the plate with the fish, spoon the sauce over the fish, sprinkle with chives, and serve.

SERVES 4

NOTE: To make the coconut cream, open a can of unsweetened coconut milk and place in the refrigerator. The solid "cream" will rise to the top. Gently remove the desired amount and put in freezer for 15 to 20 minutes.

ANDY'S OVEN-BRAISED BUTTERY FISH

PORTSMOUTH, NEW HAMPSHIRE

"Growing up in the south end of Boston, fish was Friday, fish was Lent, and fish was always fried. The frying told you what day of the week it was—everything else we ate was boiled," Andrew Bulger said. "When I first started practicing law, I went to cooking school at Madeleine Kamman's Modern Gourmet out in Newton, Massachusetts. I wanted to meet women, which was not a bad idea, except that as soon as I walked in the door, all I could think about was food. Ms. Kamman was lightening French classics, using cream reductions, cold butter or vegetable purees instead of flour to thicken sauces. I tasted something like this dish my first day in class and it changed my life. My wife—whom I met at Fenway Park, not at cooking school—has never stopped asking me to make it for company meals. You can put the whole thing together before guests arrive, have it in and out of the oven in ten minutes." Cod, haddock, scrod, or a thick cut of flounder are the best fish for this dish. Mr. Bulger serves the dish with steamed asparagus and boiled potatoes or a potato puree.

4 tablespoons (½ stick) unsalted butter, cold

4 leeks, white parts only, sliced into ½-inch rings, cleaned well and drained

Kosher salt and freshly ground white pepper

1½ cups dry white wine or vermouth

2 cups water

Four 6- to 8-ounce cod fillets, 1 inch thick

2 tablespoons minced fresh parsley

1 tablespoon minced fresh chervil

1 tablespoon fresh lemon juice

1. Preheat the oven to 400°F. Melt 2 tablespoons of the butter over medium-low heat in a shallow, ovenproof pan with a tight-fitting lid. Add the leeks, a handful at a time, stirring between each addition until they are all in the pan. Add a pinch of salt and a pinch of white pepper and cook, stirring often, about 3 minutes, until the leeks begin to soften. Add 1 cup of the wine, raise the heat to medium-high, and simmer until nearly evaporated. Combine the remaining ½ cup wine and water, add half of the mixture to the pan, and bring to a simmer. Remove the pan from the heat and set aside.

2. Pat the fillets dry with a paper towel and season with ½ teaspoon salt and ⅛ teaspoon white pepper. Arrange them on top of the leeks and pour in the remaining liquid until it reaches halfway up the sides of the fish. (Add additional water if necessary.) Divide 1 tablespoon of the remaining cold butter into four pieces and place one in the center of each piece of fish. Sprinkle with half of the parsley and half of the chervil, cover, and place in the oven for 10 minutes.

3. Remove the pan from the oven and carefully transfer each fillet to a warm dinner plate. Using a slotted spoon, remove the leeks, draining them well into the pan, and place on each piece of fish. Strain the remaining cooking liquid through a fine-mesh strainer into a saucepan and boil over high heat until reduced to about ½ cup. Remove from the heat and, working quickly, whisk the remaining 2 tablespoons butter into the sauce. Stir in the remaining parsley and chervil, and the lemon juice, and season with salt and white pepper to taste. Spoon the sauce over the fish, and serve.

SERVES 4

NEW BEDFORD: THE UNITED NATIONS OF FISH

SINCE THE EARLY 1700S, NEW BEDFORD, MASSACHUSETTS, HAS OFFERED UNLIMITED opportunities for people willing to labor as stevedores or deckhands or as cutters or packers in the fish-processing plants. Emissaries from a dozen different cultures drifted along the town's slippery cobblestones even before the young Herman Melville boarded his whaling ship. The Native American Wampanoag were joined by the British, who were in turn joined by West Africans, Irish, and Portuguese; and from Cape Verde; Poles and Scandinavians soon followed. And in addition to the steady hard work of harvesting whale oil, there was reason to dream of the geysering fortune that could be made with the perfectly aimed harpoon. When steam power and kerosene began replacing whale oil, Eastern European Jews flocked to the area to help build and run the textile mills that sprouted along the Acushnet River.

Today, the fishing industry is a shadow of its former self, but New Bedford remains the most diverse fishing town in America. Demographers estimate that 36 percent of the population in New Bedford are Portuguese, and that French, Bosnians, Russians, West Africans, Guatemalans, Mexicans, and Puerto Ricans comprise another 39 percent. Like the immigrants who preceded them, most arrived ready for backbreaking labor and made the most of whatever they found or could afford.

Although much commercial fishing has collapsed, enough seafood is landed locally to supply an affordable, pristine staple to the town's 90,000 citizens. In New Bedford, unlike many places in the United States, the cultural groups remain distinct. The local cooking tended to remain "old country" for at least a generation before New World ingredients, concepts, and techniques began to change it—sometimes for the better and sometimes not. "People who want to be like everyone else go someplace else," says Laura Orleans, the founder and director of the Working Waterfront Festival held every fall. Under the hands of New Bedford's best home cooks, fillets or steaks cut from the same fish are a quick course in food anthropology as well as a dizzying—and delicious—world tour.

LOAF

SALAD

A LA AIDA

NEW ENGLAND DINNER

EN CASSEROLE

PIE

A LA KING

SANDWICHES

One Big Table

BARBARA MEDHAUG'S NORWEGIAN SEI BIFF, REDUX

Barbara Medhaug is the daughter and granddaughter of Norwegian fishermen. Her cousin, uncle, and husband are also fishermen. "All the Norwegians in New Bedford are related," she says. "Everyone fishes, everyone cooks, everybody goes to the Lutheran church over on the hill."

They also enjoy tucking into a plate of sei biff, fried Atlantic pollock in a beef gravy enriched with sour cream. But Mrs. Medhaug, who is 82 years old and one of the grande dames of New Bedford's Norwegian community, does not. "I came to hate fish because that's most of what we ate," she says. She wasn't big on Norwegian cooking, either, and so, nearly seventy years ago began collecting more adventuresome recipes.

At first each magazine clipping and handwritten index card was a postcard from a world larger than the one she knew. After she married, each was a challenge: Just how daring could she be before local tongues began to wag? She dared a little, attitudes toward food loosened, and eventually Mrs. Medhaug was regarded as one of the best cooks in town. But today she is increasingly drawn to the recipes she once disdained. Here, for instance, Mrs. Medhaug imagines a modern iteration of sei biff that is stylish enough for a company meal, yet robust enough to make a fisherman eager to get home for dinner.

FOR THE ONIONS

2 tablespoons (¼ stick) unsalted butter

2 large onions, halved and sliced thin

Kosher salt and freshly ground black pepper

FOR THE SAUCE

2 cups homemade beef broth or low-sodium store-bought beef broth

2 tablespoons sour cream

Kosher salt and freshly ground black pepper

FOR THE FISH

1 cup all-purpose flour

Four 6- to 8-ounce skinless Atlantic pollock, cod, hake, or halibut fillets

Kosher salt and freshly ground black pepper

2 tablespoons olive oil

1. To make the onions: Melt the butter in a large skillet over medium-low heat. Add the onions, a handful at a time, ½ teaspoon salt, and ¼ teaspoon pepper. Cook, stirring occasionally, for 15 to 20 minutes, until the onions are light brown. Transfer to a bowl, cover, and keep warm.

2. Bring the broth to a simmer in a saucepan over medium-high heat. To cook the fish: Place the flour in a shallow dish. Pat the fish dry with a paper towel and season with ½ teaspoon salt and ¼ teaspoon pepper. Heat the oil in a large nonstick skillet over medium heat. Working with one fillet at a time, dredge in the flour, shaking to remove any excess, then carefully slide the fish into the skillet. Cook the fish for 3 to 5 minutes on each side, until golden brown. Transfer the fish to individual shallow bowls.

3. To serve, return the beef broth to a boil, then remove from the heat. Combine 2 tablespoons of the hot broth with the sour cream, then whisk the mixture into the remaining broth and season with salt and pepper to taste. Spoon the sauce over the fish, top with the caramelized onions, and serve.

SERVES 4

Armando and Cila Estudante's Portuguese Caldeirada

Unlike the Portuguese watermen who jumped ship in New Bedford nearly 200 years ago, Armando Estudante is not from the Azores; he grew up in Averia, once the largest fishing port in Portugal, where the cooking is considered lighter and more sophisticated. Unlike previous generations of immigrants, Mr. Estudante had graduated from college and was a captain in the merchant marine by the time he, his wife, Cila, and their infant daughter followed his parents to the United States in 1978.

Even so, he says softly, he remembers "walking the dock in the snow looking for work like the Central American guys do today." He struggled mightily to earn the money to buy his own fishing boat, which he named *Endurance*. Both at home and on the boat, he and his wife never stopped cooking the food they grew up on.

"We tried pizza once, but we are not big fans. We're the kind of people who stick to our food and our religion for life." The family version of caldeirada—the Portuguese equivalent of bouillabaisse—is, he says, unchanged. But then he catches himself and admits to having changed at least one ingredient.

"I fell in love with striped bass in America. It is wonderful. It is outrageous. It is one of the best fishes in the world. If I hadn't come to America I might not have ever known how delicious caldeirada made with striped bass could be." (The dish is also delicious made with mackerel, monkfish, cod, scup, or black sea bass.)

Portuguese Dory Fisherman, 4:30 in the morning (JOHN COLLIER, 1942).

236

One Big Table

2 cups dry white wine

2 cups water, fish broth, or clam broth

1 cup olive oil

2 teaspoons hot sauce (preferably homemade, or Frank's RedHot Sauce)

1 teaspoon paprika (preferably a Portuguese brand)

½ teaspoon ground turmeric

Kosher salt and freshly ground black pepper

3 large onions, sliced into ¼-inch-thick rings

5 medium potatoes, peeled and sliced ¼-inch thick

Four 6- to 8-ounce bone-in striped bass steaks

4 large ripe tomatoes, diced

12 garlic cloves, minced

3 bay leaves, crumbled

1 cup chopped fresh parsley

½ cup chopped fresh mint

1. Whisk together the wine, water, ¾ cup olive oil, hot sauce, paprika, turmeric, ¼ teaspoon salt, and ⅛ teaspoon pepper.

2. Heat the remaining oil over medium heat in a Dutch oven or a low, wide, heavy-bottomed pot with a tight-fitting lid. Add the onions, a pinch of salt, and a pinch of pepper and cook about 8 minutes, stirring occasionally, until soft. Pat the onions into a single layer in the bottom of the pan, arrange the potatoes on top, and season with salt and pepper.

3. Pat the fish dry with a paper towel and season with ½ teaspoon salt and ¼ teaspoon pepper. Carefully lay the fish on top of the potatoes, then sprinkle the tomatoes, garlic, and bay leaves over the fish. Stir the wine mixture, and then add enough of the liquid to reach above the middle of the fish, but not to cover.

4. Cover the pan and bring to a simmer. Reduce the heat to low and cook for 35 to 45 minutes, depending on the thickness of the fish, until the fish is flaky. While the fish is cooking, shake the pan vigorously a few times to even the cooking and add additional liquid as necessary to maintain its level.

5. When the fish is flaky, season the sauce with salt and pepper to taste, sprinkle the chopped parsley and mint over the top, and serve.

SERVES 4

From Sea to Shining Sea: Fish and Shellfish

Debra Ramirez's Guatemalan Tapado

Debra Ramirez was the only woman in the first group of Guatemalans to arrive in New Bedford. She cuts fish in a seafood processing plant, where she tries to ignore the heckling of more seasoned immigrants, and lives in constant fear of the "immigration men." She sends most of her earnings back to Guatemala for the care of her young daughter. She also watches the Food Network. Previous generations learned how to be Americans by reading newspapers and attending night school; today, English as a Second Language is often supplemented by regular doses of Cooking as a Second Language. If pressed, Ms. Ramirez will talk about her harrowing two-year journey from Latin America to New England. ("I suffered a lot. I went through hunger, I walked a lot, I slept on the sand in the desert when it was really cold, and terrible things happened that I would not desire on anyone.") But she prefers to talk about food—the daily wonder of having enough, the joy of cooking for her neighbors, the pleasure of being able to re-create dishes that she remembers from a happy week in her childhood when her family traveled to the beach.

In Guatemala, tapado, the classic fish stew, is a mix of seafood simmered in a coconut milk broth, seasoned with achiote, and generally served on mashed green plantains. In New Bedford, Ms. Ramirez reimagined the dish using ingredients she found in her adopted home.

4 tablespoons vegetable oil

1 pound extra jumbo shrimp (16 to 20 per pound), peeled and deveined, shells reserved

1 small onion, halved and sliced thin

1 red bell pepper, stemmed, seeded, and diced

2 celery stalks, diced

1 teaspoon smoked paprika

Kosher salt and freshly ground black pepper

3 medium tomatoes, peeled, seeded, and diced

2 tablespoons lemon juice

½ pound octopus or squid, cleaned and cut into bite-size pieces

1 pound mild white fish fillets, such as cod, hake, or a large flounder

½ pound fresh crab or lobster meat, or additional mild white fish

1 green banana, peeled and sliced into 1-inch chunks (optional)

1 to 2 teaspoons chili sauce (optional)

2 cups grated fresh coconut (optional)

¼ cup unsweetened coconut milk (optional)

¼ cup minced fresh cilantro

Cooked rice, for serving

1. Heat 1 tablespoon of the oil in a Dutch oven or other heavy-bottomed pot over high heat until very hot. Add the shrimp shells and cook, stirring frequently, for 2 to 4 minutes, until the shells are toasted. Add 2 quarts cold water, reduce the heat to low, and simmer uncovered for 30 minutes, until reduced to about 3 cups. Strain through a fine-mesh strainer, discard the shells, and reserve the remaining 6 cups broth.

2. Heat the remaining 3 tablespoons oil in the Dutch oven over low heat. Add the onion, bell pepper, celery, paprika, ¼ teaspoon salt, and ⅛ teaspoon pepper and cook for 3 minutes.

3. Stir in the shrimp broth, 2 of the tomatoes, and the lemon juice. Bring to a boil, reduce the heat to medium-low, and simmer for 10 minutes.

4. Add the octopus, stir, and simmer for 5 to 10 minutes, until it is tender. Add the fish and cook for 5 to 10 minutes, depending on its thickness, until octopus is tender and warm throughout.

5. Add the crabmeat, banana, if using, and the remaining tomato and cook for 3 minutes. Season with salt, pepper, and chili sauce to taste, then remove the pot from the heat, cover, and let sit for 5 minutes.

6. If using the fresh coconut and coconut milk, whisk them into the stew just before serving, along with the cilantro. Ladle the stew into bowls and serve with rice.

SERVES 4 TO 6

Lee Nakamura's Miso Slather

BERKELEY, CALIFORNIA

Lee Nakamura and Larry Fujita have owned the Tokyo Fish Market, a Berkeley institution, since 1963. This miso slather is one of their standbys. It highlights, rather than masks, the natural taste of fish and lends a subtle Japanese flavor. Mr. Nakamura invented the concoction for salmon steaks and fillets, but it is delicious on almost any fish that is to be broiled, grilled, or baked, and it does wonderful things for eggplant and summer squash as well. Mr. Nakamura serves miso-slathered fish with Matsutake Gohan (page 637), an equally simple rice and mushroom dish.

½ cup white miso

2 tablespoons mayonnaise

2 tablespoons sugar

2 tablespoons mirin

½ yuzu, juiced, or 2 tablespoons fresh lemon or lime juice

1 tablespoon grated fresh ginger

1 tablespoon rice vinegar

In a small bowl, stir together all of the ingredients. Slather generously on fish fillets or steaks and refrigerate overnight. Wipe most of the miso mixture off the fish, leaving just a thin layer, before broiling or grilling.

MAKES ABOUT 1¼ CUPS

GABE'S SPICY FISH RUB

Gabriel Ainslie's father was the cook in the family, and that didn't change when he divorced and started raising his sons alone. When Gabriel was very young, he would sit nearby and listen as his father made pork chops or salmon or pasta or sourdough bread. When Gabriel and his older brother could stand on a stool and reach the counter, they cooked with him. Gabriel learned to chop and mince and gradually "advanced through my dad's knife collection." He also advanced to more complex dishes, "usually dishes with prodigious amounts of garlic." Now a student, Gabriel uses this rub on shrimp, fish, and chicken, though most often on fish. "Fish is a good back note," he says, for a riff like this Middle Eastern–inspired spice mix that he makes fresh each time he uses it.

2 teaspoons whole cardamom pods

2 teaspoons whole cumin seeds

1 teaspoon whole fennel seeds

2 tablespoons red curry powder or paste

2 teaspoons cayenne pepper

1. In a medium dry skillet, toast the cardamom pods and cumin seeds over low heat, stirring constantly, for 3 minutes, until the spices are fragrant. Stir in the fennel seeds and toast, stirring constantly, for 30 seconds to 1 minute longer, until the spices are a shade darker. Pour the warm spices onto a plate and cool to room temperature.

2. In a spice grinder or clean coffee grinder, grind the toasted spices, red curry powder, and cayenne into a fine powder. Sprinkle onto fish fillets, fish steaks, or shrimp 5 minutes before grilling or broiling.

MAKES ABOUT ¼ CUP

CAJUN FISH RUB

Before Paul Prudhomme, there were two kinds of cooking in Louisiana. The Cajun cooking that the chef was raised on came from southern France. "The Acadians adapted their dishes to use ingredients that grew wild in the area—bay leaves from the laurel tree, file powder from the sassafras tree, and an abundance of different peppers . . . that grow wild in southern Louisiana," he writes in *Chef Paul Prudhomme's Louisiana Kitchen*. Creole cooking, on the other hand, "began in New Orleans and is a mixture of the traditions of French, Spanish, Italian, American Indian, African, and other ethnic groups. Seven flags flew over New Orleans in the early days, and each time a new nation took over . . . most of their cooks and other servants stayed behind . . . those cooks, most of whom were black . . . learned how to cook for a variety of nationalities, and they incorporated their own spicy, home-style way of cooking into the different cuisines of their employers."

There is still a distinction between Cajun and Creole cooking in Louisiana homes, but Mr. Prudhomme began referring to the two together as "Louisiana cooking." His primary messenger was blackened redfish, a small drum fillet that was pan-fried in butter with a whole lot of spices until it was almost black. By the mid-1980s, blackening wasn't a dish, it had become a concept. Chicken, pork, beef, vegetables—everything was blackened, which, in places other than K-Paul's kitchen, often meant burned beyond redemption.

This adaptation of his spice mix is designed to be rubbed into fish before adding a thin pat of butter and grilling or broiling.

2 tablespoons paprika

5 teaspoons kosher salt

2 teaspoons onion powder

2 teaspoons cayenne pepper

1 teaspoon minced fresh thyme

1 teaspoon dried oregano, crumbled

In a small bowl, stir together all of the ingredients. Sprinkle onto fish fillets, fish steaks, or shrimp 5 minutes before grilling or broiling.

MAKES ABOUT ⅓ CUP

EPHRAIM O'NEILL

"I GOT TO HAVE MY FISH. YOU TAKE MY FISH AWAY AND I AM going to starve. Mullet in the summer when they are fat. Boil it, bake it, fry it. And ole drum? You can make anything out of ole drum, you can even make codfish cakes out of that fish," says Ephraim O'Neill, a former fishing boat captain in Hatteras, North Carolina. "Drum stew's my favorite. My wife makes the best in the world. You eat her drum stew and you want to holler for a pillow and slide under the table. It's like a shot of ether to have a belly full of drum stew."

Sicilian Braised Monkfish

Mary Ann Genovese, a marketing executive in Boston, still lives in Gloucester, where her parents, Dominic and Angela Sanfilippo, settled in the early 1960s. Like many Sicilian émigrés, they worked tirelessly to re-create the daily rhythms and meals of their hometown, Porticello. Mr. Sanfilippo fished just as his ancestors had and, like thousands of Sicilian wives before her, Mrs. Sanfilippo produced extraordinary feasts for her family every day. Her American-born children were not always impressed. "I thought that I wanted peanut butter and jelly instead of salumeria on bread for lunch," says Ms. Genovese, adding, "and hamburger instead of fish for dinner."

Her parents even brought Sicily with them on vacations. "When they took us to Bermuda, my father brought his rod and reel and fished off the pier. He came back with a full bucket and filled the bathtub in our fancy hotel with these tiny fish. Then he talked the chef into cooking up a fritto misto for our dinner."

Mrs. Sanfilippo was the driving force behind the Gloucester Fishermen's Wives Association, which has become a vibrant activist group. Her recipe for braised monkfish, a wintertime staple of her childhood home, is in the association's cookbook, *The Taste of Gloucester: A Fisherman's Wife Cooks,* which she edited.

But Mrs. Sanfilippo learned that the association's success could be bittersweet. Their efforts in the 1980s to promote "garbage fish" like then-plentiful monkfish caused overfishing; today monkfish is considered a collapsing fishery. Her recipe is now a special-occasion dish, and at the Fishermen's Wives' fund-raisers, it draws crowds. Mrs. Sanfilippo expects her daughter, Ms. Genovese, to cook at her side.

Ms. Genovese is happy to comply. Once a fisherman's daughter, always a fisherman's daughter. She is inflexible about her ingredients—"I won't buy fish from somebody I don't know, and I won't buy farmed fish, it's got no flavor"—but easygoing in the kitchen. "In our family, we don't use recipes or measures, we just throw things in there and see how it comes out." The other lesson she's learned from her mother is "the simpler the better. Our monkfish takes only a few ingredients, but once people taste it, they just can't get enough."

1 tablespoon extra virgin olive oil

2 celery stalks, chopped fine

1 medium onion, chopped fine

1 large carrot, chopped fine

Kosher salt and freshly ground black pepper

½ cup minced fresh parsley

1 ripe plum tomato, chopped fine

2 pounds monkfish tail, cut into 1½-inch chunks

Italian bread, cooked rice, or risotto, for serving

1. Heat the oil in a large skillet over medium heat. Add the celery, onion, carrot, ¼ teaspoon salt, and ⅛ teaspoon pepper and cook about 6 minutes, until the vegetables are soft. Stir in the parsley and tomato and cook for 2 to 3 minutes longer.

2. Pat the fish dry with a paper towel and season with salt and pepper. Add to the pan with the vegetables, cover, and braise the fish in its own juices over medium-low heat for 10 to 12 minutes, until it begins to flake apart. Serve with a good loaf of Italian bread, or over rice or risotto.

SERVES 4 TO 6

PAULO'S MONKFISH MOQUECA

MARTHA'S VINEYARD, MASSACHUSETTS

Since the eighteenth-century whaling days, there has always been seasonal work on Martha's Vineyard, and for almost that long, those jobs have been claimed every summer by an ever-changing cast of immigrants. Young Brazilians began to arrive in 1993, and 17-year-old Paulo Sergio Ferreira was among that first group. Like many, he washed dishes and bussed tables; unlike many, he fell in love with cooking (and Vineyard life) and quickly rose through the restaurant ranks. More than fifteen years later, he is the chef of the Vineyard Haven Yacht Club, where he and his staff turn out traditional Yankee fare. The real cooking, of course, happens when Mr. Ferreira builds dishes at home, such as his country's famous braised fish. He got the recipe from a relative in Bahia and adapted it to the fish from northern waters. Monkfish tail makes such a delicious moqueca that he wonders if the fish might have gotten lost in New England on its way home to Brazil.

One Big Table

One 2-pound monkfish tail, cleaned and scaled

6 garlic cloves

Kosher salt

¼ cup olive oil

¼ cup minced fresh parsley

¼ cup minced fresh cilantro

2 scallions, green and white parts, minced

1 teaspoon minced red chiles

2 red onions, diced

4 tomatoes, peeled, seeded, and diced

1½ cups unsweetened coconut milk

2 tablespoons fresh lemon juice

Steamed white rice, for serving

1. Use a sharp knife to make 12 evenly spaced ¼-inch incisions in the fish. Slice 4 of the garlic cloves into 3 slices each and insert them into the incisions. Pat the fish dry with a paper towel and season all over with 1 teaspoon salt.

2. Using a mortar and pestle, grind the remaining 2 garlic cloves with 2 teaspoons salt to make a paste. Moisten with a splash of the oil and stir in 2 tablespoons of the parsley, 2 tablespoons of the cilantro, 1 scallion, and the chiles.

3. Heat a Dutch oven or flameproof covered clay baking dish over low heat. Add the garlic mixture and cook for a few seconds, until fragrant, then quickly add the remaining oil. Add the onions and cook, stirring occasionally, for 5 minutes, until soft. Stir in the tomatoes, coconut milk, and lemon juice, place the fish on top of the vegetables, and cover. Simmer for 15 to 20 minutes, until the fish begins to pull away from the center bone.

4. Remove from the heat, sprinkle with the remaining 2 tablespoons parsley and 2 tablespoons cilantro, and season with salt to taste. Serve with steamed white rice.

SERVES 4

BOOMBASTIC'S SCALLOPS

Brian Borgeson grew up in Wayland, Massachusetts, and began fishing and digging clams when he was 4 years old. He sold his first striped bass when he was 17—"and it's been downhill ever since," he says. The owner (and seasonal resident) of the thirty-eight-foot charter boat *Absolute* is known as "Boomer," or "Boombastic." He is also a teller of tall tales, a hard-core bon vivant, an "extreme" sport fisherman, and a fine cook. "Being a cook is like being a fisherman: It's not something you want to be, it just happens." This dish just happened. "I think there wasn't much in the house except for the scallops. I drag for bay scallops in the fall. The grapefruit was a little out there. But when I tasted it—outrageous, over the top, a classic." The dish is so delicious that he's made it in the summer when bay scallops are not available, using sea scallops instead.

1½ pounds Nantucket Bay scallops or sea scallops

Kosher salt and freshly ground black pepper

4 tablespoons (½ stick) unsalted butter, cut into small pieces

Juice and grated zest of 1 grapefruit

1 tablespoon drained capers

1. Pat the scallops very dry with a paper towel and season with salt and pepper. In a medium nonstick skillet, melt 1 tablespoon of the butter over high heat until beginning to brown. Add the scallops without crowding and cook for 2 minutes on each side, until they form a rich golden brown crust. Transfer the scallops to four individual plates.

2. Remove the pan from the heat and stir in the grapefruit juice, scraping up any residue from the bottom of the pan. Return the pan to medium heat and whisk in the remaining butter, a few pieces at a time. Stir in the zest and the capers, pour the sauce over the scallops, and serve.

SERVES 4

245

From Sea to Shining Sea: Fish and Shellfish

JOSEPH AGRESTA'S STRIPED BASS ALLA VASSA

Joseph Agresta says, "My policy is do no harm. Catch the bass, fillet the bass, cook the bass. It's not hard. You can add a little something. My wife and I tried cutting small slits and slipping a slice of garlic in and then giving the fillet a little soak. Delicious. Couldn't be simpler. People were suspicious of that dusting of Parmesan. Heck, so was I—cheese and fish? Especially great fish?—but one taste and we were sold. It's perfect, just one of those things, don't ask. We make it all the time."

Four 6- to 8-ounce skin-on wild striped bass fillets

4 garlic cloves, thinly sliced

¾ cup fresh lemon juice (about 6 lemons)

2 tablespoons olive oil

1 tablespoon unsalted butter, melted

4 teaspoons grated Parmesan cheese

1. Preheat the oven to 450°F. With the tip of a paring knife, cut a few small slits in each piece of fish, then press a slice of garlic into each slit.

2. In a large shallow bowl, stir together the lemon juice, 1 tablespoon of the oil, and the butter. Place the fish in the marinade, turning to coat, then cover the bowl and refrigerate for 15 minutes.

3. Heat the remaining 1 tablespoon oil in a large, ovenproof nonstick skillet over medium-high heat. Remove the fillet from the marinade, letting the excess drip off. Cook them, skin side down, for 3 to 5 minutes, until crisp and golden brown. Sprinkle the Parmesan over the tops and bake for 5 to 7 minutes, until the flesh is opaque and a paring knife or skewer inserted into the thickest part penetrates with little or no resistance. Serve warm.

SERVES 4

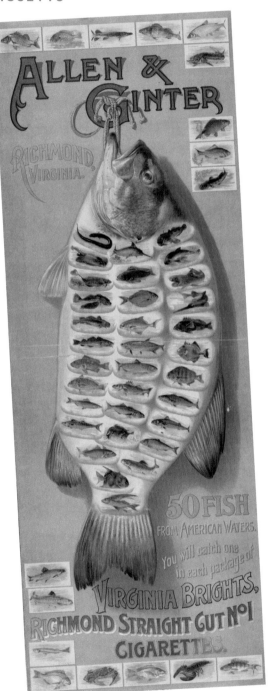

246

One Big Table

Tomas Obraitis's Armenian Mackerels

"Somebody said that if there were only twenty Armenians in the country, we'd find each other and create a world of our own. It is the way we are. There are over a million Armenian Americans in the United States. Sometimes I think they are all here in Fair Lawn; in fact, when we have dinner parties, I think that they are all in my house," says Tomas Obraitis, a stock analyst. "Usually, my wife and I cook more American food, but we cook Armenian and Middle Eastern food when we have company. This dish was originally for small whole mackerel: You stuffed them and then fried them. We changed the recipe because after you've lived in the United States for a generation you don't know what to do with a whole fish."

Bluefish, striped bass, and black bass also like this preparation, which Mr. Obraitis usually serves with sautéed eggplant and rice or couscous.

1 cup olive oil

3 large onions, chopped

Kosher salt and freshly ground black pepper

½ cup walnuts, crushed

2 tablespoons pine nuts

2 tablespoons currants

½ teaspoon ground cinnamon

½ teaspoon ground allspice

Five 4- to 6-ounce skinless mackerel fillets, 1 fillet finely chopped

2 large eggs

2 cups fine dry bread crumbs

½ cup minced fresh parsley

½ cup minced fresh dill

1. Preheat the oven to 400°F. Grease a shallow baking dish large enough to hold the fish in one layer.

2. Heat ¾ cup of the olive oil in a straight-sided skillet over low heat. Add the onions, ½ teaspoon salt, and ¼ teaspoon pepper and cook about 10 minutes, stirring occasionally, until light brown.

3. Stir in the walnuts, pine nuts, currants, cinnamon, and allspice and cook about 1 minute, until fragrant. Stir in the chopped fish and cook for 2 minutes, until no longer raw. Cover and keep warm.

4. In a shallow dish, lightly beat the eggs with a pinch of salt and a pinch of pepper. Place the bread crumbs in another shallow dish and toss with 2 more tablespoons of the oil, 1 tablespoon of the parsley, ¼ teaspoon salt, and ⅛ teaspoon pepper. Dip each fillet in the egg, the bread crumbs, and place in the baking dish. Bake about 10 minutes, until the bread crumbs are crisp.

5. Stir the remaining parsley and dill into the onion mixture and season with salt and pepper to taste. Spoon the warm onion mixture over the fish, and serve.

SERVES 4

DANIEL'S SEA BASS
WRAPPED IN CRISPY POTATO

NEW YORK, NEW YORK

By the late twentieth century, America's chefs, ingredients, and evolving cuisine were less easily dismissed by European masters. The response to Daniel Boulud's sea bass recipe was an early sign of the shift. Inspired by Paul Bocuse's red mullet fillet wrapped in a crust of shaved potatoes, Mr. Boulud created a dish using black sea bass and a sauce made from Barolo wine. In an earlier era, a chef who adapted a Gallic classic to American taste and ingredients—even a French-born one like Mr. Boulud—might have been greeted with disdain. Ah, but au contraire! Mr. Bocuse was so impressed that he dispatched the staff from his restaurant kitchen at Disney's Epcot Center to New York to learn Mr. Boulud's adaptation of his recipe.

"It was a turning point," says Mr. Boulud. "After the shock, I was flattered." The dish is a good one for company. The preparation is time consuming, but the entire dish can be assembled ahead of time, refrigerated, and then cooked after guests arrive.

FOR THE SEA BASS

Four 6- to 8-ounce skinless sea bass fillets, trimmed into 5- x 2-inch rectangles

1 teaspoon minced fresh thyme

Kosher salt and freshly ground black pepper

2 very large russet potatoes, peeled

3 tablespoons unsalted butter, melted

FOR THE SAUCE

1 tablespoon olive oil

3 shallots, minced

1 cup thinly sliced white mushrooms

1 sprig fresh thyme

1 cup homemade chicken broth or low-sodium store-bought chicken broth, plus more as needed

One 750-ml bottle dry red wine, such as Barolo

1 tablespoon heavy cream

8 tablespoons (1 stick) unsalted butter

Pinch of sugar

Kosher salt and freshly ground black pepper

FOR THE LEEKS

2 tablespoons (¼ stick) unsalted butter, melted

2 leeks, white parts only, thinly sliced

1 tablespoon minced fresh chives

1. To make the fish: Pat the fillets dry with a paper towel and season with the thyme, ¼ teaspoon salt, and ⅛ teaspoon pepper. Trim each potato lengthwise to remove the rounded sides, but leave the tips of the potatoes intact. Using a mandoline, slice each potato lengthwise into 16 very thin, long slices. Toss the potato slices with the melted butter, ¼ teaspoon salt, and ⅛ teaspoon pepper.

2. Place a 10-inch-square piece of parchment paper on the counter. Arrange 8 of the potato slices on the parchment paper to make a rectangle at least 5 inches wide, overlapping the slices by about ½ inch. Place the fish in the middle of the potato rectangle and fold the edges of the potatoes over the fish to enclose it completely. Repeat the same process for the remaining fillets. Refrigerate for at least 2 hours.

3. To make the sauce: Heat the oil in a medium saucepan over high heat. Add the shallots, mushrooms, and thyme sprig and cook, stirring often, for 8 to 10 minutes, until the mushrooms are golden brown. Add the chicken broth, bring to a boil, and cook until the pan is almost dry.

4. Add the wine, bring to a boil, and simmer about 30 minutes, until the liquid is reduced to 2 tablespoons.

5. Stir in the heavy cream, butter, and sugar and season with salt and pepper as needed. Strain the sauce through a fine-mesh strainer and keep warm. (If the sauce is too thick, add a little chicken broth to thin it.)

6. To cook the leeks: Melt the butter in a large nonstick skillet over medium heat. Add the leeks, ¼ teaspoon salt, and ⅛ teaspoon pepper and cook for 4 minutes, until softened. Transfer to a bowl and keep warm while cooking the fish.

7. To cook the fish, wipe out the skillet with a paper towel, then melt the butter over medium-high heat. Add the fish packets and cook for 3 to 5 minutes on each side, until golden brown.

8. To serve, place a bed of leeks in the middle of four warm serving plates and ladle about 2 tablespoons of the sauce around the leeks. Place a piece of fish on the leeks and sprinkle each plate with minced chives. Garnish with fresh thyme sprigs. Serve.

SERVES 4

BLACK SEA BASS

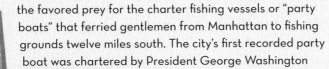

BLACK SEA BASS CAN BE FOUND FROM CAPE COD TO FLORIDA, but the densest populations have long been around New York, where it was the favored prey for the charter fishing vessels or "party boats" that ferried gentlemen from Manhattan to fishing grounds twelve miles south. The city's first recorded party boat was chartered by President George Washington and became so popular that woodcut posters like these were distributed. The fish, which typically weighs between one and three pounds, has a firm texture, a fine flake, snow-white flesh, and a rich, delicate flavor. It is surprisingly affordable and has long been the most common choice for whole-fish preparations in many Chinese restaurants. Two hundred years later, as fresh, wild-caught fish became sought after, chefs who had formerly been partial to Dover sole and wild-caught salmon began to discover the charms of sea bass.

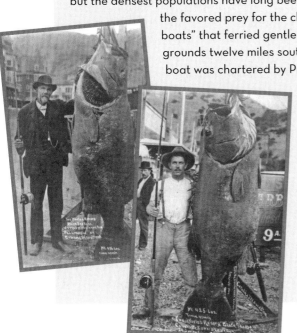

MRS. SUN'S BRAISED NEW YEAR'S SEA BASS

Cong Jingming Sun moved from China's Liaoning Province to Jackson Heights, Queens, nearly sixty years ago. She worked as a beautician and later as a seamstress and fitter in the Garment Center. In her neighborhood, where she is the girl who gave Eleanor Roosevelt a manicure and dressed "all the movie stars," she is also known for her cooking, and is especially famous for the sea bass that she makes for the Lunar New Year. She stuffs the fish with fatty Chinese ham and braises it until its flesh is warm and spicy and its skin has a shiny glaze that looks like wet lacquer.

"I didn't keep much from Liaoning Province," Mrs. Sun says. "I didn't want to. But I was careful with the things that I kept. I kept my grandmother's braised New Year's fish. If I hadn't left Liaoning Province, maybe it wouldn't be important. My sister stayed there and she makes the fish different every time. If I had stayed, I would be like my sister, I would not be so crazy to keep the bass exactly the same. But far away makes details matter more."

One 2-pound whole sea bass, cleaned

¼ pound Chinese ham or bacon, cut into 2-inch strips or chunks

2 cups sweet potato flour or cornstarch

½ to 1 cup peanut or vegetable oil

4 scallions, green and white parts, cut into 2-inch pieces

2 garlic cloves, smashed

1-inch piece fresh ginger, peeled and thinly sliced

¼ cup shaoxing wine or medium-dry sherry

3 tablespoons light soy sauce

1 tablespoon dark soy sauce

2 teaspoons sugar

1 piece star anise

1. Pat the fish dry with a paper towel. Use a sharp knife to make 3 to 4 diagonal 2-inch slices on each side of the fish. Stuff the ham or bacon into the cavity of the fish. Dredge the fish in the flour, coating evenly on both sides.

2. Heat a large wok or large skillet over medium heat. Add enough oil to reach a depth of ¼ inch. When the oil begins to smoke, carefully slide the fish into the wok and cook about 1 minute, until browned. Flip the fish over and cook for 1 minute longer, until browned on the second side. Transfer to a plate.

3. Pour off all but 1 tablespoon of the oil from the wok, add the scallions, garlic, and ginger, and stir-fry over high heat for 1 minute, until fragrant. Return the fish to the wok and add the wine, soy sauces, sugar, and star anise. Pour in enough water to cover the fish, bring to a simmer, and cook for 15 minutes, until the flesh of the fish is opaque. Transfer the fish to a large serving platter, pour the sauce over the top, and serve.

SERVES 4 TO 6

RACHELE'S HAITIAN SHAD
IN GREEN PEPPER SAUCE

Rachele Berthoumieux's recollections of her childhood in Haiti do not include warm memories of learning to cook in her mother's kitchen. In 1969, she said, her father, Roland, a captain in the Haitian Army, unsuccessfully attempted to stage a coup against the Duvalier dictatorship and was exiled to Guantánamo Bay; her mother, Solange, who was in the United States on vacation at the time, was not permitted to return home to her young daughter and son. "Aunt Lucienne hid us," Ms. Berthoumieux says. "We were lucky we weren't killed." The family was united eight years later in Brooklyn, New York. But Ms. Berthoumieux didn't learn her way around the kitchen until she was 20 years old, when she married a man whom she describes as "a really old-fashioned Haitian person" who made everything from scratch.

Today, she lives in a duplex in Baldwin, Long Island, with her parents, her two daughters in their twenties, and her 11-year-old son. Her mother prepares Haitian cuisine every day, but Ms. Berthoumieux, who is a nurse in Manhattan, cooks the traditional dishes to relax on the weekend with her children. One of their favorite dishes is Poisson Rose en Sauce, red snapper marinated in green peppers. In New York, however, the family likes to use Hudson River shad. "You can get red snapper anytime," she says, "but you can only get shad in the spring so it is special and also very delicate and delicious."

At home, Haitians abide by a single, island-wide rigid menu: Fish is always eaten with white rice and a pea porridge made from red beans or pureed pigeon peas. In America, Ms. Berthoumieux serves the dish with long grain white rice (she prefers the Madame Gougousse brand) and boiled plantains.

One 2- to 2½-pound side of shad

1 lemon, halved

½ green bell pepper, stemmed, seeded, and cut into 2-inch chunks

3 scallions, green and white parts, roughly chopped

1 garlic clove, peeled

Kosher salt and freshly ground black pepper

2 tablespoons olive oil

1 medium onion, chopped

1 tablespoon tomato paste

4 sprigs fresh thyme, tied in a bundle with kitchen twine

3 whole cloves

1 small dried red chile

1. Pat the fish dry with a paper towel. Place the fish in a shallow baking dish. Squeeze lemon juice over the fish, then rub with a lemon half.

2. In a blender or food processor, puree the green pepper, scallions, garlic, ½ teaspoon salt, and ¼ teaspoon black pepper until smooth. Pour scallion mixture over the fish and cover with plastic wrap. Marinate in the refrigerator for 2 hours or up to overnight.

3. In a large skillet, heat the oil over medium-high heat. Add the onion and cook for 5 minutes, until soft. Stir in the tomato paste. Place the fish on top and pour the marinade over the fish. Add the thyme, cloves, and chile, cover, and simmer over low heat for 20 to 25 minutes, until the fish is opaque. Discard the thyme, cloves, and chile, and serve.

SERVES 4

BERNIE'S PEELERS WITH FRIED TOMATOES

MACHEPONGO, VIRGINIA

Until the late nineteenth century, soft-shell crabs were strictly a regional specialty. Rising from their winter burrow in the crab grounds that run north from Tangier Island in Virginia to the Eastern Shore of Maryland, young blue crabs shed their outgrown shell. For a few weeks in late April or early May, the nascent new shell would remain thin, pliant—and edible. Cooking the crabs was a rite of spring on the Eastern Shore. Today, "peelers" are caught as far south as the Gulf of Mexico and as early as February, but these early risers have yet to alter the calendars of connoisseurs, who maintain that the sweetest, softest crabs with the cleanest taste come from the spongy, shallow flats along the eastern shore of the Chesapeake in Virginia and Maryland. Bernie Herman spent his summers in Northampton County on Virginia's Eastern Shore, and for him and his wife, Becky, soft-shell crabs on fried green tomatoes is a specialty in the 1720 farmhouse where they spend weekends and vacations. Instead of the conventional cornmeal, Dr. Herman likes the lightness of brown rice flour on his crabs. Using Sichuan peppercorns adds a sweet note to the fire. He's substituted canola oil for most of his preferred crab-fry medium—bacon fat. He omits the sugar from the fried green and fried red tomato recipes, and to get a thin, unbroken crust, turns his tomatoes only once.

12 slices fried green tomatoes or red tomatoes

12 small soft-shell crabs, apron and gills removed

2 cups brown rice flour

½ teaspoon ground Sichuan peppercorns

⅛ teaspoon fine sea salt

1 cup canola oil, plus more if needed

1 tablespoon bacon grease (optional, for flavor)

1. Prepare the fried tomatoes according to the chosen recipe but omit the sugar, and set aside. In a flat pan, combine well the brown rice flour, ground peppercorns, and sea salt and set aside. Place enough canola oil and, if using, a little bacon fat, in the bottom of a large cast-iron skillet to reach ¼ inch up the side. Place the skillet over medium-high heat.

2. When the oil is hot enough to cause a sprinkling of flour to sizzle immediately, quickly drag a crab through the flour mixture, turn over, repeat, and then shake gently to remove all excess flour. Immediately slide the crab into the oil and then continue dusting and frying. Work in batches; do not overcrowd the skillet. Sauté on one side for 2 minutes, turn, sauté on the second side for 1–2 minutes, and remove; place on top of brown paper bags or paper towels.

3. Place 3 fried tomato slices on each plate, top with a crab, and serve immediately.

SERVES 4

THE CEREMONY

AT THE DAY AT THE DOCKS FESTIVAL IN
Hatteras, a group of soft-spoken elders wearing bifocals and designer running suits were eager to talk about the fish they had caught, the fish they had cooked, and the fish they had eaten over the past eighty years on the Outer Banks of North Carolina. Their stories were dappled with references to "Mama," "Daddy," "the cook," "our girl." But when one of the women said, "But ole drum, now that just isn't right," the happy mood at the picnic table changed.

Red drum is North Carolina's state saltwater fish. It is also called redfish, channel bass, drum, and spot-tail, one of a big family of fish whose best-known members include black drum, croaker, kingfish, saltwater silver perch, white sea bass, and weakfish. Red drum that weighs less than ten pounds and is less than three years old is called redfish or puppy drum. Puppy drum is meaty and delicately flavored, and was the cheapest and most plentiful fish in the surf along the south Atlantic and Gulf coasts until Paul Prudhomme invented blackened redfish at his restaurant in New Orleans. Once it became famous, the cost of the fish jumped from pennies to dollars a pound, and within a decade, the wild stocks were seriously diminished.

Farmed versions helped fill the demand for smaller redfish. But generations of Outer Bankers considered the older, bigger drums to be the real prize. The reason for this is unclear. Old drum is a big, tough, sinuous fish, fine for slow-cooked soups or stews but otherwise not great eating. The passion for old drum may be historic. Or maybe it is born of the American belief that bigger is always better.

The fish generally weighs twenty to thirty pounds, but the largest on record (caught off Hatteras Island) tipped the scale at just over ninety-four. In 2007, George W. Bush designated redfish a protected game

fish and encouraged a ban on commercial harvest. To its aficionados, the president might as well have outlawed apple pie.

In the Outer Banks, people of a certain age speak longingly of old drum. Some are sad; others are angry; all considered eating the big old fish an inalienable right as well as an act of patriotism. Many have a Robin Hood tale of full moons and secluded coves and outrunning game wardens in order to bring "the old people" the fish they loved.

"We would like you to join us for The Ceremony," one courtly gentleman whispered. I didn't ask for details, but the following evening, as I approached his grand house, I wondered precisely what sort of "ceremony" this was. As I walked up to the back door, I heard muffled sounds not unlike the suck-giggle-shush noises that are sometimes overheard outside a room in which illegal substances are being smoked. Were the Elegant Elders up to no good?

Au contraire. "Welcome," whispered the Courtly Gentleman, who opened the door before I knocked. I stepped inside and an intense odor rolled over me. The place smelled like low tide and fried pig. The aroma became more pronounced as I followed my host through a long, darkened hallway toward a glowing doorway. The dining room was lit with at least 100 small candles. Dressed in evening attire, they were standing behind their chairs around the Chippendale banquet table looked as bright and expectant as they must have been at their first midnight cotillion. The chargers were silver, as were the eight pieces of flatware that flanked each place, and in the center of the table, a huge silver platter proudly held twelve thick white slabs of old drum. The platter was surrounded by bowls of boiled potatoes, chopped raw onion, chopped hard-cooked egg, and cubed and fried pork fatback. Six gravy boats contained hot grease; four silver castor sets held salt, pepper, and white vinegar. The precision of the table felt like an altar.

"I don't appreciate a society that outlaws my fish," murmured the Courtly Gentleman after helping me to my place near him at the head of the table. "Do we look like criminals? Should we have to worry about going to jail? Worry that our grandchildren would see our names in the paper? We're just a bunch of geezers keeping The Ceremony alive."

The gentleman on my right leaned toward me and whispered: "His daddy had a speakeasy. That old acorn hasn't fallen far from the oak."

The scrupulously scripted ritual of eating old drum began. Each person placed two boiled potatoes on his or her plate and used the fork at the far left to mash it. The next fork in was used for flaking the fish over the potato. This deconstructed fish cake was then topped with raw onion, chopped egg, and a mound of cracklings. Finally, a river of pork grease was poured over the entire arrangement. Some people sprinkled vinegar on old drum; others used salt and pepper. When everyone had completed building his stack of fish, a short prayer of thanksgiving was offered.

It took about the same time to eat old drum as it does to boil it: 90 to 120 minutes.

After all the evidence of the crime had been cleared from the table and the chess pie and demitasse had been served, the Courtly Gentleman said, "The driver will take you home." When I reminded him that I had my car, he smiled patiently and said, "You should not operate heavy machinery after The Ceremony."

Hidden dinners are a long tradition in the United States.
Here, a banquet table is set in the big new sewer in Waterloo, Iowa.

A WHARF OF THEIR OWN

THE OUTER BANKS OF NORTH CAROLINA IS A STRING OF FOUR BARRIER ISLANDS THAT
lie between Pamlico Sound and the Atlantic Ocean. Ocracoke, a dash of rock, dune, and sand, is the
southernmost island, accessible only by water and air. For hundreds of years it provided wayfarers from
Sir Walter Raleigh's colonists to the infamous pirate Blackbeard with a sheltered inlet. Many nationalities
have shaped the island's style, its distinct language (Ocracoke brogue), and its British-inspired, not-quite-
southern cuisine. As in many isolated corners of the United States, its home cooks are held to a high
standard.

About 800 people live on the island. Traditionally they caught grouper, croaker, snapper, bluefish,
flounder, cobia, tuna, mullet, old drum, puppy drum, mahimahi, sea trout, king mackerel, and shrimp—as
much as 50,000 pounds of seafood a day was brought to each of the town's four fish landing and cutting
houses—and they kept Ocracoke's buccaneer spirit alive. In the late nineteenth century, tourists began to
take the ferry from Hatteras to Ocracoke's charming fishing village, which curls almost completely around
its harbor, Silver Lake.

By 2005, with 1 million tourists arriving in Ocracoke each year, the cost of real estate soared, and
fishermen could no longer pay for the waterfront property needed to unload boats and cool, cut, and ship
each day's catch. The price of the last fish house was $425,000, far beyond even the collective means
of the island's seventy-five watermen. In December of that year, the last of the island's four fish houses
closed. Most of the fishermen got out of the business. The twelve who remained got creative: They formed
the Ocracoke Foundation. The fishing industry that beckoned a million tourists turned to the tourists to
save it. "Ocracoke is marketed as a traditional fishing village," said Vince O'Neal, a waterman who also
owns a restaurant on the island. "Even people who don't understand fishing have to realize that losing the
fish house is going to hurt tourism," he said, adding that "people come here to see the boats in the water,
crab pots stacked in the yard, the floats hanging in the trees, the gulls swooping down for scraps and
bycatch—and local fish on the menu."

The foundation members held fish fries and barbecues and ran raffles, wrote grant proposals, stalked
small business loans, worked second jobs, and used their boats to squire day-tripping sport fishermen out
to the fishing grounds. Their children collected donations at the Fourth of July Parade.

And within six months, the watermen had bought the last fish house in Ocracoke. They began landing
fish the next day, and several months later opened a retail shop to help support the operation. And
to the best of anyone's knowledge, they became the first group of commercial fishermen in the United
States to finance the purchase of a landing dock and cutting house in an area where waterfront property
commands top dollar from second-home buyers.

Even with their own fish house, the number of full-time commercial fishers on the island has dwindled
to ten. Twenty more have other jobs and work the water part time. All spend nearly as much time fund-
raising and retailing as they do hauling pots and setting nets. But at a time when fishing communities are
dwindling all around America, the "Hoi Toiders" of Ocracoke still share a common lineage and shared
destiny, and a taste for stewed blue crabs with "pie bread" (a kind of dumpling), pickled shrimp, and
barbecued mullet.

James Berry Gaskill's Barbecued Mullet

Every waterman has his own way to barbecue mullet, and this recipe, which was served at many of the fund-raisers that helped save the last fish house in Ocracoke, comes from waterman James Berry Gaskill. His wife, Ellen, calls barbecued mullet "a gathering recipe," one that is made for parties. "The men do the cooking outside," she says, "it's not a female job. We differentiate here."

The essential accompaniment, according to Mrs. Gaskill, is alcohol. Sliced cucumbers in vinegar and potato salad are the other traditional companions to barbecued fish. Whole smelts, sardines, or even small mackerel can be used in place of mullet. The recipe can also be used for fillets of full-bodied fish such as bass, bluefish, cod, haddock, or halibut. In this case, the fillet should be basted on both sides, wrapped in a foil packet, and grilled.

FOR THE VINEGAR

1¼ cups water

6 tablespoons white wine vinegar

¼ teaspoon cayenne pepper

⅛ teaspoon kosher salt

4 jalapeño chiles, quartered

FOR THE SAUCE AND FISH

½ cup ketchup

½ cup steak sauce, such as A1

2 tablespoons Worcestershire sauce

12 garlic cloves, peeled

Kosher salt and freshly ground black pepper

4 jalapeño chiles, quartered

Six 2-pound striped mullets (see Note), gutted and headed but not scaled

1. To make the vinegar: Bring the water, vinegar, cayenne, and salt to a boil in a nonreactive saucepan. Remove from the heat, add the jalapeños, cover, and cool to room temperature.

2. Transfer the vinegar to an airtight container and refrigerate overnight. Strain through a fine-mesh strainer into a clean container. (This makes about 1½ cups of hot pepper vinegar, enough to make three batches of fish barbecue sauce. The remainder can be refrigerated almost indefinitely and used as needed.)

3. To make the sauce and fish: Process ½ cup of the hot pepper vinegar, the ketchup, steak sauce, Worcestershire, garlic, ½ teaspoon salt, ¼ teaspoon pepper, and jalapeños in a food processor or blender to make a smooth paste.

4. Build a charcoal fire in the grill. While the charcoal is heating, split the mullets and press them flat, flesh side up, on a baking sheet.

5. Use a brush to slather both sides of the fish with the barbecue sauce. Place the fish on the grill, skin side down, cover partially, and cook for 5 to 15 minutes, until the fish is done. Serve the fish flesh side up and advise guests to remove the skin and pick the meat off the bones.

SERVES 6

NOTE: Striped mullets are also called "jumping" mullets.

SHRIMP

SHRIMP IS THE NATION'S FAVORITE SEAFOOD. AMERICANS EAT
1.5 million pounds of it a year, or 4.4 pounds per person. It is boiled,
breaded and fried, stuffed, baked, grilled, braised, and sautéed. Shrimp
are easy to overcook, but almost impossible to offend and adaptable
to almost any flavor. By most accounts, the nation's primary wild shrimp
fishery—a huge arc of ocean that runs from the Carolinas and across the
Gulf of Mexico—is healthy. Imported shrimp, however, cost far less. Nearly
90 percent of the shrimp eaten in the
United States comes from Thailand, China,
Indonesia, Ecuador, and Mexico, but
shrimp farming is growing in the
United States. Last year Arizona
produced more than 1 million pounds
of saltwater shrimp.

CREOLE SHRIMP

CHARLESTON, SOUTH CAROLINA

Everybody talks about the Creole shrimp in Charleston. A friend from the city had given me a list of great cooks and each told me, "Why, the best Creole shrimp is at my house," and then invited me to dinner. Usually, finding the "golden fleece" of an iconic recipe is a matter of tasting and listening. Americans have a weakness for the "new and improved," especially if the change puts their individuality and creativity on display. In New England, I tasted scores of different versions of chowder. In San Francisco, no two cioppinos were remotely alike. But every Creole shrimp I was served in Charleston tasted exactly like every other.

In an effort to explain this unusual phenomenon, I talked to local historians, food historians, and residents with long Charleston roots. Mrs. Vereen Huguenin Coehn, called "Miss Vereen" according to the custom, is 75 years old, and she is only a second-generation Charlestonian. But she has lived in the same house in the city's historic district since she was 5 years old. She knows the genealogy of all the old families and the dates of every ball and oyster roast, as well as who was there and what they wore. She also knows the origin of Charleston's singular shrimp.

"Why, that recipe came from Mrs. Herbert McNulta, née Kathryn Deeds, who owned the Brewton Inn with her husband!" she says. "The building is right there in historic Charleston downtown! It was a wonderful inn and it was quite famous for shrimp Creole. Mrs. McNulta gave the recipe to the Junior League to put in *Charleston Receipts*, their cookbook. Everybody uses *Charleston Receipts*. We just love to serve our local food and that book helps us maintain our traditions. We are just so fortunate."

Indeed, *Charleston Receipts* is the oldest Junior League cookbook in the country still in print. It was not the nation's first charity cookbook; the genre appeared during the Civil War and was usually an effort to raise money for widows and orphans. The first Junior League cookbook was published by the Minneapolis group in 1943 and the Charleston collection didn't appear until 1950. But the Charleston group marketed their book aggressively, and the attention it got sparked the growth of regional Junior League cookbooks across the country. No one is sure how many Junior League cookbooks have been published, but Susan Danish, the executive director of the Association of Junior Leagues International, says that together, the various books have sold at least 20 million copies.

Miss Vereen buys six copies at a time. "It tells about our lifestyle, our history, and really, the way we live through food," she says, adding, "we are so very fortunate and I just love to share our way of living."

Did her mother cook from the community book?

"She wrote it! She was the president of the Junior League! My mother was Mary Vereen Huguenin. Her people were French Huguenots and she wrote the book with one of her wonderful friends. I remember the committee in our kitchen. Even in those days many of the men loved to cook, and Mr. Elliot Hudson had a wonderful receipt for venison. Mrs. Stevens, who was in charge of testing the recipes, lived around the corner. There was a little brick wall between her house and our house, and the ladies joked about how they should cut a little gate in that wall for all the running back and forth they did. There are 750 recipes in that book!

"They got our Gullah artists to make drawings, they wrote poems. And they were totally committed to what used to be called 'getting the word out,' and is now called 'marketing.' Those women sent that book to every food editor and magazine in the country.

"Creole shrimp is another way to remember. We are so blessed to have such wonderful shrimp right here in our water. And the rice, of course, our rice is world famous. We are so fortunate to know how to cook our food just right. Mrs. McNulta was a wonderful lady."

4 tablespoons bacon fat or vegetable oil

Kosher salt and freshly ground black pepper

3 pounds extra jumbo shrimp (16 to 20 per pound), peeled and deveined

2 medium onions, finely chopped

2 celery stalks, finely chopped

1 green bell pepper, stemmed, seeded, and finely chopped

3 tablespoons tomato paste

One 28-ounce can diced tomatoes

1 teaspoon sugar

Cooked white rice, for serving

1. Heat 2 tablespoons of the bacon fat in a large skillet over medium-high heat. Pat the shrimp dry with a paper towel. Season with salt and pepper. Add the shrimp to the fat and cook for 2 minutes, until they begin to turn pink. Transfer the shrimp to a bowl.

2. Add the remaining 2 tablespoons bacon fat to the pan and heat over medium heat. Add the onions, celery, bell pepper, ½ teaspoon salt, and ¼ teaspoon pepper and cook for 15 to 20 minutes, stirring occasionally, until light golden.

3. Stir in the tomato paste and cook for 1 minute. Add the diced tomatoes and sugar, bring the sauce to a simmer, and cook, stirring occasionally, for 30 to 40 minutes, until thick.

4. Stir the shrimp into the sauce and cook for 1 minute, just until the shrimp are hot. Season with salt and pepper to taste, and serve with white rice.

SERVES 6 TO 8

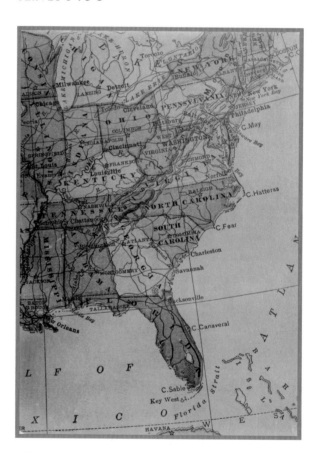

Map showing oyster and shrimp canneries of the Gulf and South Atlantic coasts (LEWIS HINES, 1913).

THE ONE AND ONLY, EVER-EVOLVING, LEGENDARY BARBECUED SHRIMP

Rare is the shrimp lover who has tasted barbecued shrimp at Pascal's Manale in New Orleans and not declared it the best shrimp dish in America. Its copious amounts of pepper and grease notwithstanding, however, there is nothing "barbecued" about the dish. Pascal Radosta, the restaurant's owner, based it on the description of a shrimp recipe that a regular customer tasted in Chicago in the early 1950s. Chances are, the customer tasted "scampi" (shrimp sautéed with garlic), and Mr. Radosta could not resist adding a Creole touch.

The family has guarded the recipe closely, but reliable sources (including me) have glimpsed the big pot at Pascal's Manale containing at least ten pounds of melted margarine that smelled as if it contained about a pound of black pepper, about half a cup of paprika (both sweet and hot), some bay leaves, and some whole garlic cloves. Unlike butter, some brands of margarine will stay emulsified and opaque when kept over low heat, and the stainless-steel vat appeared to be on a very low heat. There was a dipping basket nearby, which led me to conclude that the shrimp were dipped in the margarine and cooked only when they are ordered. Shrimp fat and the flavor from the shells and heads—Manale uses only shrimp with the heads still attached—gave more flavor to the oily bath. More oil was ladled over the shrimp after it was plated.

The best plate of Manale barbecued shrimp I ever had contained about a cup of oil. And over the past twenty-five years, as Americans have developed a taste for garlic, the amount used in the barbecued shrimp seems to have increased.

Many have tried to duplicate the recipe. Most have met with scorn, but two are credited with improving the dish as well as one's chances of avoiding coronary artery disease long enough to enjoy a second helping. The New Orleans restaurant Mr. B's Bistro uses butter instead of margarine, whisked in a little bit at a time to create an emulsion. And in an attempt to deliver flavor without cardiac arrest, chef Emeril Lagasse uses a concentrated broth made from shrimp shells to give the dish a deep flavor, and enriches it with heavy cream. More butter could, of course, be used instead of the cream.

This recipe borrows from those and other sources and has met with more approval than disapproval from Manale regulars. And that is about as good as it gets.

FOR THE SPICE BLEND

2½ tablespoons sweet paprika

2½ tablespoons hot paprika

2 tablespoons kosher salt

1 tablespoon garlic powder

1 tablespoon onion powder

1 tablespoon freshly ground black pepper

1 tablespoon cayenne pepper

1 tablespoon dried oregano

1 tablespoon dried thyme

FOR THE SHRIMP AND SAUCE

3 pounds extra jumbo shrimp (16 to 20 per pound), peeled and deveined, shells reserved

Freshly ground black pepper

6 tablespoons olive oil

1 small onion, chopped

6 garlic cloves, 2 left whole and 4 minced

3 bay leaves

Kosher salt

½ cup dry white wine

Juice and pulp of 3 lemons

3 cups water or shrimp broth

1 cup Worcestershire sauce

2 cups heavy cream

4 tablespoons (½ stick) unsalted butter, cut into 4 pieces and chilled

Biscuits, toast points, or fluffy white rice, for serving

1. To make the spice blend: In a small bowl stir together all of the ingredients. Measure out 2 tablespoons for the recipe. (The remainder can be stored in an airtight container for up to 6 months.)

2. To make the shrimp: Toss the shrimp with 1 tablespoon of the spice blend and 2 teaspoons pepper, cover, and refrigerate while making the sauce.

3. To make the sauce: Heat ¼ cup of the olive oil in a large skillet over medium heat. Add the reserved shrimp shells and cook, stirring constantly, about 30 seconds, until toasted. Stir in the remaining 1 tablespoon spice blend, the onion, all the garlic, the bay leaves, ½ teaspoon salt, and ¼ teaspoon pepper. Cook for 1 minute. Add the white wine and lemon juice and pulp, bring to a simmer, and cook for 3 minutes. Add the water and Worcestershire and bring to a boil. Reduce the heat to low and simmer for 1 hour, until the liquid is reduced by half.

4. Strain the sauce through a fine-mesh strainer, pushing on the solids with a wooden spoon to extract as much liquid as possible. Discard the solids. (The sauce can be refrigerated in an airtight container for 2 days or frozen for up to 2 months.)

5. About 20 minutes before serving, bring the sauce to a boil in a saucepan over high heat and cook until it is syrupy and reduced to about ¼ cup. Remove from the heat.

6. To serve, heat the remaining 2 tablespoons oil in a large skillet over medium-high heat. Add the shrimp and cook, stirring frequently, for 2 minutes, until just cooked through. Stir in the cream and the reduced sauce, then remove the pan from the heat. Using a slotted spoon, transfer the shrimp to a platter. Return the sauce to medium-high heat and whisk in the butter, 1 piece at a time. Pour the sauce over the shrimp and serve with biscuits, toast points, or fluffy white rice.

SERVES 6 TO 8

Peter's Saigon-Biloxi Shrimp

In 1975, Peter Nguyen's family left Vietnam and traveled a circuitous route, landing wherever church groups and missions offered housing to refugees—Guam, Oklahoma, Minnesota, Texas, Louisiana, and finally Biloxi, Mississippi. Like hundreds of others, they were drawn to the familiarity of fishing. Working as hands or headers, cutters or gutters, families like the Nguyens labored as French, Polish, and Slavic immigrants did before them.

Language barriers and suspicion from the local community made it hard to earn enough to live, much less to realize the dream each father had for his son: owning a boat of his own. But when he was 20, Mr. Nguyen made his father proud. The 1990s brought rich harvests that commanded high prices. Then in 2005, Hurricane Katrina devastated piers and boats, and, like many, Mr. Nguyen could not afford to rebuild and fish again. He went to work at the Mississippi-Alabama Sea Grant Consortium. Vietnamese fishers make up 70 percent of the state's shrimp industry, and Mr. Nguyen translates their concerns to the consortium, which is working to maintain Mississippi's fishing industry.

When it comes to Gulf shrimp, Mr. Nguyen is a true believer. "You won't get better, sweeter-tasting shrimp anywhere else. You do a recipe with Gulf shrimp and some other shrimp. Same recipe, different shrimp. You see with your own eyes, taste with your own mouth which is better." This recipe he just "made up" based on memories, and it has become a family favorite.

2½ pounds extra colossal Gulf shrimp (about 10 per pound)

⅓ cup palm or granulated sugar

¼ cup fish sauce

¼ cup fresh lime or lemon juice

¼ cup minced fresh Thai basil, mint, or cilantro

1 tablespoon vegetable oil

1 garlic clove, minced

1 to 2 Thai chiles, stemmed, seeded, and minced

1. Using a paring knife, cut through the back shell of each shrimp and remove the dark vein. Run your forefinger between the shell and flesh of each shrimp, separating but not removing shell from flesh.

2. In a large bowl, whisk the sugar, fish sauce, lime juice, basil, oil, garlic, and chiles together until the sugar is dissolved. Place shrimp and marinade in a large zipper-top plastic bag. Squeeze out the air, seal, and shake to coat the shrimp evenly. Refrigerate for 4 hours, turning the bag every 30 minutes.

3. To cook the shrimp, heat a charcoal or gas grill to high. Remove the shrimp from the marinade. Grill, turning frequently, for 2 to 3 minutes, until evenly pink and golden on both sides. Serve, passing a bowl for the shells at the table.

SERVES 6

George Billiris's Tastier Snapper

George Billiris has been called "the Patriarch," "the sponge man," and "the old man of the sea." Sponge diving is dangerous and exhausting, but the Greeks have sponge-fished for centuries. His grandfather, a fourth-generation sponge diver, emigrated from Piraeus in 1904, shortly after sponge was discovered in Tarpon Springs. The new opportunities brought thousands of Greeks to the Gulf coast of Florida in the decades that followed.

By the 1920s, the Billirises were among the leading spongers in Tarpon Springs; they built a sponging exhibition for tourists, a deep-sea fishing company, and a cruise boat company called the St. Nicholas Boat Line. Disease has since wiped out sponge beds, and synthetic sponges have greatly diminished demand, but Mr. Billiris is still involved in the distribution of natural sponges all over the world.

But if the sponges have diminished, the Greeks have multiplied: 10 percent of Tarpon Springs is said to be Greek—one of the highest percentages of any American city. "Obviously all your restaurants are Greek," Mr. Billiris says. "All the homes, the Greek homes, they stay with their Greek food." Like this fish recipe that has been passed down through his family for generations, the cooking is simpler than other cuisines. And yet, he says, "For some reason or another, it's tastier."

⅓ cup extra virgin olive oil

10 garlic cloves, chopped

2 tablespoons fresh lemon juice

1 tablespoon fresh oregano

2 teaspoons fresh mint

½ teaspoon kosher salt

¼ teaspoon freshly ground black pepper

Four 6- to 8-ounce red snapper fillets

1. Preheat the oven to 400°F. Grease a baking dish large enough to hold the fish in one layer. In a blender or food processor, process the oil, garlic, lemon juice, oregano, mint, salt, and pepper until smooth.

2. Pat the fish dry with a paper towel, then arrange in an even layer in the baking dish. Spoon all but 1 tablespoon of the oil mixture over the fish, turning the fish to coat evenly. Bake for 10 minutes. Baste the fillets with the pan juices, flip them over, and bake for 5 to 10 minutes more, until the fish is still firm but starting to flake. Spread with the reserved 1 tablespoon oil mixture, and serve.

SERVES 4

Shanaz Haghanifar's Persian New Year Fish

GAINESVILLE, FLORIDA

Shanaz Haghanifar says that she learned to cook by trial and error. The errors occurred in the kitchen; the trials involved facing the world outside her door. She followed her husband to the United States, and initially, "You didn't want to go into a store—even an Indian or Arab store—and ask for ingredients that might mark you as Iranian," she says, referring to items like zereshk, the barberries eaten by Persians in one of the many pollos, or layered rice dishes, that are a key part of the cuisine. Even making rice—the hallmark of nearly every Iranian meal and the measure of a cook—became a challenge because basmati rice was hard to come by. "For us, if you haven't eaten rice that day, you haven't eaten."

Three decades later, Mrs. Haghanifar is living with her second husband, a Cuban American, in Gainesville, Florida, home to one of the most vibrant Iranian expatriate communities in the United States. Every year the community hosts a weeklong celebration of Noruz, the Iranian New Year. The holiday is observed on the spring equinox, and hearkens back to the Zoroastrian religion that predated Islam. Noruz is both secular and ecumenical and remains the single holiday that all Iranians share: everyone has a place around the ceremonial table set with dishes that signify happiness, health, and wealth. Sabzi Pollo ba Mahi (herbed rice and fish) is always at the center of that table, and Mrs. Haghanifar, now an accomplished cook, is revered for the dish.

Because this dish was traditionally made with Caspian whitefish, Iranian Americans choose a sturdy white fish, such as red snapper or grouper. It is a simple recipe, great for a crowd. For Iranians, the saffron, garlic, and black pepper signify (and beckon) a new year and rebirth.

Four 6- to 8-ounce white fish fillets, each cut in half

Kosher salt and freshly ground black pepper

½ cup all-purpose flour

½ teaspoon garlic powder

¼ teaspoon ground saffron

3 tablespoons olive oil

Red lettuce leaves, for garnish

10 sprigs fresh parsley, for garnish

Lemon slices, for garnish

1 teaspoon minced fresh parsley, for garnish

1. Pat the fish dry with a paper towel and season with salt and pepper. In a shallow dish, combine the flour, garlic powder, saffron, ¼ teaspoon salt, and ⅛ teaspoon pepper.

2. In a large skillet, heat the oil over medium-high heat until hot. Dredge each piece of fish in the flour, then add to the pan and cook for 3 to 5 minutes, until golden brown. Flip the fish and cook for 3 to 5 minutes longer, until golden and still firm but starting to flake.

3. While the fish is cooking, arrange the lettuce leaves on a large platter, overlapping slightly and just hanging over the edge of the platter. Alternate the sprigs of parsley between the lettuce leaves so that you have an alternating red and green pattern.

4. Gently place the fish on the leaves, forming a row down the middle of the platter. Place one or two lemon slices on each piece of fish and sprinkle with minced parsley. Serve.

SERVES 4 TO 6

Mrs. Fernandez's Spanish Salt Fish

Ernie Fernandez, 16, said that his grandmother still believes that her family should not eat any food that she hasn't prepared herself. But after she turned 80, she couldn't cook alone anymore, and the other family members were either working or away at school; Ernie was the only one on hand to help. So for the past five years, they have spent every afternoon together. "At first she would not let me," Ernie explains. "Her family came from Spain and she is refined and religious and traditional and she thought it was wrong for a male to help her in the kitchen. But then she had a small stroke and after that she would let me help stir and lift things.

"My family always lived next door to my grandparents, but cooking together is how I really got to know my grandmother. Before that, I thought it was weird that she goes to mass every day and won't speak English. Now I understand that she was raised to live in a world that is gone. So she lives like everything is the same. The cooking is the same. Every Friday night we have Spanish fish for dinner. Last year she said, 'Ernesto, your Spanish fish is my Spanish fish.' I will never forget that."

FOR THE SAUCE

3 ripe plum tomatoes

2 large red bell peppers

1 medium onion, unpeeled

4 tablespoons olive oil

1 dried ancho chile

½ cup sliced almonds

¼ cup extra virgin olive oil

3 garlic cloves

2 tablespoons sherry vinegar

1 slice high quality bread, toasted, cut into ½-inch cubes (about ½ cup)

1 teaspoon pimentón or sweet paprika

Kosher salt

FOR THE FISH

Two 2-pound whole red snappers, cleaned and gutted

6 pounds kosher salt

3 cups water

1. To make the sauce: Preheat the oven to 400°F. Toss the tomatoes, bell peppers, and onion with 2 tablespoons of the olive oil in a small baking dish. Roast about 45 minutes, until partially charred, turning every 15 minutes. Cover with foil and let sit for 15 minutes.

2. Meanwhile, heat 1 tablespoon olive oil in a small skillet over medium-high heat. Add the chile and cook about 30 seconds, turning once, until darkened and slightly puffed. Transfer to a small bowl and add enough hot water to cover. Let sit for 30 minutes, then drain and discard the water.

3. Peel and seed the tomatoes, bell peppers, and chile. Peel and coarsely chop the onion. Heat the remaining 1 tablespoon olive oil in the skillet over medium-high heat. Add almonds and cook about 1 minute, until lightly toasted. Process the tomatoes, bell peppers, onion, chile, almonds, extra virgin olive oil, garlic, vinegar, bread, and paprika together in a blender to a coarse puree. Transfer to a bowl and season with salt to taste. (The sauce can be made one day ahead. Cover and refrigerate. Bring to room temperature before serving.)

4. To make the fish: Preheat the oven to 450°F. Pat the fish dry with a paper towel and place each in a separate 9 x 13-inch metal baking dish. Cover each fish with 3 pounds salt. Drizzle 1½ cups of the water over the salt in each pan. Using your hands, pack the salt over the fish to cover completely. Bake the fish about 30 minutes, until an instant-read thermometer inserted into the center registers 135°F.

5. Gently rap the salt crust with the back of a spoon to crack, then carefully remove it. Use a pastry brush to remove any remaining salt. Carefully transfer the whole fish to a large platter and serve with sauce.

———

SERVES 4

THE FRESH WATER FISHING HALL OF FAME

ABOUT 1,500 VARIETIES OF FISH PLY THE FRESH WATERS OF the United States. Some, like shad, as well as certain varieties of salmon and trout, are anadromous, ocean dwellers that are born and spawn in rivers and creeks. Others never leave fresh water. Until the late nineteenth century, the Great Lakes were one of the more important commercial fisheries in the United States.

When the Erie Canal connected those waters to the Atlantic, however, aggressive species invaded the lakes and along with overfishing, initiated a decline that was accelerated with pollution. By the twentieth century Lake Erie and many other Great Lake areas were closed to fishing. Decades of protection, purification, and restocking spawned an all-but-miraculous healing, but no significant commercial fishing returned to the lakes.

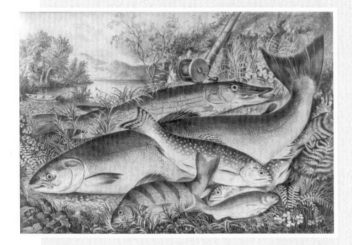

Sport fishermen are not unhappy. They have to compete with weather, the water, and the wily ways of their prey and can do without an additional challenge. Centuries removed from necessity, angling is an atavistic thing, a battle between man and nature. (There are a few women, but sport fishing is mostly a male activity.) The most legendary anglers are enshrined at the Fresh Water Fishing Hall of Fame, a curious blend of education, preservation, and theme park in Hayward, Wisconsin.

From rods and waders and tackle to the private planes that deliver extreme anglers to inaccessible waters in the wilderness of Idaho, Colorado, and Alaska, sport fishing is a $125-billion-dollar-a-year industry. Unless you know a sport-fishing fanatic, you may never taste freshwater delicacies such as sunfish, white bass, yellow bass, or ling. A friendly angler may share wild versions of carp and catfish, sturgeon, yellow perch, pike, walleye, and whitefish, but today most of these are likely to be harvested from a fish farm.

Jodi Fouch's Campfire Trout

More than a million trout are released into West Virginia's lakes and streams each year. The sport fishermen seem to know the schedule of the stock trucks, and in March, when the season opens, they wait by the side of the stream for the trucks to arrive. They catch the fish almost as soon as they are released. The wiliest fish remain and give *real* anglers the challenge they seek. At least that is how the people in Petersburg, West Virginia, see it. The town is home to the "Centennial Gold Trout," and also home to Jodi Fouch, a passionate home cook who writes about food for the *Grant County Press* there. "Real anglers don't fish behind stock trucks," she says, and "Never cook trout without some kind of potato; this is West Virginia, after all."

269

From Sea to Shining Sea: Fish and Shellfish

4 whole trout, cleaned and scaled

Kosher salt and freshly ground black pepper

8 slices bacon

1 cup yellow cornmeal

¼ cup bacon fat or vegetable oil

1 small onion, halved and thinly sliced (optional)

1. Pat the fish dry with a paper towel and season inside and out with salt and pepper. Working with 1 fish at a time, secure one end of a bacon slice in the gill of the fish and wrap it around the fish. Attach the second slice to the end of the first and continue to wrap it around the fish, ending at the tail. Use a toothpick to secure the bacon to the tail.

2. In a shallow dish, combine the cornmeal, ½ teaspoon salt, and ¼ teaspoon pepper. Roll each fish in the cornmeal until evenly coated. In a large skillet, heat the bacon fat until very hot. Add two of the fish and cook about 4 minutes on each side, until golden brown and still firm but starting to flake. Transfer to a platter and repeat with the remaining 2 fish. If desired, add the onion to the skillet and cook for 5 minutes until soft, then spoon over the fish. Serve.

SERVES 4

CARRIE WIENER'S ALSACE TO MISSISSIPPI WHITE FISH

One spring day when he was 5 years old, Jay Wiener caught a five-pound bass using his cane pole at the lake near his grandmother's home. He was a hero! A provider! The fish was gutted and frozen, and a few weeks later it was the star of his grandmother's Passover seder.

"It made me proud," says Mr. Wiener. It also forged his first link to this family recipe. The original version called for the carp that were thick in the rivers of the Alsatian Rhineland where Carrie Wiener's ancestors had lived since the 1700s. Her grandparents brought the recipe to the United States in the 1840s, and it remains a Wiener family Passover tradition.

"It is not as much a recipe as it is variations on a theme," says Mr. Wiener. It was passed along, adapted to the fish of various regions, adjusted to suit each cook's tastes. Any white-fleshed fish will do, and in addition to the classic Great Lakes whitefish, Mr. Wiener has used snapper and has his sights set on richer fish, a wild salmon perhaps. A splash of dry white wine does well in the sauce; so does lemon zest. His cousin Isabel Wile Goldman of Shreveport, Louisiana, uses red snapper and cider vinegar. His younger sister sometimes uses cayenne. The recipe's malleability has kept it alive in his family for more than 150 years in America.

"My grandmother's whitefish is like a jazz riff," he says.

FOR THE FISH

1 tablespoon unsalted butter

3 celery stalks, finely chopped

1 green bell pepper, finely chopped

½ cup finely chopped onion

1 tablespoon all-purpose flour

1 cup water

1 tablespoon Worcestershire sauce

Four 6- to 8-ounce skinless sea bass or other
    white fish fillets

Kosher salt and freshly ground black pepper

FOR THE SAUCE

2 cups mayonnaise

One 3.5-ounce jar capers, drained, brine reserved

2 tablespoons fresh lemon juice

2 hard-boiled eggs, cooled and peeled

Kosher salt and freshly ground black pepper

1. To make the fish: In a large skillet, melt the butter over medium heat. Add the celery, bell pepper, and onion and cook about 5 minutes, stirring occasionally, until soft. Stir in the flour and cook about 1 minute, until incorporated. Add the water and Worcestershire and bring to a simmer.

2. Pat the fish dry with a paper towel and season with salt and pepper, then add to the skillet and cook for 8 to 10 minutes, until the fish begins to flake apart. Using a slotted spoon, transfer the fish to a platter, and let cool to room temperature.

3. To make the sauce: In a small bowl, stir together the mayonnaise, capers, and lemon juice. Remove the yolks from the eggs and mash them with a fork. Reserve 1 teaspoon of the mashed egg yolk for garnish, then stir the remainder into the sauce. Mince the egg whites. Reserve 1 teaspoon for garnish, and stir the remainder into the sauce. Stir in some of the reserved caper brine to thin the sauce, if desired. Season with salt and pepper to taste, cover, and refrigerate until the fish has cooled completely. (The reserved garnish can be refrigerated as well.)

4. Pour the sauce over the fish. Refrigerate until chilled. Sprinkle with the reserved egg yolks and whites, and serve.

———

SERVES 4

MEANWHILE, BACK ON THE (FISH) FARM

ANGELA CAPORELLI WORKED HER WAY THROUGH COLLEGE ON COMMERCIAL FISHING
boats and then, armed with a degree in aquaculture and fishing science from the University of Rhode Island, she left the ocean for the farm. Fish farming is seen as the work of the devil by food lovers and fishermen, but Ms. Caporelli considers herself on the side of the angels. Wild fish are increasingly scarce, imports continue to skyrocket, and with the cost of land rising in the United States, more and more growers are looking for a more efficient cash crop.

"I can grow 5,000 catfish on an acre," she says, "I'd need four acres to grow one head of beef."

Ms. Caporelli, who has the passion of a reformed sinner, insists that there is a place on the nation's menu for farmed fish. "It's fine for people who live next to the ocean to talk about how wild stripers taste better than farmed bass," she says, "but what about the millions of people who don't have an ocean in their backyard?"

Comparing farmed fish to wild fish is like comparing veal to aged Kobe beef, she says. "Farmed fish will never have the intense wild flavor of a wild fish. It has less muscle because it doesn't swim as much, and it doesn't have to fight for food. But if it is grown carefully and processed right, farmed fish cooks and eats well."

Ms. Caporelli has taught dairy farmers in Massachusetts and chicken farmers in Rhode Island how to build and manage fish farms on their land. In 2002 when she was named Kentucky's aquaculture coordinator, the state had almost no fish farms, but it was looking for something to replace its ravaged tobacco industry. Kentucky's bourbon produced a steady stream of nutritious distiller's grains. The state's limestone water proved to be as beneficial to fish as it is to racehorses. Today, local largemouth bass, hybrid striped bass, paddlefish (both meat and caviar), catfish, freshwater prawns, tilapia, and trout are being sold at farmers' markets throughout the state.

Fish farming is not new. Oysters have been farmed in Long Island Sound since the eighteenth century, and trout and salmon fisheries have been stocked with spat from hatcheries for more than a hundred years. In the 1940s, man-made catfish ponds began to appear in Arkansas and the Mississippi Delta. Today, *nearly 50 percent* of fish eaten in America is farmed; more than half of that is imported. Food analysts and economists, as well as fish dealers and many fishermen, believe that farmed fish are the future of fish in America.

The greatest risk in farmed fish is its vulnerability to certain diseases, but that vulnerability can be managed. Ms. Caporelli, who could well become the Johnny Appleseed of fish farming, says, "Organic standards are just as enforceable in tiny backyard operations as they are in industrial settings."

By all accounts, farmed fish are energy-efficient and highly sustainable; they also have an insignificant carbon footprint. These facts make it difficult—even for a wild-fish lover—to dismiss fish farming as a sin against taste.

Traveling around the country, I've visited fish farms made from pens in the ocean, fish farms made by flooding fields, and fish farms that resemble aboveground swimming pools. Farmed fish are low on flavor, so they demand more from the cook. But from what I've seen and tasted, farmed fish, like farmed beef or farmed chicken, tend to be as good as their farmer.

Bluegrass Bass with Kentucky Caviar

This recipe, which uses two of the state's farmed fish—bass and paddlefish caviar—was one of the winners of the Great Kentucky Seafood Cook Off held in Louisville, Kentucky, in June 2008. It shows what it takes to make farmed fish taste delicious: serious cooking. This dish is fancy enough to impress company. It is so delicious that several chefs who were judging the contest suspected that wild fish had been used.

FOR THE BEURRE BLANC

1 cup Champagne or dry white wine

2 shallots, peeled and thinly sliced

1 tablespoon Champagne vinegar

2 sprigs fresh thyme

1 garlic clove, peeled and thinly sliced

½ teaspoon whole black peppercorns

¼ cup heavy cream

8 tablespoons (1 stick) unsalted butter, cut into 8 pieces, at room temperature

Kosher salt and freshly ground black pepper

1 tablespoon paddlefish roe, plus more to taste

FOR THE STRIPED BASS

Four 6- to 8-ounce skin-on striped bass fillets

2 teaspoons Fire and Spice Mustard Spice Blend or kosher salt and freshly ground black pepper

2 tablespoons olive oil

1 tablespoon unsalted butter

2 tablespoons minced fresh chives

1 teaspoon grated lemon zest

1. To make the beurre blanc: Combine the Champagne, shallots, vinegar, thyme, garlic, and peppercorns in a small saucepan and cook on high heat until the wine is nearly evaporated and reduced to about 1½ tablespoons of liquid. Add the cream and cook until the liquid is reduced to about 1½ tablespoons again. Strain the mixture through a fine-mesh strainer into a blender.

2. With the blender running on low speed, add the butter, 1 tablespoon at a time, until fully incorporated. (Alternatively, you can return the strained liquid to the saucepan and whisk in the butter, 1 tablespoon at a time, or use an immersion blender.) Season with salt and pepper to taste. Keep warm, but not hot, while cooking the fish.

3. To cook the striped bass: Cut shallow diagonal slashes through skin at 1-inch intervals. Line a plate with paper towels. Pat the fish dry with a paper towel and season with the mustard spice blend. Heat the oil in a large nonstick skillet over medium-high heat. At the first sign of smoke, add the fillets skin side down. Cook for 3 minutes, gently pressing on them with a spatula to keep them from curling. Flip the fish over, add the butter, reduce the heat to medium, and cook about 2 minutes longer, until the fish is just beginning to flake apart. Transfer to the paper-towel-lined plate.

4. To serve, place the fillets skin side up on warmed plates. At the last moment, stir the roe into the beurre blanc. Spoon the sauce over the fillets, taking care to evenly distribute the roe over each portion. Sprinkle with the chives and lemon zest, and serve.

———

SERVES 4

EDNA SCOTT'S HUSH PUPPIES AND CATFISH

"Everybody fried catfish," Mrs. Scott says. But few have the perfect, crisp finesse of her versions and few have had the chance to test their recipes with cooks from *Saveur* magazine.

One Big Table

FOR THE HUSH PUPPIES

¾ cup stone-ground cornmeal

1½ teaspoons baking powder

½ teaspoon seasoned salt, preferably Lawry's

½ teaspoon fresh ground black pepper

½ cup milk

1 egg, lightly beaten

½ cup minced onion

2 tablespoons minced scallion greens or chives (optional)

FOR THE CATFISH

1½ cups stone-ground cornmeal

½ cup extra-fine stone-ground cornmeal (sometimes called corn flour), preferably, or all-purpose flour

2 tablespoons seasoned salt, preferably Lawry's

1 tablespoon garlic salt

½ teaspoon onion powder

1 teaspoon freshly ground black pepper

½ teaspoon lemon pepper

1 teaspoon paprika

½ teaspoon cayenne pepper

2 pounds catfish fillets cut into 3- to 4-ounce sections

Peanut oil, preferably, or other vegetable oil for deep-frying

Hot pepper sauce, such as Texas Pete or Tabasco, for serving

Lemon wedges, for serving

1. To prepare the hush puppy batter: Combine the cornmeal, baking powder, and salt and pepper in a bowl. Combine the milk and egg, pour into the batter, and stir well to combine. Add the minced onion and, if using, the green onion and stir to combine. Set aside.

2. To prepare the catfish coating: Combine cornmeal, flour, and seasonings in a shallow dish.

3. To cook the hush puppies and the fish: Pour several inches of oil into a heavy pot or deep skillet and warm over medium-high heat until a pinch of flour sizzles when sprinkled on the oil and the oil temperature reaches 350°F on a deep-fat thermometer. While the oil is heating, coat the catfish fillets in the cornmeal mixture, and set on a tray lined with waxed paper. Add about 4 tablespoons of the remaining cornmeal mixture to the hush puppy batter, a tablespoon at a time, stirring vigorously between each addition. Continue adding until the batter is thick enough to spoon and hold its shape. Discard any remaining cornmeal mixture. Roll the batter or spoon it into 1-inch balls; larger ones will get too brown on the outside before the interior is cooked.

4. Working in batches, fry the fish until it is a deep golden brown color and crusty, 6 to 8 minutes. Drain each fillet on brown paper. After frying the fish, fry the hush puppies. Serve immediately, with hot pepper sauce and lemon wedges.

SERVES 6 TO 8

SAVING THE FARM

ED SCOTT'S DADDY MOVED TO THE MISSISSIPPI DELTA IN 1919. HE FARMED CORN, COTTON, and beans. When it became impossible to make a living on row crops, he became the first African American to grow rice in the Delta. When the elder Mr. Scott died in 1957, he had amassed 1,800 acres around Drew, Mississippi. His son, Ed, worked the same land and in the early 1980s, when neighboring farmers began digging their way back from the brink of bankruptcy by converting from vegetables to aquaculture, Ed Scott and his son dug eight ponds on their land.

When it came time to stock them, Mr. Scott says, "the local banks wouldn't loan money to a black man looking to grow some fish." He secured a government loan. When it came time to process his grain-fed catfish, none of the local white-owned processing plants would buy his crop. He and his son built a processing plant.

By 1989, Ed Scott's Pond Raised Catfish employed eighty-five people and processed more than 60,000 pounds of fish a day. Edna Scott, his wife of fifty-seven years, opened a cafeteria to feed the employees. Eventually, a cartel of huge competitors in the area forced Mr. Scott to close his processing plant. But by then Mrs. Scott's catfish breading was famous, and another farm-saving cottage industry had been born.

Vicinity of Natchitoches, Louisiana (MARIAN POST WOLCOTT, 1940).

JoJo Petty's Chipotle Tartar Sauce

"Some old boy at the fish house over by Calcasieu Lake in Louisiana made a Tabasco tartar sauce and used it on shrimp and oyster po'boys," says Jojo Petty, a fourth-generation shrimper. "It was good, darned good if you like all that vinegar with your chile. I'd rather some smoky flavor and you can give me lime over vinegar any day and twice on Sunday. This makes a mean sauce for fried shrimp and fried fish—I like using a beer tempura batter or just the lightest dust of cake flour or rice flour on mine. It's a mean sauce for french fries or fried onions, too."

One 7-ounce can chipotle chiles in adobo sauce (see Note)

¾ cup mayonnaise

¼ cup minced fresh cilantro

2 teaspoons fresh lime juice

Kosher salt and freshly ground black pepper

In a blender or food processor, process the chipotles in adobo sauce until smooth. In a small bowl, whisk the mayonnaise with the 2 tablespoons of the chipotle puree. Add more puree, 1 teaspoon at a time, to reach the desired spiciness. Whisk in the cilantro and lime juice, and season with salt and pepper to taste.

MAKES ABOUT 1 CUP

NOTE: The remaining chipotles can be refrigerated in an airtight container for up to one month.

TARTAR SAUCE

BEFORE 1929, WHEN THE HELLMANN'S COMPANY INTRODUCED A JARRED VERSION— and well before it appeared in plastic squeeze bottles—sauce tartare was an elite condiment. It was thought to be a Turkish sauce—"Tartar" is a medieval word that refers to Turkish culture—and the earliest recorded versions (1685) used hard-boiled eggs, butter, orange juice, and mustard to form a semi-cooked mayonnaise. By 1889, when sauce tartare appeared on the menu of Delmonico's, New York's legendary

Banquet at Delmonico's, 1906.

restaurant, it was a concoction of homemade mayonnaise, gherkin pickles, and spices, primarily cayenne. The sauce lost its spice somewhere on the journey from sauce tartare to tartar sauce. It did not, however, lose its favorite companion, fish—particularly fried fish. Today, in public, tartar sauce is pretty much just mayonnaise and minced pickles; in private homes, however, the sauce is not always so predictable. Regionalism—the blast of chile peppers in the tartar sauce at a Garden District home in New Orleans, the addition of minced green tomato pickles at a fishing cabin in the mountains of western Tennessee—accounts for some variations. Others are generational or idiosyncratic or both.

AMERICAN FRIED (FISH)

IF YOU'RE DRIVING THROUGH THE GREAT LAKES REGION OR THE
Deep South during warm weather, you don't need a road map to know
that you are approaching a river, creek, bay, lake, or pond. You see signs
advertising fried fish, fish shacks, and hand-lettered posters announcing a
fund-raising fish fry. Both regions claim a special relationship to the happy
combination of fish, flour, and a pot of hot cooking oil. If the fish fry as a
social form was perfected in the Great Lakes region, fried fish was elevated
to an art form in Mississippi. In Greenwood, William Leflore is a poet of fried
catfish. Just as fishermen can read the water, he can read the surface of hot
peanut oil. He knows the roil, sheen, and smell that announce 375°F. He has
a feel for dusting catfish fillets in seasoned cornmeal, lowering them into the oil, and removing them
in the breath that divides done from overdone. The crust that he gives his fish is so delicate that even as
one's teeth itch to bite into it, one's heart shudders at the thought of breaking something so fine.

Some think that Mr. Leflore's instinct is genetic. Others think that growing up in the Delta—which has
both the lowest standard of living in the country and the highest standard for fried catfish—shaped his
genius. Like most sons of the Delta, he started fishing with his daddy shortly before he began to walk.
When he was 13 he jumped into the lake with an axe handle after one of his friends shot a stump and
the water boiled with startled catfish. He bagged a dozen fish and fried them for his friends.

In 1980 his friend Parker Johnson, who runs the local farm equipment store and also fries a mean
fish, invited Mr. Leflore to fry for a fund-raising party. Since then, the two men have fried fish for the
same reason that others fish: for fun and relaxation. They fry for about eight events each year, with

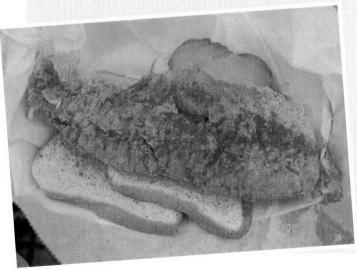

as many as 1,500 guests each. About five
nights a week, when he needs additional
fun and relaxation, Mr. Leflore goes to
Giardina's, the fanciest restaurant in town,
and fries catfish. So far he's fried about
750,000 pounds of it.

In addition to the axe handle he has
caught catfish with a cane pole, a trotline,
a yo-yo, a rod and reel, and a gill net; he
has even grabbed the suckers with his
hand. But he has never fried catfish in
anything but peanut oil or dusted it with
anything other than Martha White yellow
cornmeal, lightly salted.

CATFISH À LA KENNY

Yui Chow was born in Hong Kong and when he was 2 moved to New York with his parents and four siblings. "First we lived in the Spanish section, then in the Jewish section," he says.

Mr. Chow remembers his mother cooking a variety of fish dishes, all very simple, by poaching or deep-frying the fish in seasoned oil. Though he did not learn to cook at home, he is now an avid cook because he likes to entertain. "When I'm alone I don't cook for myself. It takes me longer to cook than it does for me to eat."

His favorite fish preparation is a catfish recipe he learned and adapted from his brother-in-law Kenny, who is also of Chinese descent. It combines traditional Chinese ingredients like ginger, scallions, and soy sauce with balsamic vinegar—a beloved staple in his pantry. Mr. Chow says he likes clean-tasting food that's simple and straightforward: "I serve this with a salad of baby greens with a balsamic vinaigrette, or with asparagus spears that I cut into two-inch pieces and blister in hot oil and sprinkle with sea salt."

½ cup soy sauce

½ cup balsamic vinegar

¼ cup olive oil

One 1-inch piece fresh ginger, peeled and thinly sliced

3 garlic cloves, thinly sliced

1 scallion, green and white parts, thinly sliced

½ teaspoon freshly ground black pepper

Four 6- to 8-ounce skinless catfish fillets

1. In a large bowl, combine the soy sauce, vinegar, oil, ginger, garlic, scallion, and pepper. Add the catfish, cover, and refrigerate for at least 30 minutes or up to 2 hours.

2. Preheat the broiler.

3. Remove the catfish from the marinade, letting the excess drip off. Arrange the fillets in an even layer on a slotted broiler pan or a wire rack set over a rimmed baking sheet. Broil for 3 to 5 minutes, until it starts to brown. Flip over and broil for 2 to 4 minutes longer, until they start to brown and flake apart. Serve.

SERVES 4

CATCHING FISH, CATCHING POEMS

DAVE DENSMORE IS A POET AND A FISHERMAN. THE TWO activities are similar, neither art nor labor, but a way of life. Mr. Densmore believes that the culture will lose more than a wild food source if it becomes impossible to fish for a living.

"I was raised, until my midteens, in Alaska. We lived a very subsistence lifestyle. I started hunting with my father when I was 7. By the time I was 9, I was hunting on my own as well. I had a skiff and outboard of my own by the time I was 10, and purchased my first commercial fishing boat at 13. Although I have lived in Astoria, Oregon, for many years, I fish summers out of Larsen Bay; Kodiak, Alaska, has always felt like hometown to me. As a teenager, I gill-netted and purse seined on the Columbia River in Oregon, but by the time I was in my early twenties I was back in Alaska, king-crabbing out of Dutch Harbor and Unalaska.

"In 1971 a king crab boat I was running caught fire and burned, forcing my crew and me to abandon ship. We spent four nights adrift in the Bering Sea. It was before the days of survival suits. High wind and waves, driving snow and numbing cold, made our survival a miracle. But early the fourth morning our life raft was run down by a Japanese trawler. They hadn't seen us, but someone aboard heard us yelling and we were rescued.

"I spent a month in the hospital and two years recovering from frostbitten feet. During that time I took up scuba diving commercially to keep my family fed. Couldn't walk very well, but I could swim all right. We also ate a *lot* of venison. I helped pioneer the Prince William Sound herring roe dive fishery during that time, and once I was able to walk and be on my feet again, I bought a salmon trawler to fish off the Oregon and Washington coasts. I'd noticed there were lots of family operations in that area. By then I had a son and I liked the idea of fishing closer to home. My wife, Pat, and I fished salmon and albacore tuna. The winter my son Skeeter was 7, I took him out of school for several months to be on the boat with us. He loved the water. When he was 10, we moved back to Kodiak. On his fourteenth birthday, June 28, 1985, he and my father drowned in a skiff accident on Uyak Bay.

"Poems come floating toward me. They are like fish. When they are there, you catch them. My wife is a poet, too. Catching fish, catching poems. Commercial fishing is not a job to most of us. It's an identity, it is who we are. Most of us are lifers who never 'retire'; we stop when forced to by time and health issues. Although you'll probably never hear anyone but a poet say it, commercial fishing is a love affair. The real value is not in dollars and cents. It's an act of faith—faith in ourselves, in our industry, in the power of hard work. If you fish, you live close to nature. Once I was setting with the bow of a seiner against the beach, my net was stretched out to intercept a salmon run, and I was watching the water and watching some young fox playing in the grass a few feet away, I was just living right there in nature's shirt pocket."

And such moments continue to be inspired by his wife's, Pat Densmore's, perfectly cooked fish.

From Sea to Shining Sea: Fish and Shellfish

Pat Densmore's Roasted Lemon Sturgeon

ASTORIA, OREGON

Like most people who've ever fished for a living, Pat Densmore believes that there is nothing finer than a perfectly fresh, plain-cooked fish. Once in a while, she'll "dress a fish up for company or maybe a special occasion." Fresh ginger gives a wonderful warmth to her creamy lemon sauce, and the dish is wonderful with aromatic rice or boiled potatoes and steamed vegetables.

6 tablespoons sake or dry vermouth

4 teaspoons grated fresh ginger

Kosher salt and freshly ground black pepper

Four 6- to 8-ounce sturgeon fillets, or salmon if sturgeon is unavailable

¼ cup dry white wine

1 shallot, thinly sliced

6 whole black peppercorns

2 cups heavy cream

3 tablespoons fresh lemon juice

One 2-inch piece fresh ginger, grated over a fine-mesh strainer, squeezed, and juice reserved

1 teaspoon grated lemon zest

2 tablespoons unsalted butter

1. In a medium bowl, combine the sake, grated ginger, ¼ teaspoon salt, and ⅛ teaspoon pepper. Add the fish and turn to coat. Cover and refrigerate for 30 minutes.

2. Meanwhile, preheat the oven to 400°F. In a small saucepan, bring the wine, shallot, and peppercorns to a simmer over medium heat and cook for 4 to 6 minutes, until the pan is almost dry. Stir in the heavy cream, return to a simmer, and cook until the cream is reduced by half. Strain the mixture through a fine-mesh strainer into a clean saucepan, pushing on the solids to extract as much liquid as possible. Stir in the lemon juice, ginger juice, and lemon zest. Season with salt and pepper to taste and keep warm while cooking the fish.

3. Remove the fish from the marinade, letting the excess drip off, and discard the marinade. In a large ovenproof skillet, melt the butter over medium-high heat. Add the fillets and cook for 2 to 3 minutes on each side, until light golden. Transfer the skillet to the oven and cook for 8 to 10 minutes, until the fish is still firm but starting to flake. Serve with the warm sauce.

SERVES 4

Senator F. Ryan Duffy of Wisconsin with a 35-pound sturgeon.

Dallyn Leiniani Duggan's Macadamia-Crusted Swordfish

Dallyn Leiniani Duggan's mother is Hawaiian, her father was a military man. When her father was called to serve in Vietnam, her mother moved the family back to her home. Ms. Duggan, who is 45 years old, now lives in Arlington, Virginia, but as far as food goes, "home" still means Hawaii.

"Like most Hawaiians, I am preoccupied with Hawaiian ingredients," she says. "I pack one suitcase whenever I go back so that I can carry two coolers full of essentials back to Virginia." Essentials like lu'au leaves, inamona [a condiment made from ground kukui nuts], limu [a sea vegetable], saimin [noodle soup], and, of course, poi.

In her years on the mainland, however, Ms. Duggan has also developed dishes that can be cooked even without the "suitcase." This swordfish encrusted with macadamia nuts is just that. "Hawaiian cuisine is basically using the state's best natural resources in the simplest way, often in preparations that fuse some of the different cultures that traded, visited, and continue to live on the islands."

One 13.5-ounce can unsweetened coconut milk

Four 6- to 8-ounce swordfish steaks

¼ cup roasted unsalted macadamia nuts

¼ cup panko (Japanese bread crumbs)

2 tablespoons unsweetened shredded coconut

Kosher salt and freshly ground black pepper

8 tablespoons (1 stick) unsalted butter

¼ cup vegetable oil

1. In a large bowl, whisk the coconut milk to combine the cream and water. Add the fish, cover, and refrigerate for 1 hour, turning every 20 minutes to coat evenly.

2. Preheat oven to 425°F. In a food processor, process the nuts, panko, coconut, ½ teaspoon salt, and ¼ teaspoon pepper until the mixture is the texture of course meal. Transfer the mixture to a shallow dish.

3. Remove the steaks from the coconut milk, letting the excess drip off. Coat them evenly with the nut mixture, pressing gently so the coating adheres, then set on a wire rack until ready to cook.

4. In a large skillet, heat the butter and oil together over medium-high heat until the butter is melted and beginning to brown. Carefully add the fish to the pan and cook for 2 to 4 minutes, until golden brown.

5. Transfer the fish a baking dish and bake about 10 minutes, until it is still firm but starting to flake. Season with salt and pepper to taste, and serve.

SERVES 4

Annette Di Nunzio's Swordfish Rolls

Fried zeppole with anchovies, baked stuffed prawns, fillet of sea bass with herbs, stuffed clams, swordfish rolls, linguine with blue crab sauce, shrimp fra diavolo . . .

Annette Di Nunzio has eaten these seven seafood dishes every Christmas Eve since she was old enough to hold a fork. When she was a child in Brooklyn, her father traveled to the Jersey shore to catch the crabs and dig the clams. Later, living on the West Coast, she made the "seven fishes" every Christmas Eve for her own family and friends.

When she moved to North Beach in 1981, she found the community she had been missing ever since she had left the East Coast years before. "I moved there for my Italian connection," she says. "I wanted to go into the little stores, speak some Italian." But long before she arrived the Chinese were moving in and the Italians were moving out, taking many of the little stores with them. "Things change," she says with a philosophical shrug. But not her swordfish rolls.

FOR THE FISH

10 very thin pieces swordfish (about 2 pounds), skin removed

2 ounces caciocavallo cheese or imported provolone, grated (about ½ cup)

5 tablespoons olive oil

¼ cup chopped fresh basil

2 tablespoons minced fresh parsley

2 tablespoons fine dry bread crumbs

Kosher salt and freshly ground black pepper

FOR THE SAUCE

2 tablespoons olive oil

1 small onion, finely chopped

1 celery stalk, thinly sliced

One 28-ounce can whole tomatoes, drained and chopped

1 cup black Gaeta olives, pitted and halved

2 tablespoons rinsed and drained capers

1. To make the fish: Trim each piece into a rough rectangle, reserving the trimmings. Place each piece between two pieces of plastic wrap and use a meat pounder to carefully flatten it to about a 1⅓-inch thickness.

2. In a bowl, combine the fish trimmings, cheese, oil, basil, parsley, bread crumbs, ¼ teaspoon salt, and ⅛ teaspoon pepper. Lay the fish slices on the work surface and divide the filling mixture evenly among them. Roll the fish around the filling and secure with a toothpick or kitchen twine.

3. To make the sauce: In a large skillet, heat the oil over medium heat. Add the onion and celery and cook for 5 minutes, until soft. Stir in the tomatoes, olives, and capers and cook for 15 minutes.

4. Place the swordfish rolls in the sauce and cook for 10 to 12 minutes, until the meat is opaque and firm to the touch. Serve hot, or cool to room temperature.

SERVES 4 TO 6

Sam Popkin's Sichuan Tuna Loin

LA JOLLA, CALIFORNIA

Sam Popkin grew up working in the family kitchen with his mother who, he says, was "a phenomenal Romanian Jewish cook." They lived in Superior, Wisconsin, in a huge extended family where everybody helped make dinner—there was never a sense that real men didn't cook. When he left Wisconsin for MIT, he went armed with a basic set of cooking skills and an instinct for making good food, but no recipes. Those skills were vital to his social success, which was substantial. "You can really get more action if you can cook," says Dr. Popkin, who is now a professor of political science at the University of California, San Diego.

This particular cause and effect may have led Dr. Popkin to call himself a "social cook." His annual Tuna Orgy showcases his social cooking skills. Ten to forty of his closest friends are invited to the extravagant day-long feast, and everyone contributes. Philippe Charat, who owns Maricultura del Norte, a deep-water feedlot dedicated to fattening bluefin tuna on sardines, contributes tuna that could inspire a sushi master to sharpen his knife.

Every year the menu begins with two kinds of sashimi (toro and maguro), followed by two tartares and then a little sorbet. Sometimes Dr. Popkin sears the toro in the style of foie gras; sometimes the group makes tuna pasta, a dish so beloved by his family that his son and daughter now make it in college.

Your children are carrying on the family tradition?

"Ah, well," says Dr. Popkin, "mastering the basics really can take you anywhere."

½ cup Sichuan peppercorns, crushed

1½ teaspoons kosher salt

3 pounds skinless bluefin tuna loin, in 1 piece

Sam's Soy Dipping Sauce (recipe follows)

Heat a gas or charcoal grill until hot. In a shallow dish, combine the peppercorns and salt, then roll the fish in the mixture, pressing so that it adheres. Grill the fish about 2 minutes on each side, until the outside is seared but the center is still rare. Slice the fish crosswise into ½-inch-thick pieces, and serve with the dipping sauce.

SERVES 8

Sam's Soy Dipping Sauce

½ cup Dijon mustard

½ cup soy sauce

3 tablespoons vegetable oil

1 tablespoon grated fresh ginger

½ jalapeño chile, finely chopped

In a small bowl, stir together all of the ingredients. The sauce can be refrigerated in an airtight container for up to three days.

MAKES ABOUT 1¼ CUPS

NOT UNCLE ROCCO'S TUNA

Rocco DiMassa would not give his niece Cara Mia Constantine his tuna recipe. Not even when she began wheedling, browbeating, and begging him. Like many of the Italians who settled in the San Pedro section of Los Angeles to create the largest Italian community in California, Mr. DiMassa owned a thirty-five-foot boat and fished for sardines, flatfish, and occasionally crab, sword, and tuna. When he was 70, after an accident on deck, he sold his boat and took up gardening. For nearly thirty years, Mrs. Constantine played to his pride, she played to his heart, she played to his ego: She pleaded that even in a family of extraordinary cooks like theirs, his tuna was in a class by itself.

"You're right," Uncle Rocco replied.

Eventually, Mrs. Constantine duplicated the roasted tomatoes and onions that he served with the tuna, but she couldn't figure out how to cook the fish loin to get it so succulent and silky. But Uncle Rocco wasn't talking. In her desperation, she even tried to spy on him.

"Get out of here," he said without looking up, his body blocking her view of the stove in his small, immaculate kitchen. When she was 55 and Uncle Rocco was 90, Mrs. Constantine sat him down for a serious chat.

"You have no children," said Mrs. Constantine. "In cases like this, secrets are traditionally passed to the closest living relative."

"Only applies if the elder is gonna pass down the secret," replied Mr. DiMassa, adding, "That tuna is going to die with me."

Mrs. Constantine was stricken. She loved her uncle too much to allow him to go without leaving behind something that kept his memory alive. She also loved the tuna. So, she decided, two can play the break-with-tradition game. Deploying a strategy that included novenas, old cookbooks, aging family friends, and calls to Sicily, Mrs. Constantine cracked the tuna code.

FOR THE TOMATOES

4 medium-size ripe tomatoes, cored, halved, and seeded

6 garlic cloves, minced

1 teaspoon minced fresh thyme

½ teaspoon sugar

Kosher salt and freshly ground black pepper

1 teaspoon olive oil

2 teaspoons chopped fresh tarragon

FOR THE ONIONS

1 quart water

½ cup white wine vinegar

½ cup sugar

Kosher salt and freshly ground black pepper

1 large onion, halved and thinly sliced

½ teaspoon olive oil

FOR THE TUNA

1 quart extra virgin olive oil

2 bay leaves

1½ pounds skinless bluefin tuna loin, cut into
    4 equal pieces

Kosher salt and freshly ground black pepper

1. To make the tomatoes: Preheat the oven to
300°F. Place the tomatoes on a baking sheet and
sprinkle with half of the garlic, the thyme, sugar,
¼ teaspoon salt, and ⅛ teaspoon pepper. Bake
for 3½ hours, until shriveled. Cool to room
temperature.

2. Coarsely chop the tomatoes. In a medium
skillet, heat the olive oil over medium heat. Stir
in the tomatoes, the remaining garlic, and the
tarragon, and cook for 2 minutes. Season with salt
and pepper to taste.

3. To prepare the onions: Meanwhile, bring
the water, vinegar, sugar, ½ teaspoon salt, and
¼ teaspoon pepper to a boil in a medium saucepan
over medium-high heat. Add the onion and cook
for 5 minutes. Drain and cool to room temperature.
Toss the onions with the olive oil.

4. To make the tuna: In a medium saucepan,
heat the oil and bay leaves to 140°F (check with an
instant-read thermometer). Pat the fish dry with a
paper towel and season with salt and pepper. Slide
the fish into the oil and cook about 5 minutes,
maintaining the temperature at 140°F. Use a slotted
spoon to remove the fish.

5. To serve, divide the onion mixture evenly
on four plates. Place the tomatoes on top of the
onions, then arrange the tuna on top. Season the
tuna with salt, and serve.

SERVES 4

Pat McQuillister's Adobong Pusit
Tangy Filipino Squid

Growing up in California, Pat McQuillister often watched her Filipina mother cook the traditional squid dish adobong pusit. In the Tagalog language, *adobong* means stewed in its own juices and *pusit* means squid. When she left home and made the dish, Ms. McQuillister would always call her mother for advice if it didn't taste quite right. She eventually wrote down the recipe and was able to make it after her mother was no longer around to advise her.

A few years ago, Ms. McQuillister visited the Philippines and altered her recipe to more closely resemble the version that her cousin makes. It's a dish typical of Cavite, a province south of Manila, where her family still lives. "With any ethnic dish," she says, "you can cook it so-so, or take it to the next level, so it tastes authentic." To get that authentic taste, she recommends making sure the squid is sautéed long enough to lose its "raw squid taste" but not so long that it dries out or browns. She claims that the dish is even better the next day.

⅓ cup white vinegar

¼ cup water

3 garlic cloves, crushed

1 teaspoon sugar

1 bay leaf

Kosher salt and freshly ground black pepper

1½ pounds squid, cleaned, tentacles removed and reserved

3 tablespoons vegetable oil

1 small onion, halved and thinly sliced

1. In a medium bowl, combine the vinegar, water, garlic, sugar, bay leaf, ½ teaspoon salt, and ¼ teaspoon pepper. Add cleaned squid and tentacles, cover, and refrigerate for 1 hour.

2. Remove the squid from the marinade, letting the excess drip off. Strain the marinade through a fine-mesh strainer and reserve. In a large skillet, heat the oil over medium heat until hot. Add the onion and cook about 5 minutes, stirring occasionally, until soft. Add the squid, cover, and cook about 10 minutes. Stir in the strained marinade and cook for 5 to 7 minutes more, until the squid is tender. Serve.

SERVES 4

KAREN STEVENSON'S CIOPPINO

SAN FRANCISCO, CALIFORNIA

Karen Stevenson says, "When we lived here as a kid, Mom's best friend was the daughter of an old Italian restaurateur. While she was never a pro cook, she was one helluva home cook. Fearless and astute. She listened to her dad's buddies and developed recipes around their stories.

"My first taste of cioppino was hers. She papered her dining room table with the *Chronicle* and gave everyone bibs and Handi Wipes, then served it with a rich red wine, crispy green salad, and crusty sourdough. We each had our own wide, flat bowl. No matter how many people were around the table, it was always a great party. This is my modified version of her original recipe.

"When we lived in Houston, one day I was hankering for good, messy cioppino. I went to my favorite fishmonger—he was a Gulf Coast man, drawl and all—and ordered the ingredients. When he asked what I was making, and I told him, his immediate response was, 'You must be from San Francisco.'"

From Sea to Shining Sea: Fish and Shellfish

FOR THE SAUCE

3 tablespoons olive oil

1 medium onion, coarsely chopped

2 garlic cloves, minced

½ teaspoon dried thyme

½ teaspoon dried rosemary

½ teaspoon dried oregano

½ teaspoon dried basil

¼ teaspoon red pepper flakes

1 bay leaf

Kosher salt and freshly ground black pepper

Two 8-ounce cans tomato sauce

Two 14.5-ounce cans whole tomatoes, drained and coarsely chopped

1½ cups dry red wine, plus more as needed

One 8-ounce bottle clam juice

FOR THE SEAFOOD

4 dozen clams, preferably Manila, scrubbed

3 pounds extra jumbo shrimp (16 to 20 per pound), peeled and deveined

1 pound crabmeat, picked over for shells and cartilage

¼ cup chopped fresh parsley

1. To make the sauce: In a Dutch oven, heat the oil over medium heat. Add the onion and cook for 5 minutes, stirring occasionally, until soft. Stir in the garlic, thyme, rosemary, oregano, basil, pepper flakes, bay leaf, ½ teaspoon salt, and ¼ teaspoon pepper and cook for 1 minute, until fragrant. Stir in the tomato sauce, chopped tomatoes, wine, and clam juice, and bring to a simmer. Reduce the heat to low, cover, and cook for 3 hours, stirring occasionally. If the sauce becomes too thick, thin it with more wine. (The sauce can be made 2 days ahead and refrigerated.)

2. To make the seafood: Reheat the sauce over medium-low heat. Add the clams, cover, and cook about 15 minutes, occasionally spooning the sauce over the top of the clams, until they open. Stir in the shrimp and cook until just pink, 3 to 5 minutes. Stir in the crabmeat and cook for one minute. Add the parsley, and serve.

SERVES 8

MY FISH, MYSELF

HALIBUT COVE IS A COMMUNITY OF ABOUT 100 HOMES THAT ARE BUILT ON THE PILINGS of vanished fish houses and docks in the fjord lands of the Kenai Peninsula. Wooden sidewalks connect the houses with the local businesses—several galleries, a restaurant that is located in an old saltery, several oyster farms—and in the summer, when the local population grows to about 150, day-trippers promenade that boardwalk. But locals get around by boat. The cove sits on the protected stretch of waterway that runs between Ismail Island and the south shore of Kachemak Bay. Clem Tillion, whom many credit with saving Alaska's fishing industry, loves this spot with the same unwavering ferocity that he loves his family and the waters that he worked for half a century.

Alaska was not yet a state when he landed there in 1947. A Navy Seabee from New England, Mr. Tillion was recovering from the malaria that he'd picked up in Guadalcanal, and had gone to the territory to check out the land that the government was offering servicemen. Coming over a hill in what is now Katmai National Park, he found a ghost town that remained after the collapse of the local herring industry. Mr. Tillion figured that he'd died and gone to heaven. What else could explain the holy silence and majestic beauty of the place or the grace of Diana Rutzebeck, the daughter of the local family that invited him to dinner.

"I fell for the whole package. The place, the water, the fish, the woman I have loved for sixty-two years," he said. The couple married, started a family, and began amassing land and reclaiming the ghost town. They named it Halibut Cove.

He watched his sons and a grandson wrangle the thirty-pound cod they'd landed that afternoon onto the kitchen counter. "You never know who's coming to dinner here. There's about forty year-round residents, and seventeen of them are members of our immediate family. We all fish, we all cook. If you catch it and clean it and cook it, you know it's done right. People who don't feed themselves aren't taking responsibility for themselves. That's what food is, that's what family is, that's what love is."

When he began as a commercial fisherman, the havoc wreaked by Alaska's old salmon canneries was already obvious. But when he began challenging the traditional fishing method of take-everything-you-can-get, he infuriated his fellow watermen, and he did it again when, instead of fishing for profit, he began pulling crabs and tagging them for the biologists who were monitoring the health of the fishery.

Nevertheless, Mr. Tillion, who has the look of an ancient mariner and is fond of quoting Shakespeare and Psalms, was elected to the state legislature in 1964 and served for sixteen years. He frequently quoted his friend, the former Governor Jay Hammond: "If you err on the side of conservation, you can always make a correction later," and added, for emphasis, "but not vice versa."

"*National Geographic* named Alaska, New Zealand, and Iceland the three most sustainable fisheries in the world," he said. "We have a state constitution that *mandates* sustainable yield. Allocation will always be political, so we gave biologists the final say in protecting our fisheries. Scientists are sometimes wrong, but politicians are always wrong."

Cinnamon Halibut

The Tillions have a fish preparation for every day of the year, most of them simple roasts with olive oil and herbs. The paterfamilias, Clem Tillion, prefers cod (it has more flavor than halibut) and likes it best simmered with potatoes in cream: "I'm very New England." His family is more adventuresome. In addition to being an artist, his daughter, Marian Beck, a former commercial boat captain, owns the restaurant in Halibut Cove, and ideas and ingredients (such as the cinnamon oil that she uses to prepare shrimp) inevitably drift a few hundred yards upshore to her family's home.

¼ cup cinnamon

1 cup vegetable oil

1 tablespoon toasted sesame oil

2 teaspoons Chinese chili paste, plus more to taste

2 pounds center-cut halibut fillet, skin removed (cod, bass, and other thick, large-flake white fish also work well)

1 tablespoon grated fresh ginger

1 cup seeded fresh tomato, fresh or high quality canned, chopped

2 scallions, green and white part, minced

Kosher salt and freshly ground black pepper to taste

1. The day before serving, make the cinnamon oil: Use water or additional vegetable oil to moisten a paper coffee filter and arrange the filter in a strainer set over a bowl. Place the cinnamon in the strainer. Warm the oil over medium-high heat until hot, 3 to 5 minutes. Pour slowly over the cinnamon. Allow to drain for an hour, occasionally using a rubber spatula to gently push the cinnamon, pressing out any remaining oil. Add the sesame oil and chili paste, and cool the mixture completely in the refrigerator.

2. Four hours before serving, place the cod fillets in a shallow dish. Pour half the oil over the fish, rubbing each side well. Spread the minced ginger over the fish, cover with plastic wrap, and place in the refrigerator.

3. Preheat the oven to 400°F. Remove the fish from the pan, scrape off the ginger, and discard the ginger and the oil. Place the fish in a baking dish, season lightly with salt and pepper, and spread the tomato and scallions evenly over the fish. Cover with foil and bake until the fish is firm and flaky, 10 to 15 minutes depending on the thickness of the fillet. Serve with lemon and additional cinnamon oil on the side.

SERVES 4 TO 6

New York's Mayor LaGuardia with a 300-pound halibut.

Makah Indian Slow-Cooked Salmon

For at least 10,000 years, wild salmon was the mainstay of First Nations cultures, a fish so prized that most of the land now called the "Pacific Northwest" was given away in exchange only for the right to catch salmon at will. Indigenous peoples on both the Atlantic and the Pacific coasts celebrated the fish for its courage, perseverance, even transcendence—qualities called "salmon medicine." When the fish began their leaps upriver, it meant that spring had arrived. Several weeks of hooking, harpooning, and bow-fishing; and cutting, curing, drying, and sometimes smoking filled a larder for a year. Then the fresh salmon feasting began.

Native Americans commonly recall their ancestors cooking the fish slowly on wooden grills assembled close to—but not on top of—hot coals. After listening to these accounts and watching Makah elders on the Olympia Peninsula cook salmon in this way, Jon Rowley, a former commercial fisherman who lives in Seattle and works as a consultant to both the fishing and wine industries, developed this method for slow oven roasting. It yields a tender, succulent fish.

The Makah generally season salmon with only salt and black pepper or spiceberry. To Mr. Rowley, however, part of the miracle of salmon is how it flourishes when paired with big flavors, such as the Asian-inspired sweet-sour-salty wine glaze in this recipe, a version of which appeared in *Gourmet* magazine. A larger side of salmon makes a wonderful party meal, although smaller cuts can be used. A forager, Mr. Rowley loves to serve the dish with sautéed morels, roasted asparagus, fiddlehead ferns (page 518), and boiled new potatoes or steamed white rice.

2 cups dry red wine

1⅓ cups mirin

1 cup soy sauce

¼ cup packed dark brown sugar

One 2-inch piece fresh ginger, grated over a fine-mesh strainer, squeezed, juice reserved

3 whole black peppercorns

2 teaspoons fresh lime juice

One 4½-pound wild king salmon fillet

1 tablespoon vegetable oil

Lime wedges, for serving

1. In a medium saucepan, bring the wine, mirin, soy sauce, sugar, ginger juice, and peppercorns to a simmer over medium-high heat. Cook about 45 minutes, until thick and reduced to about 1 cup. Transfer to a bowl, stir in the lime juice, and cool completely.

2. Preheat the oven to 225°F. Grease a baking dish large enough to hold the fish flat, or a rimmed baking sheet.

3. Pat the fish dry with a paper towel. Rub the skin with the oil and place skin side down in the baking dish.

4. Spread 2 tablespoons of the glaze evenly over the fish and let sit for 5 minutes. Spread 2 more tablespoons over the fish, then place in the oven. Bake for 1 to 1½ hours, glazing the fish every 15 minutes, until the fish has a temperature of 130°F (for medium-rare) on an instant-read thermometer.

5. Transfer the fish to a serving platter, brush with the glaze and serve with the lime wedges.

SERVES 8

SALMON

SALMON HAS ALWAYS BEEN AN ODE TO SPRING. FOR MANY YEARS, THE FIRST NORTH
Atlantic salmon caught in Maine would be ceremoniously shipped to the White House, where it would be prepared simply—seasoned lightly, poached or baked whole—and served with the season's first asparagus, sweet peas, or new potatoes. But salmon was never particularly chic; it was too abundant, and too inexpensive to capture the culinary imagination.

The fish's social status rose a little in the 1960s, when America renewed its love affair with classic French cooking. Poaching a whole salmon was a benchmark in the classic repertoire, and the dish became a fixture first at elite dinner parties, then in restaurants. By the 1990s, a chef's way with salmon was a measure of her or his genius. When caught at the perfect moment—after surfacing, fat and fierce, from the depths of the ocean and before being depleted by its fated journey upstream to the riverbeds where it was born—salmon is a perfect expression of itself. Its flesh is dense and thickly ribbed with pure white fat, allowing it to self-baste on a grill, over a fire, or in a smoker, a poaching pan, a slow oven (below 350°F), a fast oven (400-500°F), or a sauté pan. An additional sheet of fat beneath the skin, like an alabaster layer of thermal wear, melts while cooking and crisps the skin.

The combination of juicy flesh and crunchy skin alone would be enough. But salmon at that moment has an extraordinarily complex flavor. It tastes of the ocean, plus the mineral herbaceous hints of the river. That balance, of course, cannot be predicted or controlled. Nine hundred and ninety-nine servings of salmon might be marvelous eating; one might change your life.

Industrial pollution, river damming, and overfishing have long since reduced the wild salmon population from 1.5 million to fewer than a half million. Wild North Atlantic salmon has been gone for decades, but there are still five viable wild varieties in the Pacific: chum, coho, pink, sockeye, and king salmon. Climate shifts have made the runs less predictable, but each is harvested sometime between April and September. Currently, king salmon from Alaska's Yukon region, with its dense, fatty flesh and fine flake, reigns supreme.

Farmed salmon, like most species, lacks the flavor the wild fish have. However, growing methods are improving constantly and when well farmed, it is becoming firmer, fatter, and more versatile in the kitchen.

DICK YOSHIMURA'S SAKE SALMON

SEATTLE, WASHINGTON

Dick Yoshimura was born into the Japanese American community in Seattle in 1912. Like many others, he grew up in the fishing industry and married young; like most, he and his wife, Misao, were placed in an internment camp during World War II. Returning to Seattle after the war, Mr. Yoshimura went to work in the fish markets and learned how to cut fish and how to judge it, buy it, and sell it. Mutual Fish Company was the market of choice among the city's Asian seafood connoisseurs, and when the opportunity to buy the market presented itself, Mr. Yoshimura leaped at the chance.

For the next half-century, he spent the predawn hours pacing Seattle's waterfront, purchasing the best fish he could find. He watched as non-Asians began to understand the difference between most fish and his fish. By the late 1970s, anyone who knew anything shopped at Mutual Fish—and they still do. Mr. Yoshimura's son, Harry Yoshimura, daughter, Lisa Duff, and his grandson Kevin now manage the family business. Mr. Yoshimura is now 94 but still visits the store every day. He needs to check the fish, he says, and maintain his prodigious knife skills.

"It's sort of a feel, an art," explains his son, Harry. "He's still one of the best there is. I learned it by osmosis; we each have our own quirks."

Each generation has its quirks when it comes to cooking fish, as well. The patriarch is most likely to delicately fry fish and serve them with a ponzu sauce made of soy and lemon. The son tends to bake the fish en papillote. Inspired by preparations he's tasted in restaurants, Harry has added sake, ginger, lemon juice, and butter over the years. In the iteration here, he adds clams and shrimp to the fish packages. "I like to keep the seasoning subtle and the flavors clean so you taste the fish," he says. His own son, Kevin, is all about big flavors and spice. Harry Yoshimura remains philosophical. "When we are young, we complicate; then we spend the rest of our lives simplifying and paring things down to their essential nature." Although Kevin is 43, his father says, he "is a little bit of a late bloomer. He'll learn."

This dish is best served with rice and steamed vegetables. Wasabi-flavored mashed potatoes are also a delicious accompaniment.

4 pieces dried kelp (dashi kombu), about the size of each fillet

4 tablespoons sake or dry vermouth

Four 6- to 8-ounce salmon fillets

Kosher salt and freshly ground white pepper

2 tablespoons olive oil

1 tablespoon grated fresh ginger

1 small shallot, minced

1 teaspoon fresh lemon juice

1. Preheat the oven to 375°F. Cut four 15 x 20-inch sheets of parchment paper.

2. In a shallow dish, soak the kelp in 2 tablespoons of the sake for 5 minutes. Place a piece of soaked kelp on each of the parchment paper sheets. Pat the fish dry with a paper towel. Season with salt and white pepper and place on top of the kelp, skin down.

3. In a small bowl, combine the remaining 2 tablespoons sake, the oil, ginger, shallot, and lemon juice, then divide the mixture evenly over the salmon. Fold the parchment paper around the fish to form a tidy package, crimping the paper at the top to seal.

4. Place the parchment packages on a baking sheet and bake for 14 minutes, until the fish has a temperature of 130°F (for medium-rare) on an instant-read thermometer. Transfer the packages to individual plates, open carefully, and serve.

SERVES 4

From Sea to Shining Sea: Fish and Shellfish

Ellen Keyes's Salmon on Creamy Leeks

EMMONAK, ALASKA

In the winter of 2005, Humphrey and Ellen Keyes flew from their home on the Yukon-Kuskokwin Delta to Boston. A treeless tundra roughly the size of the state of Oregon, the delta juts into the Bering Sea and is frozen about nine months of the year. The delta is called "the cradle of Eskimo civilization," and the 20,000 Yup'ik people who live there constitute the largest single group of Native Americans living continuously on their land on the North American continent. Like their ancestors, Mr. and Mrs. Keyes forage, hunt, and fish to feed their family. Before this trip, they had never flown or slept away from their two daughters. Most of all, they had never believed that the mainstay of their diet—a massive local salmon called Yukon king—could become a gourmet gold mine.

But as the wild salmon stocks in the Pacific Northwest have dwindled, the quest for the perfect wild salmon pushed into increasingly remote and unlikely spots. The Yukon king travels more than 2,000 miles upriver in the spring and, near the outset of its journey, it contains 34 percent body fat, the highest of any salmon in the world. Yukon king is unctuous and juicy; it is the Kobe beef of the salmon world.

Until recently, the Yup'ik pulled purse nets to catch the fish. They cut it and hung it to dry, and fed their families for the rest of the year. But as the cost of fuel and heating oil and other necessities soared, the traditional subsistence society needed more cash than could be made working seasonal jobs in local fish canneries and processing plants. The Yup'iks learned that salmon fisheries on other far-flung rivers were successfully branding and marketing their salmon, and they knew that their salmon was better. They also knew that, by dint of treaties, they were the only people allowed to land the fish. And so in 2002, they formed a cooperative to fish, market, and sell their salmon to chefs and connoisseurs willing to pay four times the going rate for extraordinary fish from pristine waters. And their salmon were caught in an environmentally sound manner that made overfishing all but impossible.

A year later, Mr. and Mrs. Keyes made their first trip to the Boston Seafood Show, the most important show of its kind in the country. At the baggage claim area of Logan Airport, they hoisted onto their shoulders a frozen Yukon king that they had brought for Gordon Hamersley, the chef and owner of Hamersley's Bistro, who had been commissioned to create a multicourse Yukon king tasting menu for a small group of chefs and food writers.

Mrs. Keyes told the guests about the tiny boats, the fish, and the waters in which they are caught. Mr. Keyes described a way of life that revolves around foraging the tundra for berries in the summer, stalking game and wild mushrooms in the fall, and waiting, always waiting, for the king salmon to arrive in June.

The guests were so entranced that the arrival of the chef's slow-cooked salmon with creamy leeks and red wine butter failed to distract them as Mr. Keyes described the Yup'ik hope that salmon could save their civilization. Mrs. Keyes, however, bent toward her plate and inhaled deeply. Waiting anxiously for the guests to pick up their forks, she whispered, "I am learning so much about cooking salmon. We don't eat much fresh salmon, we dry it and use it to make fish cakes or soup. You should taste the recipe I learned from a chef in San Francisco! My daughters love it. And I think that this one is going to be even better! Just smell it. It smells like salmon, but better and more."

1 cup red wine

2 shallots, minced

8 tablespoons (1 stick) unsalted butter, softened

3 tablespoons chopped fresh parsley

Kosher salt and freshly ground black pepper

3 medium leeks, white and light green parts only, cut into matchsticks

1½ teaspoons minced fresh marjoram

1½ teaspoons minced fresh thyme

1 teaspoon fennel seeds, crushed

⅓ cup dry vermouth

2 cups heavy cream

1 tablespoon fresh lemon juice

3 tablespoons extra virgin olive oil

1 garlic clove, minced

Four 6- to 8-ounce skinless salmon fillets

1. In a small saucepan, bring the wine and 1 of the minced shallots to a simmer over medium-high heat and cook for 4 to 8 minutes, until the wine is syrupy and reduced to about 1 tablespoon. Strain the mixture through a fine-mesh strainer, pushing on the solids to extract as much liquid as possible. Discard the solids and cool the wine reduction to room temperature.

2. In a small bowl, combine the cooled wine reduction, 6 tablespoons of the butter, 2 tablespoons of the parsley, ¼ teaspoon salt, and ⅛ teaspoon pepper. Shape the mixture into a log, roll it in plastic wrap, and refrigerate until firm, at least 1 hour or up to 1 week.

3. Preheat the oven to 225°F. Melt the remaining 2 tablespoons butter in a large skillet over medium-high heat. Add the leeks, marjoram, thyme, fennel seeds, and ¼ teaspoon salt and cook, stirring occasionally, about 2 minutes, until the leeks are slightly wilted. Stir in the vermouth and cook about 5 minutes, until almost all of the liquid has evaporated. Add the cream and lemon juice and cook, stirring occasionally, for 15 to 20 minutes, until the leeks are soft and the cream has thickened. Season with salt and pepper to taste, cover, and keep warm.

4. In a small bowl, combine the remaining shallot, the oil, and the garlic. Pat the fish dry with a paper towel, then rub with the shallot mixture and season with salt and pepper. Place the fish flesh side down on a rimmed baking sheet and roast for 15 to 20 minutes, until the fish reaches a temperature of 130°F (for medium-rare) on an instant-read thermometer.

5. Cut the red wine butter into ¼-inch slices, and place a piece on top of each fish fillet. Turn off the oven and let the fish sit for 1 to 3 minutes, until the butter is melted.

6. Spoon some of the leeks onto the center of four plates. Place a fish fillet on top, sprinkle with the remaining parsley, and serve.

SERVES 4

CRABS, CRABS, AND MORE CRABS

ABOUT A DOZEN DIFFERENT SPECIES OF HARD-SHELL CRABS scurry around the nation's waters. Of these, four are the best known and each is associated with a different region. Blue crab is the country's third most popular crustacean, following shrimp and lobster. It ranges from Cape Cod to Florida but is most famous in the Chesapeake, where it is the basis of three regional dishes: crab boil, crab cakes, and between shedding and acquiring its shell, soft-shell crabs. Its meat is the basis of Charleston's she-crab soup, and in North Carolina, the entire crab is boiled with dumplings called "pie bread." Stone crab is found primarily in South Florida and Key West and is prized for its sweet, firm claw meat, typically boiled or steamed, cracked, and eaten with melted butter or other dipping sauces. The gigantic king crab, also known as Alaskan king, can weigh up to twenty pounds and is prized for its leg meat, which is usually sold cooked and frozen, then reheated and eaten from the shell. Dungeness crab can be found from Alaska to Mexico, but is most dense around the San Francisco Bay. It is bought fresh and can be steamed, boiled, baked, or roasted. In addition to being sold in the shell, most sizable crabs are also picked for meat. There are three grades: snow-white "lump meat" is solid meat from the body; "flake meat" is small pieces picked from the body; and "claw" meat tends to be slightly spongier and often brown-tinged.

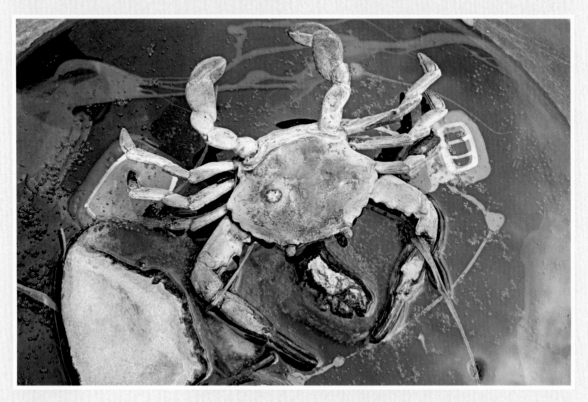

DON WONG'S DUNGENESS CRAB

When Don Wong was growing up in Oakland, California, his family owned a small Chinese restaurant. "But they never brought food from the restaurant home," he says. "That was for Americans. We ate real Chinese food." Dungeness crab is native to the American Pacific coast, but the Wongs still considered it "real Chinese"–perhaps because making the dish began with a trip to Chinatown, for the crabs and the vegetables that would be stir-fried with it. Stir-fried Dungeness crab was "weekend food." Mr. Wong learned how to make this dish by standing next to his mother as she prepared it; now he makes it at home on the weekends, flanked by his two young sons. The key to success is to keep the cooking oil hot enough when frying the crabs, to reduce the amount of juice that seeps from them. In lesser heat, the crabs will steam and be less succulent and tender.

Three 2½-pound live Dungeness crabs, cleaned

½ cup peanut oil or vegetable oil

12 garlic cloves, chopped

One 2-inch piece ginger, peeled and thinly sliced

½ cup shaoxing wine (Chinese rice wine)

1 cup chopped fresh cilantro leaves and stems

6 scallions, green and white parts, cut into 3-inch-long pieces

¼ cup soy sauce

¼ cup sesame oil

1. Bring a large pot of water to a boil over high heat. Add the crabs and cook for 10 to 15 minutes, until the meat flakes easily from the shell. Remove the crabs from the water and cool to room temperature. Twist the legs and claws from the crabs, then cut each crab body in half following the horizontal ridge of the carapace. Place the pieces of crab in a large zipper-top plastic bag and use a mallet to lightly crack the shells.

2. Heat ¼ cup of the peanut oil in a large wok or skillet over high heat until very hot. Add half of the garlic and ginger and stir-fry for 15 seconds, then add half of the crabs and cook, stirring constantly, for 2 minutes. Add ¼ cup of the rice wine, cover, and cook for 5 minutes. Uncover, stir in half of the cilantro and scallions, and cook for 2 minutes longer. Stir in 2 tablespoons of the soy sauce and 2 tablespoons sesame oil and transfer to a serving platter.

3. Pour off any oil in the pan, then return to high heat, add the remaining ¼ cup peanut oil, and repeat the cooking with the remaining crabs. Serve.

SERVES 4

DEVI JAMESON'S CURRIED DUNGENESS CRAB

OAKLAND, CALIFORNIA

When Devi Jameson piles a mound of her curried crab on a big metal dish and serves it to company, she gives each of her guests a large towel. "You have to lose your inhibitions to eat this crab," she says, "and shouldn't feel bad about using your fingers and getting nice and messy." Born in Shanghai, Ms. Jameson grew up in India prior to moving to San Francisco. Her mother was famous for her cooking. She made a small book of her Chinese and Indian recipes before she died, and Ms. Jameson, who works as a musical director in a public school, credits her for the seasoning and technique in this dish. The crab, however, is pure California.

The recipe is good for a crowd. The gravy can be made well ahead of time and then the crabs cooked in it just before serving. She serves the crabs with white rice and raita. The recipe is for one crab and should be multiplied for each crab used.

One 2½-pound live Dungeness crab, cleaned

8 whole black peppercorns

1 tablespoon coriander seeds

1 teaspoon cumin seeds

3 dried red chiles

½ teaspoon ground turmeric

2 tablespoons vegetable oil

1 medium onion, finely chopped

1½ teaspoons grated fresh ginger

2 garlic cloves, minced

1 tablespoon tomato paste

¾ cup water

1 teaspoon tamarind paste or 1 tablespoon fresh lemon juice

Kosher salt

1. Bring a large pot of water to a boil over high heat. Add the crab and cook for 10 to 15 minutes, until the meat flakes easily from the shell. Remove the crab from the water and cool to room temperature. Break the crab into pieces and use a mallet to lightly crack the shell.

2. In a small dry skillet, cook the peppercorns, coriander seeds, cumin seeds, chiles, and turmeric over medium heat for 2 to 3 minutes, stirring constantly, until toasted and fragrant. Cool completely, then grind to a powder in a spice grinder or with a mortar and pestle.

3. In a large skillet, heat the oil over medium heat until hot. Add the onion and cook about 10 minutes, stirring occasionally, until golden brown. Stir in the ginger and garlic and cook for 2 minutes longer, until fragrant. Add the ground spices and cook for 1 minute. Stir in the tomato paste and cook for 3 minutes longer. Add the water, bring to a simmer, and cook for 3 to 5 minutes, until slightly thickened.

4. Stir in the crab pieces and cook for 2 minutes, until hot. Stir in the tamarind paste and season with salt to taste. Serve.

SERVES 1

XINH'S MUSSELS IN CURRY SAUCE

OLYMPIA, WASHINGTON

Xinh Dwelley was born on a rice farm near Saigon, but she learned to cook in an American mess hall. When she was 14 years old, she began working as a dishwasher at an army base; before her fifteenth birthday, she made respectable fried chicken, meatloaf, macaroni, and hamburgers. "The officers' club loved my cooking," she says. "I did delivery." After marrying an American soldier and moving to Olympia, she shucked oysters for the Taylor Shellfish Farms. When her employers asked her to cook the staff meal, however, they wanted Vietnamese cooking, not American mess-hall cuisine, and Mrs. Dwelley greeted this as she does most challenges: "I just did it. Our rice farm was in tidal swamps; we had a lot of fish. That is what my mother cooked, that is what we ate. I have no culinary training, I have memory. I make curry sauce from memory." Her memory is acute. Her curried mussels took first prize (and $500) in the first cooking contest that she entered, and they were the most popular dish she made for the staff at Taylor Shellfish Farms. Soon, with the help of her employers, she moved from shucking oysters to cooking them—along with other seafood and fish—at her own restaurant, Xinh's Clam and Oyster House. Her curried mussels have become an institution in Seattle.

Xinh Dwelley
with giant geoduck.

5 pounds fresh mussels, scrubbed and debearded

3 cups water

¼ cup vegetable oil

1 medium onion, coarsely chopped

1 tablespoon curry powder

2 garlic cloves, minced

½ teaspoon sugar

¼ teaspoon cayenne pepper (optional)

1 cup unsweetened coconut milk

2 tablespoons soy sauce

½ cup roasted unsalted peanuts, crushed

¼ cup chopped fresh cilantro

2 scallions, green and white parts, thinly sliced

1. In a Dutch oven, combine the mussels and water, cover, and cook over medium heat for 5 to 7 minutes, until the mussels begin to open.

2. Remove the pan from the heat and let sit, shaking the pan occasionally, for 5 minutes, until the mussels have opened completely. Drain the mussels, remove the meat from the shells, and discard the shells.

3. Wipe out the pan. Add the oil, and heat over medium heat until hot. Add the onion and cook about 5 minutes, stirring occasionally, until soft. Stir in the curry powder, garlic, sugar, and cayenne (if using) and cook for 1 minute, until fragrant. Stir in the coconut milk and soy sauce and bring to a simmer. Stir in the mussels, peanuts, cilantro, and scallions, and serve.

SERVES 4 TO 6

From Sea to Shining Sea: Fish and Shellfish

Acadian Mussels

When Claudine Theirault Steffano's Acadian ancestors fled Canada in 1785 and settled near Aroostock in northern Maine, they brought with them a French approach to cooking. The retired elementary school teacher tells me that when her family moved to New Hampshire a century later, "their French kitchen sense was inseparable from Maine ingredients." These fragrant steamed mussels were the centerpiece of many festive winter meals in her own childhood. Her mother served them in the pot, with "ship's biscuits," or croutons, for dunking. Later, after she married an Italian American, Mrs. Steffano added a few tomatoes to the pot and served the mussels with bread. She also steamed the mussels, tossed pasta with the broth, and served the soupy result garnished with the shelled mussels. "My grandmother was appalled," she says, and she sympathizes. Her great-granddaughter uses olive oil instead of butter and adds lemongrass and fresh ginger to the pot. That, says Mrs. Steffano, "is taking things a little too far."

2 tablespoons (¼ stick) unsalted butter

3 shallots, minced

4 garlic cloves, thinly sliced

1 cup dry white wine

2 ripe tomatoes, chopped

1 tablespoon minced fresh thyme

1 bay leaf, crumbled

3 whole black peppercorns

5 pounds fresh mussels, scrubbed and debearded

¼ cup minced fresh parsley

2 tablespoons fresh lemon juice

1. Melt the butter in a Dutch oven over medium heat. Add the shallots and garlic and cook, stirring occasionally, for 3 minutes, until soft. Add the wine, tomatoes, thyme, bay leaf, and peppercorns, and bring to a boil. Add the mussels, cover, and cook for 5 to 7 minutes, until the mussels begin to open. Remove the pan from the heat and let sit, shaking the pan occasionally, for 5 minutes, until the mussels have opened completely.

2. Use tongs to transfer the mussels to a serving bowl, discarding any unopened mussels. Stir the parsley and lemon juice into the broth, and then pour it over the mussels, and serve.

SERVES 4

DEBORAH JOY COREY'S PICNIC LOBSTER

CASTINE, MAINE

Deborah Joy Corey, the author of *Losing Eddie* and *The Skating Pond*, grew up in rural Canadabut. She has never felt that she really belonged anywhere: "It's always seemed to me that my real life surely must be taking place somewhere else." Even though she and her husband and two daughters have lived in the small coastal town of Castine, Maine, for fifteen years, she still feels like an outsider there and she uses cooking—especially cooking lobster for her family's annual reunion—to give her daughters a sense of place.

"For me, preparing a meal for our yearly family gathering is like my younger daughter's description of knitting. She says it is tying knots together to make something beautiful, and that is just what a summer picnic is. It is a thing of beauty. A table displayed with everyone's best effort. That is what I remember the best.

"I remember the aunts trying to outdo themselves and each other. When a woman brought the most admired dish to the picnic, she tended to bring it again the following year. I remember those repeats, a tangy three-bean salad, a potato salad seasoned with a homemade mustard and trimmed with radishes, a freshly grated horseradish sauce, plump garden snow peas in a fruit vinaigrette, white dinner rolls that had risen like castles, strawberry-rhubarb pies with latticed crusts, lemon squares, meringues, and

a multitude of shiny iced delights. I remember the uncles cooking lobster and steak and hot dogs outdoors. In my favorite photograph they are young fathers, lined up and holding trays of T-bone steaks. It was what they cooked best: meat. And now it is what my brothers do best as well.

"I do lobster. My family in Canada thinks that I live south of the border; that is how my lobster dish got its name. I wonder if my daughters will remember the name or the taste or the hours we spend picking lobster meat together. It doesn't matter. When they are cooking or picking or eating lobster, they are at home."

Four 1¼- to 1½-pound steamed lobsters, meat picked and cut into ½-inch pieces

⅓ cup extra virgin olive oil

½ cup finely chopped red onion

¼ cup chopped fresh cilantro

2 tablespoons fresh lime juice

½ teaspoon kosher salt

¼ teaspoon freshly ground black pepper

Lime wedges, for serving

In a medium bowl, combine the lobster meat, oil, onion, cilantro, lime juice, salt, and pepper. Cover and refrigerate for 2 hours, until chilled. Serve with lime wedges.

SERVES 4 TO 6

Taming Fire
A SOCIAL HISTORY OF AMERICAN STOVES

Today's $10,000.00 La Cornue, Aga, and Viking ranges are not the nation's first "trophy stoves." Fireplaces were the original measure of status and wealth. Preparing dinner on an open hearth without burning the house down, however, was smoky, dirty work that required strength and skill. Hooks hung at various lengths from the top of the fireplace provided "low," "medium," and "high" flames, and cooks heaved forty-pound forged-iron pots from hooks as routinely as their modern-day counterparts turn a knob. Some of the nation's iconic dishes—clam chowder, baked beans, chicken and dumplings, Kentucky burgoo, pepper pot, and gumbo—were probably born of the ingredients on hand and the vicissitudes of fireplace cookery. But the open flame is a limited medium.

"Let's face it," said Ed Semmelroth, the founder of antiquestoves.com, "it's hard to do a nice Béarnaise sauce in a fireplace."

By the late eighteenth century, the roaring fireplace was a symbol of hearth, home, safety, prosperity, and the goodness of family life in the American imagination. Nevertheless, the dream of an easier future certainly included cooking fuel that did not require chopping and a cooking medium that was less arduous and had greater finesse. The evolution of that dream explains a lot about why we cook how we cook. In addition, stoves embody the culture's complicated relationship with progress: the national passion for the new and improved is matched only by the fear of how progress could affect private life. Perhaps for this reason, the once tiny subculture of stove worshipers has gained numbers enough to support a magazine as well as an annual conference. Each summer, several hundred stove scholars, stove restorers, and antique stove collectors—each specializing in and cooking on the stove of a discrete era—gather throughout the country to debate the merits and often the moral superiority of each.

OPPOSITE: *The Asian elements then in vogue were used by the Rathbone Company in the 1888 exhibit to communicate the luxury of its ranges.*

ABOVE: *The luxury of stoves soon gave way to amber-hued domesticity, and over a century would elapse before Viking's minimalist stainless-steel range created a market for high-end professional-gauge ranges for the home. The stainless design of the Viking range evokes the ease and utilitarianism of the professional restaurant kitchen.*

By 1790, "close stoves"—metal boxes that contained the fire and conserved fuel such as the one at left—were already being used for heating in Germany. In the United States, Benjamin Franklin was experimenting with a three-sided fireplace. Both versions offered a flat top for rudimentary cooking. And one—or perhaps both—inspired the first cookstoves as well as a new industry of stovetop cooking equipment as round-bottomed pots gave way to skillets and saucepans with flat bottoms and utensils with short handles.

Shortly before the Civil War, technological advances allowed iron to be melted and "cast" (or "formed") to create early "step stoves" like the one at right from about 1820. The second level contains the firebox with a damper that allows the cook to regulate the heat of the cooking surface. The hot air is drawn up into the chimney and this heats the tank-shaped baking chamber at the top of the stove. Step stoves allowed searing, braising, and skillet griddling, and brought steaks, chops, and other smaller cuts of meat to the American table. And with more control over oven temperature, cooks could bake delicate cake batters with beaten egg whites. It was the death knell for heavy American fruitcakes and puddings.

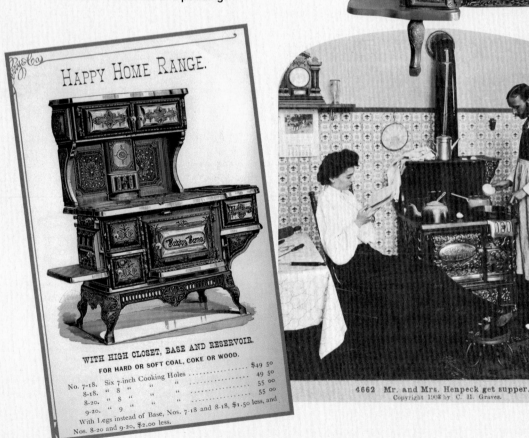

HAPPY HOME RANGE.

WITH HIGH CLOSET, BASE AND RESERVOIR.
FOR HARD OR SOFT COAL, COKE OR WOOD.

No. 7-18. Six 7-inch Cooking Holes $49 50
8-18.   " 8   "   "   " 49 50
8-20.   " 8   "   "   " 55 00
9-20.   " 9   "   "   " 55 00
With Legs instead of Base, Nos. 7-18 and 8-18, $1.50 less, and
Nos. 8-20 and 9-20, $2.00 less.

4662 Mr. and Mrs. Henpeck get supper.
Copyright 1902 by C. H. Graves.

An 1837 issue of the *Maine Farmer* called the cookstove "a pretty effectual cure for 'smoking houses and scolding wives.'" The "cure" was quickly taken, but as is often the case, the improvement begat nostalgia. As Catharine Beecher said in 1869, "We can not but regret, for the sake of our bread, that our old stead brick ovens have been almost universally superseded by those of ranges and cooking-stoves, which are infinite in their caprices and forbid all general rules."

Some regions of the country were plagued by wood shortages as early as 1790, but the first stoves that burned coal were summarily rejected. Many claimed that food cooked in kerosene emerged from the oven saturated with the taste of the fuel. Others worried about the toxicity of the cooking fumes and warned that abandoning wood was anti-American and a threat to family life. Gas did not affect the flavor of food, but its vapors were suspect. Still, much to the delight of bakers and dessert lovers, it provided a steadier oven temperature. City dwellers on both coasts quickly made the switch, but in the interior of the country, marketing gimmicks were still necessary.

I mages of the domestic idylls that would most certainly result from a clean, modern, efficient kitchen were used to market gas ranges. With its multiple burners, the ranges allowed the cook to bake, broil, sauté, and simmer simultaneously and, in theory, to spend less time cooking. In fact, the multitask range gave rise to fussier multicourse meals. In *More Work for Mother: The Ironies of Household Technology from the Open Hearth to the Microwave*, Ruth Schwartz Cowan writes: "The only person who saved labor was the husband, who no longer had to split so many logs."

I n 1893, the Michigan Stove Company displayed the Great Stove at the World's Columbian Exposition in Chicago. The unit, which is two feet high, thirty feet long, and twenty feet across, was carved from oak and weighs twenty-two tons. Today it resides at the Michigan state fairgrounds.

The early Magic Chef were majestic ranges used in grand homes. Rescued and restored by Ed Semmelroth of antiquestoves.com, a vintage Magic Chef such as this can fetch up to $30,000.

The Chambers Fireless Gas Range, an enameled gas stove, was invented by John Chambers in 1910. By surrounding the oven in thick rock wool insulation on all sides and using a system of internal dampers, John Chambers created an oven that heated quickly and retained its heat, thus conserving fuel and reducing food shrinkage. Mother of the modern trophy stove, the iconic Chambers Fireless Gas Range was manufactured in Shelbyville, Indiana, from 1912 to 1955, where a huge home economics department fastidiously created stylish, no-fail recipes to help market the stove. The resulting book, *The Idle Hour Cookbook*, remained in print until the 1960s. Mr. Chambers's most powerful marketing tool, however, was his daughter, Alma, who began touring the country in the 1930s giving large cooking shows to demonstrate recipes and explain how to use the stoves and didn't stop for the next twenty-five years.

Taming Fire: A Social History of American Stoves

To ensure the adaptation of electric stoves, local power companies sponsored cooking classes for women and young girls in cities and dispatched armies of power company cooks to more remote areas.

CHAPTER 6

POULTRY IN EVERY POT, OVEN, BROILER, AND GRILL

THE PATRON SAINT OF POULTRY

LINDSBORG, KANSAS

The Kansas prairie is a flat forever. On a late winter afternoon, the end-of-day sounds—the whinny of gears in a pickup, the bullish snort of a combine turning frosty dirt—seem bigger than anything mortal, and as the shadows grow ominous in the changing light, the little town of Lindsborg seems like the only safe place.

From an early age, Frank Reese's job was to usher the turkeys on his family's farm from the barn to the open range to peck for insects. When the other children in his first-grade class wrote adoring sonnets to their cats and dogs, Mr. Reese turned in a personal essay entitled "Me and My Turkeys." Even today, he has no memory of ever *not* loving turkeys and chickens.

In his well-pressed flannel shirt, Mr. Reese looks as if he could have stepped off a page of the 1954 Sears, Roebuck catalog. But to food lovers, animal lovers, and many family farmers, Frank Reese is a saint. He is

the man who saved American poultry. He has devoted his life to the genetic preservation of American pure-bred poultry.

Layers, fryers, roasters, stewers—since the American colonial era, there have been different birds for every season and different uses for every bird.

When it was published in 1874, the American Poultry Association's *Standards of Excellence* recognized five distinct varieties of turkeys, fifty-four varieties of chicken, and hundreds of variations on these basic themes. In subsequent editions, the title of the handbook was changed to *Standards of Perfection*, but the volume continued to detail the traits that comprise an ideal example of a given variety.

The differences between the chickens can be as dramatic as those between a Great Dane and a dachshund, and for nearly a century, farmers and hobbyists bred for the qualities that distinguished one

OPPOSITE: *Correct way to bake turkey, demonstrated by Uncle Sam's expert cooks, Washington, D.C., 1937.*

purebred bird from another. Doing so generally resulted in increased hardiness, better meat quality, greater reproductive prowess, and physical beauty. Winning was good for business: Growers wanted to buy chicks from champion stock.

In remote regions like Mr. Reese's patch of Kansas, a "best in show" fever raged well into the late twentieth century. It was a milieu in which hair dryers were aimed at feathers rather than fur. Mr. Reese won his first blue ribbon with a Jersey Giant chicken at the McPherson County Fair when he was 6 years old.

"They didn't have any junior category back then, but I had the champion and the reserve champion for ten years running," he says.

His winning streak ended when he was old enough to manage turkeys and began to show them. "I was up there with all the legendary turkey breeders; Sadie Caldwell and Gladys Hanssinger with their Bourbon Reds, Martha Walker and her

Bronzes, Norman Kardosh and his White Hollands. I got beat a lot."

He also got an education. "They taught me the history of each variety, told stories about the culture that grew up around purebred birds. It was a world that respected individuality and rewarded excellence. They had me sitting on the ground with my standards book, studying each bird, imprinting the ideal of each variety so I could look at a flock and know immediately which bird to breed."

After he'd learned to appraise dozens of varieties of chickens, ducks, geese, and turkeys, the young bird man was adopted by the legendary Norman Kardosh of Alton, Kansas. Before him, Mr. Reese understood what a perfect bird was. Under Mr. Kardosh's tutelage, he says, "I learned what a well-bred bird *means*.

It ensures the survival of the strongest, healthiest bloodlines, it ensures diversity. Without those two things, any creature is doomed."

Between earning his nursing degree, completing his military service, and his first decade as an anesthesiology nurse, Mr. Reese realized that American standard-bred birds were in big trouble.

Shortly after Herbert Hoover promised Americans "a chicken in every pot," big business began breeding more chickens and growing them faster and cheaper. The result was Big Chicken: Corporations that own every aspect of their business from research facilities, hatcheries, and feed production to factory farms, processing plants, marketing, and distribution supply American markets with more than 9 million pounds of low-cost chicken a year.

"The commercial industry developed a couple varieties that cost less to feed, fattened up faster, and sold well, and they raised these to the exclusion of all others," says Mr. Reese. "This means that one flu could wipe out every chicken, or turkey, or duck, or goose in this country. I always competed against fifty to a hundred birds at every show. Suddenly it was just me, and the pure bloodlines were dying out."

In 1989, he bought a hundred-year-old farm that he named Good Shepherd Turkey Ranch, and began restoring the populations of standard-bred birds. By 2002, his populations of American Standard Bronze, White Holland, Narragansett, Bourbon Red, and Black turkeys were strong enough to allow him to begin marketing the birds.

"The only way to save these birds was to get people to eat them," he says.

Mr. Reese has saved a dozen varieties of American purebred chickens—Jersey Black Giant and Jersey White Giant; Barred Plymouth Rock; Dark, White-Laced, Red, and White Cornish; beautiful golden Buff Orpingtons; Silverlaced Wyandotte with their silver and black feathers; Dark Brown and Light Brown Leghorns.

In 1972 Americans ate about forty-two pounds of chicken a year. In 2007 the figure had more than doubled, to eighty-seven pounds. "They don't think of chicken as anything special," says Mr. Reese. "They see chicken as an inalienable right.

"They all look the same! They all taste the same! They've lost their individuality. They've lost their dignity! When I was growing up, you ate fried chicken in the summer because that's when the little fryers were ready, you roasted chicken in the fall, you stewed it in the winter.

"Chickens used to tell you the time of year, they let you know where you stood. When you appreciate the differences between chicken, you value what makes you special and unique. You don't spend all your time trying to be just like everybody else. You go ahead and make your contribution to the world, the one you were created to make."

Helena Litke Longhofer's Midday Chicken

Frank Reese says: "I'm fourth-generation poultry farmer on my father's side, a fifth-generation poultry farmer on my mother's side, and second-generation German and English stock. It's a common combination in the Midwest prairie. When the railroad was being built, you could get your own land by clearing it, and many immigrants did just that. Most were big on simple, hearty food. My grandmother and great-grandmother fixed chicken this way for large groups, like the harvesters who came to the early spring and the late fall. Previous generations used lard for the first frying, but I use Crisco with a little pat of butter added for flavor. Over time, the homemade poultry spice blend gave way to a commercially made one, but making a fresh blend gives a better flavor. And you can use it in dressings, to season birds for roasting, even in chicken soup. This chicken recipe comes from a friend's grandmother. The meat can be served sliced and cold in sandwiches, or hot with mashed potatoes and a green vegetable. You can make Midday Chicken out of just about any breed of chicken, and frozen chicken works real well, so it's a year-round favorite and oh-so-good."

312

One Big Table

2 cups all-purpose flour

1 teaspoon Poultry Seasoning (recipe follows)

1 teaspoon kosher salt

½ teaspoon freshly ground black pepper

½ teaspoon sweet paprika

One 4-pound chicken, cut into 8 pieces and trimmed

1 cup vegetable oil or vegetable shortening

2 tablespoons (¼ stick) unsalted butter or lard

½ cup water

1 cup heavy cream

½ cup milk

1. Place an oven rack in the center position and preheat the oven to 325°F. Set a wire rack over a baking sheet and a roasting rack in a roasting pan, and line a plate with paper towels.

2. In a shallow dish, whisk together the flour, poultry seasoning, salt, pepper, and paprika. Coat each piece of chicken in the flour mixture and transfer to the wire rack.

3. Heat the oil and butter in a large cast-iron skillet over medium-high heat until a deep-frying thermometer registers 365°F to 375°F or a pinch of flour bubbles and sizzles in the oil. Carefully add half of the chicken to the skillet and cook for 8 to 10 minutes, until golden brown on both sides. Transfer the chicken to the paper-towel-lined plate to drain briefly, then transfer to the roasting pan. Repeat with the remaining chicken.

4. Carefully strain the oil through a fine-mesh strainer into a heatproof container. (Discard the oil when cool.) Return the browned bits in the strainer to the skillet and add the water. Bring the water to a simmer, scraping and stirring constantly, and cook for 1 minute. Pour this mixture, along with the heavy cream and milk, into the bottom of the roasting pan. Cover the pan with aluminum foil and bake for 2 to 2½ hours, until the chicken is tender. Serve.

_____

SERVES 4 TO 6

Poultry Seasoning

3 tablespoons dried thyme

2 tablespoons dried rosemary

2 tablespoons dried marjoram

1 tablespoon dried savory

1 tablespoon dried sage

2 teaspoons celery seeds

½ teaspoon dried oregano

½ teaspoon ground fennel

½ teaspoon ground allspice

⅛ teaspoon cayenne pepper

In a small bowl, stir together all of the ingredients. The spice blend can be stored in an airtight container for up to three months.

_____

MAKES ABOUT ⅔ CUP

Danny's Spring Chicken and Dill Noodles

Danny Williamson says: "I grew up in Douglas, Kansas. My father did the cattle and wheat, my mother had the vegetables and chickens. My older brother helped my father; I helped my mother and my grandmother. This was back in the 1960s. My mother enjoyed cooking so she took her time with it. Her attitude melted into me. She didn't season food much, but she let me experiment. Once in a while I ruined dinner. We were so poor that losing a meal was a big thing.

"I hated the farm. I hated getting up early. I wanted to play. I didn't want to work all the time. I couldn't wait to get off that farm. When I was seven, I tied the babysitter to a big old tree and left her all day. I was already feeding and watering the chickens. I loved those chickens. One of the best moments of my life was sitting under that big old tree plucking chickens with my grandmother. Another shining moment was Sunday dinner. My mother always fixed chicken, sometimes fried, sometimes roasted, sometimes stewed, it depended on the time of the year.

"I really wanted to be a chef. I went to school for it but I only lasted a year. I'm not the chef type. I'm a home cook. After school I worked in construction, I worked at H&R Block. Then one day I saw Frank Reese's birds at the state fair and it changed how I looked back at my childhood and how I imagined my future. I realized how much I'd learned growing up the way I did. I learned how to respect chickens, and that naturally carries over to how you treat people. Those chickens were teaching me to be responsible and independent and decent. I was back on the farm within a month. My partner and I put in wheat, soy, and milo and I started breeding bantams. They're tough. I had to study a lot just to keep them alive. After a while, I started keeping some of Frank's birds. I have about five hundred birds on my farm. I also judge poultry shows.

"I can tell you one thing for sure: There is no such thing as a spring chicken. In the spring, you have baby chicks in the barn and you are cooking up the last of your frozen birds. The first chickens of the year come in July. In the spring I like to make chicken and noodles. The Eastern European immigrants in the Midwest of my grandmother's generation made fresh dill noodles and when I can take the time, I do, too. I always add lemon to give the soup a bright flavor and fresh dill and spring onions because they are the first green things I get in the spring. I use a six-quart Crock-Pot. It comes out perfect every time."

FOR THE CHICKEN

One 3½- to 4-pound chicken, cut into 8 pieces and trimmed

1 medium onion, peeled and quartered

1 lemon, quartered

½ teaspoon kosher salt

6 whole black peppercorns

2 bay leaves

4 fresh dill sprigs

4 quarts water

3 spring onions or scallions, green and white parts, finely chopped, or ⅓ cup minced fresh chives, for garnish

FOR THE NOODLES

3 large eggs

2 tablespoons olive oil

2 tablespoons water, plus more as needed

2½ cups all-purpose flour

¼ cup minced fresh dill, plus more for garnish

1 teaspoon kosher salt

1. To make the chicken: The day before serving, in a 6-quart slow cooker, combine the chicken, onion, lemon, salt, peppercorns, bay leaves, and dill. Pour the water into the cooker, set on the lowest setting, cover, and cook for 12 hours. (Chicken can also be cooked on the stove. To do so, place the chicken and the aromatics in cold water over medium-low heat, bring to a boil, reduce heat to low, and simmer uncovered for 3½ hours or until the meat is cooked and the vegetables are very tender.)

2. Strain the broth through a fine-mesh strainer into a tall container, cover, bring to room temperature, and refrigerate. Transfer the chicken pieces to a plate and cool to room temperature. Remove and discard the skin and bones, keeping the pieces of meat as large as possible. Cover and refrigerate the chicken.

3. To make the noodles: In a small bowl, whisk together the eggs, oil, and water. In a large bowl, whisk together the flour, dill, and salt. Make a well in the center of the flour, add the egg mixture, and stir until a rough dough forms. If the dough does not come together, add water, 1 tablespoon at a time, until it does. Transfer the dough to a lightly floured work surface and knead about 3 minutes, until smooth. Shape the dough into a ball, cover, and refrigerate for 2 hours.

4. If using a pasta machine, follow the directions for rolling noodles about ⅛ inch thick, ⅓ inch wide, and 8 inches long. If rolling by hand, roll the dough on a floured work surface until ⅛ inch thick, then cut the dough into strips about ⅓ inch wide and 8 inches long. Hang the noodles on the back of a chair to dry slightly.

5. To serve, skim the fat from the chicken broth. Bring the broth to a simmer in a large Dutch oven. Add the noodles, stir gently, cover, and cook for 4 to 6 minutes, until tender. Stir in the chicken and cook about 30 seconds, until warmed through. Season with salt to taste.

6. Ladle into bowls, sprinkle each serving with the chopped spring onions and dill, and serve.

SERVES 6

Pech Khunn's Spring Pot-au-Feu

"Cambodians like to poach poultry in a fragrant broth," says Pech Khunn, a pianist and music teacher whose parents and grandparents fled Southeast Asia when Ms. Khunn was less than a year old and ended up in Montana. "Even at Thanksgiving, my grandmother refused to roast turkey—she poached it. So naturally I loathed and despised poached poultry until I left to go to school in Wisconsin. When I didn't have my grandmother's pot-au-feu to turn my nose up at, I missed it like crazy. Living in a group house, I understood how sensible the dish is. You can stretch a bird a long way if you have lots of vegetables and rice and a very flavorful broth. I draw a line at turkey, but no other bird is safe from my pot."

FOR THE BROTH

Two 5- to 6-pound chickens, each cut into 8 pieces

6 stalks fresh lemongrass, bottom 5 inches only

1 tablespoon coriander seeds

2 teaspoons kosher salt

3 whole black peppercorns

FOR THE SAUCE

¼ cup fresh lemon juice

2 lemons, peel and pith removed, segmented

8 garlic cloves, minced

½ cup reserved chicken broth

½ cup sugar

½ cup fish sauce

1½ teaspoons chili-garlic sauce, plus more to taste

FOR THE CHICKEN AND VEGETABLES

Four 11-ounce bone-in, skin-on chicken breast halves, trimmed and quartered

8 small red potatoes, scrubbed and halved

2 fennel bulbs, trimmed and cut into 6 wedges

30 fiddlehead ferns, cleaned well and trimmed of woody parts

8 medium carrots, peeled, and halved lengthwise, then crosswise

16 asparagus tips with 2 inches of stalk

16 white mushrooms, stemmed

16 ramps or scallions

1. To make the broth: The day before serving, place the chickens in a large Dutch oven. Cover with water by 2 inches and bring to an active simmer, skimming off the foam as it rises. Add the lemongrass, coriander, salt, and peppercorns and gently simmer for 6 to 8 hours.

2. Strain the broth through a fine-mesh strainer into a tall container. Reserve ½ cup for the sauce, then cover, bring to room temperature, and refrigerate. Discard the solids.

3. To make the sauce: Pulse the lemon juice, lemon segments, and garlic in a food processor to make a coarse puree. Transfer to a bowl and stir in the reserved chicken broth, sugar, fish sauce, and chili-garlic sauce. Cover and refrigerate.

4. To make the chicken and vegetables: About an hour before serving, remove the sauce from the refrigerator. Skim the fat from the remaining chicken broth. Place the chicken pieces bone side down in a large Dutch oven and pour the broth over the chicken. Bring to a simmer over medium-low heat and cook for 25 to 30 minutes, until the chicken is firm to the touch and registers 165° on an instant-read thermometer.

5. Transfer the chicken to a warm platter. Remove the skin, drizzle a little broth over the meat, cover loosely with foil, and keep warm.

6. Return the remaining broth to a simmer. Add the potatoes and cook about 8 minutes, until tender. Use a slotted spoon to transfer the potatoes to the platter with the chicken. Cook each vegetable separately and transfer to the platter when tender.

Strain the broth through a fine-mesh strainer into a serving bowl or tureen.

7. To serve, invite guests to place chicken and vegetables in their warm bowls, ladle the broth over the top, and stir in some of the sauce to taste.

SERVES 6 TO 8

GREEK CHICKEN AND ARTICHOKE STEW
WITH AVGOLEMONO

After getting married on a construction site more than thirty years ago, Laurie Constantino and her husband, Steve, set up housekeeping in a Quonset hut jacked twelve feet in the air, so the second floor offered a 360-degree view of the tundra. In their home office, they practiced law, much of their work on behalf of Yu'pik Eskimos. After a decade, the couple decamped to the Greek island of Limnos to thaw out in Steve's grandmother's house. There, Laurie learned Greek by listening to the local women talk about cooking. A year later, they returned to Alaska where Laurie became the state's chief prosecutor as well as an author. *Tastes Like Home: Mediterranean Cooking in Alaska*, which she wrote to benefit her church—the only Greek Orthodox church in the state—has sold fifteen hundred copies. This recipe, which she serves with "crusty bread, a light green salad, oil-cured black olives, and lots of napkins," is one of her family's favorites.

FOR THE STEW

Eight 6-ounce bone-in, skin-on chicken thighs, trimmed

Kosher salt and freshly ground black pepper

2 tablespoons olive oil

3 medium onions, coarsely chopped

2 celery stalks, coarsely chopped

1 cup dry white wine

2 cups homemade chicken broth or low-sodium store-bought chicken broth

2 cups water

8 scallions, green and white parts, thinly sliced

¼ cup minced fresh parsley

¼ cup minced fresh dill

¼ cup fresh lemon juice

4 large artichokes, trimmed to hearts and quartered

FOR THE AVGOLEMONO

2 large eggs, separated

¼ cup fresh lemon juice

¼ cup minced fresh parsley

1 tablespoon minced fresh dill

4 scallions, green and white parts, thinly sliced, for garnish

1. To make the stew: Pat the chicken thighs dry and season with salt and pepper. Heat the oil in a Dutch oven over medium-high heat. Add half of the chicken and cook for 8 to 10 minutes, until golden brown on both sides. Transfer the thighs to a plate. Return the pot to medium-high heat and repeat with the remaining pieces.

2. Pour off all but 1 tablespoon of the fat from the pot. Add the onions, celery, ½ teaspoon salt, and ¼ teaspoon pepper and cook, stirring occasionally, until soft and beginning to brown, about 8 minutes.

3. Stir in the wine and scrape up any browned bits. Bring to simmer and cook about 4 minutes, until reduced by half. Stir in the broth, water, scallions, parsley, dill, and lemon juice. Nestle the chicken pieces into the vegetables, skin side up. Bring to a simmer, cover, reduce the heat to medium-low, and cook for 30 minutes.

4. Stir in the artichoke hearts, making sure they are completely submerged and the chicken thighs remain on top. Bring to a simmer, cover, and cook for 35 to 40 minutes, until the artichoke hearts are tender.

5. To make the avgolemono: In a medium bowl, whip the egg whites with an electric mixer until soft peaks form. Beat the egg yolks into the egg whites until just incorporated, then beat in the lemon juice, parsley, and dill.

6. Beat in 1 cup of the cooking liquid from the stew into the egg mixture, then quickly stir the mixture into the stew. Cook over low heat until the sauce thickens slightly. (Do not boil or the eggs may curdle.)

7. Season with salt and pepper to taste and serve, sprinkling each portion with scallions.

SERVES 4

ARLENE'S LEMON-GARLIC ROAST CHICKEN

HILLSBORO, KANSAS

In 1873, Mennonite leaders in Russia made arrangements with the Santa Fe Railroad to purchase central Kansas land in Marion and McPherson counties, and tidy farms soon sprang up like winter wheat. Growing up there in the 1940s, Arlene Hett learned to cook from her mother, a traditional Mennonite cook. This recipe, which she found in a Mennonite cookbook published in North Newton, Kansas, is well suited to heritage and free-range birds because of its long, slow cooking. Mrs. Hett votes for using "cast iron or something heavy that holds the heat better." If you use a commercially produced bird for this recipe, you must reduce the cooking time by approximately 10 percent. Use a meat thermometer to register the internal temperature. The USDA recommends an internal temperature of 165 degrees for chicken, but many people prefer their birds less well done. Begin checking the bird's internal temperature after 45 minutes. The pan juices are wonderful and best served with a potato dish.

FOR THE COMPOUND BUTTER

4 tablespoons (½ stick) unsalted butter, softened

2 tablespoons olive oil

2 tablespoons minced fresh parsley

3 garlic cloves, minced

2 teaspoons grated lemon zest

½ teaspoon kosher salt

¼ teaspoon freshly ground black pepper

FOR THE CHICKEN

One 3½- to 4-pound whole chicken, trimmed

4 garlic cloves, peeled

1 lemon, halved

Kosher salt and freshly ground black pepper

1. Place an oven rack in the center position and preheat the oven to 450°F. Set a rack in a roasting pan.

2. To make the butter: Process all of the ingredients in a food processor until smooth. Transfer the butter to a small bowl.

3. To make the chicken: Starting at the neck, use your fingers to loosen the skin from the breast, thighs, and drumsticks. (Do not completely detach the skin.) When the skin is loose, spread all but 1 tablespoon of the garlic butter between the skin and the flesh of the bird. Stuff the cavity with the garlic cloves and the lemon halves and truss the chicken.

4. Pat the chicken dry. Rub the reserved 1 tablespoon butter over the skin and season with salt and pepper. Place the chicken on the rack and roast for 20 minutes.

5. Reduce the oven temperature to 350°F, baste the chicken with the fat from the bottom of the pan, cover with aluminum foil, and cook for 45 minutes to 1 hour, until an instant-read thermometer registers 175°F in the thigh and 165°F in the breast.

6. When the chicken is done, remove from the oven and let rest, still covered, for 15 minutes. Carve and serve with the pan juices.

SERVES 4

Mrs. Lombardo's Lemon Chicken with Potatoes

"This simple dish was one of my family's favorites when I was growing up," says Tom Lombardo. "It's a great meal for a crowd, and it's delicious. But the reason I love to make it is that it reminds me of my mother and Sunday, and all of us at the table with so much to look forward to and also the feeling that nothing could be better than being right where we were."

Twelve 6-ounce all-natural bone-in chicken thighs or two 3½-pound chickens, cut into 8 pieces each

Kosher salt and freshly ground black pepper

½ cup good olive oil

6 red potatoes, quartered

1 pound pearl onions, peeled

8 garlic cloves, peeled and smashed

2 lemons, cut into ¼-inch rounds

2 bushy sprigs fresh rosemary, leaves removed from stems and bruised

1. Preheat the oven to 350°F.

2. Season the chicken pieces with salt and pepper. In a heavy-bottomed casserole with a tight-fitting lid, heat ¼ cup of the olive oil over medium heat. When the oil is hot, add the pieces, skin side down. Cook until golden, about 5 minutes, then flip and repeat on the other side. (If the casserole isn't big enough to hold all the chicken in one layer, cook in batches and return all the browned chicken to the pot before proceeding.)

3. Add the potatoes and onions. Combine the garlic, lemons, and rosemary with the remaining olive oil and pour over everything. Cover, place in the oven and bake until the potatoes are tender and the chicken is done, about 40 minutes. Adjust seasoning with additional salt and pepper if desired and serve immediately.

SERVES 4 TO 6

321

Poultry in Every Pot, Oven, Broiler, and Grill

Ramona Padovano's Chicken Thighs with Creamy Morel and Ramp Sauce

ALEXANDRIA, VIRGINIA

Ramona Padovano has wowed her family with her Polish mushroom soup and impressed her father-in-law with her rendition of his mother's Italian meatball recipe, but what she loves best about cooking is relying on her ability to respond to ingredients. For her, spring has been the greatest challenge. The ingredients that announce the demise of winter—morel mushrooms and wild ramps—were daunting to her at first. But over the years, she's refined this chicken dish, which is best made the day before and refrigerated overnight so that the flavors can marry. She likes to serve the dish with noodles, parsley potatoes, or herb gnocchi to soak up the sauce, and steamed asparagus on the side.

Eight 6-ounce bone-in, skin-on chicken thighs, trimmed

Kosher salt and freshly ground black pepper

½ cup all-purpose flour

3 tablespoons (⅜ stick) unsalted butter

2 tablespoons olive oil

½ cup cleaned and trimmed fresh morel mushrooms

12 ramps, trimmed and roughly chopped (bulbs and leaves)

2 garlic cloves, minced

1 teaspoon dried marjoram

1 teaspoon dried thyme

1 ⅓ cups dry white wine

1 cup homemade chicken broth or low-sodium store-bought chicken broth

1 cup half-and-half or light cream

1. Place an oven rack in the lower-center position and preheat the oven to 325°F.

2. Pat the chicken dry and season with salt and pepper. Place the flour in a shallow dish. Lightly coat the chicken in the flour and shake off the excess.

3. Melt 2 tablespoons of the butter with the oil in a Dutch oven over medium heat. Add half of the chicken and cook for 8 to 10 minutes, until golden brown on both sides. Transfer the chicken to a plate. Return the pot to medium heat and brown the remaining chicken. Transfer the chicken to a plate.

4. Add the remaining 1 tablespoon butter to the drippings in the pot and let melt. Add the morels and ramps and cook for 4 to 6 minutes, stirring occasionally, until soft. Stir in the garlic, marjoram, and thyme and cook about 1 minute, until aromatic. Transfer the vegetables to the plate with the chicken.

5. Increase the heat to high, add the wine, and scrape up any browned bits. Bring to a simmer and cook about 4 minutes, until reduced by one-third. Stir in the broth.

6. Return the chicken and vegetables to the pot. Cover, place the pot in the oven, and bake about 1½ hours, until the chicken is tender.

7. Transfer the chicken and vegetables to a warm platter and skim any fat off the surface of the sauce. Stir the half-and-half or cream into the sauce and season with salt and pepper to taste. Heat until hot but not boiling. Pour the sauce over the chicken and serve.

SERVES 4

Morels, those crenellated, conical mushrooms that evoke visions of hobbits, magic, and dollar signs, thrive in the moist soil around the Great Lakes. For the past half century, nearly twenty thousand people have gathered each year at the National Morel Mushroom Festival in Boyne City, Michigan, on Lake Charlevoix to compete in foraging, cooking, and, of course, eating. Morels with scrambled eggs, in custards, on pasta, pizza, lake fish, and chicken abound.

Mike Whisante's Chicken with White Barbecue Sauce

Like most north Alabamans, Mike Whisante believes that white barbecue is the real barbecue. The sauce, a tangy concoction of mayonnaise, spices, lemon juice, and vinegar, was created at Big Bob Gibson Bar-B-Q in Decatur, Alabama, in 1925. Mr. Whisante likes it on just about any meat that can be grilled, but his favorite is split chickens, and he has developed his own version of the local favorite that he says has a high "tang." "I've never even tasted a red barbecue sauce. For me, white barbecue sauce and chicken is like ketchup and french fries."

FOR THE SAUCE

¾ cup mayonnaise

¼ cup fresh lemon juice

2 tablespoons distilled white vinegar

1 tablespoon sugar

½ teaspoon barbecue spice rub, preferably Wizzy's SmokinRub

½ teaspoon kosher salt

½ teaspoon freshly ground black pepper

FOR THE CHICKEN

One 3½- to 4-pound whole chicken, backbone removed, split in half, and trimmed

¼ cup barbecue spice rub, preferably Wizzy's SmokinRub

1. To make the sauce: In a small bowl, whisk together all of the ingredients. Cover and refrigerate for 12 to 24 hours.

2. To make the chicken: The day before serving, coat the halves evenly with the spice rub. Transfer to a large plate, cover, and refrigerate for 12 to 24 hours.

3. Heat one side of a grill to medium-high and the other side to low. Place the chicken halves on the hotter side of the grill, cover, and cook about 1 hour, turning often, until an instant-read thermometer registers 175°F in the thighs and 165°F in the breast.

4. Wrap each chicken half in aluminum foil and place on the cooler side of the grill. Cover and cook for 30 minutes more, until the chicken is falling off the bones.

5. Brush the chicken with some of the barbecue sauce and serve, passing the remaining sauce on the side.

SERVES 4

THE BENDOLPH PETTWAYS' BARBECUED CHICKEN

GEE'S BEND, ALABAMA

Tucked into a curve of the Alabama River, Gee's Bend is surrounded on three sides by water, and since the antebellum era when it was mostly occupied by the Gee brothers' ten-thousand-acre cotton plantation, the place has been isolated from the rest of the country. In 1845, in order to settle a debt, the two Gee brothers gave their plantation with its forty-some slaves to their cousin Mark Pettway, who subsequently walked to Alabama from North Carolina with ten slaves who bore his name. After emancipation, most of the black Pettways remained in the Bend, working as tenant farmers. It was not until the 1930s that a New Deal relief project stemmed starvation and replaced the area's local log-

and-mud cabins with the clapboard dwellings that locals call "Roosevelt Houses." Isolated from the rest of the country, "Benders" developed their own distinct handicrafts, as well as a remarkably well-preserved version of "soul food," the traditional poverty dishes of the rural American south. Both the crafts and the cooking express the local moral code, a make-do ethic that deplores waste. Mary Lee Bendolph, the 76-year-old descendant of a slave whose hand-stitched quilts were discovered by an Atlanta collector and displayed at the Whitney Museum of American Art in New York City, cooks and quilts from scraps and leftovers that might otherwise have gone to waste. In her own words:

"It hurts me to see people waste up things the way they do these days. That is a change in the world. I had sixteen sisters and brothers, we had to be careful and creative and smart or we were going to be hungry and cold.

"Gee's Bend represents not merely a geographic configuration drawn by the yellow pencil of the river. Gee's Bend represents another civilization. Gee's Bend is an Alabama Africa. There is no more concentrated and racially exclusive Negro population in any rural community in the South than in Gee's Bend."

—Reverend Renwick Kennedy,
The Christian Century, 1937

I started my first quilt when I was twelve, and it took me a whole year because I kept running out of the flour sacks and old skirts and shirts we used. My last piece I found was a raggedy old shirt in the mud that some wagon had run over. Oh! I was so happy, so excited. I couldn't wash that old rag fast enough to finish my quilt. We didn't have electricity, the dogs and the hogs lived under the house, you could see them through the floorboards, and it was cold, real cold. We made quilts to keep warm. There was nothing that couldn't be made into something to keep people warm. When they forget what it is like to be cold and hungry, people start throwing things out and buying new. Some of the quilters even buy new fabric, but not me. Old clothes have a spirit in them. I see that scrap of apron in a quilt and I remember the woman who wore that apron thin. Cooking is like that too. I make my cornbread to remember all the cornbread that was made for me.

(continued)

Most of the young peoples had to leave the Bend to find work. There's about seven hundred of us left here, and most of us are real old or real young. I'm lucky, my daughter, Essie, is right next door. My sons, seven of them and their wives and my grandchildren, come on the weekends and I cook. Yes, Essie and I make the cornbread, the greens, the chicken, the potato salad, the pies. We could go to the store and buy things, but then we'd just be eating. We wouldn't be caring, we wouldn't be remembering. The first thing I did when people started calling our blankets "great modern art" and our quilting collective started to make money was build me a kitchen, with running water and a refrigerator and an electric range. That's all I wanted was my kitchen. Otherwise, I want what I have.

Some people have easy lives, but I had a hard life. I had my first baby when I was fourteen, before I knew where babies come from; that's how it was back then, nobody told you. They made me leave school; I loved school, and, oh, I cried. But I got to meet Dr. King and to see him up there right next to Jesus. I sang and marched with Dr. King. I took in all that tear gas, they beat us up, threw us in jail, but we got the vote. Once I saw Dr. King drink from the white folks' water fountain and I thought I'd get me some of that white water. I found out that water's water. Your life is your life. On Sunday Essie and I make this grilled chicken. Everybody comes."

One Big Table

"[The quilts of Gee's Bend are] . . . some of the most miraculous works of modern art America has produced."
—Michael Kimmelman,
The New York Times, 2002

Old cable ferry between Camden and Gee's Bend.

Gee's Bend Barbecued Chicken

5 pounds chicken legs, thighs, and wings

2 teaspoons salt

2 teaspoons black pepper

4 cups ketchup

¾ cup brown sugar

1 cup molasses

1 cup Worcestershire sauce

½ cup soy sauce

¼ cup vegetable oil

¼ cup sesame oil

¼ cup grated fresh ginger

1 tablespoon garlic powder

2 teaspoons onion powder

3 teaspoons ground cumin

3 teaspoons chili powder

¼ teaspoon chili pepper sauce, plus more
   if desired (optional)

1. Four hours before serving the chicken, rinse it off, pat dry with paper towels and arrange pieces in a baking pan. Sprinkle the chicken with half the salt and half the pepper and place in the refrigerator for half an hour.

2. Combine the remaining salt and pepper with the ketchup, brown sugar, molasses, Worcestershire and soy sauces, the oils, ginger, garlic and onion powders, cumin, and chili powder. Remove the chicken from the refrigerator, pat dry, and slather the meat with 3 cups of the sauce. Reserve the remaining sauce to serve with the chicken. Refrigerate and let the chicken rest for three hours to soak up the sauce, turning occasionally to keep it all the pieces well coated.

3. Prepare a charcoal grill and allow to burn until the fire is medium low. Place the grill as far above the fire as possible. Remove excess sauce from the chicken so that it doesn't burn and place pieces on the grill, cover and cook for 20 minutes. Turn over and cook for 20 to 30 minutes more until the meat is firm. Slather the meat again with the sauce and cook, uncovered, for 5 to 10 minutes, turning often, to get a nice shiny glaze and a crisp skin. Serve immediately with extra sauce on the side.

SERVES 8

Mika Garnett's Southwest Chicken and Green Chile Stew

Mika Garnett has two giant three-ring binders filled with six hundred recipes, the earliest of which were handwritten by her great-aunt Eva in the 1950s. Each recipe has been rated by her family and carries a dateline from points around the United States as well as India, Europe, and Asia, especially Korea, where her daughter was born. When leafing through her notebooks to select a favorite, Ms. Garnett was surprised to discover something missing: the Oklahoma Mexican dishes that she and her two sons and daughter call dinner at least two times a week. "I guess you just don't think about the dishes that are second nature to you," she says. As in many of her Okla-Mex recipes, green chiles take the place of tomatoes. When she doesn't have time to roast and peel her own chiles, she's found that high quality canned chiles work fine. She serves this stew garnished with sour cream, cheese, and blue corn chips or packaged corn tortillas that she blisters over her stove.

1 tablespoon vegetable oil

1 medium onion, finely chopped

1 red bell pepper, stemmed, seeded, and coarsely chopped

1 carrot, coarsely chopped

1 jalapeño chile, stemmed, seeded, and finely chopped (optional)

One 4-ounce can chopped green chiles, drained

4 garlic cloves, minced

½ teaspoon ground cumin

Kosher salt and freshly ground black pepper

2 tablespoons all-purpose flour

2¼ cups homemade chicken broth or low-sodium store-bought chicken broth

1½ pounds boneless, skinless chicken breasts, trimmed and cut into 1-inch chunks

1 cup corn kernels

2 tablespoons fresh lime juice

2 tablespoons chopped fresh cilantro

1. Heat the oil in a Dutch oven over medium heat. Add the onion, bell pepper, carrot, and jalapeño (if using) and cook about 4 minutes, until the vegetables are soft. Stir in the green chiles, garlic, cumin, ½ teaspoon salt, and ¼ teaspoon pepper and cook about 1 minute, until aromatic. Stir in the flour until incorporated.

2. Stir in the broth and chicken, bring to a simmer, and cook for 5 minutes. Stir in the corn and cook for 5 to 10 minutes more, until the corn is tender and the chicken is no longer pink.

3. Stir in the lime juice and cilantro and season with salt and pepper to taste. Serve.

SERVES 4

Doris Lum's Ginger Macadamia Chicken

Unlike most of the Chinese who came to Hawaii in the mid-nineteenth century, Doris Lum's family did not leave Canton to work the sugarcane fields. They were an educated lot who took jobs as merchants and bookkeepers, and their descendants bought taro and sugar plantations. In a state where a third of the population is Chinese Hawaiian, they became part of the elite. She was not encouraged to cook as a child—her father didn't have patience for amateurs in his kitchen—but after moving to California, Ms. Lum, a workers' compensation researcher, became an accomplished cook. She has a weakness for macadamia nuts, lotus seeds, and coconut. This dish, she says, is a "variation on a family recipe for lotus-stuffed chicken from the old days, one of those simple dishes that tastes divine." Ms. Lum managed to trim the traditional cooking time of four hours to ninety minutes, but she still makes the original for holidays and other special meals.

329

Poultry in Every Pot, Oven, Broiler, and Grill

¾ cup dry sherry or dry white wine

¾ cup homemade chicken broth or low-sodium store-bought chicken broth

2 tablespoons soy sauce

2 tablespoons honey

1 teaspoon kosher salt

½ teaspoon light brown sugar

¼ cup peanut or vegetable oil

2 tablespoons grated fresh ginger

2 garlic cloves, minced

1 scallion, green and white parts, cut into ½-inch pieces

One 3½- to 4-pound whole chicken, trimmed

8 fresh cilantro sprigs

3 scallions, green and white parts, thinly sliced

2 tablespoons shredded unsweetened coconut

2 tablespoons chopped macadamia nuts

Half-circles of fresh or canned pineapple

Maraschino cherries

1. In a small bowl, whisk together the sherry, broth, soy sauce, honey, salt, and sugar.

2. Heat the oil in a wok or Dutch oven over medium-high heat. Stir in the ginger, garlic, and ½-inch-cut scallion and cook, stirring, about 1 minute, until aromatic. Add the chicken and cook for 6 to 8 minutes, turning as necessary, until golden brown on all sides. Carefully pour off any oil in the pot.

3. Pour the sherry mixture over the chicken and bring to a simmer. Cover and cook, basting and turning the chicken occasionally, for 50 to 60 minutes, until an instant-read thermometer registers 175°F in the thighs and 165°F in the breast.

4. Transfer the chicken to a plate and let rest for 20 minutes. Using a cleaver, chop the chicken into 3-inch pieces.

5. To serve, transfer the pieces to a serving platter and arrange in the shape of a whole chicken. Pour over the sauce and top with the cilantro, sliced scallions, coconut, and nuts. Place the pineapple around chicken and put a cherry in the middle of each slice. Serve.

SERVES 4

Cat Sentz's Chicken Paillards with Tomato, Goat Cheese, and Arugula

MOSCOW, IDAHO

Cat Sentz calls herself a "devoted eater," which she became after moving from her family's Ohio horse farm to New Orleans to attend Tulane University. Several weeks before Hurricane Katrina, Ms. Sentz and her new husband, Adam, relocated to Moscow, Idaho, to start a family. Their worries of living behind a "culinary Iron Curtain," were quickly dispelled. In addition to open space and friendly neighbors, their corner of Idaho offers wonderful artisanal ingredients such as the tangy goat cheese and spicy baby arugula that inspired this dish, which is a favorite of her dinner guests.

Kosher salt

Four 6-ounce boneless, skinless chicken breast halves, trimmed and pounded to ⅓ inch thick

1 cup yellow or red cherry tomatoes, halved

1 cup red grape tomatoes, halved

3 ounces mild goat cheese, crumbled (about ¾ cup)

3 tablespoons extra virgin olive oil

Freshly ground black pepper

4 cups lightly packed baby arugula

2 tablespoons minced fresh chives, for garnish (optional)

1. In a large bowl, dissolve 2 tablespoons salt in 3 cups cold water. Add the chicken, cover, and refrigerate for 30 minutes. Remove the chicken from the brine, rinse, and pat dry.

2. Meanwhile, in a colander set over a bowl, toss the cherry tomatoes, grape tomatoes, and ½ teaspoon salt. Let sit for 15 minutes.

3. Whisk 2 ounces of the goat cheese, 2 tablespoons of the oil, and ⅛ teaspoon pepper into the tomato juices in the bowl. Gently fold in the remaining 1 ounce goat cheese.

4. Heat a grill to medium-high or a grill pan over medium-high heat. Brush the chicken with the remaining 1 tablespoon olive oil and season with salt and pepper. Grill the chicken for 8 to 10 minutes, until well browned on both sides, firm, and an instant-read thermometer registers 165°F.

5. Divide the arugula evenly among 4 dinner plates, place a chicken paillard on top, then spoon the tomato and goat cheese over the chicken. Sprinkle with the chives (if using), and serve.

SERVES 4

WHO DOES CHICKEN RIGHT?

SOME GET THROUGH THE WINTER MONTHS DREAMING OF THE first pitch on opening day, others long for the afternoon when the tennis courts are playable or the morning when the earth is warm enough for planting again. John T. Edge, the intrepid stalker of iconic American food, looks forward to July Fourth and the start of fried chicken season with the fervor of a founding father.

On traditional farms, the first chubby fryers were ready in early July, which may be why fried chicken became a staple of the Independence Day table. But the man known as John T has another theory. July Fourth tends to mean "picnic," and that means "cold fried chicken."

America's fried chicken recipes define families, regions, and eras. Variations have caused feuds and created heroes. Dusting, battering, or breading chicken and frying it in hot oil may not be indigenous to America, but who else besides Americans declare where they came from simply by ordering "extra crispy," "hot," or "batter-fried"? Fortunes were made when Colonel Harlan Sanders and George W. Church created a version that could be mass produced, and sold it back to the people who invented it in the first place: home cooks.

John T has spent several decades decoding fried chicken, driving several hundred thousand miles and eating more than two thousand pounds of fried chicken. His first true love was Maymee Lee Robinson's chicken. Mrs. Robinson worked for his family in Clinton, Georgia, for decades and made a fried chicken so crisp that its edges were frilled with a nearly translucent coating that shattered on first bite.

After leaving home, he fell under the sway of the chicken that Deacon Burton fried in gigantic cast-iron skillets at Burton's Grill, a gathering spot for neighborhood folks, politicians, civil rights activists, and, as word got out, food lovers. John T's first bite was shocking.

"It wasn't crisp. It didn't shatter and fall apart; the crust and the meat underneath were one. It was soft, comfortable chicken, the kind you get when you cover the skillet, and maybe he did, but what would he have used? A manhole cover? Maybe the magic was the steam table." At Prince's in Nashville and Gus's in Mason, he found chicken that "packed a roundhouse punch of cayenne, enough to knock you in the dirt. This was not comforting chicken. This was not your mother's fried chicken. It was late-night, sober-you-up-from-a-twelve-pack-stupor kind of chicken. But it wasn't a fast-food chain, it was somebody's life work; it had somebody's name on it. There were men standing by the skillets who cared, artisans." John T romanced deep-fried chicken, Chinese fried chicken, Bosnian fried chicken, and Caribbean fried chicken. Nearing the half-century mark, he finally understood his taste in chicken.

"I personally believe it's better cold than right from the skillet." And there is no cold chicken better than his friend John Fleer's sweet tea–brined chicken. Working as the chef at Blackberry Farm in Walland, Tennessee, Mr. Fleer perfected a recipe that uses Southern iced tea to both tenderize the meat and supply a puckery-tannin counterpoint to the richness of the dish. The thick coating is reminiscent of Maryland-style batter-fried chicken and it keeps the meat moist while providing a crunch.

"You bite into it and this cold chicken consommé dribbles down your chin," he says. "It is a thing of beauty."

BLACKBERRY FARM'S TEA-BRINED BATTER-FRIED PICNIC CHICKEN

When he was the chef at Blackberry Farm, John Fleer developed this recipe with the day after in mind. The Maryland-style batter creates a next-day cold chicken that can even make Southern purists a little weak at the knees. The recipe is still served at the farm, one of the nation's premier garden-to-table inn and restaurants.

FOR THE CHICKEN

1 quart freshly brewed tea

Zest of 1 lemon, removed with a vegetable peeler

1 cup sugar

½ cup kosher salt

1 quart ice water

8 whole chicken legs, thighs and legs separated

FOR THE COATING

5 cups all-purpose flour

2 cups buttermilk

2 large eggs

2 cups finely ground cornmeal

2 tablespoons seasoning, such as Old Bay

1 tablespoon chili powder

1 tablespoon fine sea salt

1 teaspoon freshly ground black pepper

6 cups vegetable oil, for frying

1. To brine the chicken: Two days before serving the chicken, combine the tea, lemon zest, sugar, and salt in a saucepan and simmer for 2 to 3 minutes, until the salt and sugar are dissolved. Remove from heat, add the ice water and cool completely. Submerge the chicken pieces in the liquid, cover, and refrigerate for 48 hours.

2. At least 1 hour before serving, remove the chicken from the brine and drain in a strainer for 10 minutes.

3. To make the coating: Place 3 cups of the flour in a large bowl. Whisk together the buttermilk and eggs in a second bowl. Whisk together the remaining flour, the cornmeal, Old Bay, chili powder, salt, and pepper in a third bowl. Set two wire racks over two separate rimmed baking sheets.

4. Pat the chicken dry with paper towels. Coat each piece lightly the plain flour and shake off the excess. Dip in the buttermilk and egg batter, and finally roll the chicken in the cornmeal mixture. Transfer the pieces to a rack and let sit 20 to 30 minutes before frying.

5. Pour the oil into a large cast-iron skillet and heat over high heat until a pinch of flour sprinkled into the oil immediately bubbles or a deep-frying thermometer registers 365°F. Working in batches, fry the chicken pieces, adjusting the heat as necessary to maintain the oil temperature. Cook for 8 minutes, flip, and cook for 7 minutes more. The chicken should be golden brown. The juices should run clear when the thickest part is pierced, and an instant-read thermometer should register 165°F.

6. Transfer the pieces to the clean wire rack; blot them with paper towels. Cool for a few minutes or cover lightly and place in the refrigerator overnight before serving.

SERVES 8

Ardia Herndon's
Kentucky Home-Fried Chicken

Mrs. Herndon makes a classic, unembellished fried chicken with a shatter-crisp crust. Her sister-in-law Lavon Yates taught her how to make it, fifty years ago, shortly after she married. Not long after, Mrs. Herndon and her husband took over a six-hundred-acre farm close to Taylorsville. The farm had seventy-five dairy cows, eight acres of tobacco, and a passel of farmhands. The most-requested midday dinner was fried chicken. She made it as often as three times a week and served it with coleslaw, green beans, mashed potatoes, gravy, biscuits, and sweet tea.

Mrs. Herndon is firm in her approach. She prefers the flavor of a whole chicken and cuts it up herself. She uses only White Lily self-rising flour. "Lots of people put pepper in their flour," she says, but she only adds salt, and fries the pieces until they are dark brown and crisp. Lately she has made one change: "I used to use the lard from my own pigs but after my husband passed, I started to use Wesson oil." She adds, a little wistfully, "His favorite piece was the back."

One 3½- to 4-pound chicken, cut into 10 pieces and trimmed

1 tablespoon kosher salt

Vegetable oil, for frying

1½ cups self-rising flour (preferably White Lily brand)

1. Set two wire racks over two separate rimmed baking sheets. Pat the chicken dry and season with salt. Place the pieces on one of the wire racks and refrigerate uncovered for 1 hour.

2. Place an oven rack in the center position and preheat the oven to 200°F. Line a plate with paper towels.

3. Heat 2 inches of oil in a Dutch oven over medium-high until a deep-frying thermometer registers 350°F. Do not pat the chicken dry, as the moisture the salt draws from the chicken will help make the crust crispy. Coat half of the chicken in the flour, shake off the excess, carefully add to the hot oil, and cook for 10 to 12 minutes, until golden brown on the first side. Flip the chicken and cook for 10 to 12 minutes more, until an instant-read thermometer registers 175°F in the thighs and drumsticks and 165°F in the breast.

4. Transfer the chicken to the plate to drain briefly, then transfer to the clean wire rack. Keep warm in the oven.

5. Return the oil to 350°F and repeat with the remaining chicken. Serve.

SERVES 4

CHALFONTE FRIED CHICKEN

Dot Burton and Lucille Thompson learned to fry chicken from their mother, Helen Dickerson, who worked at the Chalfonte Hotel in Cape May for seventy-seven years. Her version has a firm but soft crust more often found in the "covered skillet" fried chickens of the Midwest. Her daughters say that Winifred Jones of Philadelphia, Pennsylvania, gave Mrs. Dickerson the original recipe. The sisters believe that the secret to their chicken lies in their skillets, which came from Virginia, where the family lived during the school year. More than likely, another factor is the thick onion slices that Mrs. Burton and Mrs. Thompson allow to caramelize in the skillet to create a subtle steam and a haunting, sweet flavor. The greatest secret, of course, lies in the hands of a family of women who have gently shaken the skillets fourteen hours a day from Memorial Day to Labor Day for the past eighty years.

One 3½- to 4-pound chicken, cut into 10 pieces and trimmed

Kosher salt

2 tablespoons lemon pepper

1 cup all-purpose flour

Freshly ground black pepper

Peanut oil, for frying

2 medium onions, cut into ½-inch-thick rounds

Ice water

1. Set two wire racks over two separate rimmed baking sheets. Pat the chicken dry and season with 1 tablespoon salt and the lemon pepper. Place the chicken on one of the wire rack sets and refrigerate uncovered for 1 hour.

2. In a brown bag, combine the flour, 1 tablespoon salt, and ½ teaspoon black pepper. Do not pat the chicken dry as the moisture that the salt draws from the chicken will help make the crust crispy. Working with two pieces at a time, add the chicken to the bag and shake to coat with the flour. Remove the chicken from the bag, shake off the excess flour, and return to the wire rack. Let the chicken sit for 10 minutes. Save the flour in the bag.

3. Place an oven rack in the center position and preheat the oven to 200°F. Line two plates with paper towels.

4. Heat 1½ inches of oil in a large cast-iron skillet over medium-high heat until a deep-frying thermometer registers 350°F. Carefully add half of the onion and cook for 3 to 4 minutes, until soft and golden. Use a slotted spoon to remove the onions and discard. Place the remaining onions in a bowl of ice water.

5. Return the oil to 350°F. Carefully add half of the chicken pieces to the hot oil and cook for 10 to 12 minutes, until golden brown on the first side. Flip the chicken and cook for 10 to 12 minutes more, until an instant-read thermometer registers 175°F in the thighs and drumsticks and 165°F in the breast.

6. Transfer the chicken to the plate to drain briefly, then transfer to the clean wire rack. Keep warm in the oven. Return the oil to 350°F and repeat with the remaining chicken.

7. Drain the onions and separate into rings. Shake half of the onion rings in the flour bag until well coated. Return the oil to 350°F. Carefully add the onion rings and cook about 4 minutes, until golden brown. Transfer to the other plate to drain briefly, then transfer the wire rack with the chicken. Return the oil to 350°F and repeat with the remaining onion rings.

8. Season the onion rings with salt and black pepper and serve on top of the chicken.

———

SERVES 4

Reverend Wayne Lee's Piping Hot Chicken

CHATTAHOOCHEE, FLORIDA

"When I was a young man serving a temporary post in Tennessee, I had occasion to become familiar with hot chicken," says Wayne Lee. "I grew up on sweet lard-fried chicken in the Florida panhandle. The first time I tasted hot chicken in Tennessee I thought there had been some kind of mistake, a cook perhaps had mistaken an entire bottle for a drop of hot pepper sauce. I was like to die of that chicken, but the gentlemen who took me to the hot chicken joint couldn't get enough of it. What was a visiting seminarian to do? I developed a taste for hot chicken and in the past fifty years, worked on cracking the hot chicken code. It comes down to a balance of the tart, the sweet, and the hot. A lot of it depends on your bird. We pretty much use grocery store chicken here and this is the best I've come to getting it right. I prefer to use lard in the fry bath—it makes it lighter and crisper."

2½ cups buttermilk

One 12-ounce can evaporated milk

½ cup kosher salt

¼ cup hot sauce, preferably Tabasco

Eight 4-ounce chicken drumsticks, trimmed

Eight 6-ounce bone-in, skin-on chicken thighs, trimmed

4 cups all-purpose flour

¼ cup sweet paprika

3 tablespoons freshly ground black pepper

1 tablespoon cayenne pepper

Peanut oil, lard, or bacon grease, for frying

1. The day before serving, in a large bowl, combine the buttermilk, evaporated milk, salt, and hot sauce. Add the chicken pieces and turn to coat evenly. Cover and refrigerate for 12 hours, turning the chicken occasionally.

2. Set two wire racks over two rimmed baking sheets. In a medium bowl, whisk together the flour, paprika, black pepper, and cayenne. Working with two pieces at a time, remove the chicken from the marinade and let the excess drip back into the bowl. Coat the chicken in the flour and shake off the excess. Transfer the chicken to one of the wire racks.

3. Place an oven rack in the center position and preheat the oven to 200°F. Line a plate with paper towels.

4. Heat 2 inches of oil in a large cast-iron skillet until a deep-frying thermometer registers 350°F. Carefully add half of the chicken to the hot oil and cook for 10 to 12 minutes, until golden brown on the first side. Flip the pieces and cook for 10 to 12 minutes more, until an instant-read thermometer registers 175°F in the thighs and drumsticks and 165°F in the breast.

5. Transfer the chicken to the plate to drain briefly, then transfer to the clean wire rack. Keep warm in the oven. Return the oil to 350°F and repeat with the remaining pieces. Serve.

SERVES 6 TO 8

Debbie Page-Pfetcher's Huntingdale Fried Chicken

Debbie Page-Pfetcher says: "Our father, a construction worker, would have the family travel with him during the summer to the areas of Missouri where he was working. Once we lived in a small (almost minus population) town called Huntingdale. My father leased a home that had belonged to the Squire Paul Henry family for which the county was named. The house was an old, magnificent structure with an upstairs full-front porch with a swing and a 'summer kitchen' in the back. In the kitchen sat our mother's delight, the original wood stove of the Henry family and it worked beautifully. On that stove were created some of the most unforgettable meals of my life. One of the many foods created by my mother on that stove was her fried chicken. It was cooked in a cast-iron skillet cleaned each time with cornmeal and, with her more-than-adept skill of moving the skillet to various areas of the stove's heat, she managed to create the unexplainable.

"I returned to Clinton some years later and married. I worked with a friend who married into the Henry family and became more aware of the magnificent history that revolved around the house. I did some research at the local library and discovered that Squire Paul enjoyed a good cook and a good meal. I can't help but think that the pleasures of him, his wives, their children, and their friends were revived each time the old cookstove was loaded with wood and the scent of food wafted throughout the house."

2 cups buttermilk

Kosher salt

1 tablespoon green hot sauce, preferably Tabasco

One 3½- to 4-pound chicken, cut into 10 pieces and trimmed

1 cup all-purpose flour

1 teaspoon freshly ground black pepper

Vegetable oil, vegetable shortening, or lard

1. In a shallow baking dish, combine the buttermilk, 3 tablespoons salt, and the hot sauce. Add the chicken, cover, and refrigerate for 2 hours, turning the chicken pieces every 30 minutes.

2. In a second shallow dish, whisk together the flour, 2 teaspoons salt, and the pepper. Set a wire rack over a rimmed baking sheet. Working with two pieces at a time, remove the chicken from the marinade and let the excess drip back into the bowl. Coat the chicken in the flour and shake off the excess flour. Transfer the chicken to the wire rack and let sit for 20 minutes.

3. Line a plate with paper towels. In an electric skillet, heat 1½ inches of oil to 375°F. Add the chicken to the skillet and cook for 10 minutes, until just beginning to brown. Flip the chicken pieces, cover, and cook for 20 to 30 minutes more, until the chicken is cooked through and deep golden brown, and an instant-read thermometer registers 175°F in the thighs and drumsticks and 165°F in the breast.

4. Transfer the chicken to the plate to drain briefly. Serve hot.

SERVES 4

Austin Leslie's
Legendary Chicken Persillade

NEW ORLEANS, LOUISIANA

"*The first time I cut up a chicken I was working at Portia's. The chef there, Bill Turner, asked me where I learned how to do it. I said I learned from my mother at home. He taught me how to get twelve pieces from a whole chicken; my mother was able to get thirteen pieces from the same chicken because she broke the back into two parts. When you cut it properly you won't loosen the skin.*

You start by cutting it down the back. Take a sharp cleaver and place the chicken firmly on a block and hold it down. After you split it down the back, open it up and take out the insides and put them aside. Then you cut straight through the breast. Cut it into quarters with the cleaver, separating the thighs from the breast. Then disjoint it at the wings, and disjoint the legs from the thighs. If you use a cleaver, be careful. Always move all other knives away from the board when you use a cleaver because you can mis-strike, and if that cleaver hits a knife, it can jump up and hit you. After the chicken is cut up, salt and pepper it, mixing the pieces around so the salt and pepper get all over the chicken.

I learned all about fried chicken from Bill Turner, too. It's the easiest job in the kitchen. You can tell by the sound when fried chicken is done. If you listen to it, you can hear how the sound of the grease crackling in the fryer changes. Then you know it's time to bring it up. I never cook it well done; I never cook any meat well done. What I do is take the blood out of it first. While the chicken is frying, take a pair of tongs and squeeze each piece. Squeeze it till it bursts to let the blood out. You can look right down there by the bone and see if there is any blood there. When it's ready, the chicken will float to the top, a part of it will stick up. Then you take it and check it over. If you cook it properly you can keep your guests or customers from ever seeing any blood. That's what they object to, when they prefer well-done meat—not the taste, but the blood.

Alice Curtis and her poultry, LEWIS HINE, 1921.

If you use an electric fryer, set it at 350°; if you pan-fry, wait till the oil is beginning to bubble. I use peanut oil for frying. Put the heavy pieces in first (thigh, leg, and breast), making sure you don't crowd the chicken. If you put too much in at one time the heat and oil can't get all around the meat and it will cook unevenly. You have to watch the flour that falls to the bottom of the pan very carefully. After each set of pieces gets done, strain the oil out and clean the pan, otherwise the flour at the bottom is going to burn. You've heard people say the first chicken looks good, the second so-so, and the third you can forget. That's why. Never fry anything else [meat, fish, or sausage] along with the chicken, because it will give it a bad taste. It's like frying hot sausage on a grill and then following it up with steak or ham. You see that a lot in restaurant kitchens and that's why the food has a strange taste.

—Austin Leslie in *Creole Feast*, compiled by Nathaniel Burton and Rudy Lombard (Random House, 1978)

Like many people in New Orleans, Mr. Leslie went to his attic as the waters rose after Hurricane Katrina. He was trapped there for two days in 98-degree heat and died of a heart attack in Atlanta several days after being evacuated.

FOR THE CHICKEN

One 3½- to 4-pound chicken, cut into 10 pieces and trimmed

Kosher salt and freshly ground black pepper

2 tablespoons Cajun seasoning

One 12-ounce can evaporated milk

1 cup water

1 large egg, beaten

½ cup all-purpose flour

Peanut oil

FOR THE PERSILLADE

1 cup minced fresh parsley

12 garlic cloves, minced

10 dill pickle slices

1. To make the chicken: Place a wire rack set over a rimmed baking sheet. Pat the chicken dry and season with salt, pepper, and Cajun seasoning. Place the chicken on the rack and refrigerate uncovered for 1 to 24 hours.

2. Place an oven rack in the center position and preheat the oven to 200°F. Line a plate with paper towels and place another wire rack over a second rimmed baking sheet.

3. In a large bowl, combine the evaporated milk, water, and egg. In a shallow dish, whisk together the flour, 2 teaspoons salt, and 1 teaspoon pepper. Working with two pieces at a time, add the chicken to the milk mixture and turn to coat evenly. Remove the chicken from the marinade and let the excess drip back into the bowl. Coat the chicken in the flour and shake off the excess. Return the chicken to the wire rack.

4. Place an oven rack in the center position and preheat the oven to 200°F. Line a plate with paper towels and place another wire rack over a second rimmed baking sheet.

5. Heat 2 inches of oil in a large cast-iron skillet over medium-high heat until a deep-frying thermometer registers 350°F. Carefully add half the chicken pieces to the hot oil and cook for 10 to 12 minutes, until golden brown on the first side. Flip the pieces and cook for 10 to 12 minutes more, until an instant-read thermometer registers 175°F.

6. Transfer the chicken to the plate to drain briefly, then transfer to the clean wire rack. Keep warm in the oven. Return the oil to 350°F and repeat with the remaining pieces.

7. To make the persillade: In a small bowl, combine the parsley and garlic. Top each piece of chicken with a slice of pickle, sprinkle with the persillade, and serve.

SERVES 4

Poultry in Every Pot, Oven, Broiler, and Grill

THE COLONEL'S SECRET

IN ADDITION TO BEING INDIVIDUALIZED AND REGIONALIZED, A DISH NEEDS TO BE
commodified to assure its status as an American food icon. Harlan Sanders was the poster child for this phenomenon. He began serving fried chicken from his gas station and motel in 1930, and when he sold his business in 1964, there were six hundred franchises in the United States. Today there are eleven thousand outlets in eighty countries.

The Colonel's "original recipe" is shrouded in mystery: It was even transported in armored trucks when the company's corporate offices moved. The Colonel claimed that the recipe contained "11 herbs and spices," but when the chicken was analyzed in the early 1980s for William Poundstone's book, *Big Secrets*, the laboratory found only flour, salt, pepper, and MSG. The formula may have been changed after the sale. The Colonel himself said that the corporate types had turned his recipe into "nothing more than a fried dough ball wrapped around some chicken."

For better or for worse, the Colonel's chicken, along with McDonald's burgers, are America's leading culinary ambassadors. In 2007, a wire service reported: "In Pakistan anti-American protesters set a Kentucky Fried Chicken restaurant on fire. The protesters mistakenly thought they were attacking a high-ranking U.S. military official—Colonel Sanders."

Etsuko Scholz's Panko Chicken

After marrying an American businessman, Etsuko Scholz moved from her native Tokyo to the Pacific Northwest where she taught English as a second language and raised three children. When she wanted to share the tastes of her past with her children, she cooked. "Japanese restaurants here are aimed at American tastes," she says. "Sauces are sweeter, and the vegetables are different." In a curious turn, her son's work eventually took him back to Tokyo, along with his three children. When she visits, her grandchildren beg her to cook "American." McNuggets, she found, take on a whole new meaning when they are breaded in panko, Japanese bread crumbs, and served with shaved cabbage, spicy Japanese mustard, lemon wedges, and tonkatsu sauce for a fine late-summer picnic (and leftovers make one mean sandwich).

FOR THE SAUCE

½ cup ketchup

2 tablespoons Worcestershire sauce

2 teaspoons soy sauce

1 teaspoon Dijon mustard

FOR THE CHICKEN

⅓ cup cornstarch

Kosher salt and freshly ground black pepper

2 large eggs

2 cups panko (Japanese bread crumbs)

1½ pounds boneless, skinless chicken breasts, trimmed and cut into ¼-inch strips

Vegetable oil, for frying

1. To make the sauce: In a small bowl, combine all of the ingredients, cover, and refrigerate.

2. To make the chicken: Place an oven rack in the center position and preheat the oven to 200°F. Place two wire racks over two separate rimmed baking sheets. Line a plate with paper towels.

3. In a shallow dish, combine the cornstarch, 1 teaspoon salt, and ¼ teaspoon pepper. In a second one, whisk the eggs until frothy. In a third, spread the panko in an even layer.

4. Pat the chicken dry and season with salt and pepper. Working with a few pieces at a time, lightly coat the chicken with the cornstarch and shake off any excess. Coat the chicken in the egg, letting any excess drip back into the bowl, and then in the panko. Transfer to a wire rack.

5. Heat 1 inch of oil in a large skillet or wok over medium-high heat until a deep-frying thermometer registers 350°F. Add half of the chicken to the hot oil and cook for 4 to 6 minutes, until cooked through and golden brown on all sides. Transfer the chicken to a plate to drain briefly, then transfer to a clean wire rack. Keep warm in the oven. Return the oil to 350°F and repeat with the remaining chicken. Serve with the sauce.

SERVES 4

ZACH AND CLAY'S BRICK CHICKEN WITH YELLOW SQUASH AND TOMATOES

WASHINGTON, D.C.

Clay Dunn and Zach Patton are both from the South, but they had very different food experiences growing up. Zach's mom was a fantastic cook who "even concocted a recipe in a dream and got up the next day and cooked it." Clay's mother's repertoire consisted of great fried chicken for community potlucks, but he can't remember a fresh herb, and never ate a tomato until college. When Mr. Patton and Mr. Dunn moved in together, neither wanted to part with a single issue of their collection of food magazines, so they cooked at least one recipe from each issue. They experienced royal flops and found flawless recipes, such as this pressed chicken, which originally appeared in *Gourmet*. "We barely had to tweak it at all," said Mr. Dunn.

Four 11-ounce bone-in, skin-on chicken breast halves, trimmed

Kosher salt and freshly ground black pepper

2 tablespoons extra virgin olive oil

1 pound tomatoes, coarsely chopped

12 ounces yellow squash, cut into ½-inch pieces

2 garlic cloves, minced

1 tablespoon minced fresh marjoram

1. Pat the chicken breasts dry and season with salt and pepper.

2. Heat the oil in a large skillet over medium-high heat. Add the chicken, skin side down. Cover the chicken with parchment paper, then a heavy pot or skillet, followed by a 3- to 5-pound weight (such as two 32-ounce cans or a brick wrapped in foil). Cook for 10 minutes, then remove the weight, pot, and parchment paper.

3. Flip the chicken and re-cover with clean parchment paper, the pot, and the weight. Cook about 8 minutes more, until the chicken is firm and an instant-read thermometer registers 165°F. Transfer the chicken to a serving platter, cover loosely with aluminum foil, and let rest.

4. Add the tomatoes, squash, and ¼ teaspoon salt to the skillet and cook over medium-high heat about 6 minutes, until the squash is tender and the tomatoes are saucy. Stir in the garlic and 2 teaspoons of the marjoram and cook about 1 minute, until aromatic. Season the vegetables with salt and pepper to taste.

5. Spoon the vegetables over the chicken, sprinkle with the remaining 1 teaspoon marjoram, and serve.

SERVES 4

André Soltner's Roast Chicken

Most cooks are perplexed by Chef Soltner's tenderizing rite: When the chicken thigh registers 158° to 160°F on an instant-read thermometer, he drops a teaspoon of water in the roasting pan, closes the oven door, turns off the heat, and waits three minutes before removing the bird. "For the soft breast," he says.

The idea of creating a mini steam room in the oven sends terror through the hearts of cooks who lust after a crisp chicken skin. Even so, most maintain an appreciative, if arm's-length, tolerance of divergent roasting techniques. After all, people are born to a certain roasted chicken: their mother's. To malign another person's chicken is to malign his past. "I can only roast chicken the way I roast chicken," Chef Soltner says softly.

343

Poultry in Every Pot, Oven, Broiler, and Grill

Two 1½- to 1¾-pound whole poussins or small chickens

Kosher salt and freshly ground black pepper

4 fresh thyme sprigs

4 fresh tarragon sprigs

1 medium onion, peeled and quartered

2 tablespoons vegetable oil

2 teaspoons water

½ cup white wine

½ cup homemade chicken broth or low-sodium store-bought chicken broth

2 tablespoon minced fresh tarragon

2 tablespoons minced fresh parsley

2 tablespoons (¼ stick) unsalted butter

1. Place an oven rack in the center position and preheat the oven to 450°F.

2. Pat the chickens dry and season with salt and pepper. Place 2 thyme sprigs, 2 tarragon sprigs, and 2 onion quarters in the cavity of each chicken.

3. Heat the oil in a roasting pan over high heat. Add the chickens and cook for 4 to 6 minutes, turning as necessary, until golden brown on all sides. Transfer the roasting pan to the oven and roast for 20 to 25 minutes, basting frequently, until an instant-read thermometer registers 160°F in the thighs.

4. Add the water to the roasting pan. Close the oven door, turn off the heat, and let sit for 3 minutes. Transfer the chickens to a carving board and let rest.

5. Pour off any fat from the roasting pan. Add the wine, scrape up any browned bits, and cook over medium heat about 2 minutes, until reduced by half. Stir in the chicken broth, bring to a simmer, and cook for 2 to 4 minutes, until flavorful. Off the heat, whisk in the chopped tarragon, parsley, and butter. Season with salt and pepper to taste.

6. Carve the chickens and serve with the sauce.

SERVES 4

Andrea Hutchinson's Rum-Washed and Marinated Chicken

Growing up in Savannah La-Mar, a small town on the western side of Jamaica, Andrea Hutchinson watched her grandmother pour love, tenderness, and intensity into her rum cake, her soups, her rice and chicken. Since moving to the United States, Ms. Hutchinson cooks to relax, to entertain, to remember who she is. Rum-washed chicken, which incorporates influences from Jamaica's Chinese community, was one of her mother's specialties. Served with Jamaican rice and peas, it remains one of her favorite dishes for family meals and company dinners.

⅓ cup Jamaican white rum

¼ cup jerk sauce, preferably Walkerswood brand

¼ cup Chinese black bean sauce

3 tablespoons char su (Asian barbecue sauce)

One 3½- to 4-pound chicken

2 garlic cloves, minced

One 3-inch piece fresh ginger, peeled and thinly sliced

¼ cup fresh lime juice

1. The day before serving, in a small bowl, combine the rum, jerk sauce, black bean sauce, and char su.

2. Place the chicken in a shallow bowl. Use your fingers to carefully separate the skin from the breast meat. Rub the garlic over the breast meat, under the skin, then place one-quarter of the ginger under the skin.

3. Brush the chicken inside and out with the lime juice. Rub the chicken with the rum mixture. Place the remaining ginger slices in the cavity, cover, and refrigerate for 12 to 24 hours.

4. Place an oven rack in the center position and preheat the oven to 300°F.

5. Place the chicken in a baking dish, breast down, and pour the marinade over it. Cover with foil and roast for 1½ hours. Remove the chicken from the oven and use two large forks or paper towels to carefully flip it breast up. Roast, uncovered, for 45 minutes more, until an instant-read thermometer registers 175°F in the thigh and 165°F in the breast.

6. Let rest for 5 minutes, then carve and serve.

SERVES 4

A MOST FASHIONABLE BIRD

CHICKEN HAS LONG BEEN A FAVORITE DINNER PARTY FOOD. HERE ARE A FEW SAMPLES:

1774: Hannah Glasse, *The Art of Cookery Made Plain and Easy,* Chicken Surprise
This loaf of cooked chicken enclosed in bacon and forcemeat was more complex than other popular colonial dishes such as smothered chicken but, said the author, it was "a pretty first course, summer or winter."

1824: Mary Randolph, *The Virginia House-Wife,* Chicken Fricassee
A perennial favorite in colonial times, chicken fricassee remained on dinner menus through the nineteenth century. For the most part, the dish resisted outside influences and stayed close to its French roots as a white braise with a sauce of cream, egg yolk, parsley, and lemon juice.

1869: Chef Pierre Blot, Chicken Marengo
A dish of chicken cooked with mushrooms and garlic, Chicken Marengo was said to have first been served to Napoleon by his camp cook after the battle of Marengo in northern Italy. Sixty years passed before it was resurrected as fashionable fare in Britain, by which time white wine and tomatoes had been added to the dish. The recipe was a hit in the United States, where additional permutations such as using fried eggs, roasted peppers, or crayfish to garnish the dish flourished. The recipe was introduced to *le tout* New York by French chef, cookbook author, and teacher Pierre Blot.

1877: *Buckeye Cookery and Practical Housekeeping: Compiled from Original Recipes,* Jellied Chicken
Boxed gelatin was first introduced when the British J and G Company began exporting it to America in 1845. By the 1870s its use in the home kitchen was well established in both sweet and savory dishes such as jellied chicken.

1900: Chicken à la King
Craig Claiborne in *The New York Times Food Encyclopedia,* wrote, "Over the years I have speculated about the origin of the dish called chicken à la king, Curiosity about the source has to do with a possible sea change that may have occurred when the dish arrived here, as I supposed from France." James N. Keen, a professional photographer in Louisville, Kentucky, was given a brochure forty years ago by E. Clark King 3rd, whose father was a restaurateur, which describes the genesis of the name. "It was in the early 1900s that chicken à la King was first served to the public," the brochure says. "My father was the proprietor of the Brighton Beach Hotel, a fashionable summer resort outside Manhattan. One night his head chef, George Greenwald, sent word he had concocted a dish he would like to serve my parents. It was enjoyed immensely and they asked for seconds.... The next morning, the chef asked permission to place it on the menu.... The next day the bill of fare carried the following: Chicken à la King—$1.25 a portion." In another version, "The French Chef" of Hotel Bellevue-Stratford in Philadelphia is credited with inventing a la King in 1907

1937: Chicken Kiev
The Yar restaurant in Chicago, owned by Russian immigrant Colonel Vladimir Yaschenko, was credited by the *Chicago Daily Record* with creating this dish of pounded chicken breast rolled around a compound butter, then breaded and fried. The dish later enjoyed a surge in popularity during the cold war when Russian cuisine was a source of curiosity.

1945: Chicken Francese
Everyone agrees that this dish of chicken breasts in a lemon-caper sauce was created in the mid-1940s, but there is little evidence that it was created by New York City Italians and named francese (or "French").

1950s: Chicken Divan
New York City's Divan Parisienne restaurant is said to have created this casserole of chicken, broccoli, cream, and cheese, which fits easily into the dinner party repertoire of the casserole-loving 1950s housewife.

1960s: Chicken Cordon Bleu
Often incorrectly thought of as a classic French dish of high style, Chicken Cordon Bleu was created in America during the 1960s to mimic roulades of French, Austrian, and Italian origin. While a European version may have featured prosciutto and Parmesan, here in America deli ham and Swiss cheese were more to taste. It was often found on airline menus—when air travel was still an elegant affair. The earliest reference to the concept of "cordon bleu" was in a *Los Angeles Times* description of the trendy dishes to be served at a high-end event: "Veal cordon bleu will be the pièce de résistance on the menu."

1973: Paula Wolfert, *Couscous and Other Good Food from Morocco*, Chicken Tagine with Chick-Peas
Typical of Wolfert's recipes collected at the source, this became a standard dish for a particular stratum of up-to-the-minute 1970s hostesses.

1982: Julee Rosso and Sheila Lukins, *The Silver Palate Cookbook*, Chicken Marbella
This somewhat unexpected combination of chicken, prunes, green olives, and capers cut a huge swath through company dinners in the 1980s and is still served.

LILY NG'S SALT-ZAPPED CHICKEN

When Lily Ng moved from Malaysia to live with her daughter in Denver, she spent six months watching the Food Network. She graduated from food television to recipes and food writing, and before you could say sauté, she was a blogger, exchanging recipes and making "good buddies" around the world. Her Chinese salt-baked chicken recipe not only cuts down on the usual ten pounds of salt "that costs more than the chicken," but steams the chicken Malaysian style—in the microwave.

2 tablespoons oyster sauce

2 tablespoons shaoxing wine (Chinese rice wine) or dry sherry

1 tablespoon fish sauce

1 teaspoon toasted sesame oil

1 teaspoon grated fresh ginger

½ teaspoon Chinese five-spice powder

½ teaspoon turbinado or light brown sugar

¼ teaspoon freshly ground black pepper

Eight 6-ounce bone-in, skin-on chicken thighs, trimmed

Vegetable oil, as needed

3 pounds natural coarse sea salt or kosher salt

1. The day before, whisk together in a large bowl the oyster sauce, wine, fish sauce, sesame oil, ginger, five-spice powder, sugar, and pepper until the sugar is dissolved. Add the chicken thighs, turn to coat them, cover, and refrigerate for 12 to 24 hours.

2. Place two 10-inch parchment squares on the work surface, overlapping them by about 2 inches to make a rectangle. Lightly brush the paper with oil, and then place a chicken thigh in the center. Bring the sides of the paper over the chicken and roll them down the top of the chicken. Fold the ends toward the center of the chicken and secure with butcher's twine to form a tight package. Repeat with all of the parchment paper and chicken pieces.

3. Line a large microwave-safe bowl or baking dish with several layers of parchment paper. Pour half of the salt into the bowl, arrange the chicken packages on top, and cover with the remaining salt. (Make sure that the packages are covered with the salt.)

4. Cover the bowl with a large sheet of parchment and place a large microwave-safe plate upside down over the parchment. Carefully turn the bowl over onto the plate. Fold the parchment paper up around the bowl and secure with butcher's twine to form a tight package.

5. Place the parchment-wrapped bowl, still on the plate, in the microwave and cook on medium power for 20 to 25 minutes.

6. Let the chicken sit for 10 minutes, then turn the bowl over so the plate is on top. Remove the plate. Brush away the salt from the parcels. Using kitchen shears, carefully cut the twine and tear open the parchment paper. (Use caution, as the chicken and salt will be very hot.) If serving cold, let the parcels cool to room temperature, then refrigerate. Serve hot or cold.

SERVES 4

DIANE REINER'S SAGE ROASTED CHICKEN

In the Flamingo West mobile home park near Las Vegas, Diane Reiner opened a box belonging to her adored father that she'd had since he died. She could almost taste the memories that spilled out. A chef who'd worked in Las Vegas casinos and California restaurants, he had taught her all the important things in life, like how to thicken a cream sauce with roux and how to clean a grill. Now she could almost see him again—prepping vegetables, setting up steam tables, and scribbling recipes, often on paper placemats. In the box with the Hilltop Café placemat with the roast chicken recipe are his instructions: If you cook a whole chicken, make it last for three meals—the first night eat it hot, the next day make chicken salad, then throw any chicken and bones that are left in a pot and make soup.

3 tablespoons olive oil

1 tablespoon dried sage, crumbled

2 teaspoons sweet paprika, plus more for garnish

1 teaspoon kosher salt

½ teaspoon freshly ground black pepper

One 5- to 6-pound chicken

1 medium onion, coarsely chopped

½ cup chopped fresh parsley, plus more for garnish

6 garlic cloves, peeled and smashed

1. Place an oven rack in the center position and preheat oven to 475°F. Set a rack in a roasting pan.

2. In a small bowl, combine the oil, sage, paprika, salt, and pepper to make a paste. Starting at neck, use your fingers to loosen the skin from the breast, thighs, and drumsticks. (Do not completely detach the skin.) Rub all but 1 tablespoon of the spice paste between the skin and the flesh of the bird. Place the onion, parsley, and garlic in the cavity and truss the chicken.

3. Pat the bird dry. Rub the reserved 1 tablespoon of the oil mixture over the skin and place on the rack breast up. Roast for 45 minutes. Reduce the oven temperature to 350°F and roast for 45 minutes to 1 hour more, until an instant-read thermometer registers 175°F in the thighs and 165°F in the breast.

4. Transfer the chicken to a carving board and let rest for 15 minutes. Carve, sprinkle with paprika and parsley, and serve.

SERVES 6

James Beard's Chicken
with Forty Cloves of Garlic

This recipe was adapted from *Beard on Food* (1974). Garlic was not yet America's sweetheart when this recipe was published, but the slow cooking mellowed the taste of the garlic and, according to the James Beard Society in New York City, it turns the cloves into "a buttery, mild paste perfumed with garlic that is wonderful spread on crusty toast."

One Big Table

4 celery stalks, cut into long strips

2 medium onions, coarsely chopped

6 fresh parsley sprigs

1 tablespoon chopped fresh tarragon

⅔ cup vegetable oil

Eight 4-ounce chicken drumsticks

Eight 6-ounce bone-in, skin-on chicken thighs

Kosher salt and freshly ground black pepper

Freshly grated nutmeg

½ cup dry vermouth

40 garlic cloves, unpeeled

1 baguette, sliced thin, for serving

1. Place an oven rack in the center position and preheat the oven to 375°F.

2. In a large baking dish or casserole with a lid, combine the celery, onions, parsley, and tarragon and spread in an even layer. Pour the oil into a shallow dish. Pat the chicken dry, coat with the oil and arrange over the vegetables in the baking dish. Season the chicken with salt, pepper, and nutmeg.

3. Pour the vermouth into the baking dish and arrange the garlic cloves around the chicken pieces. Cover with aluminum foil, then the lid, and bake for 1 hour to 1 hour 20 minutes, until an instant-read thermometer registers 175°F.

4. Squeeze the garlic cloves from their skin and spread on the bread slices, and serve with the chicken and pan juices.

SERVES 8

Pat Atteberry's King Ranch Chicken

When Pat Atteberry, who was born in Oklahoma and grew up in New Mexico, thinks of casseroles she thinks of the community dinners and potlucks at the First Presbyterian Church of San Angelo, Texas, that her family has attended for many years. None of the covered dishes served there is more popular than the King Ranch Chicken Casserole, a soft, spicy, cheesy mixture of tomatoes, corn tortillas, chicken, cream, and pepper that Mrs. Atteberry describes as "an enchilada in a dish." The origin of King Ranch Chicken is a bit foggy and no direct tie has been found to the sprawling West Texas ranch in its name, but when it comes to this casserole, it's better to not let the truth stand in the way: "Everybody has a recipe and everyone says theirs is the original and the best," says Mrs. Atteberry. *Feast of Good News,* the cookbook that our church published has a recipe and I was probably inspired by that version. I've been told that it's good enough to cure a lost soul."

6 ounces pepper Jack cheese, shredded (1½ cups)

6 ounces cheddar cheese, shredded (1½ cups)

½ cup vegetable oil

Ten 6-inch corn tortillas

1½ pounds boneless, skinless chicken breast halves, trimmed

Kosher salt and freshly ground black pepper

¼ cup olive oil

4 teaspoons fresh lime juice

4 teaspoons ancho chile powder

4 tablespoons (½ stick) unsalted butter

½ cup finely chopped onion

1 red bell pepper, stemmed, seeded, and coarsely chopped

1 poblano chile, stemmed, seeded, and coarsely chopped

3 garlic cloves, minced

1 teaspoon ground cumin

½ teaspoon cayenne pepper

2 tablespoons all-purpose flour

1 cup homemade chicken broth or low-sodium store-bought chicken broth

One 10-ounce can Ro-Tel tomatoes or 1¼ cups canned diced tomatoes with jalapeño chiles

½ cup half-and-half

½ cup chopped fresh cilantro, plus more for garnish

⅓ cup sour cream, plus more for serving

1. Place an oven rack in the center position and preheat the oven to 350°F. Line a baking sheet with paper towels. In a medium bowl, combine the two cheeses.

2. Heat the vegetable oil in a medium skillet over medium heat. Add 1 tortilla and cook about 1 minute, until crisp, flipping halfway through. Transfer to the baking sheet. Repeat with the remaining tortillas.

3. Pat the chicken dry and season with salt and pepper. Heat the olive oil in a large skillet over medium heat. Add the chicken, 2 teaspoons of the lime juice, and 2 teaspoons of the ancho chile powder and cook for 10 to 15 minutes, until the chicken is firm and cooked through, flipping halfway through. Transfer the chicken to a carving board and let cool slightly, then shred into bite-size pieces.

351

Poultry in Every Pot, Oven, Broiler, and Grill

4. Melt the butter in a medium saucepan over medium heat. Add the onion, bell pepper, and poblano and cook about 4 minutes, stirring occasionally, until soft. Stir in the remaining 2 teaspoons ancho chile powder, the garlic, cumin, and cayenne and cook about 1 minute, until aromatic. Stir in the flour. Stir in the broth, bring to a simmer, and cook about 3 minutes, until slightly thickened. Stir in the tomatoes and half-and-half, bring to a simmer, cover, and cook about 15 minutes, stirring occasionally, until the flavors have blended.

5. Off the heat, stir in the remaining 2 teaspoons lime juice, ¼ cup of the cilantro, and the sour cream. Season with salt and pepper to taste.

6. Spread ½ cup of the sauce evenly over the bottom of an 11 x 7-inch baking dish. Evenly layer half of the tortillas over the sauce, breaking them as needed to fill any gaps. Top with half of the chicken, half of the remaining sauce, half of the remaining cilantro, and half of the cheese. Repeat the layering with the remaining tortillas, chicken, sauce, cilantro, and cheese.

7. Bake the casserole about 30 minutes, until brown and bubbling.

8. Let cool for 10 minutes. Sprinkle with additional cilantro and serve with sour cream.

SERVES 6 TO 8

Thomas Jefferson's Chicken Fricassee

Charles Insler, a law clerk for a federal judge in St. Louis, brings the same mental precision to cooking that he does to his work: He compiles evidence, clues, and insights into each dish he tries. Having grown up in the land of culinary delights that is New Orleans, Mr. Insler had no reason to believe the food in the "rest of the country was so lackluster" until he went to Princeton University, where there was nary a beignet in sight.

While researching the food preferences of the American presidents, Mr. Insler first learned of Jefferson's penchant for fine food. Jefferson's chicken fricassee is a perfect demonstration of how, says Insler, he "brought America into the modern food era." Using the traditional French technique of fricassee, the dish calls for olive oil, which the president imported from Italy, along with mustard from France. "Of all the items in his garden Jefferson deemed his olive tree 'the most worthy of being known.'"

Not averse to revising the original, which calls for a little butter to finish the dish, Mr. Insler prefers the richness of cream for his fricassee sauce.

One 3½- to 4-pound chicken, cut into 8 pieces

½ teaspoon freshly grated nutmeg

½ teaspoon sweet paprika

Kosher salt and freshly ground black pepper

2 tablespoons olive oil

2 tablespoons all-purpose flour

1 cup water

½ cup dry white wine

2 tablespoons (¼ stick) unsalted butter

1 small onion, finely chopped

5 ounces white mushrooms, stemmed and halved

2 teaspoons minced fresh sage

½ cup half-and-half

1 tablespoon chopped fresh parsley

1. Pat the chicken pieces dry and season with the nutmeg, paprika, salt, and pepper. Heat the oil in a large skillet over medium-high heat. Add the chicken and cook for 8 to 10 minutes, until golden brown on both sides. Transfer to a plate.

2. Stir the flour into the fat remaining in the skillet and cook about 2 minutes, until lightly browned. Whisk in the water and wine and scrape up any browned bits.

3. Return the chicken to the skillet, bring to a simmer, cover, and cook about 45 minutes, until an instant-read thermometer registers 175°F in the thighs and drumsticks and 165°F in the breast. Transfer the chicken to a serving platter and cover to keep warm. Strain the sauce through a fine-mesh strainer into a liquid measuring cup.

4. Wipe out the skillet with paper towels. Melt the butter in the skillet over medium heat. Add the onion and mushrooms and cook for 6 to 8 minutes, until the vegetables are lightly browned. Stir in the reserved sauce, half-and-half, and sage. Bring to a simmer and cook about 5 minutes, until slightly thickened. Pour the sauce over the chicken, sprinkle with the parsley, and serve.

SERVES 4

Myra Carreon J. Mondzac's
Chicken Adobo

When Myra Carreon Mondzac moved to New York City from her native Philippines in 1988 the "chaotic, and stimulating beat" of her new life was everything the 28-year-old wanted, yet she still longed for the familiar rituals of her country. Eventually, she was able to visit friends in the suburbs for weekends of home cooking, eating, and talking. Nothing brought the émigrés as close to home as adobo, the Filipino national dish of soy-and-vinegar-marinated chicken. Adobo reflects the Chinese influence on the Philippines, and the use of garlic and the "pickling" of the meat in vinegar are Spanish.

Some add coconut milk or sugar, pineapple or tomatoes, but this adaptation is the perfect expression of the multicolonial influences that helped create the unique Filipino culture. Ms. Mondzac uses adobo to introduce non-Filipinos to the polyglot that is her home cuisine.

354

One Big Table

1 cup sukang paombong (palm vinegar), cider vinegar, or red wine vinegar

6 tablespoons soy sauce

6 garlic cloves, peeled and smashed

Kosher salt and freshly ground black pepper

1 bay leaf

One 3½- to 4-pound chicken, cut into 8 pieces and trimmed

1. In a Dutch oven, combine the vinegar, soy sauce, garlic, 1 teaspoon salt, 1 teaspoon pepper, and the bay leaf. Add the chicken and turn to coat. Cover and refrigerate for 2 hours.

2. Place the pot on the stove, bring to a simmer, and cook 20 minutes. Transfer the chicken, skin side up, to a wire rack set over a foil-lined rimmed baking sheet.

3. Preheat the broiler. Broil the chicken for 10 minutes, until golden brown. While the chicken broils, simmer the sauce for 5 to 10 minutes, until reduced by half. Discard the bay leaf.

4. Return the chicken to the sauce and turn to coat. Season with salt and pepper to taste, and serve.

SERVES 4 TO 6

LUPE PEACH'S CHICKEN IN CHILE-PEANUT SAUCE

Forced to support herself from the time she was an orphaned teenager in Mexico, Jesse Banderas worked as a maid and later a cook in a private home. Her specialty was tortillas, which she made by hand, a technique she taught her daughter, Lupe Peach, the proprietor of a Mexican *tienda* (shop) in Seattle. This dish, another specialty Ms. Banderas passed on to her daughter, originated in Michoacán, the state where she was raised, and it makes a fine meal when served with fresh tortillas.

6 cups water

One 3½- to 4-pound chicken, cut in 8 pieces and trimmed

2 garlic cloves, halved

Kosher salt and freshly ground black pepper

4 plum tomatoes, cored and halved lengthwise

6 tablespoons vegetable oil

4 dried pasilla chiles, stemmed, seeded, and halved lengthwise

½ cup thinly sliced onion

¾ cup shelled and skinned raw peanuts

1 tablespoon sesame seeds

½ cup homemade chicken broth or low-sodium store-bought chicken broth, plus more as needed

½ teaspoon cayenne pepper, plus more to taste

1. Place an oven rack in the center position and preheat the oven to 450°F. Lightly oil a rimmed baking sheet.

2. In a large Dutch oven, bring the water, the chicken, garlic, 1 teaspoon salt, and 1 teaspoon pepper to a simmer. Cook for 30 to 45 minutes, until an instant-read thermometer registers 175°F in the thighs and drumsticks and 165°F in the breast. Transfer the chicken to a plate to cool. Discard the cooking liquid.

3. While the chicken simmers, place the tomatoes cut side down on the baking sheet and bake about 20 minutes, until the skin starts to bubble and separate from the flesh. Remove the tomatoes from the oven and, while still hot, use tongs to remove the skin. Transfer the tomatoes and any juice to a blender.

4. Heat 2 tablespoons of the oil in a large skillet over medium-high heat. Add the chiles and cook for 15 seconds on each side, until aromatic. Transfer the chiles to the blender.

5. Add the onion to the skillet and cook about 4 minutes, stirring occasionally, until soft. Transfer the onion to the blender.

6. Wipe out the skillet with a paper towel. Add the peanuts and sesame seeds and cook over medium-high heat for 2 to 4 minutes, stirring constantly, until aromatic and just beginning to brown. Transfer the peanuts and sesame seeds to the blender. Add the broth and cayenne. Process until smooth, about 1 minute.

7. Heat the remaining ¼ cup oil in a large saucepan over medium-high heat. Add the sauce, bring to a simmer, and cook about 5 minutes, stirring occasionally. If the mixture is very thick, add more chicken broth, 2 tablespoons at a time, until it is a sauce-like consistency.

8. When the chicken is cool enough to handle, remove and discard the skin and bones, keeping the meat in large pieces. Stir them into the sauce and cook about 2 minutes, until warmed through. Season with salt and cayenne to taste and serve.

SERVES 4

355

Poultry in Every Pot, Oven, Broiler, and Grill

The Alvarezes' Pollo Criollo
Home-Style Chicken

Novelist Julia Alvarez spent her early years in the Dominican Republic and moved to New York when the political situation there became untenable. Her husband, Bill Eichner, a surgeon, is the son of Nebraska tenant farmers. "His whole family spent every Sunday afternoon sitting around the table, comparing the flavor of this year's carrots with last," says Alvarez, who grew up talking culture and politics, not cooking. Eichner spent hours coaxing his wife's mother, aunts, and cousins, and Ana, the family cook, into giving him the outlines of their family's dishes and he translated them through his own sturdy Midwestern fare. Pollo criollo is a family favorite, which they usually serve with red beans and rice (page 643) and sweet-and sour carrots (page 584).

356

One Big Table

FOR THE MARINADE AND CHICKEN

½ cup dry white wine

1 tablespoon cider vinegar

3 garlic cloves, minced

Kosher salt and freshly ground black pepper

¼ teaspoon freshly grated nutmeg

5 tablespoons olive oil

One 3½- to-4-pound chicken, cut into 8 pieces and trimmed

1 cup all-purpose flour

FOR THE SAUCE

¼ cup olive oil

1 large onion, finely chopped

2 shallots, finely chopped

3 garlic cloves, minced

1 cup water

1 cup tomato puree or crushed tomatoes

½ cup pitted green olives, chopped

1 tablespoon chopped sun-dried tomatoes

1 tablespoon drained capers, rinsed

Kosher salt and freshly ground black pepper

1. To make the marinade and chicken: In a large bowl, combine the wine, vinegar, garlic, ½ teaspoon salt, ½ teaspoon pepper, and the nutmeg. Whisk in 3 tablespoons of the oil. Add the chicken pieces, turn to coat, cover, and refrigerate for 3 hours.

2. In a shallow dish, combine the flour, 1 teaspoon salt, and 1 teaspoon pepper. Remove chicken from the marinade and pat dry. Coat in the flour mixture and shake off the excess. Heat the remaining 2 tablespoons oil in a Dutch oven over medium-high heat. Cook the chicken for 8 to 10 minutes, until golden brown on both sides. Transfer to a plate.

3. To make the sauce: Heat the oil in the Dutch oven. Add the onion and shallots and cook about 4 minutes, stirring occasionally, until soft. Stir in the garlic and cook about 1 minute, until aromatic. Add the water and scrape up any browned bits. Bring to a simmer and cook for 2 to 4 minutes, until reduced by half. Stir in the tomato puree and simmer about 5 minutes more.

4. Stir in the olives, sun-dried tomatoes, and capers, then return the chicken to the pot, skin side up. Bring to a simmer, cover, and cook for 40 to 50 minutes, until an instant-read thermometer registers 175°F in the thighs and drumsticks and 165°F in the breasts. Season with salt and pepper to taste and serve.

SERVES 4 TO 6

Mahin Rajabi's Khoreshte Fesenjan
Persian Chicken Stew

Mahin Rajabi was a law student in Iran before she immigrated to the United States with her husband in 1984. There had always been a cook in her parents' home and it was not until after her marriage that her mother taught her several dishes including fesanjan, a rich stew of ground walnuts and pomegranate that is often made for special occasions. It is now one of her family's favorites. For variety, she sometimes uses small lamb meatballs rather than the traditional chicken. She serves the traditional condiments on the side, including plain yogurt, pickled vegetables, and a large plate of mixed herbs that are munched between mouthfuls of stew.

One 3½- to 4-pound chicken, cut into 8 pieces and trimmed

3 cups water, plus more as needed

1 small onion, halved and thinly sliced

Kosher salt

1 pound shelled walnuts

¼ cup pomegranate molasses, plus more to taste

2 tablespoons sugar, plus more to taste

Shala's Torshi-e Litteh (Persian Giardiniera; page 80)

1 bunch radishes, trimmed

1 cup fresh basil leaves

1 cup fresh mint leaves

1 cup fresh tarragon leaves

1 cup chopped fresh chives

½ cup plain yogurt

1. In a Dutch oven, bring the chicken, water, onion, and 1 teaspoon salt to a simmer, cover, and cook for 30 to 40 minutes, until the chicken is cooked through and an instant-read thermometer registers 175°F in the thighs and 165°F in the breasts.

2. Transfer the chicken to a plate. When it is cool enough to handle, remove and discard the skin and bones, keeping the meat in large pieces. Strain the broth into a large measuring cup and add water, if needed, to equal 2 cups. Return the chicken and broth to the pot.

3. Pulse the walnuts in a food processor until finely ground. Add the ground walnuts, pomegranate molasses, and sugar to the pot and bring to a simmer. Cook over low heat for 30 to 40 minutes, stirring occasionally, until the sauce is thick and the oil from the walnuts has risen to the top. Add water as needed if the pot looks dry. Season with salt, sugar, and pomegranate molasses to taste.

4. Serve with bowls of giardiniera, radishes, basil, mint, tarragon, chives, and yogurt.

SERVES 4

Dawn Kita's Shoyu Chicken

Dawn Marumoto Kita remembers shoyu chicken as a standard entry in her Japanese American family's dinner repertoire. A simple, homey dish, it could be tossed on the stove or in a slow cooker while her mother rushed her and her four siblings to baseball games and dance classes. Ms. Kita's grandfather Kumitoshi Marumoto, the child of Hawaiian sugarcane laborers, was educated in Japan in the 1930s. When he returned to Hawaii as a *kibei* (a U.S. citizen of Japanese descent who is educated in Japan) and became a manager in the sugar plantation, he was, says Ms. Kita, "the nail that sticks out and must be pounded down." He and his family, including Ms. Kita's father, were among the two thousand people from the Hawaiian community of 150,000 ethnic Japanese sent to internment camps on the mainland during World War II. He spent three years imprisoned in Arizona. Once free, Mr. Marumoto vowed never to return to Hawaii, and worked in Utah as a farm laborer picking cherries and beets so he would never stick out again.

Ms. Kita's shoyu chicken is a family standard that remained a constant despite all the uprooting. She has become a community cookbook collector with a particular fondness for the Japanese Hawaiian cookbooks that help her understand the place her grandfather once called home.

Eight 6-ounce bone-in, skin-on chicken thighs, trimmed

1 cup soy sauce

1½ cups water

¼ cup packed brown sugar

2 tablespoons mirin (optional)

1 teaspoon grated fresh ginger

1 garlic clove, minced

2 scallions, green and white parts, thinly sliced, for garnish

1. In a Dutch oven, bring the chicken, soy sauce, water, sugar, mirin (if using), ginger, and garlic to a simmer, cover, and cook for 30 to 40 minutes, flipping the chicken halfway through, until the chicken is cooked through and an instant-read thermometer registers 175°F.

2. Transfer the chicken to a serving bowl and pour the sauce over the top. Sprinkle with the scallions and serve.

SERVES 4

Mori Nakashima, Manzanar Relocation Center,
ANSEL ADAMS, 1943.

One Big Table

Jonathan Rosenberg's Coconut-Marinated Chicken over Coconut Rice

AKRON, OHIO

In 2007, Jonathan Rosenberg decided that he could wait no longer to fulfill his dream of becoming a father. He adopted his infant son, Parker An, after he learned that Vietnam was one of the few countries that allowed single men to adopt. "I don't want Parker to see Vietnam as separate from me. It's part of our family now." Mr. Rosenberg is teaching himself to cook Vietnamese dishes via Internet cooking videos and cookbooks, and he and Parker love this chicken dish.

2¼ cups unsweetened coconut milk

1 tablespoon sugar

1 tablespoon fish sauce

2 tablespoons grated fresh ginger

2 garlic cloves, minced

1 teaspoon freshly ground white pepper

1 teaspoon chili paste or chili oil (optional)

1 stalk lemongrass, white part only, smashed (optional)

2 star anise pods

1½ pounds boneless, skinless chicken breasts, trimmed and cut into ¼-inch-thick slices

1 tablespoon coconut or vegetable oil

1 recipe coconut rice

6 sprigs fresh cilantro

1. Bring the coconut milk to a simmer in a medium saucepan over low heat. Stir in the sugar, fish sauce, 1 tablespoon of the ginger, garlic, pepper, chili paste (if using), lemongrass (if using), and star anise. Cover and let sit off the heat for 3 to 5 minutes, until the star anise is fragrant. (For a stronger star anise flavor, let sit for longer.) Transfer the marinade to a large bowl and cool to room temperature.

2. Add the chicken to the marinade, cover, and refrigerate for 2 to 4 hours, turning the chicken halfway through.

3. Heat the oil in a large nonstick skillet or wok over medium-high heat. Remove the chicken from the marinade and let any excess drip back into the bowl. Cook for 2 to 4 minutes, stirring occasionally, until no longer pink. Stir in the remaining 1 tablespoon ginger and cook about 1 minute, until aromatic.

4. Serve the chicken on top of the coconut rice, garnished with the cilantro.

SERVES 4

Poultry in Every Pot, Oven, Broiler, and Grill

CAROLYN TRAN'S
ROASTED LEMONGRASS CHICKEN

ATASCADERO, CALIFORNIA

Carolyn Tran lives on a desert island within the sea of California's Asian American culture. In San Francisco, where as an infant Ms. Tran and her mother joined her father who had immigrated, the young woman lived in a pan-Asian community of Japanese, Chinese, Filipino, Korean, and Vietnamese populations, including some seventh-, eighth-, and ninth-generation families as Americans. After moving to Atascadero, she was astonished to find few Asians and no Vietnamese restaurants, not even in the large city of San Luis Obispo, less than twenty miles away.

A managerial economist, Ms. Tran dreams of becoming a professional cook who brings Vietnamese culture to Atascadero plate by plate. She often rents the kitchen of a local café to do small catering jobs featuring her native cuisine. Part of winning hearts and stomachs is, she knows, keeping food light and easy, so she adapted one of her mother's signature Sunday supper dishes, grilled lemongrass pork ribs, substituting chicken for the ribs. She serves it with steamed jasmine rice, pickled vegetables, and vegetable broth or sliced fresh vegetables and seasoned rice noodles.

¼ cup fish sauce

3 stalks lemongrass (white parts only), minced

2 scallions, green and white parts, minced

1 teaspoon honey or sugar

¼ cup vegetable oil

Four 6-ounce boneless, skinless chicken breast halves, trimmed

1. In a large bowl, combine the fish sauce, lemongrass, scallions, and honey. Whisk in the oil, then add water, 1 tablespoon at a time, as needed, to make a thick marinade. Add the chicken, cover, and refrigerate for 2 to 12 hours.

2. Place an oven rack in the center position and preheat the oven to 350°F.

3. In a large baking dish, arrange the chicken breasts at least 1 inch apart. Bake for 30 to 45 minutes, flipping chicken halfway through, until the chicken is firm and an instant-read thermometer registers 165°F.

4. Slice the chicken into ½-inch-thick strips and serve.

SERVES 4

CHICK BE TOUGH

One Big Table

Americo Angelo's World-Famous African Chicken

Ricardo Ribeiro was 12 years old when he left Macau, then a Portuguese outpost, after his father, a Standard Oil Company executive, was transferred to California in 1956. He said goodbye to his uncle, Americo Angelo, the chef at the Macanese restaurant Lisboa, known for his African Chicken, which he'd improvised while working in Mozambique, and which had virtually become a Macanese national dish. The last time Mr. Ribeiro saw his famous uncle was in 1979, and he still remembers the meal they had together: "We were served in a private booth at the Lisboa. I ordered his African Chicken and he ordered a bottle of chilled vinho verde. It was one of the most memorable meals of my life." Mr. Angelo died soon after. Today, there are hundreds of versions of his famous recipe, but this one, say Mr. Ribeiro, is as close as he's gotten to the original.

361

Poultry in Every Pot, Oven, Broiler, and Grill

FOR THE MARINADE AND CHICKEN

¼ cup extra virgin olive oil, preferably Portuguese

¼ cup chopped fresh cilantro or basil

1 small shallot, finely chopped

2 garlic cloves, minced

2 teaspoons Chinese five-spice powder

1 teaspoon red pepper flakes

1 teaspoon kosher salt

½ teaspoon freshly ground black pepper

One 3½- to 4-pound chicken, backbone removed, split in half, and trimmed

FOR THE POTATOES AND SAUCE

2 large Yukon gold potatoes, peeled and cut into ¾-inch chunks

4 tablespoons vegetable oil

Kosher salt and freshly ground black pepper

4 large shallots, finely chopped

1 red bell pepper, stemmed, seeded, and finely chopped

12 garlic cloves, minced

1 tablespoon sweet paprika

1½ cups homemade chicken broth or low-sodium store-bought chicken broth

1 cup grated fresh coconut or 1 cup coconut milk

½ cup natural peanut butter

2 bay leaves

1. To make the marinade and chicken: In a small bowl, combine the oil, cilantro, shallot, garlic, five-spice powder, pepper flakes, salt, and pepper. Place the chicken in a baking dish and rub with the marinade. Cover and refrigerate for 3 to 24 hours.

2. To make the potatoes and sauce: Place an oven rack in the center position and preheat the oven to 350°F.

3. In a roasting pan, toss the potatoes with 1 tablespoon of the oil, ½ teaspoon salt, and ¼ teaspoon pepper. Spread in an even layer.

4. Heat 1 tablespoon oil in a medium saucepan over medium heat. Add the shallots and bell pepper and cook about 4 minutes, until soft.

5. Stir in the garlic and paprika and cook about 1 minute, until aromatic. Stir in the broth, coconut, peanut butter, and bay leaves, bring to a simmer, and cook about 10 minutes, until slightly thick. Season with salt and pepper to taste.

6. Heat the remaining 2 tablespoons oil in a large skillet over medium-high heat. Add the chicken and cook for 8 to 10 minutes, until golden brown on both sides. Arrange the chicken, skin side up, on top of the potatoes. Pour 1 cup of the sauce over each chicken half, reserving the remaining sauce. Bake for about 1 hour, until the potatoes are tender and the chicken is cooked through and an instant-read thermometer registers 175°F in the thigh.

7. Transfer the chicken to a carving board and let rest for 5 minutes. Discard the bay leaves. Carve the chicken and serve with the potatoes and the sauce.

SERVES 4

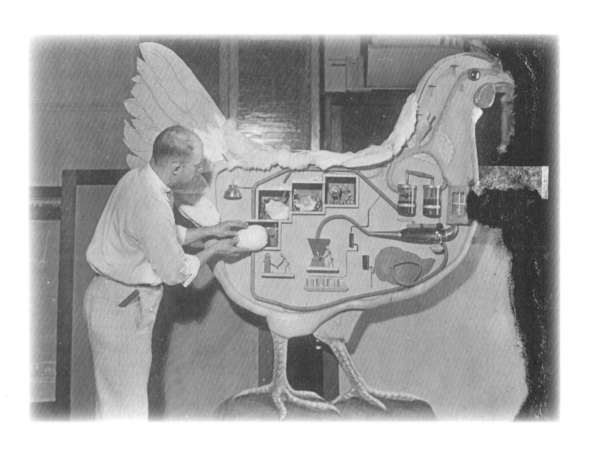

MRS. YOLANDA HO'S "CANTONESE-STYLE" MARINATED GRILLED CHICKEN

Yolanda Ho is the fourth of eight children born to Chinese immigrants who settled in Jamaica in the 1930s to work as shopkeepers. She grew up enduring the traditional Chinese gender restrictions and the even tighter class restrictions typical of the post-colonial Caribbean, but then left for nursing school in England. On her way home to Jamaica, a layover in New York turned into a job at Beth Israel Hospital and the opportunity to socialize among the many ethnic Chinese in New York City's Chinatown neighborhood, which was established in the 1840s. There, she met Anthony Ho at a dance at the Transfiguration Catholic Church. The couple moved to California and cooked outside year-round, and Mrs. Ho incorporated Jamaican and Chinese flavors in her barbecued chicken. She serves it with Jamaica's staple side dish of rice and peas.

1 cup soy sauce

¼ cup honey

2 tablespoons ketchup (optional)

1 tablespoon dry sherry

2 garlic cloves, minced

One 3½- to 4-pound chicken, cut into 8 pieces and trimmed, or 3 pounds chicken wings, wingtips removed

1. In a large bowl, combine the soy sauce, honey, ketchup (if using), sherry, and garlic. Add the chicken, cover, and refrigerate for 2 to 4 hours, turning the chicken halfway through.

2. Heat a grill to medium-high. Remove the chicken from the marinade and grill for 15 to 20 minutes, flipping occasionally, until the chicken is well browned and an instant-read thermometer registers 175°F in the thighs and 165°F in the breast and wings.

3. Transfer the chicken to a serving platter and let rest for 5 minutes before serving.

SERVES 4

AGGIE HEJJA GEOGHAN'S PAPRIKÁS CSIRKE
Chicken Paprikas

Aggie Hejja Geoghan's family fled Hungary during the 1956 revolution, when she was five years old. Their escape began as she ran with her parents across the fields behind their Budapest home, her eighteen-month-old brother in her father's arms and "sleeping" people on the ground all around them. They were smuggled across the border to Austria in the back of a supply truck, then went to Belgium, and from there sailed to America. Dishes like this one remind her of the miracle of her family's escape and the good fortune of landing where they did.

Authentic Hungarian paprika is an absolute necessity in this recipe. She prefers the sweet or mild Szeged brand, now available in most major supermarkets. She serves this dish over wide egg noodles or spaetzle.

One 3½- to 4-pound chicken, cut into 8 pieces and trimmed

Kosher salt and freshly ground black pepper

5 tablespoons olive oil

2 medium onions, coarsely chopped

2 green bell peppers, stemmed, seeded, and chopped

¼ cup Hungarian sweet paprika

1 cup plus 2 tablespoons water

1 tablespoon cornstarch

¼ cup sour cream

1. Pat the chicken dry and season with salt and pepper. Heat 3 tablespoons of the oil in a Dutch oven over medium-high heat. Add the chicken and cook for 8 to 10 minutes, until golden brown on both sides. Transfer the chicken to a plate.

2. Add the onions and bell peppers to the pot and cook about 4 minutes, stirring occasionally, until soft. Stir in the remaining 2 tablespoons oil and the paprika and cook about 1 minute, until aromatic. Stir in 1 cup of the water, ½ teaspoon salt, and ¼ teaspoon pepper. Return the chicken to the pot and bring to a simmer over medium-high heat. Reduce the heat to medium-low, cover, and cook for 1 to 1½ hours, until the chicken is tender and just falling off the bone.

3. In a small bowl, whisk together the remaining 2 tablespoons water and the cornstarch until smooth, then whisk in the sour cream. Stir the mixture into the pot, bring to a simmer, and cook about 2 minutes, until the sauce is thick. Season with salt and pepper to taste and serve.

SERVES 4

NINA CHANPREET SINGH'S CHICKEN TIKKA

Nina Chanpreet Singh, a first-generation Punjabi Sikh, grew up in the Amish country of Schuylkill County, Pennsylvania. Her family belonged to a small fellowship of Sikhs there, but she was also influenced by the simple lifestyle and the reverence for community and family of the Amish. Like them, the Sikhs preserved their tradition through the joy of communal cooking for religious events. Ms. Singh's father drives more than two hours every week to the Sikh temple in Bridgewater, New Jersey, so that his family can participate in the langaar or "open kitchen" where hundreds of the faithful are served. Chicken tikka masala is as basic to Mrs. Singh's Northern Indian roots as chicken and dumplings are to the Amish. Instead of using measuring spoons, Ms. Singh prefers her method of "smidgeons," as much spice as she can pinch between her thumb and third finger and rub together to release its essence. Serve the chicken with white rice.

FOR THE MARINADE AND CHICKEN

3 tablespoons plain low-fat yogurt

1½ teaspoons cayenne pepper

1 teaspoon ground cumin

1 teaspoon amchur powder (green mango powder)

½ teaspoon sweet paprika

½ teaspoon kosher salt

¼ teaspoon ground turmeric

1½ pounds boneless, skinless chicken breasts and/ or thighs, trimmed

FOR THE SAUCE

2 tablespoons vegetable oil

1 medium onion, finely chopped

½ teaspoon cumin seeds

1 tablespoon tomato paste

2 teaspoons grated fresh ginger

1 teaspoon ground turmeric

½ teaspoon garam masala

¼ teaspoon cayenne pepper

Kosher salt

1½ cups canned crushed tomatoes

¼ cup half-and-half

1. To make the marinade and chicken: In a small bowl, whisk together the yogurt, cayenne, cumin, ½ teaspoon of the amchur powder, the paprika, salt, and turmeric. Place the chicken in a large baking dish, evenly coat with the marinade, cover, and refrigerate for 2 to 12 hours.

2. Place an oven rack in the center position and preheat the oven to 325°F.

3. Bake the chicken for 10 to 12 minutes, until it is partially cooked and somewhat firm. Remove from the oven and sprinkle with the remaining ½ teaspoon amchur powder.

4. To make the sauce, heat the oil in a Dutch oven over medium heat. Add the onion and cumin and cook about 4 minutes, stirring occasionally, until the onion is soft. Stir in the tomato paste, 1 teaspoon of the ginger, the turmeric, garam masala, cayenne, and 1 teaspoon salt and cook about 1 minute, until aromatic. Stir in the crushed tomatoes, bring to a simmer, and cook about 15 minutes.

5. Add the chicken to the sauce, bring to a simmer, and cook for 15 to 20 minutes, until the meat is firm and an instant-read thermometer registers 175°F in the thigh and 165°F in the breasts. Stir in the remaining 1 teaspoon ginger and the half-and-half, season with salt to taste, and serve.

SERVES 4

POTPIES

THE BEST USE FOR THE TRADITIONAL CHICKENS OF WINTER—FLAVORFUL OLD ROOSTERS and hens that need to be baked, boiled, or stewed long and slow to tenderize them—is in chicken potpies. The meat pies of the British Isles were made in tin pots lined with crusts that were not meant to be eaten, but protected the meat filling from the metallic taste. In *American Cookery,* the country's earliest recipe book, Amelia Simmons provides a recipe for chicken pie that calls for six chickens, one and a half pounds butter, and a thick crust. The first record use of the term "pot pie," however, wasn't until 1839 in *The Kentucky Housewife.* The shredded-chicken-gravy-and-dough concept probably inspired other American folk dishes—chicken and biscuits and chicken à la king—and until the mid-twentieth century, the recipes for the creamy poultry pie reflected the cook's taste, family background, and region. In 1951, the Swanson Company became the first to mass-produce and sell frozen chicken potpies, and in the decades since, chefs have attempted to reclaim and elevate the dish with herbed crusts or puff pastry bonnets. But chicken potpie is a country dish, and the refined urban versions rarely compete with those from Midwestern farm kitchens.

El Tonayense Chicken Burrito

Benjamin Santana has made his fortune feeding street dwellers, hipsters, and newly minted foodies from his taco truck in San Francisco's Mission District. In its early days, the truck offered fellow Mexican Americans an outpost of home where they could get an authentic meal for less than two dollars. But over the years his clientele has widened and taco trucks have become the darling of Mexican food purists throughout the city. The more open-minded order the specialty fillings like tripitas (grilled tripe). Today Mr. Santana and his brother-partner, Esquival, own four trucks and a restaurant, El Tonayense, named after Tonaya in Jalisco, Mexico, where their family is from. Mr. Santana's pollo asado filling for burritos and tacos served with red and green salsas (see recipes for similar versions on pages 83–87) made the brothers famous.

1½ cups orange juice

3 tablespoons fresh lemon juice

1 tablespoon garlic powder

½ teaspoon dried oregano

Kosher salt and freshly ground black pepper

2 pounds boneless, skinless chicken thighs, trimmed and cut into 1-inch chunks

8 ounces dried pinto or black beans, soaked in cold water overnight or in boiling water for 3 hours

2½ cups long-grain white rice, preferably Mexican

2 tablespoons vegetable oil

6 large (12-inch) flour tortillas

¾ cup tomatillo salsa (page 83)

¾ cup lightly packed cilantro leaves

1 small onion, finely chopped

Lime wedges, for serving

1. The day before serving, in a large bowl, combine the orange juice, lemon juice, garlic powder, oregano, 1 teaspoon salt, and 1 teaspoon pepper. Add the chicken, cover, and refrigerate for 8 to 24 hours.

2. In a medium saucepan, cover the beans with water by 2 inches and add ½ teaspoon salt. Bring to a simmer and cook for 1 to 1½ hours, until tender. Drain the beans and keep warm.

3. Bring 6 cups water to a simmer in a large saucepan. Add the rice and ½ teaspoon salt, reduce the heat to low, and cook about 20 minutes, until all the water is absorbed and the rice is tender. Use a fork to fluff the rice, cover, and keep warm off the heat.

4. Heat the oil in a large skillet over medium heat. Add the chicken and cook for 4 to 6 minutes, stirring occasionally, until golden brown on all sides and no longer pink in the middle. Transfer to a medium bowl, cover, and keep warm. Wipe out the skillet with a paper towel.

5. To wrap the burritos, heat the skillet over low heat. Working with one tortilla at a time, cook for 30 seconds to 1 minute, until warm, flipping halfway through. Place about 1¼ cups rice in the center of the tortilla, leaving a 1½-inch border on each side. Spoon about ½ cup of the beans over the rice, followed by ⅔ cup of the chicken, 2 tablespoons of the salsa, 2 tablespoons of the cilantro leaves, and 2 tablespoons of the onion. Fold the sides into the center, then roll the tortillas around the filling to form a tight cylinder. Serve with the lime wedges.

SERVES 6

Katarina Longhofer's Chicken and Butterballs

DERBY, KANSAS

Katarina Longhofer brought this recipe from Russia to the Great Plains in the early 1900s. Twenty years later, when her son married, she instructed his bride, Helena Litke, in the proper preparation of the decadently rich yet light dumplings that her son had eaten growing up. They were served for family meals, and were added to "sickbed soup" which, according to her great-great-granddaughter, Marcia Quincy, "gets the body back to how it should be." According to Ms. Quincy, allspice gives the butterballs their unexpected flavor, and success depends on their size. "They should be small and tight, and after you drop them in the broth, you know they are done when they float."

FOR THE BROTH

One 3½- to 4-pound chicken, cut into 8 pieces
    and trimmed

2 quarts water

2 teaspoons kosher salt

1 celery stalk with leaves, coarsely chopped

1 carrot, peeled and coarsely chopped

1 medium onion, coarsely chopped

1 sprig fresh rosemary

1 sprig fresh thyme

1 bay leaf

1 garlic clove, peeled and halved

½ teaspoon whole black peppercorns

FOR THE BUTTERBALLS

10 slices best-quality white sandwich bread
    (about 9 ounces), quartered

1 teaspoon kosher salt

½ teaspoon ground allspice

½ cup heavy cream, plus more as needed

8 tablespoons (1 stick) unsalted butter, cut into
    1-inch pieces

2 large eggs, lightly beaten

FOR THE SOUP

2 celery stalks, cut into ½-inch pieces

2 carrots, peeled and cut into ½-inch pieces

1 medium onion, coarsely chopped

Kosher salt and freshly ground black pepper

2 tablespoons minced fresh parsley

1. To make the broth: In a large Dutch oven, bring the chicken, water, and salt to a simmer and cook for 30 minutes, skimming any foam that rises to the surface. Add the celery, carrot, onion, rosemary, thyme, bay leaf, garlic, and peppercorns and simmer about 2 hours more, until the meat falls off the bone.

2. Transfer the chicken to a plate. When it is cool enough to handle, remove and discard the skin and bones, keeping the meat in large pieces. Strain the broth into a clean large Dutch oven and discard the solids in the strainer.

3. While the broth simmers, make the butterballs: Place an oven rack in the center position and preheat the oven to 325°F.

4. Arrange the bread slices in a single layer on a large baking sheet. Toast for 15 to 20 minutes, until very dry and lightly browned. Let cool to room temperature.

5. Process the bread to fine crumbs in a food processor, or crush with a rolling pin. (You should have about 1¾ cups bread crumbs.) In a large bowl, mix them with the salt and allspice.

6. Heat the cream and butter in a small saucepan over medium heat about 5 minutes, until the butter is melted and the mixture is hot but not boiling. Stir the cream mixture into the bread crumbs until combined. Let the mixture cool about 5 minutes, then stir in the eggs until well incorporated and a large ball forms. (If the mixture doesn't hold together, add heavy cream, 1 tablespoon at a time, until it does.)

7. Form the dough into 1 tablespoon-size balls, about 1 inch in diameter. Place the butterballs on a baking sheet and cover.

8. To make the soup, bring the reserved broth to a simmer. Add the celery, carrots, and onion to the soup and simmer about 10 minutes, until the vegetables are almost tender. Stir the chicken into the broth and season the soup with salt and pepper to taste.

9. Carefully drop the butterballs into the soup and simmer about 5 minutes, until they rise to the surface. Sprinkle each portion with parsley and serve.

———

SERVES 6

THE UNITED STATES OF DUMPLINGS

DUMPLINGS IN AMERICA HAVE ALWAYS BEEN A POLYGLOT. EARLY SETTLERS ON THE Outer Banks and barrier islands of North Carolina dropped biscuit-like dough in one-pot dishes to turn a soup into a meal: "clams with pie bread," or "chicken with pie bread." Farther inland, cornmeal dumplings turned chicken or ham-hock soup into a meal of serious substance. In Midwestern settlement houses, immigrants from Eastern Europe dropped free-form dumplings into chicken and vegetable stews; Chinese laborers following the railroad west made carefully shaped dumplings. If the word *dumpling* confuses a New York City native, say "matzo ball." Eventually, the Pennsylvania Dutch made a name (and a market) for their chicken and dumplings, but the best versions come from family kitchens, not from roadside restaurants.

Proclamation Crew's Brunswick Stew

BRUNSWICK COUNTY, VIRGINIA

Stews such as Brunswick stew and its spicier Kentucky cousin, burgoo, were a nineteenth-century hodgepodge of whatever was at hand, including small game such as squirrel and rabbit, beans, and shoe-peg corn. More than an amalgam of available ingredients, they became points of regional pride and, in the case of Brunswick stew, ongoing rivalry. Brunswick County, Virginia, has claimed that the stew was invented there by African-American camp cook Jimmy Matthews in 1825. Back then the primary ingredient was squirrel. Brunswick, Georgia, also claimed it, and after 160 years, the rivalry was laid to rest in 1987 when Georgia conceded that Virginia had the more rightful claim.

The Virginia General Assembly promptly proclaimed Brunswick County "The Original Home of Brunswick Stew" and hosted a cook-off on the capitol grounds. Today, Brunswick stew is the fund-raising food of choice in that part of Virginia and stew masters make the circuit of cooking competitions to benefit their firehouses and other charities. One of them, John Clary of the Lawrenceville Volunteer Fire Department, who trained as an apprentice stew master in 1973, has traveled the country with his Proclamation Stew Crew cooking Brunswick stew in the iron cauldron the fire company acquired in the 1930s. They have gone to Brunswick, Georgia, for numerous competitions and as far north as New York City for the annual Big Apple Barbecue. Mr. Clary's recipe no longer uses squirrel, but it does contain "bacon, fatback, hog jowls, or smoked midlin meat." It is rarely cooked in small enough quantities for home use, but Mr. Clary has adapted the firehouse recipe here for less than a crowd.

Kosher salt and freshly ground black pepper

1½ tablespoons sugar

¾ teaspoon red pepper flakes

2¼ pounds boneless, skinless chicken thighs, trimmed

3 ounces pork fatback, coarsely chopped

2 pounds Yukon gold potatoes, scrubbed and cut into 1½-inch chunks

1 large onion, coarsely chopped

One 28-ounce can crushed tomatoes

Three 15-ounce cans small green butter beans (lima beans), drained and rinsed

Two 11-ounce cans white shoe-peg corn, drained and rinsed

4 tablespoons (½ stick) unsalted butter

1. In a small bowl, combine 2 tablespoons salt, ¾ teaspoon black pepper, the sugar, and red pepper flakes.

2. Place the chicken and fatback in a Dutch oven and cover with water. Bring to a simmer over medium heat. Reduce the heat to medium-low and cook for 45 minutes to 1 hour, until the chicken is tender.

3. Add the potatoes, onion, and 1 tablespoon of the spice mixture. Return to a simmer and cook about 15 minutes, until the potatoes are tender. Stir in the tomatoes, butter beans, and 1 tablespoon more of the spice mixture, and cook for 5 minutes more, until the beans are soft.

4. Stir in the corn, butter, and remaining spice mixture and simmer for 10 to 15 minutes more. Season with salt and pepper to taste and serve.

SERVES 6 TO 8

Bubba Frey's Famous Rooster Stew

W est of the Atchafalaya Basin, where the swamp gives way to prairie, small communities such as Frey, Robert's Cove, and Mowata rise out of the rice fields. The German work ethic and Old World food traditions thrive in the hands of folks like Bubba Frey.

Mr. Frey, of Frey, Louisiana, about thirty miles west of "Hub City" (Lafayette), operates his own country store on Highway 13, which he has turned into a specialty meat shop. Most days he is working by 3:00 A.M., "to boil the boudin meat, fix the rice, hang sausages in the smokehouse, and cook the hog cracklin's. It's nothing to make four hundred pounds a day now." Mr. Frey's immaculate meat case is packed with smoked spareribs, hog's head cheese, jalapeño pork sausage, garlic pork sausage, beef sausage, even stuffed beef tongue. Seasonally, the case might also hold guinea fowl, turkeys, ducks, roosters, quail, or geese from Mr. Frey's chicken yard.

371

It's not surprising that Bubba Frey makes a terrific Rooster Sauce or Rooster Brown Gravy. "It's not a stew," insists his great-nephew and godson, Lawrence. "The only time my uncle made a stew, he made it with a hen. If he cooked it on the carport outside, it was a rooster brown gravy. My old uncle called it sauce du bois because he cooked it on a wood fire." Whether stew, sauce, or brown gravy, it is best served over white rice.

One 6- to 8-pound rooster (6 months to 1 year old)

Kosher salt

⅛ teaspoon cayenne pepper

Garlic powder

1 to 2 tablespoons fresh hog lard

2 medium white onions, chopped

1 celery stalk, chopped

½ green bell pepper, stemmed, seeded, and finely chopped

2 garlic cloves, chopped

One 10-ounce can Ro-Tel tomatoes or 1¼ cups canned diced tomatoes with jalapeño chiles (optional)

1 gallon pork broth, beef broth, or chicken broth; low-sodium store-bought beef or chicken broth or water can be substituted

1. Rinse the rooster under cold running water, cut into 8 serving pieces, and drain well in a colander. Pat dry. Season with salt, cayenne, and garlic powder to taste.

2. Melt some lard in a large cast-iron pot over medium heat. Use just enough lard to cover the bottom of the pot. (The amount of lard depends on the size of the rooster and the size of the pot.) Once the lard is hot, brown the rooster pieces well on both sides. Once the meat has sufficiently browned and all the "good sticky stuff" is on the bottom of the pot, transfer the meat to a platter. (Once the chicken has browned, you will get a rich gravy and rooster meat with sticky skin.)

3. Add the onions, celery, bell pepper, and garlic to the sticky stuff and cook, stirring from time to time, until the vegetables are wilted and slightly browned. If you prefer a reddish gravy, add the tomatoes and juice as the vegetables wilt.

4. Once the vegetables have browned, return the rooster meat to the pot and cover by half with broth. Cook over low heat. (Add the remaining broth as needed during the cooking and tenderizing process. Additional broth will be needed to prevent the rooster from scorching.) As the broth evaporates, the meat will stick to the bottom of the pot. At that point, add more broth. This process should be done 5 times and will take from 1½ up to 3 hours until meat is tender. Keep adding broth as necessary to maintain a stew-like consistency.

SERVES 4 SOUTHWEST LOUISIANANS

NOTES: Cooking time depends on the size of the rooster; the older the bird, the tougher (but better-tasting) the meat. Because of the long cooking time, you will need to begin with a gallon of broth and add more as needed.

Mr. Frey uses what he calls "boudin broth." This is the water in which he boils his boudin but he says it's basically pork broth.

Mrs. Batali's Guinea Hen Cacciatore

SEATTLE, WASHINGTON

Pollo alla cacciatore is a "hunter's-style" chicken. The recipe may have started with guinea hens, rather than the chickens we know and love today. And it's never been clear whether the dish refers to the meal Italian hunters eat after they've brought home the game, or the one they have while they are out in the woods.

The chicken has a nice brown crust, and braising the meat makes the chicken so moist that it's sinful. The broth, full of tomatoes, mushrooms, and white wine, has an earthy, sweet taste.

¼ cup vegetable oil

¼ cup plus 2 tablespoons olive oil

4 ounces pancetta, diced

One 3½- to 4-pound chicken, cut into 8 pieces and trimmed, or two 2-pound guinea hens, quartered

Kosher salt and freshly ground black pepper

½ cup all-purpose flour

1 medium onion, halved and thinly sliced

3 garlic cloves, minced

½ cup dry white wine

One 28-ounce can whole tomatoes with their juices, crushed with your hand

2 teaspoons minced fresh oregano

Red pepper flakes

8 ounces shiitake mushrooms, stems removed, caps halved or quartered if large

1 green bell pepper, stemmed, seeded, and sliced

1 red bell pepper, stemmed, seeded, and sliced

1. Place a heavy-bottomed soup pot over medium heat. Add the vegetable oil and ¼ cup of the olive oil. When the oil is warm, add the pancetta. Cook, stirring occasionally to avoid burning, about 3 minutes, until brown. Transfer to a plate with a slotted spoon.

2. Season the chicken liberally with salt and pepper. Coat the pieces lightly in flour and tap off any excess.

3. Place the chicken pieces in the pot, being careful not to crowd them. (It's okay to brown the chicken in batches.) Brown the chicken on both sides. Transfer to a plate.

4. Add the onion and garlic to the oil in the pot and cook for 5 minutes, stirring occasionally. Add the white wine and bring to a boil. Allow the wine to reduce by half, about 4 minutes. Add the tomatoes, oregano, red pepper flakes to taste, and the pancetta and return to a boil. Return the chicken to the pot, pushing it down so it's covered by the sauce. Lower the heat to a simmer and cover. Cook for 20 minutes.

5. Heat the remaining 2 tablespoons olive oil in a large skillet over medium-high heat. Add the mushrooms and peppers, and toss until the peppers start to lose their crunch. Season with salt. Add to the chicken, stir, cover, and cook for 15 to 20 minutes more.

6. Check the level of the liquid as the chicken cooks. It should just cover the chicken. If necessary, add small amounts of water to maintain the level of liquid as the chicken cooks.

SERVES 4 TO 6

LISA LAWLESS'S SMOKED PHEASANT MOLE

AUSTIN, TEXAS

Lisa Lawless grew up in an idyllic suburban community in central Illinois, the sort of place that her grandparents—farmers descended from Irish immigrant farmers—might have dreamed of as "a better life." There is no doubt in Ms. Lawless's mind that the best part of that life came from her grandmothers, "very generous" cooks, who gardened, canned, and froze so that no family holiday feast was ever made from food other than their own. In a smaller way, she and her father have continued that tradition: he hunts the game birds that she prepares, according to family recipes or others she has discovered. Her pheasant mole was inspired by a dish she had at one of Rick Bayless's restaurants in Chicago. She serves it for Christmas dinner, accompanied by corn tortillas, green beans with fresh nopales (cactus paddles), and purple potatoes roasted with ancho chile powder. She is sure that her grandmothers, who never lost their enthusiasm for exotic dishes, would approve.

3 medium tomatillos, husks removed and rinsed

½ cup sesame seeds, toasted

½ cup vegetable oil

6 medium dried guajillo chiles, stemmed, seeded, and torn into flat pieces

5 medium dried ancho chiles, stemmed, seeded, and torn into flat pieces

5 medium dried pasilla chiles, stemmed, seeded, and torn into flat pieces

Boiling water

½ cup blanched almonds

4 garlic cloves, peeled

½ cup raisins

1 slice white bread, toasted and broken into pieces

1 ounce Mexican chocolate, roughly chopped

Kosher salt and freshly ground black pepper

½ teaspoon ground cinnamon

⅛ teaspoon ground cloves

One 2- to 2½-pound smoked pheasant (available at specialty grocers and gourmet supermarkets)

Warm corn tortillas, for serving

1. Place an oven rack in the highest position and preheat the broiler. Line a plate with paper towels.

2. Place the tomatillos on a baking sheet and broil about 10 minutes until soft and the skins are blackened, flipping them halfway through. Transfer the tomatillos to a large bowl. Add 6 tablespoons of the sesame seeds.

3. Heat the oil in a Dutch oven over medium heat. Working with a few pieces of the guajillo, ancho, and pasilla chiles at a time, add the chiles to the pot and toast for 20 to 30 seconds, until aromatic (don't let them smoke). Drain the chiles briefly on the plate, then transfer them to a large bowl.

4. Cover the toasted chiles with boiling water and let them sit for 30 minutes, covered with a small plate to keep them submerged. Drain the chiles and reserve the soaking liquid. (If it tastes bitter, discard.)

5. Meanwhile, remove any chile seeds from the oil and return to medium heat. Add the almonds and garlic and cook, stirring frequently, for 3 to 5 minutes, until lightly browned. Using a slotted spoon, transfer the almonds and garlic to the bowl with the tomatillos. Stir the raisins into the oil and cook 20 to 30 seconds, until puffy, then add to the tomatillos.

6. In a blender or food processor, process the chiles with 2½ cups of the reserved soaking liquid (substitute water if the soaking liquid is too bitter) about 2 minutes, until smooth, adding more liquid as needed. Press the mixture through a fine-mesh strainer into a bowl and discard any remaining solids. (Don't rinse the blender.)

7. In the blender, process the tomatillo mixture, 1 cup of the reserved soaking water (substitute water if the soaking liquid is too bitter), the bread, chocolate, 1 teaspoon salt, ½ teaspoon pepper, and the cinnamon and cloves until smooth, adding more liquid as needed. Press the mixture through a fine-mesh strainer into another bowl and discard any remaining solids.

8. Pour off all but 1 tablespoon of the fat from the Dutch oven and heat over medium-high heat. Add chile mixture and cook, stirring frequently, for 10 to 15 minutes, until darkened and thickened to the consistency of tomato paste. Stir in the tomatillo mixture and cook, stirring frequently, for 5 to 10 minutes, until thickened again to the consistency of tomato paste.

9. Stir in 1 quart water, bring to a simmer, cover partially, and cook for 45 minutes to 1 hour, until thickened. Season with salt and pepper to taste.

10. Carve the pheasant and serve with the sauce and warmed tortillas.

————

SERVES 6

DONALD'S HOT-BLOODED GAME HENS AND PEPPER JELLY

LAUREL, MARYLAND

Donald Kinney said: "During World War Two, I was in the Navy and landed in Guam. I was a cook and one of my mates found a patch of Spanish chile peppers growing wild. We put a bunch in small-mouth bottles with vinegar and in a few days we had a nice spicy sauce to add to our drab food. One day I decided to pick some myself. In short order my hands broke out in fine beads of perspiration. I left that pepper field with a trip to sick bay. One hot-blooded Texas cook would eat those peppers by the bowl, half beans, half peppers, use them in anything, inside chicken, pork, you name it. We made a sauce like Tabasco for the tables. While we were making a batch a fellow saw us and asked what we were doing. We put some on a plate to taste and he started gasping for air and water.

"I figured out this chile pepper jelly. It's real good with chicken and pork, sweet and hot at the same time. I like it with the hot-blooded Texan game hens."

Two 1½- to 2-pound whole Cornish game hens

2 tablespoons Chile Pepper Jelly (recipe follows), plus more for serving

Kosher salt and freshly ground black pepper

4 jalapeño chiles, stemmed and halved

6 slices bacon

1. Heat one side of a grill to high heat and the other side to medium-low. Soak wooden toothpicks in water for 20 minutes.

2. Pat the hens dry, brush each with 1 tablespoon of the jelly, and season with salt and pepper. Place 4 jalapeño halves in the cavity of each hen. Arrange 3 slices of bacon over the breast of each hen and secure with toothpicks.

3. Place the hens on the hotter side of the grill and cook about 10 minutes, until well browned on all sides. Move them to the cooler side of the grill, cover, and cook for 30 to 40 minutes more, until an instant-read thermometer registers 175°F in the thighs and 165°F in the breast.

4. Transfer the hens to a carving board and let rest for 5 minutes. Remove the toothpicks, split each hen in half lengthwise, and serve with chile pepper jelly.

SERVES 4

Chile Pepper Jelly

3 jalapeño chiles, stemmed, seeded, and finely chopped

3 red (cayenne) or yellow (guero or Hungarian wax) chiles, stemmed, seeded, and finely chopped

2 habanero chiles, stemmed, seeded, and finely chopped

½ cup finely chopped red onion

5 cups sugar

1½ cups cider vinegar

3 ounces liquid fruit pectin

1. In a medium saucepan, combine the chiles, onion, sugar, and vinegar. Bring to a boil over low heat, stirring frequently, and cook for 2 to 4 minutes, until the sugar dissolves.

2. Boil for 2 minutes more, then remove from the heat and skim any foam from the surface.

3. Stir in the pectin, return the saucepan to low heat, bring to a boil, and cook for 1 minute.

4. Remove the pot from the heat and skim any foam from the surface. Pour the mixture into three half-pint jelly jars and refrigerate for 24 hours, until set.

MAKES ABOUT 3 CUPS

Mill Pond Plantation's Beer and Bacon Quail

THOMASVILLE, GEORGIA

Before the Civil War, in the red clay hills of southwest Georgia, just outside Thomasville, there were seventy-one cotton plantations, with more than three hundred thousand acres in all. By the 1880s wealthy northern industrialists bought the estates for fishing and quail hunting and built retreats where they came to inhale the "pine air cure." Twentieth-century billionaires such as Ted Turner and Warren Buffett have long since acquired most of these gilded-age "winter cottages," but a few are still owned and used by the descendants of their Victorian-era owners.

"My great-great-grandfather, Jeptha Homer Wade, cofounded Western Union and lived outside Cleveland, Ohio," says Wendy Curtis. "At that time, Thomasville was the last train stop south. In 1900 he bought up a bunch of farms, put together thirteen thousand acres, and built Mill Pond. We kept chickens, cows, a huge vegetable garden, and orchards. It was paradise for the children. We were outdoors and free in all those pine woods. There was a big, black wood-burning oven in the kitchen. The cook's name was LouLou. She made prune soufflé and cheese soufflé and sticky buns. We dressed for dinner. LouLou made a lot of game. It had to be wild. Farm-raised quail especially was beneath contempt. She made it with bacon, or with oranges and wine, or barbecued, or spit-roasted, plain—simple, delicious cooking."

Eight 4-ounce whole quails

16 slices bacon (about 1 pound)

1½ cups beer

2 tablespoons (¼ stick) unsalted butter

1 tablespoon fresh lemon juice

Kosher salt and freshly ground black pepper

1. Heat a grill to high. Soak wooden toothpicks in water for 20 minutes.

2. Wrap each quail with 2 slices of bacon and secure with toothpicks. Arrange in a single layer in a 13 x 9-inch disposable aluminum baking pan.

3. Heat the beer, butter, and lemon juice in a small saucepan over medium heat until the butter is melted. Season with salt and pepper to taste. Pour the mixture over the quail and place the pan on the grill. Cover and cook, basting frequently, for 8 to 10 minutes, until the meat is firm and pink (cut one open to check).

4. Transfer the quail to a serving platter and let rest for 5 minutes. Season with salt and pepper to taste, and serve.

SERVES 4

Poultry in Every Pot, Oven, Broiler, and Grill

BILL PURDY'S PHEASANT IN A BLANKET

Bill Purdy says: "I had most of my Christmas menu picked out, but I couldn't decide on a main course. My mother suggested pheasant, and when I stared at her blankly, she reminded me of her old stories about the hard Nebraska winters when wild pheasant was often the only meat around. Rummaging through my mother's old cookbook, we found her grandmother's pheasant recipe on a piece of old, worn paper. Dinner was a hit, and it reminded me to tell the story of my ancestors and their tough lives on the plains and how my great-great-grandmother developed a quick and tasty way to cook the game bird."

3 tablespoons unsalted butter

2 carrots, peeled and coarsely chopped

2 celery stalks, coarsely chopped

1 medium onion, finely chopped

2 tablespoons chopped fresh parsley

Kosher salt and freshly ground black pepper

One 2-pound whole pheasant

1½ cups all-purpose flour

2 tablespoons vegetable shortening

½ cup water

1. Place an oven rack in the center position and preheat the oven to 350°F. Set a roasting rack in a roasting pan.

2. Melt the butter in a medium skillet over medium heat. Add the carrots, celery, and onion and cook for 4 to 6 minutes, until soft. Transfer the mixture to a bowl, stir in the parsley, ¾ teaspoon salt, and ¼ teaspoon pepper, and cool to room temperature.

3. Pat the pheasant dry and season with salt and pepper. Spoon the vegetable stuffing into the cavity and tie the legs together with butcher's twine. Refrigerate the pheasant until ready to cook.

4. In a large bowl, whisk together the flour and 1 teaspoon salt. Using a knife and fork, cut the shortening into the flour until pea-size pieces form. Slowly stir in the water until a dough forms.

5. Place dough onto a lightly floured work surface and using a rolling pin, flatten into a 15 x 10-inch rectangle about ¼ inch thick. Place the pheasant in the middle of the rectangle, breast down, and wrap the bird in the dough. Moisten the edges with water and pinch them together to seal.

6. Transfer the wrapped pheasant, breast up, to the roasting rack. Bake for 1½ to 2 hours, until the pastry is deep golden brown and an instant-read thermometer registers 175°F in the thighs and 165°F in the breast.

7. Transfer the pheasant to a carving board and let rest for 5 minutes. Break the crust into pieces. Carve the pheasant and serve with the crust.

SERVES 2

LONG ISLAND DUCKS

THE LETTERS AND JOURNALS OF EARLY EXPLORERS AND SETTLERS IN THE NEW WORLD enthuse about the profusion and variety of small, plump wild duck. In cookbooks until the late nineteenth century, duck recipes could outnumber those for chicken, goose, or turkey and generally called for a specific breed. The American conviction that "bigger is better" waddled into the domestic duck business in 1873, when, Ed McGrath, on a trip to China, mistook a big, white Pekin duck for a goose. He shipped back a batch of Pekins to the United States, but only nine survived. When the breed flourished on Long Island, it was bye-bye Pekin, hello Long Island duckling.

In 1931, Martin Mauer, a duck farmer, constructed "Big Duck," a twenty-foot-tall building in the shape of a Pekin Duck "to house his retail store and boost sales during the Great Depression." By then Long Island was the center of the national duck industry, and at its peak in the early 1950s, 60 million were bred there. Weather, the high cost of land and labor, and environmental issues pushed the industry to the Midwest, but, as the chicken industry produced a cheaper bird, the taste for duck shifted away from the mainstream to exclusive French restaurants and ethnic enclaves. Long Island now produces about 2 million ducks. Discerning and adventurous American eaters prefer ducks with a gamier flavor than are grown here, so today in an ironic shift, Long island ships two-thirds of its ducks to China. Today, Big Duck is a national landmark and it maintains its Sphinx-like position on the landscape, as cheery as its Egyptian counterpart is enigmatic.

200 Years of Black Duck and Dumplings

MACHIPONGO, VIRGINIA

In nasty weather, the cast-iron lighthouse constructed on the south end of Hog Island in 1896 was a lifesaver to sailors near the natural barrier island between Virginia's Eastern Shore and the Atlantic Ocean. However, the flashing tower light has had the opposite effect on black ducks. In wind, rain, and snow thousands of ducks—also called black brants or just brants—slammed into the edifice and met their doom. In February 1896, Margaret Doughty wrote a letter from her home overlooking the Great Machipongo River and Atlantic marshes: "Papa . . . says the new light house has lighted the last day of January and it's scared the birds out of the bay, close by the island . . . two fellows at Cobb Island killed 50 tomorrow, one week ago." Eighty years later, two of her grandnieces, Gertrude and Viola Bell, recalled the rewards of the stormy nights of their youth. "The next morning there would be nothing but ducks!" said Gertrude. "Ducks and geese," agreed Viola, "the ground would just be covered with them. And the ones that wasn't [sic] dead, people would just go get them. They used to kill them and clean them and eat them."

The sisters' grandnephew, Buck Doughty, remembers the aftermath of such hauls: "Black duck and dumplings! Ahhh! Pop-pop used to get them all the time . . . Everybody would bring them over. He ate everything that wouldn't eat him!" Black ducks were boiled with plenty of black pepper, but the miracle of the dish was his mother's dumplings.

"You just roll them out really, really thin . . . don't know how she would get the dough that thin. But they are really tight, and they would stick your teeth together. She knew they were just right when you didn't have a doughy effect inside of them. They didn't go to pieces in the water."

FOR THE DUCK

Two 2-pound whole black ducks or one 4-pound
 whole mallard duck

10 cups water

4 medium onions, finely chopped

2 tablespoons whole black peppercorns

Kosher salt

2 bay leaves

3 allspice berries

Freshly ground black pepper

½ cup all-purpose flour

4 tablespoons (½ stick) unsalted butter

4 carrots, peeled and cut into ½-inch pieces

2 parsnips, peeled and cut into ½-inch pieces

2 potatoes, peeled and cut into ½-inch pieces

1 teaspoon cider vinegar, plus more to taste

FOR THE DUMPLINGS

2 cups all-purpose flour

1 teaspoon baking powder

¼ teaspoon kosher salt

1 cup water, plus more as needed

1. To make the duck: In a large Dutch oven, combine the ducks, water, half of the onions, the peppercorns, 1 teaspoon salt, the bay leaves, and allspice. Bring to a simmer and cook 45 minutes. Transfer the ducks to a carving board and let cool slightly. Strain the broth and reserve. Wipe out the Dutch oven with a paper towel.

2. Carve each duck into 10 pieces. Pat the duck dry and season with salt and pepper. Place the flour in a shallow dish. Lightly coat the duck pieces in flour and shake off the excess. In the Dutch oven, melt the butter over medium heat. Add half of the pieces and cook for 8 to 10 minutes, until golden brown on both sides. Transfer the duck to a plate. Return the pot to medium heat and repeat with the remaining pieces.

3. Add half of the remaining onions, half of the carrots, half of the parsnips, and half of the potatoes to the pot and cook for 8 to 10 minutes, stirring occasionally, until the vegetables begin to brown. Stir in the reserved broth and the vinegar, then return all the duck to the pot. Bring to a simmer, skim any foam from the surface, and cook about 3 hours, until the meat is falling off the bones.

4. Strain the broth through a fine-mesh strainer into a tall container, cover, and refrigerate until ready to serve. Transfer the duck pieces to a plate and cool to room temperature.

5. Remove and discard the skin and bones, keeping the meat in pieces as large as possible. Cover and refrigerate the duck.

6. To make the dumplings: In a large bowl, whisk together the flour, baking powder, and salt. Make a well in the center, add the water, and stir until a rough dough forms. If the dough does not come together, add water, 1 tablespoon at a time, until it does. Transfer the dough to a lightly floured work surface and knead about 3 minutes, until no longer sticky. Shape into a ball, cover, and refrigerate for 2 hours.

7. Roll the dough on a floured work surface until ⅛ inch thick, then cut the dough into dumplings about 1 inch wide and 2 inches long. Transfer them in an even layer to lightly floured baking sheets. Cover with a kitchen towel.

8. When about to serve, skim ¼ cup of the fat from the duck broth, transfer to a Dutch oven, and heat over medium heat. (Discard the remaining fat or reserve for another use.) Add the remaining onions, carrots, parsnips, and potatoes to the pot and cook for 8 to 10 minutes, stirring occasionally, until they begin to brown. Stir in the reserved broth, bring to a simmer, and cook for 20 to 30 minutes, until the vegetables are just tender.

9. Add the dumplings to the broth, one at a time. Stir gently, cover, and cook for 6 to 8 minutes, until tender. Stir in the duck and cook about 30 seconds, until warmed through. Season with salt, pepper, and vinegar to taste.

10. Serve in warmed, shallow bowls.

SERVES 4

Poultry in Every Pot, Oven, Broiler, and Grill

MARCEL R. ESCOFFIER'S DUCK BREASTS IN CURRIED MANGO SAUCE

FORT LAUDERDALE, FLORIDA

The late Marcel R. Escoffier maintained that he was not a chef. His great-grandfather immigrated to the United States from France to cook at the St. Regis Hotel in New York City in 1892 and his great-granduncle, Auguste Escoffier, is credited with codifying French cuisine. Marcel R. Escoffier, who answered to the name of Marty, worked in, managed, and owned restaurants in New York, New Jersey, Colorado, Hawaii, and California before settling in Fort Lauderdale, where he taught in the hospitality program at Florida International University. Nevertheless, he argued that he was merely a "cooking enthusiast, verging on the obsessive, but of course, I am French."

His striking resemblance to his ancestors ran deeper than his carefully trimmed white mustache and beard. He shared the zeal of discovery and an instinct for picking up where previous generations left off: "Twenty-five years ago when I got down here, I realized that the farms in Florida were growing exotic things that you never heard about. Mangos were still exotic back then! I'm not trying to sound pretentious, but to eat well, I had to develop my own cuisine. My apology to A. Escoffier and his caneton à l'orange, but I must say that mango does the job quite nicely. It's a matter of evolution. Of where you are." And of course, where you came from.

Mallard duck breasts are wonderful in this full-flavored recipe. The dish is served with steamed rice.

Four 6-ounce boneless, skin-on duck breasts

Kosher salt

4 stalks lemongrass, white parts only, finely chopped

4 lemon leaves, or 4 bay leaves plus four 2-inch strips lemon zest

One 13.5-ounce can unsweetened coconut milk

2 onions, finely chopped

6 shallots, finely chopped

6 garlic cloves, minced

1 tablespoon grated fresh ginger

½ teaspoon saffron threads

1 tablespoon mild curry powder, plus more to taste

1 tablespoon unsalted butter

1 ripe mango, peeled, pitted, and cut into ¼-inch cubes

1 banana, peeled and sliced into ¼-inch rounds

1 star anise pod

1 quart homemade chicken broth or low-sodium store-bought chicken broth

1 cup dry white wine

½ cup Cointreau or other orange-flavored liqueur

2 tomatoes, cored, seeded, and coarsely chopped

Freshly ground black pepper

4 scallions, green and white parts, thinly sliced

1. The day before serving, pat the duck breasts dry and season with salt. Place half of the lemongrass in an even layer on a large plate. Place the breasts, skin side up, on the plate and gently press them into the lemongrass. Place a lemon leaf (or a bay leaf and a strip of lemon zest) on top of each breast, wrap tightly with plastic wrap, and refrigerate for 12 to 24 hours.

2. Remove the top of the can of coconut milk and refrigerate until the cream rises to the top. Use a spoon to carefully lift off the cream, transfer to a bowl, and freeze. (Discard the remaining liquid or use for another dish.)

3. In a food processor, grind the onions, shallots, garlic, ginger, and saffron into a fine paste.

4. Brush the lemongrass and lemon leaves off the duck breasts. Pat the duck dry and season with curry powder. Melt the butter in a large skillet over medium heat. Add the duck breasts, skin side down, and cook for 5 to 7 minutes, until light golden brown. Transfer the duck to a plate.

5. Pour off all but 1 tablespoon of the fat from the skillet and return to medium heat. Add the onion paste and cook for 6 to 8 minutes, until soft. Stir in the remaining lemongrass, half of the mango, the banana, and the star anise and cook about 7 minutes, until the mixture is almost dry.

6. Stir in the broth, wine, Cointreau, and tomatoes, bring to a simmer, and cook about 15 minutes, until slightly thickened. Return the duck breasts to the pan skin side up, and spoon the sauce over the top. Partially cover and cook about 15 minutes, until the meat is firm and an instant-read thermometer registers 130°F.

7. Transfer the duck breasts to a serving platter and let rest for 5 minutes. Off the heat, whisk the coconut cream into the sauce. Season with salt, pepper, and curry to taste. Spoon the sauce over the duck breasts and serve, sprinkling with the remaining mango and the scallions.

———

SERVES 4

"What is sauce for the goose may be sauce for the gander but is not necessarily sauce for the chicken, the duck, the turkey or the guinea hen."
—Alice B. Toklas

Noelia Rosenthal's Duck with Root Vegetables

Born in Brooklyn, Robert Rosenthal is a man of great enthusiasm and singular focus. For reasons that neither he nor Noelia, his Puerto Rican–born wife, understand, he was seized in 1982 by an unexpected desire to run away to the country. From their nineteenth-century stone church-turned-farm-and-home in Sullivan County, New York, Mr. Rosenthal, who was determined to make a living from the land, asked chefs, "What do you need, what is missing?" The reply was unanimous: "Great duck." Duck had become too mild and too mushy, but customers were unhappy when they did not find it on a menu. Mr. Rosenthal began growing heritage breeds of duck, and soon he wanted to find the gold standard, the duck by which all others would be measured. "I kept asking, 'What is it? Where is it?' I read, I studied. If you saw my office you would understand the mind of a madman."

Noelia Rosenthal's approach is simpler. She cooks the meat slowly, primarily in its own fat. "Only the best duck can be made this simply," says Mr. Rosenthal. "From Normandy, an aged Duclair. Now, that's a duck! A cross between a white male and a domestic female—I got a French Pekin and a wild mallard together! So rich and gamey that it needs to be hung and aged like beef. No sane person would do something like à l'orange to a duck like Duclair." The Duclair, in other words, needs proper cooking but nothing that might mask its extraordinary flavor.

FOR THE DUCK

5 tablespoons olive oil

2 garlic cloves, minced

Kosher salt and freshly ground black pepper

One 4- to 5-pound whole Normandy, mallard, or Duclair duck, cut into 8 pieces, fat trimmed and reserved

2 carrots, peeled and coarsely chopped

1 parsnip, peeled and coarsely chopped

1 medium onion, finely chopped

FOR THE VEGETABLES

12 ounces red potatoes, scrubbed and cut into ½-inch pieces

12 ounces carrots, peeled and cut into ½-inch pieces

12 ounces parsnips, peeled and cut into ½-inch pieces

Kosher salt and freshly ground black pepper

1 cup frozen green peas, thawed

1. To make the duck: The day before serving, in a shallow baking dish, combine 3 tablespoons of the oil, the garlic, ½ teaspoon salt, and ½ teaspoon pepper. Add the duck breasts and turn to coat. Cover and refrigerate for 12 to 24 hours. Season the duck legs, thighs, and wings with salt and pepper, cover, and refrigerate for 12 to 24 hours.

2. Heat the remaining 2 tablespoons oil in a Dutch oven over low heat. Pat the duck legs, thighs, and wings dry, place in the Dutch oven in a single layer, and cook for 15 minutes, flipping once, until light golden brown on both sides.

3. Add the trimmed and reserved duck fat, carrots, parsnip, and onion, and enough water to cover the duck and vegetables by 1 inch. Bring to a bare simmer and cook over low heat about 3 hours, skimming and reserving the fat from the surface, until the fat is completely rendered and the duck is tender.

4. Transfer the duck pieces to a plate and keep warm. If desired, strain the broth through a fine-mesh strainer and reserve for another use. Discard the vegetables. Wipe out the Dutch oven with a paper towel.

5. Heat 1 tablespoon of the reserved duck fat in the Dutch oven. Add the duck breasts and cook for 10 to 15 minutes, flipping once, until golden brown on both sides and an instant-read thermometer registers 130°F. Transfer them to a carving board, cover with foil, and let rest.

6. While the duck breasts cook, make the vegetables: Heat ¼ cup of the reserved duck fat in a large skillet over medium heat. Add the potatoes, carrots, parsnips, ½ teaspoon salt, and ¼ teaspoon pepper and cook for 15 to 20 minutes, stirring occasionally, until tender and golden brown on all sides. Stir in the peas and cook for 1 minute, until warm. Season with salt and pepper to taste.

7. To serve, slice the duck breasts and arrange on a platter with the legs, thighs, and wings. Spoon the vegetables over the duck, drizzle with 2 tablespoons of the reserved duck fat, and serve.

SERVES 4

Releasing ducks at waterfowl sanctuary.

ONE NATION UNDER TURKEY

WHEN CONGRESS NAMED THE BALD EAGLE THE NATIONAL bird, Thomas Jefferson wrote to his daughter, saying that he wished they'd chosen the wild turkey. Americans are still inspired by soaring eagles, but at the center is a huge, deeply bronzed turkey. The bird is treasured, anticipated, disparaged, romanticized, and frequently overcooked.

Wild turkey were abundant in seventeenth-century New England, and the bird quickly replaced the English goose as the festive fowl of choice in the New World. "The turkey is certainly one of the handsomest gifts the New World made to the Old World," noted the French gastronome Brillat-Savarin, after shooting and preparing a wild turkey near Hartford, Connecticut, in 1794. M. Brillat-Savarin might not recognize the shape, size, or taste of most American turkeys today, but he would appreciate the passion and opinions aroused by the big, modern Thanksgiving bird. The most common questions today are fresh or frozen? Organic or conventional? Factory- or farm-raised? Industrial-hybrid or purebred—rise from a desire to have "the best" Cooks are offered factory birds, free-range birds, and "self-basting" birds, and all sorts of advice on how to cook them. One expert advises a 500°F oven for a short time, while another insists on slow roasting at half that temperature. Some brine, some inject the meat with marinade, some cover the bird with foil, or bake it in a brown paper bag, or slow the roasting by packing its breast in ice prior to putting it in the

oven. Some roast breast down, others roast breast up. Turkey is barbecued, smoked, and deep-fried.

Given the chance, each side attempts to convert the other by cooking a tastier bird. The basic techniques remain the same—and most of them are roasted, barbecued, grilled, or deep-fried, but all are tweaked to accommodate different provenance, different region, or the cook's taste and family tradition.

KATHLEEN CURTIN'S MODERN ROAST TURKEY

PLYMOUTH, MASSACHUSETTS

During her twenty-two-years as Plimoth Plantation's food historian, Kathleen Curtin, has developed historical menus to bring alive not only New England's first Thanksgiving but feasts through the centuries. She knows of only one eyewitness account of the 1621 harvest celebration, found in a letter from Edward Winslow. For the feast, four men were sent "fowling," and likely bagged turkeys that were plentiful in the New England woods. "We assume that turkey was part of the legendary groaning board," Ms. Curtin says, "and we know that it was a small, gamier, wild bird that, like a goose, had no white meat and was cooked by spit roasting if young or braised if older."

Whether using a free-range organic or a heritage Narragansett, Ms. Curtin tries to adapt the spirit of the early technique to accommodate all the changes in cooking technology and turkey breeding. This recipe, she says, "was born out of my desire to create a consistently juicy bird. The one thing that can ruin Thanksgiving is an overdone turkey breast that shreds instead of slices and turns to sawdust in the mouth. There just isn't enough gravy to cover that problem! But I am pretty sure that if I had the chance to serve this version to a member of the original colony they'd be able to identify the bird they were eating."

8 tablespoons (1 stick) unsalted butter, melted

One 18- to 20-pound whole turkey, neck, giblets and liver reserved, and brined (see Dr. Starkloff's Cider-Brined Grilled Turkey, page 393, for brining instructions)

2 medium onions, coarsely chopped

2 carrots, peeled and coarsely chopped

2 celery stalks, coarsely chopped

3 tablespoons chopped fresh parsley, or 1 tablespoon dried

3 tablespoons chopped fresh thyme, or 1 tablespoon dried

2 tablespoons chopped fresh sage, or 2 teaspoons dried

Freshly ground black pepper

¼ cup unbleached all-purpose flour

Kosher salt

1. Place an oven rack in the lower-center position and preheat the oven to 325°F. Lightly grease a large V-shaped roasting rack with some of the melted butter and set it inside a shallow roasting pan.

2. Remove the turkey from the brine, rinse well under cold running water, and pat dry. Using metal skewers or toothpicks, secure the neck skin to the back of the turkey, then tuck the turkey's wings behind its back.

3. In a large bowl, combine the onions, carrots, celery, 1 tablespoon of the melted butter, the parsley, thyme, sage, and pepper to taste. Stuff one-third of the vegetable mixture into the turkey cavity. Tie the legs together with butcher's twine. Brush the skin with the remaining melted butter.

4. Place the turkey breast down on the prepared rack. Sprinkle half of the remaining vegetable

mixture around the bottom of the pan and pour in 1½ cups water. Roast the turkey for 2½ hours, basting every 30 minutes with pan drippings and adding more water to the pan as needed to keep the vegetables moist and to prevent burning.

5. Remove the turkey from the oven and using kitchen towels or oven mitts, flip it breast up. Baste the turkey, return it to the oven, and roast for 1 to 2 hours more, basting every 45 minutes, until an instant-read thermometer registers 165°F in the thighs and drumsticks and 155°F in the breast.

6. Increase the oven to 400°F and roast for 10 to 20 minutes, until the skin is well browned and an instant-read thermometer registers 175°F in the thighs and drumsticks and 165°F in the breast. Transfer the turkey to a serving platter or carving board and let rest for 30 minutes to 1 hour.

7. While the turkey roasts, make the broth for the gravy. In a large saucepan, combine the reserved neck and giblets, the remaining vegetable mixture, and 5 cups water. Bring to a simmer and cook for 1 hour.

8. Add the liver and simmer for 5 minutes more. Strain the broth through a fine-mesh strainer. Reserve the neck, giblets, and liver and discard the remaining solids. Pick the meat from the neck and finely chop the giblets and liver. (The neck meat, giblets, liver, and broth can be refrigerated until you are ready to make the gravy.)

9. To make the gravy, transfer the pan juices from the roasting pan to a fat separator or a liquid measuring cup and let sit about 5 minutes, until the fat floats to the top. Reserve ¼ cup of the fat and discard the rest or reserve for another use.

10. Return the reserved ¼ cup fat to the roasting pan and heat over medium-low heat. Whisk in the flour and cook for 2 minutes, until it begins to brown. Whisk in the broth and scrape up any browned bits. Stir in the reserved neck meat, giblets, and liver, bring to a simmer, and cook for 5 to 10 minutes, until thick. Season with salt and pepper to taste.

11. Carve the turkey and serve with the gravy.

SERVES 20 TO 22

Thanksgiving turkey for the President, 1929.

Aunt Vestula's Buttermilk-Marinated Wild Turkey

FILBERT, SOUTH CAROLINA

Wild turkey is a point of pride, a pledge to Southern tradition, a man thing. For decades Vestula Sanders's way with the wild bird protected her large family from the ugly truth that the local wild turkeys were tough. Aunt Vestula's buttermilk brine made the bird succulent and tasty. She herself always gave credit to the wild birds, but her nieces and nephews, who are grandchildren of a freed slave and still farming the land their father purchased in 1915, credit their aunt, and buttermilk.

FOR THE TURKEY

One 13- to 15-pound whole wild turkey

Kosher salt and freshly ground pepper

2 quarts buttermilk

3 celery stalks, finely chopped

1 medium onion, finely chopped

2 slices white bread, torn into small pieces

1 cup dry sherry

2 teaspoons sweet paprika

4 tablespoons (½ stick) unsalted butter, melted

FOR THE GRAVY

¼ cup all-purpose flour

2 cups whole milk

Kosher salt and freshly ground pepper

1. To make the turkey: The day before serving, pat the turkey dry and season with salt and pepper. Place the turkey in a baking dish and pour the buttermilk over the top. Cover and refrigerate for 12 to 24 hours, turning several times.

2. When ready to cook, place an oven rack in the lower-center position and preheat the oven to 350°F.

3. In a medium bowl, combine the celery, onion, bread, ½ cup of the sherry, and the paprika. Transfer the turkey to a shallow roasting pan and pour in the remaining ½ cup sherry. Stuff the onion mixture into the turkey cavity and tie the legs together with butcher's twine. Brush the turkey with the melted butter.

4. Roast the turkey, breast up, for 3 to 4 hours, basting every 30 minutes, until an instant-read thermometer registers 175°F in the thighs and drumsticks and 165°F in the breast.

5. Transfer the turkey to a serving platter or carving board and let rest for 30 minutes to 1 hour. Pour off all but ¼ cup of the fat from the roasting pan (leave the drippings).

6. To make the gravy: Heat the drippings in the roasting pan over low heat. Whisk in the flour and cook for 2 minutes, until beginning to brown. Whisk in ¼ cup of the milk and scrape up any browned bits. Remove the pan from the heat and slowly whisk in the remaining milk. Return to medium heat, bring to a simmer, and cook about 5 minutes, until thick. Season with salt and pepper to taste.

7. Carve the turkey and serve with the gravy.

SERVES 14 TO 16

Circa 1776 Beacon Hill Chestnut Stuffing

BOSTON, MASSACHUSETTS

Lorraine Stern's family owned a home on Beacon Hill in Boston from the early 1700s until about 1999, when, as the last surviving direct descendant, she stopped fighting the snow and moved to Miami. This recipe was as integral to life in that house as the Revere drawings and Audubon watercolors. The original called for more meat and created a decidedly British pudding-like stuffing. Small notes on the recipe show a steady lightening, the subtraction of meat and the addition of more bread, and the arrival of modern appliances to mince and chop in place of knives.

2 tablespoons (¼ stick) unsalted butter

2 medium onions, finely chopped

2 pounds bulk sweet sausage

1 carrot, peeled and coarsely chopped

1 celery stalk, coarsely chopped

1 parsnip, peeled and coarsely chopped

8 cups cooked, shelled, and peeled chestnuts

1 cup homemade beef broth or low-sodium store-bought beef broth

2 cups homemade chicken broth or low-sodium store-bought chicken broth

3 cups dry white bread crumbs

3 cups dry cornbread crumbs

1 cup chopped walnuts

1 tablespoon minced fresh parsley

1 teaspoon dried thyme

½ teaspoon dried marjoram

½ teaspoon dried sage, crumbled

½ teaspoon freshly ground black pepper

½ teaspoon kosher salt

1 large egg, lightly beaten

1. Melt the butter in a large skillet over medium heat. Add the onions and cook about 4 minutes, stirring occasionally, until soft. Increase the heat to high, crumble the sausage into the skillet, and cook, breaking up the meat with a wooden spoon, about 6 minutes, until no longer pink. Transfer the mixture to a large bowl.

2. Pulse the carrot, celery, and parsnip in a food processor until finely chopped. Stir the vegetables into the sausage mixture. In the food processor, process 2 cups of the chestnuts with the beef broth until a loose puree forms. Stir the puree into the sausage mixture.

3. Finely chop the remaining 6 cups chestnuts and stir into the sausage mixture along with the chicken broth, bread crumbs, walnuts, parsley, thyme, marjoram, sage, pepper, salt, and egg. Cover and refrigerate until needed.

MAKES ABOUT 12 CUPS, ENOUGH TO STUFF A 20-POUND TURKEY

Mollie Shimelovich Chester's Turkey Stuffing

When she enters her kitchen at dawn on Thanksgiving, Joann Bander's battle between her childhood tastes and the current cooking trends begins. Her Grandmother Mollie, her Aunt Goldie, and her mother beckon from her file box and from the pages of the 1950 *Young Hebrew Association Cookbook*. While raising her two children, she tried sausage-and-fruit stuffing, oyster stuffing, cornbread stuffing, and countless other variations, before returning to the recipe that her grandmother created when she had a little restaurant in Brockton, Massachusetts. Most of the handwritten recipes Mollie Shimelovich left behind combine Ukrainian Old Country tastes and local New England ingredients. Her stuffing is made from old-fashioned common crackers, cornflakes, and egg, enriched with sautéed onions and mushrooms. But her granddaughter has also gotten inspirations from food magazines and has been known to replace the domestic cultivated mushrooms with shiitake, oyster, and porcini varieties.

One 7.5-ounce box common crackers (also called pilot crackers)

8 cups cornflakes

2 large eggs, lightly beaten

½ pound (2 sticks) unsalted butter

8 ounces white mushrooms, finely chopped

2 large onions, finely chopped

¾ cup warm water

½ teaspoon kosher salt

½ teaspoon freshly ground black pepper

1. In a large bowl, combine the crackers and cornflakes. Using your hands, gently crush the ingredients so that some large pieces still remain. Stir in the eggs.

2. Melt the butter in a large skillet over medium-high heat. Add the mushrooms and onions and cook for 10 to 12 minutes, stirring occasionally, until golden brown. Stir the vegetables, water, salt, and pepper into the cracker mixture until evenly combined. Cover and refrigerate until needed.

MAKES 8 CUPS, ENOUGH TO STUFF ONE TURKEY (12 TO 15 POUNDS)

Frances Butler's Texas Tamale-Stuffed Turkey

SAN ANGELO, TEXAS

Frances Butler grew up on the family ranch and continues to preside over the dry, windy land. The lonesomeness of ranch life, she says, was offset by "group cooks" such as the annual Thanksgiving tamale making: "Wild turkey hunting has been a West Texas sport for as long as anybody remembers, and tamale-stuffed turkey may have been an early tip of the hat to the Mexican ranch hands who've been around for at least as long as the turkey. This recipe dates back to the early 1900s. I got it from a family whose grandmother was German but had been raised in Mexico. I make it most often in the cold months, but I've been known to put a tamale-stuffed turkey in the roasting pit in my time, as well. You can use commercial tamales, of course, but I like the two-day ritual of making tamales and then making the turkey. I always double or triple the tamales and freeze the extra. These days people use more barnyard turkey than they do wild. Before you go thinking that's a sorry thing, let me tell you this. You feed your chickens or turkey some chile peppers before you decide. That spicy-sweet flavor gets into the meat and you know what they mean when they say it doesn't get any better."

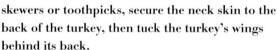

This stuffing is also delicious in chicken and squab. Serve with high quality corn chips, salsa (pages 83 to 87), and sour cream.

4 shallots, peeled

2 garlic cloves, peeled

2 jalapeño chiles, stemmed and seeded

Kosher salt and freshly ground black pepper

8 tablespoons (1 stick) unsalted butter, cut into 8 pieces and chilled

30 medium pork, chicken, or chile tamales (page 6), husks removed and discarded

1 cup frozen corn, thawed

One 8- to 10-pound whole turkey, giblets removed

1. Place an oven rack in the lower-center position and preheat the oven to 350°F. Set a large V-shaped roasting rack inside a shallow roasting pan.

2. Pulse the shallots, garlic, chiles, 1 teaspoon salt, and ½ teaspoon pepper in a food processor until finely chopped. With the food processor running, add the butter, one piece at time, and process until a paste forms.

3. In a large bowl, crumble the tamales and using a fork, stir in the corn. Season with salt and pepper to taste.

4. Pat the turkey dry. Using metal skewers or toothpicks, secure the neck skin to the back of the turkey, then tuck the turkey's wings behind its back.

5. Stuff the tamale mixture into the turkey's cavity and tie the legs together with butcher's twine. Place the turkey in the prepared rack, breast up, and rub with the butter mixture. Cover the turkey loosely with foil and roast for 1 hour, basting with pan drippings every 20 minutes.

6. Uncover and roast for 30 to 45 minutes, until the skin is well browned and an instant-read thermometer registers 175°F in the thighs and drumsticks and 165°F in the breast and stuffing.

7. Transfer the turkey to a serving platter or carving board and let rest for 30 minutes to 1 hour.

8. Carve the turkey and serve with the tamale stuffing.

SERVES 10 TO 12

Dr. Starkloff's
Cider-Brined Grilled Turkey

Max C. Starkloff, M.D., the health commissioner of St. Louis, was a serious cook, as was his son, Gene B. Starkloff, M.D. When Gene Starkloff heard that his father's sister, Irma von Starkloff Rombauer, was writing a cookbook, he was appalled. "But Aunt Irma can't cook!" he exclaimed, and his father agreed. Their descendants do not remember when this conversation took place, but they do know that Aunt Irma's cookbook, *The Joy of Cooking*, has sold more than 19 million copies. They also remember this turkey, which was usually served with apple or mango chutney, plum sauce, whole-grain mustard flavored with maple syrup, or Aunt Irma's Cumberland sauce.

2 gallons apple cider

2 cups kosher salt

10 garlic cloves, peeled and crushed

One 13- to 15-pound whole turkey

1 bunch fresh sage, rosemary, or thyme, or a combination

1. The day before serving, heat 1 quart of the cider and the salt in medium saucepan over medium heat, stirring constantly, until the salt has dissolved. Set aside to cool to room temperature.

2. In a container large enough to hold the turkey and brine, combine the cider-salt mixture, the remaining cider, and the garlic. Stuff the turkey cavity with the herbs and tie the legs together with butcher's twine. Place the turkey in the brine and weight with a plate to keep submerged. Cover and refrigerate for 8 to 12 hours.

3. When ready to cook, remove the turkey from the brine, rinse well under cold running water, drain well, and pat dry. Transfer half of the brine to a large disposable aluminum roasting pan and reserve the remaining brine. Place 3 cups of apple or hickory wood chips in water to soak.

4. Heat one side of a charcoal grill to high. Add 1½ cups of the wood chips to the coals. Place a disposable aluminum pan on the hotter side of the grill and the turkey on the cooler side, breast up. Close the lid vents, cover the grill, and cook for 45 minutes. (If you have a grill thermometer, it should read 350°F to 400°F.)

5. Add another 1½ cups of wood chips to the coals and pour the reserved brine into the roasting pan, to replace the brine that has cooked away. Rotate the turkey 180° and cook for 45 minutes more, until deeply browned. (If the wing tips or breast darken too rapidly, cover them with foil.)

6. While the turkey is on the grill, place the oven rack to the lower-center position and preheat the oven to 325°F. Set a roasting rack in a shallow roasting pan.

7. Transfer the turkey to the prepared rack, place in the oven, and roast for 20 to 40 minutes, until an instant-read thermometer registers 175°F in the thighs and drumsticks and 165°F in the breast.

8. Transfer the turkey to a serving platter or carving board and let rest for 30 minutes to 1 hour.

9. Carve the turkey and serve.

SERVES 14 TO 16

Janet Trent's Award-Winning Cajun Deep-Fried Turkey

SANFORD, NORTH CAROLINA

A descendant of Scots who received land grants from King George III to settle North Carolina, Janet Trent grew up just outside of Raleigh. North Carolina is the country's second-largest producer of turkeys—39 million birds are raised a year, creating a state farm income of more than half a billion dollars. Ms. Trent, like most folks, ate roast Thanksgiving turkey growing up, but when she was in her thirties she deep-fried her first turkey, and over the last sixteen years, she has developed her own seasoning rub. In 1996, her mother received a flyer tucked into her utility bill promoting the North Carolina Poultry Federation's deep-fried turkey contest. Ms. Trent entered and was one of five winners—and from then on her deep-fried turkey became a Thanksgiving tradition for her family.

To prevent burns from spattering oil, most cooks wear oven mitts or gloves, long sleeves, heavy shoes, and even safety glasses. They deep-fry outdoors, never leave the pot unattended, and always keep a fire extinguisher handy. Having two people lower and raise the turkey makes the job easier. Ms. Trent's husband designed and built a special extension hook that allows her to lower the bird into the boiling oil from a safe distance.

¼ cup kosher salt

1½ tablespoons onion powder

1½ tablespoons garlic powder

1½ tablespoons freshly ground black pepper

1½ tablespoons freshly ground white pepper

1 tablespoon dried basil

1½ tablespoons sweet paprika

1½ teaspoons cayenne pepper

1 teaspoon ground bay leaves

1 teaspoon filé powder

One 10- to 12-pound whole turkey

4 to 5 gallons peanut oil, for frying

Cayenne Cornbread Dressing (recipe follows), for serving

1. The day before serving, in a medium bowl, stir together the salt, onion powder, garlic powder, black and white peppers, basil, paprika, cayenne, bay leaves, and filé. Pat the turkey dry and rub the interior and exterior with the salt rub. Place the bird in a shallow roasting pan, cover, and refrigerator overnight.

2. When ready to cook, heat the oil in a 7- to 10-gallon turkey fryer over medium-high heat until a deep-frying thermometer registers 375°F. Pat the turkey dry, and place in the fryer basket or on the turkey rack, neck down. Slowly and carefully lower the turkey into the oil. (The level of the oil will rise with the weight of the turkey, and the oil will bubble from moisture.) Immediately check the temperature and adjust the heat so the temperature remains at 350°F. Cook for 35 to 45 minutes, until an instant-read thermometer registers 175°F in the thighs and drumsticks and 165°F in the breast.

3. Carefully remove the turkey from the fryer and let drain for a few minutes. Transfer to a serving platter or carving board and let rest for 30 minutes to 1 hour.

4. Carve the turkey and serve with the dressing.

———

SERVES 12 TO 14

Cayenne Cornbread Dressing

FOR THE CORNBREAD

2 cups all-purpose flour

2 cups stone-ground cornmeal

¼ cup sugar

2 tablespoons baking powder

1 teaspoon kosher salt

3 cups buttermilk

6 tablespoons (¾ stick) unsalted butter, melted

5 large eggs, lightly beaten

FOR THE DRESSING

½ pound (2 sticks) unsalted butter

1 medium onion, finely chopped

8 scallions, green and white parts, finely chopped

1 cup finely chopped fresh parsley

½ cup chopped fresh basil

6 garlic cloves, minced

1 tablespoon kosher salt

4 teaspoons dried oregano

2 teaspoons freshly ground black pepper

2 teaspoons cayenne pepper

2 teaspoons onion powder

2 teaspoons dried thyme

2 cups homemade chicken broth or low-sodium store-bought chicken broth

2 cups evaporated milk

7 large eggs, lightly beaten

1. To make the cornbread: Place an oven rack in the center position and preheat the oven to 375°F. Grease a 13 x 9-inch baking pan.

2. In a large bowl, whisk together the flour, cornmeal, sugar, baking powder, and salt. In a medium bowl, whisk together the buttermilk, melted butter, and eggs. Gently whisk the egg mixture into the flour mixture until combined. Pour the batter into the prepared pan. Bake about 55 minutes, until golden brown and a toothpick in the center comes out clean.

3. Let the cornbread cool completely, then crumble into small pieces.

4. To make the dressing: Preheat the oven to 350°F. In a large skillet, melt the butter over medium heat. Stir in the onion, scallions, parsley, basil, and garlic and cook about 4 minutes, stirring occasionally, until the onion is soft. Stir in the salt, oregano, pepper, cayenne, onion powder, and thyme and cook about 1 minute, until aromatic.

5. Add the broth, bring to a simmer, and cook about 5 minutes. Stir in the crumbled cornbread until well combined. Remove the pan from the heat and stir in the evaporated milk and eggs. Return the skillet to low heat and cook, stirring constantly, about 2 minutes. Transfer stuffing to a large baking dish, cover with foil, and bake 30 minutes. Remove the foil and bake 15 minutes, until the top is browned.

———

SERVES 12 TO 14

Ruth Fertel's Plaquemines Parish Oyster Dressing

Ruth Fertel, a biologist and former thoroughbred horse trainer who turned a corner steakhouse into an international empire, was a "force of nature," says her son, the writer and professor Randy Fertel. This "force" acquired hurricane velocity around the holidays. Her turkey stuffing, unlike the Yankee version, has a peppery bite—and more oysters than stale bread.

3 loaves French bread, cut into 1-inch cubes (about 12 cups)

1 gallon oysters with liquid

1¼ pounds (5 sticks) unsalted butter

1 pound hot sausage, casing removed and minced

1 pound smoked sausage, minced

4 celery stalks, finely chopped

3 medium onions, finely chopped

1 green bell pepper, stemmed, seeded, and finely chopped

1 red bell pepper, stemmed, seeded, and finely chopped

12 garlic cloves, minced

12 chicken bouillon cubes

Kosher salt and freshly ground black pepper

Red pepper flakes

12 large eggs, lightly beaten

1. Several days before serving, spread the bread cubes out on two baking sheets and let dry at room temperature.

2. Place an oven rack in the center position and preheat the oven to 350°F.

3. Strain the oysters over a large saucepan. Heat the oyster liquor over high heat until almost boiling. Stir in the oysters and cook for 1 to 2 minutes, until the edges begin to curl. Strain the oysters and reserve the liquid. Set the oysters aside to cool to room slightly, then coarsely chop.

4. Melt 1 stick of the butter in a large Dutch oven over medium-high heat. Crumble in the hot sausage and add the smoked sausage and cook, stirring frequently to break up the hot sausage, for 6 to 8 minutes, until just beginning to brown. Stir in the celery, onions, bell peppers, and garlic and cook about 8 minutes, stirring occasionally, until the vegetables are soft. Stir in the oysters, the reserved liquid, and the bouillon cubes. Bring mixture to a simmer and cook about 5 minutes. Season with salt, pepper, and pepper flakes to taste. Stir in the bread cubes, 2 cups at a time, until enough bread has been added to absorb the liquid but the mixture remains moist.

5. Melt the remaining 4 sticks butter in a small saucepan, then stir into the stuffing with the eggs. Transfer stuffing to a large baking dish, cover with foil, and bake for 1 hour. Remove the foil and bake about 15 minutes more, until stuffing is brown. Serve.

SERVES 18 TO 20

SUSAN SHIRK'S TURKEY MAPO DOUFU

Asia scholar Susan Shirk went to Japan as an exchange student after high school and fell in love with the place. "I always felt bad for the other scholars," she says, because "Asian food is great—better than the rest of the world." Living in Hong Kong in the 1970s, she joined Chinese housewives in cooking lessons sponsored by the gas company. The experience was fun but she knew that elaborate dishes such as duck feet in licorice sauce were not recipes she'd make at home. Home cooking, she says, should be simple and tasty. Her version of mapo doufu is a good example. She acquired the recipe thirty years ago when doing research in Chengdu, the capital of Sichuan Province.

1 tablespoon vegetable oil

1 tablespoon grated fresh ginger

2 garlic cloves, minced

1 pound ground turkey

¼ cup mapo doufu sauce

¼ cup water

1 small head napa cabbage, coarsely chopped

One 14-ounce block tofu, cut into 1-inch cubes

1. Heat the oil in a wok or large skillet over high heat. Add the ginger and garlic and cook for 30 seconds to 1 minute, stirring constantly, until aromatic. Add the turkey and cook, stirring constantly, for 3 to 5 minutes, until no longer pink.

2. Stir in the sauce and water until combined. Add the cabbage, 1 handful at a time, and cook about 3 minutes, until tender but still crunchy. Gently stir in the tofu and cook about 3 minutes, until warmed through. Serve.

SERVES 4

SUNDAY DINNER
CAMP McKIBBIN

No 8 CRUIKSH
PHO
MARSHALL
HALL 1897

Cooking for Crowds

Cooking alone in the kitchen has the delicious feeling of a stolen moment, and there are evenings when a quiet, cozy table for one is an unsurpassed luxury. But the charm of solitary meals is mostly considered un-American. Cooking and eating in the United States have long been social activities. Beginning in our early history, building and tending the fire as well as gathering and preparing the food with the rough tools that were available required a group effort. Maybe the sense of hard-won accomplishment made food taste better, or perhaps the numbers of people gathered at the table created warmth, well-being, and excitement and turned meals into feasts. At church suppers and firehouse dinners, the regional community feeds and festivals, we regularly sense being part of something greater than ourselves, or at least something greater than a TV dinner.

In-ground cooking made a giant leap forward after the Europeans introduced iron pots to the new world. Emblematic in-ground meals—the New England clam bake, lobster bake, beanhole beans and hasty pudding; pit-barbecued pig in the Southeast; lamb in the Midwest, beef in the Far West; and luaus in Hawaii—seemed to spring from the soil of different regions.

One Big Table

Orchard Beach, Maine, Clambake c. 1861–80.

The Wampanoag Indians—"people of the first light"—who greeted the Massachusetts Pilgrims, had a long tradition of giving an *appanaug*, or clambake, to honor tribal events and seasonal changes. But the colonists reviled clams, eating them only as starvation rations and using them to fatten pigs. By the late nineteenth century, mass transportation had turned clambakes into a tourist opportunity.

Allen's Neck Clam Bake

The annual Allen's Neck Clam Bake, perhaps the most fabled and authentic community clambake, began in 1887 as a gathering of the Quakers living in the Westport, Massachusetts, area. The Friends now host over 500 paying guests lucky enough to get a ticket. They line their two-foot-deep Allen's Neck pit with a ton and a half of cannonball-sized rocks, and count on a truckload of seaweed and a cord of four-foot, split wood to cook over 20 bushels of clams, 200 pounds of sausage, 75 pounds of fish, 150 pounds of tripe, and 75 dozen ears of corn—a celebration of community, cooperation, and historically good eating.

Washington State Oyster toast.

HOW TO PREPARE THE IDEAL NEW ENGLAND CLAMBAKE, NO MATTER WHERE YOU LIVE

Arrange for fair weather.

Find yourself a legal beach, yard, or maybe a vacant lot where you won't set the trees on fire.

Shovel out a pit; line it with big, round rocks.

Build a rousing wood fire that will burn for a couple of hours while you tie up steamers, quahogs, and mussels into cheesecloth bundles.

When the rocks glow hot, let the fire burn out.

Rake the searing coals between the rocks.

Strew the pit with sopping wet seaweed and listen to it pop and crackle.

Quickly place the shellfish packets onto the seaweed.

Pile on glorious lobsters, don't skimp, get plenty.

Between blankets of dripping seaweed, layer sweet corn, new potatoes, and onions.

If you like, add salted, peppered chicken parts, and firm linguica or chorizo sausage.

A final layer of soggy seaweed and you're set.

Cover the great pile with a canvas tarp or lots of gunnysacks.

Wet them down nicely so they won't burn up.

Seal the cover edge with stones for in-ground steaming.

Assemble your good and hungry group.

Open a beer, pop a bottle of champagne, or pour some iced tea.

Prepare to chat or play ball with the kids for a couple of hours.

At long last, swoop off the canvas cover and remove the clambake.

Arrange on great platters, or dole a little of everything onto plates.

Serve with melted butter and lemon slices.

Maynard Stanley's Beanhole Beans

OWL'S HEAD, MAINE

Maynard Stanley is a third-generation "critter catcher," the founder of a special effects production company, and the king of beanhole "suppahs," the traditional staple of church suppers, firehouse dinners, and family reunions throughout the state of Maine.

On the family business:
"People go crazy when raccoons or skunks or bats or little black bears or even moose—I've handled a couple moose in my time—move into their homes. They need a critter catcher to make sure that they don't do anything unnecessary, such as blow the critter's head off. They don't understand that critters can get lost or confused and they just need a little help relocating. I resolve conflicts between people and animals in a safe and humane way. I feel blessed."

On Beanhole Beans: "The smoke and the Maine dirt are what make a bean worth eating. The Native Americans had that all figured out and they passed their knowledge along to the settlers. Now here in Maine we've honored that gift. It didn't hurt that beans grow well here. The logging camps did their bit keeping the tradition alive, too. There's nothing like in-ground cooking to feed a slew of hungry men with minimal effort and cost.

"The only change we made from the original is using a big iron pot instead of something made from clay. Why someplace else got to be called Beantown is beyond me, and I could tell you stories about what they do to their beans, but I don't like to speak ill of others. It's better to set an example, and that's what my wife, Norma, and I have been doing for near forty years.

"Beanhole beans are not a spur-of-the-moment kind of thing. You have to soak your beans the day before and you have to dig your pit. Then I line it with flat stones. Then I find my wood—I like oak and maple—and by evening I'm ready to build my fire. The bonfire of all bonfires. You have to watch it all night till it dies down. It can be real pretty with the sparks and smoke, but it can put you to sleep, so Norma and I don't sit around. I put together my beans and get my pork all set. Norma does the slaw and biscuits, we make the pies. When the fire has died down to about a foot of coals, we pull out any remaining logs and lower in our beans and everything else. I cover the whole show with a big heavy piece of metal; a few friends have to help me lift and lower it. Then I shovel the coals and heap them up on top of the metal and then I bury the whole thing.

"It's basically an in-ground oven. The beans boil like the dickens for the first four hours and then they'll simmer for six more hours. All that time they are drawing in the flavor from the ground and the wood and the smoke and getting tasty.

"When people taste our beanhole beans, there's no going back. The only place they are going is home to try to make their own beanholes." Mr. Stanley does not give recipes: "Because I don't use them. You cook something enough, it becomes part of you, your hands know what to do. That's the way it is with me and beans." Nevertheless, the following recipe is a good place to start.

Beanhole Beans for 100 People

10 pounds Maine yellow eye beans (Jacob's Cattle beans and soldier beans can also be used)

5 pounds salt pork

5 medium-size yellow onions, chopped

1 cup molasses

1 cup maple syrup

4 tablespoons mustard powder

2 tablespoons ground cinnamon

1 tablespoon ground clove

½ cup Maine sea salt

2 tablespoons freshly ground black pepper

1. Twenty-four hours before serving, place the beans in a large pot and cover with cold water for 8 hours. Drain. Cover with enough water to reach two inches above the beans, place on low heat, cover, and bring to a boil. Boil five minutes, reduce heat to low, and simmer for 40 minutes. Remove from heat. Drain, reserve half the water, cool the beans under cold running water, and set the beans and the reserved cooking water aside.

2. Eighteen hours before serving, dig a pit that is 3 x 4 feet and about 2½ feet deep. Line the pit with flat rocks. Build a bonfire in the pit, light it, and allow it to burn until one foot of hot ash and coal has

been formed on the bottom of the pit. Remove any remaining pieces of logs.

3. Ten hours before serving, place the beans in the bottom of a big iron pot with a tight-fitting lid. Lay the fat back on top of the beans, add the onions, molasses, maple syrup, mustard, cinnamon, clove, sea salt, and black pepper. Add the reserved cooking water. Cover the beans with cold water that reaches 2 inches above the top of the beans. Cover the pot, lower into the pit. Use a shovel to completely cover the pot with hot coals. Bury with dirt and allow to cook, undisturbed, for 10 hours.

4. Remove the dirt. A few strong people wearing fire gloves should use metal hooks to lift the pot from the pit. Carefully remove the lid, add the sea salt, and use a wooden canoe paddle to stir the beans in order to distribute the salt. Recover, allow to sit for fifteen minutes, and then serve.

—

MAKES 100–120 CUPS

Before barbecue acquired little wheels and began strutting its stuff around the patio, the barbecue pit was a hole in the ground, and barbecue involved an entire animal. Going to a barbecue was a daylong event for dozens, if not hundreds, of people.

ROAST BULL

EAT DRINK AND BE MERRY

When a Navajo girl reaches puberty, her family may conduct a kinaaldá for her; this is a traditional five-day, four-night ceremony to prepare her for womanhood. The girls run three times a day, and in between, they are groomed, bejeweled, and enrobed in special outfits whose colors reflect the four sacred directions. Her hair is bound, then washed in yucca root. She is

Kinaaldá Ceremony

molded in the image of Changing Woman, one of the most important deities in Navajo culture. She participates in an all-night sing (or blessing ritual) conducted by a medicine man—and through it all prepares a 100-pound corn cake that will be baked directly in the earth and distributed to all guests at the end of the ceremony.

On the first day, the men in the family dig the hole in which the cake will be baked. Too shallow, and the batter will overflow it; too deep, and the cake won't cook through; too crooked, and the cake won't bake evenly. Once the hole is perfectly shaped—about the width of a standard garden shovel and about 8 inches deep—the men cut dry piñon and juniper and haul it to the pit. There has to be enough to keep the fire burning for three days and nights.

Over the next three days, they spread 100 pounds of dry white corn on a tarp and check each kernel by hand. The corn is then roasted and ground, some by hand with a traditional grinding stone. After the women sift the cornmeal three times, through progressively finer screens, the strenuous work of mixing 100 pounds of meal with boiling water begins. Mixing the batter is both celebration and endurance test. When an elder declares the batter ready, the action moves back outdoors.

The family removes wood and ashes from the pit and lays wet paper bags on the bottom, topped with a specially constructed corn husk cross. They pour in the batter, bless it, top with another corn husk cross and more wet paper bags, then rebury it with sand, hot ashes, and more wood. They relight the fire and watch all night as the cake steams in the hot earth. On the fifth morning, after the kinaaldá's last predawn run, the family uncovers the cake as ceremoniously as they put it in the ground. The young woman cuts small pieces and offers them to the elder supervising the baking and the medicine man. If they agree it's perfect—moist, sweet, the adobe color of the earth in which it was baked—legend says the young woman will have a good life—and more important, always have enough food to share with her family and the tribe.

Green Chili Cholent

Filipe Ortega, potter, medicine man and impassioned connoisseur of slow-cooked pinto beans, was born fifty-eight years ago in La Madera, a small bump in the isolated, dusty high plains about an hour north west of Santa Fe. His father's people are Apache. They have lived in the area for longer than written history, are observant Catholics, and greet each day by tossing cornmeal in the four directions. His mother's family arrived in New Mexico from Spain in the late 1700s and brought with them a peculiar habit of lighting a candle at dusk on Friday night, giving their children four-sided tops to play with at Christmastime, and baking unleavened bread at Easter. They too are observant Catholics.

Mr. Ortega was far too consumed with his own passions to notice the multiple spiritual skeins in the family. He has always been deeply in love with mud--"anything mud was for me. My grandmother taught me to build hornos, the outdoor mud ovens, and to make bricks and build adobe walls and mud floors." In addition, he was always in love with beans. He seemed to possess an innate understanding of the Platonic ideal of pinto beans and was bitterly disappointed in beans that fell short.

"My mother made them in a metal pressure cooker with so much salt. I knew that this was not the way of beans. My grandmother had two clay pots, like the Spanish cozuela, or the Arabic tian, and somehow I knew the beans needed to be cooked in them. But the pots had been in the family for several hundred years and she would not allow me to cook in them. If I wanted to make perfect beans, I had to make my own pots. That is what I did and that is how I understood the Apache saying for delicious. They say 'da-likao-go-lni,' meaning it comes out sweet. Everything cooked in micaceous clay pots comes out sweet. Our clay is alkaline and we don't use glazes, so it reacts and neutralizes the acid. "I do not need to use salt. Everybody else in my family has high blood pressure, but not me."

Mr. Ortega's early success with pots and beans may have stoked his particular brand of can-do-ism. Scornful of a weak sermon one Sunday when he was seventeen, he told the priest that he himself could preach better. "The priest told me I'd have to go to seminary first. That is what I did. I went to seminary in Detroit. Soon after I got there, I heard two students talking the way that my mother and grandmother talked to each other. That's when I knew that my grandmother and mother were Crypto Jews, the Spanish Jews who publically converted during the Inquisition and secretly continued their traditions. That's when it all made sense, the shredded apple relish and cracker pudding they made at Easter made sense, the meat and vegetables that they began cooking on Friday morning to eat throughout the weekend. 'Oy vey, Maria,' I thought, 'green chili cholent!'"

"I learned Hebrew, Latin, and Greek. I got a master's in Biblical studies and a master's in Divinity. But I knew that I wasn't priest material. I am Catholic, oh yes. Just not Roman Catholic. I went home. My family wasn't surprised. Apparently, my father's side had known when I was born that I am a two-spirit, both male and female. Gay, bi people who don't fit into the heterosexual definition are often two-spirits. Two-spirits are supposed to heal. My grandmother told me that I had no choice, if I didn't heal, I'd die. I made pots. I've been accused of using a wheel, my pots are so uniform. But I coil and scrape, that is the traditional way. My pots are uniform because I've been making them for forty years. I've been tooting the horn for micaceous clay pots since 1979. I never put out a shingle that said 'shaman for hire,' but people find me. I work with them, I make my pots, I teach at a junior college. I've made my family's adobe house into a bed and breakfast, though there is no place around here to eat, so really it is a bed and breakfast, lunch and dinner. I cook beans every day. I suppose I don't need to tell you what I cook for Friday dinner."

2 tablespoons vegetable oil, chicken fat,
or beef fat

1 (5-pound) flat-cut (or "first cut") beef brisket,
trimmed

Kosher salt and freshly ground black pepper

4 medium onions, coarsely chopped

6 garlic cloves, peeled

2 tablespoons chili powder

2 teaspoons dried oregano, preferably Mexican

2 teaspoons ground coriander

2 (14.5-ounce) cans fire-roasted diced tomatoes
with green chilies, with juice

1 (12-ounce) can dark Mexican beer, such as
Dos Equis or Negro Modelo

1 (7-ounce) can diced green chilies, with juice

6 large ancho chiles

1 tablespoon honey, preferably "chili honey,"
plus more to taste

½ cup chopped fresh cilantro stems

1 (3-pound) butternut squash, peeled, seeded,
and cut into 2-inch chunks

1 cup dried hominy, soaked for 1 hour and
drained

1 cup dried cranberry beans, soaked for 1 hour
and drained

2 carrots, peeled cut into 2-inch chunks

1 pound beef marrow bones, cut in 1- to 3-inch
lengths

Water, as needed

Fresh lime juice, to taste

Fresh cilantro leaves, for garnish

Warm corn tortilla, optional

1. The day before serving, place an oven rack in the center position and preheat the oven to 225°F.

2. Pat the brisket dry and season with salt and pepper. In a large Dutch oven, heat 2 tablespoons of the oil over high heat. Add the brisket and cook for 12 to 14 minutes, until well browned on both sides. Transfer the brisket to a platter.

3. Add the onions, garlic, and ½ teaspoon salt to the fat in the pot and cook over medium heat for 10 to 15 minutes, until the onions are beginning to brown. Stir in the chili powder, oregano, and coriander and cook for about 1 minute, until aromatic. Add the tomatoes and their juice, beer, green chiles, ancho chiles, and honey and bring to a simmer.

4. Remove the pot from the heat and place the cilantro stems in the center of the pot. Place the brisket on top of the cilantro stems, then scatter the squash, hominy, cranberry beans, and carrots around it. Lay the beef bones on top of the meat and add enough cold water to cover the roast by four inches.

5. Cover the pot and place in the oven for 8 hours, until the brisket is tender, adding water as needed to keep the meat covered by at least 1 inch of liquid.

6. Remove the pot from the oven, discard the beef bones, and season with salt, pepper, honey, and lime juice to taste. Cool the brisket to room temperature, then cover the pot and refrigerate until ready to serve.

7. When ready to serve, place an oven rack in the center position and preheat the oven to 350°F.

8. Cut the brisket across the grain into ¼-inch-thick slices. Transfer the sliced brisket to a large baking dish and pour the sauce over the top. Cover with foil and put in the oven for about 20 minutes, until heated through.

9. Garnish with the cilantro leaves and serve with the tortillas on the side (if using).

————

SERVES 8

Ruth Kendrick's Winning Dutch Oven Salmon in Black and White

OGDEN, UTAH

No self-respecting pioneer headed West without an iron pot, skillet, and Dutch oven. These utensils were of central importance to the 70,000 Mormons who moved west to escape persecution between 1847 and 1869. After they circled their wagons at night, the pots were set over the fires to feed hundreds of travelers. Ruth Kendrick, whose paternal great-grandfather, Robert Sweeten, was the last surviving member of the pioneers of 1847 when he died in the 1930s, stays close to this history by collecting iron pots and cooking in them. Large ones can be filled and buried in a fire pit; these will feed an army. Smaller versions can be buried in the coals of a backyard grill and will feed a family. In either event, the work is done far ahead of the meal. Kendrick's search for family tradition lead her to Dutch ovens, but she found that cooking historic recipes in the ovens took the quest for tradition a little bit too far. One year she won the World Championship Dutch Oven Cook-off, and she notes that wagon train food will not earn accolades from friends and family or win contests. "That is the irony of cooking in iron," said Mrs. Kendrick. "You can't use the old-time recipes if you want to win. Those people had no sugar, no salt, no spices. If you want to win, you have to go gourmet." The fish fillets are dramatic looking and deliciously succulent, with a hint of smoke. The recipe can be expanded to feed a crowd.

FOR THE DIP

½ cup white sesame seeds

1 teaspoon vegetable oil

⅓ cup mayonnaise

1 teaspoon onion salt

2 teaspoons salt

3 tablespoons white vinegar

⅓ cup lemon juice

2 teaspoons crushed red pepper

¼ teaspoon liquid smoke

3 tablespoons milk

FOR THE COATING

2½ cups white sesame seeds

2½ cups black sesame seeds

4 to 6 fresh salmon fillets, skin removed, trimmed into serving pieces

1 tablespoon salt

2 tablespoons vegetable oil for cooking

2 to 4 tablespoons lemon juice to taste

1. To make the dip, mix seeds and oil together in a blender until well combined. Add mayonnaise, onion salt, salt, white vinegar, lemon juice, crushed red pepper, liquid smoke, and milk and blend until smooth. Refrigerate overnight to thicken and blend flavors.

2. To make the sesame seed coating, place a line of white sesame seeds about 2 inches wide and 10 inches long on waxed paper. Next to the white seeds, place a line of black sesame seeds about 2 inches wide and 10 inches long.

3. Lightly salt each salmon fillet. Dip fillet into chilled dip mixture and set aside. One by one, press fillets onto the sesame seeds. Turn over carefully, covering entire fillet with seeds. Be careful not to mix the colors as you press the seeds onto the salmon. Set coated fillets aside.

4. Heat a 14-inch Dutch oven over 15 briquets. Pour in enough oil to lightly coat bottom, approximately 2 tablespoons. Heat oil. Carefully place fillets in Dutch oven. Place lid on oven and ring lid with 20 briquettes. While cooking, occasionally sprinkle fillets with lemon juice. Cook approximately 20 minutes, depending on thickness of fillet. Remove carefully to serving dish.

SERVES 4 TO 6

Iron pots set above the fire gave birth to regional specialties that, like in-ground meals, showcase local ingredients, are an ode to the cultural history of a place. Chowder still means New England, Kentucky is burgoo, and the low country is Frogmore stew. If the church supper is jambalaya or a crawfish or shrimp boil, you know you are in Louisiana. Cioppino still smacks of San Francisco, and chili—well, you need to taste it before you can use that dish as a GPS.

Wayne Calk's Gold Star Chuckwagon Chili

EL PASO, TEXAS

Wayne Calk can fix a mean batch of chili as easily as he can fix up an old chuckwagon. A retired industrial arts teacher and school administrator in El Paso, Texas, he got interested in chuckwagon cooking about fifteen years ago. Since then, he has restored two old wagons, and he and cooking partner Skip Clark use their John Deere/Moline Wagon Works wagon for cooking competitions and to do catering for wedding receptions, graduation parties, and church socials. "I just want people to come out and enjoy

what we do with the chuckwagons," he says. "It's about keeping the cowboy heritage alive." In 2005, when the Texas state legislature voted to make the chuckwagon the Texas state vehicle, the Calk-Clark wagon was parked on the capitol grounds in Austin, along with Don and Shirley Creacy's Wild Cow Ranch wagon. "We were cooking two-inch rib-eye steaks in the Senate chambers," Calk recalled. "I believe that's the only time that's ever happened."

Calk and his partner have cooked for

groups from 25 to 1,200 people, and he enjoys the competitions and the prizes they've won. But his favorite experience is taking his chuckwagon each fall to a ranch in South Texas to cook for hunting parties.

Calk created his spicy Gold Star Chili recipe for a school fund-raiser a number of years ago. In addition to beef, it contains buffalo meat because one of his neighbors donated it to the cause. Designed for a Dutch oven and an open fire, this chili is easily prepared on a kitchen stove—as long as you've got a very large pot.

5 tablespoons bacon grease

One 2 ½-pound sirloin steak, trimmed and cut into 1-inch cubes

One 8-ounce buffalo steak, trimmed and cut into 1-inch cubes

2½ pounds lean ground beef

1 large onion, coarsely chopped

3 garlic cloves, minced

2 jalapeño chiles, stemmed, seeded, and finely chopped

4 Anaheim chiles, stemmed, seeded, and coarsely chopped

¼ cup chopped fresh cilantro

¼ cup gold tequila (preferably José Cuervo)

One 12-ounce bottle beer (preferably Lone Star)

Two 14.5-ounce cans stewed tomatoes, coarsely chopped

1½ cups tomato sauce

½ cup chili powder

½ cup tomato paste

2 tablespoons honey

1 tablespoon red pepper flakes

1 tablespoon ground cumin

1 tablespoon cider vinegar

1 teaspoon ground allspice

1 tablespoon hot sauce

Kosher salt

1. Heat the bacon fat in a large Dutch oven over medium-high heat. Brown the meats in batches, transferring each to a large bowl when done.

2. Return all the meats and their juices to the pot and stir in the remaining ingredients. Bring to a simmer and cook, uncovered, stirring frequently, about 2 hours, until the meat is tender.

3. Season with salt to taste and serve.

———

SERVES 10 TO 12

Leah Chase's Famous Gumbo des Herbes

MADISONVILLE, LOUISIANA

Born to Creole parents in Madisonville, Louisiana, Leah Chase moved to New Orleans when she was fourteen years old to live with relatives and attend St. Mary's Academy. New Orleans was still a segregated town when she graduated and when she went to work in restaurants, first as a waitress and then as a cook—opportunities afforded few African Americans at that time— she began learning about fine dining. "There were a few small black places, but they didn't even have menus," she said. Dooky Chase Restaurant was one such place, and a few years after marrying its scion, Edgar "Dooky" Chase II, Leah Chase began working there, spreading white tablecloths over the tables, replacing the ketchup bottles with fresh-cut flowers, and bolstering the fried chicken with her family's fine Creole recipes—shrimp Clemenceau, chicken breast stuffed with oyster dressing, and gumbo des herbes.

"I was teaching my people to enjoy the finer things like the white people did on the other side of town," she said. Soon after politicians, writers, and musicians like Nat King Cole and Duke Ellington began to show up for dinner, the other side of town arrived. Later, Dooky Chase became the "neutral ground" of the civil rights movement and Mrs. Chase was alternately referred to as the Queen of Creole Cooking and a Louisiana culinary legend. If she had to choose a single title, it would most likely be the former. "Being a legend just means you're old," she said.

It's not surprising that Ms. Chase, whose "daddy was more Catholic than the Pope," has become best known for the annual pilgrimage to Dooky Chase for Holy Thursday gumbo des herbes. The event is as sacrosanct as receiving ashes the first day of Lent; and everyone leaves the cathedral of Creole cuisine feeling blessed to have been among that year's chosen. Loaded with ham, sausage and brisket, this green gumbo was always simmered with an odd number of greens, since among the Creoles, odd numbers are thought to be lucky. Mrs. Chase scoffs at this theory. "We Creoles aren't superstitious," she said, "we're just careful."

1 bunch mustard greens

1 bunch collard greens

1 bunch turnip greens

1 bunch watercress

1 bunch beet tops

1 bunch carrot tops

1 bunch spinach

1 head lettuce

1 head cabbage

2 medium onions, chopped

4 cloves garlic, chopped and mashed

Water

1 pound smoked sausage

1 pound smoked ham

1 pound brisket stew meat

1 pound boneless brisket

1 pound hot chaurice sausage

5 tablespoons flour

1 teaspoon thyme leaves

1 tablespoon salt

1 teaspoon cayenne pepper

1 tablespoon filé powder

1. Clean all vegetables, removing bad leaves and rinsing away all the grit.

2. In a large pot place all greens, onions, and garlic. Cover with water and boil for 30 minutes.

3. While the greens are boiling, cut all the meats and sausages into bite-size pieces and set aside.

4. Strain the vegetables after boiling, reserving the liquid.

5. In a 12-quart stockpot place smoked sausage, ham, and brisket meats, adding 2 cups of the reserved liquid. Steam for 15 minutes.

6. While steaming the meats, place the chaurice in a skillet and steam until the fat is rendered. Set the chaurice aside, reserving the grease.

7. Puree all vegetables in a food processor or in a meat grinder.

8. Heat the skillet of chaurice grease; then add the flour, stirring constantly, for about 5 minutes, or until a light-colored roux is achieved. (The roux does not have to be brown.) Pour the roux over the steamed meats, stirring well. Add the vegetables and two quarts of the reserved liquid.

9. Simmer for 20 minutes. Add the chaurice, thyme, salt, and cayenne pepper. Stir well.

10. Simmer for 40 minutes. Add filé powder, stir well, and remove from heat. Serve over steamed rice.

—

SERVES 8

Helen Griffin Williams' Macaroni and Cheese

MILLWOOD, NEW YORK

Helen Griffin Williams, mother of three including a former Miss America and grandmother of four, is a retired music teacher as well as a fine and adventurous cook. Her culinary innovations, however, do not extend to macaroni and cheese:

"It does not matter where you go or how much you achieve, if you are African American, macaroni and cheese is part of your life. You never have a gathering without macaroni and cheese. The tradition may have started because it's cheap—you can feed hundreds at a church social or a family reunion out of a few trays of macaroni and cheese—but I think people appreciate it because it's good and because it's something that a working mother can make ahead of time. My mother figured that out early on. She was born in Buffalo in 1921, got her degree to teach Head Start, taught in that program her entire working life, and raised four children. My father was a porter on the railroad. We knew we would get educated, we knew we would make them proud, we knew that there would always be macaroni and cheese at family gatherings.

"Macaroni was a side dish, not a main meal. White people ate macaroni as an entrée, but we ate it with meat or what have you. You always made a lot of it, always froze some. At Thanksgiving my mother made enough so that we could take trays home and freeze them. I have some macaroni in the freezer now, in case one of my children or grandchildren stops by. I was a music teacher, and after I retired, I spent more time cooking. I've seen three macaroni and cheese cookoffs on the Food Network. One lady baked her macaroni and cheese like individual soufflés in muffin tins, and another one added artichokes. I don't know anyone who would do a thing like that. Everybody I know likes their macaroni and cheese pure, just plain and unadulterated.

"That doesn't mean you don't make changes to get your recipe just how you like it. As soon as I had a home of my own, I started using both mild and sharp cheddar in my macaroni and eggs instead of flour to thicken the sauce. My mother used flour to thicken her sauce and she added the cheese right in. I like to cut my cheese in cubes and layer them. I also like to use bread crumbs to give a little crust on the top. My daughter Vanessa uses lots of different fancy cheeses and has gone back to the cream sauce. The pendulum swings, but never past good sense. You want people to know what they are looking at when they see a pan of your macaroni and cheese on the buffet."

4 tablespoons butter

2 eggs

1 teaspoon salt

1 teaspoon mustard powder

1 teaspoon white pepper

2½ cups milk

8 ounces elbow macaroni

½ pound of mild cheddar cheese, cut into half-inch cubes

½ pound of sharp cheddar cheese, cut into half-inch cubes

¼ cup bread crumbs

¼ teaspoon paprika

1. Preheat the oven to 375°F, use a small dab of the butter to grease an 8-inch square baking dish, and place a pot of lightly salted water to boil. In a small bowl, whisk together the eggs, salt, mustard, white pepper, and milk and set aside. When the water is boiling, add the macaroni, stir to keep from sticking, and cook until barely tender. Drain into a colander and cool under running water.

2. Combine the cubes of mild and sharp cheddar. Place a layer of the macaroni on the bottom of the dish, scatter a layer of cheese cubes over it. Continue making layers until all the macaroni and cheese have been used. Pour the egg and milk mixture over the layers and jiggle pan to distribute evenly. Combine the bread crumbs and the paprika and sprinkle evenly over the top, then dot with thin slices of the remaining butter. Bake until brown and bubbly, about 20 minutes.

SERVES 4 TO 6

INVENTING TRADITION: GREEN BEAN CASSEROLE

THE CAMPBELL'S SOUP COMPANY ESTIMATES THAT 30 million green bean casseroles are made in the United States each year. Twenty million of these are prepared on Thanksgiving. The dish, which contains green beans, Campbell's condensed cream of mushroom soup, and French's French Fried Onions, has no connection to colonial history; the recipe was created in 1955 at the Campbell's test kitchen. It was then under the management of home economist, Dorcas Reilly, who remains mystified by the recipe's iconic stature.

"I have no memory of that recipe," she said shortly after her eightieth birthday in 2006. "It was one of three to five hundred recipes we did that year. We'd take a few ingredients, go into the kitchen, and come up with recipes that would fit on a label. We taste tested them. It usually took four or five trials before you got one that rated 5 out of 5 on our taste scale. I don't remember anything special about the green bean casserole. It didn't start out to be a winner. That happened later, and I still don't know why. It's versatile, it's easy, it's attractive, and I guess after fifty years, people feel they can count on it."

Indeed, attempts to upgrade Green Bean Casserole with fresh cream sauce, wild mushrooms, tiny haricots vertes, by making fried onions from scratch, tend to be greeted with outrage. The recipe worked beautifully in the glass and lightweight metal cookware that was introduced in the 1950s, and it was perfectly pitched for the casual buffet-and-brunch entertaining style that took root in midcentury.

In 2002, Mrs. Reilly traveled to Ohio to present the original copy of the Green Bean Casserole recipe to the National Inventors Hall of Fame. The well-worn recipe card was placed between Enrico Fermi's invention of the first controlled nuclear reactor and Thomas Alva Edison's two greatest hits: the lightbulb and the phonograph.

CHAPTER 7

Everything but the Squeal: Beef, Buffalo, Game, Lamb, and Pork

BUILDING BETTER BEEF

McALLEN, TEXAS

Heading south from San Antonio on Highway 281, the temperature rises steadily, the leafy horizon flattens to a hard line, the countryside fades from green to brush brown. Soon only patches of dried grass, cactus, Texas persimmon, and scruffy mesquite punctuate the vast sweep of hard-baked red dirt. It is 105 degrees dry. In the Rio Grande Valley, you do what the land demands: You eat meat.

The Wild Horse Desert, the tract of land that stretches from the Nueces River to the Rio Grande, was the birthplace of the American cowboy. With the help of Hollywood, this iconic image—a curious composite of Mexican *vaquero*, Civil War veteran, freed slave, and assorted desperados—remains deeply lodged in the American imagination. Beef plays a large role in the cowboy myth. Some visitors start to swagger and develop a lonesome prairie–size bloodthirst at the scent of sizzling meat and smoke. Locals, many of whom are descendants of the original cowboys, see meat-eating as a crucial link in the dance between a harsh land and survival.

"We are not salad people," says Melissa McAllen Guerra, firmly. "Pound for pound, it takes a heck of a lot more water to grow tomatoes than it does to grow cattle around here. Vegetable gardens are a luxury."

The daughter of a seventh-generation cattle rancher, Melissa now lives on a corner of her husband's family ranch. She hosts a television series, *The Texas Provincial Kitchen*, owns her own culinary store, and is the author of two cookbooks. A freckle-faced redhead, she looks far more Mount Holyoke (where she studied music) than Wild West. She drives a soccer mom's SUV, is the wife of a Mexican-born artist who grew up on the ranch next door, and is the working mother of three adolescent sons. But the closer she gets to her childhood home—the McAllen Ranch, a few miles east, which was settled by her ancestors in 1791 and is the oldest continuously operating cattle farm in the United States—the more she becomes a daughter, a sister, a McAllen.

"Nobody wants to be the generation that loses the ranch," she says. "We'll do about anything to avoid that. Turn Grandma's house into a B&B, work day jobs, learn to manage the mineral rights, put up forty miles of game-proof fence and offer hunting parties, run birding trips, write cookbooks, give cooking classes.

"Cattle's been a losing proposition for as long as I can remember. Heck, ranches like ours would have been gone if people hadn't found oil on their land in the 1940s. But oil's not a renewable resource and it's not a way of life. Someday it'll dry up. My father believed in Beefmaster. Now my brother's breeding Japanese Akaushi into the line. They can't help it. They were raised to believe that no matter what happens, the solution is breeding better beef."

"You could ranch a thousand acres to death and still be broke," says Melissa's father, Jim McAllen, as he sits in his daughter's big kitchen with its hand-painted Mexican tiles and polished mesquite cabinetry. Like a coach assessing the odds, Mr. McAllen Sr. is just stating the facts, and after six decades, he still expects to beat them. Barrel-chested, with fair hair and skin, he favors his great-grandfather, John McAllen, who came from Glasgow in 1848, more than he does his great-grandmother, Salome Balli, who was the daughter of a Mexican colonel and the owner of a 95,000-acre Spanish land grant. Mr. McAllen

Sr. is a well-polished and well-pressed cowboy and one of the best beef breeders and traders of his generation.

The quest for breeding perfect beef is a constantly shifting calculus between the land and climate, the realities of business and, increasingly, marketing and food fashion. Given the time it takes to breed cattle for a specific characteristic, a successful breeder is a cross between soothsayer and scientist. Mr. McAllen Sr. is thought to have a sixth sense for beef trends. By the time the public was demanding highly marbled meat, bigger rib-eyes, heftier ribs, or lean meat, he had long since honed his herd for those characteristics.

The story of beef in America was written first by the land, then by transportation, then by centralization, and now, he says with a hint of sneer, "by marketing." The iconic Texas longhorn—a descendant of European draft and dairy cattle and the wild Spanish fighting bull, introduced to the desert that was then known as

Norteño or "north" of Mexico—had been bred to thrive in heat and drought.

Fences were few, and feral cattle were considered public property. Between 1866 to 1890, nearly 10 million longhorns were herded up to New

Mexico, Colorado, and the Midwest. The longhorn's popularity did not come from the taste of its beef, but rather from the toughness of the breed. Its meat is stringy—"You have to salt it, hang it, and dry it and make macacado, dry shredded beef," says Mrs. Guerra—but there was a high demand for longhorn beef, hides, and tallow. If they managed to avoid the Comanches, thievery, shoot-outs, rattlesnakes, wolves, hunger, sunstroke, dehydration, and short change, cowboys stood to make a small fortune.

"Had the railroad never come, we'd still be eating longhorn," says Jim Sr. "It's the only breed that could tolerate the long cattle drives." But the train arrived in 1904 and the cowboys switched from herding and trailing cattle to buying and breeding. Since it was no longer necessary to hone the breed for hiking ability, ranchers such as Mr. McAllen's grandfather began crossing shorthorns and longhorns to create meatier cattle.

Even as feedlots and processing plants began springing up in the Midwest at major railroad junctions, and profits and sovereignty over beef breeding and feeding shifted from ranchers to industrialists, cattlemen in the Wild Horse Desert remained convinced that if they could breed better beef, they could stem the tide of industry and restore the proper order of civilized carnivorousness: land, cattle, dinner.

"Breeding for a particular characteristic takes twelve generations," Jim Sr. said.

"We're a little slow," drawled his daughter, sliding a plate of puffy tacos onto the kitchen table.

When Jim Sr. was five years old, his father made the daring move of buying a new breed of cattle called Beefmaster. They were bred from the unlikely cross of Indian Brahman with Hereford and milking shorthorn. For young Jim McAllen, it was love at first sight—"I don't know what it is about those motley-faced fellas, but I still can't stop looking at them" he says—and for at least the past half-century, he has been honing the breed to the local landscape, the market, and food fashions. It's always a gamble. "You could invest all that time, effort, and money, breed a magnificent animal and it won't be what the industrial cattle buyer wants that year."

You can also be blindsided, as the dean of Beefmaster was by the rage for Certified Angus.

"That's not a cattle breed, it's a cattle brand and it's got no business in Texas. Would you walk around out there in a black coat? I bought twelve Certified Angus and a year later only six were alive. They can't take this heat!" he says. Pausing, he adds, "You got to hand it to them. These guys invented a brand that is basically nothing but a black cow with a trace of Aberdeen-Angus genetic matter and they marketed it to the point that it's all Angus, all the time, everywhere you look."

If he has his way, choice Certified Angus beef will fill up the grocery stores and leave a hole at the high end of the beef market that he and his son, James McAllen Jr., can fill. "James is working with the Akaushi breed from Japan, real rare, real risky, and real interesting. One of my bulls made cover boy of *Beefmaster Cowman* magazine."

Melissa McAllen Guerra shares her father's squared-jaw determination and love of the Rio Grande Valley. A superb publicity wrangler, she is rapidly becoming the Martha Stewart of the Wild Horse Desert. She opened a culinary store in San Antonio to market the charm and style of the Rio Grande's Norteño culture—a meld of Mexican and Texan traditions—to the masses. She also wanted a place to sell her brother's beef.

"The Akaushi consistently grade prime or above prime," she shouts from the backseat as her brother James Jr. chauffeurs us in his big Ford pickup. We bounce across the desert on our way

to see cattle. We are searching for the McAllens' single longhorn and Mr. McAllen Sr.'s motley-faced Beefmasters. His best bulls have sold for upwards of $35,000, ten times the typical price. Barbecue, a small calf who was the sole survivor of a recent grassfire that claimed fifty thousand acres, earned himself a lifelong dispensation as well as a close and affectionate relationship with the McAllen patriarch. We are also looking for James McAllen Jr.'s redheaded Akaushi.

The youngest of Jim McAllen's five children and the only son, James Jr. is tall and dark, but he wouldn't stand a chance as a Hollywood cowboy. His profile is too finely chiseled, his voice too gentle, his manner too considered. A talented painter, he had a double major—fine arts and business—at Texas Christian University. He was an entrepreneur for ten years, but when his first child was born in 2008, he suddenly felt an irresistible pull back to the ranch and to the dream that began more than three hundred years ago.

Mr. McAllen Jr. is a modern rancher. His cattle have electronic monitoring tags that contain their description and pedigree. Using a mobile ultrasound machine and infrared scanner, he collects and stores dozens of facts, including the animal's average daily weight gain and measurements of the carcass, rib-eye, and intramuscular fat.

Like Japanese Kobe, which sells for $150 to

$500 a pound and melts in the mouth like foie gras, Akaushi are densely packed with fine layers of fat. Unlike Kobe, Akaushi have a high percentage of monounsaturated fat, the highest of any beef in the United States today.

"The hope is to keep the incredible carcass, heat resistance, and consistency characteristics of our Beefmaster and breed an animal that consistently produces prime grade meat with healthy fat," says Mr. McAllen Jr., steering around rattail cacti. It is late afternoon and he is driving through a 15,000-acre pasture to a watering hole. A covey of startled vermilion flycatchers rise from a grove of gnarled mesquite as he pulls close to the trees and stops the truck. Next to him on the seat is an orderly stack of graph paper. "At this point we have data on about fifteen thousand animals."

Across the horizon, a line of his first Akaushi-Beefmaster cattle mosey away from the sunset and toward the water. They look like a living landscape painting—straight backs, staunch legs, firm muscles, coats the color of the desert sand.

"Aren't they gorgeous? Dad and I are blown away by these calves, they're way beyond anything we dreamed of. But we are way, way out there. This breeding is either lunatic fringe or cutting edge."

Copyrighted 1895 by THE CALVERT LITHO CO. DETROIT, MICH.

Kiko Guerra's Norteño Fajita

When Kiko Guerra's family came from Spain to ranch the land they'd been granted by the crown, their property between the Nueces River and the Rio Grande was considered northern Mexico. After the border war of 1846, the land became part of south Texas. Mr. Guerra cannot imagine living anywhere else, and he cannot imagine cooking meat over anything but mesquite. The dense, oily wood burns very hot and issues a mellow, spicy smoke that is to Norteño cooking what olive oil is to Italian cuisine.

Mr. Guerra, an artist, is a fire master. He uses two fire pits, which allows him to control the size and intensity of his cooking fire. In one he builds a mesquite fire and when the flames die to glowing embers, he transfers them to the other pit for cooking.

Fajita is his favorite meal for a crowd. Long before it was a trendy restaurant concept, fajita was simply the cuts of belly meat that cover a cow's rib; they are also called skirt or hanger steaks, and are usually about eighteen inches long and an inch thick. "It was cheap and good, so fajita cooked over an open fire was cowboy food long before it was party food. Some people like the inside cut, which tends to be tougher and needs a lime or beer marinade. The outside skirt is tender and needs only to be seasoned. You should turn the meat six to eight times as you cook it, remove it from the grill, rest it a little, slice it thin and on a diagonal and serve it with nothing more than pico de gallo and corn tortilla." He adds, "Though we sometimes put out a pot of beans, sliced tomatoes, shredded lettuce, guacamole, even a couple extra salsas. It's not traditional, but I love to eat steak or fajita with the Texas peach chutney I make, too."

One 2-pound skirt or hanger steak

Sea salt and freshly ground black pepper

1 white onion, minced

2 medium-size ripe tomatoes, or 8 tomatillos, or a combination of the two, chopped

½ avocado, peeled, pitted, and cut into bite-size cubes

2 to 4 serrano chiles, stems removed, minced

2 tablespoons minced cilantro

12 fresh corn tortillas, warmed

Guacamole, salsa, hot sauce, lemon wedges, or other desired garnishes

1. Build a mesquite fire. While you are waiting for the flames to die down (20 to 30 minutes) remove the meat from the refrigerator, and season well on all sides with salt and pepper.

2. When you have burning embers, grill the steak for approximately 10 minutes per side, turning often. When the internal temperature reaches 135°F on an instant-read thermometer, remove from heat, loosely cover on a platter and allow to rest for 20 minutes.

3. While the meat is resting, make the pico de gallo by combining the onion, tomatoes and/or tomatillos, avocado, chiles, and cilantro in a bowl. Start with 2 chiles and add more if you want a hotter sauce.

4. Slice the steak, set it out surrounded by the pico de gallo, tortillas, and garnishes, and allow guests to make their own tacos.

———

SERVES 4

FAJITA, INC.

WHEN JUAN ANTONIO "SONNY" FALCON WORKED AT THE OLD AUSTIN MEAT PACKING
Company, in Austin, Texas, he and his fellow employees were always looking for ways to use the meat that otherwise got ground up. One day he was hit with an idea, a variation on *taco al carbon* that he called "frajita." He invented and named the dish on his own, but he has since heard from reputable scholars that a similar dish was prepared as early as 1930 in the Rio Grande Valley. "The first time I looked at that cut of meat," he says, "I saw a thick belt. That is how I came up with the name. *Frajita* means 'little girdle.'"

In 1973 he suggested to his mother-in-law, who ran Guajardo's Cash Grocery, the family's business, that he offer his creation. He also began grilling at rodeos and county fairs across the state, attracting lines so deep that other concessionaires also began grilling skirt steak and wrapping slices in soft flour tortillas. "By the time I thought to trademark the name, they wouldn't give me 'frajita,'" he says, "but I did trademark 'Fajita King.'"

In 1982, George Wiedemann, the German-born chef of the Hyatt Regency in Austin, put "sizzling fajita" on the menu, and the sizzling platter presentation found a permanent place on restaurant menus throughout the world. Since there are only four skirt steaks per carcass, the current appetite for fajita is filled by using other cuts of beef (sliced sirloin is popular) or shrimp and chicken.

Zhey Yang's Korean Bulgogi

LINCOLN, NEBRASKA

Korean barbecue is known as bulgogi or bool kogi and comes from two words meaning "fire" and "meat." The bulgogi grill is perforated tin and looks like a half-globe or an inverted wok, and can easily be improvised. Says Zhey Yang, "That was the first thing I noticed when I came to this country: Korean people punching holes in tin cans and cookie sheets, even one metal light shade, and then making fires under them and making bulgogi." The grill can be used indoors over a gas flame or outdoors over a coal fire.

Unlike Western barbecue, which tends to cook slowly, the Korean version, of marinated wafers of beef, chicken, shrimp, squid, or tofu is seared quickly on the brazier. The meat or fish is served with dozens of condiments, dips, hot sauces, pickled vegetables, fish or crab, sticky rice, soups, and kimchi (Korea's pickled cabbage dish that is said to have more than two hundred variations). The bite-size pieces of meat or seafood are rolled in rice pancakes or lettuce leaves. Peppery greens, particularly meenari (Korean watercress), add crunch. Medium-grain white rice, completely unseasoned, is an essential buffer to the hot, fermented chili paste, gochu jang, which is as important to the Korean table as salt is elsewhere.

Four 14-ounce pieces beef short ribs, cut flanken style (across the bone), or four 9-ounce rib-eye steaks, sliced into very thin strips

1 medium papaya, peeled, seeded, and pureed

3 tablespoons soy sauce

1 tablespoon honey

1 tablespoon fresh ginger juice

1 onion, coarsely chopped

¼ cup peeled and chopped pear

¼ cup chopped pineapple

2 tablespoons dry sake

2 garlic cloves, minced

1 teaspoon freshly ground black pepper

4 scallions, green and white parts, coarsely chopped

1 teaspoon sugar

1 teaspoon sesame seeds

¼ cup toasted sesame oil

1. In a large bowl, cover the meat with cold water and refrigerate for 8 to 12 hours. Remove the meat from the water, dry well, and transfer to another large bowl. Strain the soaking water, reserving ⅓ cup.

2. In a small saucepan, bring the reserved ⅓ cup water, the papaya, soy sauce, and honey to a simmer over low heat and cook about 10 minutes, until thickened. Transfer to a medium bowl and cool to room temperature.

3. In a blender, process ¾ cup of the papaya mixture, the onion, pear, pineapple, sake, garlic, pepper, scallions, and sugar together until smooth. Return the mixture to the saucepan. Bring to a simmer, and cook, stirring occasionally, for 30 minutes, until thick. Stir in the sesame seeds.

4. Pour ¾ cup of the marinade and the sesame oil over the beef, toss to coat, and let sit for 10 minutes.

5. Heat a grill over high heat. Place the meat on the grill and cook about 4 minutes per side, until well browned and serve.

SERVES 4

Angela Warnick Buchdahl's Brisket

TACOMA, WASHINGTON

Born in Korea, Angela Warnick Buchdahl was 5 years old when her parents moved to Tacoma, Washington. She grew up in the city's Jewish community in the 1980s and eventually became the first Asian American to be ordained in North America as a cantor and a rabbi.

A pioneer in celebrating her two heritages, she is now passing on her biculturalism to her three children in dishes such as this one, which adapts her mother's traditional recipe for Korean bulgogi marinade to the brisket cut often favored by American Jewish cooks. Ms. Buchdahl has replaced her mother's mirin with a sweet kosher wine and added Korean-style heat with jalapeño peppers.

Everything but the Squeal: Beef, Buffalo, Game, Lamb, and Pork

¾ cup soy sauce

⅓ cup kosher sweet wine, such as Manischewitz

⅓ cup water

¼ cup toasted sesame oil

¼ cup honey

2 tablespoons sesame seeds

6 garlic cloves, minced

1 tablespoon freshly ground black pepper

One 5- to 7-pound flat-cut (or "first cut") kosher beef brisket, trimmed

1 large onion, halved and thinly sliced

2 celery stalks, thinly sliced

2 jalapeño chiles, stemmed, seeded, and thinly sliced (optional)

1. Place an oven rack in the center position and preheat the oven to 375°F. In a medium bowl, whisk the soy sauce, wine, water, sesame oil, honey, sesame seeds, garlic, and pepper together.

2. Place the brisket fat side up in a roasting pan and cover with the onion, celery, and jalapeños. Pour the soy sauce mixture over the brisket and cover with foil. Bake for 1 hour.

3. Uncover, reduce the oven temperature to 350°F, and cook about 5 hours longer, until the brisket is tender.

4. Transfer the brisket to a carving board and let rest for 15 minutes. Skim the fat from the pan juices. Cut the brisket across the grain into ¼-inch-thick slices. Return the sliced brisket to the roasting pan and spoon the juices over the top. Cover with foil and bake about 20 minutes, until heated through. Serve.

SERVES 8 TO 10

THE MEDIUM IS THE MEAL: DAVID KLOSE

IT WAS PROBABLY GERMAN AND CZECH IMMIGRANTS WHO ELEVATED BRISKET—
a stringy, fatty cut from the lower chest of beef—from ground meat for hamburger to an icon of Texas barbecue. The Germans and Czechs who arrived in west Texas in droves in the eighteenth century operated the meat shops, built smokers for their sausages and hams, and likely made the short leap from long, slow simmering (as in sauerbraten or cholent) to long, slow smoking (as in Texas brisket).

The legendary pit masters of Texas reign over wood-fired brick furnaces that seem large enough to forge steel. They say that the "art" of barbecue lies primarily in maintaining a consistent temperature of 250°F for the eight to fourteen hours required to slow-smoke a brisket. Competitors on the national barbecue circuit also require mobility. Smart money tends to be on "offset pits," enclosed ovens that resemble oil drums with a firebox on one end. The heavy-duty log-burning pits made by David Klose are considered "da bomb." A former welder, Mr. Klose builds everything from simple kettle grills and drum smokers to gigantic catering rigs. His offset pits are as sculptural as they are functional. Rarely seen without his cowboy hat, he can keep you laughing until the brisket is done. "I built my first pit out of self-defense. I was sick of eating Wendy's hamburgers. I built a pit so I could barbecue in my welding shop. Family and friends asked me to build them pits. This was early on, 1986. The barbecue industry was in its infancy. The Aztecs have been doing it for two thousand years, the Mexicans have done it for a thousand, Texans have

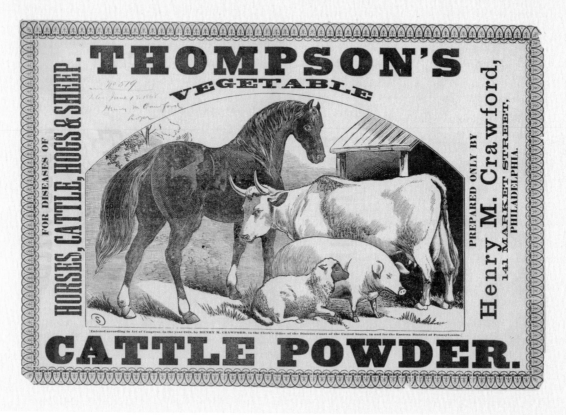

done it for two hundred, and they've been doing it for about six years in Oklahoma. I just delivered a rig to California and, I'm telling you, it'll be another twenty years before it catches on big out there.

"It was a lot more fun to make barbecue pits than fences and gates. I started with making three-eighths-inch steel offset drum smokers. I made one-of-a-kind pits because, well, because I could, I guess. I made a giant beer bottle pit, a chuckwagon pit. People gave me things and I turned them into pits. An 1806 metal baby carriage, a phone booth from Bosnia with bulletproof glass doors. A friend of mine recently got her husband a $100,000 custom-built Orange County chopper. I built him a pit sidecar. His ribs can go a hundred and forty miles per hour.

"I went to my first cookoff to sell my pits, I went back for fun. Barbecue cookoffs are like family reunions for dysfunctional families. You need a twelve- to fourteen-hour attention span to cook good barbecue—that's not possible if you are not drinking. I learned from the masters. Paul Kirk, seven-time world champion. He was one of the three guys who set up in a parking lot for the first Kansas City Royal competition. I knew him ten years before I knew he could read, and it turns out the guy's got degrees in history, food science, he's a teacher. He has me reading books to get the basics and then he tells me I know as much as he does and just get out there, listen to your body and cook. If it's hot, add salt. If it's cold, add pepper. Listen, smell, watch, feel it. You have to know it in your bones.

"Many Texas barbecue fanatics have a strong belief in the beneficial properties of accumulated grease."
—Calvin Trillin

"Barbecue is basically three waves of flavor. The first delivers the smoke, the second wave is comprised of your seasonings, the third is a tidal wave, the full body of the meat, it brings it all together. I use oak mostly—hickory is getting hard to find. There's thirty-two kinds of oak, I like white oak and post oak, nice steady heat, red oak gives a nice color. Pecan's nice for chicken.

"When competitive barbecue took off, competitors needed solid, movable pits and I started making custom rigs. Trailer-mounted pits, pits in train cars, trucks. I've done a few semi-tractor trailers that can do twenty thousand pounds of meat at a time. If you are catering an event for over a million people, you need a bunch of those. Somebody challenged me to do the tallest grill in the world and I did, twenty-three feet tall. I don't look at the world the way most people do. Most people look at a water tower and see a water tower. I see an elevator up to a pit. The prettiest pit I ever built was the one I made for Continental Airlines. It is a perfect ten-to-one scale model of a 777 wide-body. Does five hundred pounds of meat at a time. I don't think I can do better. You give me a million dollars and ask me to do better, I am going to have to give you your money back.

"If you know how to barbecue, you don't need a hundred-thousand-dollar rig. You need a hole in the ground and a grate. But you know, boys and their toys. I can't tell you how many times I've delivered a pit to somebody and the next thing, his neighbor calls: 'Hey, you know that pit you made for that old boy? I want the same thing. Except two inches bigger.' Fine with me. I got about twenty-six guys working for me now. They're all ironworkers and they're all artists."

DAVID KLOSE'S TEXAS BRISKET

One Big Table

Most home cooks use the flat of the brisket, which weighs around five pounds. When choosing your meat, Mr. Klose says, "pick it up and see if you can roll it. The more flexible the meat, the more tender it will cook up. The briskets with a thicker small end tend to cook more consistent." Paul Kirk taught Mr. Klose to reverse the usual order of flavoring the meat: mop it first, then season it. Leftover mop and rub can be stored separately and well covered in the refrigerator for later use.

1. Remove the meat from the cooler and lay it out on a pan or platter to warm up to room temperature. Make a fire using the wood of your choice. Hickory and oak are the traditional choices. Make the mop by combining the mustard, water, and fat. To make the rub, combine the ingredients well.

2. When the fire has died down to 250°F, mop the mustard mixture on the nonfat side of the brisket in a ⅛-inch-thick layer. Place the meat, fat side up, on the grill and then apply a ⅛-inch layer of mop to the fat side. Close the lid.

5 pounds beef brisket in one piece

FOR THE MOP

2 cups prepared yellow mustard (preferably French's)

¼ cup water

¼ cup melted beef fat

FOR THE RUB

½ cup sea salt

¼ cup granulated sugar

¼ cup brown sugar

½ cup coarsely ground black pepper

½ cup ground white pepper

½ cup sweet paprika

½ cup chili powder

½ cup garlic salt

½ cup onion salt

3. After 1 hour, sprinkle about ¼ cup of the rub on top of the meat and allow it to absorb for 30 minutes.

4. Turn the meat over and apply ¼ cup of the rub to the other side. Cook for approximately 1 hour per pound of meat, until the meat has reached an internal temperature of 175°F, as registered on an instant-read thermometer. Remove from the smoker, wrap in foil, and allow to rest for 30 minutes.

5. Slice the meat at a 45-degree angle against the grain for serving. The remaining mop can be diluted to a milk-like consistency and served on the side for dipping. Or serve the meat with your favorite sauce.

———

SERVES 8 TO 12, DEPENDING ON WHERE YOU ARE FROM

DR. BARBECUE: CAROLYN WELLS, PhB.

CAROLYN WELLS, BARBECUE CHAMPION AND CONTEST JUDGE, IS the cofounder and longtime president of the Kansas City Barbecue Society. She figures that she has eaten an average of 150 pounds of barbecue a year for the past thirty years. Her voice is as smoky as a Texas brisket. "I grew up in Tennessee, fell in love, moved to Kansas City to marry the guy, and fell in love again. Kansas City is the crossroads of American barbecue, a big railroad crossing, where the Southerners and Texans and beef cattle all came together and decided to be friends. That sort of open-mindedness was an eye-opener to me. I grew up in the mountainous south where everybody is pigheaded [and] barbecue is pork, hickory, and vinegar sauce—the end. In Texas, it's mesquite in the south, hickory in the north, and nobody can do it but us. Kansas City is tolerant of all styles of barbecue except bad barbecue.

"That's why we formed the Kansas City Barbecue Society. A few of us had competed in the American Royal Barbecue competition in 1987—I won the only category I entered, which was ribs, and all I had was two borrowed grills—and we decided we needed a governing body for the study and preservation of fine barbecue. Well, ten thousand members later, we sanction between seven hundred and eight hundred cookoffs a year, we're international, and we educate and test candidates for PhBs (Doctors of Barbecue Philosophy). It's a rigorous test. There are only fourteen PhBs alive today. If you let your standards slip, the next thing you know, you'll be eating barbecued pasta and that's just not right. This is about meat, and America.

"People barbecue to tell you who they are and where they came from and what's important to them. It's all there on your plate, or all over your fingers or down the front of your shirt. You can be a socialite or a plumber and make a mark in American barbecue. It is democratic. It's the summer game for people who don't play baseball. On a competitive level, it's a close world. I never had children, my husband died last year, but the barbecue people are my family. I retired from competition about fifteen years ago. I still judge, but only on special occasions. I never want barbecue to be a job. I never want barbecue to be anything but wild and crazy amateurs having a whole lot of fun."

Carolyn Wells's Kansas City Ribs

Kansas City is the melting pot of American barbecue. People use beef, pork, lamb, game, hot links. They use fruitwood and hardwood. They tend toward a thick, slightly sweet, tomato-based sauce that is not as tangy as a Southern vinegar-based sauce or as aggressively smoky or peppery as Texas sauces. Because of the city's history as a big beef-packing town, beef ribs are especially popular. Store extra rub in a well-covered container for later use.

2 large racks beef ribs, about 3 pounds each
   (or 4 racks baby back ribs)

FOR THE DRY RUB

½ cup granulated sugar

½ cup brown sugar

½ cup smoked paprika

¼ cup sea salt

¼ cup celery salt

3 tablespoons onion powder

3 tablespoons chili powder

2 tablespoons ground cumin

1 tablespoon freshly ground black pepper

2 teaspoons mustard powder

1 teaspoon ground chile
   or cayenne pepper

FOR THE SAUCE

1 teaspoon sea salt

1 teaspoon chili powder

1 teaspoon ground cumin

1 teaspoon sweet paprika

½ teaspoon ground allspice

½ teaspoon ground cinnamon

½ teaspoon ground nutmeg

½ teaspoon ground black pepper

½ teaspoon cayenne pepper

1 teaspoon Tabasco sauce

2 cups ketchup

¾ cup molasses

½ cup cider vinegar

1. Pat the ribs dry and let them come to room temperature.

2. To make the dry rub: Combine all the ingredients in a glass jar and shake well. Coat the ribs on all sides with the rub, wrap tightly in plastic wrap, and refrigerate for 1 day.

3. To make the sauce: Combine all ingredients in a 1-quart glass jar, shake well, and store in the refrigerator overnight.

4. To barbecue the ribs, remove them from the refrigerator, brush off the excess dry rub, and bring to room temperature. Meanwhile, prepare a wood fire or preheat the oven to 250°F.

5. Brush the ribs with the sauce and place on the grill over indirect heat. Cover and grill for 2½ to 3 hours, turning and brushing with sauce several times until the meat has shrunk away from the bone and is very tender. (If cooking in the oven, place the ribs on a rack in a roasting pan. Cover and roast for 2½ to 3 hours.)

6. Ten minutes before the meat is finished, slather generously with the sauce. Serve with additional sauce for dipping.

SERVES 4

THEY'VE GOT THE BEEF

THE COLEMAN FAMILY HAS BEEN RANCHING CATTLE SINCE 1870, WHEN THE CLAN traveled in covered wagons from Altoona, Pennsylvania, to Saguache, Colorado. Mel Coleman Jr., the eighth-generation steward of the family's spread in the San Luis Valley, remembers his father saying "a ranch is a great place to raise cattle, kids, and hell." By 1979, as the ranch was teetering on the edge of bankruptcy, Mel Coleman Sr. had an epiphany: He would sell grass-fed beef that was naturally raised without hormones or antibiotics. Soon, father and son were selling their high-quality beef to some of the best restaurants in the world. At one of those restaurants, Ardio in Japan, they had the best steak of their lives. "A six-ounce top sirloin cut an inch and a half thick, grilled on a hot, flat grill, dusted with a large pinch of fresh-grated wasabi," Mel Jr. says. "Top sirloin is not as tender as many cuts, but it has the most flavor. It's my favorite cut."

Logan Wilkes's Fast Fire Flank Steak

SALT LAKE CITY, UTAH

Growing up in Portland, Oregon, Logan Wilkes was a typical northwestern jock—but shortly after arriving at Brigham Young University, he discovered he had a voice, dance moves, and a serious way with meat. At BYU he became part of a dining group in which each member was required to prepare a meal once a week. With the help of his mother's recipe blog, he could find recipes at the click of a mouse and began cooking for friends. As he continued to perfect his skills at the grill, he says, he discovered how both music and dance and the preparing and sharing of food break down barriers. This flank steak is his favorite recipe, and the one most requested by fellow diners and girlfriends.

1½ tablespoons brown sugar

2 tablespoons sesame seeds

6 garlic cloves, minced

1½ tablespoons soy sauce

1 tablespoon dry sherry

1 tablespoon toasted sesame oil

1 teaspoon grated fresh ginger

2 scallions, green and white parts, thinly sliced

One 1¼-pound flank steak

1. In a large baking dish, mix together the sugar, sesame seeds, garlic, soy sauce, sherry, sesame oil, ginger, and scallions. Lightly score the flank steak on each side in a 1-inch crosshatch pattern. Place the meat in the baking dish and rub the marinade into the scoring. Cover and refrigerate for at least 3 and up to 12 hours.

2. Remove the steak from the refrigerator and let sit at room temperature for 30 minutes. Meanwhile, heat a grill to medium-high.

3. Remove the steak from the marinade and let any excess drip off. Place the steak on the grill and cook for 7 to 12 minutes on each side, until browned and an instant-read thermometer registers 125°F for medium rare.

4. Transfer the steak to a carving board and let rest for 10 minutes. Thinly slice the steak against the grain and serve.

SERVES 4

William Fiorino's Modiga Steak with Peppermint Sauce

Rosalie Fiorino Harpole's father, William, came from Rome and worked as a butcher his whole life for Italian shops such as Cuccione's Italian Meat Market and Rallo Meats, and big companies, such as National Foods and Kroger. "My mother was a fabulous baker and my father a terrific cook," she says. "We ate a lot of meat, had wonderful bread and sweets, and we listened to a lot of baseball on the radio. My father was as committed to the St. Louis Cardinals as he was to his modiga steak." Once, the Cardinals made him so mad that he turned off the radio three times during the game.

FOR THE SAUCE

¼ cup lightly packed fresh peppermint leaves

1 garlic clove, minced

1 large ripe tomato, cored, peeled, seeded, and finely chopped

¼ cup olive oil

2 tablespoons water

Kosher salt and freshly ground black pepper

FOR THE STEAKS

1 cup plain dry bread crumbs

1 ounce Parmesan or pecorino Romano cheese, grated (about ¼ cup)

¼ cup chopped fresh parsley

3 garlic cloves, minced

1 teaspoon kosher salt

¼ teaspoon ground black pepper

½ cup olive oil

Four 8- to 12-ounce strip sirloin steaks, about 1 inch thick

Garlic salt

1. To make the sauce: Crush the mint and garlic to a paste with a mortar and pestle. Transfer the mixture to a medium bowl and stir in the tomato, olive oil, and water. Season with salt and pepper to taste.

2. To make the steaks: In a shallow dish, combine the bread crumbs, cheese, parsley, garlic, salt, and pepper. Pour the oil into a second shallow dish. Pat the steaks dry and season with the garlic salt. Coat the steaks first in the oil and then the seasoned bread crumbs. Transfer to a wire rack set over a rimmed baking sheet.

3. Heat a grill to medium-high. Grill the steaks for 4 to 6 minutes per side, until an instant-read thermometer reads 125°F for medium-rare.

4. Transfer the steaks to a carving board and let rest for 10 minutes. Slice and serve with the peppermint sauce.

SERVES 4

ELLEN SULLIVAN'S LAVENDER TENDERLOIN

VALLEY CENTER, CALIFORNIA

In 1998, Ellen Sullivan purchased land in northern San Diego County, California, named it The Lavender Fields, and planted, grew, and harvested fields of lavender. She also searched for culinary uses for the plant, which is still considered more of an aromatic flower than a herb. "The first modern culinary use I saw was a chef's recipe for lavender crème brûlée, and that got me thinking. Lavender's flavor is both tangy and floral, so it works as well in savory dishes as it does in sweet ones—I love what it does to beef tenderloin." This recipe remains one of Ms. Sullivan's favorite company meals.

2 tablespoons dried food-quality lavender buds

2 tablespoons fennel seeds

1 tablespoon whole black peppercorns

1 tablespoon whole white peppercorns

1½ teaspoons dried thyme

1 teaspoon kosher salt

One 4½-pound whole beef tenderloin, trimmed and silverskin removed

2 tablespoons olive oil

1. The day before serving, grind the lavender, fennel, peppercorns, thyme, and salt to a powder with a mortar and pestle or in a spice grinder. Rub the tenderloin with the spice mixture, wrap tightly in plastic wrap, and refrigerate for 8 to 24 hours.

2. Remove the tenderloin from the refrigerator and let sit at room temperature for 30 minutes. Place an oven rack in the center position and preheat the oven to 425°F. Place a rack inside a roasting pan.

3. Remove the plastic wrap, brush off the spices from the tenderloin, and rub with 1 tablespoon of the oil. Place the tenderloin on the rack and roast for 15 minutes, turning once halfway through.

4. Reduce the heat to 325°F and roast for 5 to 15 minutes longer, to the desired doneness (an instant-read thermometer will read 125°F for medium rare).

5. Transfer the roast to a carving board and let rest, loosely covered with foil, for 10 minutes. Meanwhile, add the remaining olive oil to the roasting pan, scrape well, and stir to combine the drippings.

6. Cut the tenderloin against the grain into ½-inch-thick slices and transfer to a serving platter. Drizzle the pan drippings over the meat and serve.

SERVES 8 TO 10

MARY LASATER'S UNBELIEVABLE ROAST BEEF

MATHESON, COLORADO

The Lasater family of Matheson, Colorado, has been raising beef cattle since 1882. Today, the family's thirty thousand acres of prairie land is a study in eco-habitation. Beefmaster—the family's trademarked breed of cattle—roam the flatlands feeding on the grass, fertilizing it with their droppings, and tilling the land with their hooves, just as the buffalo herds once did. Dale Lasater says this sensibly gentle approach to cattle ranching shows the hand of his mother, Mary. She was an avid horsewoman who loved

any work involving cattle, he says. She also ran the house, raised six kids, and put a sizable dinner on the table every night.

To keep up with it all, she devised a unique method of making roast beef. She would partially cook the roast in the morning, leave it in the oven with the door closed during the day, then finish the cooking in the late afternoon. Mr. Lasater thinks his mother's no-fuss cooking method is perfect for the modern working cooks who don't have the time or energy at the end of a long day for a major cooking project even if it doesn't involve cattle. That said, this method does keep the meat at a temperature the USDA considers a health risk and should be attempted with only the freshest, cleanest, organic meat available.

One 3-pound beef chuck-eye roast, trimmed
Kosher salt and freshly ground black pepper

1. Place an oven rack in the center position and preheat the oven to 375°F.

2. Pat the roast dry and season with salt and pepper. Transfer to a rack in a roasting pan. Roast for 1 hour.

3. Turn off the oven and let the roast sit for 4 to 6 hours. (Do not open the oven door.)

4. Forty to 50 minutes before serving, turn on the oven to 300°F. Cook the roast for 25 minutes longer for rare (120°F on an instant-read thermometer) and up to 35 minutes for medium rare (125°F).

5. Transfer the roast to a carving board and let rest for 15 minutes.

6. Cut the roast thinly against the grain and transfer to a serving platter. Serve with any accumulated juices.

SERVES 6

Mrs. Pfluger's Sauerbraten

HANNIBAL, MISSOURI

"My grandmother's family came to Missouri because they knew people there," says Mrs. Gertrude Pfluger. "They ran a boarding house right here in Hannibal, saved, and got some land over by Sedalia—you could get land by clearing it, grazing or planting it, and living there. The women went into town once a week to buy what they didn't grow or trade for. It was their social life and it was still going on when I was a girl in the 1920s.

"You went to the Italian for your veal and chicken, the German put your hogs up for you and made the sausage, bacon, and ham and such, the Bohemian did most of the beef cattle. His wife would pickle up your Sunday roast if you wanted and you could pick it up, just like that, all ready to cook overnight," she says. "The women swapped recipes while they waited for their meat. They did not think of the recipes as ethnic. My grandmother died thinking that veal Parmesan was an American dish. Her neighbor, Roma McBride, thought that sauerbraten was American because she got the recipe from the butcher. They were all in America and everything they ate after they got here was American."

This version of sauerbraten is distinguished by its warm spices and long, slow marinating. Mrs. Pfluger allows the meat to sit in the liquid for three or four days prior to cooking it. She serves the meat sliced, with potatoes, noodles, or dumplings.

2½ cups water

1½ cups red wine vinegar

1 cup apple cider vinegar

3 tablespoons granulated sugar

½ teaspoon grated fresh ginger

3 bay leaves

15 whole black peppercorns

1 large onion, halved and sliced ¼-inch thick

One 4-pound beef chuck-eye or rump roast, trimmed

1 teaspoon kosher salt

¾ teaspoon freshly ground black pepper

2 tablespoons vegetable oil

3 carrots, peeled and cut into 2-inch chunks

⅔ cup packed brown sugar

2 tablespoons (¼ stick) unsalted butter

2 tablespoons all-purpose flour

¾ cup raisins

Hannibal, Missouri, 1912.

1. Two to 3 days before serving, combine the water, vinegars, granulated sugar, ginger, bay leaves, and peppercorns in a medium bowl. In a large bowl, arrange the onion in an even layer. Pat the roast dry and rub with the salt and pepper. Place the roast on top of the onion, pour over the marinade and refrigerate for at least 48 hours, up to 4 days.

2. Remove the beef from the marinade and pat dry. Strain the marinade and reserve both the liquid and the onion.

3. Place an oven rack in the center position and preheat the oven to 300°F.

4. Heat the oil in a large Dutch oven over medium heat. Add the roast and cook for 8 to 10 minutes, until well browned on all sides. Transfer the roast to a plate.

5. Add the reserved marinated onion and the carrots to the Dutch oven and cook for 4 to 6 minutes, until soft. Stir in reserved marinade and the brown sugar and bring to a simmer.

6. Return the beef to the pot, cover, and transfer to the oven. Cook for 3½ to 4 hours, until the meat is tender.

7. Transfer the beef to a carving board and the carrots to a serving platter. Cover both loosely with foil.

8. Melt the butter in a medium saucepan over medium heat. Whisk in the flour and cook for 2 to 4 minutes, until golden brown. Whisk in the cooking liquid, onion, and raisins and cook for 4 to 6 minutes, until thickened.

9. Cut the roast against the grain into ½-inch-thick slices and transfer to the platter. Pour the sauce over the beef and serve.

SERVES 8

Jan Mohr's Marinated Chuck Roast

When Jan Mohr was a teenager in the fifties, she had to be home for Saturday night dinner. "If we had a date, we could either go out later or invite our date to come for dinner," she says. There was a standard menu for Saturday night: grilled steak, Caesar salad, and some type of potato. "We used chuck-eye steak and it was marinated in a sauce that my father had made up. He even sent it in to *Gourmet* magazine and they printed it. My mother always made the marinade in the same ceramic beer stein. The steak marinated for twenty-four hours. My father's formula for timing the cooking of the steak was the amount of time it took him to drink two Old Forester bourbons and soda."

440

One Big Table

¾ cup red wine

½ cup soy sauce

3 tablespoons steak sauce

2 tablespoons Worcestershire sauce

2 tablespoons fresh lemon juice

8 garlic cloves, minced

Pinch of celery salt

Pinch of sweet paprika

Pinch of seasoning salt

One 1½-pound chuck-eye steak, trimmed

2 tablespoons vegetable oil

1. The day before serving, in a large bowl, combine the wine, soy sauce, steak sauce, Worcestershire, lemon juice, garlic, celery salt, paprika, and seasoning salt. Add the steak, cover, and refrigerate for 24 hours, turning once.

2. Before cooking, pat the steak dry. Heat the oil in a large skillet over medium-high heat. Add the steak and cook for 6 to 10 minutes per side, until well browned on both sides and the desired doneness.

3. Transfer the steak to a serving platter and let rest for 5 minutes. Slice and serve.

SERVES 4 TO 6

MEMERE DUSSAULT'S SUNDAY POT ROAST

D r. Al Dussault is a psychoanalyst and a photographer—both fields, he says, that "have to do with values, exposure, and intensity." He and one of his sisters are the keepers of the flame for their third-generation French Canadian clan. His grandparents owned a corner grocery store and his grandmother's pot roast—one part French and one part Yankee boiled dinner—is the sort of an expansive, inexpensive dish that kept friends and family fed during the Great Depression.

"My grandmother would put it on in the morning before church," he says. "Every time somebody else stopped by, she added another potato or more carrots. It all cooks so long that you can't really tell what's meat and what's potato, anyway. And no matter how far you stretch it, Memere's Sunday pot roast always tastes rich and meaty. We serve it with white bread and mayonnaise. I don't know why."

441

One 4- to 5-pound chuck-eye or rump roast, trimmed

Kosher salt and freshly ground black pepper

1 cup all-purpose flour

½ cup olive oil

2 large onions, finely chopped

5 garlic cloves, minced

8 cups homemade beef broth or low-sodium store-bought beef broth

2 cups red wine

One 14.5-ounce can diced tomatoes, drained

1 teaspoon dried oregano

1 teaspoon dried sage

1 bay leaf

½ teaspoon ground allspice

1½ pounds small red potatoes, scrubbed

1 pound carrots, peeled and cut into 2-inch chunks

3 parsnips, peeled and cut into 2-inch chunks (optional)

3 turnips, peeled and cut into 2-inch chunks (optional)

1. Pat the roast dry, season with salt and pepper, and lightly dredge in the flour. Heat ¼ cup of the oil in a large Dutch oven over medium-high heat. Add the roast and cook for 8 to 10 minutes, until well browned on all sides. Transfer to a plate.

2. Add the onions and cook over medium heat about 4 minutes, until soft. Stir in the garlic and cook about 1 minute, until aromatic. Stir in the broth, wine, tomatoes, oregano, sage, bay leaf, allspice, ½ teaspoon salt, and ½ teaspoon pepper. Bring to a simmer, then return the roast to the pot, cover, and cook for 1½ hours, adding water as needed to keep the meat covered by 1 inch.

3. Add the potatoes, carrots, parsnips (if using), and turnips (if using). Cover and simmer about 1½ hours longer, until the meat and vegetables are tender.

4. Transfer the roast to a carving board and let rest for 15 minutes. Using a slotted spoon, transfer the vegetables to a serving platter and loosely cover with foil. Return the sauce to a simmer and cook for 10 to 15 minutes, until slightly thickened. Season with salt and pepper to taste.

5. Cut the roast against the grain into ½-inch-thick slices and transfer to the serving platter with the vegetables. Pour the sauce over the beef and vegetables and serve.

SERVES 8 TO 10

Everything but the Squeal: Beef, Buffalo, Game, Lamb, and Pork

Hoover's Night Hawk Chicken-Fried Steak and Cream Gravy

"Texas cuisine may be separated into three distinct divisions—barbecue, Mexican food, and that rare and wonderful piece of bucolic fancy, the chicken-fried steak," claimed the late travel writer Jerry Flemmons.

The dish has its own inherent contradictions. It is, for instance, neither chicken nor exactly steak. It is always served with a white sauce that is called "cream gravy" but made of milk. Like any icon, the finer points of the dish Texans call "CFS" are fiercely debated. The history of the dish has conflicting versions: It may have been inspired by breaded wiener schnitzel and pioneered by the huge German population that arrived in Texas in the late nineteenth century; it may have been a chuckwagon invention—or perhaps it was shaped by both cultures. There is also debate about the precise cut of meat: Most Texans can't imagine anything but pounded round steak, while a privileged few say that CFS must be made from pounded beef fillet. The proof, of course, is in the CFS itself.

"Everybody's mama's got a recipe," says Hoover Alexander, a fifth-generation Texan and the impresario of Hoover's Cooking in Austin. In his own home, the finer points of CFS are drawn from his parents' backgrounds—his mother grew up on a farm in the Texas blackland prairie, his father on a ranch in Pilot Knob—and his experience in the cooking corps at Harry Akin's Night Hawk Restaurants, Austin landmarks from 1932 to the late 1970s and the first restaurants in the city both to serve African-American customers and to offer career-track training to women and people of color. By the time Mr. Alexander began cooking at the Night Hawk, its CFS was the distillation of hundreds of family recipes. This recipe uses the Night Hawk seasonings, but unlike the restaurant, which deep-fries its CFS, Mr. Alexander fries it in a cast-iron skillet as his mother did.

Bob Lemmons, born a slave around 1850, Texas.

FOR THE STEAKS

4 cups all-purpose flour

4 teaspoons baking powder

1 tablespoon kosher salt

1 tablespoon freshly ground black pepper

2 teaspoons granulated garlic

1 teaspoon onion powder

1 teaspoon cayenne pepper

2 cups milk

4 large eggs

½ cup vegetable oil

Four 6-ounce beef cube steaks, pounded
to ¼ inch thick

FOR THE GRAVY

2 cups milk

2 cups homemade chicken broth or low-sodium
store-bought chicken broth

2 tablespoons bacon grease or vegetable oil

½ cup all-purpose flour

½ teaspoon garlic powder

½ teaspoon onion powder

Kosher salt and freshly ground black pepper

1. To make the steaks: Place an oven rack in the center position and preheat the oven to 200°F. Place a wire rack over a baking sheet and place in the oven. Line a plate with paper towels.

2. In a shallow dish, whisk together the flour, baking powder, salt, pepper, granulated garlic, onion powder, and cayenne. In a second shallow dish, whisk together the milk and eggs.

3. Heat the oil in a large cast-iron skillet over medium heat until a deep-fry thermometer registers 350°F. Meanwhile, working with one steak at a time, dredge in the flour mixture and shake off

the excess. Dip the steak into the egg mixture, and then back into the flour mixture. Add two of the steaks to the skillet and cook for 4 to 6 minutes, until golden brown on both sides.

4. Transfer the steaks to the paper towel–lined plate to drain briefly, then to the wire rack and keep warm in the oven. Return the oil to 350°F and repeat with the remaining steaks.

5. To make the gravy: In a medium saucepan, bring the milk and broth to a simmer. Pour off all but 2 tablespoons of the oil from the skillet. Whisk in the bacon grease and flour and cook over medium heat about 2 minutes, until the flour is lightly browned. Slowly whisk in the milk mixture, garlic powder, and onion powder. Bring to a simmer and cook about 20 minutes, until thickened. Season with salt and pepper to taste.

6. To serve, place a warm chicken-fried steak on a plate and pour the gravy over the top.

SERVES 4

Grandma Telly's Oxtail

I n 2001, when her husband got a promotion that moved the family from Jamaica to Chicago, Natalie Marshal-Rose could not boil an egg. While she hunted for work as a paralegal, she decided to teach herself how to cook. "I was raised by my grandparents. My grandmother encouraged schooling and discouraged housekeeping, except cooking, which she promoted as a way to lure a husband, but by then, I would have none of it." Once in the kitchen, she was amazed to find that she had channeled her grandmother. "I'd get a flash of memory, see her cooking something, saw what she did, smelled the kitchen and from those memories, I taught myself how to cook." She cooked until her rum cakes were perfect, her coconut drops flawless, her jerk pork pitch-perfect. In addition to her day job, she soon had a sideline selling rum cakes and other Jamaican sweets to Chicagoans. But in her own kitchen, now in Texas, her favorite dish is still her grandmother's oxtail stew. "This is my gift to her, sharing Jamaican cooking with non–West Indians. She would be amazed."

Although oxtail can be cooked more quickly in a pressure cooker, Mrs. Marshal-Rose says that the flavor and texture are best when cooked à la Grandma Telly—simmered in a Dutch oven for hours, then served with pigeon peas, rice, carrots, and fried plantains.

2 pounds oxtail

Kosher salt and freshly ground black pepper

½ teaspoon onion powder

¼ cup soy sauce

2 medium scallions, white parts only, finely chopped

1 garlic clove, minced

2 fresh thyme sprigs

1 tablespoon olive oil

2 cups water

2 carrots, peeled and cut into 1-inch chunks

One 14-ounce can butter beans, drained and rinsed

½ Scotch bonnet chile, stemmed, seeded, and finely chopped

1 teaspoon sugar, plus more to taste

1. In a large bowl, season the oxtail with salt, pepper, and onion powder. Add the soy sauce, scallions, garlic, and thyme and toss to combine. Cover and refrigerate for 1 to 12 hours.

2. Heat the oil in a Dutch oven over medium-high heat. Add the oxtail and cook about 6 minutes, until well browned on all sides. Stir in the water, bring to a simmer, and cover, and cook about 2 hours, until the meat is tender.

3. Stir in the carrots, beans, Scotch bonnet, sugar, 2 teaspoons salt, and ½ teaspoon pepper and cook for 20 to 30 minutes, until the carrots are tender. Season with salt, pepper, and sugar to taste and serve.

SERVES 4 TO 6

EDMUND COLGAN'S MIDCENTURY SWISS STEAK

"Both of my parents were wonderful cooks," said Lydia Shire, the chef of Boston's venerable Locke-Ober's. "They say the Irish can't cook. But my father, Edmund Colgan, was one of the exceptions. He would cut recipes from the newspaper, and when I came home from school, the kitchen would be full of the most amazing smells.

"He died before I learned his recipes and it took me a long time to reconstruct his Swiss steak. But here it is, the old 1950s standby, with a couple of flourishes of my own. And now my children swoon for it the same way that my siblings and I did." Seven-bone chuck roasts (named for the shape of the bone within, not for the number of bones) are hard to find, she notes, but essential to this dish, "important enough to ask your market to order one special for you. The reason I love this cut," she says, "is because of the proportion of meat to fat, which is perfect for braising."

Two 2½- to 3-pound 7-bone chuck roasts, trimmed

Kosher salt and freshly ground black pepper

½ cup all-purpose flour

6 tablespoons olive or vegetable oil

2 large onions, halved and thinly sliced

One 6-ounce can tomato paste

1 tablespoon canned chipotle chiles in adobo sauce

One 750-milliliter bottle cream sherry

12 garlic cloves

1 cup chopped fresh parsley

2 teaspoons grated lemon zest

1. Place an oven rack in the center position and preheat the oven to 325°F.

2. Pat the roasts dry, season generously with salt and pepper, and dredge in the flour. Heat 2 tablespoons of the oil in a large Dutch oven over medium-high heat. Add one of the roasts and cook until well browned on all sides, 8 to 10 minutes. Transfer the roast to a plate. Add 2 tablespoons more oil to the pot and repeat with the remaining roast.

3. Add 2 tablespoons more oil to the pot and lower the heat to medium. Add the onions and cook for 8 to 10 minutes, stirring occasionally, until lightly browned. Stir in the tomato paste and chipotles and cook about 2 minutes, until beginning to darken. Stir in the sherry and 6 of the garlic cloves, scrape up any browned bits, and bring to a simmer. Return the roasts to the pot and add enough water to come halfway up the sides of the roasts.

4. Cover the pot, transfer to the oven, and cook for 2 to 2½ hours, until the roasts are tender, adding water as needed.

5. Transfer the roasts to a carving board and let sit for 15 minutes. Season the sauce with salt and pepper to taste. Mince the remaining 6 garlic cloves, transfer to a small bowl, and stir in the parsley and lemon zest. Cut the roasts into ½-inch-thick slices and transfer to a serving platter. Sprinkle the parsley mixture over the top and serve with the sauce.

SERVES 6 TO 8

445

Everything but the Squeal: Beef, Buffalo, Game, Lamb, and Pork

Jackie Mintz's Stir-Fried Beef

BALTIMORE, MARYLAND

Jackie Mintz's family arrived in Bronxville, New York, from Shanghai in 1941, intending to remain only until the war in China ended. Having grown up in a privileged household, her mother knew nothing about cooking, and there was no Chinese community or Asian grocery near their home. "We both learned to cook Chinese in Bronxville from my older cousin," says Mrs. Mintz. "My husband, Sid, is an Eastern European Jew who was born in New Jersey. His father was a cook and owned a restaurant. I taught my husband our family's recipes. He does most of the cooking in our home."

One 1-pound flank or tenderloin steak, cut across the grain into 1- by 1½-inch strips

½ cup light soy sauce

6 tablespoons dry sherry

4 teaspoons cornstarch

2 teaspoons brandy

2 tablespoons peanut or vegetable oil

1 teaspoon Sichuan peppercorns, toasted and crushed

1 bunch scallions, green and white parts, cut into 2-inch lengths

12 garlic cloves, thinly sliced

1 cup chopped fresh cilantro

1. In a medium bowl, toss the beef with ¼ cup of the soy sauce, 2 tablespoons of the sherry, and 3 teaspoons of the cornstarch and let sit for 15 minutes. In a small bowl, combine the remaining ¼ cup soy sauce, remaining ¼ cup sherry, remaining 1 teaspoon cornstarch, and the brandy.

2. Heat the oil in a wok or large nonstick skillet over high heat. Drain the marinade from the beef, add the beef to the wok in an even layer, and cook until well browned on the first side, 1 to 2 minutes. Stir the beef and cook until no longer pink, 30 seconds to 1 minute longer.

3. Stir in the peppercorns, scallions, and garlic and cook about 1 minute, until soft. Mix in the cilantro and soy sauce mixture and cook, stirring constantly, about 30 seconds, until the sauce is thickened. Serve.

SERVES 4

AMERICAN ICON: MEATLOAF

IN AMERICA, WHERE THE PANTRY AND THE CULINARY IMAGINATION TEND TO BE GLOBAL, anyone can create the world as he or she wishes it to be in one glorious dish. Variations on meatloaf are a portrait of America. By changing the meats or the seasonings, one can change its nationality, its regionality, and its family of origin. Local permutations reflect an area's ethnic heritage. The Italian and Portuguese influence is big in the Northeast, while the South tends toward Creole and barbecue flavors. There is a strong German influence on meatloaf in the Midwest, and Mexican flavors show up in Southern California.

Peter Kaufman, who organized a national meatloaf contest and in 1994 published his findings in *The Great American Meatloaf Contest Cookbook: Great Meatloaf Recipes by Great Americans*, says that meatloaf remains constant generation to generation because "it's never been in style, so it never goes out of style."

MR. MEATLOAF'S PERSONAL FAVORITE

The most interesting thing Peter Kaufman learned from tasting three thousand versions of meatloaf in his national meatloaf contest was the secret of great Midwestern meatloaf: "People with German backgrounds told me that if you add a little applesauce, your meatloaf will never dry out," he says. This addition, plus a mixture of beef, pork, and lamb, Middle Eastern seasonings, and a rich onion and mushroom gravy make his meatloaf "better than anybody else's."

Mr. Kaufman uses a Chicago Metallic meatloaf pan, which drains the fat into a pan below.

1¼ pounds 85% lean ground beef

½ pound ground lamb

½ pound ground veal

¼ cup cornflake crumbs

3 tablespoons ketchup

1 tablespoon Dijon mustard

¼ cup unsweetened applesauce

½ teaspoon ground cumin

½ teaspoon ground cardamom

½ teaspoon freshly ground black pepper

¾ teaspoon kosher salt

1 large egg

1¼ cups fresh bread crumbs

Peter's Onion and Mushroom Gravy (recipe follows), for serving

1. Place an oven rack in the center position and preheat the oven to 350°F.

2. In a large bowl, mix together the beef, lamb, and veal. With your hands, mix in the cornflake crumbs, ketchup, mustard, applesauce, cumin, cardamom, pepper, salt, and egg. Slowly mix in the bread crumbs. Transfer the mixture into a 9-inch loaf pan and even it out.

3. Bake for about 1½ hours, until an instant-read thermometer registers 155°F.

4. Let the meatloaf rest for 10 minutes before slicing and serving with gravy.

SERVES 6 TO 8

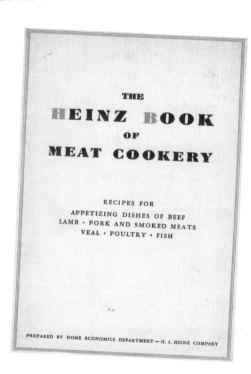

THE
HEINZ BOOK
OF
MEAT COOKERY

RECIPES FOR
APPETIZING DISHES OF BEEF
LAMB · PORK AND SMOKED MEATS
VEAL · POULTRY · FISH

PREPARED BY HOME ECONOMICS DEPARTMENT — H. J. HEINZ COMPANY

Everything but the Squeal: Beef, Buffalo, Game, Lamb, and Pork

448

Peter's Onion and Mushroom Gravy

This is an upscale spin on the creamy, beefy gravy that makes "blue-plate" meatloaf and mashed potatoes so popular. It also makes a good sauce for roast beef, meatballs, or chopped steak.

½ cup dried mushrooms, such as porcini, candy cap, or morel, chopped

1 cup boiling water

4 tablespoons (½ stick) unsalted butter, cut into ½-inch chunks and chilled

1 medium onion, finely chopped

1 garlic clove, minced

Kosher salt and freshly ground black pepper

1 teaspoon apple cider vinegar

10 ounces white mushrooms, thinly sliced

½ cup crushed tomatoes

3 cups homemade beef broth or low-sodium store-bought beef broth

½ cup heavy cream

1. In a small bowl, cover the dried mushrooms with the boiling water and let sit for 20 minutes.

2. Melt 2 tablespoons of the butter in a large skillet over medium heat. Add the onion and the garlic. Season lightly with salt and pepper and cook for 2 minutes, stirring constantly. Reduce the heat to low and continue cooking, stirring frequently to avoid burning, until the onion is medium gold in color. Add the apple cider vinegar, raise heat to medium and cook, stirring constantly, for 1 minute.

3. Drain the dried mushrooms and reserve the liquid. Add the rehydrated mushrooms and the white mushrooms to the pan, stir, and season with salt and pepper. Add the reserved mushroom liquid, the tomatoes, and the broth. Reduce the heat to low and simmer until reduced by half, about 15 minutes.

4. Add the cream and cook for 5 minutes. Just before serving, increase the heat to high and bring the sauce to a boil. Remove from heat, whisk in the remaining 2 tablespoons butter, and season with salt and pepper to taste. Serve.

MAKES ABOUT 2 CUPS

Anne Rosenzweig's Old-Fashioned Meat-and-Rice Loaf

Throughout American history, restaurant chefs have looked to home cooks for inspiration and home cooks have aspired to cook like chefs. Meatloaf is a particular crucible. If elevated too much beyond its roots, it ultimately becomes "pâté." For chefs like Anne Rosenzweig, whose New York restaurant Arcadia was in the vanguard of the New American Cuisine movement in the 1980s, the challenge of meatloaf is restraining the haute impulse. By using fatty sirloin and lean veal, she gives her version of an old-fashioned, Eastern European rice-and-meat pie a finer texture. Fresh ginger and pistachio nuts enrich the flavor and provide an unexpected twist. The surprises are subtle, but they create a loaf that is special enough for a company dinner and homey enough to sidle up to mashed potatoes and gravy.

1 medium onion, chopped

2 garlic cloves, peeled

One 1-inch piece fresh ginger, peeled

1 tablespoon unsalted butter

1 pound ground veal

1 pound ground sirloin

1 cup cooked white rice, cold

1 large egg

½ cup shelled unsalted pistachios

2 teaspoons kosher salt

1 teaspoon freshly ground black pepper

1. Place an oven rack in the center position and preheat the oven to 350°F.

2. In a food processor, process the onion, garlic, and ginger until smooth. Melt the butter in a large skillet over medium-high heat. Add the onion mixture and cook about 5 minutes, until soft. Remove from the heat and cool.

3. In a large bowl, combine the onion mixture with the veal, sirloin, rice, egg, pistachios, salt, and pepper by hand, taking care to mush the meat as little as possible. Place the mixture in a nonstick 9-inch loaf pan and form into a solid loaf.

4. Bake the meatloaf about 1 hour, until an instant-read thermometer registers 155°F. Let the meatloaf rest for 20 minutes before serving.

SERVES 6 TO 8

Helen Gianacakes's Ouzo Meatballs

LOUISVILLE, KENTUCKY

Helen Gianacakes grew up in Cincinnati, Ohio, where her father owned a restaurant. She helped make ice cream, candy, and Greek pastry when she was a young girl, but she learned to make fast family meals after she married, moved to Kentucky, and began a family. Like many, her interest in cooking—as opposed to getting dinner on the table—blossomed after her three children were off on their own. Visiting her son in Dallas, she met Evelyn Semos, who worked at Neiman Marcus for twenty-seven years, rising from sales clerk to one of the store's leading tastemakers. This recipe for meatballs was inspired by Mrs. Semos, who has since passed away. Mrs. Gianacakes serves it as an appetizer or as an entrée in the traditional Greek feasts she prepares at Thanksgiving and Christmas.

The meatballs can be served plain or in a casserole with tomato sauce.

2 slices white sandwich bread, crusts removed

¼ cup ouzo

3 tablespoons vegetable or olive oil

½ cup finely chopped onion

1 pound lean ground beef

1 large egg

1 teaspoon minced fresh mint

1 garlic clove, minced

1 teaspoon minced fresh oregano,
   or ¼ teaspoon dried

1 teaspoon kosher salt

½ teaspoon freshly ground black pepper

1 cup all-purpose flour

1. Place an oven rack in the center position and preheat oven to 450°F. Lightly grease a rimmed baking sheet.

2. In a small bowl, soak the bread in the ouzo for 5 minutes. Squeeze the bread dry and discard the liquid.

3. Heat the oil in a large skillet over medium-high heat. Add onion and cook about 4 minutes. Using a slotted spoon, transfer the onions to a large bowl. Cool to room temperature.

4. Add the bread, ground beef, egg, mint, garlic, oregano, salt, and pepper to the onions. Mix and knead until smooth.

5. Shape into 1-inch balls. Roll the balls in the flour and put on the baking sheet.

6. Bake about 20 minutes, shaking the pan to turn the meatballs halfway through, until no longer pink on the inside.

SERVES 4

Max Menendez's Mexican Meatballs

"We have a big Mexican community here," Max Menendez says. "The first generation immigrants tend to stay close to their roots, and each other. Their children assimilate and their grandchildren, like me, are interested in the culture that got lost along the way." When he was in graduate school, Mr. Menendez spent a lot of time in his grandmother's kitchen, learning her recipes. "These meatballs," he says, "are great party food, and if you serve them with rice and beans, they are a fine meal."

FOR THE MEATBALLS

¼ cup fine dry bread crumbs

½ cup milk

½ cup olive oil

1 medium onion, finely chopped

1 green bell pepper, stemmed, seeded, and finely chopped

2 pounds 85% lean ground beef

1 pound ground pork

½ cup cooked white rice, cold

2 large eggs, lightly beaten

2 teaspoons kosher salt

1 teaspoon freshly ground black pepper

¼ teaspoon freshly grated nutmeg

FOR THE SAUCE

1 tablespoon olive oil

4 garlic cloves, minced

One 28-ounce can whole tomatoes

1 cup water, plus more as needed

¾ teaspoon dried oregano (preferably Mexican)

Kosher salt and freshly ground black pepper

1. To make the meatballs: In a small bowl, combine the bread crumbs with the milk.

2. In a large skillet, heat 2 tablespoons of the oil in a heavy skillet over medium-low heat. Add the onion and bell pepper and cook about 4 minutes, until soft. Transfer to a large bowl and cool to room temperature.

3. Squeeze the milk from the bread crumbs and add them to the onion mixture. Add the beef, pork, rice, eggs, salt, pepper, and nutmeg. Use two forks to combine, working quickly and delicately in order to avoid overworking the meat. Form the mixture into 1-inch balls. Place on a tray, cover with plastic wrap, and refrigerate for 1 hour.

4. Meanwhile, make the sauce: In a medium saucepan, heat the oil over low heat. Add the garlic and cook, stirring constantly, about 1 minute until aromatic. Using your hands, crush the tomatoes and add them to the pan. Add the water and oregano, bring to a simmer, and cook for 10 minutes. Season with salt and pepper to taste, cover, and keep warm.

5. To cook the meatballs, heat the remaining 6 tablespoons oil in a large skillet over high heat. Add the one-third of the meatballs and cook for 6 to 8 minutes, until well browned on all sides. Transfer to a large plate and repeat with the remaining meatballs in two batches.

6. Pour off the fat left in the skillet and return all the meatballs to the pan. Add the sauce. Bring to a simmer, cover, and cook over low heat for 20 to 30 minutes, until the meatballs are no longer pink on the inside, adding water as needed if the sauce gets too thick. Serve.

SERVE 8 TO 10

Everything but the Squeal: Beef, Buffalo, Game, Lamb, and Pork

MICHELLE COMPARETTI ZEIKERT'S
REAL ITALIAN MEATBALLS

Michelle Comparetti Zeikert says her German mother learned how to make Italian meatballs and sauce from her mother-in-law, Mary Comparetti—and she learned so well that people in their Italian neighborhood on Long Island never suspected that a non-Italian hand was at work. When she and her husband moved to Chicago, the Italian shopkeepers sized up Ms. Zeikert as one of them, she says, but the things they gave her to taste were different from what she was accustomed to in New York. "We roast chicken with herbs and garlic; in Chicago, they stew chicken with lemon and potatoes on top and call it chicken Vesuvio, which I love." Meatballs and gravy are more about family than they are about region, she says. "Whenever I get homesick for New York Italian, I make a big pot of my mother's Sunday 'gravy' and a hundred meatballs. I've added a few things. I use fresh basil rather than dried, shallots rather than onions, adobo seasoning, anise, and the best grated cheese I can afford. We are on a budget, just as my family was when I was growing up," Ms. Zeikert says, "but I have learned that spending on cheese is always worth the investment."

FOR THE BREAD CRUMBS

Two ½-inch slices stale Italian bread

3 tablespoons (³⁄₈ stick) unsalted butter

1 shallot, finely chopped

1 garlic clove, minced

1 teaspoon dried Greek oregano

½ teaspoon kosher salt

¼ teaspoon cayenne pepper

FOR THE MEATBALLS

Milk, as needed

½ cup plus 1 teaspoon olive oil

½ cup finely chopped onion

2½ pounds mixed ground beef, veal, and pork

1 to 2 large eggs, lightly beaten

½ cup chopped fresh basil

½ teaspoon ground fennel seeds

1 teaspoon garlic powder

1½ teaspoons kosher salt

½ teaspoon freshly ground black pepper

Pinch of freshly ground white pepper

1 teaspoon adobo seasoning

½ teaspoon tomato paste

¼ cup grated Parmesan or pecorino Romano cheese

1. To make the bread crumbs: In a food processor, pulse the bread until medium-fine crumbs form. In a large skillet, melt the butter over medium heat. Add the shallot and garlic and cook about 1 minute, until aromatic. Stir in the bread crumbs, oregano, salt, and cayenne and cook for 5 to 7 minutes, until golden brown. Transfer the bread crumbs to a small bowl and cool to room temperature.

2. To make the meatballs: Add milk to the bread crumbs 1 tablespoon at a time at 1-minute intervals, until the crumbs are soft but not soupy. (The mixture should be the consistency of thick Cream of Wheat.)

3. Heat 1 teaspoon of the oil in a small skillet over medium heat. Add the onion and cook about 4 minutes, until soft. Cool to room temperature.

4. In a large bowl, break up the meat with a spoon. Put the onion and 1 of the eggs in the center of the meat along with the basil and gently incorporate. Add the fennel, garlic powder, salt, black and white peppers, adobo seasoning, and tomato paste to the meat and mix gently.

5. Gently add the cheese and the bread crumb mixture, adding crumbs only as needed until it is cohesive and smooth. You may not need all the bread crumbs. (If you have added all the crumbs and the mixture is still crumbly or loose, add the remaining egg.) Cover the bowl and let the meat rest in refrigerator for up to 30 minutes.

6. Place an oven rack in the center position and preheat the oven to 350°F.

7. With wet hands, form the meat into 2-inch-balls.

8. Heat the remaining ½ cup oil in a large skillet over medium heat. Add half of the meatballs and cook for 6 to 8 minutes, turning until browned on all sides. Transfer the meatballs to a rimmed baking sheet. Repeat with the remaining meatballs.

9. Bake the meatballs about 25 minutes, until they are no longer pink on the inside.

———

SERVES 6 TO 8

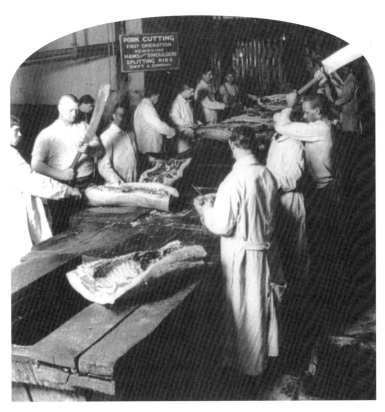

Swift & Co. packing house, Chicago, 1905.

MIKE MAGNELLI'S RIFF ON ITALIAN "GRAVY"

The son of Sicilian immigrants, Michael Magnelli grew up thinking that "gravy" is red and meaty and is generally served over pasta. After graduating from the Boston Conservatory, he played guitar for Frank Sinatra Jr. and in Broadway shows, and he continues to travel and perform—and cook. "Give me a crowd and a stove and I am going to cook," he says. "Both my parents cooked. I learned the basics from my mother. After that, my tastes were shaped by living on the road and eating with a lot of different people." The result has often been riffs on the dishes of his youth, like this gravy. He omits ground beef and pork and uses sliced steak to create a light but intensely meaty tomato sauce.

1 whole head garlic

3 tablespoons olive oil

1 pound sirloin or flank steak, sliced thinly

Kosher salt and freshly ground black pepper

4 large Roma (plum) tomatoes, chopped

2 teaspoons red pepper flakes

3 tablespoons capers, rinsed

1 cup water

1 bunch fresh basil, leaves only, finely chopped

1. Preheat the oven to 350°F.

2. Trim the stem end and remove about ¼-inch from the top of the garlic head. Place the garlic on aluminum foil and drizzle with 1 tablespoon of the olive oil. Wrap tightly and bake for 30 minutes or until the cloves are soft to the touch. Remove from the oven and let cool.

3. Heat the remaining olive oil in a large, deep pot. Season the steak slices with salt and pepper and add them to the pot in one layer. Cook on medium-high heat, turning occasionally, until lightly browned on all sides, 3 to 4 minutes.

4. Add the tomatoes, red pepper flakes, and capers and lower the heat to medium-low. Simmer for 15 minutes.

5. While the meat is simmering, separate the roasted garlic cloves. Peel them and add to the meat. Stir well.

6. Add the water and simmer 20 minutes more.

7. Remove from the heat and stir in the basil. Serve over your favorite pasta.

SERVES 4 TO 6

One Big Table

Olga Peters's Transylvanian Goulash

One Sunday a month, Olga Peters's thirteen grandchildren (give or take a child) and occasionally their parents descend upon her kitchen to learn her Hungarian recipes. Standing in her small kitchen, a tiny, white-haired beacon in a blizzard of activity, she delights in the chaos. Her wobbly pots that were grocery give-always in the 1950s hold goulash for an army. The steam fogs the window, obscuring the half-acre garden Mrs. Peters has tended since she was married in 1938.

"We see each other regularly now," says one of Olga's grandsons, Marty Cingle Jr., who teaches math and coaches basketball at a local junior high and organized the family's cooking lessons. "It's become automatic. You don't have to think about it, you just show up." But show up hungry. A dozen sets of hands can produce a feast.

2 tablespoons lard

1 medium onion, finely chopped

1 garlic clove, minced

1 tablespoon sweet Hungarian paprika

3 cups homemade chicken broth or low-sodium store-bought chicken broth

2 pounds pork shoulder, trimmed and cut into 1-inch cubes

2 cups drained sauerkraut

½ teaspoon caraway seeds

¼ cup tomato juice

2 tablespoons all-purpose flour

1 cup sour cream

Kosher salt and freshly ground black pepper

1. Melt the lard in a large pot over medium heat. Add the onion and garlic and cook, stirring occasionally, until the onion is translucent, about 6 minutes.

2. Add the paprika and ½ cup of the broth and bring to a boil. Add the pork and simmer, covered, for 1 hour.

3. Add the sauerkraut, caraway seeds, tomato juice, and the remaining broth to the pot. Return to a simmer, cover, and cook for 1 hour more, until the meat is tender.

4. Whisk the flour and sour cream together and carefully stir into the pot. Simmer for 10 minutes. Season with salt and pepper to taste and serve.

SERVES 4 TO 6

Everything but the Squeal: Beef, Buffalo, Game, Lamb, and Pork

Shahnaz Ahmad's Keema Mattar
Pakistani Ground Meat

PHOENIX, ARIZONA

Growing up in a Punjabi household in Pakistan, Shahnaz Ahmad was a reluctant cook. "My mother forced me to learn. She says that you can't survive if you can't cook, but cooking was my least favorite thing to do." When she moved to the United States and began a family of her own, however, she was so frustrated by her "second rate" dishes that she corresponded with her mother and cooked from the letters she received in return. "When my children were young, their favorite dish was keema mattar. It's easy to make, and if you use a pressure cooker, it can be quick, too. The dish is more like my mother's when I make it on top of the stove—and now that my children are grown, I cook it that way when they come home to visit. I am still not in love with cooking, but I love to make my family and friends happy—and for some reason, my cooking does that and that is why I cook."

You can use any sort of ground meat—goat, lamb, even chicken—for this dish.

2 pounds lean ground beef

1 large onion, finely chopped

4 garlic cloves, minced

2 teaspoons kosher salt

1 teaspoon cayenne pepper

Pinch of ground turmeric

¼ cup vegetable oil

2 cups shelled fresh or frozen green peas

2 plum tomatoes, cored and finely chopped

1 serrano chile, stemmed, seeded, and finely chopped

1½ teaspoons grated fresh ginger

1½ teaspoons ground cumin

1 teaspoon ground coriander

½ cup chopped fresh cilantro, for garnish

1. Combine the ground beef, onion, garlic, salt, cayenne, and turmeric in a heavy-bottomed pot and cook over medium-high heat, stirring constantly and breaking up clumps of ground beef. When the texture is fine, cover, and reduce the heat to medium-low. Cook for 15 to 20 minutes, until the liquid from the meat and onion has cooked away.

2. Add the oil and cook about 5 minutes, stirring to keep it from sticking.

3. Add the peas, tomatoes, chile, and ginger. Cover and cook over medium-low heat for 5 to 7 minutes, until peas are done and tomatoes are incorporated.

4. Stir in the cumin and coriander and remove from the heat. Garnish with cilantro and serve.

SERVES 6 TO 8

456

One Big Table

AMERICAN ICON: HAMBURGER

WHEN AMERICANS SAY "HAMBURGER," THEY MEAN THE sandwich, not just the meat patty, and they mean something deeply and uniquely American. In fact, many lay claim to the creation of the hamburger. The Akron County Fair theory, for instance, wherein a 27-year-old concessionaire named Frank Menches supplemented

his dwindling supply of sausage by using ground beef in his patties in 1892, ignores the fact that ground beefsteak was popular in Hamburg, Germany, more than fifty years earlier. It also overlooks a similar dish that appears on an 1836 menu from Delmonico's restaurant in New York City. And what are we to make of the butter-fried beef patty sandwiches that were allegedly served at a fair in Seymour, Wisconsin, in 1885? Locals insist that butter burgers are the *ur*-burger. People in New Haven, on the other hand, claim that one Louis Lassen served the "first" burger at his New Haven lunch counter in 1900. The people of Missouri insist that burgers were minted at the St. Louis World's Fair of 1904, while the first White Castle (1921) in Wichita, Kansas, seems to give the Jayhawks bragging rights.

George Motz, whose documentary film and book, *Hamburger America*, established him as one the nation's preeminent philosophers of burgers, believes that context, more than history, explains the variety in the nation's burger experience. The

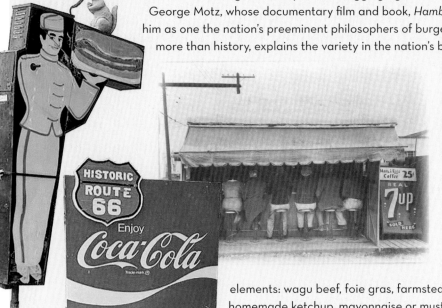

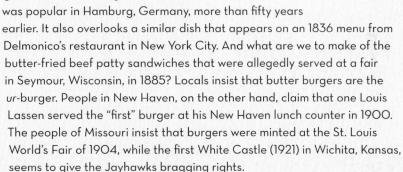

exigencies of a backyard grill beg for a thick burger, while the demands of the democratic challenge of feeding the most people the fastest naturally led fast-food chains to develop thin patties and sliders. And what serious chef could lend his name to a burger without first supplying one or more of the following elements: wagu beef, foie gras, farmstead cheese, artisanal bread, homemade ketchup, mayonnaise or mustard, and microgreens.

BILL AND CHERYL JAMISON'S GREEN CHILE CHEESEBURGERS

TESUQUE, NEW MEXICO

Of the hundreds of regional burger variations nationwide, New Mexico's green chile cheeseburger is the most enduring and irresistible celebration of place. A staple of diners, drive-throughs, filling stations, food trucks, and upscale restaurants, the burger is as ubiquitous as it is audacious. In 2008, Cheryl Jamison studied over 8,000 nominations for the state's best version, sampled each and then charted her course through the "Land of Enchantment" to create a map of the green chile cheeseburger trail. She also helped inaugurate the Governor's Green Chile Cheeseburger at the state fair. In addition to writing award-winning cookbooks, such as *Smoke & Spice* and *The Border Cookbook*, Mrs. Jamison, along with her husband Bill, teach cooking in their home in Tesuque and claim that the best green chile cheeseburgers are made from hand-cut beef chuck, cheddar cheese, and freshly roasted New Mexico green chiles, the long green Anaheim variety that are sometimes called Hatch for the town where many are grown and roasted. Purists insist that the patty with melted cheese and roasted peppers should be served on a plain bun and state that those who wish to have lettuce or tomato should order a salad. Condiments such as catsup and mayonnaise are, in the green chile cheeseburger ontology, referred to as adulterants.

Winner of 2009 Green Chile Cheeseburger Challenge, Badland's Burger, Grants, New Mexico.

FOR THE SAUCE

½ cup mayonnaise

½ cup prepared barbecue sauce

FOR THE BURGERS

2¼ pounds freshly ground beef chuck

1 teaspoon salt

½ teaspoon ground black pepper

3 ½-inch-thick onion slices

Vegetable oil for basting

3 New Mexico green chiles

12 thin slices cheddar cheese, room temperature

6 hamburger buns, split

1. **Prepare a wood-fired barbecue. Whisk mayonnaise and barbecue sauce in small bowl to blend. Cover and chill for thirty minues.**

2. **Mix the ground chuck with 1 teaspoon salt and ½ teaspoon pepper just to blend (do not overmix). Form the meat into six 1½-inch-thick patties. Cover and let stand at room temperature 30 minutes.**

3. **Run a metal skewer horizontally through center of each onion slice. Brush the onion slices lightly with vegetable oil to coat lightly. Rub the chiles with oil. Transfer the onions and chiles to barbecue. Grill onions until softened and browned, about 5 minutes per side. Remove skewers from onions. Chop onions; transfer to small bowl. Char chiles until blackened on all sides. Enclose chiles in paper bag 10 minutes. Peel, seed, and chop chiles, combine with the onions, and season to taste with salt and pepper.**

4. **Sprinkle the beef patties with salt and pepper and grill until cooked, about 4 minutes per side for medium. Top each burger with 2 cheese slices during the last minute of cooking. Place bottom halves of rolls on work surface. Divide chile-onion mixture among rolls. Place cheese burgers on top of the chile-onion mixture. Spread 1 tablespoon mayonnaise-barbecue sauce over cheese, cover with bun tops, and serve, passing remaining sauce.**

MAKES 6 BURGERS

Everything but the Squeal: Beef, Buffalo, Game, Lamb, and Pork

Mamie Meyer's Veal Milanese

Mamie Meyers, a retired elementary school teacher recalls: "When I was growing up in the 1930s, it was all Italian up on the hill, the tallest point in the city. Back then, you might go to the Italian butcher and vegetable man, but that was the extent of interaction. The lady who helped my mother, Nel Faida, that was her name, went up the hill on Thursday to provision. She got this recipe from the meat cutter up there. Sometimes she served the chop with spaghetti, but I liked it best with salad. Mother had a vegetable garden. We thought it was exotic to have, basically, a schnitzel with the bone on it. When I went to Italy on my honeymoon I was served arugula and I looked at it and said, "Oh, dear, they know we are Americans and they are serving us weeds," but I liked it better than the red-leaf lettuce we had at home and I've used it ever since."

FOR THE VEAL

1 cup fine dry bread crumbs

3 tablespoons chopped fresh parsley

2 tablespoons grated Parmesan cheese

½ teaspoon kosher salt

¼ teaspoon freshly ground pepper

½ cup buttermilk

½ cup milk

Four 8-ounce bone-in veal loin chops, pounded thin

1 cup olive oil

FOR THE SALAD

1 tablespoon fresh lemon juice

¼ teaspoon kosher salt

⅛ teaspoon freshly ground black pepper

3 tablespoons olive oil

8 cups lightly packed baby arugula

3 ounces Parmesan cheese, thinly shaved

1. To make the veal: Place an oven rack in the center position and preheat the oven to 450°F. Place a wire rack on a rimmed baking sheet.

2. In a shallow dish, combine the bread crumbs, parsley, cheese, salt, and pepper. In a second shallow dish, combine the buttermilk and milk. Dip the chops in the milk, then coat with the crumbs. Set aside in a single layer on a large piece of waxed paper until all the chops have been coated.

3. Heat the oil in a large skillet over medium heat. Add the chops, working in batches if necessary, and cook about 8 minutes, until golden brown on both sides. Transfer the chops to the wire rack.

4. Bake the chops for 10 minutes, until rosy in the middle. Remove from the oven and let rest on the rack for 5 minutes.

5. To make the salad: In a large bowl, combine the lemon juice, salt, and pepper. Slowly whisk in the oil. Add the arugula and toss to coat with dressing. Add the shaved cheese and combine.

6. To serve, place a veal chop on each dinner plate and a portion of salad on top of the chop.

SERVES 4

Helena Litke's Schnitzel with Paprika Cream and Dumplings

Lena Litke was born Helena Doroty Knopff in 1900 in Whitehorse, Yukon, Canada, one of four children. Her parents were of German and Russian descent. She worked as a nurse most of her life and married Gustav Litke in 1918. The couple moved first to Gothenburg, Nebraska, then to Shaddock, Oklahoma, where their descendants still farm and still prepare this rich family recipe.

FOR THE VEAL

4 slices bacon

Four 6-ounce veal sirloin steaks

Kosher salt and freshly ground black pepper

½ cup all-purpose flour

1 small onion, finely chopped

1 teaspoon sweet paprika

1 cup sour cream

½ cup tomato sauce, fresh or high quality canned

FOR THE DUMPLINGS

2 cups sifted all-purpose flour

4 teaspoons baking powder

1 teaspoon kosher salt

¼ teaspoon freshly ground black pepper

1 large egg, well beaten

3 tablespoons (⅜ stick) unsalted butter, melted

⅔ cup milk

1. To make the veal: Fry the bacon in a large skillet over medium-low heat about 10 minutes, until crisp. Using a slotted spoon, transfer the slices to a paper towel—lined plate.

2. Pat the veal dry and season with salt and pepper. Dredge the meat in the flour and shake off the excess. Reheat the bacon fat in the skillet over medium heat. Add the veal and cook for 4 to 6 minutes, until well browned on both sides.

3. Add the onion and paprika and cook for 6 to 8 minutes, until golden brown. Stir in the sour cream, and tomato sauce. Season with salt and pepper to taste. Remove from the heat.

4. To make the dumplings: In a large bowl, whisk together the flour, baking powder, salt, and pepper. Stir in the egg, melted butter, and milk to make a moist but stiff batter.

5. Return the skillet to medium-low heat. Drop tablespoon-size portions of the dumpling batter on top, cover, and cook about 18 minutes, until the dumplings are cooked through. Crumble the bacon and sprinkle it over the top. Serve.

SERVES 4

461

Everything but the Squeal: Beef, Buffalo, Game, Lamb, and Pork

THE CHILI COOKOFF

FOUNDED IN 1967 BY RACE CAR DRIVER AND AUTOMOTIVE
designer Carroll Shelby, the three-thousand-member International
Chili Society is a nonprofit organization that sanctions chili cookoffs
around the United States by providing rules,
regulations, and judges. It supports about two
hundred qualifying cookoffs a year, in three
categories—red chili, salsa, and *chili verde* (green chili)—all leading up
to its World's Championship Chili Cookoff. The Society felt that comparing green and
red chilies was like comparing apples with oranges, so the first Chili Verde competition
was organized in New Mexico. Several years ago the chili world was rocked when a
chili head from Massachusetts took first place in the annual cookoff.

Traditionally, the chili belt ran from California and Texas, through Arizona, New
Mexico, and Nevada, then across the Midwest, but like many regional dishes in the
post-Food TV era, chili is less about a place than a state of mind. Preferences vary
by region: In Florida, the dish is sweeter than others and sports lots of tomato sauce;
in Cincinnati, sweet spices like cinnamon and allspice take the stage. Texas, New
Mexico, and California like it hot, often adding cayenne and habanero peppers to
their brew; while in northern Minnesota, the Dakotas, and Nebraska, chilis are more homey and less
spicy. Colorado and New Mexico use peppers that are still green, and green chili is usually made with
chicken, lamb, or pork, instead of beef.

ROD OKUNO'S GREEN CHILI

DENVER, COLORADO

Before World War II, when they were sent to a relocation camp in Arizona, the Okuno family owned a thriving restaurant, the Holly Ho in Los Angeles. When they were released, in 1945, the family moved to Denver, a city that was working hard to welcome Japanese families. They began rebuilding their life by opening a diner on Twentieth Street and selling roasted nori (seaweed) to fellow Japanese people and slowly wooed the general population with the classics from their Holly Ho days. As the clientele grew, so did requests for meatloaf, macaroni, and chicken fried steak to the menu of the Twentieth Street Café. Today the walls of the café, hung with sixty years' worth of pictures of politicians, sports figures, and other local heroes, read like a history book. And the huevos rancheros and other dishes inspired by the increasing number of Latino people who have moved into the neighborhood are a testament to how alive and constant history is. Rod Okuno, the third generation at the helm of the café, perfected this green chili, which is a perennial winner of the local Best Cheap Eats Award. Mr. Okuno sees the accolades as less about chili than they are about family—had there been a "best of nori" award, his great-grandfather would certainly have claimed it. His humble opinion does not, however, change the fact that this is a great version of green chili. The recipe makes a large amount and makes a great meal for a crowd. It is also good for smothering burritos, eggs, or other grilled meat.

20 cups water

1 4–5-pound pork butt (bone in)

Salt and pepper to taste

1 large yellow onion, diced

6 cups roasted and diced green chiles

2 cups tomato sauce (fresh or high quality canned)

1 cup minced jalapeño chiles

1 tablespoon garlic powder

1 teaspoon dried oregano

1 teaspoon powdered cumin

1 teaspoons chicken bouillon

Cornstarch for thickening

1. The day before serving, preheat the oven to 400°. Season the pork butt on all sides with salt and freshly ground black pepper and roast for 3½ hours. Remove from the oven and cool, then use a sharp knife to roughly chop the pork. Reserve the meat and the bone.

2. Bring the water and the bone to a simmer in a tall pot. Add the pork, onion, chiles, tomato sauce, jalapeños, garlic powder, oregano, cumin, and bouillon. Bring to a boil, reduce the heat to simmer and simmer, uncovered, for one hour. Remove the bone and discard, refrigerate over night.

3. Remove the pot from the refrigerator and lift off excess fat. Return to low heat. Combine one tablespoon of cornstarch with ½ cup of the cool broth and beat well to create a smooth mixture. When the chili is simmering, slowly whisk in the cornstarch, stirring well between each addition, to desired thickness. The Twentieth Street Café prefers the chili soupy.

SERVES UP TO 20

Everything but the Squeal: Beef, Buffalo, Game, Lamb, and Pork

Jerry Buma's Booma's Revenge Chili

NORTHBRIDGE, MASSACHUSETTS

Jerry Buma was the first northeasterner to win the International Chili Society's World's Championship. "I got a lot of e-mails asking if I put lobster in my chili," says the former marine. Lobster, indeed. He caught the chili bug thirteen years ago when he was working as a bartender. "A buddy of mine was a member of the International Chili Society and asked me to go to a cookoff in New Haven." After sampling a variety of chilis, he decided he could do better.

Mr. Buma, who taught himself how to cook using electric skillets and hot plates in his barracks while serving in the Marine Corps, says that if you plan to serve his prize-winning chili with salted crackers or corn chips, you should add a half teaspoon less salt to the spice mix. And allow the chili to cool down slightly before you serve it. If it's served steaming hot, he says, some of the complexities of the chiles will be lost. If you prefer your chili with beans, serve them on the side.

One 4-ounce can whole roasted green chiles, drained and seeded

3 garlic cloves

One 10.5-ounce can double-strength beef broth (preferably Campbell's Condensed Beef Broth)

1½ teaspoons cayenne pepper (or less if you want mild chili)

2 tablespoons mild California or Anaheim chile powder

2 tablespoons hot New Mexico chile powder

2 tablespoons mild New Mexico chile powder

2 tablespoons ancho chile powder

2½ teaspoons kosher salt

1½ teaspoons sugar

2½ teaspoon garlic powder

3 tablespoons onion powder

3 tablespoons freshly ground cumin

1 teaspoon dried Mexican oregano

Salt-free store-bought chicken broth, as needed

3 pounds beef tri-tip, cut into ⅜-inch dice

One 8-ounce can tomato sauce (preferably Hunt's)

Tabasco sauce

1. Combine the roasted chiles, garlic, beef broth, cayenne, chile powders, salt, sugar, garlic and onion powders, cumin, and oregano in a blender and liquefy, adding enough chicken broth to keep the process going.

2. Sauté the meat in several batches, stirring almost constantly, until cooked through and no longer pink. Do not brown. Drain and rinse the meat well to remove all cooking solids and ensure a smooth gravy.

3. Transfer the meat to a large, heavy pot and add half of the spice mixture and enough chicken broth to just cover the meat. Cover the pot and cook slowly over low heat for 1 hour, stirring occasionally. Add chicken broth as needed to just cover the meat with liquid.

4. Add the rest of the spice mixture and simmer for 30 minutes, again adding broth as necessary.

5. Add tomato sauce and simmer 30 minutes more. The meat should be tender but if necessary, cook a little longer. Add Tabasco to taste.

SERVES 6 TO 8

NOTE: Unlike the chili powders generally found at the grocery store, pure ground chiles make the meal. See Resources for suppliers.

SAM ARNOLD'S BUFFALO BURGERS

In the late 1950s, Samuel P. Arnold, an advertising executive in New York City, caught the Wild West bug. The origins of his infatuation have never been clear, but its effect was profound. He left New York City, purchased an ugly, old motel on a gorgeous plot in the red sandstone about an hour outside Denver, built a sprawling adobe replica of Bent's Fort, Colorado's first fur-trading post, and began to champion the region's history, indigenous culture, and cooking with the passion that only an outsider can summon. He soon opened a restaurant that became famous for its buffalo, elk, and other game, and for its historical menus. The food cognoscenti made regular pilgrimages: James Beard and Craig Claiborne and Julia Child sucked on the restaurant's broiled buffalo marrow bones in the dining room, while upstairs in Arnold's home, his young daughter, Holly, played with Sissy Bear, their adopted Canadian black bear. After school, Holly made flour porridge with butter, cinnamon, and honey for Sissy Bear and herself. She and her brother, Keith,

spent hours scavenging for arrowheads and listening to her father's friend, Big Cloud, a Lakota Indian chief who lived with the family and was known to most as Toothless Charlie.

When Ms. Arnold was ten, she made her debut as tortilla maker in the restaurant kitchen. By then, her mother was deeply involved with preserving and protecting Native American culture and was building the Tesoro Cultural Center at the Fort. Her father studied with James Beard, amassed three thousand cookbooks, and became the country's foremost authority on the cooking of the Santa Fe trail.

Since her parents passed away, Holly Arnold Kinney has been running the restaurant and Tesoro Cultural Center. "The Fort serves more than seventy thousand buffalo dinners a year, steaks, prime rib, buffalo hump, tongue, sausage, and 'Rocky Mountain oysters,'" she says, "but upstairs we ate mostly burgers. Buffalo burgers, with my father's secret sauce."

465

Everything but the Squeal: Beef, Buffalo, Game, Lamb, and Pork

1 cup mayonnaise

½ cup chili sauce

1½ pounds 88% lean ground buffalo

Kosher salt and freshly ground black pepper

4 hamburger rolls (preferably sourdough onion)

4 green chiles, roasted, peeled, and stemmed

½ sweet onion such as Vidalia, Walla Walla, Maui, or Texas Sweet, thinly sliced into rings

1. Heat a grill or cast-iron skillet over medium-high heat.

2. In a small bowl, combine the mayonnaise and chili sauce.

3. Form the meat into four equal burgers by hand or using a clean tuna can with the top and bottom removed. Season with salt and pepper.

4. Cook the burgers for 6 to 8 minutes, until well browned on both sides and cooked to the desired doneness. Transfer the burgers to a plate.

5. Grill the buns for 1 to 3 minutes, until lightly browned.

6. Transfer the buns to four individual plates and slather with the sauce. Place a burger on each bun, top each with a green chile and some onion, and serve.

SERVES 4

SEBASTIEN BONNEAU'S GRILLED RABBIT WITH PARSLEY BUTTER

Sebastien Bonneau grew up on the outskirts of Bordeaux, France. Like most of their neighbors, his parents had a kitchen garden and raised chickens, rabbits, and pigs. His father was a pastry chef, and after Mr. Bonneau completed his own pastry training, he was offered a job in Texas. Life on the Rio Grande was substantially different from on the Garonne River in southwest France, but after marrying a Texan, his life began to echo that of his parents. Along with his wife, Esther, and their young daughter, Margaux, he moved to an eight-acre farm outside Austin, and the Old World began sliding into the Wild West. The ducks came first. "We wanted a healthy, kind, humane way of life," says Mr. Bonneau, who speaks country-boy English with a French accent. "Free-range, nonmedicated, hormone-free poultry and rabbit." Two years later, rabbits, guinea hens, geese, turkey, quail, pheasant, and peacocks joined the ranks, and the couple's Creekside Farm had become a fixture in the Austin farmers' market.

"You can panfry the rabbit pieces in a cast-iron skillet in this recipe," he says, "but grilling is more fun."

One 3- to 3½-pound rabbit, cut into 6 pieces
Kosher salt and freshly ground black pepper
¼ cup olive oil
¾ cup chopped fresh parsley
4 tablespoons (½ stick) unsalted butter, melted
4 garlic cloves, minced
1 tablespoon fresh lemon juice

1. Preheat a grill to medium. Liberally sprinkle the rabbit with salt and pepper.

2. When the fire is ready, rub the rabbit pieces with olive oil and place on the grill. Cook on one side for 5 to 10 minutes until they begin to brown, turn pieces and grill other side for 5 to 10 minutes. Cook until meat is browned and cooked through. (Smaller pieces such as the front legs will take less time than larger loin pieces.)

3. Transfer the rabbit to a platter, cover loosely with foil, and let rest for 5 minutes.

4. In a small bowl, combine the parsley, butter, garlic, lemon juice, and 1 teaspoon salt. Spoon the sauce over the rabbit and serve.

SERVES 4

Guy Hymel Jr.'s Smothered Rabbit with Brown Gravy and Onions

WHITE CASTLE, LOUISIANA

"What others use as bait or try to exterminate," Guy Hymel Jr. says, "Louisianans use as the main ingredient in bayou delicacies" such as crawfish, opossum, raccoon, nutria, and tree perch [squirrel, for the uninitiated]. "We cook it all, Boo! If we don't know what it is, we just heat up a pot of rice and put it on top. I grew up, went to school, learned to hunt, and I learned to cook from Guy Sr.; I taught Guy III; and he's teaching Guy IV. Wild game cooking in Louisiana is generational. It's in our DNA."

He grew up eating squirrel, wood ducks, and deer. Though Mr. Hymel prefers to hunt deer because he "gets more for the bang," everything is fair game. Smothered rabbit with brown gravy and onions, rabbit sauce piquant, and rabbit spaghetti are just a few of his specialties. But he only cooks swamp rabbits, he says, not the cottontails, because he prefers the larger size.

One 3- to 3½-pound rabbit, cut into 6 pieces, backbone reserved and cut into 4 pieces

6 garlic cloves, peeled

Creole seasoning (preferably Tony Chachere's)

1 cup vegetable oil

½ cup all-purpose flour

1 medium onion, finely chopped

2 celery stalks, finely chopped

¼ cup finely chopped green bell pepper

1 quart water

1 tablespoon tomato paste (optional)

Kosher salt and freshly ground black pepper

1. Make a small slit on each piece of meat and stuff it with garlic. Pat the rabbit dry and season with the Creole seasoning.

2. Heat ½ cup of the vegetable oil in a cast-iron pot over medium-high heat. Add the rabbit and cook for 4 to 6 minutes, until dark brown on both sides. Transfer to a plate. Pour off the oil in the pan.

3. Heat the remaining ½ cup oil in the pot over medium-high heat. Whisk in the flour and cook about 10 minutes, stirring constantly, until dark brown.

4. Add the onion, celery, bell pepper, water, and tomato paste (if using) and bring to a simmer.

5. Return the rabbit to the pan, cover the pan with foil and the lid, and cook for 45 minutes to 1 hour, until tender. Season with salt and pepper to taste and serve.

SERVES 4

One Big Table

Bow Hunter's Venison Loin with Savory Wine Sauce

ELDORADO SPRINGS, MISSOURI

Like his father, Mike Longerhofer is a self-proclaimed cowboy who spent twenty-five years herding cattle in the rolling hills of western Missouri. He's lived in rural areas most of his life and started hunting as a child. It's always been about survival, not sport. Bow hunting, he says, equalizes the hunter and the hunted. His voice becomes emotional as he continues. "By its very nature, [it] forces the hunter to step back in time, to rely on his hunter-gatherer instincts. I am far more dependent upon my skills for my success and safety, more vulnerable than when I rifle hunt. Bow hunting makes me appreciate the vastness and power of the natural world, how small, yet connected, I am. I feel the woods on a misty morning the way a surfer feels waves on the ocean or a climber feels the mountain. Bow hunting teaches you who you are. I bow hunted for three years before I got my first kill. You feel like you earn the kill when you hunt with a bow; you also feel connected to something primal, an ancient rite. Dressing the animal is part of the ritual, an act of respect. I don't kill unless I am going to eat it.

"I've started to teach bow hunting and a few of us now are hunting and taking the meat to food banks. This crisis in unemployment, more people need food, but food donations are down. What a privilege it is to make a difference that way. I don't believe I've ever dressed an animal that wouldn't be proud to feed hungry people."

Mr. Longerhofer adds this advice: "I don't cook venison unless I've marinated it. My wife Carla and I figured that out. We cook together."

FOR THE VENISON

1 cup olive oil

2 carrots, finely chopped

2 celery stalks, finely chopped

½ cup finely chopped onion

4 garlic cloves, minced

2 fresh thyme sprigs

2 bay leaves

One 3-pound bone-in venison loin

Kosher salt and freshly ground black pepper

2 tablespoons clarified butter or vegetable oil

FOR THE SAUCE

3 cups homemade beef broth or low-sodium store-bought beef broth

2 tablespoon (¼ stick) unsalted butter

1 shallot, finely chopped

1 garlic clove, minced

1 fresh thyme sprig

2 tomatoes, cored and coarsely chopped

¼ cup port

3 tablespoons sherry vinegar

2 tablespoons red currant jelly

Kosher salt and freshly ground black pepper

1. To make the marinade: The day before serving, combine the oil, carrots, celery, onion, garlic, thyme, and bay leaves, in a large baking dish.

2. Bone the venison loin. Trim and discard the fat and sinew. With a cleaver, chop the bone into 1-inch pieces and reserve for the sauce. Slice the loin against the grain into six pieces. Arrange them in a single layer in the baking dish, turn to coat with the marinade, cover, and refrigerate for 24 hours.

3. To make the sauce: In a small saucepan, bring the broth to a boil, reduce the heat, and cook until reduced by half.

4. Melt the butter in a large saucepan over high heat. Add the reserved bones and cook for 8 to 10 minutes, until well browned. Add the shallot, garlic, and thyme and cook until soft and lightly colored. Add the tomatoes and cook for 2 minutes. Add the port and vinegar, bring to boil, and reduce by half. Add the reduced broth and the currant jelly. Reduce the heat to low, cover, and cook for 1 hour, skimming as necessary.

5. Remove from the heat and strain. Season with salt and pepper to taste. Refrigerate until needed.

6. To cook the venison, place an oven rack in the center position and preheat the oven to 400°F.

7. Remove the venison from the marinade, pat dry, and season with salt and pepper. Heat the clarified butter in a large ovenproof skillet over medium-high heat. Add the venison and cook for 6 to 8 minutes or until well browned on both sides. Transfer the pan to the oven and roast for 5 to 7 minutes, to the desired doneness (110°F on an instant-read thermometer for rare; 120°F for medium rare).

8. Transfer the venison to a carving board and let rest for 5 minutes. Gently reheat the sauce. Slice each piece of meat against the grain into three or four pieces and serve with the sauce.

SERVES 6

Mico and Josip Jakšic's Croatian Venison Gulaš

Josip Jakšic was born in Wisconsin, but his license plate reads CROAT. Croatian music booms through the cab of his pickup when he drives to his hunting grounds about forty-five minutes outside Milwaukee. The fields are inhabited by the same type of whitetail deer as those found in Croatia, and like most Croatian ex-pats, Josip hunts in November and December. His father, Mico, stays in town to run Domines Deer Processing, one of the few shops that can still skin, cut, grind, and wrap deer, bear, elk, caribou, moose, and antelope. Samples of each usually show up at the Croatian Eagles Soccer Club's annual wild game banquet, often as goulash. "It is the ultimate comfort food," says Josip. "You can use about any cut of tough meat, make it in big quantities for big parties—and it freezes well, too." He likes venison best of all and enjoys stirring the simmering pot to keep the gulaš from burning. The stew is best served over soft polenta. But he wouldn't complain about gulaš on mashed potatoes or egg noodles.

Vegeta (a product of Podravka, a company from Koprivnica, Croatia) is a universal seasoning.

3 pounds venison roast, trimmed and cut into 1-inch cubes

3 large onions, finely chopped

6 garlic cloves, minced

¾ cup olive oil

2 bay leaves

Water, as needed

¼ to ⅓ cup Hungarian sweet paprika

¼ cup Vegeta

2 carrots, peeled and thinly sliced

2½ pounds wild and domestic mushrooms, thickly sliced (optional)

1½ teaspoons freshly ground black pepper

1½ teaspoons freshly ground white pepper

½ teaspoon cayenne pepper

Kosher salt

1. The day before serving, in a large bowl, combine the venison, onions, garlic, oil, and bay leaves. Cover and refrigerate for 8 to 12 hours.

2. Transfer the meat and its marinade to a large Dutch oven and bring to a simmer. Cover and cook, stirring occasionally and adding water as needed, about 2 hours, until the meat is almost tender.

3. Stir in the paprika, cover, and continue cooking over the lowest possible heat until the meat is tender, about 30 minutes. Discard the bay leaves. Stir in the Vegeta, carrots, mushrooms, black and white peppers, and cayenne. Cover and cook for another hour, adding water as needed, until the vegetables and meat are very tender. Season with salt to taste and serve.

SERVES 6 TO 8

Nick and Kathy Forrest's Road Show Roast Leg of Lamb

OXFORD, OHIO

Nick and Kathy Forrest do not live far from the dairy farm where he grew up in the southwest corner of Ohio. But today their five-acre spread is surrounded by suburbs—and back in 1985, when several of the couple's seven children lobbied to raise lambs to show at the county fair, other parents (most of whom were former city dwellers) had certain "aesthetic concerns." Livestock-showing quickly became the Forrest family sport. With the children raising up to thirty animals at a time from infancy to county fair time, the family had to rent two additional five-acre plots and was producing several thousand pounds more meat than they could eat—but the children refused to send the animals to auction. "The lamb is all grass-fed, it's too good for that," says Mr. Forrest.

So the couple tried to find an appreciative audience, and when that failed, they began to build one, and started a lamb-cooking road show. "People around here had no idea of all the things that can be done with lamb," says Mr. Forrest. He and his wife were among the lamb ignorati at first, but their earliest customers taught them. "There were hundreds of people from Italy, Greece, Jordan, West Africa, the Middle East who had come to Ohio to work or study or teach—and they were so desperate to find the sort of lamb they had back home that they would drive around looking for grazing lamb. Eventually they found us." Mr. Forrest became the president of the first grass-fed lamb society in the country.

The Forrests don't tour much anymore. "We don't have to," he says. "I could sell ten times the lamb I can raise here. And now, when spring comes, all the soccer parents are calling, asking when the lambs are coming. They want to see them running around and jumping. It's good for property values! They can't wait to stand on their decks and watch the view."

One 3½- to 4-pound boneless half leg of lamb

Kosher salt and freshly ground black pepper

20 garlic cloves, thinly sliced

2 cups basil leaves

1¼ cup olive oil

¼ cup high quality grated Parmesan cheese

1. Place an oven rack in the center position and preheat the oven to 425°F.

2. Pat the lamb dry and season with salt and pepper. Use a sharp knife to make ½-inch diagonal slits that are about 2 inches apart all over the lamb. Press half of the sliced garlic into the slits.

3. In a food processor, pulse the remaining garlic with the basil, olive oil, cheese, ½ teaspoon salt, and ¼ teaspoon pepper to form a paste. Rub this paste all over the lamb. Place the meat on the rack in the roasting pan and roast for 30 minutes.

4. Reduce the temperature to 325°F and roast for 40 to 50 minutes more, until the desired doneness (125°F on an instant-read thermometer for medium-rare; 135°F for medium).

5. Transfer the roast to a carving board and let rest for 10 minutes. Carve and serve.

SERVES 6 TO 8

Road Show North African Grilled Lamb

OXFORD, OHIO

This is another Forrest road show recipe, inspired by a customer, Eli Ahmed, that brings rave reviews.

One 4- to 5-pound bone-in leg of lamb, trimmed

4 garlic cloves, minced

¼ cup Greek-style yogurt

¼ cup chopped fresh mint leaves

1 scallion, green and white parts, finely chopped

2 teaspoons ground turmeric

1 teaspoon ground cardamom

1 teaspoon grated fresh ginger

1 teaspoon sweet paprika

½ teaspoon kosher salt

½ teaspoon freshly ground black pepper

1. Cut ½-inch, diagonal slits about 2 inches apart on all sides of the lamb. Combine the garlic, yogurt, mint, scallion, turmeric, cardamom, ginger, paprika, salt, and pepper and rub two-thirds of it into the meat, massaging it well into the slits. Cover loosely and refrigerate for 1 to 2 hours. Refrigerate the reserved marinade.

2. Bring the meat to room temperature. Heat a charcoal grill with a rotisserie to medium or preheat the oven to 325°F. If using a grill, skewer the lamb securely on the rotisserie rod and set it medium distance from the coals. Grill, turning from time to time and basting with additional marinade, for 1½ to 2 hours, until the meat is well browned and cooked to the desired doneness (125°F on an instant-read thermometer for medium rare; 135°F for medium).

3. If using the oven, place the lamb in a baking dish, cover with foil, and bake for 2 to 2½ hours, to the desired doneness.

4. Transfer the lamb to a carving board (if you have used the oven method, rub it with the reserved marinade) and let rest for 10 minutes. Carve and serve.

SERVES 6

THE SAFFRON KING'S PERSIAN KEBABS

NEW YORK, NEW YORK

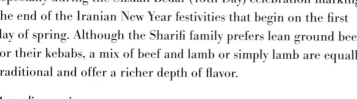

Behroush Sharifi is a large man with a small ponytail. His bulk belies his agility on the mountain bike that he races through Manhattan, delivering small packets of Persian saffron to chefs at the city's elite restaurants. At $88 an ounce, the spice is precious stuff. He was a child émigré who fled Iran with his mother, a nurse, just after the Iranian Revolution, landing first in England and then in Arkansas. In Mr. Sharifi's mother's kitchen, like that of most Iranians, saffron played a large role no matter how hard it was to procure.

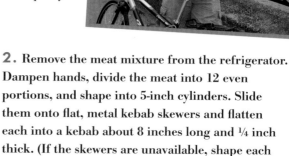

Now, Mr. Sharifi mixes saffron with butter to finish off the grilled kebabs that are Iran's most popular fast food or picnic fare, especially during the Sizdah Bedar (13th Day) celebration marking the end of the Iranian New Year festivities that begin on the first day of spring. Although the Sharifi family prefers lean ground beef for their kebabs, a mix of beef and lamb or simply lamb are equally traditional and offer a richer depth of flavor.

4 medium onions

¾ pound 90% lean ground beef (preferably ground twice)

¾ pound ground lamb (preferably ground twice)

3 large egg yolks

½ teaspoon kosher salt

¼ teaspoon freshly ground black pepper

12 long, flat, metal kebab skewers

Pinch of saffron threads

Pinch of sugar

1 tablespoon unsalted butter, melted

1 tablespoon ground sumac

Pita bread or lavash, for serving

1. Grate the onions on the large holes of a box grater. Squeeze out excess liquid by hand or press out in a strainer with a wooden spoon. Transfer the onions to a medium bowl and add the ground beef and lamb, egg yolks, salt, and pepper. Using your hands or an electric mixer, blend the ingredients until the mixture is sticky. Cover and refrigerate for 4 to 5 hours.

2. Remove the meat mixture from the refrigerator. Dampen hands, divide the meat into 12 even portions, and shape into 5-inch cylinders. Slide them onto flat, metal kebab skewers and flatten each into a kebab about 8 inches long and ¼ inch thick. (If the skewers are unavailable, shape each portion of meat into an 8 x 1½-inch rectangle.)

3. In a mortar and pestle, grind the saffron and sugar together until the saffron threads are pulverized. Stir into the butter.

4. Heat a grill to high. (If not using skewers, heat a grill pan over high heat.) Grill the kebabs—or unskewered portions—for 2 to 3 minutes, brush with saffron butter, and flip. Grill on the second side for 2 to 3 minutes more, until the meat is cooked through.

5. Brush with saffron butter, remove from the skewers, sprinkle with the sumac, and serve with the bread.

SERVES 6

PAUL ANGELO'S SEARED LAMB CHOPS WITH OLIVES AND POLENTA

EUREKA SPRINGS, ARKANSAS

Paul Angelo's great-grandfather was a stonemason who came to New York to build bridges. He developed rheumatism at a young age and moved to Eureka Springs to "take the cure." Unable to work stone, he cooked and gardened. After he'd saved enough to buy a little farm, he moved his family to the Ozarks and their healthier way of life. But, says Mr. Angelo, "they hated it and as soon as he could, my grandfather moved up to Ohio to learn butchering there." The family went back to the Ozarks in the summer, and he and his sisters loved it, as do his children now.

"My great-grandfather was pretty busted up and gnarled but he lived to be eighty-seven years old and he was one heck of a cook. All the men in my family cook. Whenever we get together, all we do is cook—cook and drink and sing."

His great-grandfather used a lot more olive oil and made these chops in a skillet, partially covered. His grandfather and father started them on the stove and finished them in the oven. He adapted the recipe to use on the grill.

Eight 4-ounce thick-cut lamb loin chops, tied with string

1 cup oil-cured black olives, drained, pitted, and coarsely chopped

¾ cup olive oil

1 teaspoon grated lemon zest

¼ teaspoon red pepper flakes

Kosher salt and freshly ground black pepper

Soft polenta (such as Arthur Zampaglione's Polenta, page 618), for serving

1. Place the chops in a shallow dish. In a small bowl, combine the olives, oil, zest, and pepper flakes and pour over the chops. Cover and refrigerate for at least 2 hours and up to 24.

2. When ready to cook, remove the chops from the marinade and place on a plate. Transfer the marinade to a small saucepan.

3. Heat a grill or the broiler to medium-high heat. Season the chops with salt and pepper and grill or broil 4 inches from the heat, for 6 to 10 minutes, until well browned on both sides and cooked to the desired doneness (125°F on an instant-read thermometer for rare; 130°F for medium-rare).

4. Meanwhile, place the marinade over medium heat and cook just until the oil bubbles. Place a mound of warm polenta on each of four plates and top each with two chops. Using a slotted spoon, remove the olives from the warmed oil and sprinkle them over the chops. Serve.

SERVES 4

4-H Club member, Pocahontas County, West Virginia, 1921.

Everything but the Squeal: Beef, Buffalo, Game, Lamb, and Pork

STILL AT HOME ON THE RANGE

TIERRA AMARILLA, NEW MEXICO

MOLLY AND ANTONIO MANZANARES RANCH SHEEP MUCH AS THEIR ANCESTORS DID, riding horseback to move their flock from one high desert pasture to another to graze on lush mountain grasses and mountain mahogany and snowberry. While on summer pasture, the flock and the shepherd's camp are moved to a new location weekly, allowing the ewes and lambs to have access to fresh feed at all times and ensuring the long-term health of the range.

Although there are now few full-time sheep ranchers in this part of northern New Mexico, the area used to be the world's lamb capital. "Once upon a time, there were more lambs shipped out on the railroad from Chama than from anywhere in the world," Mr. Manzanares says. Then lamb consumption in the United States began to drop. To survive, ranchers with small flocks needed to find markets for both the wool and the meat from their animals. To preserve tradition as well as make ends meet, Mr. and Mrs. Manzanares helped found Ganados del Valle, a community-based economic development organization for the primarily Hispanic, low-income community. Mrs. Manzanares, a master weaver, is a founding member of Tierra Wools. Shepherd's Lamb, their family business, is the first certified organic lamb supplier in New Mexico. She has little time to cook but when she makes chili she uses lamb for the traditional beef in green chili. (See recipe for green chili, page 463.)

RICK JARRETT'S SHEPHERD'S STEW

Rick Jarrett is a fifth-generation Montana rancher whose ancestors homesteaded in Sweet Grass County in the late 1880s. His Norwegian ancestors rode from Illinois to Big Timber, and 120 years later the Jarretts continue to farm and shepherd there. Mr. Jarrett is convinced that where you eat a meal affects the way it tastes, or at least the memory of its taste. He remembers going to sheep camp once a week during summers with his father. The gatherings were one of the few opportunities that sheepherders had to talk to anyone but their four-legged charges. There was always a communal meal, and he loved the lamb stew. "Just as soon as we opened the door of the sheep wagon, the smell of the lamb stew would make my mouth water," he says. Part of the ritual was eating the stew on chipped enameled tin plates and drinking coffee from tin cups. It seemed to echo the untamed roughness of the country. Shepherd's stew served on Limoges china doesn't taste the same.

477

1½ pounds boneless lamb shoulder, trimmed and cut into 1-inch cubes

Freshly ground black pepper

Garlic salt

½ cup all-purpose flour

2 tablespoons vegetable oil

2 rutabagas, peeled and cut into ½-inch pieces

3 potatoes, peeled and cut into ½-inch pieces

1 pound carrots, peeled and cut into ½-inch pieces

1 large onion, finely chopped

8 ounces shiitake mushrooms, stemmed and thinly sliced

8 cups homemade chicken broth or low-sodium store-bought chicken broth

1 tablespoon chopped fresh basil

1 tablespoon red pepper flakes

2 bay leaves

Kosher salt

1. Season the lamb with pepper and garlic salt. Dredge the lamb in the flour and shake off the excess. Heat the oil in a large Dutch oven over medium-high heat. Add the lamb and cook for 6 to 8 minutes, until well browned on all sides.

2. Add rutabagas, potatoes, carrots, onion, mushrooms, broth, basil, red pepper flakes, and bay leaves. Bring to a simmer, cover, and cook about 3 hours, stirring occasionally, until the lamb is tender.

3. Remove the bay leaves, season with salt and pepper to taste, and serve.

SERVES 4

Everything but the Squeal: Beef, Buffalo, Game, Lamb, and Pork

Gwen Tabor's African Lamb Tagine with Sweet Tomato Jam

ANN ARBOR, MICHIGAN

Attending graduate school, Gwen and John Tabor lived in Morocco for several years before. "Learning to cook from the women helped me get to know them, and so that is what I did," Gwen says. "This particular dish is so rich and sweet that even our children, who normally are not big on lamb, look forward to it. We generally serve it with couscous or rice. But John also keeps a winter garden and we love serving kale sautéed in olive oil with a few drops of balsamic vinegar with this lamb dish as well."

Olive oil

2½ pounds boneless lamb shoulder, trimmed and cut into 1½-inch pieces

Kosher salt and freshly ground black pepper

2 garlic cloves, minced

½ teaspoon crushed saffron threads, steeped in ½ cup hot water

2 teaspoons ground cinnamon

1 teaspoon ground ginger

1 medium onion, grated

1½ cups homemade chicken broth or low-sodium store-bought chicken broth or water

One 28-ounce can whole tomatoes, pureed with their juices

2 tablespoons tomato paste

¼ cup dark honey, such as buckwheat

3 tablespoons toasted sesame seeds

1. Heat a film of olive oil in a skillet or sauté pan over high heat and brown the lamb pieces, sprinkling each with salt and pepper as you go.

2. Combine the lamb, garlic, saffron infusion, 1 teaspoon of the cinnamon, the ginger, onion, and broth in a tagine or large Dutch oven. Bring to a boil over medium heat. Reduce the heat to low, cover and simmer for 1 hour.

3. Add the tomatoes, tomato paste, and season with salt. Simmer uncovered until the lamb is tender and the sauce has thickened, about 30 minutes. Add the honey and the remaining 1 teaspoon cinnamon and cook for 2 minutes.

4. Season with salt and pepper to taste, sprinkle with the sesame seeds, and serve.

SERVES 4 TO 6

Sheep on White House lawn, 1910.

Freda Cenarrusa's Basque Lamb Shanks

BOISE, IDAHO

Mr. and Mrs. Cenarrusa are living history books of the Basque experience in Idaho. Mrs. Cenarrusa, the progeny of English, Scots, Danish, and Cherokee Indians, grew up on an Idaho ranch where her family raised and herded sheep, milked cows, and harvested crops. Pete Cenarrusa, ten years her senior, is the child of Basque immigrants. He served nine terms in the Idaho House of Representatives and was Idaho's secretary of state for thirty-five years. The family runs sheep, and Mrs. Cenarrusa has managed the business for the past half century.

To raise money to support Basque historical projects such as the restoration of one of the boardinghouses that became "home away from home" for sheepherders as well as the social center of the Basque immigrant community, the couple give a lamb barbecue each year. In the colder weather, they serve guests these slow-simmered lamb shanks.

Nonstick cooking spray

4 lamb shanks, fat trimmed

2 to 4 garlic cloves, minced

1 large onion, finely chopped

Kosher salt

Seasoned pepper (preferably Lawry's)

½ cup fruity red wine, like beaujolais

Water or chicken broth

Cooked rice or noodles, for serving

1. Spray a Dutch oven with nonstick cooking spray and brown the shanks over medium heat. Stir in the garlic and onion and sauté until brown. Add salt and seasoned pepper to taste.

2. Turn the heat to low, add the wine, and cover. Cook on low heat for at least 4 hours, stirring occasionally and adding water or meat broth if necessary to keep the shanks barely covered.

3. After 4 hours, remove from the heat. Transfer the lamb shanks to a plate, and when they are cool enough to handle, remove the bones and the gristle and discard. Defat the meat juices, return the meat and juices to the pot, and simmer over low heat uncovered for about 3 minutes to allow the gravy to thicken. Taste and adjust the seasoning with additional salt or black pepper. Serve the meat and gravy over rice or noodles.

SERVES 4

MARINA MARKOS KLUTER'S MACEDONIAN LAMB

A wave of Macedonian immigrants coming to North America began in the late 1880s. Marina Markos Kluter's family emigrated to Toronto, and worked in restaurants and eventually opened one of their own. Her mother's simple recipes made a lot for a little. "She cooked the way she'd been shown," Ms. Kluter says, "and that is the way she showed me." Knowing that the recipes she makes embrace her family history each time they are prepared is something Ms. Kluter finds comforting, especially after she moved to Massachusetts as a young bride.

She likes keeping her lamb recipe "as is," and prepares it only occasionally, primarily at Easter. "What I have discovered in the course of the years is that if you have a dish once in a while, it is really special. If you make it more often, it is not so special anymore."

One 6- to 8-pound bone-in leg of lamb

3 garlic cloves, thinly sliced

1 tablespoon kosher salt

⅛ teaspoon freshly ground black pepper

1 tablespoon dried oregano

1 teaspoon dried thyme

1 tablespoon dried mint

¼ cup fresh lemon juice

3 cups boiling water

8 potatoes, peeled and quartered lengthwise

4 carrots, peeled and cut on the bias into 1½-inch lengths

1. Place an oven rack in the center position and preheat the oven to 425°F. Pat the meat dry and place in a roasting pan or shallow baking dish, fat side up. Use a small knife to make incisions into the top of the lamb and insert the sliced garlic cloves in each one.

2. Mix the salt, pepper, oregano, thyme, and mint in a small bowl. Rub this on the surface of the lamb and into the slits with the garlic.

3. Place roasting pan with the lamb in oven and roast for 30 minutes. Reduce the heat to 350°F and roast for 2 hours more. Thirty minutes before the end of the roasting period, mix together lemon juice and boiling water and pour over the lamb.

4. While the lamb finishes cooking, place the potatoes and carrots in a large pot, cover with water, bring to a boil, and cook about 10 minutes, until almost tender.

5. Transfer the lamb to a carving board to rest for 20 minutes. Skim most of the fat that accumulated in the pan. Increase the oven temperature to 400°F.

6. Drain the partially cooked vegetables and add to the pan juices, spooning the juices over the vegetables. Return to the oven and cook for 20 minutes, until golden brown.

7. Carve the lamb and serve with the vegetables and gravy.

SERVES 8 TO 10

PIG'S PROGRESS

MADISONVILLE, TENNESSEE

ALAN BENTON MEANT TO BE A HIGH SCHOOL TEACHER. BUT IN 1973, THE REALITY OF raising a family on a teacher's salary and the sight of a for sale sign in front of a local roadside ham- and bacon-making operation changed his life. The confluence may also have saved bacon and restored the dignity of American country ham: Mr. Benton's dry-aged ham and smoky bacon are considered by connoisseurs to be the best of their kind. "There are two crucibles of country ham," he says. "Patience and good pork are what it's really about. You cannot make an incredible ham out of a sad little skinny pig and you can't rush it."

As he explains, there are some false distinctions in American country ham. "We're all lying when we call those hams 'Virginia' or 'Kentucky' or 'Tennessee' hams. The current point of origin of a particular American country ham doesn't describe the meat. Understanding that all American country hams are descended from the European Black Forest, prosciutto, and Serrano hams tells you that the hams are dense, well-aged, with nutty, salty tones."

Christopher Columbus brought pigs to the New World on his second voyage. Within a decade, pork was raised in every Spanish settlement throughout the Caribbean. The Jamestown colony in Virginia had so many pigs and such difficulty penning them that they relocated the porcine population offshore and created Hog Island. Pigs wandered the streets of Philadelphia, New York City, and Boston until departments of sanitation were established in the latter half of the nineteenth century. By then, slave ships had long since delivered African pigs to the United States. Thomas Jefferson may (or may not) have imported pigs from Calcutta, and Yorkshire pigs from England were taking Pennsylvania and Ohio by storm.

There were different pigs for different people, but most households raised and slaughtered a few each year. Fresh pork was a luxury of "hog killing time," usually late fall, when neighbors gathered to butcher the animals and turn the meat into hams, sausages, bacon, pickled meat, and lard, often the most important protein in the rural inland winter diet.

The Ohio River and a strong German community made Cincinnati a great hog-trading, sausage-making town and earned it the name Porkopolis. Because there are different pigs for different purposes, a number of distinct breeds—Berkshire, Duroc, Gloucestershire Old Spot, Large Black, Tamworth, or Red Wattle—were raised and traded.

Mr. Benton is a native Virginian. "My mom's people built the first house in Scott County in the southwestern hills of the state, and they cured things in straight salt," he says. "My father's family built on the adjoining piece of land and they used salt, brown sugar, and black and red pepper. And that is how I cure my hams to this day. But I live in Tennessee and I'm proud of it and I call my hams 'Smoky Mountain Country ham.'

"When I started out in 1973," Mr. Benton continues, "you could still get some pretty good pork from a processor right in Knoxville, all grown within a hundred-mile radius of my shop. Not long after that it started to change. The local processor went broke, and I had to go to the other side of the state. It happened again and again. I'd find a good little processor and a year later they'd close, and I'd have to move farther away and every time I did, the pork got a little worse. By the 1980s, I

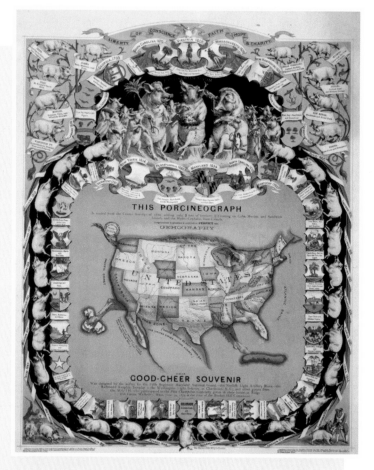

was going all the way to the Midwest to buy, and that meat was bad. It was all quick-buck pork. I am not saying it would make you sick, but I'll tell you, it wouldn't make good ham."

But just before he threw in the towel, a group of pig farmers across the country began to raise and revitalize the classic American breeds. "The first time I tasted Berkshire pork was an epiphany. It was tender and silky and tasted like pork," Mr. Benton says. "I know the heritage hogs are better. I can't tell you that pasture raising really makes a difference and I don't know whether or not using antibiotics affects the character of pork, but I want natural pork, just in case it does."

Crouched over a small campfire on the bank of a mountain stream, the Prince of Pigs was warming a cast-iron skillet the size of a manhole cover. It was Sunday, and he and his wife, Sherry, and their daughter had spent the afternoon hiking and digging wild ramps. Mrs. Benton was cleaning the wild leeks in the stream, and Mr. Benton was cooking the fat from some of his bacon and peeling potatoes. Between potatoes, he glanced at the chunk of twenty-four-month-old country ham that he'd brought in his knapsack. Soon he would slice the meat thin, fry it in the skillet, and serve it over the potatoes and ramps.

"You taste that and you know two things for sure," he says. "You know it's spring in the Smoky Mountains and you know that ol' hillbillies can make a country ham that's right up there with the ones made by our European cousins."

The Bentons' Spring Ham and Ramp Hash

MADISONVILLE, TENNESSEE

2 slices thick-cut bacon (preferably Benton Bacon), cut into ½-inch pieces

4 large russet potatoes, peeled and cut into ¾-inch chunks

Kosher salt and freshly ground black pepper

2 pounds ramps, cleaned, trimmed, and coarsely chopped

1½ to 2 pounds 24-month dry-aged country ham, thinly sliced

1. Cook the bacon in a large cast-iron skillet over medium heat until the fat has rendered. Transfer the bacon to a plate.

2. Increase the heat to high, add the potatoes, ½ teaspoon salt, and ¼ teaspoon pepper. Cook for 6 to 8 minutes, until golden brown on all sides. Reduce the heat to low, add the ramps, and shake the pan. Continue shaking and cooking about 10 minutes, until the ramps and potatoes are soft. Remove from the heat, adjust the seasoning with additional salt and pepper if desired and divide among 6 plates.

3. Return the skillet to the fire and when it is very hot, lay the ham slices in the skillet for less than a minute to warm, then place over the hash on each plate and serve.

SERVES 6

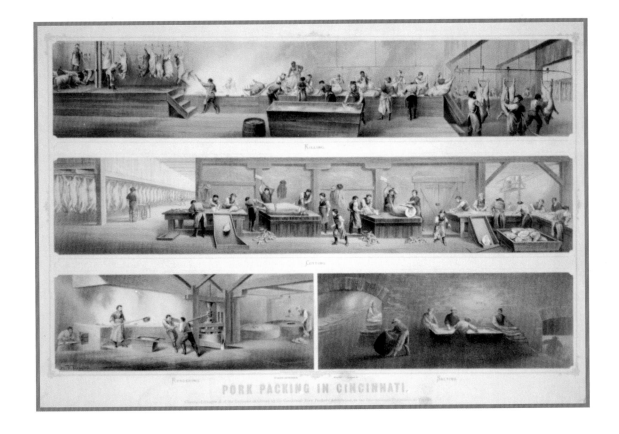

PORK PACKING IN CINCINNATI.

Everything but the Squeal: Beef, Buffalo, Game, Lamb, and Pork

HOME-CURED HOLIDAY HAM

The southeast United States, particularly the hills of Virginia, Kentucky, and Tennessee, have been the epicenter of the nation's hams for more than three hundred years. The mild winters and hot summers are ideal for dry-curing. After a long, slow cure, the hams are smoked and hung to age. The finest of these are hung for nearly two years and have a flavor and texture that is like Italian prosciutto. The artisans who create the country's finest hams tend to call well-aged hams "country hams," and regard the sweeter, more familiar brine-cured ham as "city hams." Like Alan Benton in Tennessee, Sam Edwards, of S. Wallace Edwards and Sons in Surry County, Virginia, and Nancy Newsom, whose family makes Colonel Bill Newsom's Aged Kentucky Ham, prefer not to boil or bake a whole country ham.

Putting a quick (three-week) cure on a fresh ham is another option. This recipe is the result of dozens of interviews with ham makers and ham bakers. The slow poaching, bourbon-honey glaze, and baking work well for store-bought brine-cured ham as well. (This recipe uses pink salt, a curing salt that contains nitrites to protect from botulism.)

FOR THE CURING SOLUTION

1 gallon spring water

½ cup kosher salt

2 cups brown sugar

2½ tablespoons pink salt, such as DQ Curing Salt or Insta Cure No. 1

One 5- to 8-pound bone-in fresh ham (½ rear leg of pig), skin on if possible

FOR THE HAM

1 quart water

2 quarts unfiltered apple juice or cider

1 teaspoon apple cider vinegar

6 whole black peppercorns

3 cups bourbon

FOR THE GLAZE

2 tablespoons sorghum

2 tablespoons honey

1½ tablespoons Dijon mustard

½ pound (2 sticks) unsalted butter

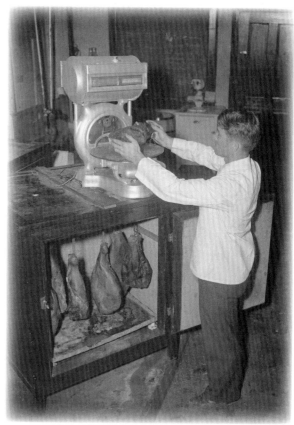

1. To cure the ham: Three weeks before serving, combine the water, kosher salt, brown sugar, and pink salt in a large nonreactive pot and bring to a simmer over high heat until the salts and sugar are dissolved. Remove from the heat and cool completely.

2. Add the pork, weight down with a heavy plate in order to cover the meat completely, and refrigerate for 2 weeks.

3. Rinse the cured pork under cold running water. Place in a smoker or over cooling hardwood coals for 12 to 24 hours. Then hang the ham to dry in a cool, well-ventilated place for 3 to 5 days.

4. To cook the ham: The day before serving, rinse the ham and put it in a large stockpot. Add the water, apple juice, vinegar, peppercorns, and 1½ cups of the bourbon and bring to a boil. Lower the heat to a bare simmer and cook uncovered for 3 to 4 hours, until an instant-read thermometer inserted in the thickest part of the ham registers 150°F.

5. Remove the pot from the heat and cool the ham in the broth to room temperature. Refrigerate in the broth for 8 to 24 hours, until chilled.

6. About 4 hours before serving, preheat the oven to 450°F. Remove the ham from the broth. Discard the broth. Place the ham on a rack in a large roasting pan, skin (or fat) side up. Use a sharp knife to remove the skin from the ham, leaving as much fat as possible on the meat. Score the fat in a diamond pattern.

7. To make the glaze: Simmer the remaining 1½ cups bourbon in a medium saucepan over medium-low heat until reduced to ½ cup. Stir in the sorghum, honey, mustard, and butter. Bring to a simmer, then remove from the heat. Brush the glaze on all sides of the ham, taking care to dab the brush into the cuts.

8. Roast the ham for 20 minutes.

9. Baste the ham with the glaze, reduce the oven temperature to 300°F, and roast, basting every 30 minutes, for 2 to 3 hours, until the surface has a brown crust and an instant-read thermometer inserted into the thickest part of the ham registers 150°F.

10. Transfer to a carving board and let rest for 30 minutes before carving and serving.

SERVES 12

7UP Ham

Carbonated water with fruit juices and herbal distillations were first sold on street corners in large American cities during the late eighteenth century, but it wasn't until the 1870s—when doctors, dentists, and pharmacists began experimenting with various flavor and curative compounds—that soda pop became big business.

A Philadelphia pharmacist, Charles E. Hires, created root beer, and after being challenged by prohibitionists, succeeded in building an empire by advertising it as "The National Temperance Drink." By the 1880s, two new ingredients—an extract from the coca plant and an extract of the cola, or kola, nut— appeared, and by 1886, John Stith Pemberton, a pharmacist in Atlanta, Georgia, compounded a syrup from caffeine, cola nut extract, and several other oils, called it Coca-Cola, and marketed it as a headache cure. The syrup was a hit and soon Mr. Pemberton was using an oar to stir up vats of it in his backyard.

Fizzy pops provide a natural lift to baked goods and extra muscle to marinades. Soda pop cakes and marinades seem to have risen from the American South, although the precise time and point of origin for the latter use is debated. Dr Pepper and Coca-Cola are used with baby back ribs and tough cuts of beef. Marinades like this one with 7UP are used to tenderize pork and give it a hint of spice and lemon.

1 cup soy sauce

1 cup oil (vegetable, safflower, or canola)

2 cups 7UP

1 teaspoon powdered horseradish

1 teaspoon garlic, minced

Combine all ingredients. Pour over meat—fresh ham, cured ham, large joints of lamb, or beef brisket—and marinate in the refrigerator overnight. If using sliced turkey breast, marinate for 2 hours prior to barbecuing. Remove from the marinade— discarding the liquid—and pat dry. Bake, grill, or roast the meat according to taste.

MAKES ENOUGH TO MARINATE
3 TO 5 POUNDS OF MEAT

Laurent Roffe's Pork Roast

Laurent Roffe loves to make this pork roast. It can be served year-round, and is easy to prepare, forgiving of mistakes, and great for sandwiches the next day. "It just keeps on giving," he says. But most of all, he likes the rich, sweet, spicy smell that fills the house while the roast cooks, and the kudos he gets every time he serves it.

Mr. Roffe was born in Casablanca, spent his childhood in Paris, moved to Israel as an adolescent, and served time in the Israeli army before attending Pratt Institute in New York. He cannot remember a time that he was not interested in food. But it was not until he left home for college that his talents began to emerge. A recipe from Jacques Pépin inspired this, his number one meal for company.

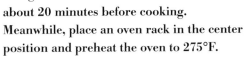

1 cup balsamic vinegar

⅓ cup soy sauce

3 tablespoons olive oil

½ cup honey

2 tablespoons Dijon mustard

2 teaspoons cayenne pepper

1 tablespoon sweet paprika

1 tablespoon ground cumin

1 tablespoon ground turmeric

One 2½- to 3-pound boneless center-cut pork loin, trimmed

1. In a large bowl, mix 2 tablespoons of the vinegar, the soy sauce, oil, honey, mustard, cayenne, paprika, cumin, and turmeric. Score the loin all over very lightly in a crisscross pattern with a sharp knife and place it in the marinade, turning until it is all coated. Cover and let rest for at least 1 hour in the refrigerator, turning several times.

2. Remove the loin from refrigerator about 20 minutes before cooking. Meanwhile, place an oven rack in the center position and preheat the oven to 275°F.

3. Lightly oil a roasting pan and place the loin in the pan. Spoon the marinade on top and place in the oven. Cook, turning and basting the loin every 20 minutes, for about 2 hours or until the inside is slightly pink but not bloody and an instant-read thermometer registers 145°F.

4. Transfer the pork to a carving board, cover loosely with foil, and let rest for 15 minutes.

5. Pour any juices into the roasting pan, along with any leftover marinade. Add the remaining vinegar, bring to a simmer, and cook, scraping up any browned bits, until thickened slightly.

6. Slice the pork, transfer to a serving platter, and spoon some of the sauce on top. Serve, passing the remaining sauce at the table.

SERVES 6

LILLIE LOUVIERE DELPHIN'S
ROAST WHILE YOU REST

Few words in American English are as misunderstood as "Creole." For eighteenth-century Louisianans, "Creole" meant born native to the soil. Both black and white children born in the colony were designated as Creole to distinguish them from Louisiana's European and African settlers. Later, "Creole" referred to children of mixed blood. Today, "Creole" is defined as anyone born on Louisiana soil from the intermarriage of Europeans, Africans, and Native Americans.

Lillie Delphin is a soft-spoken Creole who grew up in the little community of Frilot Cove, near Opelousas, Louisiana. "It was a rural community with the church being the center of the activities," she says. "It was very rural and very independent." Yeast cakes were handmade and sun-dried on rooftops, then used to bake fresh bread. Some meats hung in the smokehouse while others dried in the sun to create tasso, a seasoning ham. Butter was churned and preserved in jars filled with brine. "We put clabbered milk in a cheesecloth and hung it from the clothesline to drip for a day," she says, "and you had what we now call cream cheese." A cream and sugar sauce was poured on top to create a wonderful breakfast food.

At least five meats were prepared for every holiday or special occasions. "This was tradition for everyone in the community," Ms. Delphin says. "The meats were usually roasted in the oven. We didn't have any barbecuing or grilling. We had the pork roast, the beef roast, the lamb roast, some type of poultry, turkey usually, and either duck or geese. Back then eating was taken very seriously. There was no fast food. Everything was cooked slowly and everyone ate slowly. A holiday dinner lasted from noon on."

Ms. Delphin learned the technique of roasting meat overnight from her parents and grandparents, who oven-roasted at least four meats at a time. "The size of the roast was so much larger back then than what I use. I guess it required more heat and a longer cooking time. It was using the heat more efficiently. The meats were always cooked at night. They would not open the oven door at all, but the next day they were just perfect."

(NOTE: The contemporary food-safety standards that were largely developed to safeguard against microbes that can be found in industrial-raised and processed meat that is shipped great distances condemn this traditional, slow-heat technique. For more information on meat-cooking safety, see www.fsis.usda.gov/factsheets/meat...fact_sheets/index.asp. If purchasing fresh, naturally raised local meat from a known source, discuss cooking methods with the grower.)

2 tablespoons kosher salt

4 teaspoons freshly ground black pepper

2 teaspoons sweet paprika

1 teaspoon cayenne pepper

One 5-pound boneless beef or pork roast, trimmed

6 garlic cloves, thinly sliced

2 jalapeño chiles, stemmed and thinly sliced

6 tablespoons (¾ stick) unsalted butter, cut into 6 pieces

1. Place an oven rack in the center position and preheat the oven to 500°F. Line a roasting pan with aluminum foil.

2. In a small bowl, combine the salt, pepper, paprika, and cayenne. Sprinkle a tablespoon of the mixture over the bottom of the pan. With a sharp knife, pierce about 36 holes 1 inch deep in the roast. Place an equal amount of the seasoning in each slit, followed with the garlic and jalapeños, divided evenly.

3. Place roast in the pan and dot with the butter. Cover the pan with aluminum foil and bake about 2 hours if using fresh meat from a known source or follow the meat safety cooking instructions on the link at left.

4. If using the overnight method, turn off the oven and leave the roast inside for 8 to 12 hours.

5. Transfer the roast to a carving board and thinly slice against the grain. Transfer to a serving platter. Skim any fat from the juices in the pan, transfer to a saucepan, and reheat. Pour over the meat and serve.

SERVES 6 TO 8

RITA NEWMAN'S CUBAN PORK ROAST

MYRTLE, MISSOURI

Near the top of the Ozarks just above the Arkansas border, past a big sign on the gate—NEWMAN'S HERITAGE—is the lush green haven of Mark and Rita Newman's pig farm. The Newmans are true believers in the value of small family farms, and breed some of the most succulent heirloom pork around. This dish is one of Rita Newman's childhood favorites. Her mother used the pan drippings to make the gravy that accompanied the tenderloin and a batch of biscuits.

1 garlic clove, minced

1 tablespoon ground cumin

1 tablespoon dried oregano

2 teaspoons kosher salt

1 teaspoon freshly ground black pepper

Olive oil

One 7-pound boneless, skin-on Berkshire pork shoulder roast

2 tablespoons fresh lemon juice

1. The day before serving, in a small bowl, combine the garlic, cumin, oregano, salt, and pepper. Stir in oil as needed to make a paste.

2. Poke holes in the flesh side of the roast. Fill the holes with the paste. Pour the lemon juice on the roast and rub it in all over.

3. Let the roast sit on a platter or pan in the refrigerator, skin side up, uncovered, to infuse with the spices about 24 hours.

4. About 1 hour before you want to cook the roast, take it out of the refrigerator to warm up. Place the roast on a rack in a roasting pan. Preheat the oven to 350°F.

5. Roast skin side up until the skin is crispy, about 20 minutes, then turn over.

6. Continue cooking until an instant-read thermometer registers 185°F—about an hour and 20 minutes.

7. Transfer the roast to a cutting board and let rest 20 minutes before carving and serving.

SERVES 12

Roy Balmilero's Hawaiian Kalua Pork

Luau is the Hawaiian Islands' clambake, beanhole dinner, and barbecue: the primordial outdoor feast of a pig roasted in the ground in an imu oven, kalua pork. "You don't learn to cook it as much as you absorb it," says Roy Balmilero. "It is part of growing up in Hawaii." When lacking a pit or visiting his daughter on the mainland, Mr. Balmilero makes kalua pork with pork butt that he rubs with salt and liquid smoke, then roasts about two hours. It isn't traditional kalua, but the seasoning and slow cooking make the meat tender and full of flavor. With a bit of rice one can almost hear the surf and smell the puakenikeni flowers.

491

4 to 5 pounds boneless pork butt, trimmed

2½ tablespoons Hawaiian red salt or kosher salt

2 tablespoons liquid smoke or smoked paprika

1 large banana leaf, or 4 to 5 unpeeled bananas

4 to 6 ti leaves or large piece of aluminum foil

1. Place an oven rack in the bottom position and preheat the oven to 325°F.

2. Make several shallow, long cuts along the roast and rub with the salt and liquid smoke. Wrap the roast with the banana leaf. (If using bananas, place them on top of the roast.) Wrap the pork in the ti leaves or foil and place in a roasting pan.

3. Roast for 3 to 4 hours, until the meat is tender and registers 185°F on an instant-read thermometer.

4. Transfer the meat to a carving board and let rest for 20 minutes. Remove the outer wrapping and the banana leaves or bananas. Shred pork into large pieces. Serve.

SERVES 8 TO 10

Everything but the Squeal: Beef, Buffalo, Game, Lamb, and Pork

LANA CHEN'S SLOW-BRAISED PORK SHOULDER

Lana Chen is from Beijing, where she grew up in a traditional courtyard house and was raised by her grandmother. When she was 16, she began medical school and met the man who would become her husband. When they graduated, the couple decided to leave China. After an arduous journey through the south of China, they made it to Macau and then Hong Kong, where Dr. Chen worked as a doctor for a church clinic. In the mid 1960s, the Chens immigrated to the United States, eventually settling in rural New England where they raised three children and built their medical practice.

In her early years in the States, when she was home with her young children, Dr. Chen turned her attention to the kitchen. Having no first-hand experience cooking, she relied on memories of her grandmother, who spent all her waking hours cooking and caring for their traditional Chinese household. She was able to re-create many of her grandmother's dishes through trial and error—and some ingenuity, since the nearest Asian grocery was in Boston's Chinatown, about an hour's drive away.

This dish is a Chinese classic often attributed to Su Dongpo, a Sung dynasty poet and statesman. It's a favorite recipe of Dr. Chen's because it's pretty much foolproof. Once everything's in the pot, she says, all the work is done. The braising liquid and fat of the pork shoulder create a self-basting system that always results in tender, fall-off-the-bone meat.

1½ cup dark soy sauce

¼ cup hoisin sauce

1 teaspoon garlic powder, or 1 clove garlic, minced

1 teaspoon onion powder, or 1 tablespoon minced onion

One 6-pound bone-in pork shoulder, trimmed

3-inch piece fresh ginger, cut into 7 pieces

¼ cup shaoxing wine (Chinese rice wine) or dry sherry

¼ cup vegetable oil

4 scallions, green and white parts, cut into 2-inch lengths

3 star anise pods

4 Sichuan peppercorns

1 garlic clove, peeled and smashed

1. In small bowl, combine ½ cup of the soy sauce, the hoisin, garlic powder, and onion powder. Pat the pork dry and rub with 3 slices of the ginger. Brush the pork shoulder with the wine then generously brush with the soy mixture and set aside about 15 minutes to dry.

2. Heat the oil in a wok or large skillet over high heat. Carefully add the roast to the wok and cook for 8 to 10 minutes, turning frequently, until well browned on all sides. Transfer the roast to a large pot, skin side up.

3. Add the remaining 1 cup soy sauce, 4 slices ginger, the scallions, star anise, Sichuan peppercorns, and smashed garlic. Fill the pot with enough water to cover the pork shoulder completely. Bring to a simmer over high heat, reduce the heat to medium, and cook for 30 minutes.

4. Reduce the heat to low, cover, and cook about 4 hours more, until the meat is tender and nearly falling off the bone.

5. Transfer the meat to a carving board and let rest for 20 minutes. Shred the meat into large pieces and serve.

SERVES 6 TO 8

VERNON'S JERKED PORK

Allan Vernon says, "I grew up in Jamaica and when I moved to New York, I noticed a distinct lack of jerk. It was difficult to believe. You could get anything in that city but jerk chicken or pork. I opened a stand and then a restaurant. After a while, I started to bottle my sauce in this little plant in New Haven where they had some lady doing kosher salad dressing on Monday morning, some guy doing salsa that afternoon, a family doing their Italian tomato sauce, and me doing my jerk. All of us immigrants, trying to do it right, get the kids through school, make a little business, trying to get an edge. Before I went there, I thought the world was divided into Jamaicans and everybody else.

"They called me the King of Jerk; it stuck. I moved to Atlanta because so many of my family has. There is a big Caribbean community here. At home, for my kids and grandchildren, I make this jerk. You can use the sauce on chicken or fish, but I like pork the best. My grandkids call me the King of Jerk, too."

3 tablespoons whole allspice berries

1 teaspoon ground cinnamon

½ teaspoon ground nutmeg

4 teaspoons ground coriander

6 scallions, green and white parts, finely chopped

3 garlic cloves, chopped

1 Scotch bonnet chile, with seeds

2 tablespoons dark rum

6 tablespoons water

1½ teaspoons kosher salt

Freshly ground black pepper

Two 1-pound pork tenderloins, trimmed

1. Grind the allspice berries in a spice grinder and transfer to a blender. Add the cinnamon, nutmeg, coriander, scallions, garlic, chile, rum, water, salt, and pepper to taste. Blend until a smooth paste forms, scraping down the sides of the jar as needed.

2. Place the pork tenderloins in a shallow baking dish. Wearing rubber gloves, rub the paste all over the pork. Cover and refrigerate for 2 to 12 hours.

3. Preheat the broiler. Place the pork 4 inches under the broiler and broil, turning once, for 12 to 15 minutes, until the pork is only slightly pink in the center and registers 145°F on an instant-read thermometer.

4. Transfer to a carving board and let rest for 5 minutes. Cut into ¼-inch-thick slices and serve.

SERVES 4 TO 6

493

Everything but the Squeal: Beef, Buffalo, Game, Lamb, and Pork

Ivy Henz's Bacon-Roasted Pork with Prunes

CINCINNATI, OHIO

Mrs. Ivy Henz was born on a horse farm in southern Ohio in 1921. After marrying and moving to Cincinnati, she became part of a small group of wealthy men's wives who supervised their children, debated literature, theater, and politics, lobbied for equal rights and against segregation, and hosted Eleanor Roosevelt. Mrs. Henz says: "Don't ask me where I got the recipe. I remember that Emma Lazarus, God rest her soul, made a pork loin stuffed with prunes for some of her fancy parties. There were a few years, after the war I think it was, everybody was making pork with prunes. I added bacon, it changed the dish considerably and everybody wanted the recipe. That must have been when I wrote it down, but it wouldn't have been my recipe. It was my idea, that I grant you, but the recipe would have come from Twinkie, the country girl who cooked for us. Twinkie cooked for my mother and came with me when I married Mr. Henz. When she got the cancer, her daughter took over. Her name was Winnie, but we called her Twinkie Too. She came every day for about twenty-five years and then a few days after Mr. Henz's funeral in 1988, she stopped coming. Never heard a word. I was sixty-six years old and I'd never cooked a thing in my life. I liked it right away.

"I made this pork for holidays until a couple years ago. I'll be ninety soon. I still make myself two lovely meals every day and then I drive over to the cemetery. That's where all my friends are. That's what happens when you get to be my age. You might want to think about that the next time you go cutting calories, starch, and fat.

"Personally, I would advise doubling the bacon."

FOR THE PORK

½ teaspoon rubbed dried sage

¼ teaspoon dried thyme

¼ teaspoon crumbled dried rosemary

½ teaspoon mustard powder

1 teaspoon kosher salt

½ teaspoon freshly ground black pepper

One 4-pound boneless pork loin, trimmed and tied

16 pitted prunes

12 slices bacon

FOR THE SAUCE

3 tablespoons finely chopped red onion

½ cup ruby port

2 cups red wine

1 cup pitted prunes, quartered

1 cup dried figs, quartered

½ cup golden raisins

1 cup homemade chicken broth or low-sodium store-bought chicken broth

⅛ teaspoon ground cinnamon

Kosher salt and freshly ground black pepper

1. To make the pork: The day before serving, combine the sage, thyme, rosemary, mustard, salt, and pepper in a small bowl. Pat the pork dry and rub the seasoning blend onto all sides. Wrap tightly in plastic wrap and refrigerate for 8 to 24 hours.

2. About 2 hours before serving, preheat the oven to 350°F. Remove the pork from the refrigerator. Scrape the seasoning blend off the pork and discard.

3. Run a skewer lengthwise through the center of the pork. Remove the skewer and insert the handle of a wooden spoon into the hole, halfway through the meat. Twist the spoon to enlarge the hole enough to insert the prunes. Repeat at the other end. Push 8 of the whole prunes into the hole from one end and repeat with the remaining prunes at the other end until a tightly packed line runs the length of the pork.

4. Wrap the bacon widthwise around the pork and place in a large roasting pan. Roast about 1½ hours, until an instant-read thermometer registers 145°F. Transfer the roast to a carving board and let rest for 10 minutes.

5. To make the sauce: While the pork is roasting, in a medium skillet, bring the onion and port to a simmer and cook until the port has evaporated. Add 1 cup of the red wine and cook until the wine is almost evaporated. Add the quartered prunes, figs, raisins, broth and the remaining wine, and cinnamon and cook, stirring frequently, to thicken. Season with salt and pepper to taste.

6. To serve, slice the pork, transfer to a serving platter, and spoon the sauce over the top.

SERVES 8 TO 10

Everything but the Squeal: Beef, Buffalo, Game, Lamb, and Pork

LUG POCHE'S SMOTHERED PORK CHOPS

BREAUX BRIDGE, LOUISIANA

In the old African-American churches of Louisiana, after the congregation has contributed to the collection plate, a preacher dissatisfied with the offering might encourage greater donations by saying, "Thank y'all so much for bringing me the pig tails and feet, but we need to get a little higher up on that hog." Well, a pork chop is about as high on the hog as you can get.

Floyd Poche's great-grandparents immigrated to New Orleans in 1859 from the German-French border. They moved west to settle in the village of Poché Bridge, an isolated farming community near the Atchafalaya Swamp. Their grandson Lug Poche established a slaughterhouse there in 1962. Today, Lug's son Floyd operates the family business, which includes a USDA processing plant that makes and ships specialty meats such as chaurice (spicy pork sausage, similar to chorizo), hog head cheese, marinated pork, marinated turkey, stuffed chaudin or ponce (stuffed pork stomach), stuffed pork chops, tasso ham, boudin, smoked sausage, and andouille.

While Monday is red beans and rice day in New Orleans, Tuesdays in Poché Bridge is dedicated to smothered pork chops. Though pork chops are flavorful and need little to tenderize them, smothering (or étouffléeing) them is a favorite Cajun preparation technique.

Locals refer to the smothered pork chop gravy as sauce brûlée or "burned sauce," because you "kind of let the gravy stick on the bottom," Mr. Poche says. "The more you stick and unstick, the better the gravy is going to be."

Four 8-ounce bone-in pork rib chops, ½ to ¾ inch thick

Poché Bridge Cajun Seasoning, or kosher salt, freshly ground black pepper, red pepper flakes, garlic powder, onion powder, and celery salt

¼ cup vegetable oil

2 medium onions, finely chopped

1 medium green bell pepper, stemmed, seeded, and finely chopped

3 garlic cloves, minced

1 quart homemade chicken broth, low-sodium store-bought chicken broth, or water, plus more as needed

Kosher salt and freshly ground black pepper

1. Pat the pork dry and season with Poché Bridge Cajun Seasoning or suggested mix. Heat the oil in a large cast-iron skillet over medium-high heat. Cook the chops until golden brown on both sides, then transfer to a plate.

2. Add onions, bell pepper, and garlic to the fat in the pan. Cook for 3 to 5 minutes, stirring occasionally, until the vegetables are wilted. Add ½ cup of the broth to deglaze the bottom of the skillet, scraping up the brown bits.

3. Return the meat to the skillet, add the remaining 3½ cups broth, bring to a simmer, cover, and cook for 1 hour, until the chops are tender. Add more broth as needed. Season to taste and serve.

SERVES 4

Mrs. O'Brien's Brined Pork Chops

"It's tiresome to hear about how we can't cook. Of course some Irish can't cook, but neither can some French," said Mrs. Janet Tilden O'Brien. She grew up on the "Irish Gold Coast" in New Jersey and moved to Las Vegas twenty years ago. "Cooking is not about nationality, it's about ingredients or the absence of them, fuel or a shortage of it, time or the lack of it. The Irish like a good meal as well as the next nationality, and a lot more than the English, I might add. It's just that so many came after the great famine and got stuck in a joke that they can't get out of. This pork chop recipe came with my great-great-grandmother who migrated from Mayo just after the Civil War. She used lard, I use olive oil. She served it with butter mashed potato and turnip, I like garlic mashed potato and some nice crisply steamed greens."

½ cup packed dark brown sugar

¼ cup kosher salt

10 whole black peppercorns

5 juniper berries

5 bay leaves

2 tablespoons fennel seeds

1 cup mixed fresh herbs (rosemary, thyme, sage, oregano)

Peel of 1 orange

1 quart boiling water

3 quarts cold water

Twelve 4-ounce bone-in center-cut pork chops

2 tablespoons extra-virgin olive oil

1. In a large bowl, combine the sugar, salt, peppercorns, juniper berries, bay leaves, fennel seeds, herbs, orange peel, and boiling water. Stir to completely dissolve the sugar and salt. Stir in the cold water to cool the brine.

2. Lay the chops in a single layer in a large nonreactive pan and completely cover them with the brine. If a chop floats to the surface, weigh it down with a plate. Cover and refrigerate for 12 to 24 hours.

3. Heat a grill or broiler. Drain the pork chops, discarding the brine, and pat dry. Brush with oil and grill or broil for 10 to 12 minutes, until well browned on both sides and an instant-read thermometer registers 145°F. Transfer the chops to a serving platter and let rest for 5 minutes before serving.

SERVES 6

THALIA'S TAMARIND-CHILI CHOPS

SPOKANE, WASHINGTON

"You cannot understand the importance of having one showstopping recipe unless you have a Filipino mother and an African-American Jewish father," said Thalia Pe-Benito Freidan. "Without a dish that makes them all greedy and glassy-eyed, you are a ghost at family gatherings. Aunts and cousins are nice to you, but no one remembers your name because it's all about the food and who makes the best chicken and whose noodles are gone first and whose cake is the envy of all. We have over a hundred people when both sides of the family converge, and word of brownies made from a mix travels fast. When I was in college, I dated an Indian pre-med guy, which to my family was as bad as brownies from a box, though I do not really understand why, but his mother was an amazing cook. I learned these pork chops from her and brought them the year I brought Saleem to the family picnic back in 2001. One whiff and the whole crowd was ready to announce my marriage, which never happened mostly because one afternoon with my tribe was enough for him. Eventually he married an only child! I still make the pork chops. The same recipe works well for lamb chops, too."

FOR THE BRINE

1 quart water

¼ cup fresh orange juice

2 teaspoons grated orange zest

¼ cup kosher salt

2 tablespoons brown sugar

2 tablespoons soy sauce

1 tablespoon grated fresh ginger

1 tablespoon honey

1 teaspoon whole black peppercorns

⅛ teaspoon red pepper flakes

Eight 4-ounce bone-in center-cut pork chops

FOR THE GLAZE

¼ cup malt vinegar

¼ cup cider vinegar

½ cup dark brown sugar

½ cup homemade chicken broth or low-sodium store-bought chicken broth

1 plum tomato, cored and chopped

1 tablespoon tamarind paste

Raise your own

Security Administration

1. To make the brine: Combine the water, orange juice, orange zest, salt, brown sugar, soy sauce, ginger, honey, peppercorns, and red pepper flakes in a large saucepan. Bring to a simmer and cook until the sugar and salt have dissolved. Cool to room temperature.

2. Arrange the chops in a shallow glass or ceramic baking dish and cover with the brine. Cover with plastic wrap and refrigerate for 3 hours.

3. To make the glaze: Combine the vinegars, brown sugar, broth, tomato, and tamarind paste in a small saucepan and cook over medium heat about 15 minutes, stirring occasionally, until thick and syrupy. Remove from the heat, strain through a fine-mesh strainer, and cool to room temperature. Reserve ½ cup of the glaze for serving.

4. Preheat the broiler. Remove the chops from the brine and discard the brine. Pat the chops dry and brush with the glaze. Place the chops on a broiler pan and broil about 6 minutes, turning once, until deep brown on both sides and just cooked through but still moist in the center.

5. Transfer the pork chops to a serving platter and let rest for 5 minutes. Spoon the reserved glaze over the top and serve.

SERVES 4

Susan Rosenburg's Pork Chops and Pickled Peppers

"My grandmother kept rabbits in hutches behind her house. No one else had rabbits behind their large Victorian houses on Harvard Street right in the middle of Cambridge. Nobody else had chickens or gardens or grapevines or apple, cherry, pear, peach, and fig trees," Susan Rosenburg recalled. "The food I ate at my friends' houses was pallid and limp. Nothing crunched. At home we had vivid green beans that had been cooked briefly with small round new red potatoes, a little chopped onion, a little olive oil, a little water. We had risi e bisi—peas from the garden mixed in with rice just before it had finished cooking. We had potatoes roasted with a chicken. We had peppers, fried quickly in olive oil so hot that their skins blackened. We could peel the skin off and eat them with our fingers, the way we ate the crisp skin from the chicken."

The idea of using the juice from pickled peppers to marinate pork chops also came from Ms. Rosenburg's grammy.

¼ cup fine dry bread crumbs

Four 8-ounce bone-in pork rib chops, pounded to an even thickness

Kosher salt and freshly ground black pepper

2 tablespoons olive oil

1 cup pickled peppers plus 2 tablespoons pickled pepper juice

¼ cup dry white wine or water

1. In a shallow dish, spread the bread crumbs in an even layer. Pat the pork chops dry and season with salt and pepper. Press all sides of the meat into the bread crumbs and pat them to get the crumbs to stick.

2. Heat the oil in a large skillet over medium-high heat. Add the pork chops and cook for 4 to 6 minutes, until browned on the first side.

3. Flip the pork chops over, add the pickled peppers and their juice and cook for 4 to 6 minutes more, until the second side is browned and an instant-read thermometer registers 145°F.

4. Transfer the pork chops and peppers to serving dish and let rest for 5 minutes. Pour the wine into the pan, scrape up any browned bits, and simmer for 1 minute. Pour the mixture over the pork chops and serve.

SERVES 4

501

Everything but the Squeal: Beef, Buffalo, Game, Lamb, and Pork

Bianca Garcia's Pork and Chicken Adobo

BOSTON, MASSACHUSETTES

"My family moved from the Philippines to Boston in 2000, and our go-to dish, like so many other Filipinos living abroad, is adobo," says Bianca Garcia, who is studying marketing at Harvard. "It does not matter that the dish takes hours to cook and that the smell of it stays in the apartment complex for days—it brings us a taste of home. All Filipino families each have their recipes for adobo. Basically, it is any meat or any combination of meats that is braised and simmered in vinegar, soy sauce, lots of garlic, black peppercorn, and bay leaves. Every family claims their version to be the best. Of course, that cannot be true since my family's version is the best."

2 pounds bone-in, skin-on chicken thighs

2 pounds pork belly

1 cup white vinegar

½ cup soy sauce

4 bay leaves

10 cloves garlic, crushed

2 tablespoons olive oil

Salt and pepper to taste

Red pepper flakes to taste (optional)

1. Put the chicken, pork, vinegar, soy sauce, bay leaves, and 7 garlic cloves in a shallow pot over low heat. Add one cup water, plus more if necessary, to barely cover the meat, bring to a boil, then reduce the heat and simmer for 1 hour.

2. Use slotted spoons to remove the chicken and the pork and set aside. Allow the broth to continue simmering. Warm the olive oil in a large skillet over medium-high heat. Add the rest of the garlic. Pat the pork and the chicken dry and sear each piece in the olive oil on all sides until golden brown. Return the chicken and pork to the pot, reduce the sauce by simmering for another hour to an hour and a half, stirring occasionally, until the sauce thickens.

3. Serve with fried rice.

SERVES 6

DAN THE PIG MAN'S BABY BACK RIBS

YORK, NORTH CAROLINA

Dan Huntley, former political columnist for the *Charlotte Observer*, winces, rubs his temples, and says, "Meat hangover." Then he pours himself a tankard of mint sweet tea.

He is sitting on a concrete slab in front of his Pig Palace, the three-thousand-square-foot "classy man cave" that his wife had built for him out of pine "bacon-slab siding." The Pig Palace houses his library, computers, music collection and files on the right side. But on the other side is a makeshift kitchen where, he says, "the left side of my brain lives." There, in his current life as itinerant caterer, he prepares the cauldrons of bastes and rubs and sauces that he uses to "spread the love." He also refers to his business as "insane," and "a bad living but a nice way of life." His card reads: DAN HUNTLEY, BARBECUE PROVOCATEUR, OUTDOOR FEAST CATERING, WHOLE HOG/OYSTER ROASTS/CRABMEAT GUMBO.

"I'm seventh-generation North Carolina and the first generation who ever went to college. When I was growing up, barbecue was the lowest of the low. It was poor blacks and whites making the most of poor cuts of meat, tenderizing them with vinegar and pepper and smoke. They had cinder blocks, a fire pit, and an iron grate. The come-lately rich white boys all have meat thermometers. Real barbecue guys don't take their pig's temperature. They listen to the meat, they don't want the pork cooking in its own grease. A 120-pound pig has about two gallons of grease in it. You don't want to heat it too high so that the grease cooks the flesh and you don't want it accumulating at the bottom of your rig and starting a fire.

"After college, my wife and I moved to Key West and lived in a conch shack with no refrigerator. I worked as a fisherman. I wanted to be the Ernest Hemingway of the drug generation but I ended up learning to barbecue meat from the Cubans. I turned the mailbox into a firebox, hooked it up to an old busted refrigerator with a stovepipe and smoked fish and meat. It preserved it as well as a refrigerator and it tasted better.

"When the kids came along, we moved back [to North Carolina]. I went to work at this itty bitty weekly, the *Pineville Pioneer*. After about three years, I heard that the *Charlotte Observer* was hiring photographers, so I bought a camera and turned myself into one. When the paper figured out I knew a lot of people, they let me write. The local guys all talked to me. But the national guys, the senators, presidential candidates? The only way they are going to talk to some non-Ivy, non–*New York Times* guy is if I distinguish myself in my first question. I started asking: 'When you were growing up, who did the cooking in your house?' They were expecting some question on policy or platform and they'd stop for a second and then they'd start telling me their life stories.

"For five years, I worked in a restaurant with this wonderful chef, a woman from France. She taught me the universality of cooking pork. Doesn't matter if it is cochon or carne, it's all about fire and iron. I went to barbecue cookoffs and watched. Eventually I won some pig trophies.

"Barbecue is an expression of life, an American art form. Now, I love a Weber grill, but the Weber has been the great homogenizer. Pound for pound, you are going to eat better if the cook is a contraption maker. I've seen some junkyard serendipity you wouldn't believe. My rig? I put it together for a hundred and sixty-five dollars and it's built like a Sherman tank. Why would you want to pay more for your rig than you paid for your pig? I've seen cooking rigs made out of a satellite dish found by the side of the road, smokers made out of old refrigerators, galvanized trash cans, a backhoe bucket, and a seven-foot rotisserie that one guy put together with the chain from his grandson's bicycle. You can't find that in the Yellow Pages. You can't learn how to do that on the Web. It's not about a recipe as much as it is about knowing what to do when something happens, like your rig catches fire in four lanes of traffic going seventy miles an hour.

"I invented a barbecue sauce, my Pig Pucker. I studied barbecue formally. I wrote a business plan. When the paper downsized, I started to make sauce and create feasts for people. It's tough. I don't want to deliver barbecue to someone I don't know or don't like. I put too much of myself into it. That's not good for business. But you know, this morning at five, I came out here and got the fire going and that smoke, it's like an aura. It takes me into another zone, some place between, you know, primal man hunting and the shade tree mechanic."

4 racks baby back pork ribs, 4 to 6 pounds

1 teaspoon fine sea salt

1 teaspoon chili powder

1 teaspoon ground cumin

1 teaspoon sweet paprika

½ teaspoon ground allspice

½ teaspoon ground cinnamon

½ teaspoon ground nutmeg

½ teaspoon ground black pepper

½ teaspoon cayenne pepper

1 teaspoon Tabasco sauce

2 cups ketchup

¾ cup molasses

½ cup cider vinegar

1. Dry the ribs and let them come to room temperature while you prepare the dry rub.

2. To make the dry rub, combine all the dry spices in a glass jar and shake to combine well. Coat the ribs on all sides with the rub, wrap tightly in plastic wrap, and refrigerate for 24 hours.

3. Make the sauce by combining the Tabasco, ketchup, molasses, and vinegar, in a 1-quart glass jar. Shake well and store in the refrigerator overnight.

4. Three hours before you intend to serve the ribs, remove them from the refrigerator, brush off the excess dry rub, and bring them to room temperature. Prepare a wood fire or preheat the oven to 250°F.

5. Brush the ribs with sauce and place over the heat. Cover and cook for 2½ to 3 hours, turning and brushing with sauce several times until the meat has shrunk away from the bone and is very tender.

6. Ten minutes before the meat is finished, slather generously with the sauce. Serve with additional sauce for dipping.

SERVES 4

INTINERATE CUE MASTERS

JIMMY HAGOOD OF CHARLESTON, SOUTH CAROLINA, HAS VIP SEATING ON the top of the barbecue RV that he drives around the country, spreading the gospel of Carolina 'Cue. While friends and fellow Carolinians sip and savor above, he offers tastes on the asphalt at the annual Big Apple Barbecue Block Party.

TONY TSUJIKAKA'S SMOKED BABY BACKS AND SAUERKRAUT

SEATTLE, WASHINGTON

In Seattle, in the 1940s Torakichi ("Tony") Tsujikaka's business partner, and one of his first friends in the United States, was a German man named Bert Mieks. Mr. Mieks taught him everything he needed to know to get started in ceramics manufacturing, and perhaps equally important, how to make these smoked baby back ribs with sauerkraut. Now, Mr. Tsujikaka's daughter, Grace Boyd, serves the dish with potatoes, mashed or baked, but nothing too rich, as the ribs and sauerkraut are almost a meal in themselves. She has a propane smoker, and adds mesquite wood chips to the lava rocks for flavor.

Two 1½- to 2-pound racks baby back pork ribs, cut into slabs that can fit into your smoker

1 tablespoon garlic powder

2 tablespoons seasoning salt (preferably Johnny's Seasoning)

8 ounces thick-cut bacon, cut into ½-inch pieces

1 medium onion, finely chopped

4 cups sauerkraut, drained well, excess moisture squeezed out

1½ tablespoons brown sugar

2 bay leaves

1½ tablespoons whole black peppercorns

1 cup water

1½ teaspoons caraway seeds

Kosher salt and freshly ground black pepper

1. Preheat the smoker to medium-high heat. Lightly sprinkle the slabs of ribs on both sides with garlic powder and seasoning salt. Place the slabs of ribs on the smoker racks. Smoke about 5 hours, until the meat pulls away from the bone. Remove from the smoker and keep warm.

2. Cook the bacon in a Dutch oven over medium-low heat about 10 minutes, until crispy. Drain the bacon on paper towels. Add the onion to the fat and cook over medium heat about 4 minutes, until soft.

3. Stir in the sauerkraut, brown sugar, bay leaves, peppercorns, and water. Bring to a simmer, cover, and cook for 30 minutes. Add caraway seeds and stir to combine.

4. Add the ribs and cook for 5 to 10 minutes, until the liquid is thickened. Season with salt and pepper to taste and serve.

SERVES 4 TO 6

GEORGE CHEW'S JUSTIFIABLY FAMOUS RIBS

George Chew came up with this simple recipe when he was in law school and helping to raise money for the Asian American student group: It is one part bean sauce and three parts hoisin sauce with garlic. "As my cooking evolved, I started to riff on the recipe, adding other ingredients. It is still changing depending on the availability of ingredients, but the essentials remain the bean and hoisin sauces and making people happy that they showed up to eat."

507

FOR THE MARINADE

6 tablespoons hoisin sauce

3 tablespoons ketchup

2 tablespoons maple syrup

2 tablespoons mirin

2 tablespoons Chinese black bean sauce

2 tablespoons dark soy sauce

2 tablespoons toasted sesame oil

1 tablespoon rice vinegar

1 tablespoon Asian chili sauce

2 garlic cloves, minced

1 teaspoon minced fresh ginger

1 teaspoon freshly ground black pepper

Four 2½- to 2-pound racks pork spareribs, trimmed

1. One to two days before serving, combine the marinade ingredients in a large glass, ceramic, or enameled baking dish and let sit for 1 hour.

2. Lightly score the meat side of the ribs. Add the ribs to the marinade and rub it in well. Cover, and refrigerate for 1 to 2 days, rubbing the ribs with the marinade every 8 hours.

3. Place the oven racks in the bottom-center and top-center positions and preheat oven to 350°F. Line two large rimmed baking sheets with foil.

4. Place the ribs in a single layer on the baking sheets and roast for 50 minutes. Flip the ribs and cook for 20 minutes, then flip again and cook for 20 to 30 minutes more, until the meat pulls away from the bone.

5. Transfer to a carving board, cut into individual ribs, and serve.

SERVES 6 TO 8

Everything but the Squeal: Beef, Buffalo, Game, Lamb, and Pork

Ermita Campos's Red Chile Pork

Ermita Campos farms a strip of dusty land outside Santa Fe. She and her daughter Margarite grow many vegetables but are most famous for the tomatoes that they sell at farmers' markets and serve with the family's red chile pork. "I am not sure where the recipe came from, it's older than dirt, simple, full of flavor. You can use any cut of meat. When we make it for the young chefs and serve it with warm corn tortillas and a nice pot of beans they act like we invented water, like red chile is new," she says. Looking past the parched riverbanks that frame her fields to the rocky hillside, she smiles. "I guess you could say its new every time you make it. Yes, you could say that."

2 pounds boneless pork shoulder or butt, trimmed

4 or 5 garlic cloves

1 teaspoon kosher salt

1 quart water

2 tablespoons bacon drippings or vegetable oil

1 tablespoon all-purpose flour

½ cup pure red chile powder

Cooked pinto beans, for serving

1. Rinse the meat and pat dry.

2. Put 2 garlic cloves through a press and rub on the all sides of the pork. Sprinkle with ½ teaspoon salt.

3. Place the pork in a slow cooker or pressure cooker and pour in the water. Set the slow cooker for 6 hours or pressure cook for 30 minutes.

4. Cool the meat in the broth.

5. Discard any excess fat from the meat and broth. Shred the meat. Set aside the broth.

6. Finely chop or press the remaining garlic. Heat the bacon drippings in a 2-quart skillet over medium heat. Add flour and stir until smooth. Stir in the garlic and shredded pork and brown lightly.

7. Stir in the chile powder and brown lightly, being careful not to scorch it.

8. Mix in the broth slowly and check that all the chile powder has dissolved. Reduce the heat to very low and simmer until the broth thickens.

9. Serve with beans and as much of the red chile sauce as the eater will brave.

SERVES 4

Christy Spackman's Meat Pie

When Christy Spackman was a child in Utah her mother taught her to cook. "At one point," she says, "I realized that I can actually trace this pie recipe back to my great-great grandmother Josephine Giggar, who was born in Sioux City, Iowa. The pie was passed down from her paternal grandfather, Wayne Line, who married into the Church of the Latter-Day Saints, and his daughter Norma made it her own."

Ms. Spackman says she's added "a bit more seasoning here, another little flavor there, but this pie defines me as a daughter, granddaughter, sister, and cousin."

1 recipe Pie Day Committee's Crust (page 693) or store-bought pie dough

8 ounces boneless pork shoulder, trimmed and cut into ½-inch pieces

1 small onion, finely chopped

1¼ pounds red potatoes, peeled and cut into ¼-inch pieces

½ teaspoon ground cloves

2 teaspoons ground cinnamon

¾ teaspoon ground allspice

½ teaspoon ground cumin

½ teaspoon ground coriander

¼ teaspoon cayenne pepper

Kosher salt and freshly ground black pepper

1. Divide the dough in half and roll each piece out on a lightly floured work surface to a 12-inch circle, about ⅛ inch thick. Fit one dough round into a 9-inch pie plate and transfer the second one to a lightly floured parchment-paper-lined baking sheet. Cover both and refrigerate until needed.

2. Place an oven rack in the center position and preheat the oven to 425°F.

3. Bring the pork and 3 cups water to a simmer in a large saucepan. Cook for 30 minutes.

4. Add the onion and cook for 5 minutes, until the onion is tender.

5. Drain the pork and onion, reserving ½ cup of the cooking water. Transfer the pork and onion to a large bowl.

6. Meanwhile, in a separate pot, bring the potatoes and 1 quart water to a simmer. Cook for 5 to 7 minutes, until tender. Drain.

7. Add the cloves, cinnamon, allspice, cumin, coriander, and cayenne to the meat and toss to combine. Stir in the potatoes. Season with salt and pepper to taste, then stir in the reserved ½ cup of liquid.

8. Pour the pork mixture into the dough-lined pie plate. Top with a second dough round and crimp the edges. Cut a couple of slits in the top crust. Bake for 30 minutes, until the crust is golden brown.

9. Let sit for 10 minutes before serving.

SERVES 8

ELANA GARCES'S STEAMED PORK LOAF

MIAMI, FLORIDA

Elana Garces's great-grandfather moved from South China to Cuba in 1930 to work the sugarcane, and married the daughter of a Cuban coworker. "They moved to Miami before World War Two and sold vegetables in the market," Ms. Garces says. "They also sold rice and beans and meat pies and carne. Later, they had a little store and some rental apartments." Ms. Garces's great-grandfather played the ukulele and loved to eat everything from Cuba and Miami—but not beef meatloaf, which he said was disgusting.

"One Thanksgiving he made a Chinese steamed meatloaf from a recipe he found in a Chinese American cookbook," she says. "Then my mother made it better. And I made it better again. My great-grandfather was very proud when I became an ophthalmologist," she says, "but he was most proud of my Chinese steamed pork loaf. He said that if I didn't make it for his funeral, he would come back and haunt me. He died last year when he was a hundred and one years old and I have not seen him since."

2 duck or large chicken eggs

2 tablespoons soy sauce

½ teaspoon rice vinegar

1 pound ground pork

1 pound fresh water chestnuts, scrubbed and peeled, or two 8-ounce cans, rinsed and drained, coarsely chopped

4 scallions, green and white parts, finely chopped

2 tablespoons minced fresh cilantro

1 tablespoon rice wine

2 teaspoons kosher salt

½ teaspoon Chinese red chili oil

2 teaspoons toasted sesame oil, plus more for the pan

1 teaspoon sugar

2 teaspoons cornstarch

1 tablespoon dry sherry

2 tablespoons fermented black beans

1 tablespoon toasted sesame seeds

1. The day before serving, place the eggs in a small pot and cover with cold water by ½ inch. Add 1 tablespoon of the soy sauce and the vinegar and bring to a boil over medium heat. Remove from the heat, cool the eggs in the soy water completely, and refrigerate overnight.

2. Peel and halve the eggs, discard the whites, and chop the yolks.

3. In a large bowl, combine the remaining 1 tablespoon soy sauce with the pork, water chestnuts, scallions, cilantro, rice wine, salt, chili oil, sesame oil, and sugar. Use your hands to combine well. In a small bowl, stir together the cornstarch and sherry, add to the meat, and combine well.

4. Place half the meat on a large sheet of plastic wrap and shape into an 11 x 5-inch rectangle. Sprinkle the egg yolks down the center of the meat. Place the black beans in a column along either side of the egg, then sprinkle the sesame seeds over the meat.

5. Cover with the remaining meat mixture and press gently to seal the edges, then wrap tightly in the plastic wrap, put on a heatproof plate that will fit into a steamer, and refrigerate for 2 hours.

6. If you have a steamer, pour 1 quart of water in the bottom of it and arrange the rack. Or make a steamer by placing a rack or heatproof plate in the bottom of a large pot with a tight-fitting cover. Add enough water to almost reach the bottom of the rack and bring to a boil. Carefully add the meatloaf, cover the pot, and steam over high heat for 20 minutes, until an instant-read thermometer registers 150°F.

7. Transfer the meatloaf to a carving board and let cool. Remove the plastic wrap and slice the pork loaf. Serve.

——

SERVES 6 TO 8

"THE BEST IN THE MARKET."

CHAPTER 8

EAT YOUR VEGETABLES

When Eat Your Vegetables Day was established in 1991, it was a declaration of courage and evidence that the nation's traditional meat-and-potato mentality had begun to falter. Cattlemen roared in protest. Vegetarians exulted. Medical experts heralded the designation as a giant step toward healthful eating. In all the din, the deeper significance of Americans celebrating vegetables by eating them all day—went all but unnoticed.

No robust, work-a-day American quakes in the face of say, spinach, but most would agree with the famous 1928 *New Yorker* cartoon, with E. B. White's succinct caption: "I say it's spinach and I say the Hell with it." Several years later, in one of the songs that he wrote for *Face the Music*, Irving Berlin labeled all trouble, disappointment, or inconvenience as "spinach," and echoed Mr. White in the refrain: "And the Hell with it!"

This history of suspicion and revulsion has simmered beneath the surface of American life for more than three centuries.

One of the first vegetables European settlers were offered in the New World—fresh corn, which they

called "maize"—was something they'd been raised to view as animal fodder. So they quickly shifted their attention to propagating the livestock they'd brought from the Old World. Alas, their early attempts floundered. On the other hand, the vegetable seeds they'd brought—carrots, beets, turnips, onions, cabbages, peas, endive, shallots, spinach, chives, cucumbers, lettuce, cresses, and leeks—flourished.

Massachusetts' Bay Colonists rejoiced that the New World soil produced better "garden fruit" than Europe's. Conscientious housewives served vegetables year-round by partially cooking and sealing some with fat in crocks, sun-drying others, and packing others in straw and storing them in root cellars. In the fall, the last pickings were turned into winter's pickles, preserves, sauces, and catsups. But as soon as they had a steady supply of meat, red-blooded Americans pushed fresh and preserved vegetables to the sides of their plates.

Like meat and game, highly durable vegetables such as pumpkins, cabbages, and other root crops were suited to the harshness and constant motion of frontier life. The more delicate vegetables were a

lot of work to grow and even more work to keep, and for nearly a century, they were the province of landowners who had both the space—and, until after the Civil War, the free labor—to cultivate and preserve the bounty.

In a culture that proclaims all people to be equal, small distinctions loom large. Fresh vegetables were one of the first foods to carry a social distinction between "us" (the majority who labor) and "them" (the upper class who did not). The latter were disgusted by crude cabbages and roots; the former considered slender asparagus and little peas suspiciously dainty. Even in the late twentieth century, when "real men" did not eat quiche, eating vegetables was mocked as being "unmasculine."

Overcooking was the nation's answer (and perhaps another expression of vegetable hatred). One 1895 cookbook called for a three-hour cook time for string beans and two hours for carrots. In the late nineteenth century, Juliet Corson, the famed founder of The New York Cooking School, said that following such instructions yielded brown-green masses of fiber with no taste or nutritional value.

But ambition and starvation are strong currents in American cuisine. By the late nineteenth century, however, the emerging middle class dreamed of even further ascent and mimicked the styles and tastes of those who had already arrived. Grand restaurants opened in large cities, and chefs turned out superb vegetable dishes. Increasingly the public didn't need to be force-fed peas. "British peas"—or *petit pois*, thank you very much—became a sign of high class.

The wider market for produce prompted Southern states to grow early- and late-season tomatoes, radishes, cucumbers, cauliflower, onions, and salad greens and to ship them north. By the roaring '90s, refrigerated rail cars, along with increased market gardening and truck farming brought fresh vegetables to city dwellers every month. But the demand pushed growers to

produce greater quantities of sturdier goods, and taste was an early casualty.

When the Great Migration of the 1890s brought thousands of Italians and Greeks with strange varieties of broccoli, eggplant, green beans, tepary beans, tomatoes, greens, garlic, and even parsley, vegetable fear found a new target.

In her 1881 book *Fifty Years in a Maryland Kitchen*, Jane Grant Gilmore Howard noted "a very general prejudice" against fresh garlic.

As late as 1927 Ida Cogswell Bailey Allen, star of *The National Radio Homemaker's Club*, wrote that the United States was the only country where vegetables were more "accessories than real foods," and were seen as "necessary evils."

Among upper- and middle-class urbanites, the view on "new" vegetables was that they were "scary and disgusting until proven otherwise by a famous chef." In the meantime, they clung to their familiar peas and carrots. No such adjustment was needed in rural areas, where vegetable love hadn't made many inroads. A survey of rural families in Ohio between 1926 to 1928, writes Richard Hooker in *Food and Drink in America*, showed that of the thousands of varieties of vegetables available in the nation, "only potatoes, cabbages, lettuce, tomatoes, onions, corn, sweet potatoes and string beans" were commonly used. Even more worrying: "A home demonstration agent in South Carolina regretted that farmers felt they were 'too busy' to bother with gardens, poultry and dairy products and instead concentrated on cotton and other major crops."

Large-scale canning and freezing technology arrived just in time. Without a way to mass-market vegetables (and fruit), the United States could have ended up with a big cotton patch.

Both canned and frozen food were sold as early as the 1870s, but neither became big business until after the mechanics of canning improved and Clarence Birdseye, a former field naturalist, invented an industrial flash-freezing method, and began to exercise his genius for product development and marketing.

He called his products "frosted," and used Eskimos and sled dogs to evoke the wholesome

Thornton Dial, 2005.

naturalness of the spinach and peas he introduced in 1930. People loved them, but it took fifteen years to convince retailers to buy freezers for his frozen delicacies when they already displayed cans of the same vegetables on their shelves. World War II made the decision for them.

"Tin went to war; frozen foods stayed home," wrote E. W. Williams, the president of the Quick Frozen Food Association in his book *Frozen Foods*.

By the time he died in 1956, the industry that Mr. Birdseye invented was flourishing. Rare was the home without at least a package of frozen peas in the freezer. Mr. Birdseye claimed that his frozen vegetables were better than fresh, and with farmers increasingly developing vegetables to survive long shipping and storage times, his claim was plausible. Early on, the larger frozen food companies established regional processing stations so that vegetables destined to be frozen often traveled far fewer miles than those shipped long distances, held in cold storage, and sold as "fresh." The convenience of vegetables that required no washing, peeling, slicing, or dicing was indisputable. By creating fancy, freezable vegetable preparations he saved cooks even more time, and gave them panache as well.

The most powerful thing that the former field naturalist supplied, however, was the knowledge and authority of the company that bore his name. There he was, an exacting and protective shield, between the dangerous, bumpkin-tended earth and the vulnerable consumer with his clean white collar. There was nothing to fear in Mr. Birdseye's vegetables. Flash-freezing was the final answer to vegetable fear.

It was also a great democratizer. It was difficult to meet the demand for cheap vegetables using old-fashioned farming techniques, but quick freezing allowed the geographically remote and the economically challenged to eat nutritionally intact, almost-fresh vegetables 365 days a year. After 1954, when TV dinners were introduced and became an instant sensation, after fast food began to sprawl alongside highways and neighborhoods, more and more fertilizers, pesticides, and soil-distressing farming techniques were required to fill the vegetable compartment in the aluminum trays, the cardboard french fry container, the plastic salad bar boxes, and the tomato center of frozen pizzas.

But in mid-century, frozen vegetables were young and anything seemed possible. Home cooks used

PRODUCE OF U.S.A. arrowhead ranches, inc., GLENDALE, ARIZONA

an arsenal of convenience foods to prepare creative, economical, all-American family-style dishes such as green bean and mushroom casserole in a jiffy.

Did people learn to love vegetables enough to rise up and defend them against culinary malfeasance? Was it ambition to save the planet or the eternal need of different generations to distinguish themselves that caused the food revolution? Or was it a nutritional imbalance as serious as scurvy on the western frontier that turned these creations, along with frozen, canned, and otherwise processed food, into public health enemy number one.

We do not know. We know that National Eat Your Vegetable Day, which fell in National Candy Month, and shared its date with Watergate Day and National Apple Strudel Day, disappeared. We know that after the San Francisco board of supervisors voted to declare Mondays as Vegetarian Day, the public response was divided. One local citizen criticized the image of a tea leaf salad as "technically . . . not vegetarian—note the dried shrimp flakes . . ." Another citizen said: "Let's forbid eating tofus once a week in this town. I'm sick of the veggie/vegan hipster holier than thou attitude. Let's hear it for tofu-free Tuesdays!"

SHELLY BONHAM'S FIDDLEHEAD FERNS

Shelly Bonham's grandmother learned the lessons of the Great Depression and taught her to forage, can, and freeze. But Ms. Bonham was slow to adopt these traditions. "I am a Gen Xer and I got lost in the good life for a while. But now that I have children of my own, I want to teach them the same self-sustaining values that were instilled in me . . . that wonderful and delicious things do not have to be expensive, that acting resourcefully pays dividends, and that sometimes, trudging through the mud takes you to the greatest treasures." Fiddleheads, the young coiled sprout of the ostrich fern that grow in the newly warm ground in early spring in northern New England, have become emblematic of her return to the simple life. She named the magazine that she founded and dedicated to sustainable living *Fiddlehead Loop*. And in addition to gathering, cooking, and preserving this spring delicacy, she has debriefed her grandmother for recipes. This is one of her favorites.

One Big Table

2 tablespoons fresh lemon juice

¾ teaspoon kosher salt

Freshly ground black pepper

2 tablespoons olive oil

4 cups fiddleheads, cleaned and trimmed

1. Bring a medium pot of water to a boil.

2. In a large bowl, combine the lemon juice, salt, and pepper to taste. Whisk in the olive oil.

3. When the water is boiling, add the fiddleheads. Boil until tender, 5 to 7 minutes.

4. Drain, shake dry, and add to the lemon and olive oil dressing. Toss to coat well and serve as you would asparagus, as a first course or side dish.

SERVES 4

Simpson Wong's Sichuan Pea Greens

When he was forty years old, Simpson Wong owned two restaurants in New York City. He was a runner—lean, fit, and health conscious. Then, one morning at the gym, the Malaysian-born chef suffered a heart attack. "There are heart issues in my family, I smoked and probably consumed two cups of butter a night just tasting dishes before they went out to the dining room," he said. He scaled back to one restaurant and lowered the fat content of his cooking. The result is light, vivid dishes such as these fresh pea greens with a hot, jalapeño bite and a hint of sesame.

Kosher salt

6 quarts fresh pea greens, or watercress (about 16 bunches), heavy stems removed

2 teaspoons canola or vegetable oil

4 garlic cloves, finely chopped

2 jalapeño chiles, seeded and finely chopped

1 teaspoon toasted sesame oil

1 tablespoon soy sauce

1. Bring a large pot of water to a boil. Lightly salt the water, add the pea greens, and boil for 30 seconds. Quickly drain and rinse under cold running water. Pat dry.

2. Heat the oil in a large heavy skillet or wok over medium-high heat. Add the garlic and jalapeños and cook, stirring constantly, until fragrant, about 30 seconds. Add the pea greens and stir for 1 minute.

3. Transfer to a large bowl and add the sesame oil and soy sauce. Toss to combine. Divide among four plates and serve immediately.

SERVES 4

Marge Klindera's German-Style Spinach

In the twenty-six years that Marge Klindera has been part of Butterball University's fifty-five-member team that fields about two hundred thousand calls a year for turkey-cooking advice, she has talked thousands of home cooks through their holiday recipes.

This "old-time German recipe for creamed spinach from my mother" remains her favorite holiday dish. Reminiscent of the creamed spinach served in traditional American steakhouses, it can be further enriched by substituting heavy cream for half the milk.

6 slices bacon

3 pounds fresh spinach, stemmed, or two 10-ounce packages of frozen chopped spinach, thawed

2 tablespoons all-purpose flour

2 cups milk

1 tablespoon minced onion

Kosher salt and freshly ground black pepper

1. Bring a large pot of lightly salted water to a boil.

2. Fry the bacon in a large skillet over medium heat until crisp. Using a slotted spoon, transfer the bacon to a paper towel to drain.

3. When the water is boiling, drop in the spinach, working in batches if necessary. Boil until tender. Drain and cool completely under cold running water. Squeeze it dry and coarsely chop. (If using frozen spinach, just drain and squeeze dry.)

4. Return the skillet with the bacon grease to low heat. Add the flour and whisk until smooth. Slowly add the milk, whisking until smooth.

5. Add the onion and season lightly with salt and pepper. Add the spinach. Cook, stirring occasionally, until the sauce thickens, about 10 minutes.

6. Remove from the heat, and taste and adjust with additional salt and pepper if desired. Crumble the reserved bacon on top and serve.

SERVES 6

One Big Table

JILL WENDHOLT SILVA'S
AFTER THE SPINACH FESTIVAL SPINACH

LENEXA, KANSAS

During the 1930s, Lenexa, Kansas, was known as "the spinach capital of the world" and home to a sizable community of émigrés from Brussels who first introduced the crop. When Jill Wendholt Silva moved to the little town just south of Kansas City, she was eager to attend the annual spinach festival. It boasted an appearance of Popeye and Olive Oyl, as well as the world's largest spinach salad and Ms. Silva, the food editor of the *Kansas City Star*, had visions of finding spinach growers and spinach cooks coming home with recipes. Instead, she returned home with a desire to cook spinach, and then more spinach. This dish, a variation on the traditional Italian dish, is probably too simple to enter in the spinach festival cooking contest, but as Popeye can attest, simple is better when it comes to spinach.

1½ pounds fresh spinach

2 tablespoons olive oil, plus more to taste

2 tablespoons pine nuts

Salt to taste

4 garlic cloves, thinly sliced

Freshly ground black pepper to taste

Juice from ½ fresh lemon, about 1 tablespoon

1. Trim away stems from spinach and rinse in two changes of cold water. Drain and dry in a salad spinner and set aside. Warm 1 teaspoon of the olive oil in a skillet over medium-low heat. Add the pine nuts and cook, tossing and stirring constantly until golden, 1 to 2 minutes. Remove the nuts to paper towels, season lightly with salt, and return the skillet to the heat.

2. Add 1 tablespoon of olive oil and when it is warm, add the garlic and cook, stirring frequently, until just golden, about 2 minutes. Add a handful of spinach and toss. Raise the heat to high and, as the spinach wilts and makes room in the pan, add more. When all the spinach is cooking, toss it in the pan, and season lightly with salt and black pepper. Cover the pan, cook for 1 minute, remove from heat and allow to sit for 3 minutes to finish cooking. Add the lemon juice, adjust seasoning with salt, pepper, and olive oil, if desired. Sprinkle with the pine nuts and serve.

SERVES 4 AS A SIDE DISH

"*I do not like broccoli. And I haven't liked it since I was a little kid and my mother made me eat it. And I'm President of the United States and I'm not going to eat any more broccoli.*"

—George H. W. Bush

Roli Khare's Nouveau Saag Paneer

JERSEY CITY, NEW JERSEY

Roli Khare, a government attorney and Hindu vegetarian, sees cooking as a meditative practice, an offering for both the diner and the divine. She began cooking while she was an exchange student living in her parents' native India. The intensity of her experiences there shaped not only her worldview but also her cooking style. "Like navigating the streets of Delhi," she says, "a little bit of luck and eccentricity is required." This variation on the saag paneer of north India was an accident. "I grabbed broccolini instead of spinach at the market and my mother, who is a wonderful cook, encouraged me to work with it, adding some collard greens to the mix. The results were a far cry from the heavy saag paneer that many Indian restaurants serve their American customers. To lighten her version further and create a dish that can serve as a main course or a side dish, Ms. Khare uses tofu instead of paneer (a fresh, pressed cheese). Either—or even both—make a fine variation on the classic theme.

Kosher salt

1 bunch fresh broccolini, trimmed

1 bunch fresh collard greens or mustard greens, heavy stems removed

1 tablespoon ghee or vegetable oil

2 teaspoons ground coriander

½ teaspoon ground turmeric

¼ teaspoon cayenne pepper or 1 small fresh chile, finely chopped

1 teaspoon chopped fresh ginger

2 pinches of asafetida

3 tablespoons water

⅔ cup crème fraîche

½ pound firm tofu, cut into 1-inch cubes, or ½ pound paneer or queso fresco, cut into 1-inch cubes

½ teaspoon sugar

1 teaspoon fresh lemon juice

Chapatis or whole-wheat pita bread, for serving

1. Add 2 teaspoons salt to a large pot of water and bring to a boil. Add the broccolini and collard greens and simmer until very tender, about 1 hour.

2. Drain the vegetables, reserving about ⅓ cup of the cooking water. Transfer to a blender or food processor and blend until slightly chopped; do not overblend to a puree.

3. Heat the ghee in a large saucepan over medium heat and fry the coriander, turmeric, cayenne, ginger, and asafetida for 30 seconds. Add the vegetables and the water. Cover and cook over medium-low heat for 10 minutes.

4. Stir in the crème fraîche. Add the tofu, 1 teaspoon salt, and the sugar, stir well, and simmer over low heat for 5 minutes more.

5. Transfer to a serving dish and mix in the lemon juice. Adjust the salt to taste. Serve with chapatis or whole-wheat pita bread.

SERVES 4

FARM FUTURES

IN THE 1960S, WOMEN IN JAPAN WHO WERE CONCERNED ABOUT FOOD SAFETY AND THE
industrialization of food sources created partnerships with farmers to pre-buy their harvest. A
quarter century passed before Community Supported Agriculture began appearing in the United
States. Today, CSA members purchase "shares" and receive weekly deliveries of what is ripe, typically
picking up bags and boxes of food from church basements. Cooking in response to the produce as it
appears reverses the modern American cooking paradigm—find recipe, buy ingredients, cook—and this
responsive cooking is a significant challenge for some. But it may be a sign of cooking to come. There
are more than 3,000 community supported farms nationwide, and some individual farms have begun
to collaborate on weekly deliveries of locally grown vegetables, meat, chicken, fish, dairy, and eggs.
One, the Good Natured Family Farms, a cooperative of 150 family farms located within 100 miles of
Kansas City, created a partnership with Hen House grocery stores and nearly 1,500 members pick
up their weekly grocery orders at one of the store's twelve locations. "It takes an intense amount of
organization," said Diana Endicott, who along with her husband Gary sold a landscaping business in
Texas to return to their childhood home in Kansas, where they farm over 400 acres, "and you always
have to be thinking of the next need." In addition to their CSA at Hen House, Ms. Endicott created a
workplace CSA and delivers a refrigerated truck to a large business for weekly pickups. Employees at
Hallmark Cards in downtown Kansas City, for instance, can pick up their weekly delivery in the parking
lot after work. "Every box keeps another family on their land," she says.

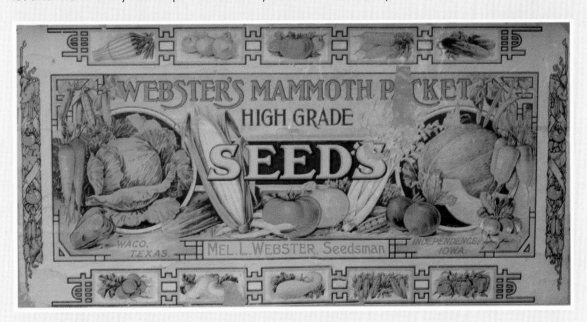

CHRIS DUVAL'S QUICK-BRAISED COLLARD GREENS WITH BACON AND SWEET ONIONS

SEATTLE, WASHINGTON

Growing up in Dallas, Chris Duval loved helping his dad cook Mexican food. "I still have a scar from cutting lettuce" says the software tester. Mr. Duval's heritage includes "a little French and Russian"; his wife, Lisa, is Armenian. Cooking is their idea of a good time.

Although collard greens are considered Southern, they grow well in Seattle. Inspired by something he saw on the Food Network, Mr. Duval figured out a way to use some of his favorite things—peppery bacon and the local sweet Walla Walla onions—with the thick-leaved, cold-weather greens.

1 pound collard greens (1 large bunch), stalks trimmed, roughly chopped

¼ pound thick-sliced pepper bacon, cut into ½-inch strips

1 small Walla Walla or other sweet onion, finely chopped (about ¾ cup)

1½ cups homemade chicken broth or low-sodium store-bought chicken broth

Kosher salt and freshly ground black pepper

1. Bring a large pot of salted water to a boil. Add the collards and cook until they are wilted, about 5 minutes. Drain.

2. Cook the bacon in a large skillet over medium-high heat, stirring occasionally, until crisp and brown and the fat is rendered, 3 to 4 minutes. Add the onion and cook until softened, about 4 minutes.

3. Add the greens and turn to coat well. Add the chicken broth to cover the collards. Cook until the liquid is reduced by half and greens are very tender, about 15 minutes. Season to taste with salt and pepper, and serve.

SERVES 4 AS A SIDE DISH

Grading and packing onions, ARTHUR ROTHSTEIN, 1939.

SHAHEEN SHAHNAZ'S
COLLARD GREEN THORAN

Thoran is a traditional lunch side dish in Kerala, India, where Shaheen Shahnaz grew up. It is served, says Ms. Shahnaz, now an architect, whether the household is "Muslim, Christian, or Hindu, carnivores or vegetarians." Just about any green vegetable can be used. On the weekends, she loves to serve her husband and two children ghee rice, chicken or lamb stew, a dry lentil curry, and a thoran of spinach, collard greens, or kale. Served with rice, fish or lentil curry, pickles, and pappadam (crisp lentil wafers), thoran makes a quick, tasty weekday meal.

1 bunch collard greens

¼ cup grated fresh coconut

2 shallots, sliced

2 garlic cloves

1 tablespoon vegetable oil

½ teaspoon yellow mustard seeds

2 whole fresh red chiles

¼ teaspoon ground turmeric

¼ teaspoon ground red chile (optional)

Sea salt or kosher salt

Steamed rice (preferably basmati), for serving

1. Soak the greens in lots of water for 5 to 10 minutes to get rid of the sand. Rinse well. Drain thoroughly, then blot dry with paper towels. Remove the thick central stem and slice the leaves into thin ribbons.

2. Pulse the coconut, shallots, and garlic in a food processor until the mixture looks scrambled.

3. Heat the oil in a large skillet or wok over medium heat and add the mustard seeds and whole chiles. Fry until the mustard seeds begin to pop. Add the collard greens, turmeric, and ground chile, if using. Add 2 to 3 tablespoons water, cover, reduce the heat to low, and cook about 5 minutes until leaves are wilted. (They take longer to cook than other greens, so check the pan after 5 minutes, add water by spoonfuls, and cook longer, if needed.)

4. Make a well in the middle of the greens, add the coconut mixture, then cover it with the greens. Cook uncovered over medium heat for 5 to 10 minutes more, until all the water evaporates. Add salt to taste. Serve with rice.

SERVES 4 TO 6

Bernadette Grosjean's Endive Gratin

LOS ANGELES, CALIFORNIA

Growing up in Belgium, Bernadette Grosjean took her mother's creamy gratin of endive-stuffed ham for granted. Now a psychiatrist at the University of California Los Angeles, Dr. Grosjean realizes how rare a dish it is. She spends her days treating the indigent and homeless in L.A. and says, "After a day of giving therapy on the street, in abandoned buildings, the back seat of my car, I'm hungry for the familiar, for something comforting. Nothing does the job as well as this dish, which happens to be one of the few things I can cook. At home we served it as a main course with buttered mashed potatoes. My friends here think that is a little excessive."

3 tablespoons (³⁄₈ stick) unsalted butter, plus more for the baking dish

8 heads Belgian endive, about 2 pounds

Salt and freshly ground white pepper

2 teaspoons all-purpose flour

½ cup milk

1 cup grated Gruyère cheese

½ cup heavy cream

⅛ teaspoon freshly grated nutmeg

16 thin slices ham

Mashed potatoes, for serving

1. Preheat the oven to 350°F. Lightly butter an 8-inch square flameproof baking dish.

2. Slice the endive crosswise into ¼-inch pieces. Melt 2 tablespoons of the butter in a large skillet over medium heat. Add the endive, season lightly with salt and white pepper, and cook, tossing gently, until it is nearly soft. Pour into a colander and drain while preparing the sauce.

3. To make the sauce, melt the remaining butter in a small saucepan over low heat. Whisk in the flour to make a smooth paste. Whisk in the milk a little at a time and simmer gently until the sauce is beginning to thicken, about 5 minutes. Add half the cheese a little at a time, stirring well between each addition. Season with salt and white pepper and stir. Stir in the cream and season with the nutmeg. Cook for 5 minutes more, stirring constantly. Remove from the heat.

4. Place a ham slice in the baking dish, add a drizzle of cream sauce and a spoonful of endive. Carefully roll the ham into a firm cylinder. Use a toothpick, if necessary, to secure the roll. Continue until all the ham and endive are used. Spread the remaining cream sauce over the endive rolls, sprinkle with the remaining cheese, cover with foil, and bake for 15 minutes.

5. Remove from the oven. Turn on the broiler and place the baking dish under it to brown the cheese. Serve immediately.

SERVES 4 AS A MAIN COURSE, 8 AS A SIDE DISH

Henrietta Cosentino's Chard Torta

The young man who courted Henrietta Cosentino in southern Nigeria, when they were both Peace Corps teachers, was attacked by marauding thieves on his way to their first date. When Donald Cosentino limped into her house, she poured him a shot of fiery gin, surveyed her almost bare larder, and fried up a yam. He broke a tooth.

Los Angeles has provided a polyglot environment for Ms. Cosentino to expand her food knowledge. She finds inspiration at Catalina's Market on Western Avenue where she picks up Argentinian sardo cheese, crème caramel, and empanadas. When she's too busy to cook, she often buys the torta, baked in a gigantic pie plate. To make it herself, she picks chard from her vegetable garden and steams it. The torta is a big hit at dinner parties, served warm or cold to accompany Italian cold cuts, grilled sausage, or cold salmon.

1 recipe dough for a double-crust pie (pages 693, 694, 695, 696, or 697)

3 large bunches chard, trimmed

3 red-skinned potatoes

3 hard-boiled eggs, peeled and chopped

½ cup chopped drained pimento-stuffed olives

⅛ teaspoon ground cumin

⅛ teaspoon ground cinnamon

1 teaspoon kosher salt

1 teaspoon freshly ground black pepper

3 large eggs, lightly beaten

1 tablespoon unsalted butter, cut into small pieces and chilled

1. Preheat the oven to 425°F. Divide the pie crust in half and roll each out to 12 inches. Circle a 9-inch pie pan with one. Refrigerate the pan and the other circle.

2. Place the chard in a large stockpot with 1 cup of water, cover, and steam until wilted and the stalks soften.

3. Drain the chard thoroughly, transfer to a large bowl or cutting board, and mince.

4. Prick the potatoes with a fork, place in a small bowl with 2 tablespoons water, and cover with plastic wrap. Microwave for 5 minutes or until just fork-tender.

5. Drain the potatoes, cool slightly, and chop into small pieces.

6. Combine the potatoes, chard, hard-boiled eggs, olives, cumin, cinnamon, salt, and pepper. Stir well. Add the beaten eggs and mix well until thoroughly combined.

7. Scrape the chard mixture into the dough-lined pie pan. Dot the butter pieces on top and lay the top pie crust over the plate. Crimp the crusts together around the rim of the pan and prick the top crust with a fork to create steam vents.

8. Bake the torta for 10 minutes, then turn down the heat to 350°F. Bake for 1 hour more, or until the crust is golden brown.

9. Remove from the oven and cool until just warm before serving.

—

SERVES 4 TO 6

Melissa Guerra's Tacos de Acelgas
Swiss Chard Tacos

MCALLEN, TEXAS

Melissa McAllen Guerra, host of the television series *The Texas Provincial Kitchen*, cookbook author, and owner of a Latin American culinary store in San Antonio, grew up on her family's cattle ranch in the Rio Grande Valley. Chard, which her Mexican-born husband calls *acelgas*, makes a delicious filling for crisply fried flauta-style tacos as a snack or as a vegetable main course.

3 pounds fresh tomatoes, peeled and seeded

1 or 2 garlic cloves

4 tablespoons corn oil, plus additional for frying

Kosher salt and freshly ground black pepper

1 pound fresh red or white chard, washed and chopped

½ cup chopped onion

1 teaspoon minced garlic

32 corn tortillas (6-inch size works best)

3 ounces crumbled *cotija* cheese or shredded Monterey Jack (about ¾ cup)

1. Preheat the oven to 200°F. Line a baking sheet with paper towels. Place a wire rack over another baking sheet.

2. Puree the tomatoes and garlic in a blender or a food processor. If necessary, add up to ½ cup water to facilitate blending.

3. Heat 2 tablespoons oil in a large skillet over medium heat. Add the puree, season with salt and pepper to taste, and bring to a simmer. Cook until thick, about 25 minutes, stirring occasionally.

4. While tomato puree is reducing, fill a large pot with water and bring to a boil. Add the chard and cook for 10 minutes, until tender. Drain thoroughly.

5. Heat 2 tablespoons oil in a medium skillet over medium heat. Add the onion and cook, stirring occasionally, until translucent. Add the chard and minced garlic, and season with salt and pepper. Cook for 10 to 15 minutes, stirring occasionally, until the filling is very dry and well flavored. Remove from the heat.

6. Wrap 8 tortillas at a time in a clean, damp kitchen towel. Heat them in the microwave for 1½ to 2 minutes on high, until they are steamy and pliable. Remove 1 tortilla from the bundle and lay out flat. (Keep the rest well wrapped in the towel.) Fill the tortilla with 1 to 2 tablespoons of the chard and roll up tightly. Place the taco on a baking sheet, with the curved edge of the tortilla underneath. Dampen, warm, fill, and shape the remaining tortillas into tacos in this fashion.

7. Heat ½ inch oil in a large skillet over medium-high heat until hot but not smoking. Place the tacos one by one in the hot oil, with the curved edge still underneath. Fry for 1 to 2 minutes, then gently turn over with tongs and fry the other side about 1 minute, until crisp. Remove from the oil and drain on the paper towel–lined sheet pan.

8. Place all the tacos on a serving platter, pour the warm tomato puree over the top, and sprinkle with the cheese.

MAKES 32 TACOS, SERVES 8

Hilda Minter's Spicy Escarole

In 1988, Hilda Minter's husband, Joe Minter, a retired construction worker, received a message from God directing him to create a sculpture park depicting the African American spiritual experience in their backyard in the Woodland Park neighborhood of Birmingham. Their property abuts a historic African American cemetery, and the notion of painting the verse from John 3:16 on the tailgate of a pickup truck or *His Word Is Real* on a defunct movie theater marquee gave her pause. When her husband paid homage to the American workingman by welding giant rusty wrenches to a cross, Mrs. Minter made her favorite spicy escarole. When Mr. Minter was heralded as a visionary genius, she made bigger pots of the escarole for the busloads who began to make pilgrimages to his sculpture park. "We were put here to make things and give them away," said Mrs. Minter, a retired nurse's aid. "People don't expect escarole to be so sweet and spicy. That's why I like it; it make me think and I like to watch what it does to people too."

3 tablespoons bacon grease or olive oil

¼ pound thickly sliced spicy pressed sausage such as pepperoni, chorizo or soppressata, cut into ¼-inch dice

2 garlic cloves, minced

½ teaspoon crushed red pepper

4 heads of escarole (2½ pounds), dark outer leaves removed, inner leaves coarsely chopped

2 cups diced stewed tomatoes, fresh or high quality canned

1 tablespoon minced oregano

1 to 2 teaspoons salt

Black pepper to taste

Cider vinegar or lemon juice to taste

Heat 2 tablespoons of the bacon grease or olive oil in a large soup pot over high heat. Add the spicy sausage and garlic and continue cooking over high heat, stirring constantly, until the garlic is golden, about 2 minutes. Add the red pepper and stir. Add the escarole in batches and cook. Add the tomatoes and oregano; season with salt and pepper and bring to a boil. Cook over low heat until the escarole is tender, 10 to 15 minutes. Remove from heat, cover, and allow to sit for 10 minutes. Season with additional salt, pepper, vinegar, or lemon juice to taste and serve with cornbread or beans or both.

SERVES 4 TO 6

ALLISON MARTIN'S ROASTED CURLY KALE

BAR HARBOR, MAINE

"This is one of the most miraculous things. You rub kale with olive oil, you roast it exactly the right amount of time, and it comes out sweet and crisp every time," says Allison Martin, who with her husband, Elmer Beal, runs a small seasonal restaurant in Maine (see Elmer Beal's Corned Haddock in Lemon Cream Sauce, page 231). "I love to roast the kale with clams and thin slices of linguiça sausage. Or serve it over steamed or roasted shellfish, but it's great with chicken or pork. My daughter, who is eleven, makes a meal of roasted curly kale."

One Big Table

2 pounds curly kale, rinsed and thoroughly dried

2 tablespoons olive oil

2 tablespoons pine nuts (optional)

½ teaspoon kosher salt

¼ teaspoon freshly ground black pepper

1. Preheat the oven to 450°F. Remove the ribs from the kale and tear the leaves into bite-size pieces. This should yield about 4 cups of kale.

2. Toss the kale in a large bowl with the olive oil, pine nuts, if using, and the salt and pepper. Let sit at room temperature for 10 minutes.

3. Spread the mixture on a baking sheet and roast for 2 minutes. Toss, roast for 2 minutes more. Remove from the oven and serve.

SERVES 4

Peter Stark's Late Summer Garden Braise

WHITMORE LAKE, MICHIGAN

A rock 'n' roller since the age of twelve, Peter Stark is, more than forty-five years later, still "connecting with people and spreading good vibes onstage." The same spirit that drives him to perform may have been responsible for his crop of eighty varieties of herbs and vegetables that he and his wife, Kristina, grow at their Renaissance Acres Organic Herb Farm. This recipe was a result of a glut of red-skinned potatoes, garlic, corn, tomatoes, beans, fresh herbs, and spinach, and has become a favorite late-summer dinner.

2 teaspoons olive oil

1 pound small red-skinned potatoes, quartered

1 medium onion, chopped

1 garlic clove, minced

1 medium zucchini, coarsely chopped

½ pound green beans, trimmed and cut into 1-inch lengths

½ cup homemade vegetable broth or low-sodium store-bought vegetable broth

½ cup fresh corn kernels

2 medium-size ripe tomatoes, coarsely chopped

1½ teaspoons chopped fresh herbs, such as thyme, oregano, or rosemary

6 ounces spinach leaves, preferably New Zealand spinach

Kosher salt and freshly ground black pepper

2 ounces crumbled feta, goat, or blue cheese, about ½ cup (optional)

Icing Spinach, RUSSELL LEE, 1939.

1. Heat a large skillet over medium-high heat and add the oil. Add the potatoes and cook, stirring occasionally, until lightly browned, about 5 minutes.

2. Add the onion, garlic, zucchini, and green beans; cook, stirring often, 2 minutes. Add the broth and cook, stirring occasionally, 2 minutes. Add the corn, tomatoes, and herbs. Cover and cook over medium heat just until potatoes are tender, about 3 minutes.

3. Add the spinach and cook until just wilted, about 2 minutes.

4. Season with salt and pepper to taste. Just before serving, sprinkle with the cheese, if desired.

SERVES 4

Carmen Johnson's Chiles Rellenos

Teresa Ortiz grew up in Mexico City and married a Minnesotan of Scandinavian descent. Political activists who loved to travel, they raised their three children in St. Paul, Guatemala City, and San Cristobal de Chiapas. Carmen Johnson, their youngest child and only girl, learned to make Danish pastries and Swedish cookies from one grandmother and northern Mexican dishes, like this orange-scented version of meat-stuffed peppers, from the other. Because the chiles can be prepared ahead, they make a marvelous meal for a crowd and are delicious served with rice, black beans, and crisp vegetables or salad.

12 medium poblano chiles

2 cups cooked white rice

½ pound thinly sliced Monterey Jack cheese (about 12 slices)

FOR THE SALSA CASERA

6 Roma (plum) tomatoes

¼ cup finely chopped onion

3 garlic cloves

2 or 3 serrano chiles

2 tablespoons chopped cilantro

2 pinches of kosher salt

FOR THE PICADILLO DULCE

1 pound lean ground beef

2 garlic cloves, chopped

1 small onion

2 tablespoons chopped fresh parsley

¼ cup chopped walnuts

¼ cup salted peanuts

½ cup raisins

2 red apples (such as Cortland), cored and cut in small pieces

2 carrots, cut in small pieces

¾ cup orange juice

2 pinches of kosher salt

1. Preheat the oven to 375°F. Arrange the poblano chiles in a single layer in a baking dish. In another baking dish, arrange the tomatoes, onion, garlic, and serrano chiles for the salsa casera. Roast until all the vegetables are charred, 40 to 50 minutes, turning frequently so the vegetables roast evenly. Remove from the oven and turn the oven down to 350°F. Put the poblano chiles in a resealable plastic bag to let them sweat until cool.

2. To make the salsa casera: Place the roasted tomatoes, onion, garlic, and serrano chiles in a blender or food processor and blend until liquefied. Transfer to a saucepan and simmer over low heat for 30 minutes, until thick.

3. Pour the salsa into a bowl and let cool. Stir in the cilantro and salt.

4. To make the picadillo dulce: Heat a large skillet over medium heat. Add the ground beef, garlic, onion, and parsley, and cook until the beef is no longer pink. Stir in the walnuts, peanuts, raisins, apples, and carrots. Add the orange juice and salt. Lower the heat and simmer about 30 minutes, until the liquid is reduced.

5. After the poblano chiles cool, wearing gloves, carefully remove the skins, keeping the chiles intact. Cut a slit along the length of each chile and carefully remove seeds and veins without removing the stems. Arrange the chiles in a single layer in a baking dish. Fill each one with 2 tablespoons rice, 2 to 3 tablespoons of picadillo dulce, and a slice of cheese.

6. Bake about 10 minutes, until the cheese melts. Serve the chiles topped with salsa casera.

SERVES 4 TO 6

JEFF BEIL'S BUTTERED RADISHES

"People don't think about cooking radishes," said Jeff Beil, a 30-year-old web producer, "and it's so good. Sometimes I add some murdered (chopped and caramelized) onions to the radishes. They are also awesome tossed with grilled peaches. But usually I just go pure and straight and serve these as a vegetable with grilled fish or chicken, or on a big salad."

4 tablespoons unsalted butter

2 bunches radishes, scrubbed, tops removed, except for a few tender decorative stems, cut in half

2 teaspoons black lava salt or kosher salt

12 teaspoons poppy seeds

Melt the butter in a heavy pan over medium-high heat and continue cooking until the foam subsides. Place the radish halves, cut side down, in the pan and cook until they begin to char, about 3 minutes. Turn the radishes and cook until the skins blister, about another minute. Use a slotted spoon to remove the radishes to paper towels to remove excess butter, plate, and sprinkle with the salt and poppy seeds.

———

SERVES 4

533

Eat Your Vegetables

Jasmin Evans's
Roasted Zucchini Provençal

COCONUT CREEK, FLORIDA

Jasmin Evans grew up near Stuttgart, Germany, but when Ms. Evans was twenty, she and her husband moved to the United States. This recipe has been in her collection for so long that she cannot remember its provenance. It is a favorite of her children, who love to eat spoonfuls of the robustly seasoned casserole on toasted French bread. Ms. Evans serves it as a main course or a side dish.

534

One Big Table

4 medium zucchini, quartered lengthwise
   and sliced

1 onion, sliced

1 tablespoon olive oil

2 tablespoons plain dry bread crumbs

1 tablespoon grated Parmesan cheese

4 niçoise olives, pitted and chopped

2 to 4 anchovy fillets, rinsed and chopped

2 garlic cloves, minced

½ teaspoon grated lemon zest

1 teaspoon minced fresh thyme

1 teaspoon minced fresh basil

½ teaspoon minced fresh rosemary

Kosher salt and freshly ground black pepper

1. Preheat the oven to 425°F.

2. Mix the zucchini and onions with the oil, spread on a rimmed baking sheet, and roast for 7 to 8 minutes. Stir and roast another 5 to 8 minutes, until golden. Remove from the oven but leave the oven on.

3. Spoon the zucchini mixture into a 9 x 9-inch baking dish. Combine the bread crumbs, cheese, olives, anchovies, garlic, lemon zest, thyme, basil, and rosemary. Add salt and pepper to taste. Spread over zucchini and bake until the topping is golden brown, about 10 minutes.

4. Let cool slightly and serve on French bread or as a side dish.

SERVES 4

VEGETARIANISM

THE FIRST VEGETARIAN SOCIETY IN THE United States was founded in 1850 by William Alcott, uncle of writer Louis May (who was also vegetarian). Abraham Lincoln, Henry David Thoreau, Ralph Waldo Emerson, Harriet Beecher Stowe, Susan B. Anthony, Dizzy Gillespie, Billie Jean King, Miles Davis, and Allen Ginsberg all eschewed meat for at least part of their lives. Today, vegetable-centric eating—be it vegetarianism, veganism, or raw foodism—is back in fashion, again.

"How can you eat anything with eyes?"

—William Kellogg, industrialist, founder of breakfast food company (1860-1951)

"I am a vegetarian for health reasons—the health of the chicken."

—Isaac Bashevis Singer, Polish American writer and Nobel Prize winner (1902-1991)

Maya Lachlan's Salted Summer Squash

Like most people in the rustic old sugar-mill town on the north shore of O'ahu, Maya Lachlan cannot pinpoint her ancestry. "People came from China, Japan, Korea, Portugal, Norway, Scotland, and the Philippines to work on the sugar plantations. My mother told me we had a little bit of each so we better be nice to everybody." Ms. Lachlan surfs, gardens, cooks, hikes, and dances a mean hula. "We call ourselves the 'anti-Waikiki.' There are wild chickens in the mango trees and more backyard barbecues than restaurants. Our idea of nightlife is sitting on the beach looking at the stars. Some friends and I made salt in pans in the backyard for a while. The iron oxide that is prevalent throughout these islands gives the salt a pink-rusty cast. We also made some black lava salt. This recipe came from those efforts, as well as the fact that one night we didn't have any olive oil to make a raw vegetable salad. We use the same technique on green papaya and not-quite-ripe mango. The crunch is great with roast pig or just about any barbecue. The trick is to make the dish one second before you serve it. If it sits, it gets watery and limp. You want the crunch."

535

Eat Your Vegetables

6 small to medium yellow summer squash

2 teaspoons highest quality coarse sea salt
(preferably Hawaiian pink or black lava variety,
ground very fine)

Cut the squash in half lengthwise, then into ⅛-inch-thick half-moon slices. In a large bowl, toss the squash with the salt. Serve immediately.

SERVES 4

"I eat a lot of tofu. You'll like it."
—Fred Rogers, educator, minister, TV host
(1928–2003)

*"I'm not a vegetarian
because I love animals;
I'm a vegetarian
because I hate plants."*
—A. Whitney Brown, writer and comedian (b. 1952)

*"Vegetarian: that's an old word
for 'lousy hunter.'"*
—Andy Rooney, radio and TV writer
and commentator (b. 1919)

*"I was a vegetarian until I started
leaning toward the sunlight."*
—Rita Rudner, comedian, writer, actor (b. 1953)

Maureen Walther's
Southern Squash Casserole

Following a grand cross-country tour of the United States, Maureen Walther met the man she would marry on her flight back home to Johannesburg. One thing led to another, and as the plane flew over Arkansas, her future husband announced that he would retire there. A year later, she was living in the hamlet of Mt. Ida. She found her fellow villagers "warm and accepting," and the squash casserole, one of the jewels of the American southern kitchen, delicious.

One Big Table

4 tablespoons (½ stick) unsalted butter, plus more for the baking dish

1 small Vidalia or other sweet onion, finely chopped

4 medium yellow summer squash (about 2 pounds), cut into ¼-inch-thick slices

¼ cup grated Parmesan cheese

1 cup grated Cheddar cheese

1 cup fresh bread crumbs

2 large eggs, lightly beaten

1 teaspoon kosher salt

½ teaspoon freshly ground black pepper

1. Preheat the oven to 375°F. Butter an 8-inch square baking dish.

2. Melt 2 tablespoons of the butter in a large skillet over medium-high heat. Add the onion and cook, stirring often, until softened but not browned, approximately 5 minutes. Add the squash and stir well. Cover and cook, stirring often, for 7 to 8 minutes, until the squash is tender but not browned.

3. Transfer the squash and onion to a large bowl, let cool for a few minutes, then stir in the Parmesan, ¾ cup of the Cheddar, and ½ cup of the bread crumbs. Stir in the eggs, salt, and pepper. Transfer the squash mixture to the prepared baking dish.

4. Melt the remaining butter. In a small bowl, combine the remaining Cheddar and bread crumbs. Toss with the melted butter. Scatter over the casserole.

5. Bake for 30 minutes, until the top is crisp and golden brown and a knife inserted into the center comes out clean. Serve hot.

SERVES 4

MARY SHAW'S VACANT LOT TOMATO DINNER

In the day care center Mary Shaw runs in her home, it is not unusual for several babies to stay for weeks on end. The day before Hurricane Katrina, a group from the Good Food Neighborhood program, which works to make good food accessible to all, helped the neighborhood doyenne plant a kitchen garden in her backyard. A year later the volunteers came back and dug a new garden in the flooded silt. They gave Mrs. Shaw seedlings and seeds—eggplant, mustard greens, spinach, tomatoes, mint, basil, green bell peppers, and green onions. "We eat everything that comes out of the ground," she says. "I don't can or preserve. I fed everybody fresh vegetables. Even the babies. I don't see vacant lots anymore, I see gardens to come."

12 large Creole tomatoes or other large tomatoes

Salt

1 pound medium shrimp

2 pounds ground beef chuck

½ large sweet onion, chopped

1 green bell pepper, stemmed, seeded, and chopped

1 garlic clove, chopped

2 green onions (scallions), chopped

3 cups fresh bread crumbs (preferably from crustless French bread)

Creole seasoning

1. Preheat the oven to 350°F. Cut a thin slice from the stem end of each tomato. Using your fingers and/or a small knife, core the tomatoes, but leave the walls intact. Discard the seeds. Roughly chop the pulp. Lightly salt inside the tomatoes, then invert them onto paper towels until ready to stuff.

2. Bring a medium saucepan of salted water to a boil over high heat. Add the shrimp and cook just until they all turn bright pink. Using a skimmer or slotted spoon, transfer to a plate to cool; reserve the cooking liquid. Peel the shrimp and roughly chop.

3. Brown the beef in a large skillet over medium heat, stirring to break up any clumps. Spoon off any accumulated grease. Return the pan to the heat and stir in the onion, bell pepper, garlic, green onions, and tomato pulp. Cook, stirring occasionally, until the vegetables have softened, about 5 minutes.

4. Remove from the heat and pour into a large bowl. Cool slightly, then stir in the bread crumbs, shrimp, enough of the shrimp cooking liquid to hold the mixture together and keep it moist, and Creole seasoning to taste.

5. Place the tomatoes, hollow side up, in a greased baking dish just large enough to hold them snugly. Spoon the filling into the centers. Bake for 25 to 30 minutes, until the skin begins to shrivel and the tomatoes are tender.

SERVES 12

MISS JEANIE'S GREEN TOMATO PIE

After a particularly calamitous early-summer gale, Miss Jeanie Claiborn, a passionate gardener and cook who is, she says, "what was once called 'a lady' and today would be termed 'a professional volunteer,'" reached the end of her green tomato repertoire. This pie was inspired in equal measure by the eggplant Parmesan she had sixty-four years ago when she went to New York City to shop for her trousseau and her love for sharp, fresh feta cheese. It can be served as an appetizer, a luncheon dish, or a main course.

1 tablespoon olive oil

2 cups freshly made fine bread crumbs

2 teaspoons chopped fresh oregano

½ teaspoon kosher salt

1 teaspoon freshly ground black pepper

1 whole egg plus 1 egg white

3 pounds green tomatoes, cut into ¼-inch slices

2 pounds ripe red tomatoes, peeled, cored, seeded, and chopped

1 teaspoon grated orange zest

1 garlic clove, minced

1 bay leaf

½ cup crumbled feta cheese

1. Preheat the oven to 350°F. Lightly coat a baking sheet and a 9-inch fluted tart pan with the olive oil.

2. In a shallow dish, combine the bread crumbs, oregano, salt, and pepper. In another dish, beat together the egg and egg white. Dip the green tomato slices in the beaten eggs then dust with the bread crumb mixture. Lay the slices on the baking sheet. Bake, flipping once, until the bread crumbs are golden, about 15 minutes per side. Remove from the oven but leave the oven on.

3. Meanwhile, combine the red tomatoes, orange zest, garlic, and bay leaf in a nonstick skillet. Cook over medium-low heat, stirring occasionally, until the sauce thickens, about 30 minutes. Remove the bay leaf.

4. Spread a thin layer of tomato sauce on the bottom of the tart pan. Cover with a layer of green tomato slices and another thin layer of sauce. Sprinkle with a small amount of the feta and repeat until all the ingredients are used up. Top with a generous layer of the feta. Cover with foil and bake for 2 hours. Let cool briefly before serving, or cool completely to serve at room temperature.

SERVES 6

The Davis Family's
Creamed Tomatoes with Biscuits

In the early 1900s when the Davis family settled there, Salem, West Virginia, was a hardscrabble sort of place. Faced with feeding a family of nine, Edna Davis stretched gifts from the garden into meals like this one, which her granddaughter, Pamela Davis, still prepares when simple comfort is the order of the day. If the tomatoes are acidic, she adds a pinch of sugar to the pot. This is a lovely side dish with grilled (or fried) chicken or fish, or a lunch or vegetable meal when topped with poached eggs.

10 to 12 large ripe tomatoes, cored

3 tablespoons all-purpose flour

1½ cups milk

Kosher salt and freshly ground black pepper

4 to 8 hot biscuits, halved and buttered

1. Lightly cut an X in the bottom of the tomatoes. Place the tomatoes in a large pot and cover with water. Bring to a boil and cook 2 to 5 minutes, until the skins come off easily. Remove from the heat. Remove the tomatoes with a skimmer or slotted spoon and slip off the skins. Reserve some of the cooking water for a soupier mixture.

2. Return the tomatoes to the pot. Add the flour and milk and cook over medium-high heat, stirring occasionally and breaking the tomatoes up with a spoon, until tomatoes reach the consistency of a stew. Add salt and pepper to taste.

3. Place the biscuits on plates. Ladle the tomatoes on top and serve.

SERVES 4

Eat Your Vegetables

ALLEN ACHTERBERG'S
SUMMER VEGETABLE CHARLOTTE

DALLAS, TEXAS

Allen Achterberg has been a third-grade teacher for twenty-three years and has attended more than his allotted share of staff meetings, PTA dinners, and potluck suppers. The barrage of congealed salads, layered salads, and pasta salads that reappears each year has inspired his endless search for something unique. One of his newfound recipes is this vegetable charlotte, which he predicts will wow the covered-dish crowd.

Olive oil

6 slices high quality white sandwich bread, crusts removed

3 Black Beauty or other large eggplants (about 1 pound each)

Kosher salt and freshly ground black pepper

½ cup dried apricots, chopped

Boiling water

3 garlic cloves, minced

2 small yellow onions, finely diced

2 small zucchini, cut into ½-inch cubes, to equal 2 cups

1 red bell pepper, stemmed, seeded, and minced

3 tablespoons toasted pine nuts

2 tablespoons honey

1 tablespoon balsamic vinegar

1 large tomato, chopped, to equal 1 cup

2 teaspoons grated lemon zest

1 teaspoon fresh lemon juice

¼ teaspoon saffron threads

2 tablespoons chopped fresh basil

1 tablespoon chopped flat leaf parsley

1. Preheat the oven to 375°F. Lightly oil a 2-quart charlotte mold or soufflé dish and a baking sheet.

2. Cut the bread into rectangles and triangles to cover the bottom, sides, and top of the mold. Once the bottom and sides are in place, brush lightly with oil. Reserve the rest of the bread for the top.

3. Peel 1 eggplant, then cut it lengthwise into ¼-inch-thick slices. Arrange them on the baking sheet, brush lightly with oil, season with salt and pepper, and bake until soft, about 10 minutes. Remove from the oven but leave the oven on. When the slices are cool enough to handle, lay them over the bread all around the sides of the mold, with enough length remaining so the slices can be folded up over the top of the mold, after it is filled.

4. Cut the 2 remaining eggplants into ½-inch cubes, salt lightly, and set in a colander to drain for 15 minutes.

5. Cover the apricots with boiling water. Let sit for 2 minutes to soften. Drain and pat dry.

6. Warm 3 tablespoons oil in a heavy-bottomed skillet over medium-low heat. Add the garlic, stir and cook for 1 minute, until fragrant. Add the onions, season lightly with salt and pepper and cook for 5 minutes, until wilted and translucent.

7. Rinse the eggplant cubes, pat dry, and add to the skillet. Stirring constantly, cook for a few minutes, until soft. Add the zucchini and red pepper, stir, and cook until the zucchini is tender. Remove from the heat. Stir in the apricots, pine nuts, honey, and vinegar.

8. Combine the tomato, lemon zest and juice, and saffron in a food processor and puree to a thick paste. Stir into the cooling vegetable mixture. When it reaches room temperature, stir in the basil and parsley. Taste and adjust seasoning.

9. Using a slotted spoon, ladle out the mixture, knocking it against the side of the pan to remove excess moisture, and spread it into the lined mold. Fold the ends of the eggplant slices up over the vegetables and brush with olive oil. Fit the reserved bread over the top, press down well, brush with olive oil, and place in the oven.

10. Bake until the bread is dark gold, 25 to 30 minutes. Let rest for 20 minutes, then invert the charlotte onto a serving dish. Serve hot or warm.

SERVES 8

VICTORY AND VEGETABLES

"The war garden was a war-time necessity. This was true because war conditions made it essential that food should be raised where it had not been produced in peace times, with labor not engaged in agricultural work . . . The author, wishing, as every patriot wished, to do a war work which was actually necessary, which was essentially practical, and which would most certainly aid in making the war successful, conceived the idea in March, 1917, of inspiring the people of the United States to plant war gardens in order to increase the supply of food without the use of land already cultivated, of labor already engaged in agricultural work, of time devoted to other necessary occupations, and of transportation facilities which were already inadequate to the demands made upon them."

—Charles Lathrop Pack,
The War Garden Victorious, 1919

IN MARCH, THEREFORE, SOME WEEKS BEFORE THE UNITED STATES entered the war, Pack organized for this work a commission known as the National War Garden Commission.

Insisting that every home garden was a munitions plant, Michigan-born Charles Lathrop Pack initiated a food-growing effort that may have boosted morale as much as it did the national pantry at the outset of World War I. By the end of the war, five million "war" or "victory" gardens were producing $1.2 billion worth of food. Much to the consternation of the Department of Agriculture, who feared that a movement of home gardening would hurt the food industry, Eleanor Roosevelt planted a victory garden at the White House. More than 20 million home and community gardens were planted in backyards, rooftops, vacant lots, public parks, and roadways and proved that the Department of Agriculture's concern was not ill founded; victory gardens produced 10 million tons of vegetables, almost the same amount that was produced commercially in the country that year. Some public gardens like the Dowling Community Gardens in Minneapolis and the Back Bay Fens in Boston continued, but the vegetable garden at the White House disappeared. However, in 2009, Michelle Obama put in a kitchen garden as part of a new war effort: the war against unhealthy eating.

KURT SPIRIDAKIS'S OVEN-ROASTED EGGPLANT

BATH, MAINE

Only a year after Kurt Spiridakis got a degree in economics and statistics at the University of Pennsylvania, he burned out. He moved to Maine to explore what would become a passion: boat building. After a yearlong apprenticeship at The Carpenter's Boat Shop, he moved to a Virginia farm, where he learned organic gardening. Still, boats beckoned, and several years later he moved to the Greek island of Spetses, exploring his Greek roots and working in a small shipyard. He and his girlfriend cooked in their tiny kitchen on two nonadjustable burners, controlling cooking temperatures by moving the skillet to the sink. The refrigerator top doubled as counter and storage space for their three skillets and a soup pot. When his sister, Nicole, came to visit she reported that their food "was not only presentable, it was better than most of the taverna food I ate."

¼ cup olive oil

1 medium eggplant, unpeeled, cut into ½-inch cubes

1 garlic clove, minced (optional)

Sea salt

2 teaspoons dried oregano

1 cup diced tomatoes (fresh or canned)

Freshly ground black pepper

4 ounces crumbled feta cheese (about 1 cup)

1. Preheat the oven to 350°F.

2. Heat the olive oil in a skillet over medium-high heat. Add the eggplant and garlic, if using, and cook, stirring occasionally, until browned and beginning to get tender. Season with ½ teaspoon salt and 1 teaspoon of the oregano.

3. Pour into an 8 x 8-inch ceramic or glass baking dish. Cover with the tomatoes, add salt and pepper to taste and the remaining oregano. Sprinkle the feta over the top. Cover with foil and bake for 25 to 30 minutes, until the feta begins to melt.

4. Remove from the oven and let rest for 5 to 10 minutes to allow the flavors to blend, or as they say in Greece, so the eggplant can "drink the liquid."

5. Serve as a hot salad, side, or part of a vegetarian meal with bread.

SERVES 4

MR. ZANGER'S VEGETARIAN CHILI

CAMBRIDGE, MASSACHUSETTS

In his guise as "Robert Nadeau, restaurant critic, Boston Phoenix," Mark Zanger has spent most evenings for the past quarter-century in restaurants. In his kitchen at home he demands as much of himself as he does from chefs. Vegetarian chili, all but an oxymoron, has been one of the greater challenges of his home cooking career. He says:

"I was fortunate to begin making chili with a 1966 book, *A Bowl of Red*, by Frank X. Tolbert. Tolbert gives conservative Texas recipes and goes into the origins of chili as a cheap dish and chuckwagon favorite using lean, low-grade beef and kidney suet. Tolbert opposed all sweet ingredients such as tomatoes, cooked onions, or bell peppers, leaving a stew with dry spices, featuring cumin. His basic attitude was: 'My chili is the best in the world; yours or anyone else's is unfit for donkeys.'

"Over the years I have adapted his recipe to all kinds of meat, including ground turkey and pressure-cooked beef heart. I had many requests for vegetarian chili, and many failures. One problem in making vegetarian chili is that one tends to think of [chili] as a meat dish with beans, and therefore is misled to substitute for the meat. This will not work, because vegetarian meat substitutes will not absorb the flavor of the spices.

"I finally got on the right track by studying a Pakistani-Punjabi chickpea stew called chole. Despite the similar sounding name, there is no connection between chili and chole. But chole has a rich chile-garlic-cumin gravy, even though contemporary recipes often use tomatoes.

"A key point is that it is the beans which must substitute for the meat in vegetarian chili, and therefore we use higher-protein red beans instead of the starchier pinto beans that are bland foils for meat chili. We also cook some of the spices into the beans. Freed of the confusion about meat substitutes, we then turn to silken tofu, which is fattier and tastes better than firm tofu. Along with vegetable oil, the silken tofu supplies the fat that carries the fat-soluble flavors of garlic, cumin, and hot pepper. I think of it as a substitute for cheese, which only became a standard garnish for chili when cooks began routinely to skim off the unhealthful beef fat. Some people go on to add sour cream, avocado, and other fatty garnishes. This detracts from the integrity of the dish.

"Other ingredient pickiness: The green enchilada sauce is currently the only such product in Boston supermarkets that isn't mostly tomato. There used to be red enchilada sauce made primarily from chiles, but brand by brand it has been tomato-fied. If you want to soak, skin, seed, and make your own chile sauce—and have a level-four biohazard lab in which to do so—that would be even better.

"Powdered cumin loses a lot. Prechopped garlic has everything but the bite. No amount of it will provide that. Oregano, a good friend of beef, is really a substitute for wild herbs of similar flavor in the Southwest, and I have sometimes cooked epazote with the beans instead. The paprika needn't taste like much; but the chile powder is mission critical."

1 pound dried red beans

4 to 6 dried hot chiles

Sea salt

2 to 4 tablespoons cumin seeds

2 to 4 garlic cloves

¼ cup vegetable oil

4 heaping tablespoons pure ancho chile powder

2 tablespoons paprika

One 14-ounce can green enchilada sauce

1 tablespoon dried oregano

Tomato sauce (optional)

One 12.3-ounce package silken tofu

Masa harina or cornmeal, to thicken (optional)

1 onion, for garnish (optional)

Cheddar cheese, for nonvegan garnish (optional)

1. Place the beans and twice their volume of water in a pot and bring to a boil. After 5 minutes, drain the beans. Cover with fresh water and soak overnight.

2. Drain the beans again, add twice their volume of water with the dried chiles and salt to taste. Cook over medium heat until they're tender, but not falling apart.

3. Toast the cumin carefully in a toaster oven until you can smell the aroma. Grind the seeds with sea salt in a mortar and pestle or fold into aluminum foil and roll a heavy jar over them. It's okay if they don't turn to powder. Chop the garlic.

4. Heat the oil in a large pot and add the cumin and garlic. Cook a minute or two, then add the chile powder and paprika. Cook a little more, letting it stick but not burn.

5. Add the enchilada sauce, beans and their cooking liquid, and the oregano. Remove the whole chiles. Cook until you can't stand not tasting the mixture, then add more chile powder and/or paprika so it looks red, salt to adjust the flavor, and possibly a few tablespoons of tomato sauce, no more.

6. Cut long slices both ways in the tofu to outline cubes, then run the knife around the inside edge of the package to loosen the tofu. Turn the package upside down so the cubes release onto a cutting board. Don't worry about some odd pieces. Add the tofu to the pot.

7. Correct the soupiness of loose stew with masa harina.

8. If you must, dice optional onion and/or Cheddar cheese as garnishes.

9. Serve over rice.

———

SERVES 6 TO 8

LENI SORENSEN'S BOLIGEE

CROZET, VIRGINIA

"My mother was 'Peck's Bad Girl,' a young white woman who joined the NAACP and married and divorced my father, a black man from Texas," said Dr. Leni Sorensen, the head of African American history at Monticello. "Growing up in Riverside, California, I didn't think of myself as black or white. I was the daughter of a single working woman, reared to be a radical and an atheist with a grandmother and a great-aunt pulling hard in the other direction. I don't need to tell you who won. Both my great-grandfathers were born in 1870. My grandmother and aunt cooked on this amazing gas and wood combination range. They taught me to make corn pone and to appreciate the theater of black churches. I left home when I was 16 and put together a band, Womenfolk; we performed all over the place from 1963 to 1966. I married and we went back to the earth on a farm in Oklahoma. Later, my husband Kip and I moved here to Crozet, raised our children. I got my doctorate and went to work at Monticello; it's right down the road. Kip and I make up for missing the farm by our garden. It gets bigger every year. On Wednesdays, I make up a pot of food and bread and sit on the porch from five to eight and talk to anyone who comes by who wants to talk about gardening or cooking or history. My grandmother and aunt made this dish. They were from Boligee, Alabama—hence the name. It's like having a garden for dinner. I make it for my grandchildren and serve it with corn pone."

6 slices thick-cut double smoked bacon, chopped

2 yellow onions, peeled and sliced into ½-inch rounds

1 to 2 teaspoons salt

Black pepper to taste

4 ripe tomatoes, sliced in ½-inch slabs

12 new potatoes, unpeeled, sliced in ½-inch slices

4 cups green beans, rinsed, ends snapped and cut in bite-size lengths

In a heavy cast-iron pot over low heat, cook the bacon until it begins to crisp, 5 to 7 minutes. Add the onions in one layer, season lightly with salt and pepper, and cook, stirring occasionally until they are limp and translucent, about 5 minutes. Add the tomatoes in layers and season with salt and pepper. Add the potatoes in layers and season each with salt and pepper. Add the green beans and season with salt and pepper. Cover, reduce the heat to lowest setting, and cook until the potatoes are tender, 40 to 60 minutes.

SERVES 6

Michael Hogue's Tajine bil Khodar
Vegetable Tagine

Michael Hogue grew up on military bases, an experience that allowed him to see—and taste—the world with no preconceived ideas. During his own tour in the navy, he learned that "kitchen duty was mandatory for newbies" and about "cooking for the masses and making do with what you have." He first tasted this dish at Al-Fassia in Marrakesh and has modified it only by increasing the lemon and cinnamon. Couscous is the traditional base for a tagine, but Mr. Hogue suggests serving it over rice or fettuccine, or even on its own. A salad of oranges and olives, accompanied by a traditional flatbread, might start the meal, followed by the tagine. Chilled melon balls would be a perfect ending.

1 tablespoon olive oil

2 medium onions, finely chopped

2 cups homemade vegetable broth or low-sodium store-bought vegetable broth

1 cup water

½ cup fresh lemon juice

1 pound carrots, peeled and cut into 1-inch chunks

½ pound turnips, peeled and cut into 1-inch chunks

½ pound Yukon gold potatoes, peeled and cut into 1½-inch chunks

½ pound sweet potatoes, peeled and cut in 1½-inch chunks

1 teaspoon ras-al-hanout spice blend

1 teaspoon ground cinnamon

Kosher salt and freshly ground black pepper

2 Meryam's Preserved Lemons (page 82), 1 chopped and 1 sliced thin

One 9-ounce package frozen artichoke hearts, thawed

1. Heat the oil in a Dutch oven or tagine over medium heat. Add the onions and cook about 4 minutes, stirring occasionally, until soft.

2. Stir in the broth, water, lemon juice, carrots, turnips, potatoes, sweet potatoes, ras-al-hanout, cinnamon, 1 teaspoon salt, and ½ teaspoon pepper. Bring to a simmer, cover, and cook about 30 minutes, stirring occasionally, until the vegetables are tender.

3. Stir in the chopped preserved lemon and artichokes and simmer for 5 minutes more. Season with salt and pepper to taste. Garnish with the sliced lemon, and serve.

SERVES 6

Mitra Stricklen's Khoresht Bademjoon
Persian Eggplant Stew

Mitra Stricklen, a graduate student in anthropology at the University of Chicago, a gardener, cook, and local food advocate, adores eggplant, particularly her mother's Persian-style sweet-and-sour eggplant. Ms. Stricklen says that she carries the recipe for khoresht bademjoon in her head to farmers' markets and modifies the basic formula to suit what is best in the market that day.

2 large eggplants

Kosher salt

2 tablespoons olive oil

3 yellow onions, sliced

¼ cup vegetable oil

One 14.5-ounce can whole tomatoes or 6 large
    tomatoes, roasted and peeled

1 tablespoon kosher salt

1 tablespoon ground cinnamon

1 teaspoon freshly ground black pepper

½ teaspoon ground nutmeg

1 cup water or vegetable stock

2 tablespoons fresh lemon juice

Persian Herbed Steamed Rice (page 631),
    for serving

1. Cut the eggplants into thick slices. Generously salt both sides of each eggplant slice and let drain in a colander for 15 minutes so the salt can pull out the bitterness.

2. Rinse the slices and pat dry.

3. Meanwhile, heat the olive oil in a skillet over low heat and add the onions. Cook until soft and golden brown, stirring occasionally, about 20 minutes.

4. Heat the vegetable oil in a wide, heavy-bottomed skillet over medium-high heat and fry the eggplant slices until golden brown on each side. Remove from the oil and drain on a wire rack set over a baking sheet or paper towels.

5. In a large saucepan, combine the tomatoes, 1 tablespoon salt, the cinnamon, pepper, nutmeg, water, and lemon juice and mix well. Bring to a boil, then reduce the heat and simmer for 15 minutes. Add the eggplant slices and cook for 5 minutes more.

6. Transfer to a serving dish and garnish with the fried onions. Serve with chelo.

SERVES 6

Roohi Choudhry's Eggplant Pakorey

Born in Peshawar, Pakistan, Roohi Choudhry came to the United States in 1999 for graduate school in Texas and "stayed on." She grew up in a traditional household where her mom, Suboohi, did all the cooking. "Most of my life," she says, "I could not even make an egg, and I had no interest in cooking." Once in America, though, she "didn't have options for good food," so she began calling her mom for recipes. Her first foray into cooking "was a disaster, a flop," but slowly and steadily she found a rhythm.

Eggplant pakorey is simple enough to make anytime, but in the Choudhry household it was synonymous with Ramadan. "When you haven't eaten all day," she says, "this is the best thing ever." Although she doesn't currently observe Ramadan, making her mother's recipe is a tradition that brings back nice memories.

To create a taste balance, she suggests serving this recipe with a cooling yogurt-based side dish or sauce. You can use this batter with a variety of seasonal vegetables. Partially cooked potato rounds and cauliflower florets are her favorites.

7 heaping tablespoons *besan* (Indian chickpea flour)

Scant ¼ teaspoon baking soda

1 teaspoon freshly ground cumin seeds

½ teaspoon kosher salt

1 teaspoon grated fresh garlic

1 teaspoon grated fresh ginger

¼ teaspoon red pepper flakes, or to taste

½ cup lukewarm water

1 medium eggplant

Olive oil, for frying

Coriander chutney or tamarind chutney, for serving

1. Sift the flour into a bowl with the baking soda, cumin, and salt and mix with a fork, mashing any lumps in the flour. Add the garlic, ginger, and pepper flakes. Add the water a little at a time, beating gently with the fork as you go until the batter reaches the consistency of a thick cream soup (add more water if necessary). Cover the bowl and refrigerate for at least 1 hour and up to 3 hours.

2. Slice the eggplant into ¼-inch-thick rounds and immerse them in a bowl of lukewarm, lightly salted water (this will prevent them from turning color).

3. Heat about ½ inch of oil in a large nonstick skillet over medium heat. One at a time, remove the eggplant slices from the water, dry, and dip in the batter, coating all sides. Fry them in small batches, flipping once, until golden brown. Using a skimmer or slotted spoon, transfer the slices to a wire rack or paper towels to drain.

4. Serve hot, while they are still crispy, with coriander or tamarind chutney.

SERVES 4

David Shield's Remarkably Light Fried Okra

Dr. David Shields developed a taste for rice as a child when his father, a CIA agent, was stationed in Japan and rice was the "daily bread." Now a professor of Southern Letters at the University of South Carolina and a cofounder of the Carolina Gold Research Foundation, Dr. Shields says his interest in repatriating heirloom grains, such as Carolina Gold Rice, was as much a result of his mother's dedication to fine food as it was to his academic interest. His research into the community identity that formed around the Carolina Rice Kitchen has led him to historic rice bread recipes and to using rice flour in southern classics, such as this fried okra. Rice flour absorbs less oil and, he says, makes a more cohesive batter than, say tempura, which can be shatter-prone. In recipes from the eighteenth century, okra was typically sliced thinner than a quarter and, he says, the diagonal cut makes the perfect flesh-to-interior ratio for deep-frying.

2 pounds young okra, preferably Clemson Spineless variety

1½ cups cold lager beer

1 egg

¼ teaspoon salt

⅛ teaspoon cayenne pepper

1½ cups rice flour, preferably Anson Mills Carolina Gold Rice Flour

1 cup cornstarch

Up to 6 cups sesame oil or vegetable oil, for deep-fat frying, plus more if necessary

1. Wash the okra, pat dry, and slice each piece diagonally into slices no thicker than a quarter and set aside in a large bowl. Place the beer, egg, salt, and cayenne in a large bowl and whisk to combine. Add the rice flour and cornstarch, and whisk to combine well. Pour the batter over the sliced okra and set aside.

2. Heat a countertop deep-fry machine or fill a pot that is equipped with a basket or strainer slightly less than half full of sesame or vegetable oil and place over medium-high heat. Bring the oil to 350°F. To check the temperature, with a slotted spoon or tongs drop one piece of okra in the oil. It should bubble immediately.

3. Remove a handful of okra slices from the batter with a slotted spoon or tongs. Tap to remove excess batter (they won't separate if you're clamping them with tongs) and then carefully lower the pieces into the oil. Fry for about 3 minutes until very dark brown and then drain on paper towels. Maintain an oil temperature between 325 and 350°F. Serve as a snack or as a side dish with meat or fish.

SERVES 8

One Big Table

Kirti Gupta's New-World Bhindi Masala
Spiced Okra

Brought up in Mumbai, Kirti Gupta moved to the United States following an arranged marriage. She was intrigued by her first taste of many ethnic foods and called her parents for help preparing her favorite Indian dishes. Eventually she created her own cultural exchange in her kitchen. Combinations such as adding a little garam masala to pasta have allowed her to venture into new territory, she says, while retaining some of her own identity. Ms. Gupta misses traditional Indian foods, like bhindi (okra) and vada pav, a patty of potatoes, peas, and herbs. "They have it here," she says, "but it's not the same. I could make it better at home."

1 pound okra

1 teaspoon red chile powder, or more to taste

1 teaspoon ground turmeric

1 tablespoon ground coriander

1 tablespoon gram flour or besan (Indian chickpea flour)

1 tablespoon garam masala

Kosher salt

¼ cup olive oil

1 teaspoon yellow mustard seeds

1 teaspoon cumin seeds

1 or 2 green chiles, stemmed and finely chopped

1 teaspoon ginger-garlic paste

2 large onions, diced

4 tomatoes, diced

½ bunch cilantro, leaves only, finely chopped, for garnish

1. Trim off any long stems from the okra, but leave the small cap on. Quarter the okra lengthwise from the tip to the stem end, but do not separate.

2. Thoroughly combine the chile powder, turmeric, coriander, gram flour, garam masala, and salt to taste. Fill each okra pod with this mixture, and press cut quarters together.

3. Heat the oil in a large skillet over medium-high heat. Add the mustard seeds, cumin, green chiles, and ginger-garlic paste. As soon as they begin to splatter, add the onions and cook them until golden brown.

4. Add the tomatoes and cook for few minutes, until they become soft. Stir frequently so the mixture doesn't stick to the pan.

5. Add the stuffed okra and cook, uncovered, for 8 to 10 minutes. Transfer to a serving dish, sprinkle with the cilantro, and serve hot.

SERVES 4

ADELE ETOCH'S STUFFED ARTICHOKES

FAYETTEVILLE, ARKANSAS

By the 1930s, Helena, Arkansas, a busy port city on the Mississippi River, had a large and well-established Lebanese population, and the late Adele Etoch was one of the home cooks whose efforts kept the community close—and vibrant. The child of restaurant owners, she enjoyed an easy grace in the kitchen, whether she was cooking for four or forty, and a half century after her death, her grandchildren still request their MaMaw's stuffed artichokes as a treat for their July birthdays.

3 globe artichokes, 1 inch trimmed off the top, leaf tips clipped

5 tablespoons fresh lemon juice

4 tablespoons olive oil

Kosher salt

½ cup finely chopped onion

1½ pounds 85% lean ground beef

4 garlic cloves, minced

¼ teaspoon red pepper flakes

½ cup toasted pine nuts

Freshly ground black pepper

One 6-ounce can tomato paste

1 tablespoon minced fresh mint

1. Cut the stem from each artichoke and trim the bottoms so they sit flat. Open the artichokes and scrape out the chokes with a spoon. Arrange the artichokes in a Dutch oven and add just enough cold water to cover them. Add 1 tablespoon of the lemon juice, 1 tablespoon of the olive oil, and 1 teaspoon salt.

2. Cover with a lid that fits down inside the pot and holds the artichokes under the water. Bring to a simmer over medium-low heat and cook for 25 to 35 minutes, until the artichokes are tender and the leaves pull out with a little resistance.

3. Reserving 3 cups of the cooking liquid, transfer the artichokes to a colander and drain upside down.

4. Meanwhile, in a large skillet, heat 1 tablespoon of the oil over medium heat. Add the onion and cook about 4 minutes, until soft. Stir in the beef, garlic, and pepper flakes and cook about 4 minutes, stirring constantly and breaking up the meat, until the meat is no longer pink. Drain off any excess fat, then stir in the pine nuts. Season with salt and pepper to taste and let cool.

5. In a blender or food processor, process the reserved artichoke cooking liquid, remaining ¼ cup lemon juice, tomato paste, and mint for about 30 seconds, until well blended.

6. Pour the remaining 2 tablespoons oil into the Dutch oven. Place the artichokes in the pot on their bases, spreading out the leaves and pushing them open. Fill the artichokes with the meat mixture, then pour the tomato sauce over the top.

7. Bring to a simmer over high heat, then reduce the heat to medium-low, cover, and cook for 20 to 25 minutes, until the sauce has thickened and the artichokes are very tender. Serve.

SERVES 6

GRACE BRUCATO'S TOMATO-BRAISED ARTICHOKE HEARTS

Eat Your Vegetables

Grace Brucato never expected to be the family cook. Coming of age in the late 1930s, she was one of the few girls in the Sicilian enclave in Rochester, New York, who was not lured to the kitchen. But years later, her husband, Salvatore's, enthusiasm for Sicilian cooking proved infectious, and he became her kitchen mentor. When Mr. Brucato died, his special artichoke dish, based on a recipe of his mother's, became her own. She's taught her granddaughter and grandson to make it, and hopes to teach her two great-grandchildren someday, too.

The dish is a wonderful accompaniment to roasted meat and hearty pasta dishes. Mrs. Brucato figures on about four baby artichokes per person, and when fresh artichokes are too expensive, she uses frozen artichoke hearts.

FOR THE TOMATO SAUCE

2 tablespoons olive oil

2 garlic cloves, minced

One 28-ounce can crushed Roma (plum) tomatoes, including juice

Kosher salt

¼ cup chopped fresh basil

Freshly ground black pepper

FOR THE ARTICHOKES

½ lemon, if using fresh artichokes

32 to 48 small artichokes, or six 9-ounce packages frozen artichoke hearts

4 large eggs

½ cup all-purpose flour

1 teaspoon kosher salt

1 teaspoon freshly ground black pepper

Olive oil, for frying

½ cup grated Parmesan cheese

1. To make the sauce: Heat the olive oil in a large saucepan over medium heat. When the oil is hot, add the garlic and cook until it begins to brown. Add the tomatoes and 1 teaspoon salt. Bring to a boil, reduce the heat to low, cover, and simmer for 45 minutes, stirring occasionally.

2. Add the basil and pepper to taste. Simmer for 15 minutes. Adjust the seasoning as desired.

3. To make the artichokes: Preheat the oven to 350°F. If using fresh artichokes, prepare an ice water bath and add the lemon juice. Trim away the tough outer leaves, slice the artichokes in half vertically, and use a teaspoon to scrape out the choke. Drop each half in the acidulated water to avoid discoloration while you prepare the remaining artichokes. If using frozen artichoke hearts, place them in a colander under running water until they are mostly thawed. Drain, pat them dry, and slice in half.

4. Beat the eggs in a small bowl. In a separate shallow bowl, combine the flour, salt, and pepper. Heat 2 to 4 tablespoons olive oil in a large skillet over medium-high heat. Dip each artichoke half in the eggs and then the flour, making sure that it is evenly coated. Working in batches if necessary, cook the artichokes, turning until lightly browned. Transfer to a wire rack set over a baking sheet.

5. Spread a bit of the tomato sauce into a large casserole and place artichoke hearts in a single layer over it. Add a bit more sauce, a layer of cheese, and another layer of artichoke hearts. End with a layer of cheese. Bake uncovered about 15 minutes, until the cheese is golden brown.

SERVES 8

Maria Latimore's Braised Green Beans

When Maria Latimore was two, her family moved from Wadley, Georgia, to Roxbury, a neighborhood in Boston. By the time she was in her early teens, she cooked the family dinner five nights a week, learning the basics from her mother. But while her mother's cooking was—and still is—very Southern, Ms. Latimore liked to experiment in the kitchen. "I cook because I like to eat food that tastes good and is healthy for me," she says. She developed this recipe for green beans as an alternative to cooking them with ham hocks or neck bones, "the way my mother would."

1 tablespoon olive oil

1 medium onion, finely chopped

2 garlic cloves, minced

½ teaspoon dried thyme

½ teaspoon dried rosemary, crushed

⅛ teaspoon red pepper flakes

2 pounds fresh green beans, trimmed and snapped into 2-inch pieces

Two 14-ounce cans low-sodium chicken broth

3 cups water

2 teaspoons kosher salt

½ teaspoon freshly ground black pepper

1. Heat the oil in a large Dutch oven over medium heat. Add onion and cook until brown, about 10 minutes, stirring a few times. Stir in the garlic, thyme, rosemary, and red pepper flakes and cook for 2 minutes more.

2. Turn up the heat to high and stir in green beans, broth, water, salt, and black pepper. Bring to a boil, then lower heat to medium, and simmer vigorously for 45 minutes, or until beans are completely tender. Serve.

SERVES 8 TO 10

Bill Best's Leather Britches (Shuck Beans)

Bill Best's family has farmed in Appalachia since before the American Revolution. There was a time, he says, when "everyone was a seed-saver" because it was the only way to grow food. He learned seed-saving from his mother and grandmother and returned to the practice twenty-five years ago, when his customers began complaining about his commercial green beans. Growing traditional regional beans from saved seed has been personally satisfying and today he sells more than four hundred varieties of heirloom beans and forty-one types of seed. "Leather Britches"—unshelled beans that were traditionally threaded together and hung to dry (at which point they look like little britches on a clothesline)—can be cooked slowly and can stay on the stove for several days, he says, and be eaten for lunch, supper, and lunch again the next day. "The dish gets better with each succeeding meal."

2 pounds green beans

½ pound salt pork, cut into cubes

1 or 2 large onions, sliced

2 large potatoes, peeled and cut into chunks

Kosher salt

Trim and string the beans and break them in half. Put in a large saucepan and add water to cover. Add the pork (more or less, to taste), onions, and potatoes. Add salt to taste. Cover and simmer over low heat on a wood stove for 1 hour.

SERVES 4 TO 6

Cheryl Shafer's Corn on the Cob

FINDLAY, OHIO

Cheryl Shafer, who grows corn with her husband, Harold, gives this advice to the steady stream of shoppers who drive to their farm for their corn fix:

"If you grow up near corn, you are moved by acres of straight, leafy rows, reassured by order and predictability. You know the difference between good and bad corn early in life and have the confidence that comes from such discernment. Along with Huck Finn, you know 'There ain't nothing in the world so good when it's cooked right,' and you know that this means rushed from the field, shucked, and plunged into a pot of boiling water before the sugar in the kernels begin to convert to starch."

To boil corn on the cob: Bring a big pot of water to a boil. Husk the corn and rub away the silk. Add the corn and boil, uncovered, until tender, 5 to 7 minutes.

To grill corn on the cob: Fill a bucket or big pot with ice water. Leave the husks and silk intact and plunge the corn in the water. Soak for 2 hours and up to 6, weighting down if necessary to keep the ears submerged. Preheat a grill. Place the corn in a single row on the grill, cover and cook, turning often, until the husks are lightly browned on all sides, 15 to 20 minutes. The corn can also be buttered prior to grilling. Pull back the corn husks and remove the silk. Spread the ears with the butter of your choice and re-cover the corn with the husks. Soak in water for 10 minutes. Grill until tender, turning from time to time, 15 to 20 minutes. Remove the husks and season with salt and pepper.

To microwave corn on the cob: Remove the husks and silk from up to 6 ears of corn. Place the corn in gallon-size resealable plastic bags. Seal the bags halfway. Set the timer for 2 minutes per ear and cook on high.

FLAVORED BUTTERS

IT IS DIFFICULT TO IMPROVE ON AN EAR OF FRESHLY PICKED CORN COOKED NOT A SECOND too long. However, this does not stop corn-on-the-cob-crazed Americans from dreaming of better butters or alternative cooking methods.

Boiling and steaming preserve the sweet innocence of corn; grilling or roasting it add a smoky element. In New Mexico, Arizona, and Texas, where smokiness is next to godliness, roasting and grilling are popular and both chile-laced and lime-accented butters bring out the sweetness of the corn.

Ancho Chile Butter

LOS RANCHOS DE ALBUQUERQUE, NEW MEXICO

2 small dried ancho chiles

8 tablespoons (1 stick) unsalted butter, softened

½ teaspoon kosher salt, plus more to taste

Stem the chiles, break them open, and shake out all the seeds. Bring a small saucepan of water to a boil. Lower the heat, add the chiles, and simmer until softened, about 5 minutes. Drain and let cool. Use a small knife to scrape the flesh of the chiles from the skins. Discard the skins and chop the chiles to a paste, and cream together with the butter and salt in a small bowl. Stir in more salt, if desired.

————

MAKES ABOUT ½ CUP

Lime Butter

TAYLOR, ARIZONA

4 tablespoons (½ stick) unsalted butter, softened

4 tablespoons mayonnaise

4 teaspoons grated lime zest

1 teaspoon kosher salt

Scant pinch of ground chile or chili powder

2 tablespoons fresh lime juice

Cream the butter with the mayonnaise, lime zest, and salt in a small bowl. Gradually stir in the ground chile and the lime juice.

————

MAKES ABOUT ½ CUP

Hannah Berman's Corn Pudding

EL CERRITO, CALIFORNIA

Hannah Berman represents the most recent generation of "glorious amateur" home cooks—young people who see cooking and eating as a great adventure they can share in their homes, or in the great electronic village of the Internet. Famous in high school for always bringing great cookies to class, Ms. Berman cooked in her college dorm, mainly to avoid cafeteria food. When she got her own apartment, she formed a monthly dinner party club and served lavish meals to twenty or more friends.

Ms. Berman described her corn pudding's texture as "almost like a soufflé." Although she made the dish in college when she was craving comfort food, and still makes it for dinner, she considers it "special food for a special occasion." The recipe works with frozen corn, but using fresh "makes a big difference," she says.

3 tablespoons (⅜ stick) unsalted butter, melted, plus more for the baking dish

2 tablespoons all-purpose flour

1 teaspoon kosher salt

4 large eggs

2 cups corn kernels (preferably fresh)

1⅓ cups half-and-half

1. Preheat the oven to 325°F. Lightly butter an 8 x 8-inch casserole or baking dish.

2. Combine the melted butter, flour, salt, eggs, corn, and half-and-half, beating to blend thoroughly. Pour into the casserole. Bake about 1 hour, stopping after 30 minutes to stir the mixture.

3. The pudding is ready when a knife inserted into the center comes out clean. Serve immediately.

SERVES 4

Leona Chalmers's
Corn and Mushroom Skillet Cake

"My mother and grandmother used cornmeal and sugar and made these cakes for breakfast," Leona Chalmers says. "They were usually served with sausage or scrapple or the like." Ms. Chalmers likes having some texture, so she added the corn kernels. She also took out the sugar and serves them for supper. They are good with pulled pork and grilled meat of any sort. "My granddaughter is now vegetarian," Ms. Chalmers says, "and she likes these cakes with grilled vegetables, black bean chili, or some pepper Jack cheese melted on top."

Unsalted butter

2 cups fresh corn kernels, cut from the cob, or 2 cups frozen, thawed and drained

2 cups wild mushrooms such as chanterelles, fresh or rehydrated dried

Kosher salt and freshly ground black pepper

1 cup coarse yellow cornmeal

⅓ cup boiling water, plus more if necessary

2 large eggs, lightly beaten

1 cup buttermilk

1 tablespoon minced scallions, green and white parts, or chives

½ cup vegetable oil or bacon grease

½ cup fresh ricotta or soft fresh goat cheese

1. Melt 1 tablespoon butter in a cast-iron skillet. When it is very hot, add the corn kernels. Cook and stir to toast the corn to a dark gold color, but stand back—those nibs can pop and make the butter splatter. Remove from the heat using a slotted spoon, transfer the corn to paper towels. Pat it dry.

2. Return the skillet to the stovetop, raise the heat to high, add more butter if necessary, then add the mushrooms, season lightly with salt and pepper, and cook just to warm, about 2 minutes, stirring and tossing constantly. Remove from heat. Transfer to the paper towels to drain.

3. Preheat the oven to 350°F. In a medium bowl, stir together the cornmeal, 1 tablespoon salt, and ⅛ teaspoon pepper. Add boiling water to the cornmeal mixture a little at a time, whisking between each addition until you have a thick paste. In another bowl, stir together the eggs and buttermilk. Add this to the cornmeal mixture and stir to combine. Add the toasted corn and minced scallions, and season lightly with additional salt and pepper.

4. Warm 8 tablespoons butter or the vegetable oil or bacon fat in a 12-inch cast-iron skillet over medium-high heat. When hot, pour the corn batter into the pan and reduce the heat to medium. Immediately scatter the mushrooms across the cake. Divide the ricotta into small pieces and dot over the top. Cook for 1 minute more. Transfer to the oven and bake until the top is lightly golden and the cake feels firm to the touch, about 15 minutes.

5. Remove from the oven, cool slightly, and turn out onto a serving plate, cut into wedges and serve.

SERVES 8

Tommy Verdillo's Stuffed Escarole

BROOKLYN, NEW YORK

The impresario of Tommaso's restaurant in Bay Ridge, Brooklyn, Tommy Verdillo has been wowing Le Tout Italian New York with his flawless renditions of southern Italian cooking as well as the operatic arias that he belts out in the dining room. Escarole is delicious as a side dish or tossed with pasta when it is chopped, sautéed with garlic, and allowed to simmer slowly in its own juices, he says. "But this dish, ah this dish, is the star, a course that humbles all others, a meal in itself."

¼ cup golden raisins

1¼ teaspoons olive oil

1 garlic clove, minced

½ cup dry bread crumbs

¼ cup coarsely chopped walnuts

½ teaspoon kosher salt

Freshly ground black pepper

1 anchovy fillet, finely chopped

1 teaspoon capers, drained and chopped

2 cups plus 2 tablespoons homemade chicken broth or low-sodium store-bought chicken broth

1 head escarole

6 garlic cloves, crushed

⅛ teaspoon red pepper flakes

1. Soak the raisins in hot water for 30 minutes. Drain and pat dry.

2. Heat ¼ teaspoon of the oil in a medium nonstick skillet over medium heat. Add the minced garlic and cook, stirring constantly, for 30 seconds. Add the bread crumbs, walnuts, salt, and pepper to taste. Lower the heat and cook, stirring frequently, until the crumbs turn golden brown, about 4 minutes. Transfer to a large bowl and toss in the raisins, anchovy, and capers. Stir in 2 tablespoons of chicken broth.

3. Carefully press open the escarole leaves like flower petals, leaving them attached at the core. Spoon the filling between the leaves. Close up the leaves and tie string around the escarole to secure.

4. Heat the remaining oil in a deep skillet. Add the crushed garlic and pepper flakes and cook, stirring, for 3 minutes. Add the remaining broth and carefully place escarole in skillet. Bring to a simmer, cover, and cook until escarole is tender, about 45 minutes. Remove the string, cut into quarters, and serve.

SERVES 4

Anthony "Tadon" Miletello's Stuffed Mirliton

Long before words such as "organic" and "sustainable" entered the American lexicon, Mary Lee and Anthony "Tadon" Miletello were working the earth. Married for forty-nine years, they plant spring and fall gardens in the fertile Louisiana soil. In mid-January, Mr. Miletello sets the seeds for his summer eggplants and tomatoes. Toward the end of March he plants the seedlings along with row upon row of okra, cucumbers, snap beans, purple hull peas, field peas, corn, and mirliton.

A member of the cucumber family, many Americans know mirliton as chayote squash or mango squash, since it originated in Mexico; in the Louisiana Bayou, Cajuns often use its French name, christophene. Some pronounce mirliton as spelled, while others say "mella-ton." The vegetable loves the subtropical Louisiana climate, and the Miletellos produce surplus crops every year. What they can't eat, they jar, freeze, or sell to passersby.

561

Eat Your Vegetables

8 to 10 mirliton or chayote squash

1 pound ground beef

1 pound medium shrimp, peeled and deveined

2 medium yellow onions, diced

1 medium green bell pepper, stemmed, seeded, and diced

5 garlic cloves, minced

¼ cup freshly grated Romano or Parmesan cheese

1 cup packaged Italian bread crumbs

1 cup plain dry bread crumbs

Kosher salt and freshly ground black pepper

½ cup shredded Cheddar cheese

1. Preheat the oven to 350°F. Bring several quarts of water to a boil in a medium stockpot.

2. Cut the mirliton in half lengthwise and boil until tender, about 15 minutes. Drain and set aside to cool.

3. Brown the beef in a skillet over medium-high heat, stirring to break up clumps, about 10 minutes. Add the shrimp and cook 10 minutes more or until shrimp turn pink. Add the onions, bell pepper, and garlic and cook, stirring, until tender, 5 to 7 minutes.

4. Discard the seeds, then scoop the pulp from the mirliton, being careful not to break the skin. Add the pulp and grated cheese to the skillet. Combine the bread crumbs and sprinkle about half into the skillet. Stir well. Season with salt and pepper to taste and cook for 5 minutes, stirring occasionally.

5. Scoop generous portions of the filling into each mirliton shell and place in a 9 x 13-inch baking dish. Sprinkle the remaining bread crumbs and the Cheddar cheese on top.

6. Bake uncovered for 30 minutes or until slightly brown.

———

SERVES 8 TO 10

Ben Herrera Beristain's Stuffed Peppers

Chiles en nogada may be the most famous dish to come out of the Mexican state of Puebla. The green poblano chiles, the white ground walnut sauce, and the red pomegranate seeds reflect the colors of the Mexican flag. Many Mexicans prepare the dish to celebrate the anniversary of the country's independence from Spain on September 16, when the three main ingredients are abundant. Mr. Herrera Beristain's grandmother also prepared it every fall in honor of his grandfather's saint's day.

Mr. Herrera Beristain has lived in the United States for ten years. The accountant-turned-translator, whose family has owned a restaurant in Mexico City for more than forty-five years, cooks because he "finds the whole process of converting ingredients into a dish magical."

FOR THE PEPPERS

12 large poblano chiles

Vegetable oil

FOR THE FILLING

3 tablespoons olive oil

1 large white onion, finely chopped

1 head garlic, cloves separated, peeled, and finely chopped

2 pounds ground beef

2 ripe plantains, peeled and cut in small cubes

4 red apples (such as Cortland), cored and cut in small cubes

1 cup raisins

6 ounces candied citron, cut in small cubes

4 ounces blanched almonds, chopped

1 tablespoon ground cumin

1 tablespoon ground cinnamon

1 teaspoon dried oregano

Kosher salt and freshly ground black pepper

2 tablespoons all-purpose flour

FOR THE BATTER

4 large eggs, separated

½ teaspoon fresh lime juice

3 tablespoons all-purpose flour

3 to 4 cups vegetable oil, for frying

FOR THE WALNUT (NOGADA) SAUCE

9 ounces walnut pieces

1 bolillo (Mexican sandwich roll) or ¼ to ⅓ loaf French bread, cut into small pieces

Milk, as needed

6 ounces queso doble crema or cream cheese

FOR SERVING

Seeds of 1 pomegranate

¼ cup chopped fresh parsley

1. Preheat the oven to 500°F.

2. To prepare the peppers: Lightly brush the skin of the poblanos with oil and place them on a baking sheet. Roast until they are blistered and black on all sides, turning them as needed.

3. When the peppers are done, place them in a clean brown paper bag. Roll the bag closed. (This will steam the peppers and make the skin easier to remove.)

4. After 15 minutes, remove the peppers from the bag and carefully peel away their skins. Wipe the peppers clean with a paper towel. Using a paring knife, carefully slice them open vertically from the stem down, open, and gently cut away and discard the seedbed.

5. To prepare the filling: Heat the olive oil in a Dutch oven over medium heat. Add the onion and garlic and cook, stirring often, until translucent. Add the ground beef and cook, stirring to break up clumps, until browned. Transfer the mixture to a strainer and drain very well.

6. Return the meat to the pot and add the plantains, apples, raisins, citron, almonds, cumin, cinnamon, and oregano. Season with salt and pepper to taste. Cook, stirring occasionally, for 10 to 15 minutes, until heated through and well combined.

7. Gently spoon the filling into the peppers so they are well filled but not overflowing. Set the stuffed peppers on a baking sheet and sprinkle with 2 tablespoons flour.

8. To prepare the batter: In the bowl of a standing mixer, beat the egg whites and lime juice on high speed until stiff, about 3 minutes. Reduce the speed to medium and add the yolks one by one. Add the flour and keep beating until well mixed.

9. Heat the oil until very hot in a large heavy skillet or deep-fryer.

10. Grabbing the peppers by the stem, dip them in the batter, coating them well. Be careful not to spill the filling. Working in batches, deep-fry the chiles until golden brown on all sides. Place the chiles on a wire rack set over a baking sheet or a tray lined with paper towels.

11. To prepare the walnut sauce: Place the walnut pieces and bread in a food processor and add milk to just cover. Add the queso doble crema and process until smooth.

12. To serve: Place the peppers on a platter, spoon sauce on top to just cover, and sprinkle with pomegranate seeds and chopped parsley.

——————

SERVES 4

Barbara Rush's Zucchini Casserole

In the summer of 2002, the people of Granville, Ohio, created a potluck to fight childhood hunger in Licking County, Ohio. The local football team set up tables on Main Street in Granville. Families came, paid $5 to rent a table, and laid out food to share. Cooks brought their best dishes. The local gourmet club

evaluated each. No one was more surprised than Barbara Rush when her zucchini casserole took the blue ribbon. "I am not a cook," said the retired schoolteacher. "This award should really go to my mother-in-law. She was a simple farm woman. Every summer night of her life, she made this casserole. Every night her husband came in from the field, said something surly, and sat down and ate without looking up. A good night was when he said nothing. When I make this recipe of hers, and everyone goes nuts for it, I like to think she's up there in heaven, hearing it all, getting her due at last."

2 cups grated sharp cheese

3 cups cubed bread crumbs

¼ cup melted butter

4 cups thinly sliced zucchini

1 large onion, thinly sliced

3 cups thinly sliced Roma tomatoes

½ cup finely chopped green peppers

½ teaspoon kosher salt

Freshly ground black pepper to taste

1. Preheat the oven to 350°F. Divide the cheese into 3 equal portions and set aside. Place the bread crumbs in the food processor with all but 2 teaspoons of the melted butter and pulse to combine.

2. Butter a 1½-quart casserole dish. Alternately layer the zucchini, onion, tomatoes, peppers, cheese, and bread crumbs in the casserole. Sprinkle each layer with salt and pepper ending with bread crumbs. Cover the casserole with tinfoil and bake for 45 minutes. Remove the foil and continue baking for 15 minutes more to brown the top.

SERVES 6 AS A SIDE DISH, 4 AS A MAIN COURSE

Patricia Greathouse's Chiles Rellenos

Patricia Greathouse, author of *Mariachi*, is descended from a long line of chile-loving New Mexicans. Her recipe for chiles rellenos (stuffed chiles) is her mother's. Suitable for vegetarians, it lets the chile shine through, unlike the more conventional heavily battered dish. First choice for the chiles in the dish is freshly roasted New Mexican green chiles, but frozen whole or canned chiles may be substituted. Chiles rellenos are excellent with juicy pinto beans, calabacitas (small squash), and warm flour tortillas. They also make a great burrito, wrapped in a warm flour tortilla.

565

Eat Your Vegetables

2 cups all-purpose flour

1 teaspoon kosher salt

2 large eggs

1 pound Monterey Jack or longhorn cheese, or
½ pound of each

12 freshly roasted New Mexico or Anaheim green chiles, peeled and seeded, stems left on

Vegetable oil

1. Preheat the oven to 250°F. Line a baking sheet with paper towels or brown paper bags. Put the flour on a plate, and mix the salt in well. Beat the eggs to combine in a shallow bowl. Cut the cheese into logs ½ inch square and as long as you can make them.

2. Lay a log lengthwise in each chile, adjusting the fit by cutting it or adding a little extra piece as needed. Wrap the chile around the cheese so none of the cheese shows.

3. Heat ¼ inch of oil in a large skillet over medium heat until hot but not smoking. One at a time, roll the chiles in the flour and then in the egg, letting any extra egg drip off. Lay a few of the chiles seam side down in the frying pan. Don't crowd them; they shouldn't touch. Fry until golden brown, then flip and cook on the second side. Transfer to the baking sheet to drain.

4. Keep the fried chiles warm in the oven while you prepare the remaining chiles, or serve them hot as soon as they're finished cooking. Add more oil to the skillet as necessary; be sure to reheat the oil sufficiently before adding the chiles.

MAKES 12 RELLENOS, SERVES 3 TO 4

Ari Feyda's Egyptian Seder Peppers

Before Ari Feyda, a croupier at one of the Las Vegas casinos and an amateur historian, passes the platter of her peppers, she will tell the origin of this delicate recipe. Even before their expulsion from Spain, Sephardic Jews were never isolationists. And when they immigrated to the Ottoman Empire in the fifteenth century, their cooking picked up traces of Turkish and Balkan influences, as well as hints of North Africa and the Middle East from Morocco, Algeria, Syria, Lebanon, and Iran. With their sweet, pungent, and spicy notes, these peppers tell that story.

8 red or yellow bell peppers

2 tablespoons sunflower oil

2 garlic cloves, minced

1 pound tomatoes, peeled, seeded, and chopped, or one 14.5-ounce can stewed tomatoes

Kosher salt and freshly ground black pepper

1 teaspoon sugar

½ pound fresh mozzarella cheese, cut in 8 pieces

½ pound fresh salty cheese, such as ricotta salata or feta, cut in 8 pieces

1. Preheat the oven to 500°F. Place the peppers on a baking sheet and roast for ½ hour, until the skins are blistered.

2. Place the peppers in a brown paper bag, seal the bag, and let the peppers rest for 15 minutes. Turn the oven down to 350°F.

3. Use a sharp knife to remove the skins and seeds from the peppers, leaving them as intact as possible.

4. Heat the oil in a skillet over high heat and cook the garlic until gold, about 1 minute. Add the tomatoes, crushing them between your fingers while allowing as few seeds as possible into the sauce. Season with salt and pepper to taste, add the sugar, and simmer for 20 minutes, stirring occasionally. Pass the sauce through a food mill to remove any remaining skins and seeds.

5. Slip a piece of mozzarella and a piece of feta or ricotta salata inside each pepper. Place the peppers in a baking dish, cover with tomato sauce, and bake for 20 minutes. Serve very hot.

SERVES 8

One Big Table

Nancy Rigg's Mammoth Zucchini "Roast" with Wild Rice Stuffing

CAMARILLO, CALIFORNIA

Nancy Rigg's Amish ancestors left Colorado after they got into trouble for serving homemade beer and wine to Civil War soldiers. This recipe literally grew out of her first vegetable garden in California. One morning in early fall she found her dog barking at a zucchini plant at the back of the plot, "a huge zucchini that had been growing, and growing, concealed by the large plant leaves," until it was "as big as a leg of lamb or a standing rib roast of beef." For an upcoming vegetarian feast, Ms. Rigg decided to core, stuff, and bake it, serving it like a roulade. The key to this presentation is to hollow out the zucchini without slicing it in half. Serve with salad, sautéed carrots, and freshly baked artisan bread.

2½ cups chicken or vegetable stock

3 tablespoons (⅜ stick) unsalted butter

¾ cup wild rice

¼ cup basmati or long-grain brown rice

1 tablespoon olive oil, plus more for the baking dish and basting

1 large Vidalia or other sweet onion, chopped

2 or 3 garlic cloves, minced

6 fresh sage leaves, minced, or 8 dried sage leaves, crushed

2 tablespoons chopped fresh thyme leaves, or 2 teaspoons dried

2 tablespoons chopped fresh marjoram leaves, or 2 teaspoons dried

1 tablespoon chopped fresh winter savory, or 1 teaspoon dried

2 celery stalks, sliced

1 pound fresh cremini mushrooms, stemmed and sliced

One 8-ounce can whole water chestnuts, drained and diced

¼ cup good quality Chardonnay

1 cup dried cranberries

1 cup fresh cranberries, washed

½ cup chopped walnuts

Kosher salt and freshly ground white pepper

½ cup chopped fresh curly parsley leaves

1 enormous zucchini, at least 12 inches long and 16 to 18 inches around

1. Bring the chicken stock to a boil. Add 1 tablespoon of the butter and the wild rice, reduce the heat and simmer, covered, for about 30 minutes.

2. Add the basmati rice and simmer for 15 to 20 minutes more, until all the liquid is absorbed, the wild rice cracks open and softens, and the basmati rice is cooked. Fluff and set aside.

3. Preheat the oven to 350°F. Lightly oil a baking dish just large enough to hold the zucchini.

4. Melt the remaining 2 tablespoons butter with 1 tablespoon olive oil in a large skillet. Cook the onion until translucent. Stir in the garlic, sage, thyme, marjoram, and winter savory. Add the celery, mushrooms, and water chestnuts and cook until golden, stirring occasionally and adding a bit more butter or olive oil if needed. Add the wine and the dried and fresh cranberries, cover, and simmer 5 minutes, allowing the sweet and tart flavors to emerge. Remove from the heat.

5. Add the walnuts, a touch of salt and pepper, and the parsley. Mix in the rice to complete the stuffing.

6. Wash the squash and trim the ends. Carefully core out the center of the squash using a long, thin knife such as a boning knife. Do not break through the skin. Discard the flesh or use it for another dish.

7. Gently fill the zucchini with the stuffing. Set the squash in the prepared baking dish and lightly baste with olive oil. Arrange any leftover stuffing around the squash. Cover with foil and bake for 40 to 60 minutes, until the squash is tender.

8. Let rest for 5 minutes, then carefully cut into 2-inch-thick slices.

———

SERVES 4 TO 6

One Big Table

Regina Safdie's
Sephardic Stuffed Zucchini

"Syrian Jews make stuffed vegetable dishes just for special occasions because the preparation is elaborate and takes a lot of time," says Regina Safdie, a psychiatric social worker. "I always went home to Los Angeles to spend the Jewish holidays with my parents. One of the benefits was that my mother made incredible muhshi kusa (stuffed squash). In 2007, I realized that I better learn how to make the dish myself. My mother demonstrated it and I got the concept. But I'd not even made it when she died unexpectedly the next year. I consulted cookbooks and other relatives to get the amounts right. I lightened my version by using ground turkey instead of beef, and made it slightly sweeter by including onion. But I believe my mother would approve of my version, and it makes me feel close to her when I make this in my own kitchen."

¼ cup long-grain white rice

¾ cup water

1 pound ground beef or ground turkey

1 teaspoon kosher salt

2 teaspoons freshly ground black pepper

1 tablespoon ground cinnamon

1 tablespoon ground allspice

⅓ cup ketchup or high-quality tomato paste

10 zucchini, 6 to 8 inches long, ends trimmed, halved lengthwise

4 or 5 green onions (scallions)

15 dried apricots

¾ cup pomegranate syrup or concentrate (preferably Sadaf or Cortas brand)

1. Put the rice and water in a small saucepan. Bring to a boil and simmer for 5 minutes. Remove from the heat and transfer to a medium bowl. Cool to room temperature. Thoroughly mix in the ground meat, salt, pepper, cinnamon, allspice, and ketchup.

2. Cut off the stem ends of the zucchini and carefully scoop out the middle of each half and leave an edge about ⅛ inch thick. Discard the flesh or use it for another dish.

3. Spoon the stuffing into the zucchini. Do not overstuff, as the rice will expand while it cooks.

4. Place green onions in the bottom of a large pot in a loose grid. (This prevents the zucchini from sticking.) Add the zucchini, also in a grid pattern. Place the apricots on top of the zucchini. Pour in the pomegranate syrup and water just to cover the zucchini. Cover with a plate or a lid that fits into the pot to keep the zucchini from moving during cooking. Bring to a boil, then reduce the heat.

5. Simmer for 1½ hours, until the filling is cooked and the zucchini are tender.

6. Transfer the apricots to a large platter. Top with the zucchini and spoon over the juices from the pot.

SERVES 10

INTO THE WOODS

VUTH OUK CAME TO THE UNITED STATES FROM CAMBODIA IN 1986. WHEN HE WAS ABOUT
19, in 1989, he started foraging for mushrooms near his home in Portland, Oregon. He was looking for work and saw people picking for a mushroom company. "They showed me which ones to pick. Now I know it and how to look for it. I know more than everybody."

Mr. Ouk travels the United States and Canada looking for mushrooms. He's combed Oregon, Montana, Idaho, California, and Alaska. He has picked in New Hampshire and Massachusetts, and found chanterelles growing under huckleberry bushes in Vermont in June. Black trumpet mushrooms grow along the California-Oregon border and all the way through San Francisco in December and January. In August, chanterelle season begins in Oregon. Morels grow a year after a forest fire. "When they have the fire there, I go to that state," he says.

"I study the ground if mushrooms are coming. If there's moss and canopies, that's a good sign. For chanterelles, we need more trees. Any kind of mushrooms, we need more trees." Because of logging, the weather has changed. It doesn't rain as much, so there are fewer wild mushrooms available.

Mr. Ouk says there are three hundred to four hundred people in the mushroom-picking community. About 30 percent are Cambodian, and a good number are Laotian. There are also Americans, but the growing majority is Mexicans. "Right now," he said, "there are no morel mushrooms. Can't do nothing about it," he says—except "stop logging."

Vuth Ouk's Samlor Kor Ko
Khmer Vegetable Ragout

Chicken, beef, or shrimp can be added to this traditional Khmer dish, but this version uses only vegetables. The delicate, woodsy flavor of the tree fungus is the star of the show, but almost any mushroom can be used.

2 slices galangal, ¼ inch thick by 2 inches long, peeled

1 stalk fresh lemongrass, woody parts removed, minced to equal 1 tablespoon

2 kaffir lime leaves (or the zest from 1 lime)

3 slices fresh turmeric root, ¼ inch thick by 2 inches long, peeled, or ½ teaspoon dried turmeric powder, toasted in a dry pan until fragrant and cooled

2 garlic cloves, roughly chopped and toasted in a dry pan until fragrant

½ teaspoon sweet paprika, toasted in a dry pan until fragrant and cooled

1 to 2 teaspoons oyster sauce (dark soy can also be used)

1 teaspoon sugar or honey

2 tablespoons toasted rice powder

1 cup coconut milk

2 cups water

1 teaspoon salt

1 tablespoon vegetable oil or coconut oil

1 Thai chile, whole

2 cups butternut or other firm winter squash, peeled, seeded, and cut into ½-inch cubes

1 Asian eggplant, cut into bite-size chunks

1 bitter melon, seeds removed, cut into ½-inch chunks

2 pounds coconi (also called tree eat fungus and cloud eat fungus)

2 cups fresh spinach or watercress leaves, rinsed well and coarsely chopped

1. Combine all the aromatics with the oyster sauce, sugar, rice powder, coconut milk, and water in a blender. Pulse until smooth, taste, adjust seasoning with salt, soy sauce, chili paste, or black pepper to taste, and set aside.

2. Warm the oil in a wok or large skillet. Add the chile pepper and cook until toasted and then remove and set aside. Add the winter squash and stir-fry until lightly toasted. Add the eggplant and stir-fry for 3 minutes. Add the bitter melon and coconi and stir to combine. Add the sauce and, stirring constantly, cook until the vegetables are tender, about 3 more minutes. Add the spinach, toss, and adjust seasoning with additional salt or some of the fried Thai chile if desired. Serve immediately with rice or French bread.

SERVES 4

KATHERINE THUNDERCLOUD'S
TUNDRA PICKER'S TART

"I was disillusioned with America when I came to Alaska in the 1970s. I thought I loved the place because it was wild and expansive. Over time, I realized that what I love about Alaska is that it is what America was meant to be, or used to be before everything got so crowded and corporate. There are people from everyplace, everyone needs each other, and if you have a dream and if you work hard enough, you can make it happen," says Katherine Thundercloud Nichols, a former wilderness guide. She describes her current calling as "seeker, body-worker, cook, healer," and there is no place she finds as pleasurable as the Yukon tundra that surrounds her best friend's home. Spending the day foraging and the long evening cooking is her idea of heaven on earth, she says.

½ recipe Anne LaFiandra's Lard Crust (page 694)

Kosher salt

2 tablespoons (¼ stick) unsalted butter

½ small onion, minced

3 garlic cloves, minced

¼ cup white wine

1 tablespoon dry sherry

1 pound wild mushrooms such as morels, chanterelles, and porcini (or a mix), cleaned and cut in bite-size pieces

3 large eggs

½ cup milk

½ cup heavy cream

1 cup sour cream

⅛ teaspoon ground nutmeg

⅛ teaspoon freshly ground white pepper

All-purpose flour, for rolling the pastry

1 cup grated Gruyère or similar cheese

1. Make the pastry, adding an additional ¼ teaspoon salt. Form into a ball, cover, and refrigerate for at least 30 minutes.

2. Preheat the oven to 300°F.

3. Melt 1 tablespoon of the butter in a medium skillet over medium-low heat. Add the onion and garlic and cook until translucent, about 3 minutes.

Add the white wine and sherry and cook until the liquid evaporates, 3 to 5 minutes. Let the mixture cool, and puree in a food processor.

4. Melt the remaining butter in the skillet over medium heat. Add the mushrooms. Season lightly with salt and cook, stirring frequently, until they begin to soften. (The length of time needed will depend on the kind of mushrooms and moisture content.) Remove from the skillet and cool.

5. Whisk together the eggs, milk, and heavy cream in a large bowl. Add the sour cream and whisk again. Stir in the onion-garlic puree. Season with salt, nutmeg, and white pepper.

6. Sprinkle a work surface lightly with flour and roll out the pastry. Place in a 10-inch pie or tart pan and crimp the edges. Prick the bottom of the crust with a fork and sprinkle with the cheese. Spread the mushrooms over the cheese and pour the egg mixture evenly over the mushrooms. Tap the pie several times on the counter to evenly distribute the contents.

7. Bake until the crust is golden and the tart feels relatively firm, about 35 minutes. The tart can be served at room temperature.

SERVES 8

Vasugi Ganeshananthan's Sri Lankan Mushroom Curry

Vasugi Ganeshananthan grew up in Bethesda, Maryland, and like many girls, learned to cook at her mother's side. She started cooking seriously when she moved to the Midwest for graduate school and realized that if she wanted curry, she would have to make it. "This gave me great social currency," she says. "The only Indian restaurant in town was bad and most of the people who lived in town had never had Sri Lankan food. It became a way to lure friends. And I realized that I was not a terrible cook." She got this recipe from her great-aunt, and often makes it without the curry leaves, which can be difficult to find. Rice is the traditional companion for this dish, but she prefers couscous. You can also use soy milk for a healthier curry or coconut milk for a slightly richer one.

A fiction writer and journalist, Ms. Ganeshananthan finds that both writing and cooking require flexibility and surprise. "If you start making curry and don't have a cinnamon stick, you have to be willing to go with it and accommodate the lack in some other way."

573

Eat Your Vegetables

8 ounces mushrooms, thinly sliced (oyster, porcini, or other wild mushroom, or domestic white or portobellos)

½ teaspoon vegetable oil

1 small onion, diced small

1 garlic clove, finely chopped

1 medium tomato, roughly chopped

Pinch of whole fennel seeds

Pinch of yellow mustard seeds

1 teaspoon curry powder (preferably Ceylon curry)

3 or 4 fresh curry leaves

Pinch of ground fennel seed

Kosher salt

½ to 1 teaspoon whole milk

1. This step is optional, but will speed up the cooking process: Place the mushrooms in a bowl, cover with plastic wrap, and microwave on high for 90 seconds. When you remove them from the microwave, they will be very mushy.

2. Put the vegetable oil in a medium nonstick skillet over medium heat. Add the onion and cook until soft, 3 to 5 minutes. Add the garlic, tomato, whole fennel seeds, mustard seeds, curry powder, curry leaves and ground fennel, and salt to taste. Cook for 3 to 4 minutes, until heated through. Add mushrooms and their liquid and cook over medium-low heat until the liquid is absorbed, 3 to 5 minutes. (If you skipped step 1, add the raw mushrooms and cook for 5 to 7 minutes, until the curry thickens.) Turn off the heat and slowly add the milk so it does not curdle. Serve warm.

SERVES 4

Marilynn Yee's Broccoli

Marilynn Yee got this recipe from her Malaysian babysitter. At one time she used light soy sauce instead of the fish sauce, but Ms. Yee found that the fish sauce adds another layer of flavor. "You can use it with almost any green vegetable," she says. "This dish has converted many children who wouldn't touch broccoli. I would bet the elder George Bush might even like it."

One 1- to 2-pound head broccoli

2 tablespoons premium oyster sauce

1 tablespoon fish sauce

¼ cup peanut oil

1½ teaspoons minced garlic

1. Cut the broccoli into bite-size florets. Bring a large pot of water to a boil. Drop the florets into the water and turn off the heat, making sure all the florets are submerged. After 4 to 5 minutes, drain the broccoli well in a colander. If you like the broccoli crisper, then drain it sooner.

2. While the broccoli is soaking, combine the oyster sauce and fish sauce in a large bowl. Heat the oil in a small saucepan over high heat until almost smoking. Add the garlic to the oil (be careful the garlic does not burn), then quickly pour into the bowl on the top of the sauce mixture.

3. Add the broccoli and stir well to coat with the sauce.

SERVES 4 TO 6

CELIA MANNESE'S
BROCCOLI RABE NAPOLITANO

HIGHLAND, NEW YORK

Ron Rozman is a freelance writer who works from his home in Highland, New York. The variety of broccoli rabe he grows—as well as the recipe for preparing it—comes from his late mother-in-law, Celia Mannese, whose parents brought the seeds from near Naples almost a century ago. Mrs. Mannese "always made sure someone in the family was growing it so she could collect the seeds every fall," he says. He also credits his mother-in-law with teaching him how to cook. Vegetables at her house were "green, not khaki," he says. This deceptively simple preparation highlights the toothsome qualities of the somewhat bitter green.

1 large bunch young broccoli rabe

1 tablespoon kosher salt

1 tablespoon extra virgin olive oil

4 garlic cloves, thinly sliced

3 ounces pancetta, fried until crisp, drained, and crumbled

1. Separate the leaves, florets, and tender stems of the broccoli rabe. Discard any woody, thick stems.

2. Bring a large pot of water to a boil and add 1 tablespoon salt. Add the broccoli rabe. Blanch for 30 to 40 seconds, then drain.

3. Heat the olive oil in a large, deep skillet over medium heat. Add the garlic and cook, stirring constantly, just until golden brown. Remove the garlic from the pan with a slotted spoon.

4. Add the broccoli rabe to the pan and cook, stirring, for 4 to 5 minutes, until heated through.

5. Transfer to a serving bowl and sprinkle with the crumbled pancetta and browned garlic. A piece of crusty Italian bread on the side is good.

SERVES 4

DESEREE ANNE KAZDA'S SPICED CAULIFLOWER

SEATTLE, WASHINGTON

Deseree Anne Kazda counts Filipino, French, and Norwegian immigrants among her ancestors—but much of her cooking style is the result of her own experimentation. "I helped Mom with big dinners like Thanksgiving," she says, "and also worked as a waitress. That inspired me to re-create restaurant dishes at home." She didn't particularly like cauliflower when she developed this recipe, she says, but she and her husband like Indian food and thought these flavors would jazz up the vegetable. If the amount of cayenne in the recipe is too much for you, cut it in half. "That way, you will still get some of the cayenne flavor, but it won't be overly spicy."

1 head cauliflower, trimmed and cut into florets

1 tablespoon olive oil

¼ teaspoon ground turmeric

¼ teaspoon ground cumin

¼ teaspoon cayenne pepper

½ teaspoon chili powder

Kosher salt and fresh cracked black pepper

1. Put the cauliflower in a large resealable plastic bag with the oil, turmeric, cumin, cayenne, and chili powder. Add salt and cracked black pepper to taste. Seal the bag and shake to coat. The cauliflower will turn yellowish.

2. Pour the seasoned cauliflower into a large skillet or saucepan. Cover and cook over medium heat until the florets are soft, about 15 minutes, stirring occasionally.

3. Uncover and cook for 2 minutes more, just to brown some of the pieces.

SERVES 4

PENNSYLVANIA DUTCH RED CABBAGE

Leona Miller's parents left the Mennonite community they'd grown up in and moved to western Pennsylvania, but returned to their family farm in the summers to lend a hand—or to drop off their children for a few weeks. "It was the best time of the year for my sisters and I. We spent the day with our grandmother in the kitchen, listening to her stories and learning how to make some of the traditional dishes.

"My grandmother used more vinegar and no wine, of course, but I figure that recipes are made for changing. I also replaced the brown sugar that she used with honey. We like to serve this with pork roast, sausages, or baked chicken."

2 slices thick-cut, very smoky bacon, thinly sliced crosswise

1 medium red onion, thinly sliced

2 garlic cloves, minced

1 head red cabbage (about 1½ pounds), outer leaves removed, cored, and shredded, to equal 8 cups

2 teaspoons caraway seeds

1 bay leaf

Kosher salt and freshly ground black pepper

3 cups dry white wine

1 tablespoon honey

¼ cup cider vinegar

1. Fry the bacon in a heavy pot or Dutch oven over medium-low heat until almost crisp, about 10 minutes, stirring and turning to avoid burning. Add the onion and garlic and cook until soft, about 10 minutes. Reduce the heat to low. Add the cabbage, cover the pot, and cook for 5 minutes, stirring frequently. Add the caraway seeds and bay leaf, season lightly with salt and pepper, and stir.

2. Combine the wine, honey, and vinegar and stir into the cabbage. Cook, stirring frequently, until the cabbage is soft, about 45 minutes. Add additional water or wine if necessary to keep the mixture well moistened.

3. When the cabbage is tender and the liquid has evaporated, transfer to a bowl, and cool to room temperature. Cover and refrigerate overnight.

4. To serve, warm the cabbage over low heat or in a microwave. Remove the bay leaf, taste, and adjust the seasoning before serving.

SERVES 8

GIANTS

"SUPERSIZED" FRIES AND BAGELS THE SIZE OF LIFE PRESERVERS MAY BE SALES PLOYS, but Bonnie Dinkel of Wasilla, Alaska, whose family is the crowned royalty of the giant cabbage world, admits that in the world of vegetables, bigger does not make better eating. "You can make pretty good sauerkraut from a ninety-pound cabbage," she says, "but mostly we feed them to livestock."

Monster vegetables have been recorded as far back as the 1850s. Rare is the county fair that does not award blue ribbons for size, and an increasing number of giant vegetable clubs have recently facilitated the exchange of growing tips—and bigger and bigger vegetables. The winner of Alaska's first cabbage weigh-off in 1941 tipped the scale at 23 pounds. In 2000, the winner weighed in at 105.6 pounds. Alaska's long summer days and the cool temperatures that like cabbage made Matanuska Valley famous for supersized vegetables. Dr. Don Dinkel, a professor emeritus of horticulture, says, "It never really gets dark here. Down in Kentucky, at the end of the day it gets dark—boom. Here the light fades very gradually and you get 430 more hours of daylight for photosynthesis."

But the Lower 48 is not immune to the urge for Bigger Vegetables. New York State, for instance, has become the epicenter of Giant Pumpkinism. One of the nation's most revered pumpkin weigh-ins is held at Cooperstown in the fall, and the New York State Giant Pumpkin Growers Association has 300 members. Randy Sundstrom, the president of the association, has a theory about the rise in popularity in giant pumpkins. He and his wife, Deb, the association's secretary, "noticed a rise in membership when gas prices jump," he said. "Fewer people are going on vacation. They are looking to relax at home."

And while the competition is fierce among Great Pumpkin growers—it was once an honor to be a member of the 700-pound club, but now there is a 1,600-pound club with three members—there is also plenty of time to simply sit and watch the gourds grow.

The Tamoreyas' Big Cabbage Gratin

In 1935, 203 Minnesota families reeling from the Great Depression relocated to Palmer, Alaska, to found the Matanuska Colony, a New Deal project. The Matanuska Valley's fertile black soil and nineteen hours of daylight in summer have made the valley Alaska's agricultural heartland. There are a number of different theories on why cabbages grow to the size of Volkswagens in the valley—the largest one recorded at the Alaska State Fair is 105.6 pounds!—but everyone agrees that giant vegetables are the region's trademark. Descendants of the original homesteaders, like the Tamoreyas, are still operating farms.

3 leeks, white and pale green parts only

2 pounds Savoy cabbage, shredded

2 tablespoons (¼ stick) unsalted butter or vegetable oil

1 shallot, minced

1 teaspoon white vinegar

⅓ cup all-purpose flour

1 cup milk

¼ cup heavy cream

1 cup sour cream

3 large eggs

2 tablespoons brown mustard

1 teaspoon yellow mustard seeds

1 teaspoon dill seeds

3 tablespoons minced fresh dill

Kosher salt and freshly ground black pepper

1. Preheat the oven to 350°F. Bring a large pot of lightly salted water to a boil. Slice the leeks in thin disks and wash in three changes of cold water, separating the layers to remove the sand and create individual rings. Drain well.

2. When the water is boiling, add the leeks and cabbage and boil for 5 minutes. Drain through a colander. Cool under cold running water and drain again, pressing a spatula against the cabbage to remove any excess water. Transfer to a bowl.

3. Use some of the butter to grease a 6-cup glass casserole, pie pan, or gratin dish. Melt the remaining butter in a saucepan over medium-low heat. Add the shallot and stir to soften, about 1 minute. Add the vinegar and continue cooking, for 1 minute more. Add the flour and stir to combine. Add the milk and stir frequently, until the mixture is smooth and very thick. Remove from the heat. Whisk in the heavy cream, sour cream, eggs, mustard, mustard seeds, dill seeds, and dill.

4. Stir the sauce into the cooled cabbage and leeks. Taste and adjust the seasoning with salt and pepper. Pour into the prepared baking dish and bake until fragrant and lightly brown, about 40 minutes.

SERVES 8

ANNIE LAU'S GARLIC STIR-FRIED BRUSSELS SPROUTS

SAN JOSE, CALIFORNIA

Annie Lau is ethnically Chinese, born in Malaysia. Her husband is ethnically Chinese, born in Hawaii. The couple moved to San Jose in the late 1990s and their kitchen is a laboratory where their regional and ethnic influences meet local ingredients. Neither had seen Brussels sprouts before moving to California, but after numerous attempts, they devised a recipe to bring out the nutty sweetness in the little cabbages. The final recipe, Ms. Lau says, "is an experiment in laziness. The less you do, the better." Try to pick similar size sprouts.

1 tablespoon extra virgin olive oil

4 garlic cloves, minced

2 cups Brussels sprouts, outer leaves trimmed, then halved

Kosher salt and freshly ground black pepper

1. Heat the olive oil in a nonstick skillet over medium heat. Add the garlic and cook until fragrant and light brown. Add the Brussels sprouts and turn the heat to medium-high. Season with salt and pepper.

2. Do not disturb for about a minute, so the edges caramelize, then toss. Leave for another minute or more. If the sprouts have not picked up enough golden color toss again. The more caramelization (browning) you get, the better the flavor (high heat is key!). Be careful not to overcook, though, which releases that nasty sulfur odor that puts people off Brussels sprouts.

3. Taste and adjust the seasoning with salt and pepper. Serve immediately.

SERVES 4 TO 6

MR. WOERNIK'S ONION RINGS

Back when Cincinnati was known as Porkopolis, Harry Woernik's father, grandfather, and great-grandfather were butchers and sausage makers. "My grandfather also fried a mean onion ring. He had a big barrel that he rigged up for deep-frying outside the back door of the shop and figured out how to give the rings the lightness that a lot of the beer-battered onions don't have, as well as some spice. He used a corn flour that a farmer friend ground real fine and a seasoning blend that is no longer made. I use a portable Fryolator that I got at a garage sale, but I've also used a countertop fryer. Heck, I even used to fry the onions in a cast-iron skillet. My grandfather used lard, of course, but I use mostly vegetable oil for frying. It's not exactly health food, but I make them once a year, for the family reunion, where we serve all the old sausage and hams, sauerkraut, hot dogs, and hot potato salad. The rest of the stuff you can make ahead, but you don't fry an onion until your cousin is standing in front of you with an empty plate and a sort of hungry look in the eye."

2 large white onions, peeled and cut into ½-inch-thick slices

1 quart buttermilk

Dash of hot sauce (preferably Frank's)

Vegetable oil, for frying

2½ cups all-purpose flour

½ cup fine corn flour, such as masa harina

¼ teaspoon celery salt

1 teaspoon sweet paprika

¼ teaspoon garlic powder

1 tablespoon Old Bay Seasoning

One 12-ounce bottle light beer

1½ cups club soda

1½ teaspoons kosher salt, plus more for sprinkling on the onion rings

½ teaspoon freshly ground black pepper

1. Separate the onion slices into rings and place in a large bowl. Combine the buttermilk and hot sauce, pour over the onions and soak at room temperature for at least 1 hour.

2. Fill a deep-fat fryer with oil and heat to 350°F.

3. While the oil is heating, sift together the flour, corn flour, celery salt, paprika, garlic powder, and Old Bay. Add the beer and whisk until smooth. Add the club soda and whisk until smooth. Season the batter with the salt and pepper and set aside.

4. Line several baking sheets with multiple layers of paper towels and keep a roll of towels handy. When the oil is the fryer reaches 350°F (hot enough to sizzle a sprinkle of flour), drain the onion rings and pat them dry with paper towels; discard the buttermilk. Place a few handfuls of rings in the batter and stir with a fork to coat them completely. One at a time, pick the rings up with the fork, shake off excess batter, and carefully slide into the oil. Do not overcrowd the fryer, and keep the temperature steady at 350°F.

5. Turn the rings once or twice to get an even golden brown, about 3 minutes. Drain on the baking sheets, sprinkle with salt, and serve immediately.

SERVES 4 TO 6

Lan Pham's Herbed-Roasted Onions

BALTIMORE, MARYLAND

Lan Pham was 2 years old when she immigrated to the United States from Vietnam with her family. Her father became a State Department official assigned to various posts in Asia and Africa and she lived in the Philippines during an earthquake and during a political uprising that closed her school. During civil unrest in Ethiopia, U.S. Marines escorted her to class. Yearly monsoons punctuated the relative calm of her high school years in Thailand. When she serves these herb-roasted allium, she tells her guests: "to taste, just one taste, and they are surprised by the sweet flavor and rich aroma. I tell them that everybody knows that slow-cooked onions don't give bad breath."

2 medium red onions

2 medium yellow onions

2 tablespoons fresh lemon juice

1 teaspoon Dijon mustard

2 garlic cloves, minced

1 tablespoon fresh thyme leaves

¾ teaspoon kosher salt

¼ teaspoon freshly ground black pepper

¼ cup extra virgin olive oil

1 tablespoon chopped fresh cilantro

1. Preheat the oven to 400°F. Cut each onion into quarters, keeping the root end still intact so wedges hold together.

2. In a large bowl, combine the lemon juice, mustard, garlic, thyme, salt, and pepper. Slowly whisk in the olive oil.

3. Add the onions to the bowl and mix well. Transfer the onions to a baking dish or sheet in a single layer. Bake for 30 to 45 minutes, until tender and browned at the edges. Toss the onions as necessary during cooking to ensure even browning.

4. Remove onions from the oven and transfer to a serving platter. Sprinkle with the cilantro.

SERVES 4

Tiffany Medeb Lee's
Algerian Roasted Beets and Greens

Mrs. Lee, a midwife, began to think about her family recipes when she had children of her own and spent more time at home. She remembered that her mother, a war bride, had arrived in Chicago from Algeria equipped with no knowledge of English—and no understanding that "Algerian Muslim" and "Black Muslim" were not the same thing. That, along with her mother's cooking, caused certain consternation in her father's family. "The first time she met a beet was the day she landed in Chicago. My father is African American, and his family couldn't believe that my mother didn't know American greens or root vegetables. They tried to teach her how to cook for my father. It was a disaster. Eventually, they realized that her way with roots and greens was not half bad. My mother boiled the beets for this recipe, but I like the flavor better when I roast them.

"Theirs was an unlikely marriage. My mother likes to say it worked out as well as the beets."

8 beets, well scrubbed, root ends trimmed but not removed, greens reserved

4 carrots, well scrubbed and cut into 1-inch-thick pieces

6 tablespoons olive oil

1 teaspoon ground cumin

½ teaspoon smoked paprika

4 garlic cloves, cut in thin slivers

2 tablespoons fresh lemon juice

Kosher salt and freshly ground black pepper

½ cup crumbled cheese, such as aged goat cheese, feta, or ricotta salata

1. The day before serving, place the beets and carrots in a bowl. Combine the ¼ cup of the oil, the cumin, and paprika. Pour over the vegetables and toss to coat well. Cover and refrigerate overnight.

2. Preheat the oven to 400°F. Remove the beets and carrots from the refrigerator and bring to room temperature.

3. Drain the beets and carrots and place on a baking sheet. Roast until tender, 20 to 30 minutes depending on the size of the beets, turning several times.

4. While the beets are roasting, prepare the greens. Remove the thickest parts of the stems and cut the leaves into ½-inch ribbons. Toss with 1 tablespoon of the olive oil.

5. Warm the remaining olive oil in a large skillet over medium heat. Add the garlic and cook until golden, about 2 minutes. Add the greens, increase the heat to medium-high and cook, stirring frequently, until the greens are tender, about 5 minutes. Remove from heat, stir in the lemon juice, and season to taste with salt and pepper.

6. When the beets are tender, remove from the oven and set aside until cool enough to handle. Cut the beets in half and place them, along with the carrots, in the center of a platter. Arrange the greens in a ring around the beets, sprinkle with cheese, and serve.

SERVES 6

583

Eat Your Vegetables

Tía Rosa and Ruth Eichner's Sweet-and-Sour Carrots

The novelist Julia Alvarez grew up in the Dominican Republic; her husband, Bill Eichner, is the son of tenant farmers in Nebraska. Dinner at the couple's Vermont home is a study in how far-flung flavors have enriched the simple sturdy fare of America.

Dr. Eichner spent hours coaxing Alvarez's mother, her aunts, and her cousins (not to mention Ana, the family cook) into giving him the broad outlines of their family's dishes—sweet-and-sour carrots, spicy Caribbean chicken, red beans and rice, and bread pudding. He tested the recipes on his parents, Ruth and John, who now live a couple of minutes away. Ruth, herself an accomplished cook, really liked the recipe for sweet-and-sour carrots.

2 pounds carrots, peeled

3 green bell peppers, cut into 1-inch squares

3 yellow onions, cut into 1-inch wedges

¾ cup cider vinegar

¾ cup sugar

1 cup tomato puree

1 teaspoon mustard powder

1 teaspoon Worcestershire sauce

Kosher salt and freshly ground black pepper

1. Boil the whole carrots until tender, then cut into ½-inch rounds. Steam the bell peppers and onions until tender. Combine all the vegetables in a large crock or bowl.

2. Combine the vinegar and sugar in a saucepan over low heat. Cook for 5 minutes, stirring to dissolve the sugar. Stir in the tomato puree, mustard, and Worcestershire. Remove from the heat. Pour over the vegetables and stir together well. Taste and adjust seasoning with salt and pepper. Cover and chill for at least 2 hours before serving.

SERVES 8

Mrs. Dubrow's Carrot "Noodles" in Buttery Chervil Sauce

IOWA CITY, IOWA

"My great grandmother, Birdie Dubrow, was a radio cook back in the day before telephones," said Emma O'Keefe. "The farms in the Midwest were so spread out that the women hung out with each other by broadcasting from their kitchens and exchanging recipes. It was their version of blogging. She gardened, and by this I mean cultivated about an acre of raised beds until several years ago when she turned a hundred and one. She did lots of inventive things with vegetables, like making 'noodles' from carrots or zucchini, in order to use what she grew, but also because she liked to confound the women who listened to her. She used lovage and parsley in this dish. I like the hint of licorice that chervil gives. It cracks me up when I see 'vegetable ribbons' and 'vegetable pasta' on the menus of fancy restaurants. My grandmother fixed this when the larder was low and she needed to economize."

Kosher salt

8 large carrots

4 tablespoons (½ stick) cold butter

1 shallot, minced

½ teaspoon celery seeds

2 cups white wine

1 tablespoon minced fresh chervil

1 tablespoon minced fresh flat-leaf parsley

1 tablespoon minced fresh chives

Freshly ground white pepper

1. Fill a large container with cold water. Add ice cubes and a pinch of salt. Using a vegetable peeler, cut thin lengthwise strips of carrot, plunging them into the ice water as you go along.

2. Bring a large pot of water to boil over high heat.

3. Melt 1 tablespoon of the butter in a medium saucepan and cut the remaining butter into small chunks and return it to the refrigerator. Add the shallot to the melted butter and cook for 1 minute, until softened. Add the celery seeds and wine and simmer until the wine is reduced by half, about 7 minutes. Remove from the heat.

4. When the water comes to a boil, drain the carrots and drop them into the boiling water for 30 to 60 seconds to heat and barely soften. Drain immediately.

5. Return the saucepan to the heat and when the reduced wine is warm, begin whisking in the cold butter, one piece at a time. Remove the pan from the heat as you add and whisk to avoid completely melting the butter. Be very careful; the point here is to create a thick sauce, which relies on butter that is not fully melted.

6. When all the butter has been added, stir in the chervil, parsley, and chives. Season with salt and pepper to taste. Toss the carrot "noodles" in the sauce and serve immediately.

SERVES 8

JOANN CALHOON'S MOLTEN SQUASH TIAN

COLBY, KANSAS

Joann Calhoon raised seven children on a farm on the western Kansas prairie. Ms. Calhoon found that both summer and winter squash varieties grew well in her garden—and filled bellies. She served them to her family and the hungry farmhands. "We grew a lot of butternut or Hubbard because it kept well in winter months," she says, "and enjoyed the more tender squash throughout the summer." This recipe can be used all year long. A clay tian (French casserole dish) gives the best results.

½ cup olive oil

4 medium delicata squash or 1 large butternut squash, peeled, seeded, and cut into 1-inch cubes, to equal 6 to 8 cups

1 garlic clove, minced

Kosher salt and freshly ground black pepper

½ cup grated Parmesan cheese

1. Preheat the oven to 450°F. Use some of the oil to grease a 2-quart clay pot or shallow ceramic casserole.

2. Toss the squash with ¼ cup of olive oil and the garlic and season lightly with salt and pepper. Place in the casserole. Season the top again lightly with salt and pepper, sprinkle with the Parmesan, and drizzle with the remaining oil.

3. Place in the oven and immediately reduce the temperature to 400°F. Bake until the top is crisp and golden and the squash is tender, 30 to 40 minutes. Serve immediately.

SERVES 4

DENA YOUNG'S APPLE-BAKED ACORN SQUASH

CLINTON, MISSOURI

Growing up with a sister and four brothers, Dena Young was her mother's deputy cook. She learned the value of cooking for a crowd. Her simple squash dish is as wonderful for large gatherings or potlucks as it is for quiet nights at home.

2 acorn squash, halved crosswise, seeds and fibers scooped out

Kosher salt and freshly ground black pepper

4 teaspoons unsalted butter

4 fresh sage leaves

2 small McIntosh apples, halved, cored and cut into ¼-inch-thick slices

1 teaspoon honey

3 cups apple cider

½ cup toasted nuts, such as pine nuts, chopped pecans, chopped walnuts, or shelled pumpkin seeds, for garnish (optional)

1. Preheat the oven to 350°F. Make a clean slice on the bottom of each squash half so that it will sit evenly, taking care not to cut into the flesh. Place in a medium roasting pan. Prick the squash with a fork.

2. Season lightly with salt and pepper. Place a thin slice of butter (about ½ teaspoon) in each and top with a sage leaf. Fan half of an apple in the cavity of each squash half. Add the remaining butter, combine the honey with the cider and pour ¼ cup of this mixture in each squash. Pour the remaining 2 cups of cider into the roasting pan.

3. Cover loosely with aluminum foil. Roast until the squash is tender, about 1½ hours.

4. Place one squash half on each of four plates, sprinkle with nuts, if using, and serve immediately.

SERVES 4

LESLIE SCOTT'S TWICE-BAKED TRUFFLE POTATO

Like wine, wild truffles require a complicated synergy of soil and temperature, sunlight and air, and just as Oregon produces fine varietal wines, the state produces a wild white winter truffle that obsessed native son James Beard, who declared Oregon's *Tuber oregonense* the equal of the legendary Italian variety. In recent decades, however, the reputation of Oregon's white truffles suffered serious damage, and to restore its rightful glow, Leslie Scott and her partner, the mycologist and truffle scientist, Charles Lefevre, founded the Oregon Truffle Festival. People, said Ms. Scott, were harvesting the truffles all wrong: "They were using rakes, tearing up the ground, pulling them up too early, before they had a chance to develop the remarkable scent that can turn a twice-baked potato into a work of art." And so while the festival offers the tastings and truffle meals and wine pairings that one would expect, it also offers a two-day intensive for training truffle dogs, like this Lagotto Romagnolo, the Italian dog bred for truffling, who commuted from Blackberry Farm in Tennessee to teach neophyte pooches how to sniff and dig the tubers.

Use fresh Oregon winter white truffles in season (December through February) for the full truffle experience. If fresh truffles are not in season, then either Oregon White Truffle oil or white truffle butter may be used in place of fresh truffles. To make white truffle butter, place one large fragrant white truffle in a Ziploc bag with one pound of sweet butter and refrigerate for one week. Wrap in ⅛-pound cubes and freeze until ready to use.

4 medium-sized russet potatoes, well scrubbed

3 tablespoons olive oil (2 tablespoons Oregon white truffle oil optional)

2 tablespoons butter (white truffle butter optional)

8 large shallots, peeled and sliced thin

2 tablespoons dry vermouth

2 ounces fresh white truffles, half shaved and half grated or finely chopped

1 cup crème fraîche or sour cream

½ cup mild fresh goat cheese

1 teaspoon sea salt, or more to taste

White pepper to taste

2–4 cups cooking-grade rock salt (optional)

1. Preheat the oven to 400°F. Pierce the potatoes in several places with a fork, rub with 1 tablespoon olive oil, and bake until tender, 45 to 50 minutes. Remove from oven and cool to room temperature. Reduce the oven temperature to 350°F.

2. While the potatoes are cooling, melt the butter in a skillet over medium heat, add the sliced shallots, season lightly with salt and pepper, and sauté, turning often, until golden on all sides, about 10 minutes. Add the vermouth, stir, and simmer until evaporated, about 5 minutes. Use a slotted spoon to remove the shallots and drain on paper towels.

3. Use a sharp knife to cut a thin slice from the narrow end of each potato and then slice each in half widthwise. Scoop out the cooked potato flesh from each half, taking care to leave at least ¼ of an inch of cooked flesh on the bottom and sides of the potato. Place the scooped potato in a bowl.

4. Combine and whip together the grated truffle, the crème fraîche, and half the goat cheese.

5. Add 1 tablespoon of olive oil to the potato, along with the truffled crème fraiche and goat cheese mix. (Use 1 tablespoon of the white truffle butter or oil at this step if fresh truffle is unavailable.) Use a rice or handheld masher to create a smooth, creamy texture. Season to taste with salt and pepper and set aside.

6. If using rock salt, arrange in a baking pan; use a teaspoon to fill each shell with the potato mixture and place each into the salt. (If not using rock salt, muffin tins will preserve the potatoes' shape.) Drizzle the remaining olive oil over the potato (truffle oil or butter optional), spread or thinly slice the remaining goat cheese over each, and bake for 20 minutes. Use the remaining truffle to shave over each potato and serve immediately.

SERVES 8

Michael Chu's Garlic Mashed Potatoes

SAN FRANCISCO, CALIFORNIA

Software designer and founder of the Web site cookingforengineers.com, Michael Chu says that "as an engineer I strive for the most efficient path to a desired result. When the desired result is creamy mashed potatoes that everybody loves, I use floury potatoes, such as the russet variety." Mr. Chu is an empiricist: "There are a variety of mashing techniques that will take you to smooth and creamy, but the handheld mixer, used quickly to avoid overbeating and overdeveloping the potato starch, is best." For classic, unembellished mashed potatoes, omit the garlic, but Mr. Chu's pan-roasted garlic technique delivers a heady, mellow garlic flavor.

20 garlic cloves, skin on

2 large russet potatoes

½ cup heavy cream

1 tablespoon sweet butter

Salt and pepper to taste

1. Place a heavy-bottomed pan with a tight-fitting lid over low heat and add the garlic cloves. Toss the garlic occasionally until dark, about 20 minutes. Remove from heat, cover the pan, and let sit for another 20 minutes. When the garlic is cool, peel, remove the woody stems, pass the cloves through a garlic press, and set aside.

2. Meanwhile, wash the potatoes, peel, cut into 1-inch chunks, and set aside. Bring a large pot of water to a boil (2 to 3 quarts), add the potatoes, cover, and boil for 10 minutes until tender.

3. While the potatoes are boiling, warm the heavy cream—do not boil. When tender, drain the potatoes. Using a ricer, masher, or for the creamiest potato, an electric mixer, mash the potatoes and garlic. Add the butter a little at a time, then the cream. Be careful not to overbeat as the potatoes will become pasty. Season to taste with salt and pepper and serve.

SERVES 4

In 2006, Steve Barone, a comic, filmmaker, and advertising executive, created the Mashed Potato Wrestling Foundation in 2006 in the then small farming community of Barnsville, Minnesota. In order to fill the "ring," a pit was built from hay bales and tarps and filled with about a ton of potato scraps from a local processing plant. The local fire department added water; about a dozen children known for their whip kicks jumped in and did the mixing. Soon other communities and fairs were establishing mashed potato wrestling meets, and Mr. Barone, the reigning world champion, retired from the ring to work on a documentary film. "I'm afraid of the ring," he said. "It's dangerous out there. I enjoy eating mashed potatoes more than wrestling in them."

John Pull's Tater Tot

"I grew up in Minnesota, home of the covered dish, throne of the casserole," said John Pull, a researcher at the Library of Congress. "Tater tot casserole, that midcentury construction of frozen tater tots, ground meat, creamed soup, and anything else you can imagine mixing into a casserole pan, occupied a special spot in my family's culinary arsenal." His culinary sights were set higher than the tater tot, and yet it was his tater tot casserole for which his stylish friends clamored. Oh, he improvised. He added wild mushrooms, ground veal, artisanal cheeses, but these revisions never reduced his dinner guests to licking the casserole or stealing from one another's plates. In desperation, he secretly fabricated his own tater tots. Over 100,000 recipes for tater tot casserole are available on the Internet, but these potato puffs, which can be deep-fried or baked, make a noble substitute for the frozen fellows. They are also sensational with roasted chicken or meat.

1 small onion

2 large eggs

¼ cup vegetable oil, plus more for deep frying

3 tablespoons cracker crumbs

1 teaspoon salt

⅛ teaspoon freshly grated nutmeg

½ teaspoon baking powder

1 garlic clove, minced

¾ pound baking potatoes, peeled

½ pound celery root, peeled

1 piece of bacon, crisply fried and minced

Freshly ground black pepper to taste

⅛ teaspoon smoked paprika

1. If baking, preheat the oven to 400°F and grease 36 1¾ x 1-inch muffin cups. If frying, set up a deep fryer and bring the oil to 375°F. Peel the onion, grate into a fine-mesh strainer, and press hard to remove as much liquid as possible. Roll onion in paper towels to remove any remaining moisture and set aside.

2. Whisk the eggs, ¼ cup oil, cracker crumbs, salt, nutmeg, baking powder, and garlic together. Grate the potatoes into the mixture and stir. Grate the celery root together and stir. Add the onion and bacon, season with black pepper, paprika, and additional salt to taste.

3. If baking, use a teaspoon to form the mixture into balls, place each in a prepared muffin tin and bake until crisp, about 20 minutes. If frying, form the mixture into "tots" and use a slotted spoon to slide them into the oil. Working in batches, fry them until they are golden and crisp, about 5 minutes, turning occasionally.

MAKES 36 TATER TOTS

The Latke Lady's Latkes

When Nancy Rothstein's children were in elementary school, she made a decision: Armed with potatoes, a food processor, and an electric frying pan, she became the emissary for this Jewish holiday tradition in her small community, and went to her children's elementary school to make her crispy, crunchy latkes. Soon enough, she became known around town as "The Latke Lady."

Now, when the three generations of Rothsteins gather every year for Chanukah, she gets to expose the youngest to her famous potato creations. "I look forward to my grandkids getting older so I can cook with them," she says. "For now, having my family together for Chanukah and sharing laughs, gifts, and potato pancakes will do." Mrs. Rothstein recommends keeping young children out of the kitchen while the pancakes cook, though, since the process involves a lot of hot, spattering oil.

Her kids and grandkids love applesauce with her latkes. Since she lives in "apple country," she makes applesauce in the fall and puts it in the freezer for Chanukah. However, she prefers her latkes with sour cream.

4 large russet potatoes

1 medium onion

2 large eggs

1 tablespoon all-purpose flour, plus more as needed

½ teaspoon baking powder

Kosher salt and freshly ground black pepper

Vegetable oil, for frying

1. Peel the potatoes and grate them on the large holes of a box grater or in a food processor, and place them in a bowl of cold water so they do not brown. Grate the onion into a separate bowl. Drain the potatoes and onion, put them in a clean kitchen towel, and squeeze out as much water as possible.

2. In a large bowl, combine the eggs, flour, baking powder, and salt and pepper to taste. Stir in the potatoes and onion and mix well. If the potato batter gets watery as it sits, add a small amount of flour.

3. Heat oil in a large frying pan over medium heat until very hot but not smoking. Drop the batter by large spoonfuls into the hot oil and flatten slightly with a spatula. Fry on both sides, flipping once, until crisp and golden. Remove from the pan and drain on paper towels. Serve immediately with applesauce or sour cream. (You can also freeze the fried latkes between sheets of foil and reheat them in the oven as you need them.)

SERVES 4 TO 6

Cecylia Roznowska's Potato Pancakes Stuffed with Bacon, Mushrooms, and Onion

CHICAGO, ILLINOIS

According to Polish tradition, a prosperous marriage begins with gifts of bread, salt, and wine, and dancing ensures happiness for the couple. For more than two decades, Cecylia Roznowska, a Polish-born dancer and choreographer, has been leading wedding dances and twirling Polish-American couples in a polonaise toward happily-ever-after. Since immigrating to Chicago in 1984, she is the founder and artistic director of the Northwest Center of Traditional Polish Dancing and the Polonia Ensemble, a youth folk dance company that performs at celebrations, festivals, parades, and—of course—weddings.

Dancing with the troupe's young people, including three of her own grandchildren, makes her feel like a girl again in the village of Rabka, learning the steps to the krakowiak and mazur. She can imagine that her stomach is full of her grandma's pierogi with sauerkraut, her pigtails flying, and her embroidered skirt whipping around her legs. When Ms. Roznowska is not dancing alongside her grandchildren, she is with them in the kitchen where she's taught them to make pacski doughnuts as well as these wonderful stuffed pancakes.

FOR THE STUFFING

1 tablespoon vegetable oil

2 slices bacon

2 large onions, diced

6 white mushrooms, thinly sliced

½ teaspoon kosher salt

Freshly ground black pepper

FOR THE PANCAKES

5 to 6 medium russet potatoes (about 2 pounds), scrubbed clean

1 large egg

1 tablespoon dry bread crumbs

Kosher salt and freshly ground black pepper

1 to 2 tablespoons vegetable oil

½ cup sour cream, for garnish

1. To make the stuffing: Preheat the oven to 250°F. Heat the oil in a large skillet over medium-low heat. Add the bacon and fry until it is cooked though but still a little pink and soft. Remove the bacon from the skillet (leave the oil and fat in the skillet) and, when cool enough to handle, chop it fine.

2. While the skillet is still hot, add the onions and place over low heat. Cook, stirring frequently, about 2 minutes. Add the mushrooms and bacon and raise the heat to medium. Season to taste with salt and pepper. Cover the skillet and cook for 15 minutes. Transfer the stuffing to an ovenproof dish and keep warm in the oven.

3. Meanwhile, make the pancakes: Grate the potatoes on the large holes of a box grater or with the grating disk of a food processor. Roll the potatoes in a clean kitchen towel and wring out any excess moisture. Transfer the potatoes to a bowl and stir in the egg, bread crumbs, and salt and pepper to taste.

4. To cook the pancakes, pour the oil into the skillet and place over medium heat. When the oil is very hot but not smoking, pour in a scant ¼ cup of batter and spread it out with a spatula until it is about 6 inches in diameter. Cook until the bottom is golden brown, about 3 minutes, then flip and cook the other side until browned and the pancake is slightly crispy, about 3 minutes more. Transfer the pancake to a plate and place in the oven to keep warm. Repeat until all the batter is used.

5. To serve, place ¼ cup of the stuffing mixture on each pancake and then fold over. Put a dollop of sour cream on the side.

SERVES 4

Palmyra Cueva's Potato Tortilla

Lee Ann Cueva regularly prepares some of her Spanish abuela's (grandmother's) favorite dishes. "I learned her techniques from the many years spent with her in the kitchen. When I moved to Charleston, I often called her for help, and she would walk me through her recipes with her own measurements, like 'a handful of this,' or 'put some in and taste it.'" Through the years, she's gotten pretty close to duplicating Abuela's specialties—"My brothers sometimes say mine are better," she says, "but I think it's because we haven't had the pleasure of her cooking for so many years."

Ms. Cueva sometimes tops this classic Spanish dish with some freshly grated Parmesan cheese, fresh parsley, and paprika.

½ cup olive oil, plus more as needed

4 medium russet potatoes (about 2 pounds), peeled and thinly sliced

Kosher salt or coarse sea salt and freshly ground black pepper

1 or 2 garlic cloves, minced (optional)

8 large eggs, beaten until foamy

1. Warm the olive oil in a large skillet over medium heat. Add the potatoes and season with salt and pepper to taste. If using the garlic, add it now. Reduce the heat to medium-low and cook the potatoes, flipping them occasionally, until tender (do not brown; the potatoes should not stick together).

2. Shake the skillet to level the potatoes. Add the eggs and season again.

3. Cook over medium heat until the tortilla starts to brown on the bottom. Invert a serving plate over the pan and flip the tortilla onto the plate. Add more olive oil to the pan and slide the tortilla back into the pan to cook the other side. When the second side begins to brown, flip the tortilla again to give it a nicer shape.

4. Serve hot or at room temperature (Abuela served hers at room temperature, cut into wedges).

SERVES 8

595

Eat Your Vegetables

Nonna Concetta's Pizza di Patate
Potato Pizza

After arriving in New York City from her hometown of Rome on the *Michelangelo* in 1969, Carla Rea searched for her professional calling for about thirty years. She was a housewife and, thanks to lengthy transatlantic calls with her grandmother, Nonna Concetta, a cooking student. She taught elementary school and Berlitz courses, owned a clothing boutique, and served as the town sheriff, delivering summons in her stiletto heels; she finally found her calling as a real estate broker. She has become famous for selling the sorts of palaces that have 5,000 square feet of marble on their counters and floors, a fame that rests, she says, on her habit of offering cooking class open houses that feature her grandmother Nonna's potato casserole.

12 Yukon Gold or 6 large russet potatoes

1 tablespoon coarse salt or to taste

½ teaspoon white pepper

2 pounds aged whole milk mozzarella cheese

2 cups finely grated Parmigiano cheese

½ cup plain bread crumbs

2 tablespoons butter, cut into ¼-inch pieces

1. Preheat the oven to 350°F and grease a 9 x 12-inch baking dish lightly with olive oil. Boil the potatoes with the salt in an 8-quart saucepan with enough water to cover the potatoes by 2 inches. Boil the potatoes until fork tender, about 20 minutes. When potatoes are cooked, remove from the water and allow to cool. Peel the potatoes and mash them in a large bowl.

2. Add the white pepper, mozzarella cheese, and Parmigiano cheese. Mix well with your hands until completely combined.

3. Pour the mixture in the baking dish and sprinkle the bread crumbs over it. Dot the top of the bread crumbs with the butter pieces and cover the baking dish with aluminum foil. Bake for 45 minutes, or until the cheese begins to bubble up around the sides of the baking dish.

4. Remove the foil and broil for 7 minutes more or until the bread crumbs are lightly brown.

5. Remove from the oven and allow to cool slightly. Serve with salad as a light lunch or a side dish with meat.

SERVES 8

Laurent Roffe's Roasted Potatoes with Chestnuts and Onions

Born in Casablanca, Laurent Roffe spent his childhood in Paris, moved to Israel as an adolescent, and served time in the Israeli army before attending Pratt Institute in New York. He cannot remember a time that he was not interested in food. But it was not until he left home for college that his talent—and passion—for cooking began to emerge.

2 pounds small white potatoes

1 pound pearl onions, peeled

2 pounds shelled, peeled fresh chestnuts, or frozen chestnuts, thawed

2 garlic cloves, crushed

2 tablespoons olive oil

½ cup heavy cream

1 tablespoon fine sea salt

1½ teaspoons freshly ground black pepper

1. Preheat the oven to 400°F.

2. Toss together all ingredients in a bowl. Transfer to a baking dish and bake about 1 hour, until the tip of a knife goes easily into the potatoes. The potatoes and chestnuts should hold their shape and not be mushy.

SERVES 6

Children gathering potatoes, Maine, JACK JELANO, 1940.

Skillet Food Truck Herbed Fries

SEATTLE, WASHINGTON

After graduating from the Culinary Institute of America, Joshua Henderson catered location shoots for photographers and got an itch for mobile food before returning to Seattle, where he grew up. There, his two retooled vintage Airstream trailers roam like nomads serving up delicious bistro cooking that has been known to incite brake-slamming high-speed chases and other unacceptable road acts. The location schedules are posted on the company's Web site, and the fries served with the trucks' Kobe beef triple crème cheese burger are not difficult to make at home. The secret is soaking the potatoes in cold water to stabilize the starch. The double frying also helps give a crisp fire. And fresh dill makes a unique—and addictive—magic.

1½ quarts vegetable oil

4 medium baking potatoes, scrubbed but not peeled and cut into ¼-inch-thick sticks

2 tablespoons chopped mixed soft herbs such as flat-leaf parsley, dill, and sage

Sea salt

Freshly ground black pepper, optional

1. Line a baking sheet with several layers of paper towels and set aside. In a large saucepan, heat the oil to 300°F. Fry the potatoes until softened but not browned, about 10 minutes. Work in batches if necessary to avoid overcrowding the pan. Use a slotted spoon or basket to remove the fries, spread them on the lined baking sheet, and drain for 5 minutes.

2. Increase the temperature under the oil until it reaches 350°F. Add the fries to the hot oil and cook until golden brown and crisp, 6 minutes. Transfer the fries to a bowl. Sprinkle the fries with the herbs, salt, and black pepper if using. Toss gently and serve immediately.

SERVES 4 TO 8

FRY ME A 'TATER

THE BIRTH OF THE COMMERCIAL POTATO CHIP IN THE UNITED STATES CAN BE TRACED back to Saratoga Springs and Cleveland, Ohio, in the mid-nineteenth century, but recipes for frying sliced potatoes circulated in France when Thomas Jefferson served as an ambassador there and, according to *The Oxford Companion to American Food and Drink*, a reference to deep-fried potatoes appeared "in a document in Thomas Jefferson's hand that clearly dates from the years 1801–1809, his years in the President's house when he had a French chef . . ." This may explain the "Frenching" of potato batons when the various shapes of deep-fried potatoes were standardized in early-twentieth-century America. Wafers became "chips" and sticks became "fries." The dish was part of the fast-food repertoire before World War I, but got a bigger role when meat shortages forced hamburger stands to think outside the bun. In the decades since, technology, growing specifications, and clever marketing have made french fries into the most popular fast food in the United States with sales of more than a billion dollars each year.

Devan Ganeshananthan's
Sri Lankan Dry Potato Curry

Devan Ganeshananthan is the vice principal at New Rochelle High School. His parents are Sri Lankan Tamils who left the country in the early 1970s. Mr. Ganeshananthan says his mother taught him to cook when he was a teenager because she was extremely concerned that he would waste away in college. "Many first-generation kids look to language, religion, or culture in terms of their identity," he says. "The main way I associate with my culture is through food." Sri Lankan dry potato curry is one of the recipes his mother taught him, although he has altered it to suit his own tastes, he says. He has made it heartier with the addition of buttermilk. It is also a little spicier than his mother's.

2 pounds red-skinned or other boiling potatoes

Kosher salt

1½ teaspoons Jaffna curry powder

1 large yellow onion

1 garlic clove

1 long green chile

1 dried red chile

2 tablespoons vegetable oil

1½ teaspoons yellow mustard seeds

1½ teaspoons fennel seeds

Up to 1 cup buttermilk or coconut milk

1. Put the potatoes in a pot of cold water and bring to a boil over high heat. Reduce the heat and simmer for 5 to 10 minutes, until the potatoes are partially cooked but not quite soft when pierced with the tip of a knife.

2. Drain the potatoes and let cool until you can handle them. Cut into ½-inch cubes. Toss the potatoes with salt and curry powder to taste, making sure they are coated well.

3. Dice the onion. Mince the garlic and green chile. Cut the dried chile into about 5 pieces.

4. Heat a couple of tablespoons of vegetable oil in a deep skillet over medium-high heat and add the onion, garlic, and chiles. Cook, stirring frequently,

until the mixture is golden brown. Add mustard and fennel seeds to taste and stir. Add the potatoes and just enough buttermilk to moisten everything. Cook and stir until the potatoes are coated by the onion mixture and tender—you may need to add a little bit of oil. Be careful not to overcook the potatoes—they should be firm and not crumbly. Serve hot.

SERVES 6

Sally Levine's Passover Crepe "Noodles"

CLEVELAND, OHIO

Sally Levine's parents were second cousins who grew up together in a little town in Romania. Holocaust survivors, they immigrated to America in 1949. Mrs. Levine considers her parents' ordeal "a typical immigrant story," a tale of tragedy, survival, and hope. And she tells her grandchildren their story when she teaches them the family's Passover recipes. Cooking, she has learned, is not only an act of cultural identity but a means of connecting with her past while creating a future.

This recipe, passed down through generations, is rarely made by modern kosher cooks. Store-bought noodles do not hold a candle to the taste and texture of homemade noodles. Mrs. Levine's mother, grandmother, and great-grandmother all made noodles from slices of potato-starch crepes.

Mrs. Levine makes the crepes on "regular" nights, too, filling them with cooked chicken left over from a pot of traditional chicken soup. If serving as filled crepes, serve at room temperature. The dish calls for a "bubbe cup" of potato starch, meaning a full, rounded cup. Share the noodle "ends" with the grandkids, as Mrs. Levine does with hers.

10 large eggs

1 "bubbe cup" potato starch

1 teaspoon kosher salt

2 cups cold water

Vegetable oil, for frying

1. In a large bowl, whisk together the eggs, potato starch, salt, and water.

2. Brush ½ teaspoon oil in a 9-inch skillet over medium-high heat. Using a ¼-cup measure per crepe, ladle the batter into the skillet, tipping the pan so that the batter covers the entire surface.

3. When the crepe starts to pull away from the sides, lift it up gently with a spatula and flip it. Cook just until the bottom is firm and golden; do not overbrown. (These fry up quickly, so keep an eye on them so they don't burn.) Transfer the cooked crepe to a plate.

4. Brush another ½ teaspoon oil in the pan and reheat it before ladling the batter for the next crepe. Remix the batter well before pouring, as the starch tends to settle to the bottom. Repeat until all the batter is used, stacking the crepes as they are cooked.

5. Refrigerate the crepes overnight if using for noodles.

6. When ready to serve take 2 or 3 crepes at a time, roll them up tightly like a cigar, and cut them into 1-inch-wide strips. Add the noodles to a pot of your favorite chicken broth. Don't forget to give the ends of the noodles to your little ones to eat!

MAKES ABOUT 22 CREPES

CHLOE'S BUTTER BEANS

Historically, shell beans and field peas were the staff of life during the cold months in the mountain South. Thousands of varieties of beans and peas grow in pods on creeping vines or pole vines and can be eaten fresh or dried. Stewed with a bit of bacon or "side meat," the dried beans kept mountain families alive between growing seasons. Chloe Porter, a gardener, pianist, music teacher, and cook in western North Carolina, inherited what she called "a reverent view of beans."

Her favorite are butter beans. The United States grows nearly one hundred varieties. Lima is one variety and to Ms. Porter, nothing is finer than baby limas stewed with bacon and milk. Dried cranberry or cannelloni beans are the best store-bought substitutes for dried butter beans. The dried beans should be covered with cold water and soaked overnight before cooking. The secret to cooking tender beans, says Ms. Porter, is a heavy pot, gentle heat, and two rounds of cooking. Salt toughens the beans, so it should be added at the end of cooking. Older, drier beans will require more water than recently picked and dried ones. Always add enough cold water to a bean pot to keep them covered by a half-inch.

3 cups dried butter beans, soaked overnight and drained

3 slices thick-cut smoked bacon

1½ cups milk

1 tablespoon unsalted butter

Fine sea salt and freshly ground black pepper

1. Combine the beans and 8 cups of cold water in a large pot. Quarter 1 slice of bacon and add to the pot. Bring to a boil over high heat, reduce the heat, and simmer, covered, until the beans are tender, 40 to 45 minutes. Drain the beans and wipe out the pot. Discard the bacon.

2. Dice the remaining bacon. Place the pot over medium heat. Add the bacon and cook about 5 minutes, stirring occasionally, until it is crisp. Add the beans back to the pot with the bacon and add the milk, butter, and 1½ teaspoons salt. Adjust the heat if necessary and simmer about 10 minutes, until the milk is reduced to a creamy glaze. Taste the beans and season with pepper and more salt if they need it. Serve warm or at room temperature.

SERVES 4 AS A MAIN COURSE, 6 AS A SIDE DISH

MADISON'S MINTED MASHED LIMA BEANS

ESTACADA, OREGON

"I had a dish like this in Israel, but it was made with fava beans," says Madison Rothman. "I'm not a big fan of favas, but I do love limas and other butter bean varieties that we had in Tennessee when I was growing up. Here, we get some interesting old varieties in the farmers' markets. I guess you could say that this recipe is the result of where I grew up, where I traveled, Oregon—where I came to attend college—and where I hope to live forever."

4 cups medium fresh or frozen lima or butter beans

½ cup extra virgin olive oil

2 garlic cloves, minced

1 tablespoon fresh lemon juice

Kosher salt and freshly ground black pepper

4 chive blades or 1 scallion (green part only), minced

½ cup chopped peppermint leaves

1. Place the beans in a pot over medium heat, and cover with cold water. Add 1 tablespoon of the olive oil and half the garlic. Simmer until tender, about 15 minutes. Drain.

2. Using a ricer or food mill, mash the beans and remove the skins. Stir in the remaining olive oil, 1 tablespoon at a time. Stir in the lemon juice. Season with salt and pepper to taste. Stir in the chives and peppermint and serve.

SERVES 4

Eat Your Vegetables

VIVIAN RICHARDSON'S LENTILS AND ROASTED VEGETABLES

"I decided that a base recipe of lentils and roasted vegetables would be just the wintry ticket for a ski weekend," says Vivian Richardson. "The first night I prepared pans of roasted vegetables: a carnival of carrots, fennel, turnips, potatoes, and an abundance of whole garlic cloves, crisp and caramelized and fragrant with olive oil. I mixed them with lentilles du puy (the lovely little green French beauties) prepared in a seasoned vegetable broth laced with lemon thyme.

"The lentils and roasted vegetables for the first night's dinner acted as a cushion for a beautiful piece of fresh halibut à la bonne femme, in a white wine and stock broth. The last night, with very little time to produce dinner, I sliced and sautéed lamb sausages while I put on a pot of rice. I added vegetable broth to the lentil and vegetable mixture to moisten it and render it saucy. Rummaging around in the cupboard, I found cinnamon and oregano. A tablespoon of this and a teaspoon of that and I soon had a fragrant salmagundi redolent with flavors that bespoke romantic evenings in Marrakech. I set aside a large portion for the one vegetarian among us and added the lamb sausage to the rest."

FOR THE ROASTED VEGETABLES

6 to 8 carrots, cut into 1-inch-thick coins

3 medium fennel bulbs, cored and cut into medium chunks

2 garlic heads, large cloves cut in half

½ pound fingerling potatoes, cut into 1-inch-thick coins

3 large turnips, peeled and cut into medium chunks

Olive oil

Kosher salt

FOR THE LENTILS

1 very small onion

1 pound lentilles du puy, examined for stones and rinsed

2 quarts water, homemade chicken or vegetable broth, or low-sodium store-bought chicken or vegetable broth

1 garlic clove

Scant ½ teaspoon lemon thyme or regular thyme leaves

1 teaspoon kosher salt

1. To make the vegetables: Preheat the oven to 400°F. Toss the vegetables with olive oil to coat, and sprinkle with salt. Spread evenly in one layer on rimmed baking sheets. Roast until they are crisp and browned around the edges, about 30 minutes. At the 15-minute mark, turn vegetables with a spatula. Turn once again if necessary.

2. To make the lentils: Cut the onion in half and skewer each half with a toothpick to hold together. Combine the onion, lentils, water, garlic, thyme, and salt in a large saucepan. Bring to a boil, reduce the heat to a simmer, and cook uncovered for 20 to 30 minutes, until lentils are tender. Drain and cool. Remove the onion and garlic.

3. Serve separately or combined.

SERVES 6 TO 8

Azalina Eusope's
Spicy Lentil and Shallot Dumplings

At 19, Azalina Eusope was already a pastry chef in her hometown of Penang, Malaysia. She fell in love with and married an American and followed him when his work called him back to San Francisco. Wowed by the pastry shops and bakeries in San Francisco—"There is so much high quality pastry there, I didn't want to compete"—she turned her attention to Malaysian savory fare, which she began selling at her local farmers' market. Americans, she said, didn't really know much about Malaysia: "It's not as familiar as Thailand or Singapore." In 2009, *Bon Appétit* named her lacy crepes with curry one of the top ten lunches to be had in the U.S. Had the magazine's editors had a chance to eat the dumplings that she makes for her family, she would most likely have won two spots on the list.

1 cup dried black lentils, soaked overnight

1 cup dried yellow lentils, soaked overnight

2 tablespoons clarified butter

2 cups diced shallots

⅓ cup minced green pepper

⅓ cup minced red pepper

1 teaspoon freshly ground black pepper

1½ teaspoons sea salt

2 tablespoons fresh coriander, minced

2 tablespoons fresh mint, minced

1 teaspoon ground cumin

1 teaspoon ground coriander

2 tablespoons rice bran oil, or other vegetable oil, plus more as needed

1. Combine the lentils and drain well in a fine-mesh strainer. Warm the clarified butter in a skillet over medium heat. Add the shallots, reduce the heat to low, and cook until the shallots are golden, about 10 minutes, stirring constantly. Add the minced green and red peppers, stir, and continue to cook until the peppers are beginning to soften, 3 minutes. Add the black pepper, salt, fresh coriander, mint, cumin, and dried coriander, stir, and cook until the spices are fragrant, about 2 minutes. Add the drained lentils, stir well, cover, remove from heat, and set aside for 1 hour.

2. Warm the rice bran oil in a heavy skillet over medium heat. Taste the mixture and season with additional salt if desired. Shape the mixture into small patties that are about 3 inches in diameter and ½ inch thick. When the oil is hot, place the patties in the skillet and fry until golden on first one side and then the other, about 2 minutes on each side. Drain on paper towels and serve with coconut sambal (see recipe below)

MAKES ABOUT 24 PATTIES; SERVES 6 AS A MAIN COURSE, 12 AS AN APPETIZER

Azalina's Coconut Sambal

Sambal is the Malaysian equivalent of salsa, a condiment that is served as a counterpoint and is sometimes used in cooking. Fresh coconut is essential to this remarkable sambal.

2 cups fresh coconut, shredded

2 cups fresh mint

2 teaspoons freshly ground black pepper

2 teaspoons sea salt

Combine all the ingredients in a bowl, stir well, and allow to sit for at least 1 hour prior to serving.

MAKES 2½ CUPS

ALICE MOREIRA HOWE'S FEIJOADA
Brazilian Black Bean Stew

The thick bean and pork stew called feijoada, which all Brazilians embrace as their national culinary symbol, has historical origins that mirror the country's cultural mix of Portuguese colonials, indigenous Indians, and African slaves who were brought to work plantations—rubber, sugar, cotton, cocoa, coffee—or mine diamonds and gold. Some Brazilians believe that feijoada had roots in the Portuguese caldeirada, a traditional stew. But most Brazilians accept the theory that slaves developed the dish and added discarded pork scraps from the Big House. The traditional topping of farofa (toasted manioc), comes straight from Indians in the rain forest.

Alice Moreira Howe, born into a distinguished Rio de Janeiro family, has a lineage from Portugal and Italy. An artist who has lived in the United States for more than twenty years, she brought with her a treasured cookbook of her grandmother's. Those recipes mingle with Ms. Howe's love of the Brazilian tastes cultivated by her childhood nanny, a direct descendant of slaves.

4 cups dried black beans

1½ pounds carne seca (Brazilian salted cured beef)

1 pound sweet sausage, cut in 1-inch pieces (preferably Portuguese chouriço; see Note)

1 rack spareribs, cut into 2-rib segments

1 bay leaf

1 onion

1 garlic clove

2 tablespoons olive oil

Farofa (optional; see Note)

1. The night before cooking, soak the beans in a large bowl with water to cover at by least 3 or 4 inches. Soak the carne seca in water to cover.

2. The next morning, drain the beans and place in a large pot with water to cover by at least 3 inches. Bring to a boil over medium heat.

3. Cut the carne seca into 1-inch pieces.

4. Add the carne seca, sausage, ribs, and bay leaf to the beans. Simmer about 2 hours, until the beans are soft and the meats are tender, stirring from time to time and adding water as necessary to keep beans covered. Keep an eye on the beans so they don't burn at the bottom!

5. Chop the onion and garlic. Heat the olive oil in a cast-iron skillet over medium heat. Add the onion and garlic and cook until golden brown. Add 2 ladlefuls of beans and mash them. Stir this back into the pot of beans. It will thicken and season the beans.

6. Simmer gently for at least another hour, adding water as necessary. A good feijoada should have a creamy consistency when done. Remove the bay leaf. Some people take the meats out at this point and serve them separately on a platter. Top with farofa, if using.

SERVES 8 TO 10

NOTE: Ms. Howe says, "When I use the Portuguese sausage, I usually prick it with a fork and simmer it for ten minutes in enough water to cover; then I cut it."

To make farofa, melt 2 tablespoons unsalted butter in a saucepan over medium heat. Add 1½ cups manioc flour and cook, stirring constantly, until the flour is toasted, 8 to 10 minutes.

RICHARD'S REFRIED BEANS

Throughout his many careers—he has worked as a hairdresser, a registered nurse, an addictions counselor, and a television talk show host—Steve Pope scheduled his work around the needs of his garden. "It began twenty years ago when my partner, Richard, and I moved to west Texas and planted a large garden. We always got a big crop of pinto beans and when they started to turn gold and to dry in their pods we started to mention 'Refried Beans Weather.' Every year, the first night that we made a pot of these beans and had them for dinner with a flour tortilla was the time when we said good-bye to summer. The beans gave us comfort and seemed to feed our souls. We separated some years back, but I always think of Richard and our younger selves when I make this dish, and I still make it every year."

607

Eat Your Vegetables

TO PREPARE THE BEANS

1 pound dried pinto beans

Water

2 smoked ham hocks or ½ pound cubed ham

One 14-ounce can tomato sauce

1 tablespoon chili powder

Salt and freshly ground black pepper

1. Soak the beans overnight in cold water to cover by 2 to 3 inches.

2. Drain the beans and cover with about 2 inches of fresh water in a large saucepan or Dutch oven. Make cuts in the ham hocks, down through the rind, and add to the pot (or add the ham). Stir in the tomato sauce and chili powder. Bring to a boil, then reduce the heat and simmer, covered, about 2 hours. Stir the beans up from the bottom occasionally, and add water if they start looking dry.

3. When beans are soft but not mushy, and still hold their shape, they are done. Taste and add salt and pepper, if desired, starting with about ½ teaspoon of each.

SERVES 4 TO 6

TO FRY THE BEANS

¼ cup bacon drippings

1 small onion, finely chopped

1 garlic clove, minced or pressed

1 recipe Richard's beans

4. Melt the bacon drippings in a large heavy skillet over medium heat. Add the onion and garlic and cook until the onion is soft and clear.

5. Drain the liquid from the cooked pintos, reserving 1 cup. Remove the ham hocks. Add the drained beans to the skillet, and mash them with a potato masher. Work the cooking liquid, ¼ cup at a time, into the mashed beans until mixture is uniformly moist and smooth. Cook and stir the beans up from the bottom of the pan, until mixture is a thick paste.

SERVES 4 TO 6

Ris Lacoste's Boston Baked Beans

Washington, D.C.

A Boston baked bean recipe is like any family recipe—everyone has his or her own version. This is Ris Lacoste's mother's recipe, which was lauded as the best in the family. "The beans were in demand and appeared at every wedding shower, baby shower, Tupperware party, family gathering, and at all holiday buffets," Chef Lacoste says. "And, of course, at every Saturday dinner and Sunday breakfast." On Saturdays, she says, they went in the pot by nine in the morning and were ready for dinner. "We had beans with ham, steak, burgers, hot dogs. On Sunday, we all loved baked beans, scrambled eggs, and toast after Mass at St. Anthony's in New Bedford, Massachusetts. A cold bean sandwich for lunch was not too shabby, either."

She has called her mother dozens of times to get the recipe, Chef Lacoste says, and her mother makes a new comment about the beans each time she calls. "One comment is always there, however, and I can't hang up the phone until I hear it: 'But your father didn't like the beans too sweet, so I don't put in much molasses.' So none of the thirty-one people in my immediate family like their beans too sweet either," Chef Lacoste laughs.

2 pounds white pea beans (navy beans)

¾ pound lean salt pork, cut into large chunks

2 large onions

2 tablespoons molasses

2 tablespoons brown sugar

2 teaspoons mustard powder

1 teaspoon freshly ground black pepper

1. Preheat the oven to 325°F. Pick through the beans by hand to remove any stones. Place the beans in a 4-quart bean pot or baking dish and bury the pieces of salt pork and the onions in them. Sprinkle with the molasses, brown sugar, mustard, and pepper.

2. Cover all with warm water. Cover the pot with the lid or foil and place in the oven.

3. Check every 1½ hours for dryness, as beans soak up the water, and add boiling water just to cover when necessary. Uncover the beans for the last hour of cooking, or after the last addition of water, to dry them a bit and to form a nice crusty topping. Cooking time is approximately 6 hours.

4. The beans are done when still firm but cooked through, beautifully browned by the long, slow absorption of the molasses and brown sugar, and the pork juices. Let rest at room temperature before serving.

SERVES 12

One Big Table

The Chile Woman's Three Sisters Chile Casserole

Detroit native Susan Welsand came to Bloomington to attend Indiana University and never left. She had her first "blissful" taste of chile at a neighbor's, became a chile aficionado and realized she would have to start growing her own. Fortunately, her students—she has been a volunteer ESL tutor for twenty-five years—started bringing her chile seeds from all over the world. Her passion is now her business. What she doesn't sell, freeze, or use fresh, she strings into ristras or dries to grind into powder. Ms. Welsand puts chiles "in anything and everything," she says, including this stew of corn, squash, and beans, a trio known in the Southwest as "the three sisters."

609

Eat Your Vegetables

1 cup mixed dried beans

1 tablespoon baking soda

1 butternut squash (about 2½ pounds), cut in half, seeds and fibers discarded

6 fresh red or green New Mexico Hatch chiles

1 small onion, chopped

1 cup fresh corn kernels

4 to 6 sun-dried tomatoes, roughly chopped

1 cup cooked amaranth, quinoa, spelt, or kamut

6 ounces garlic-herb cheese, preferably Swiss Connection, crumbled (about 1½ cups)

1. Place beans in a deep saucepan with 3 cups of water and boil for 4 minutes. Remove from the heat and add the baking soda. After the beans fizz up, place the lid lightly on the pot, and let them sit for an hour. Rinse well, add 3 cups fresh water to the beans, and simmer for 1 hour more or until tender. Drain and transfer to a large bowl.

2. While the beans are cooking, preheat the oven to 400°F. Place the squash on a greased baking sheet flesh side down, and roast until the flesh is softened, about 30 minutes. Remove and let cool. Scrape out the flesh, chop it, and add it to the beans. Discard the skin.

3. Turn the oven to broil. With a sharp paring knife, slit each chile down one side. Put on a broiler pan or baking sheet and place directly under the broiler. Roast, turning occasionally, until the skins are blackened and blistered all over, about 10 minutes. Remove from the oven and, using tongs, place the chiles in a clean brown paper bag. Fold the bag shut.

4. When the chiles have cooled to the touch, gently peel off the blackened skin using your fingers, or rub off with a paper towel. Cut the seedbed and stem from each chile and discard. Roughly chop the chiles and add to the beans and squash.

5. Turn the oven back on to 350°F. Stir the onion, corn, tomatoes, amaranth, and cheese into the beans. Spread in a large glass baking dish. Bake for 40 to 45 minutes, until thick and bubbling. Serve.

SERVES 4 TO 6

CHAPTER 9

AMBER WAVES OF GRAIN

KING OF THE MILL

COLUMBIA, SOUTH CAROLINA

Before corn transformed the Great Plains of the American Midwest and became essential to cattle, hog, and chicken farms, before it was fabricated into starch and syrup and used to make rayon, rubber tires, car fuel, explosives, shotgun shells, battery cells, aspirin, surgeon's gloves, and embalming fluid, it was the delicious crop of late summer. Parched, dried, ground, milled, baked in ashes, and boiled in lye, corn became part of distinct regional cuisines, especially in the American South. Corn bread, pone, dodgers, cakes, spoon bread, grits, and hominy stew connected generations.

In the mid-1990s, Glenn Roberts, a highly regarded restoration consultant in Charleston, went to the grocery store in his hometown of Edisto, South Carolina, and couldn't find corn grits as his mother, grandmother, and at least seven generations of Robertses had known it. And the jab of pain he felt somewhere between his heart and his stomach at the disappearance of traditional grits—stone-milled dent corn with a rich corn taste and a substantial, creamy feeling in the mouth—wouldn't go away.

With enough money and commitment, research and skill, antebellum homes and buildings can be restored or rebuilt. Re-creating their menus, on the other hand, requires ingredients produced by local mills, using crops grown on small farms from seeds saved from generation to generation—a vanished way of life. But Mr. Roberts is not easily defeated. He steered his Lexus toward country back roads, surveying fields for signs of antebellum corn. He drove hundreds of miles and spent hours hunched over antique agricultural reports, plantation ledgers, cooks' journals, antebellum cookbooks, and seed catalogs. Within two years, this Southern gentleman and erudite guardian of the past was divorced and seemed to have disappeared.

But his detective work paid off. He identified the variety of corn needed to make perfect southern grits—Carolina white seed mill, a soft, easy-to-mill dent variety that was traditionally admired for its high mineral content, floral characteristics, and, most important, its creamy texture. In 1997, he found Carolina Gourdseed White in a bootlegger's cornfield near Dillon, South Carolina. The corn had been hand-selected by a single family since the 1600s.

In addition to locating and cultivating the grain, Mr. Roberts had to figure out how the kernels were milled before industrial rollers and

sifters took over the grits and cornmeal business. The best flavor in the corn, he realized, came from larger pieces with the germ intact. "The big guys call those pieces trash and throw them out, but it's the best part of the kernel," he says. Intrigued by a reference to corn that ripened and was milled late in the fall, he experimented with freezing the grain before milling. The result was the platonic ideal of a grit.

Having decided that his lunacy could be a business, Mr. Roberts sold his homes and cars and boats, his art and antiques. He rented a warehouse behind a car wash in Columbia, South Carolina, bought four old granite mills and forty chest freezers and began saving—and milling—the corn. He named the business Anson Mills. He likes to say that he went from making a quarter million dollars a year to losing a quarter million dollars a year.

His determination to coax corn out of hiding, mill it properly, and restore it to its rightful position on the nation's table soon led to efforts to save other all-but-extinct grains. Massive cultural and scientific research, tests, false leads, and intimate work with the federal government's bank of nearly five hundred thousand plant samples were needed to save Carolina Gold rice, old-fashioned buckwheat, and the varieties of wheat that make biscuits worth eating. Mr. Roberts has also provided grants to resuscitate more than a dozen types of endangered antebellum mill corn.

Navajo farm, EDWARD CURTIS, 1906.

Properly cultivated, his heirloom corn delivers about 20 bushels an acre, as opposed to the 120 bushels a factory farmer can expect. He plants about a thousand acres a year and has contracted with certified organic farmers around the country to grow the corn for him. He spends most of his time traveling from field to field, consults with growers on his BlackBerry, fields calls about old mills all over the country that might be for sale, talks cooking with chefs such as Thomas Keller and Charlie Trotter, who buy his grains, and plans dinner with his new wife, the food writer and photographer, Kay Rentschler.

"Corn breeds its own poets, lunatics, and lovers."

—Betty Fussell, *The Story of Corn*

Kay Rentschler's Rich Spoonbread

COLUMBIA, SOUTH CAROLINA

Spoonbread, says Kay Rentschler's husband, Glenn Roberts, is the apogee of corn flavor. This recipe, which should be filed between "low-down corn mush" and "lofty corn soufflé," was a Native American specialty that Charlestonians still call "Awendaw," after the Awendaw Indians. Ms. Rentschler developed this version, which she finishes with a final glaze of heavy cream. "She was born in Vermont," explains Mr. Roberts.

Either yellow or white grits can be used in this recipe; for best results use cold-milled grits and the highest quality cornmeal you can find. Anson Mills brand is well worth the expense.

614

2 tablespoons (¼ stick) unsalted butter, at room temperature, plus more for greasing the pan

½ cup white or yellow Carolina quick grits

2 cups spring or filtered water

1¼ teaspoons fine sea salt

½ teaspoon freshly ground black pepper

2 cups whole milk

1 cup white or yellow cornmeal

3 large eggs, lightly beaten

1½ teaspoons baking powder

¼ cup heavy cream

1. Preheat the oven to 450°F. Grease a 9-inch cast-iron skillet, a 9-inch cake pan, or a 1½-quart casserole dish with butter.

2. Place the grits in a heavy-bottomed 2½-quart saucepan and cover with the water. Stir once. Let the grits settle for a full minute.

3. Tilt the pan and set over medium-high heat and bring to a simmer, stirring constantly with a wooden spoon, until the starch begins to coat the spoon, 5 to 8 minutes. Reduce the heat to low and stir frequently, until the grits are just tender and hold their shape on a spoon, about 25 minutes.

4. Beat in the butter, salt, and pepper. Whisk in one-third of the milk, and continue adding and whisking by thirds until all the milk is incorporated.

5. Cover the pot, raise the heat to medium, and bring the grits to a simmer, whisking frequently. Whisk in the cornmeal and remove the pan from the heat.

6. Ladle about 1 cup of hot grits into the beaten eggs and whisk them to warm. Pour the egg mixture back into the grits. Stir in the baking powder. Scrape the batter into the prepared pan and smooth the top. Spoon the cream over the top.

7. Place the pan in the oven and bake 10 minutes. Lower the heat to 375°F and bake until the spoonbread is nicely risen and golden brown, 15 to 20 minutes more. Remove from the oven and serve without delay.

SERVES 4 TO 6 AS A SIDE DISH

Fathiyyan Mustafa's
Creamy Grits and Chard

SUMTER, SOUTH CAROLINA

In 1974, Azeez Mustafa was a husband, the father of two children, and a highly paid steelworker in New Jersey. Then he was laid off. "That shook us up bad. Fathiyyan and I, all set up to raise our kids one minute and the next minute we didn't have enough to pay the mortgage. We started doubting everything we'd been raised to believe, how, if you work hard, you get ahead. I swore that this wasn't going to happen to me ever again. I had just enough savings to buy a little hunk of land back home in South Carolina. I figured that if we had land, we could always eat. We didn't have money, so we built a teepee. We couldn't afford to pay for chemicals and pesticides and, anyway, by then, we didn't believe everything we read about how you needed them. We were organic before that was a word. We made a co-op with other organic growers and sold our 'veg-edibles' as a group. We saved money and built our first little house. That's where we cook now. We sit down for dinner with our workers at noon every day. We have the largest organic 'veg-edible' farm in the state. I helped start the Sumter cooperative farms and mentor many farmers on organics. I have five grandchildren. We are very grateful that we had no choice but to live the life we have. It is a good life. So is my wife's chard and grits."

FOR THE GRITS

1 cup whole hominy grits (white or yellow)

2 to 3 tablespoons unsalted butter

1 teaspoon fine sea salt, plus more to taste

½ teaspoon freshly ground black pepper (optional)

FOR THE CHARD

2 pounds rainbow chard, rinsed well and spun dry (spinach, watercress, or very young kale can also be used)

4 tablespoons olive oil

4 large garlic cloves, sliced thin

¼ teaspoon cayenne pepper, plus more to taste

¼ teaspoon fine sea salt, plus more to taste

1 teaspoon cider vinegar

4 leaves youngest chard, washed, stemmed, dried, and cut into fine ribbons

1. To make the grits: Place grits in a bowl and cover with water. Stir once and let sit. When the hulls and chaff rise to the top, skim them off with a fine tea strainer. Drain the grits in a fine-mesh strainer and rinse under cold water.

2. Put 3 cups water in a saucepan over medium heat. When it simmers, add the grits, turn the heat to very low. Cook, stirring occasionally and adding water by the tablespoon as necessary, for 45 minutes, until the grits are tender.

3. Add 1 tablespoon water, cover, remove from heat, and let sit for 5 minutes.

4. Return to the heat, and beat in the butter a little at a time. Season with the salt and black pepper. Keep warm, stirring occasionally.

5. To make the chard: While the grits are cooking, cut the chard stems into ½-inch slices and cut the leaves crosswise into ½-inch ribbons.

6. Warm 2 tablespoons of the olive oil in a large skillet over medium heat. Add the garlic and cook until it begins to turn gold. Stir in half the cayenne. Add the chard stems and toss to coat well. Reduce the heat to low and continue cooking, stirring frequently, for 4 to 5 minutes.

7. When the stems begin to grow tender, raise the heat to high and add the leaves. Season with the salt and the remaining cayenne pepper. Cook for 2 minutes, stirring constantly, until the leaves are tender. Add the vinegar and more salt and cayenne, if desired. Toss to mix. Remove from heat.

8. To serve, spoon the grits onto a warmed platter and make a well in the center of the grits. Use tongs to remove the greens from the pan, squeezing out as much of the liquid as possible, and place them in a ring around the grits. Return the skillet to high heat, bring the juices to a boil and stir in the remaining olive oil. Spoon the juice into the center well in the grits. Sprinkle with the chard and serve immediately.

SERVES 4

Brenda Martin's Coush-Coush

LAFAYETTE, LOUISIANA

Any ordinary football fan can chant "De-fense! De-fense!" But when Louisiana State University's defensive line needs extra encouragement, the fans remind the players of two local specialties worth fighting for: "Hot Boudin! Cold Coush-coush! Come on Tigers! Push, push, push!"

Coush-coush is an old South Louisiana cornmeal recipe most often sweetened with cane syrup, honey, or molasses, doused with milk, and served as a hot cereal for breakfast, or on cold winter nights when rib-sticking comfort is in order. Brenda Martin prepares it in a cast-iron skillet that has been passed down through her family.

Coush-coush can be the right response to family crises. After her mother had heart surgery, she says, "we fixed her coush-coush for two weeks until her appetite came back." This version is unsweetened and makes an unusual companion to savory ragout, gravy, or stew.

2½ cups white or yellow cornmeal

¾ teaspoon kosher salt

1¼ teaspoons baking powder

1¾ cups milk

¾ cup vegetable oil

1. In a large mixing bowl, combine the cornmeal, salt, baking powder, and milk. Blend well.

2. Heat the oil in a cast-iron skillet over medium-high heat. When oil is hot, pour in the cornmeal mixture and cook approximately 5 minutes, letting a crust form at the edges.

3. Once the crust has set, stir, lower the heat to medium-low and cook, stirring occasionally to break up the new crust as it forms, until it resembles crumbled cornbread, about 15 minutes.

SERVES 6

ARTHUR ZAMPAGLIONE'S POLENTA

NEW YORK, NEW YORK

Arthur Zampaglione takes a perverse delight in serving his perfectly rendered polenta in an even layer right onto a wooden table—raw pine works best. Polenta alla spianatora—literally, polenta spread flat—is a rustic ritual that has been performed in the Tuscan hinterlands since the beginning of time. "Only foreigners and prissy people eat polenta from a dish," says Mr. Zampaglione, the New York correspondent for the Italian newspaper *La Repubblica*.

Most cooks top their polenta with big, meaty sauces. Mr. Zampaglione says that the ragù must contain at least one sweet sausage and that it must be placed in the center of the polenta "tablecloth."

FOR THE MEAT SAUCE

4 tablespoons butter

2 tablespoons olive oil

2 celery stalks, minced

3 carrots, minced

1½ medium onions, minced

4 fresh bay leaves

½ pound ground veal

½ pound ground pork

4 cups stewed tomatoes, with their juice

1 cup white wine

½ pound beef stewing meat, cut into 1-inch chunks

½ pound pork, cut into 1-inch chunks

½ pound sweet Italian sausage, skin and fennel seeds removed

Salt and ground black pepper, to taste

1 pound white mushrooms, cut into wafer-thin slices

¼ cup Italian parsley, minced

Parmesan cheese, grated

FOR THE POLENTA

2 teaspoons kosher salt

6 cups water

¾ cup coarse cornmeal, plus more for the table

1¼ cups fine cornmeal

1 tablespoon unsalted butter

1. To make the meat sauce, melt the butter with the olive oil over high heat. Add the celery, carrots, onions, and bay leaves, and sauté over medium-high heat for 5 minutes. Reduce heat to medium-low, add ground veal and pork, and simmer for 7 minutes. Add the tomatoes and their juice and cook uncovered for 15 minutes.

2. Add the wine, the beef, pork, and sausage, and cook uncovered for 20 minutes, stirring frequently. Adjust the seasoning. Add the mushrooms and parsley and stir, cover, and set aside while making the polenta.

3. To make the polenta, add the salt to the water in a heavy-bottomed pot and bring to a boil over high heat. Very slowly sift in alternating handfuls of coarse and fine cornmeal, whisking constantly.

4. Add the butter, reduce heat to low, and stir with a wooden spoon until the polenta peels cleanly off the sides of the pot, about 20 minutes.

5. Make a circle of coarse cornmeal 15 inches in diameter on a clean table or a large platter, and spread the polenta over it to a thickness of ¾ inch. Top the polenta with the sauce and serve immediately with grated Parmesan on the side.

SERVES 6

Leslie Forde's Nouvelle/ Barbadian Coo-Coo

When she was a child, Leslie Forde's parents came to the United States from Barbados to continue their educations. They gradually fell in love with America, but they made sure that their children spent a few months of each year in Barbados. Ms. Forde, now a marketing executive, is "a product of both cultures in every aspect of life," and her cooking tells the tale. A serious amateur from a young age, she attended Le Cordon Bleu in London and applies classic French techniques to Bajan ingredients and flavors, layering as many herbs and peppers as she can into most dishes. Coo-coo, the Caribbean cornmeal porridge, is not usually highly seasoned, but she adds curry and both chicken broth and coconut milk to the dish. While coo-coo is traditionally served with flying fish, Ms. Forde serves hers with tilapia or cod.

½ cup light coconut milk

3 cups homemade chicken broth or low-sodium store-bought chicken broth, or water

1 cup cornmeal

1 teaspoon kosher salt

1 teaspoon raw or brown sugar

5 okra (2 to 3 inches long), rinsed, tough stems and tails removed, sliced into thin rounds (about ½ cup)

1 tablespoon curry powder

1 teaspoon ground allspice

Hot pepper sauce

Seasoning salt

Freshly ground black pepper

5 scallions (white and light green parts only), sliced

1. In a small bowl, stir together the coconut milk, 1 cup of the broth, and the cornmeal. Make sure the cornmeal is fully integrated with the liquid.

2. In a large saucepan or stockpot, bring the remaining broth, the salt, sugar, and okra to a boil. Reduce the heat to medium and cook at a fast simmer for 10 minutes.

3. Remove the pan from the heat and stir in the cornmeal mixture until fully combined. Stir in the curry powder, allspice, and hot pepper sauce to taste.

4. Return to the heat and simmer over medium heat, stirring constantly, until mixture thickens and cleanly comes away from the pan, 10 to 15 minutes.

5. Stir in seasoning salt and pepper to taste.

6. Garnish with the scallions and serve immediately.

SERVES 4 TO 6

Maria Gallardo's Fresh Corn Casserole

SAN FRANCISCO, CALIFORNIA

As a young woman living in Ocotlan, a small city in Jalisco, Mexico, Maria Gallardo dreamed of "a ticket out of town" to a place like Guadalajara when she met a dashing man from that big city at a county fair. She did not anticipate a ticket out of Mexico, which was the dashing young man's dream. But in 1964, the newlyweds moved to San Francisco. Her husband was eager to live like an American, so she learned to make meatloaf and spaghetti and tuna salad. But in a strange city where Mexican ingredients were then scarce, her mouth watered for spicy chiles, long-stewed moles, soft tacos, and fresh tamales. For years she prepared his-and-her meals, but gradually she invented dishes like this casserole layered with fresh American corn, cornmeal, and a poblano sauce, which used American ingredients and an American sensibility while sating her hankering for home. The dish can be prepared with or without the cheese, and can also be made without the spicy sauce and served with sour cream and salsa on the side.

FOR THE CASSEROLE

¾ pound (3 sticks) unsalted butter, melted, plus more for the pan

8 ears corn, husked and all silk removed

1 cup milk

1½ cups cornmeal

1½ cups rice flour

1 tablespoon sugar

2 teaspoons kosher salt

1 cup grated Monterey Jack cheese (about 4 ounces)

1 cup grated mozzarella cheese (about 4 ounces)

FOR THE SAUCE

2 tablespoons (¼ stick) unsalted butter

3 poblano peppers, seeded and chopped

½ medium white or yellow onion, diced

1 cup tomato sauce

¾ cup sour cream

1. Preheat the oven to 350°F. Lightly butter an 8-inch-square baking pan.

2. To make the casserole mixture: With a sharp knife, cut the kernels off the cobs. In a food processor or blender and working in batches, coarsely grind the kernels with the milk.

3. In a mixing bowl, combine the cornmeal, rice flour, sugar, and salt. Add the corn mixture and stir well. Stir in the melted butter.

4. To make the sauce: Melt the butter in a large skillet over medium heat. Add the peppers and onion and sauté until tender. Add tomato sauce and simmer for 5 minutes. Remove from heat and let cool for 10 minutes before stirring in the sour cream.

5. Pour half the casserole mixture into the prepared pan, smoothing the top. Spread the sauce over it and top with the rest of the casserole mixture. Sprinkle with the cheeses. Place the pan in a 9 x 13-inch pan. Pour boiling water into the larger pan to a depth of 1½ inches.

6. Bake for 90 minutes, until the cheese is golden brown on top.

SERVES 6 TO 8

KEN BOWLING'S POSOLE

Like many products of border towns, Ken Bowling grew up eating biculturally in El Paso, Texas. His efforts in the kitchen are not, therefore, spent on melding Mexican and American flavors, but on the subtle nuance that distinguishes one family's or one region's food from another. As a young adult he moved north to larger, more cosmopolitan towns and by the time he reached Santa Fe, the Southwest's many layers of flavors had found their way into his kitchen. He takes ethnic cooking classes for fun, makes an annual pilgrimage to Hatch, New Mexico, to buy the green chiles and red chiles he hangs in his garage to use throughout the year. He travels back to El Paso to visit family—and stock up on Mexican oregano.

2 pounds posole (lime-slaked dried corn, aka hominy)

½ cup all-purpose flour

Kosher salt and freshly ground black pepper

Two 1-pound pork tenderloins, trimmed and cut into ½-inch chunks

¼ cup olive oil

3 tablespoons finely chopped onion

6 garlic cloves, minced

10 cups homemade chicken broth or low-sodium store-bought chicken broth

2 bay leaves

½ teaspoon chopped fresh oregano

1 big pinch saffron threads

¾ cup chopped fresh cilantro

4 small limes (preferably Mexican or Key limes), halved

1. Put the posole in a large Dutch oven, cover with water, cover the pot, and simmer about 3 hours, until tender. Add water as needed to keep the posole covered. Drain, rinse well, and return to the pot.

2. In a shallow dish, whisk together the flour, 1 teaspoon salt, and 1 teaspoon pepper. Dredge the pork in the flour and shake off the excess. Heat the olive oil in a large skillet over medium-high heat. Add the pork and cook for 4 to 6 minutes, stirring frequently, until well browned on all sides. Transfer the pork to the pot with the posole.

3. Add the onion and garlic to the skillet and cook about 4 minutes, until soft. Stir in about 1 cup of the broth and scrape any browned bits from the bottom of the pan. Add the onion-broth mixture to the posole and pork.

4. Add the remaining broth, the bay leaves, oregano, and saffron, bring to a simmer, and cook for 1 hour. Season with salt and pepper to taste. Ladle into warmed bowls and sprinkle with the cilantro. Serve with the limes.

SERVES 8

Harvesting corn, New Mexico.

THE GEECHEE GIRL'S RED RICE

Dr. Vertamae Smart-Grosvenor, the granddaughter of a former slave, was born in the Carolina lowlands, the marshy region that—from the late seventeenth century until after the emancipation—has been the cradle of Carolina Gold rice, one of the best rices in the world. The area developed its own culture—the Gullah-speaking Geechee people who created both the rice and the "The Carolina Rice Kitchen," a rice-centric fusion of African, West Indian, and European cooking that was America's first regional "Creole" cuisine. Like the rice and the language, the cooking has long been in diaspora, along with much of the historical detail of the Geechee people.

"People accept that Italy is pasta, but they don't understand that America was once rice," said Dr. Smart-Grosvenor, a commentator on National Public Radio and the author of three books, including *Vibration Cooking or The Travel Notes of a Geechee Girl*. Sitting on her porch overlooking marshlands that were once a four-hundred-acre rice plantation, she feels increasingly impelled to set the record straight by telling the story of early-American rice.

Carolina Gold rice was developed in the eighteenth century in South Carolina, Georgia, and northern Florida. A long-grain Asian rice was brought to the New World in the late seventeenth century by slaves from rice-growing regions in West Africa, where they had learned how to prepare the swampy fields, construct canals and dikes, flood and drain the land, and plant and tend the rice that grew in the fields. The delicate grain flourished in the lowlands of the southeastern colonies, where it developed a subtly nutty, herbaceous flavor. When Thomas Jefferson was ambassador to France, he helped cross this long-grain variety with a short-grain Asian variety (probably a cousin of today's Arborio rice) to please European tastes—and South Carolina unseated Genoa as the number one rice-exporting port in the world. Fortunes were made; Charleston was built; and untold hundreds of thousands of slaves hulled, winnowed, hand-pounded, and winnowed the grains again before screening and handpicking to exclude broken grains or "middlins." The result was one of the best rices in the world, reserved for export and the tables of the world's elite.

Along with the partially hulled brown rice, the broken middlins (basically grits made from rice instead of corn) were the staple of Geechee homes. Shrimp, crab, oysters, sausage and bacon, chicken, and beans were abundant, as were African vegetables such as hot peppers, okra, greens, sesame seeds, and peanuts. They went into dishes such as Frogmore stew (a boil that usually contains shrimp, sausage, and corn—but no frogs); chicken bog (spicy baked rice with chicken, sausage, and bacon); hoppin' John; oyster roasts; Low Country barbecue; and sweet potato pie. Recipes were rarely recorded; cooking was an oral tradition.

Dr. Smart-Grosvenor knows firsthand the toll that distance and dispersion take on culture. After her family moved to Philadelphia when she was 9 years old, her schoolmates taunted her speech. She traded Gullah for perfect English and became shy about the traditional cooking she had learned from her Geechee grandmother and her father, Frank Smart.

"At one point, when I wanted to rebel, I dreamed about growing up and having my own kitchen and not allowing one grain of rice in there," said Dr. Smart-Grosvenor. Instead, she lived in Paris and New York City (where she raised her two daughters) and traveled extensively on the trail of what she calls "Afro-Atlantic cuisine." Last year, she settled in a small cottage in Palm Key where, she says, her life is "just the opposite of anything I imagined. My kitchen is rice, rice, rice." And the quiet allows her to feel what she calls "the evidence of things unseen," the way her front-porch swing moves rhythmically on breezeless days, the scent of cooking when there are no pots on the stove, the whispers that seem to hum just beneath the cicadas at night.

"I traveled and studied, traveled and studied. Always looking for the 'Africanisms' in dishes and then trying to chart their course from Africa to the region that spreads from Charleston to New Orleans. But all I needed to do was sit here on the porch and feel the connection. No sane person can sit on my porch and say that Africans came to America with no culture. It just got scattered, absorbed, forgotten, misunderstood, and reinvented—just like the rice that was at its culinary center. The dish that tells the story the best is probably red rice, she said. A staple of traditional Geechee kitchens, it can be as simple as rice cooked with tomatoes, or as rich as her family recipe. She calls its style "Afro-Brazilian-West-Indian-Italian-Chinese-Geechee" and serves it with boiled shrimp or crabs, chicken or beef, or fresh corn on the cob.

1 cup homemade chicken broth or low-sodium store-bought chicken broth

1 cup strained pureed tomatoes or tomato juice

1 teaspoon red wine vinegar

½ teaspoon dried thyme

1 bay leaf

½ to 1 small chile pepper, minced

1 slice smoky bacon, cut fine

½ cup minced yellow onion

1 garlic clove, minced

¼ cup minced smoked beef sausage

1 celery stalk, diced

1 cup finely minced mushrooms

Kosher salt and freshly ground black pepper

1 cup Carolina Gold rice, rinsed and drained

1. Combine the broth, tomatoes, vinegar, thyme, bay leaf, and chile in a medium saucepan over low heat. Bring to a boil, then simmer for 5 minutes. Cover, remove from heat, and let sit at least 1 hour.

2. Put the bacon in a heavy-bottomed medium pot (preferably cast iron) with a tight-fitting lid over medium heat and cook, stirring frequently, until the bacon is crisp. Drain on a paper towel–lined plate.

3. Add the onion to the bacon fat and cook, stirring constantly, until the onion begins to soften, about 3 minutes. Add the garlic, stir, and cook for 1 minute. Add the sausage and celery and cook, stirring frequently, until the celery begins to soften. Add the minced mushrooms, ½ teaspoon salt, and ½ teaspoon pepper and stir once. Cover, remove from heat, and let sit for 5 minutes.

4. Return the pot to medium-high heat. Add the rice and stir to coat the grains of rice well. Strain the liquid into the pot and stir to combine. Reduce the heat to the lowest setting. Cover the pot and cook for 20 minutes without lifting the lid.

5. Remove the pot from the heat and, without lifting the lid, let sit for 10 minutes more. Fluff lightly with a fork, and correct seasoning, if necessary, before serving.

SERVES 4 TO 6

SMOKING FOR JESUS MINISTRY'S DIRTY RICE

U p in the hill country, about an hour west of Austin, Round Top, a former stagecoach stop, is little more than a wide spot on U.S. Highway 281. There is a post office, a gas station, a volunteer fire department, a branch of the National Cattleman's bank, and a cattle auction barn, and since 2005, when Hurricane Katrina drove a small, nondenominational congregation from New Orleans's Ninth Ward to higher ground, a truck stop that serves New Orleans cooking. It is called Real New Orleans Style Restaurant.

"I got the message to move my people," said Willie Monnet, the group's pastor. Two days before the levee broke, 187 members of his flock piled into twenty vehicles. It took nineteen hours to make the three-hour trip to Lone Star, Texas, where they had been offered temporary housing. "We thought we were leaving for a few days and, over time, we realized we were gone for good. We didn't fall apart because of our faith and the generosity of the Texas people," said Pastor Monnet, whose ministry has always focused on jobs, education, and community outreach. "We didn't know how we could ever thank the fine people of Texas, so we did what we know, we cooked them a big community dinner. Well, they loved it so and I knew right then that we'd found our new ministry and we weren't going home."

Five years later, the gumbo, po'boys, jambalaya, étouffée, dirty rice, and pies have made the Real New Orleans Style Restaurant a must-stop for truckers, travelers, and the food cognoscenti. Many ask how the church got its name. Pastor Monnet assures them that it has nothing to do with barbecue but is based on a passage in the Book of Revelations that castigates those with lukewarm faith. "We are hot," he says, "we are smoking for Jesus. We feed your body and your soul."

1 chicken giblet, 1 chicken liver, and
   a couple of necks, trimmed and rinsed

½ cup minced shallots

2 cups homemade chicken broth or
   low-sodium store-bought chicken broth

4½ cups water

3 or 4 sprigs fresh flat-leaf parsley

8 to 10 whole black peppercorns

Kosher salt

3½ tablespoons vegetable oil

¼ cup all-purpose flour

1 large onion, minced

2 pounds cremini mushrooms, cleaned
   and chopped

In the Rice Fields of La.

1 green bell pepper, stemmed, seeded, and
    diced small

1 red bell pepper, stemmed, seeded, and
    diced small

1 celery stalk, diced small

5 garlic cloves, sliced

1 teaspoon fresh thyme leaves

1½ cups short-grain rice (preferably
    Anson Mills Carolina Gold or basmati)

1 bay leaf

Freshly ground black pepper

½ cup thinly sliced green onions (scallions),
    green parts only

1. In a heavy saucepan, combine the giblets, shallots, chicken broth, 2 cups water, the parsley, peppercorns, and ½ teaspoon salt. Bring to a boil, reduce to a simmer, and cook for 10 minutes or until the livers are just cooked through.

2. Using a slotted spoon, transfer the livers to a bowl. Simmer the giblets for 30 minutes more.

3. Transfer the giblets to the bowl with the livers to cool. Strain the stock through a fine-mesh strainer into another bowl.

4. Remove the meat from the necks, discarding the skin and bones. Chop the giblets and livers, and return them to their bowl.

5. Combine the oil and flour in a heavy skillet, preferably cast iron, and cook over medium heat, stirring constantly for about 30 minutes, until it is the color of milk chocolate. Add the onion and cook, stirring, until the roux turns a darker mahogany color, another 20 to 30 minutes.

6. Add the chopped mushrooms, bell pepper, celery, and garlic and cook, stirring, until the vegetables are softened, about 5 minutes.

7. Add the reserved broth and the thyme and simmer the gravy for 30 minutes, skimming off any fat or foam.

8. In a heavy saucepan combine the rice, the remaining 2½ cups water, the bay leaf, and salt and pepper to taste. Bring a to boil, reduce the heat to low, cover, and cook for 15 minutes or until it is tender and the water is absorbed.

9. Remove the pan from heat and let steep, covered, for 5 minutes more.

10. Remove the bay leaf from the rice. Stir the giblets and green onions into the gravy, adjust the seasoning, and stir into the rice.

SERVES 6

ht by A.L.Barnett. Lake Charles. La. 1910. # 112.

Lonnie Holley's Jambalaya

Lonnie Holley, the visionary artist whose work has been exhibited at the Smithsonian American Art Museum, the American Folk Art Museum, the High Museum of Art, and the White House, was born in 1950, the seventh of twenty-seven children. He lived in a series of foster homes, spent time in the Industrial School for Negro Children in Mount Meigs, Alabama, and ran away to New Orleans when he was 14 years old.

Mr. Holley says: "I slept where I could and worked in restaurants, that's where you could get jobs. I learned to cook by inhaling and sweating, listening and being hungry. Gumbo or jambalaya is the sort of thing you grab from the air. It's a summer day and there are eggplant or tomatoes, it's a lucky day and there is chicken or crawfish, it's a hog-killing day and there is sausage, maybe peppers and onion, okra. When rice is in the air, that is jambalaya day. You pull a little of this and a little of that and you build, just like you do a building, a sculpture, an installation, a painting. You build layers. It's a God-given thing, you just stay out of the way and the food moves through you and there is enough to eat, oh, there is so much to eat if you watch and reach and take what God gives you.

"Cooking showed me that I am an artist. Cooking taught me how to make art. When my sister and her children were burned up in a fire in 1970, I was sick in the soul and the heart and we did not have money to make the send-off we wanted, couldn't afford headstones for the babies. There was a foundry near her house

and I found a soft sandstone-like block, something they use in metal casting then throw out, and I carved the stones. That is why some people call me 'The Sandman.' That was the beginning. Nothing is trash, there is art, there is eating. If you take what you find, the art moves through you. It is not your business; you are the tube, the wind tunnel, the empty pipe, the land that the wind sweeps up. I take the things I find. Sometimes I know what they are for. Sometimes it is years before something tells me what it wants to be.

"I worked hard and had a home outside Birmingham, behind the airport. I built a world there, collected for years, had fifteen children. They wanted to expand the airport and they condemned my property. I sued, and later they had to pay me. I moved to Harpersville. The neighbors did not like my hair, my dreads. They thought the truckloads I brought were junkyard. It is clay, it is marble, it is metal, it is paint. When people are afraid of what is given, hatred and sadness are the result. God gave me art and God gave me cooking. Jambalaya is a good thing to think about when you have a lot of folks to feed because you can always add more rice if you need to. That makes the meal bigger and bigger, depending on who stops by and wants to eat."

2 tablespoons sweet paprika

2 tablespoons garlic powder

1 teaspoon fresh ground black pepper

2 teaspoon cayenne pepper

1 tablespoon dried oregano

1 tablespoon dried thyme

1 pound medium shrimp, peeled and deveined, shells reserved

4 whole chicken legs, cut apart to make drumsticks and thighs

4 tablespoons vegetable oil or bacon fat

1 quart water

1 yellow onion, chopped

2 garlic cloves, minced

1 red bell pepper, chopped

2 celery ribs, sliced ¼ inch thick

1 large tomato, seeded and chopped

2 bay leaves

1 teaspoon Worcestershire sauce

2 teaspoons hot sauce (preferably Tabasco)

2 cups white rice

6 cups homemade chicken broth or low-sodium store-bought chicken broth

4 andouille sausages (about 1 pound), sliced in ½-inch chunks

Kosher salt and freshly ground black pepper

1. Combine the paprika, garlic powder, black pepper, cayenne, oregano, and thyme in a jar. Shake it up. Put 1 tablespoon of this spice blend in a big bowl. (The remainder can be stored, tightly covered, in the refrigerator for up to 6 months.) Add the shrimp and chicken and toss to coat each piece well. Cover with plastic wrap and put in the refrigerator for 1 to 2 hours.

2. Heat 1 tablespoon of the oil in a soup pot over high heat. Add the shrimp shells and cook, stirring

constantly, until the shells are bright pink. Add the water, bring to a boil, reduce the heat to low, and cook until the water is reduced to half, about 15 minutes. Strain the broth and set aside.

3. An hour before serving, warm 2 tablespoons of the oil a large heavy-bottomed pot over medium heat. Remove the chicken and shrimp from the refrigerator and brush the spice blend from the chicken with paper towels. Brown the chicken on all sides, about 5 minutes per side.

4. Add the onion, stir, and cook for 1 minute. Add the garlic, bell pepper, and celery, stirring after each addition. Cook until the vegetables begin to soften, about 5 minutes. Stir in the tomato, bay leaves, Worcestershire, and hot sauce. Add the rice and stir. Add 2 cups of the strained shrimp broth and the chicken broth to the rice. Reduce the heat to medium-low, partially cover the pot, and cook, stirring occasionally, for 15 minutes.

5. Add the shrimp and andouille. Add salt, pepper, and additional spice blend to taste. Cook, uncovered, about 5 minutes more, until the rice is tender. Remove from the heat and serve immediately.

SERVES 8

Mireille Fabius's Riz Djon Djon

Mireille Fabius was a prosperous Haitian woman who worked as dressmaker to the daughters of Papa Doc Duvalier. In 1964, she, her husband, and young children joined her parents who had long since immigrated to New York City. In her new country, she designed clothing for department stores and took up the cooking that back home she'd left to the family's maids.

In Haiti, cooks are measured by their ways with rice. Djon Djon is all but a national dish, and Ms. Fabius has yet to meet anyone who has not fallen for her version. To keep the spice subtle, she uses a habanero whole (rather than chopped), coupled with pungent wild mushrooms such as porcini or candy-caps. She has also substituted salted chicken or vegetable bouillon cubes for the salt. These small changes elevate an everyday Haitian dish to a company-worthy side dish that is wonderful served with chicken or pork.

1 cup dried wild mushrooms

4½ cups boiling water

¼ cup vegetable oil

2 slices bacon, coarsely chopped

1 medium onion, coarsely chopped

4 garlic cloves, crushed

Kosher salt

½ teaspoon fresh thyme leaves

1 whole Scotch bonnet or habanero chile

2 cups white rice

2 to 4 teaspoons unsalted butter

Freshly ground black pepper (optional)

1. Place the dried mushrooms in a medium saucepan, cover with the boiling water, and place over low heat. Simmer until tender, 20 to 30 minutes.

2. Remove from heat and let sit until any grit settles to the bottom. Carefully strain the liquid through a fine-mesh strainer. Discard the grit. You should have about 1 quart mushroom broth (add water if you don't). Lightly rinse the soaked mushrooms, then drain and chop.

3. Heat the oil in a large saucepan over medium heat. Add the bacon and cook, stirring occasionally, until some of the fat has been rendered but the bacon is not yet crisp.

4. Add the onion, garlic, and about 1 tablespoon of the chopped mushrooms. Cook stirring occasionally, until the bacon is crisp, about 10 minutes.

5. Add the reserved mushroom broth, 2 teaspoons salt, the thyme, and the remaining mushrooms. Float the chile on the liquid, cover, lower the heat, and simmer for 30 minutes.

6. Gently stir in the rice, being careful not to puncture the chile. Cover and cook 15 to 20 minutes, until the rice is tender.

7. Remove the chile. Stir in the butter. Taste and add salt and black pepper, if desired. Cover the pot, remove from the heat, and let sit for 10 minutes before serving.

SERVES 8

Nancy Mehagian's Armenian Rice with Vermicelli

Nancy Mehagian's mother was born in Syracuse, New York, in 1915, the year of the Armenian genocide. Her father, who had been living in the Armenian provinces of Turkey, was the last person to escape his village after the Turks set fire to it. After they married, the couple moved to Phoenix. "We were the only [Armenians] I knew," Ms. Mehagian says. "Now there are more Armenians in Southern California than in Armenia."

"Growing up, we ate pilaf all the time the way Americans eat potatoes," she says. Now pilaf has become part of the American food lexicon. This recipe, from Ms. Mehagian's mother, uses a fair amount of butter and chicken broth. "Everyone says it's the best they ever tasted," she says.

8 tablespoons (1 stick) unsalted butter

⅔ cup broken (about 1-inch pieces) vermicelli noodles

2 cups long-grain white rice

1 teaspoon kosher salt

5 cups boiling homemade chicken broth or low-sodium store-bought chicken broth

1. Melt the butter in a heavy saucepan over medium-high heat. Add the vermicelli and brown in the butter, stirring constantly. Watch carefully so the butter does not burn.

2. Add the rice and salt and stir a few minutes more.

3. Stir in the broth, cover the pot with a tight-fitting lid, and simmer over very low heat for 20 to 25 minutes, until all liquid is absorbed.

4. Fluff the pilaf with a spoon and let stand at least 10 minutes before serving.

SERVES 6 TO 8

Princesses, National Rice Festival, Crowley, Louisiana.

Abeer Abutaleb's Egyptian Beram Ruz

Abeer Abutaleb was born in Damanhour, a small city in Egypt. She and her husband immigrated to the United States after finishing their medical residencies. Once here, they completed second residencies and started a family. Dr. Abutaleb is committed to preparing special meals—such as okra in a casserole, stuffed grape leaves, stuffed cabbage, and tilapia cooked in a casserole or fried—to pass their culinary heritage on to her two daughters. She also teaches them prayers and songs, and celebrates religious occasions. She prepares this dish, which she learned from her grandmother, in a special ceramic pot she brought with her from Egypt. One could prepare the dish in a regular casserole, she says, but it would not be the same. "It wouldn't taste as much like home to me."

2 tablespoons (¼ stick) unsalted butter

2 cups rice (preferably medium grain)

½ teaspoon kosher salt

¼ teaspoon freshly ground white pepper

2 cups whole milk, plus more as needed

1 cup heavy cream

1. Preheat the oven to 450°F. Grease the bottom and sides of a 2-quart casserole with the butter. Add the rice, salt, and pepper.

2. Bring the milk to a boil. Pour the milk and cream over the top of the rice.

3. Bake until all the liquid is absorbed, about 45 minutes. Add additional milk a little at a time if the casserole seems dry before the rice is tender. Serve hot.

SERVES 8

THE ARMENIAN CONNECTION

IN 1948, TOM DEDOMENICO AND HIS NEW BRIDE, LOIS, MOVED INTO AN APARTMENT building in San Francisco owned by an Armenian woman named Pailadzo Captanian. Tom's mother's family had owned a pasta factory in Italy and his father, also an Italian immigrant, had established a pasta-making business in the Mission District. Tom and his three brothers worked at the family's Golden Grain Macaroni factory. At home, his young wife spent the afternoons listening to her landlady's stories of the Armenian genocide and learning to make yogurt, baklava, and Armenian rice pilaf. A decade later, when Lois served that pilaf, Tom's brother Vincent looked down at his plate and said, "This would be good in a box. We got rice, we got macaroni." He added dried chicken broth and herbs and in 1958, America met an Armenian dish in a box with a name that sounded Italian. From the beginning, Rice-a-Roni was advertised with the jingle that most baby boomers can still hum. Some Armenian Americans say that the only contribution they made to American cuisine is considered Italian and comes in a box.

Shanaz Haghanifar's Chelo
Persian Herbed Steamed Rice

Even plain rice, the hallmark of nearly every Iranian meal, was a challenge to Shanaz Haghanifar when she immigrated to America as a young bride. She experimented with jasmine and long-grain Carolina rices, steaming them in the way that makes Persian rice notable for its fluffiness. "For us, if you haven't eaten rice, then you didn't eat that day," she says. "It's our daily food" (and a perfect companion to Ms. Haghanifar's Persian New Year Fish recipe on page 265).

2 cups high quality basmati rice

2 teaspoons coarse sea salt

3 tablespoons plus 2 teaspoons unsalted butter, melted

Pinch of ground saffron

1. Place the rice in a deep bowl and run cold water over it, swirling the rice with your hand. Add enough water so it covers the rice by 2 inches. Drain and rinse five or six times, until the water runs clear.

2. Add enough room-temperature water to cover the rice by 2 inches and set aside for 2 hours.

3. Bring 6 cups water and the salt to a boil in a large, preferably nonstick, pot. Drain the rice and add to the boiling water. Lower the heat to a high simmer and cook, uncovered, for 10 to 15 minutes or until al dente.

4. Drain the rice in a colander. Put 3 tablespoons of the melted butter and 2 tablespoons water in the bottom of the pot.

5. Sprinkle 1 large spoonful of rice over the bottom of the pot so it is evenly covered. Spoon remaining rice into the center of the pot until you have a pyramid.

6. Mix the remaining butter with ⅓ cup warm water and pour over the rice pyramid. With a spoon or spatula re-form the pyramid if necessary.

7. Place a clean dishcloth or two paper towels over the pot and cover firmly with the lid. (The cloth will trap the steam away from the rice, preventing it from getting sticky.) Place the pot over low heat and cook undisturbed for 20 minutes.

8. Remove the lid and fluff with a fork. In a small bowl, dissolve the saffron in 3 tablespoons boiling water. Remove ¼ cup of the rice from the pot and stir gently into the saffron mixture. Ladle the remaining rice into a serving dish and sprinkle the saffron rice over it.

9. The rice at the bottom of the pot should be a solid crust that can be removed by gently prying it up with a spatula or fork or by turning the pot over onto a serving plate. The crust is called tah dig, and is considered a great delicacy in Persian cooking.

SERVES 4 TO 6

Mam Mbye's Ceebu Jen
Senegalese Fish and Rice

The eldest of thirteen children, Mam Mbye spent her early years watching her mother cook. Her mother frequently served Ceebu Jen, the Senegalese national dish, for the huge family. One day when she was preparing it, a neighbor came to call and she left the pot unattended. When her mother returned to the kitchen, 7-year-old Mam was standing on a stool, finishing the dish. "My mother had to use big iron pots . . . and she was terrified for me to ever try lifting them or to be near the stove, so she was shocked. But when she tasted the Ceebu Jen, she started yelling, 'My daughter can cook! My daughter can cook!' and I've been cooking ever since. My father was an accountant with the railroad. My mother was a seamstress and a hairdresser and had an export business. When the strikes and bad times made it impossible for me to finish my education in Senegal, I got a grant to come to the University of Wisconsin to study English literature. No one in my family had ever done that, but my husband and I loved America and we moved to Los Angeles for the weather. I taught English and African studies at UCLA. I often cooked for events, and eventually that turned into a catering business. When my family came from Africa to visit they hated it. They said that everybody worked all the time, and what sort of life is that." But it is Mam Mbye's life, and with one possible exception, she would not trade it for all the red rice and fish in the world. "In Senegal, the farmers and fishermen bring the food right to your door. Here you have to go buy the food at the grocery and it is older, even frozen. I have to use a lot more spices and seasoning to give it flavor."

FOR THE SPICE MIX

1 tablespoon dried sage

1 tablespoon cumin seeds

1 tablespoon coriander seeds

1 tablespoon dried thyme

1 tablespoon black peppercorns

FOR THE BROTH

8 ounces salt cod

1 pound medium-size shrimp

½ cup canola oil

4 cloves garlic, minced

2 yellow onions, quartered

¼ dried red chili pepper, minced, plus more to taste

3 6-ounce cans tomato paste

16 cups water

2 fish, lobster, or shellfish bouillon cubes or 2 cups clam juice or other seafood broth

2 large carrots, peeled and cut into quarters

1 medium cabbage, cut into eighths

1 small head cauliflower, cut into large flowerettes

1 large eggplant, cut into 2-inch squares

1 yucca root, peeled and cut into 1-inch squares

1 red bell pepper, cored, seeded, and cut into 1-inch wedges

1 green bell pepper, cored, seeded, and cut into 1-inch wedges

1 banana squash, cut into 2-inch pieces

2 sweet potatoes, cut into 1-inch dice

8 okra, stemmed and cut in half

1 cup minced sorrel leaves

1 sweet tamarind, peeled, pulp chopped

FOR THE FISH AND STUFFING

5 pounds whole grouper, sea bass, or black cod, scaled, gutted, head and tail removed, cut into 2-inch steaks

½ to 1 cup canola oil

2 bunches flat-leaf parsley

2 garlic cloves

1 teaspoon dried spice mixture, plus more to taste

¼ teaspoon salt, plus more to taste

FOR THE RICE

3 pounds fragrant long-grain rice such as jasmine rice

FOR THE SPICY SAUCE

¼ cup canola oil

1 yellow onion, minced

4 garlic cloves, minced

¼ to ½ dried red chile pepper, minced

1 can tomato paste

½ teaspoon salt, plus more to taste

½ teaspoon dried spice mixture

1. To make the spice mixture, place all the dried spices in a blender, coffee or spice mill and pulse to make a find powder, remove, and set aside.

2. To make the broth, cover the cod with cold water in a pan, bring to a boil, simmer for 5 minutes, drain under cold running water to remove the salt, and set aside. Peel the shrimp, save the shells, and refrigerate the shrimp for later use. Warm half the oil in a large pot. Add the shrimp shells and sauté, stirring constantly until dark pink and fragrant, about 3 minutes. Add 4 cups of cold water and simmer for 20 minutes. Strain the broth, discard the shells, and return the pot to the heat.

3. Add the remaining ½ cup canola oil and when it is warm, add the garlic, onion, and chili pepper. Season lightly with salt and freshly ground black pepper and cook, stirring frequently, until the onions are nearly translucent, about 5 minutes. Add the tomato paste and cook, stirring constantly, until the paste smells toasty and the oil and tomato separate, 3 to 5 minutes. Add the reserved shrimp broth, 12 cups of water, and all the remaining ingredients except for the cod, the sorrel, and the tamarind. Stir to combine and simmer until the sweet potatoes are tender, about 20 minutes.

4. While the broth is simmering, prepare the fish. Rinse in cold water and pat dry with paper towels. Starting at the spine, make several deep diagonal cuts in each piece and set aside. Pick the leaves from the parsley, discard stems, and place leaves in the blender. Add the garlic, the spice mixture, and half the salt and pulse to make a paste. Stuff the paste into the diagonal slashes and lightly season the fish on each side with the remaining salt.

5. Warm ½ cup of canola oil in a large skillet over medium-high heat. Fry the fish until the skin is crispy, about 3 minutes per side. Work in batches if necessary and add additional oil if needed to cover the bottom of the pan. Drain the fish on paper towels and set aside.

6. When vegetables are tender, use a slotted spoon to remove them from the broth and set aside. Add the cod, sorrel, and tamarind and simmer for 20 more minutes. Taste the broth and season with additional salt, black pepper, or chili pepper if desired. Ladle 4 cups of the broth over the vegetables and set aside. Return remaining broth to medium heat and make the rice.

7. Place rice in a colander under cold running water and toss until the water runs clear. Add the rice to the broth, raise the heat to medium-high and stir very well. The broth should cover the rice by one inch; if it does not, add cold water. Bring the rice to a boil, cover tightly, and reduce the heat to medium and cook, checking and stirring occasionally, until the rice is almost tender, about 20 minutes. Lay the fish on top of the rice, cover, and continue cooking for 5 minutes. Add the vegetables and remaining broth, cook for 2 minutes, leave covered, and remove from heat.

8. While the rice is cooking make the spicy sauce by warming 3 tablespoons of canola oil in a pan over medium heat. Add the minced onion, garlic and chile pepper, stir, and cook until fragrant, about two minutes. Add the tomato paste and stir until toasty and fragrant, about 2 minutes. Use a ladle to remove 3 cups of the broth that is covering the vegetables and stir into the sauce, along with ½ teaspoon of the spice blend and the shrimp and simmer for several more minutes until the shrimp are tender.

9. Use a slotted spoon to lift the fish and vegetable pieces from the rice onto a plate. Pour the rice onto another large platter, place the fish and vegetables on top of the rice. and cover with sauce. Scrap the crispy bits of rice from the bottom of the pot and either serve these on the side or crumble them on top of the Ceebu Jen before serving.

SERVES 10 TO 15

Teddy Myers's Minorcan Pork Pilau

ST. AUGUSTINE, FLORIDA

In 1768, more than a thousand people from different Mediterranean countries were brought to Florida as indentured servants to work on an indigo plantation south of St. Augustine. They were Roman Catholic or Eastern Orthodox and collectively became known as Minorcans, and their descendants have been an important part of St. Augustine and St. John's County for more than two hundred years. This version of Minorcan pilau (or pilaf) is well loved by the staff of St. Augustine's Lightner Museum. To make it even richer, add both smoked ham hocks and salt pork. If you prefer not to use the salt pork, use about four tablespoons of butter or margarine instead. Datil peppers can be difficult to find outside of Florida, but habaneros make an acceptable substitute. Remember to use care when handling hot peppers. If you want a less fiery stew, you can wrap the peppers in a cheesecloth pouch and remove them before serving (although some would say this is for sissies).

2 to 3 pounds bone-in pork shoulder or chops

2 smoked ham hocks (optional)

2- by 3-inch piece salt pork, cut into 1-inch cubes

2 onions, chopped

3 garlic cloves, minced

Two 28-ounce cans whole tomatoes

1 heaping tablespoon dried thyme

1 heaping tablespoon dried oregano

1 heaping tablespoon dried basil

1 heaping tablespoon dried parsley

2 bay leaves

1 pound bulk sausage (plain or Italian)

3 green bell peppers, stemmed, seeded, and chopped

2 pounds large shrimp, peeled and deveined

½ pound kielbasa or smoked sausage, diced

4 cups white rice

3 datil or habanero chiles, minced

1. Place the pork shoulder and ham hocks, if using, in a large heavy-bottomed pot and cover with water. Bring to a boil, reduce to a simmer, and cook until pork is tender and can be torn into pieces, about 2 hours. Remove the pork from the broth and, when it is cool enough to handle, tear into pieces, discarding the bones, gristle, and skin from the ham hocks. Save the broth separately.

2. In another large heavy-bottomed pot, cook the salt pork over medium-high heat until the fat has been rendered and the pork is brown. (It should look like pork rinds.) Remove and set aside.

3. Add the onions to the rendered fat and cook, stirring frequently, until they begin to soften. Stir in the garlic, tomatoes, thyme, oregano, basil, parsley, and bay leaves and mix well. Reduce the heat to medium and cook this mixture down, stirring frequently, until very thick and dark red in color.

4. Crumble in the bulk sausage. Stir in the bell peppers, salt pork pieces, 1¾ pounds of the shrimp, the torn pork, kielbasa, and rice.

5. Add enough pork broth to cover the rice by 1 inch. Reserve remaining broth. Bring to a simmer, reduce the heat to low, cover, and cook about 1 hour.

6. Stir in the chiles and more broth, if needed, to keep the rice moist. Continue cooking over low heat, stirring often. The pilau is done when the rice is tender but not mushy.

7. Steam the remaining shrimp and place on top for garnish.

SERVES 16

Ronnie Morris's
Kensington Plantation Chicken Pilau

Ronnie Morris has been helping to care for Kensington Plantation since he was a teenager. Before him, his parents and grandparents helped maintain the oak allee, the mansion, the historic overseer's house, the gardens and the woods of the 670-acre estate off the Cooper River. No one could have been happier than Mr. Morris when the plantation's current owner, Richard Stoney, a Charleston restaurateur, along with his friend Batt Humphreys, a writer, polo player, and owner of a nearby plantation, decided to plant ten acres of real Carolina Gold rice. While the public has never lost the conviction that "Carolina" means "the best," Carolina rice has only recently been brought back from the brink of extinction. Mr. Stoney and Mr. Humphreys were among a small group who dedicated the land to "repatriating" the grain. "There is nothing close to eating real Carolina Gold rice, fresh harvested from the field," said Mr. Morris, "My family's been making pilau forever. You can make it with game birds, duck, shrimp, fish, you name it. Pilau is most fun to make over a fire or at least outdoors. Great for hunting-shack meals and tailgating and fishing parties, that's where you see pilau most on these old plantations. That's how I like it best, cooked outdoors. My father taught me. You can slow-cook any kind of rice, but nothing is going to be as earthy, as nutty and delicious as the rice that belongs in this land."

4 slices thick-cut bacon

2 pounds chicken legs and thighs

Salt and pepper

4 tablespoons (½ stick) unsalted butter

1 cup finely chopped celery

1 red bell pepper, minced

1 yellow onion, minced

2 cups long-grain rice, preferably Carolina Gold

4 cups chicken broth or water

1 teaspoon to 1 tablespoon Worcestershire sauce

¼ cup green onions, minced

1. Fry the bacon in a skillet until crisp. Remove the bacon and drain on paper towels. Keep 3 tablespoons of the bacon fat, discard the rest and return the fat to the skillet to medium heat. Season the chicken pieces with salt and pepper. Add half the butter to the bacon fat and brown the chicken on each side, about 5 minutes per side.

2. Add the celery, bell pepper, and onion and continue to cook for 5 minutes, until the vegetables become fragrant. Add the rice and stir to coat each grain. Add the chicken broth or water, then cover and reduce heat to low and cook undisturbed for 20 minutes, until liquid is absorbed.

3. Add the Worcestershire to taste and whisk in the remaining cold butter. Crumble the bacon and use it to garnish the dish, along with the green onions.

SERVES 6 TO 8

LEE NAKAMURA'S MATSUTAKE GOHAN
Mushroom Rice

Lee Nakamura is co-owner with partner Larry Fujita of the Tokyo Fish Market, a Berkeley institution since 1963. He likes to serve matsutake gohan—a simple dish of matsutake mushrooms and rice—with salmon and his miso slather (page 240). These mushrooms are as highly prized in Japan as truffles are in France, and as expensive. They are somewhat less expensive in the United States, where they are found in abundance in the Pacific Northwest.

1½ cups short- or medium-grain Japanese rice

3 ounces matsutake (or any fresh wild) mushrooms

1 tablespoons shoyu (Japanese soy sauce)

1 tablespoons sake

1½ teaspoons mirin

¼ teaspoon kosher salt

½ teaspoon bonito flakes

1. Wash the rice thoroughly in cold water, changing the water until it runs clear. Drain the rice in a colander and set aside for 30 minutes.

2. Meanwhile clean and slice the mushrooms.

3. Mix together the soy sauce, sake, and mirin, and add enough water to make 3 cups.

4. Transfer the rice to a heavy-bottomed pot and add the liquid, mushrooms, salt, and bonito flakes. Bring to a boil over high heat. Lower the heat, cover the pot, and simmer until all the water has been absorbed, about 20 minutes.

5. Remove pan from heat and let rest for 10 to 15 minutes before serving.

SERVES 6

MARTINA ROSSI KENWORTHY'S
RISOTTO AI FUNGHI PORCINI

Martina Rossi Kenworthy, who was born in Bologna, Italy, has lived in New York for more than twenty-seven years. Before she arrived, she really hadn't spent any time in the kitchen, since others did the cooking in her childhood home. But "I must have absorbed so much from mothers, nannies, or grandmothers. I knew that if you can't get exceptional ingredients, you might as well not cook." This posed a major problem when she was hungry for risotto. The high quality, short-grained Carnaroli or Nano rice that is essential was impossible to find, even in New York City. She and her friend Beatrice Ughi got so sick of hearing each other complain about the lack of fresh, nutty-tasting Nano rice that they formed Gustiamo, an import company. "It's easy, but not simple. We made risotto perhaps a thousand times in the kitchen at our warehouse and realized a few things. You have to make your own chicken broth, you have to use good rice (Carnaroli and Vialone Nano are the best available commercially today), and stir often, but not obsessively. Always turn off the heat before you think the rice is finished. It will keep cooking. The final risotto should be creamy and shiny and impossible to resist."

2 ounces dried porcini mushrooms

6 cups homemade chicken broth, plus more if needed

2 tablespoons (¼ stick) unsalted butter

1 small onion, finely chopped

2 cups Carnaroli rice

½ cup Cognac

½ cup freshly grated Parmigiano-Reggiano cheese

2 tablespoons chopped fresh parsley

Sea salt and freshly ground black pepper

1. Pour 1 cup of lukewarm water over the mushrooms and soak for half an hour. Lift the mushrooms out of the soaking liquid and chop. Reserve the soaking liquid. Bring the chicken broth to a light simmer in a saucepan. Cover and keep hot.

2. Melt the butter in a heavy-bottomed pot over medium heat. Add the onion and cook, stirring frequently, until soft and translucent but not browned, 3 to 4 minutes. Add the rice and stir with a wooden spoon over high heat until toasted and opaque, about 3 minutes. Add the Cognac, stir well, and let evaporate completely.

3. Reduce the heat to medium-low and start adding a couple of ladles of hot chicken broth. Continue adding the broth one ladle at a time, waiting until the liquid is absorbed before adding more. Stir gently between each addition.

4. Add the mushrooms to the rice when it has cooked, about 10 minutes. Stir, taste, season with salt, and continue adding broth. If necessary, add the mushroom liquid. Very old rice will require more liquid, fresh rice will require less.

5. Cook until the rice is tender yet still a little al dente, 15 to 20 minutes longer after adding the mushrooms. Turn off the heat, stir in the Parmigiano, parsley, and salt and pepper to taste. Cover the pot and let rest for 5 minutes before serving.

SERVES 4 TO 6

Julie Shafer's Risotto with Lemon and Asparagus

Julie Shafer isn't sure who taught her to make risotto. As soon as she was old enough to hold a spoon her grandmother, mother, or one of her aunts would stand her on a chair so she could stir the rice. "Many people view risotto as something fancy, when it's really just a staple of Italian cooking," she says. Using these basic instructions with seasonal ingredients, she can make a variety of risotto dishes, such as risotto Milanese, primavera, pesce, funghi, and quattro formaggi. In California, the asparagus season begins in late winter and extends through the spring, which is when she makes this version.

2 lemons

2 small bundles asparagus

1 medium yellow onion, finely chopped

2 teaspoons unsalted butter

2 tablespoons olive oil

2 cups Arborio or Carnaroli rice

2 to 3 quarts homemade chicken broth or low-sodium store-bought chicken broth, heated

Finely grated Parmesan cheese

1. Grate the lemon zest, juice the lemons, and strain the juice.

2. Peel the asparagus, cutting off the woody ends. Cut the spears into 1-inch lengths and steam to al dente.

3. Cook the onion in the butter and olive oil in a large saucepan over medium heat until they are transparent and fragrant, 5 to 10 minutes. Add the rice and stir until grains are almost clear, 5 to 10 minutes.

4. Keeping the broth on a low boil, ladle 1 to 1½ cups into rice. Stir constantly, until liquid is just about absorbed. Continue adding broth in the same manner, until rice is creamy and almost al dente. (You may not need all the broth.)

5. Stir in the lemon zest, lemon juice, and asparagus with one last ladle of broth. Cook for 1 minute.

6. Take the pan off the heat and add finely grated Parmesan to taste. Cover with a lid or foil. Let sit for 5 minutes before serving.

SERVES 8

Ms. Pina's Cape Verdean Jagacida

Colleen Pina-Garron's maternal and paternal grandparents emigrated from Cape Verde in the early 1900s. Like thousands of others who left the island off the northwest coast of Africa, they came to New Bedford to work in the textile mills and lived in Bay Village, a project that more closely resembled a village in Cape Verde than it did low-income housing.

"I remember watching one grandmother walking through the projects carrying groceries on her head," said Ms. Pina-Garron. "My grandmothers only cooked Cape Verdean, but they insisted that English be spoken at the table, pushed their children to excel in school, flew an American flag, and lived to see their progeny flourish."

It wasn't until she was teaching middle school in 1984 that Ms. Pina-Garron realized that lots of "nos con nos" had been lost along the way. Roughly translated, the Creole phrase means "the us within us," and denotes Cape Verdeans' cultural soul. Appointing herself the keeper of the Cape Verdean flame, Ms. Pina-Garron, along with her husband, Christopher Garron, began working as a disc jockey and playing Cape Verdean music at parties in New Bedford. She also began gathering recipes—first from the twenty-five thousand Cape Verdeans who live in New Bedford, then from the 350,000 others scattered across the United States.

Every Cape Verdean has their own recipe for jagacida, the traditional rice-and-bean dish that Cape Verdeans call "jag," and serve with fish stews.

4 tablespoons (½ stick) unsalted butter

1 large yellow onion, minced

½ teaspoon kosher salt

½ teaspoon freshly ground black pepper

¼ teaspoon sweet paprika

2 bay leaves

1 quart cold water

2 cups long-grain rice

1 cup cooked and cooled butter beans or lima beans

1. Melt the butter over medium heat in a pot with a close-fitting cover. Add the onion, season lightly with some of the salt and pepper, and stir. Add the paprika and bay leaves and cook over medium-low heat until the onion is soft, about 5 minutes.

2. Add the cold water, stir, and bring to a boil.

3. Stir in the rice and reduce the heat to the lowest possible level. Cover the pan and cook undisturbed for 20 minutes.

4. Add the beans to the top of the rice, cover, and cook for 5 minutes more.

5. Remove from the heat. Fluff the rice, cover again, and let it settle for at least 15 minutes. Uncover and gently stir in the beans.

SERVES 4

Claudette Eugene's Riz et Pois
Rice and Beans

On a day that seems way too hot for a slow-cooked, meaty meal, Claudette Eugene is cooking one anyway. "I cooked yesterday, I cook today, I will cook tomorrow," she says. "I cook every day. The food never stays."

In Haiti, a cook learns to match the heat of the day with the chiles in a meal, to deploy bitter and sweet flavors against the languor of humidity. And an intuitive cook like Ms. Eugene naturally melds the culinary patois of Haiti—a blend of African, Spanish, French, and British influences culled from tropical produce and spices like nutmeg, allspice, and annatto—in the kitchen. The kind of safety measures crucial in a tropical climate prompt the Haitian-born cook's habit of rinsing, marinating, rubbing, cooking, and recooking. Seasoning is added at each stage, and the flavor of the dish grows incrementally more complex. "It's the healthy way to cook," she says.

And yet something more than health simmers in the battered aluminum pots crowding the stove in her Brooklyn brownstone: a spirit that, for all her matter-of-factness, the Haitian cook is not unmindful of. It's odd, she muses, "when you cook, you only eat a little and feel satisfied. In a restaurant, you eat a lot and are still hungry."

½ pound dried red beans

8 whole cloves

1 garlic clove, chopped

Leaves from 1 sprig parsley, chopped

1 scallion, green and white parts, chopped

1 tablespoon vegetable oil

One 14-ounce can coconut milk

1½ teaspoons finely chopped Spanish onion

1 teaspoon adobo seasoning (preferably Goya)

¼ green bell pepper, stemmed, seeded, and thinly sliced

2 cups long-grain rice, rinsed

Kosher salt and freshly ground black pepper

1. Place the beans and cloves in a medium pot and cover with water by 2 inches. Bring to a boil, lower the heat, and simmer until very tender, about 1 hour. Drain the beans, reserving the liquid. Add enough water to the liquid to equal 1 quart.

2. Meanwhile, with a mortar and pestle, mash the garlic, parsley, and scallion into a paste to create "picalese."

3. Heat the oil over high heat in a large kettle with a tight-fitting lid. Add the picalese and cook, stirring, until fragrant, about 45 seconds. Add the beans, coconut milk, and onion and cook, covered, for 3 minutes, stirring occasionally. Stir in the reserved liquid and the adobo, reduce the heat to low, and cook, covered, for 25 minutes.

4. Stir in the bell pepper and bring to a boil. Stir in the rice and cook, covered, until tender, about 25 minutes more.

5. Season with salt and pepper to taste. Transfer to a serving bowl and serve immediately.

———

SERVES 6

RITA PELLEGRINI'S WILD AND BROWN RICE SALAD

Rita Pellegrini was born in Brazil and spent the first decade of her working life on cruise ships. She settled in Seattle with her husband, and now says that the best thing about being on solid ground is being able to cook in her own kitchen. There are fewer than a quarter-million Brazilian-born nationals living in the United States and this may explain why she "keeps company" with Brazil by cooking with the fresh fruit juices that are so popular there.

Ms. Pellegrini's parents were, she says "macrobiotic hippy people"—wild or brown rice was a regular part of her diet. Her own wild rice salad uses fresh carrot-orange juice along with pineapple, watermelon-mint, and ginger juices.

1 quart water

¾ cup wild rice

¼ cup long-grain brown rice

1 sprig fresh thyme (optional)

Kosher salt

⅓ cup fresh orange-carrot juice, or plain orange juice

1 celery stalk, finely chopped

1 large carrot, peeled and finely chopped

¼ cup dried cranberries

¼ cup shelled pistachios, toasted

1 tablespoon vegetable oil

Freshly ground black pepper

4 cups lightly packed arugula leaves, for garnish (optional)

1. In a large saucepan, combine the water, wild rice, brown rice, thyme, if using, and ½ teaspoon salt, and bring to a boil over medium-high heat. Cover, reduce the heat to medium-low, and cook about 40 minutes, until tender. Drain the rice, transfer to a large bowl, and cool to room temperature. Discard the thyme sprig.

2. Stir the orange-carrot juice, celery, carrot, cranberries, pistachios, and oil into the rice. Season with salt and pepper to taste.

3. Divide the salad among four plates, garnish with the arugula, if using, and serve.

SERVES 4

Ann Green's Red Beans and Rice

ABEND, LOUISIANA

Early tavern owners used to set an extra place at the table in case an unexpected traveler needed a hot meal. In Louisiana, having extra food on the stove is a similar gesture. "I don't know what it is to cook a small meal," says Ann Green. "I always cook enough for ten or fifteen people on the weekend. Normally, at the end of the day there is nothing left if you have people dropping in."

Born and reared in Convent, Louisiana, the seat of St. James Parish, Ms. Green learned to cook from her mother. "When I was growing up you had to learn to cook. My uncle made me a little stool to stand at the stove and cook. If you didn't do it right, you stood there until you did."

Ms. Green grew up in a family of seven children. Her daddy earned fifty-seven dollars a week, which bought staples such as bread, rice, beans, and a piece of meat. Red beans and rice was weekly fare, as was potato stew. "The main dish on Sunday was fried chicken with potato salad, sweet peas, and baked spaghettis," she says. "The next Sunday we would have stewed chicken. Chicken was expensive, so that was a Sunday dish. Monday meant beans and rice. My aunt went to her grave cooking chicken on Sunday and red beans and rice on Monday."

Some cooks season their red beans and rice with andouille sausage, salt pork, or ham hocks. Ms. Green's family uses pickled pork.

2 pounds red beans

2 cups diced onions

2 cups sliced green onions (scallions), green and white parts

1 cup diced celery

1 cup diced green bell pepper

1 pound Cajun pickled pork or other spicy pickled meat

5 pig tails, each cut into 4 pieces

½ pound smoked sausage, sliced thin

½ teaspoon baking powder

1 large cooking spoon lard

Kosher salt and cayenne pepper

Granulated garlic

½ cup chopped parsley

Cooked long-grain rice, for serving

1. Wash the beans, cover with cold water, and soak overnight in the refrigerator.

2. Drain beans and rinse in cold water. Place them in a 12-quart Dutch oven, then add enough water to cover them by 1 inch.

3. Add onions, 1½ cups of green onions, the celery, bell pepper, and meats.

4. Cook over medium-high heat about 2 hours, stirring occasionally to prevent scorching. (Add more boiling water to keep the beans covered.)

5. About an hour and a half into the cooking process, add the baking powder. The baking powder will foam. Reduce the heat to low and add the lard. (This makes the beans really creamy.)

6. Season to taste with salt, cayenne, and granulated garlic.

7. Stir in parsley and the remaining green onions. Serve over rice.

——

SERVES 10

RED BEANS AND RICELY YOURS

BORN IN ONE OF THE POOREST SECTIONS OF NEW ORLEANS, THE JAZZ LEGEND LOUIS Armstrong ate red beans and rice every day. "It really should not be hard for you to figure out my favorite dish to eat," he wrote a fellow New Orleans native. "We were all brought up eating the same thing and it's red beans and rice with ham hocks." Mr. Armstrong, who was also known as "Satchmo" (short for "satchel-mouth") and "Pops," was known to sign his letters "Red Beans and Ricely Yours."

Rajni Hatti's Rava Dosa
Cream of Wheat Pancakes

Charlestown, West Virginia, is not a hotbed of Indian culture, says Rajni Hatti, but ever since her husband's job brought them from Chicago to this outpost about an hour west of Washington, D.C., Ms. Hatti has been surprised by how interested her neighbors have been in learning her culture. She started teaching Indian cooking and even appeared on a local-access television show.

Ms. Hatti remembers waking up on weekend mornings to the smell of her mother cooking dosas. She learned much of what she knows in the kitchen from watching and helping her mother. "I guess a lot of it is that feeling of family, whether it was waking up to the smell of something cooking or getting together with all our family or just having a really good meal," she says. "For me the food and the family closeness go hand in hand."

The quintessential dish of South India, dosas are typically made by soaking, then grinding, rice and urad dal (split white lentils). To cut down on cooking and preparation time, Hatti has tweaked the recipe to use rava (farina or Cream of Wheat) and flour. Dosas are typically cooked on a tava (cast-iron griddle), but you can use a nonstick pan.

2 cups farina (preferably Cream of Wheat)

½ cup all-purpose flour

¼ cup grated fresh coconut

⅛ teaspoon baking soda

1½ teaspoons kosher salt

⅛ teaspoon red pepper flakes

1 tablespoon ground cumin

4 to 8 curry leaves, finely chopped (optional)

½ cup chopped cilantro

1 medium green serrano chile, finely chopped

1 cup plain low-fat yogurt

2¼ cups water

Vegetable oil

Coconut chutney or mango pickle, for serving

1. Put the farina, flour, coconut, baking soda, and salt in a blender or food processor and blend until the ingredients are fully combined, about 1 minute.

2. Pour the mixture in a large mixing bowl and stir in the red pepper flakes, cumin, curry leaves, if using, cilantro, chile, and yogurt.

3. Add the water gradually until the dough is a little thinner than the consistency of pancake batter. (You may need a little more or less water to achieve this consistency.) Cover and set aside for 30 minutes.

4. Heat a tava (cast-iron griddle) or large nonstick skillet over medium heat and lightly coat with oil. When the oil starts smoking a little (after 3 to 5 minutes), use a ladle to pour about ½ cup of batter onto the griddle and spread it into a thin layer, about a ⅛ inch thick.

5. Adjust the heat, if necessary, so that the batter sizzles while cooking but does not burn. When the underside of the dosa turns golden brown, drizzle a little oil on top and then flip it. Cook until golden brown spots appear on the bottom of the dosa. Serve immediately with coconut chutney or mango pickle.

SERVES 4

Joseppi's Farro "Risotto"

Farro is emmer wheat, an ancient Mediterranean variety said to have been the staff of life of pharaohs and legions. It is pearl-shaped and cooks a little like risotto and a little like barley. Joseppi Rossi's family moved to the United States from Israel, and farro was a staple of his home growing up. His mother makes farro salads in the summer, and Mr. Rossi, an accountant, makes this risotto-like dish in the fall, when root vegetables are beginning to show up at the farmers' market.

One Big Table

1 cup farro

½ cup olive oil

8 fresh sage leaves

1 quart homemade chicken broth or rich vegetable broth or low-sodium store-bought chicken or vegetable broth

1 yellow onion, peeled and thinly sliced

Kosher salt and freshly ground black pepper

1 cup white wine

1 celery stalk, diced small

1 carrot, peeled and diced small

1 cup cubed butternut squash, cut into ½-inch pieces

2 tablespoons roughly chopped fresh sage

½ cup grated Parmigiano-Reggiano cheese

1. If you are using farro with the bran intact, place the grain in a heavy plastic bag, place on the work surface, and bang it with a rolling pin two or three times to loosen the bran.

2. Place the farro in a small bowl, cover with cold water, and set aside for 1 hour.

3. About 1½ hours before you plan to serve the farro, pour 2 tablespoons of the olive oil in a small skillet over high heat. When hot but not smoking, add the sage leaves. Cook briefly on each side to crisp. Transfer to a paper towel–lined plate.

4. Bring the broth to a simmer in a small saucepan. Skim off and discard any chaff and hulls that may have risen to the top of the soaking farro. Drain the farro with a tea strainer, then in a colander.

5. Place a heavy-bottomed 4-quart pot over medium heat. Pour in the remaining olive oil and when it is hot, add the onion. Season lightly with salt and pepper. Cook, stirring often, until the onion is lightly browned, about 5 minutes.

6. Add the farro and stir to coat it with the oil. Stir in the wine and cook until it has all been absorbed.

7. Reduce the heat to the lowest possible setting and slowly begin adding ladles of broth, letting the farro absorb it between additions. Stir once between additions. Continue this process for about 45 minutes.

8. Gently stir in the celery, carrot, and squash. Cook, adding broth as needed, about 30 minutes more. The farro should fluff up to more than twice its size and be very tender.

9. Remove the pan from the heat and stir in the chopped sage. Add the cheese and beat vigorously for a few seconds until creamy. Add salt and pepper to taste. Divide between four bowls, garnish with fried sage leaves, and serve.

SERVES 4 AS A ROBUST FIRST COURSE
OR A SMALL MAIN COURSE

DALIA'S ISRAELI COUSCOUS

Dalia Levin grew up in Israel and met her American husband, Noah, while she was serving in the Israeli army. The Levins have been a member of a monthly gourmet club in Park City for years. This is the recipe that Mrs. Levin used to introduce Israeli couscous—a dense, pearl-shaped pasta that is about the size of a barley grain—to her club and it remains one of the favorites. It will not work with conventional couscous, but pearl barley or pastina can be substituted and cooked according to the instructions on their packages.

Harissa is a spicy paste, available in tubes and jars and, like Israeli couscous, is available online.

5 tablespoons olive oil

½ cup Israeli couscous

2½ cups homemade vegetable broth or
    low-sodium store-bought vegetable broth,
    or 2 vegetable bouillon cubes dissolved
    in 2½ cups water

6 ripe plum tomatoes, seeded and cut into
    ½-inch dice

Grated zest from ½ orange

¼ cup oil-cured black olives, pitted and minced

½ red bell pepper, minced

½ cup coarsely chopped pistachio or pine nuts

¼ cup chopped fresh flat-leaf parsley

¼ cup chopped fresh basil

Kosher salt and freshly ground black pepper

¼ to ½ teaspoon red pepper flakes or harissa

1 yellow onion, diced

2 garlic cloves, minced

2 medium zucchini, diced to make 2 to 3 cups

1. Heat 2 tablespoons of the olive oil in a small saucepan over medium heat. When hot, add the couscous and toast, stirring constantly, about 5 minutes. Add 2 cups of the broth, cover, and reduce the heat to low. Simmer until tender, about 6 minutes.

2. Drain in a colander, rinse under cold running water, and drain again.

3. In a large bowl, combine 1 tablespoon of the olive oil, the tomatoes, orange zest, olives, red bell pepper, pistachios, parsley, and basil. Season with salt and pepper and red pepper flakes or harissa to taste.

4. Pour the remaining 2 tablespoons olive oil into a large, deep skillet over medium heat. Add the onion and garlic and cook, stirring often, until wilted and almost translucent, about 5 minutes.

5. Add the zucchini and the remaining broth and cook for 2 minutes.

6. Add the couscous, stir, and cook for 2 minutes until the flavors are well combined. Adjust the seasoning with salt and black pepper. Partially cover and remove from heat.

7. Stir the tomato mixture into the couscous and serve immediately.

SERVES 4

Amber Waves of Grain

Gabrielle Arnold's Couscous

Gabrielle Arnold's family came from Spain and Venezuela and she grew up in the Northeast, but she considers herself a Floridian. "Every part of me is comfortable here. Florida is an extremely diverse place and it shaped me in the most important way: It made me curious about other people and culture." She travels to eat, and the cultures she discovers inevitably end up back in her kitchen where she responds to the ingredients she finds. "I'm all about improvisation, so there are very few things that I make twice. This recipe happens to be one of them." Ms. Arnold, an advertising copywriter, describes it as "Thanksgiving stuffing meets the Middle East. The fresh herbs make the couscous so aromatic that you can't help but eat it if you're within twenty-five to fifty feet of it. It makes a wonderful meal, is terrific with sliced chicken, and holds its own at picnics, potlucks, and buffets."

Handful of fresh sage leaves

Handful of fresh oregano leaves

10 to 12 sun-dried tomatoes or 8 oven-roasted tomatoes

2 shallots, peeled

¼ red onion, peeled

1 small garlic clove

5 tablespoons olive oil

Kosher salt and cracked black pepper

2 cups water

1½ cups instant couscous

¼ cup pine nuts or crumbled feta, for garnish

1. Chop up the sage and oregano. Set aside a small amount for garnish. Dice the tomatoes, shallots, onion, and garlic.

2. Pour 4 tablespoons of the olive oil into a medium skillet over medium heat. Add the chopped sage and oregano, the tomatoes, shallots, onion, and garlic, and cook, stirring frequently, until the onion is tender. Keep partially covered about half the time so all the juice doesn't evaporate. Add 1 teaspoon salt and cracked black pepper to taste.

3. Bring the water to a boil in a medium saucepan. Add the remaining 1 tablespoon olive oil, ½ teaspoon salt, and the couscous. Cover and remove the pot from the burner right away. Keep covered for 5 minutes. When the water is fully absorbed, fluff the couscous with a fork.

4. Toast the pine nuts: Cover the bottom of a small skillet evenly with the nuts (no oil is required). Cook over medium-low heat (no higher!) and toss them around constantly until they're browned on all sides. Be vigilant: They burn easily.

5. Add the herb and tomato mixture to the couscous. Season with a little extra pepper and another dash of salt and/or olive oil if you like. Toss *really* well to remove all clumps. Top with the pine nuts or feta cheese and the fresh herbs. Toss again and serve.

SERVES 4

Vito Zingarelli's Remarkable Peasant Pasta

Vito Zingarelli says: "My father was a carpenter, and my brothers and I always worked with him. We spent a lot of time visiting relatives in New York and New Jersey—that's where I fell in love with theater. With all my construction experience, I ended up on the production side and eventually became a stage manager. I came to Whidbey to take a break, and it was home right away. After a year of creating dinners to introduce Seattle chefs to the farmers on Whidbey, I got lucky and was offered a position at Hedgebrook, the forest retreat for women writers. The position combines the things that I care most about: serious food and serious art. We grow our own fruits and vegetables and use them to make the meals that the residents share every night.

"A few years ago, I noticed that some of the residents had begun to talk about wheat intolerance and I started fooling around using spelt flour to make pasta. I found that the fine-ground spelt pastry flour makes a smooth, silky pasta that is virtually indistinguishable from wheat flour pasta. The key to this dish is soaking the noodles in the sauce. I call it 'slaking,' which is what bricklayers call it when they add just the right amount of water to cement to get a perfectly smooth, satiny texture."

FOR THE PASTA

2¼ to 2½ cups fine-milled spelt pastry flour, plus more for kneading and cutting

½ teaspoon kosher salt

3 large eggs

FOR THE PEASANT SAUCE

1 cup olive oil

4 medium onions, cut in half and sliced in ⅛-inch slices

Red pepper flakes

1 cup dry, not oil-packed, sun-dried tomatoes

Boiling water

1 cup oil-cured olives, pitted and cut into thirds

2 teaspoons dried oregano or 1 teaspoon fresh

Kosher salt and freshly ground black pepper

Freshly grated pecorino Romano cheese, for serving

1. To make the pasta: Pour 2 cups of the flour into a large bowl. Stir in the salt. Make a well in the center and crack the eggs into it. Stir with a fork to combine. Sprinkle in additional flour, if necessary, to achieve a soft, nonsticky dough. Sprinkle more flour on a work surface, turn out the dough, and knead it until it is smooth, about 10 minutes. Cover with a clean kitchen towel and let rest at room temperature for 30 minutes.

2. Line a baking sheet with a kitchen towel. Cut and shape the dough into six balls. Working with one ball of dough at a time and keeping the others covered, lightly flour the work surface and roll out a ball of dough to a sheet ⅛ inch thick. Using a hand-cranked pasta machine or a very sharp knife, cut the sheet into strips ½ inch to ¾ inch wide to create linguine or fettuccine noodles. Transfer the noodles to the baking sheet and cover with another clean towel. (It's all right if the noodles are tangled; they will come apart when they cook.) Repeat with the remaining dough.

3. To make the peasant sauce: Pour the olive oil into a skillet large enough to contain the pasta and the sauce. Warm the oil over medium-low heat, then add the onions and 1 teaspoon red pepper flakes (or to taste). Cover and cook, stirring occasionally, until the onions have exuded their liquid but are still pale, about 30 minutes.

4. Meanwhile, cover the sun-dried tomatoes with boiling water. Let them soak for 15 minutes, then drain and reserve the liquid.

5. When the onions are completely cooked (they should be soft and translucent, not browned), stir in the olives, tomatoes, and oregano. Cover and remove from the heat.

6. Bring a large pot of well-salted water to a boil. Add the pasta and cook until extremely al dente. (The noodles need to be undercooked in order to absorb the liquid of the sauce.) Reserve about 1 cup of the pasta water, then drain the noodles and carefully pour them into the sauce.

7. Return the skillet to low heat. Add the reserved tomato water and stir. Cook uncovered for 5 to 10 minutes, until the pasta is tender, has absorbed as much sauce as possible, and is "slaked." Add some of the pasta water, if necessary, to keep a saucy consistency.

8. Taste and adjust the seasoning with salt, black pepper, and red pepper flakes. Serve immediately, with grated Romano cheese on the side.

MAKES ABOUT 1 POUND NOODLES,
SERVES 4 TO 6

Jesse Kelly-Landes's Flame-charred Red Pepper–Tomato Sauce

Ms. Kelly-Landes added a hint of Texas smokiness to create a toothsome pasta sauce that is delicious on her gnocchi (see recipe page 662) as well as in lasagna or with dried pasta. This recipe makes enough for one pound of pasta.

One 28-ounce can whole peeled plum tomatoes, with juice

5 tablespoons (⅝ stick) unsalted butter

1 medium yellow onion, peeled and halved

1 small red bell pepper

Kosher salt

1. Chop the tomatoes and combine with their juices, the butter, and onion halves in a medium saucepan.

2. Place over medium heat and bring to a simmer. Cook, uncovered, at a very slow but steady simmer, about 30 minutes.

3. Meanwhile, put the pepper on a cooking fork and hold over the stove burner, turning frequently, until it's black and blistered.

4. Put the pepper in a plastic container, cover tightly, and let sit about 10 minutes. Remove the pepper and gently pull off the skin. Don't use any water; just rub the pepper in a clean kitchen towel.

5. Core the pepper and remove the seeds and stem. Chop the pepper and add it to the sauce. Stir occasionally, breaking up any large pieces of tomato. Taste and add salt as needed.

6. Remove from the heat, discard an onion half, and puree the sauce in a blender. Return to the saucepan to reheat. If it's slightly watery, cook for a few minutes to thicken.

MAKES ABOUT 3 CUPS

Amber Waves of Grain

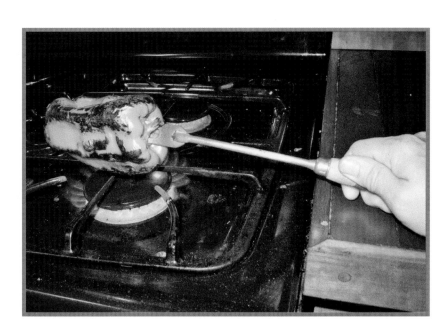

ALI REA-BAUM'S PASTA
WITH RED WINE AND MUSHROOM SAUCE

DAVIS, CALIFORNIA

"I started cooking from Marcella Hazan's cookbooks with my mother when I was ten years old, and pasta may be the first thing I ever fell in love with. I fell in love with painting not that long after," said Ali Rea-Baum, an art historian. The 27-year-old self-taught cook says that her two loves are deeply connected—"You can't know art history without knowing Italy, and you can't spend much time in Italy without being exposed to some incredible pasta"—and the improvisational nature of making pasta for dinner is, to her, akin to making a little bit of art. This particular sauce is wonderful on a cool night, and shiitake mushrooms can be substituted for their wild cousins.

¼ cup olive oil

2 tablespoons butter

2 medium yellow onions, minced to equal 3 cups

¼ teaspoon salt, plus more to taste

Freshly ground black pepper, to taste

2 garlic cloves, minced

¼ cup highest quality balsamic vinegar

2 cups white mushrooms, sliced

2 cups wild mushrooms such as porcini, hen of the woods, or candy cap, fresh or dried, sliced thin

2 cups high quality Barolo wine

2 teaspoons minced flat-leaf parsley

1 pound linguine

1. Warm the olive oil and half the butter in a skillet over medium-low heat. Add the onions. Season lightly with salt and freshly ground black pepper and cook, stirring frequently, until soft, about 5 minutes. Add the garlic, stir, and continue cooking until the onions are lightly caramelized, about 10 minutes more. Add the balsamic vinegar, turn heat to high, and cook, stirring constantly, until the vinegar is evaporated. Reduce heat to medium and add the mushrooms. Season lightly with salt and pepper and stir. Cook for 5 minutes.

2. Add the red wine, partially cover, and continue cooking until the mushrooms are tender, about 10 minutes. Meanwhile, cook the pasta in well-salted boiling water until tender and drain. Taste the sauce and adjust seasoning with additional salt and pepper if desired. Stirring vigorously, add the reminaing butter. Add the drained pasta, toss, and serve, with grated Parmesan on the side, if desired.

SERVES 4 AS A MAIN COURSE,
6 AS A FIRST COURSE

Bessie's Short Rib Ragu

"My father worked the rodeo, my mother was rodeo queen and later she cooked for the crew. We lived on the road until I was twelve," says Bessie Oakley Klose, a silversmith and mother of three who is "a decent barrel racer" and a darned fine cook. "My father said we were related to Annie Oakley, but he said a lot of things and they weren't all true. I didn't care. I loved listening to his stories. I have this memory of sitting around a campfire, eating macaroni and meat sauce, not meatballs, not ground beef, really rich meat sauce. My mother said she used to make sauce from short ribs and I more or less put this recipe together in their memory after they died, though believe me they never heard of Pinot Noir. I like to use long fusilli, it sucks up the sauce real good. This works great in a Dutch oven over a fire or buried in the ground, too. It's just right for that sort of cooking."

1 to 2 cups all-purpose flour

1 tablespoon kosher salt, plus more to taste

1 teaspoon freshly ground black pepper

2 tablespoons canola oil

4 pounds short ribs, each cut across the bone into 2 inch segments

4 small carrots, cut into ¼-inch dice

2 celery stalks, strings removed, cut into ¼-inch dice

1 medium onion, cut into ¼-inch dice

2 medium shallots, minced

1 bottle pinot noir or cabernet

1 dried bay leaf

2 juniper berries

1 sprig fresh rosemary

5 sprigs fresh thyme

2 sprigs fresh flat-leaf parsley

2 teaspoons tomato paste

1 cup high-quality canned tomatoes

6 garlic cloves

4 cups veal or beef stock, homemade or low-sodium canned

1. Preheat the oven to 250°F. Place a medium flameproof casserole over medium-low heat. Season the flour with salt and pepper. Add the oil and when it is very hot, drag the meat through the flour to dust on all sides, shake off excess, and, working in batches, brown slowly on all sides 5 to 6 minutes per side. Remove and set aside. Add half of the carrots, celery, onion, and shallots to the casserole, and cook over medium heat, stirring occasionally, until the vegetables are soft and golden, about 3 minutes. Add the red wine, bay leaf, juniper berries, rosemary, thyme, and parsley, scrape the bottom of the pan to incorporate all the bits of meat and flour, reduce heat to low, and simmer until the wine has reduced to about 1 cup, about 20 minutes.

2. Add the tomato paste and tomatoes, stir, and simmer for 3 minutes. Add the garlic and the meat stock and simmer for 30 minutes until reduced by half. Strain, discard the aromatics, and wipe out the casserole. Return the strained liquid to the casserole and return to low heat. Add the remaining half of all the vegetables and the meat. Stir to combine. Taste and adjust seasoning lightly with salt and black pepper. Cover and place in the oven for 4 to 5 hours, until the meat is falling from the bones and the sauce is bubbling. Remove from the oven, adjust seasoning with salt and pepper to taste, and set aside.

3. Boil 1 pound of pasta, preferably wide noodles such as pappardelle, in well-salted water. Drain and toss with the sauce. Serve immediately.

SERVES 4

Cookie Rooney's
Pesto and Green Bean Pasta

FRANKLIN LAKES, NEW JERSEY

"I was the oldest of eleven children from a big Italian family, and the first thing I cooked was pasta. I was about nine, my mother was pregnant and not feeling well, and I told her I'd make dinner. So I ran back and forth from the kitchen to the bedroom and made pasta fagioli," said Angela "Cookie" Rooney, a real estate agent. "With a family that size, the secret is 'stretching.' I learned a lot about how to stretch things from my mother, adding green beans and potatoes to pesto is a good example. I've added tuna, chicken, tomatoes. But my secret ingredient is lemon zest. It brightens everything."

4 medium red-skinned potatoes, cut into 1-inch dice

¼ cup extra-virgin olive oil, plus more for potatoes

Salt and freshly ground pepper to taste

2 garlic cloves, peeled and coarsely chopped

1½ teaspoons kosher salt, plus more to taste

3 cups fresh basil leaves

¼ cup pine nuts

¾ cup freshly grated Parmesan cheese

¼ cup freshly grated pecorino cheese

Grated zest of ½ lemon

1 teaspoon fresh lemon juice, plus more to taste

1 pound dried fettuccine

2 cups green beans

1. Preheat the oven to 400°F. Place the potatoes in a bowl. Add 1 to 2 tablespoons olive oil, season lightly with salt and pepper, and set aside for 30 minutes. Meanwhile, place the garlic, 1 teaspoon kosher salt, and 1 cup basil in a food processor and pulse until chopped. Add the remaining basil and process until chopped. Add the pine nuts, cheeses, and ¼ cup olive oil and process until the mixture forms a smooth paste. Remove to a bowl, fold in the lemon zest and juice, adjust seasoning with additional salt and black pepper if desired, and set aside.

2. Place the potatoes in an even layer on a baking sheet and bake, turning several times, until golden and tender, 7 to 10 minutes. Remove from the oven and cool while the pasta cooks.

3. Cook the pasta in a large pot of well-salted boiling water, according to the directions on the package. Steam the green beans until tender and set aside. When the pasta is tender, drain, reserving 1 cup of the cooking water and transfer to a large bowl. Add the pesto sauce and toss, adding pasta cooking water as needed to get a smooth sauce. Add the potatoes and green beans, season with additional salt and black pepper to taste, and serve.

SERVES 4

Nico's Bucatini with Dandelion Greens, Garlic, and Ricotta Salata

"My grandfather moved from Sicily to New Jersey," says Nick Gagliotti, a cabinetmaker. "My father moved us all to Vermont the spring I turned three years old. The first thing my grandfather did was strap a basket on his back, take me by the hand, and walk me into the woods. We came back with about a bushel of wild garlic (ramps) and then he walked up and down our road digging up people's dandelions. My grandfather, who was quite the character, said it was his public service. My best memories are of being in the woods with him, gathering things to cook. It usually took about an hour to fill up his basket. The rest of the time we spent smoking and playing cards and drinking wine from this little pouch he carried. I use regular garlic if there isn't any wild around and watercress or arugula if the dandelions aren't tender and right. It's all good."

1 pound bucatini

¼ cup olive oil

2 garlic cloves, smashed

½ teaspoon minced fresh chile or ¼ teaspoon red pepper flakes

1 pound small, tender dandelion leaves, well rinsed and cut into ½ inch ribbons

Salt and freshly ground black pepper

1 cup freshly grated ricotta salata or other tangy fresh cheese

1. Bring a large pot of well-salted water to a boil. Add the pasta, stir well, and boil until tender, about 7 minutes or according to package directions.

2. Meanwhile, warm the olive oil in a deep skillet over medium heat. Add the garlic and cook until almost gold, about 3 minutes. Remove from the heat. When the pasta is almost done, return to high heat add the chile and dandelions. Stir-fry to barely wilt the leaves.

3. Drain the pasta and toss with the dandelion mixture. Season lightly with salt and pepper, if desired. Add the cheese, toss quickly, and serve immediately.

SERVES 6 AS AN APPETIZER,
4 AS A MAIN COURSE

DIDI REA'S FAVORITE PASTA

Didi Rea, a talent manager in Hollywood, heard a client describing a dish similar to this nearly a decade ago. "I was recently divorced, had just discovered that my inheritance had evaporated under the hand of a money manager, and I was broke," said Ms. Rea, who grew up on Park Avenue in New York City. "This was the moment when Didi Debutante, Downwardly Mobile was born. I hadn't worked a paying job in years, I honestly didn't know how I was going to keep meals on the table and tuitions paid. I overheard someone describing this dish and thought it sounded yummy and knew it was cheaper than Spago. I tried it a few times and knew when I'd gotten the balance right because my girls, who are normal eaters, inhaled it. Zucchini pasta was a building block in the life we've built together. Chocolate cake helps, too."

1 pound pasta (preferably farfalle or radiatorre)

4 tablespoons high quality olive oil

4 large garlic cloves, chopped

2 to 2½ pounds fresh zucchini, sliced into ¼-inch disks

2 teaspoons kosher salt, plus more to taste

Freshly ground black pepper to taste

½ cup freshly grated Parmesan cheese

1. Bring a large pot of salted water to boil. Add the pasta and stir. While the pasta is cooking, place a large skillet over medium heat and add the olive oil. Sauté the garlic, stirring frequently, until it is translucent, 3 to 4 minutes. Add the zucchini and cook until it is soft and browned, season with salt and freshly ground black pepper.

2. When the pasta is tender, drain it, reserving a cup of the cooking water. Toss the pasta with the zucchini, along with the Parmesan cheese and enough of the reserved pasta liquid to create a creamy consistency. Serve, with additional cheese on the side.

SERVES 4 TO 6

Barbara Urban's
Fresh Tomato and Peas Pasta

Barbara Urban's great-grandfather moved from Sicily to Toledo, Ohio, in the 1920s when the Italian community there was burgeoning. This was thanks, in part, to its butchering industry and the National School of Meat Cutting, as well as its proximity to the "Hooch Highway" that ran south from the Canadian border during Prohibition and brought gangsters like Al Capone to town. "Like everyone who came, his wife brought seeds from her family's tomatoes. She told me that the first thing you have to do to make a great red sauce is plant the tomatoes. This was one of her recipes. We make it a lot in the fall when we are canning and drying tomatoes."

1 pound linguine

¼ cup olive oil

3 shallots, sliced very thin

2 garlic cloves, sliced very thin

1 carrot, peeled and diced

1 plum tomato, peeled, seeded, and diced

Kosher salt and freshly ground black pepper

¼ cup tomato paste

½ teaspoon dried oregano

1 teaspoon minced fresh parsley

1½ cups cooked and cooled fresh peas or thawed frozen

½ cup freshly grated Parmesan cheese

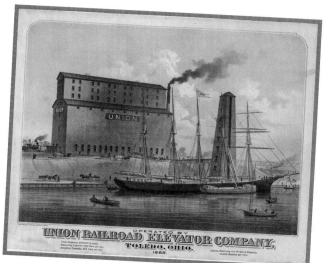

1. Bring a large pot of well-salted water to a boil over high heat. Add the linguine, stir, and cook until tender, 8 to 10 minutes, or according to package directions. When done, drain the pasta, reserving about 1 cup of the cooking water.

2. While the pasta is cooking, place a large skillet over medium heat. Pour in the olive oil and when it is warm, add the shallots and garlic. Cook, stirring frequently, until the vegetables begin to soften and become fragrant, about 3 minutes. Add the carrots, tomato, 1 teaspoon salt, and pepper to taste and cook until tender, 8 to 10 minutes.

3. Stir the tomato paste and ½ cup of the pasta water into the vegetables. Add the oregano, parsley, and pasta and stir. Add the peas and cheese and stir. Add more pasta water if necessary to coat the pasta nicely. Season with additional salt and pepper to taste, and serve immediately.

SERVES 4 TO 6

CHESTER AARON'S VERY GARLIC PASTA

I n 1997, retired college professor and author of *Garlic Is Life* (a memoir!) Chester Aaron had eighty varieties of garlic growing on his four-acre plot in Occidental, California. He credited garlic for his vitality and recites the names of his most beloved varieties—Red Toch, French Messadrone, Spanish Roja—as other artists might summon the muse. It is a passion that he inherited from his father, a Russian immigrant and Pennsylvania farmer who ate raw garlic like potato chips. Mr. Aaron continues to appraise the appearance, aroma, and taste of his bulbs with the dispassion of a sommelier. Some, he says, explode in the front of the mouth, others come alive later in the back. Some, like Xian garlic from China, are rich and mildly hot, while others, like Spanish Roja and Creole Red, are quite hot and tend to linger.

1 pound linguine

½ cup extra virgin olive oil

6 garlic cloves (preferable Spanish Roja or other hardneck garlic), minced

1 cup whole salted cashews

1 teaspoon kosher salt

1 teaspoon freshly ground black pepper

6 fresh basil leaves, shredded

1 tablespoon chopped fresh flat-leaf parsley

Freshly grated Parmesan cheese, for serving

1. Bring a large pot of well-salted water to a boil, add the linguine, and cook until tender, about 7 minutes or according to package directions.

2. While the pasta is cooking, heat the oil in a skillet over medium heat. Add the garlic and toss for 2 minutes, until lightly gold but not browned. Add the nuts and season with the salt and pepper.

3. Drain the pasta. Toss with the nut sauce. Add the basil and parsley and toss again. Adjust seasoning and serve with grated Parmesan cheese on the side.

SERVES 6

BETTY KELLER'S
CRISPY SHALLOT AND RICOTTA PASTA

The youngest of five boys, chef Thomas Keller was raised by a single mother, Elizabeth Marie "Betty" Keller, who managed restaurants in West Palm Beach, Florida. This spaghetti allowed her to feed her brood inexpensively and in a hurry. When Thomas was 16 and washing dishes at the Palm Beach Yacht Club, the club's chef quit and Thomas's mother told her son, "You are the chef." For nearly four decades, he's done his best to live up to her pronouncement and is the only chef in the United States to have two restaurants—The French Laundry in Yountville, California, and Per Se in New York City—that have earned the top Michelin star rating.

In this dish, that meant substituting fresh ricotta for the cottage cheese his mother used, creating a silky reduction sauce with butter, and including one ingredient—the tender shoots of sprouted cilantro—that was not in the 1960s culinary vocabulary and is still not common parlance.

659

Amber Waves of Grain

4 large shallots, peeled

½ cup all-purpose flour

Kosher salt and freshly ground black pepper

2¼ cups canola oil

2 sticks (½ pound) unsalted butter

1 teaspoon white wine vinegar

Stems from 4 sprigs parsley, rinsed and cut into ½-inch pieces

1 pound dried spaghetti

1⅓ cups ricotta cheese

2 tablespoons extra virgin olive oil

¼ cup finely minced flat-leaf parsley

30 cilantro shoots (young sprouts picked before leafing, optional)

1. Cut 2 of the shallots into ⅛-inch rings and set aside. Mince the remaining shallots and set aside. Put the flour into a pie plate. Season very lightly with salt and black pepper. Heat 2 cups of the canola oil in a small pot over medium heat until it registers 325°F on a deep-fry thermometer. Working in batches, toss the shallot rings in the flour to coat and shake off any excess. Fry in the oil, stirring gently, until golden brown, about

1½ minutes. Use a slotted spoon to transfer the fried shallots to paper towels to drain. Pat the rings slightly and set aside.

2. Heat the remaining ¼ cup canola oil in a large skillet over medium heat. Reduce the heat, add the chopped shallots, and cook, stirring frequently until they begin to caramelize, 3 to 4 minutes. Add the butter, vinegar, and 2 cups of water and simmer until the mixture is reduced by one-third, 15 to 20 minutes.

3. Meanwhile, bring a large pot of well-salted water to a boil. Place the parsley stems in a fine-mesh strainer, dunk into boiling water for 10 seconds, then cool completely under cold water. Add the spaghetti to boiling water and cook until al dente, 8 to 10 minutes, or according to package directions. Drain the spaghetti and add to the skillet with the shallot reduction. Add the cooked parsley stems, the ricotta, olive oil, and salt and pepper to taste and toss to combine. Divide the spaghetti among four warm bowls. Garnish with minced parsley, cilantro shoots, if using, and fried shallot rings. Serve immediately.

SERVES 4 AS A MAIN COURSE,
6 AS AN APPETIZER

Jack Czarnecki's Fabulous Fungi Pasta

DUNDEE, OREGON

In 1916, Jack Czarnecki's grandparents opened Joe's, a Polish workingman's bar in Reading, Pennsylvania. His parents put tablecloths on the tables and expanded the menu and Jack Czarnecki was named one of the top chefs in the country by the James Beard Society. Each generation foraged for mushrooms: morels and chanterelles, puffballs, hedgehogs, lobster mushrooms, candy caps, and porcini. But Mr. Czarnecki is obsessed with fungi: he got a degree in biology from the University of California at Davis, wrote three books, including *Joe's Book of Mushroom Cookery*, and moved to Oregon, where the foraging season is nearly year-round. And there are native black and white Oregon truffles. He established the Joel Palmer House in Oregon's wine country and dedicated himself to rehabilitating the public impression of Oregon truffles—"they've been maligned and misunderstood, mostly because they are picked and shipped before they are ripe," he says—and truffle oil. Until Mr. Czarnecki, no one in the United States had managed to infuse a light olive oil with a truffle in full bloom. Dishes such as this angel hair pasta in creamy mushroom sauce reach an entirely new level when finished with a drop or two of the extraordinary oil.

1 small shallot, finely chopped

1 cup dry white wine

1 cup milk

2 tablespoons fresh mascarpone or cream cheese

½ cup unsalted butter, at room temperature

2 cups clean wild mushrooms such as chanterelles, morels, candy caps, lobster mushrooms, or porcini, or white mushrooms, cleaned and sliced, if necessary

Salt and freshly ground white pepper to taste

1 tablespoon cognac

¼ cup shredded Parmesan cheese, plus up to 1 cup more for serving

1 pound angel hair pasta

8 ounces fresh lump dungeness crab, picked over

Oregon White Truffle Oil

1 fresh white Oregon truffle (optional)

1. Bring a large pot of salted water to a boil. Meanwhile, combine the shallot and white wine in a sauce pan over medium heat and cook until the liquid is reduced by half, about 5 minutes. Whisk in the milk and simmer gently for 5 minutes. Whisk in the mascarpone, remove from heat, and beat until smooth.

2. Melt the butter in a sauté pan over medium heat. When the butter is hot, add the mushrooms, season lightly with salt and black pepper, and cook, stirring constantly, until the mushrooms are tender. The time will vary depending on which varieties are used. Remove from the heat, add the cognac, stir, and add ¼ cup of the Parmesan cheese.

3. When the water boils, add the pasta and return the cheese sauce to medium-low heat. When it is warm, stir in the sautéed mushrooms. Taste and adjust seasoning. Add the crabmeat, stir gently, and continue cooking until just warm, about 2 minutes.

4. Drain the pasta, toss immediately with the sauce, add the white truffle oil and top with a shaved white truffle, if available. Serve immediately with additional Parmesan cheese on the side.

SERVES 6 AS A FIRST COURSE, 4 AS A MAIN COURSE

Barbara Damrosch's Winter Vegetable Pasta

Barbara Damrosch is a dark-eyed earth mother whose shingled farmhouse is flanked by extraordinary flower gardens. A landscape designer and the author of *The Garden Primer,* she and her husband, Eliot Coleman, a sustainable-farming expert, grow most of what they eat on their Four Season Farm and sell market vegetables and cut flowers and see themselves as revolutionary. He says: "What I do every day is the most radical thing possible. I address the cause of our troubled food system, not the symptom. The aspirin company wants you to treat your headache by taking aspirin; they don't want you to figure out that your hat is too tight. I show people how they can grow their lives and live beautifully without buying anything." They have movable, unheated greenhouses, and make creative use of cold weather vegetables. Ms. Damrosch says: "The key is cooking seasonally. But cooking with the seasons is like gardening, over time your relationship with nature becomes more collaborative. You learn to live in the moment, cook in the moment."

6 leeks, white and light green parts only

4 long carrots, peeled

1 large parsnip, peeled

4 cups shredded kale (rinsed, ribs removed, leaves cut into long, thin strips)

½ cup olive oil, plus more if desired

Kosher salt and freshly ground black pepper

1 pound linguine

Freshly grated pecorino Romano cheese, for serving

1. Bring a large pot of well-salted water to a boil.

2. Meanwhile, cut the leeks lengthwise into very thin strips. Soak in cold water, then drain in a colander, and rinse until all the grit is removed.

3. To cut the carrots and parsnip, hold the vegetable by the root end, and using a vegetable peeler, cut long thin strips, rotating the vegetable to remove the strips in an even pattern all the way around.

4. Pat the leeks dry and combine with the carrots, parsnip, and kale in a large Dutch oven or skillet.

Add the oil, ½ teaspoon salt, and ¼ teaspoon pepper, and toss to mix. Cut a circle of parchment paper to cover the vegetables, and place the pan over low heat. Cook until the vegetables are tender, 10 to 12 minutes.

5. While the vegetables are cooking, boil the linguine until tender, 10 to 12 minutes. Drain, reserving some of the cooking water.

6. Toss the pasta with the vegetables over low heat, adding pasta water if necessary to coat the noodles well. Taste and add more salt and pepper if desired. Serve immediately with grated Romano cheese on the side.

SERVES 6 AS A FIRST COURSE, 4 AS A MAIN COURSE

JESSE KELLY-LANDES'S
THREE-CHEESE GNOCCHI

AUSTIN, TEXAS

Jesse Kelly-Landes grew up in Georgetown, Texas. The daughter of an emergency room physician and a nurse and the granddaughter of Eastern European immigrants, she and her sister were outsiders. "My mother was Catholic, but my father was Jewish and in Georgetown that means you are different." They spent a lot of time at home, cooking with their mother. Ms. Kelly-Landes created these gnocchi with what she had on hand. They contain no potato, but are wonderful and light and a perfect counterpart to her roasted red pepper–tomato sauce, which was inspired by Marcella Hazan.

One Big Table

4 ounces chèvre, crumbled

6 ounces Bucheron, crumbled

¼ cup grated Gruyère

2 large eggs, lightly beaten

Kosher salt

½ teaspoon freshly ground black pepper

Slightly heaping ⅔ cup all-purpose flour

Flame-charred Red Pepper–Tomato Sauce (page 651)

1. Combine the cheeses, egg, 1 teaspoon salt, and pepper and mix well. Add the flour and mix with a fork just to combine. It should be a rather sticky dough.

2. Scoop small balls of dough with a spoon or melon baller and roll with your hands to form a tiny egg shape, about 1 inch long and ½ inch thick. Set aside in one layer on a parchment paper–lined baking sheet and cover with a clean kitchen towel.

3. Bring a large pot of salted water to a boil. Once you have a rolling boil, drop in the gnocchi. After they float to the top, cook for 1 to 2 minutes more, until tender.

4. Drain the gnocchi in a colander. Serve immediately with Roasted Red Pepper–Tomato Sauce.

SERVES 4 AS A FIRST COURSE

City Market, Austin, Texas, 1939.

Moonstone Farm's Squash-Filled Ravioli

MONTEVIDEO, MINNESOTA

In 1972, Audrey Arner and Richard Handeen, liberal arts graduates and refugees of the 1960s, went back to the land—the 240-acre piece of the Minnesota prairie that Mr. Handeen's great-grandparents homesteaded in 1872. Today, they raise grass-grazed cattle and lead a community of environmentalist farmers. In a life that's ruled by the seasons, winter is about making art, making music, and making pasta. Every year after Thanksgiving, four generations gather around the old pasta machine. Their favorite ravioli fillings use the ingredients they can find in their late-autumn garden: butternut squash and the last hardy arugula of the season. A double or triple batch is enough to freeze and serve for a big group of family and friends on Christmas Eve.

FOR THE PASTA DOUGH

4 large eggs

⅔ cup water

3½ cups semolina flour, plus more as needed (preferably Bob's Red Mill)

2 teaspoons fine sea salt

Melted butter, for brushing pasta

FOR THE FILLING

1½ cups cooked and pureed butternut squash

2 tablespoons melted butter

Pinch of ground nutmeg

Fine sea salt and freshly ground black pepper

1. To make the dough: Place the eggs and water in a 4-quart mixing bowl. Add the semolina flour and sea salt and stir until incorporated. Continue adding semolina, 2 tablespoons at a time, until you have a firm but pliable dough. Lightly flour a work surface. Knead the dough for 5 minutes, then place in a plastic bag or wrap in plastic and let rest at room temperature for at least 30 minutes. While the dough is resting, prepare the filling.

2. To make the butternut squash filling: Combine the squash, melted butter, nutmeg, and salt and pepper to taste in a medium bowl.

3. Divide dough into 24 pieces. Working with two pieces at a time and keeping the others covered, flatten each into a rectangle. Using a pasta machine, roll one piece of dough into a very thin sheet. Lay the sheet flat on a lightly floured work surface. Drop one of the fillings on the sheet by scant teaspoonfuls in two rows, spacing the mounds 1½ inches apart, for a total of 12 mounds per sheet. Brush the edges and between the mounds of filling lightly with melted butter. Roll out the second piece and cover with the second sheet, pressing down around the filling to seal. Using a pastry wheel or a knife, cut the pasta between filling, trimming the sides to form 1½- to 2-inch ravioli. Transfer the ravioli to a floured baking sheet. Repeat with the remaining dough and filling.

4. Let the ravioli dry for at least 30 minutes. To freeze, let dry overnight before freezing on baking sheets. Once frozen, they can be transferred to a heavy plastic bag and kept in the freezer for up to 6 weeks.

5. To cook the ravioli, bring a large pot of salted water to a boil. Working in batches of about 30 ravioli at a time, cook until tender, about 3 minutes. Lift out with a slotted spoon, drain, and serve with melted butter or the sauce of your choice.

MAKES ABOUT 144 RAVIOLI

Mama Fresina's Lasagna

"This is the most traditional lasagna recipe in the family. It must have come from Italy or maybe from God," says Phyllis Fresina, the matriarch of the pasta-making clan. "Somebody before me added the cottage cheese; that's America, not Italy. I made this dish a lot when my husband and I were young, but as time when on, people didn't want such a rich lasagna and I began adding more spinach and less meat. This is a great dish for a crowd. You can make it a day ahead and put it out with bread and a salad and never think about cooking after the company arrives."

Kosher salt

1 pound lasagna noodles

¼ cup olive oil

2 pounds ground beef

Freshly ground black pepper

2 cups onions, diced

8 to 12 garlic cloves, minced, to measure ¼ cup

2 cups cooked spinach, drained (or frozen spinach, thawed, drained, and patted dry)

1 teaspoon dried oregano

2 teaspoons minced fresh parsley

2 teaspoons minced fresh basil or 1 teaspoon dried

Two 6-ounce cans tomato paste

Two 14-ounce cans high-quality tomato sauce

1 cup sliced white mushrooms

1 cup cottage cheese

1 cup ricotta cheese

2 cups shredded mozzarella cheese

1. Preheat the oven to 350°F. Bring a large pot of well-salted water to boil over high heat, add the lasagna noodles carefully, so as not to break, stir gently, and cook, stirring occasionally, until tender, about 10 minutes. Drain the noodles and cool completely under cold water. Toss the noodles with some of the olive oil to prevent them from sticking and set aside.

2. Place a Dutch oven over medium-high heat and brown the ground meat, stirring to break the meat up well, about 10 minutes. Season lightly with salt and pepper. Remove the meat and set aside, discarding the excess fat. Return the pot to medium heat. Add the olive oil and, when it is warm, add the onions and garlic, cook until soft, about 3 minutes. Stir in the spinach. Add the oregano, parsley, and basil, season with salt and pepper, toss to combine, and remove from the pot and set aside.

3. Reduce the heat to low and add the tomato paste to the pot. Cook, stirring constantly to dry and lightly brown the paste; this intensifies the flavor and brings out a toasty sweet note, but be very careful not to burn it. Add the tomato sauce to the paste and stir to combine. Stir in the onion and garlic mixture. Simmer for several minutes, add the mushrooms, and simmer for 15 minutes, stirring occasionally. Add the meat and stir well. Season with additional salt and pepper if desired.

4. Remove the pot from the heat and beat in the cottage cheese and then the ricotta to make a creamy tomato sauce.

5. Preheat the oven to 350°F. To assemble the lasagna, ladle a layer of sauce in the bottom of a 9 x 13-inch baking dish. Add a layer of noodles, then top with sauce and the shredded mozzarella. Repeat three times, leaving about ½ inch of space between the top of the lasagna and the edge of the pan to avoid overflow. Top with sauce and grated mozzarella and bake, uncovered, for 30 to 40 minutes, until bubbly.

———

SERVES 6 TO 8

Steamer loading grain from floating elevator, New Orleans.

Linda Fresina's Vegetable Lasagna

BATON ROUGE, LOUISIANA

Linda Crutchfield Fresina likes to say that she is "a hundred percent Italian by marriage," a claim that no one who has eaten her cooking would dispute. She learned how to cook from her mother-in-law, and when it became clear that she was more than qualified to carry the family cooking torch, she began to adapt recipes to a world that wants more vegetables than beef. This lasagna is like a late summer garden in a pan and is wonderful made the day before serving.

2 eggplants, cut into bite-size cubes to measure 16 cups

2 tablespoons kosher salt, plus more as necessary

10 zucchini, cut into bite-size cubes

2 yellow onions, diced

2 red bell peppers, pith and seeds removed, cut into bite-size pieces

1 cup olive oil

1 teaspoon freshly ground black pepper

⅛ teaspoon cayenne pepper or chili pepper sauce, plus more to taste

1 pound lasagna noodle, or "Elene Piccolla" noodles

1 pound ricotta, or more to taste

1 large egg

1 cup heavy cream

1 teaspoon minced garlic

⅛ teaspoon nutmeg

2 cups fresh artichoke hearts or oil-marinated artichoke hearts

6 cups Flame-charred Red Pepper–Tomato Sauce (page 651)

1 cup oil-cured black olives, pitted and chopped

1 cup freshly grated Parmesan

2 pounds fresh mozzarella, sliced thinly

1. Preheat the oven to 350°F. Place the eggplant in a colander in the sink, sprinkle with salt, and allow to drain for 30 minutes. Rinse the eggplant under cold water and pat dry. Place the eggplant, zucchini, onions, and bell peppers in a large bowl, add the olive oil, and toss. Season lightly but thoroughly with salt, freshly ground black pepper, and cayenne to taste and set aside for half an hour.

2. Spread the vegetables in a single layer on baking sheets and bake, stirring occasionally, for 1 hour. Remove from the oven and place all the vegetables in a large bowl to cool. Leave the oven on. While the vegetables are cooling, bring a large pot of well-salted water to boil and cook noodles according to the directions on the package, drain, and cool completely under cold water and set aside.

Street vendor for Italian feast, 1908.

3. Combine the ricotta, egg, cream, garlic, and nutmeg in a mixing bowl, beat until smooth, and set aside. If using fresh artichoke hearts, clean them, slice thinly, and steam until tender. Cool and set aside. If using oil-marinated artichoke hearts, drain them well and pat dry. Place all the lasagna components in a row.

4. In the bottom of a 9 x 13-inch casserole, spread a thin layer of the sauce. Lay the first layer of noodles in the pan, overlapping them slightly to create a solid base. Spread one-third of the vegetable mixture over the noodles, add a thin layer of artichoke hearts, sprinkle with olives and ladle one-quarter of the remaining sauce evenly over the vegetables. Sprinkle with one-third of the Parmesan cheese and then a third of the mozzarella to create a thin layer. Add another layer of noodles and top with another third of the vegetables; smooth the ricotta mixture over the vegetables. Create another layer of noodles, cover with the remaining vegetables, add the remaining artichoke hearts and olives, spread some sauce over the vegetables, sprinkle with Parmesan cheese and top with a layer of mozzarella.

5. Add the final layer of noodles, then the remaining sauce, and top with the remaining mozzarella and Parmesan. Cover with foil and bake at 350°F for 40 minutes, or until the cheese is melted and the sauce is bubbling. Allow to cool for 15 minutes to make the lasagna easier to slice, and serve.

SERVES 8

In the eighteenth century, after the unification of Italy, poverty drove thousands of men to the United States to work. Frank Fresina's ancestors, who worked in the citrus trade in Palermo, Sicily, were among those who came to work the citrus harvest in the South. "Initially, they filled the labor shortage on the plantations after the Emancipation," said Frank Fresina. "They felt at home with the subtropical climate, the Catholicism, and the rapacious appetite for fine food in south Louisiana and they stayed and started businesses. My great-grandfather opened the family pasta factory and shop in New Orleans. When we moved to Baton Rouge in the early 1960s, we moved all the antique machinery so that our pasta would never change. There are a lot of Cajun and Creole Italo-Americans. We can't make pasta fast enough."

MU JING LAU'S PENANG BEEF WITH RICE NOODLES

Mu Jing Lau has been chef-owner of Mu Du Noodles, a small Santa Fe restaurant, for more than twelve years. She serves fresh food made with largely organic ingredients and, when she can, from sources at the local farmers' market. She was born in Canton, China, and immigrated to the United States with her parents at age 8, but cooking and serving Asian food was the last thing she thought she would be doing. "My mother was a terrible cook, so I never learned to like Chinese food."

Ms. Lau credits her move to Santa Fe—after careers as a woodworker and computer engineer—with her change of both heart and profession. "I became more Chinese when I moved here." Still, the first time someone suggested she open a noodle house, she snubbed the proposal. "I told them that I didn't eat noodles, and I certainly didn't cook noodles," she laughs. "But you never know where life will lead you. I never would have chosen this life, but I'm very grateful for it—even if I've had to eat my words."

Ms. Lau discovered this dish during a visit to Malaysia, then modified it to suit her own sense of place and taste. She cuts fresh noodle sheets to size, but dried rice noodles will work, too. She does not dry her marinated meat before searing it, but restaurant woks get much hotter than stovetop models, so you may have to experiment to get a good sear.

The red sauce is very hot, so use less if your tongue is tender, more if you are a fire-eater.

½ cup light soy sauce, or enough to cover the meat

One 2-inch piece fresh ginger, peeled, then minced or grated

2 garlic cloves, minced

1 pound beef tenderloin or flank steak, cut against the grain into ¼-inch slices

½ pound fresh or dried wide rice noodles

Vegetable or peanut oil, for cooking

1 bunch green onions (scallions), trimmed and cut into 6-inch lengths

2 to 3 handfuls bean sprouts

FOR THE BLACK SAUCE

3 tablespoons oyster sauce

3 tablespoons mushroom soy sauce or other dark soy

1 tablespoon brown sugar

3 tablespoons water or beef broth

FOR THE RED SAUCE

2 tablespoons red chile jam

2 tablespoons sambal oelek

1. Combine the soy sauce, ginger, and garlic in a shallow bowl or baking dish. Add the beef and turn to coat well. Cover and refrigerate overnight.

2. If using dried rice noodles, soak in very warm water until pliable, 10 to 30 minutes. Drain well before proceeding. (Fresh noodles need no advance preparation.)

3. To make the black sauce, combine all the ingredients in a small bowl.

4. To make the red sauce, combine all the ingredients in a separate small bowl.

5. Heat a wok as hot as you can and add a film of oil. When the oil is hot and barely smoking, drain the meat and add to the wok, spreading it flat along the bottom and sides. For the best sear, do not flip or stir the meat; let it sit undisturbed for a few minutes, until a test piece looks brown and crisp. Flip and sear on the second side. Transfer the meat to a plate and cover to keep warm.

6. Add more oil to the pan and when it is hot, gently lay the noodles in the wok. Using the same technique as you used for the meat, sear one side, then flip the noodles and sear the second side.

7. Pour the black sauce over the noodles and toss to coat. Add the red sauce to taste and quickly toss again. Add the green onions and toss a few seconds, until they've wilted. Add the bean sprouts, toss once more, and transfer to a serving bowl.

8. Add the reserved beef and any accumulated juices and serve immediately.

SERVES 4 AS A FIRST COURSE
OR PART OF A MEAL MADE OF
AN ASSORTMENT OF LITTLE DISHES

Mimi San Pedro's Philippine Pansit
Fried Rice Noodles

"My grandfather had four daughters. He sent them to the United States for college. I do not know why he chose Arkansas, but he researched it very carefully and that is where he moved the family so his daughters could go to school," said Mimi San Pedro. "They decided to stay, and my grandfather said that each of his daughters had to have a son and then a daughter—and they did! My grandfather said that each grandson had to go to medical school—and they did. He said that each daughter had to become a nurse practitioner—and they did, except for me, and I tried. I have no bedside manner. I am a businesswoman. But I had to try or my grandfather would have been upset. Then my mother would have been upset and then the entire family would have been upset." And this, she suggested, could have had a deleterious effect on the pansit and other traditional dishes that the extended family eats when they gather around one table. Ms. San Pedro calls pansit "the Filipino national noodle dish."

Three 8-ounce packages of rice noodles (bihon)

3 tablespoons vegetable oil

4 garlic cloves, peeled and crushed

1 large onion, diced

5 carrots, peeled and julienned

3 cups julienned green beans

2 cups thinly sliced cabbage

4 celery ribs, sliced into wafer-thin diagonal slices

5 tablespoons soy sauce, preferably Kikkoman brand

2 tablespoons Asian fish sauce

2 tablespoons Asian oyster sauce

½ teaspoon black pepper

3 cups shredded cooked chicken

5 cups homemade chicken broth or low-sodium store-bought chicken broth

1 cup julienned snow peas

½ cup thinly sliced scallions

2 hard-boiled eggs, sliced crosswise

1. Place the noodles in a shallow dish, cover with hot water, and soak until almost soft, 3 to 5 minutes, depending on the thickness of the noodles. Drain and cool under cold running water and set aside.

2. Place the oil in a wok over medium-high heat. When warm, add the crushed garlic and cook, tossing occasionally to avoid burning, until golden, about 2 minutes. Add the onion and stir for 2 minutes. Add the carrots, green beans, cabbage, celery, soy sauce, fish sauce, oyster sauce, and black pepper and cook and stir until the vegetables are half cooked, about 4 minutes.

3. Add the chicken and the broth and bring to a boil. Lower the heat, then stir occasionally until the chicken is warm, about 3 minutes. Add the noodles and the snow peas and continue cooking and stirring until the broth is absorbed and the noodles are tender. Transfer to a platter, top with the scallions and eggs, and serve.

SERVES 10 TO 15

Isabel Morales de Dioguardi's Quinoa a la Huancaina

Quinoa is a weekday staple in Peru, in the background of everything, the foundation that holds up each meal. "It's funny because they just add it to the food," says Maria Sanders, who came to the United States when she was 12. "It's not like 'Okay, I'm cooking with quinoa today.' It's such a basic thing there." The Incas called it chisaya mama (mother of all grains) for good reason. It can grow at altitudes up to 13,000 feet and its protein content is a whopping 15 percent, compared to 7 percent for rice.

Maria's mother, Isabel Morales de Dioguardi, remembers getting up before dawn every day to spend hours buying quinoa and other food on the black market to serve at her restaurant and hotel in Arequipa, in southern Peru. Today her son Bernard runs the Crismar Hotel. Ms. Morales de Dioguardi has lived in the desert of New Mexico since 1976, when the family, with three teenage children, fled Peru's military government. She and her husband now run a Dairy Queen because "all the food is delivered to the door prepared." But on special occasions, she still cooks traditional quinoa recipes like this one.

1 cup quinoa (husked and cleaned)

2 cups water

2 tablespoons olive oil

3 small onions, diced

2 tablespoons ground aji colorado (red chile)

2 tablespoons ground aji amarillo (yellow chile)

1 cup evaporated milk

1 cup finely diced queso fresco

Salt and freshly ground black pepper

4 boiled potatoes, hot

4 hard-boiled eggs, peeled and quartered

1. Rinse and drain quinoa at least twice. Combine the quinoa and water in a medium saucepan over medium heat, cover, and simmer for 15 to 20 minutes, until the water has been absorbed, the quinoa looks translucent, and a small white "tail" is visible on each grain. Remove from the heat.

2. Pour the oil into a medium skillet over medium-high heat. Add the onions and cook, stirring occasionally, until golden. Add the ground chiles and stir to blend. Add the quinoa and mix again.

3. Reduce the heat to low. Stir in the milk and cheese and cook until the cheese starts to melt. Season with salt and pepper to taste.

4. Arrange the potatoes and eggs on four plates. Divide the quinoa among the plates, and serve.

SERVES 4

NOTE: Quinoa grains naturally have a bitter coating, but most quinoa sold commercially in North America has been processed to remove this. Queso fresco, a Mexican cheese, is generally available in supermarkets. The special Peruvian red and yellow chiles can be found in Asian markets.

Erin Drasher's Quinoa-Cherry Pilaf

DEXTER, MICHIGAN

Erin Drasher was brought up in central Pennsylvania by parents of German descent. "My parents were raised on Pennsylvania Dutch cooking," she says, "which consists mainly of lard, meat, potatoes, and pie. They later adopted a healthier vegetarian diet." Several years ago, she moved to Michigan, the second most agriculturally diverse state in the country. "This culture has influenced the way I think about food," she says. "I now prefer to purchase food locally or grow my own fresh ingredients.

"I will sometimes start with a recipe and substitute ingredients based on what is in season and add or subtract herbs and spices to suit my palate. Reading about food, eating, and experimenting has given me confidence in my cooking and has made me a better amateur cook."

She loves the "sweetness of the cherries paired with the earthiness of the beets and spinach" in this quinoa recipe. "Combined with the tanginess of the goat cheese and the nutty texture of the quinoa and sunflower seeds, it's just delicious."

3 large golden beets

2 tablespoons olive oil, plus more for the beets

1 cup quinoa, rinsed, drained, and dried

2 cups water

⅓ cup loosely packed dried sweet cherries (preferably from Door County)

1 medium onion, chopped

2 garlic cloves, minced

2 packed cups baby spinach

Kosher salt and freshly ground black pepper

1 ounce crumbled soft goat cheese (about ¼ cup)

2 tablespoons shelled raw sunflower seeds

Chopped fresh parsley, for garnish

1. To roast the beets, preheat oven to 400°F. Trim off the tops of the beets. Brush with olive oil and wrap in aluminum foil. Roast for 45 minutes to 1 hour, until a paring knife pierces them easily. Remove from the oven and cool until you can handle them. Slip off the skins and cut into large dice.

2. Toast the quinoa in a dry medium saucepan over medium heat. Add the water and cherries. Bring to a boil, reduce the heat to low, and cover. Cook for 15 minutes, until the water has been absorbed, the quinoa looks translucent, and a small white "tail" is visible on each grain.

3. While quinoa is cooking, heat the oil in a skillet over medium heat. Add the onion and cook, stirring occasionally, until translucent. Stir in the garlic and spinach and cook until the spinach is just wilted. Add the beets and quinoa and toss.

4. Transfer to a serving bowl. Stir in salt and pepper to taste. Toss with the goat cheese. Divide among 4 plates and top with sunflower seeds and chopped parsley.

SERVES 4

Janet Crain's Kasha Varnishkes

Janet Crain's great-grandparents were Eastern European Jews who arrived at Ellis Island in the late 1800s. Her grandmother was born in the United States in 1898.

Her family eats dinner together only one day a week—on Shabbat. "It is traditional in my family to have chicken soup, chicken, kasha varnishkes, and a vegetable" for the Friday night Sabbath dinner, she says. "Shabbat is a celebration of the end of the workweek. It is a time to count your blessings, eat a slow meal, and celebrate family."

Her grandmother used to make kasha varnishkes without a recipe—"a little of this and that." Dr. Crain likes to serve hers with applesauce.

3 ounces bow tie pasta (about 1 cup)

Vegetable oil or nonstick cooking spray

½ cup whole kernel kasha (buckwheat groats)

1 cup homemade chicken broth or low-sodium store-bought chicken broth

¼ cup chopped scallions, green and white parts

One 4-ounce can mushroom pieces, drained

Kosher salt and freshly ground black pepper

1. Bring a large saucepan of salted water to a boil. Add the pasta, stir, and cook until al dente, 11 to 12 minutes. Drain.

2. While the water is heating, pour a little oil in a small saucepan or spray the pan with cooking spray. Place the pan over medium heat and add the kasha. Cook, stirring constantly, until fragrant and toasted, 2 to 3 minutes. Add the broth, bring to a boil, cover, reduce the heat to low, and cook until the liquid has all been absorbed, 10 to 12 minutes.

3. Heat 1 tablespoon oil in a large skillet. Add the scallions and mushrooms and cook until the scallions are soft and golden.

4. Stir the pasta and kasha into the scallions and mushrooms. Season with salt and pepper to taste and heat through.

SERVES 2

Ice Cream for All

Ice cream is an inalienable American right, as close as we come to one single, undivided national appetite. The initial shock of ice cream against the tip of the tongue is a mark of American childhood. In the eighteenth century, the dessert was a rare and labor-intensive luxury. But time and technology eventually delivered the "frozen dainty" to Main Street. Indeed, ice cream was the first taste of America offered to immigrants at Ellis Island. Americans each consume an average of 22 ½ quarts of ice cream a year.

Thomas Jefferson's Vanilla Ice Cream

When a group of Virginia statesmen stopped at the home of Maryland's colonial governor on their way to negotiate a treaty with the Iroquois nation in 1744, they were served an iced cream made from milk and strawberries. William Black, one of the guests, described the dish as a "dessert no less Curious," a rarity that he said "eats most Deliciously." Within twenty years, Giovanni Bosio had opened the nation's first gelateria in New York City, and by the summer of 1790, another merchant reported that President George Washington spent about $200 on ice cream for afternoon gatherings. But it was not until Thomas Jefferson served as secretary of state that ice-cream making entered the national lexicon. In his diary, Jefferson noted that "snow gives the most delicate flavor to creams, but ice is the most powerful congealer and lasts longer" and provided a recipe for a rich, custard-based "French Style" ice cream. This version of the original has been updated for modern ice-cream freezers

8 cups heavy cream

1 vanilla bean, split in half

6 large egg yolks

1 cup sugar

1. Combine the heavy cream and vanilla bean in a heavy-bottomed pot. Place over medium heat and bring to a boil. Reduce the heat and simmer, stirring often, for 5 minutes. Remove from heat and set aside.

2. Whisk the egg yolks and the sugar together until thick and light yellow, 5 to 6 minutes with a handheld whisk, 3 to 4 minutes with an electric mixer. While still whisking, add 1 cup of the hot cream to the yolk mixture in a slow, steady stream. Then gradually stir the egg mixture into the remaining cream. Continue stirring until the mixture is thick enough to coat the back of a spoon, about 5 minutes. Set aside for 10 minutes.

3. Line a fine-mesh strainer with cheesecloth and moisten with warm water. Pour the custard mixture through the strainer and into a bowl. Discard the vanilla bean, stir the mixture, cover and refrigerate for at least 1 hour or up to 12 hours. Freeze according to the instructions on your ice cream freezer, transfer to a mold or container, and freeze for 1 hour before serving.

———

MAKES 2½ QUARTS

In the nineteenth century, Philadelphia, with its public ice cream gardens, was the center of the ice-cream universe, and many accounts say that Augustus Jackson, an African-American candy maker who had worked as a chef in the White House, was the emperor of Philadelphia ice cream. Making the confection was still an arduous task. Large blocks of ice were harvested from rivers in the winter and stored in straw for the summer treat. An 1894 article in the *New York Times* claimed that Mr. Jackson invented a method for beating more air into the frozen egg and cream custards. The results were so toothsome that his ice cream fetched $1 a quart and, said the *Times*, "It immediately became popular, and the inventor soon enlarged his store, and when he died left a considerable fortune. A good many tried to follow his example, and ice cream was hawked about the streets, being wheeled along very much as the hokey-pokey carts are now, but none of them succeeded in obtaining the flavor that Jackson had in his product."

Other accounts maintain that Mr. Jackson wholesaled his ice cream to the city's ice-cream gardens, many of which were owned by African Americans. During Mr. Jackson's reign, "French style vanilla ice cream" was rechristened and became "Philadelphia style vanilla ice cream."

President Roosevelt's secretary accepts an ice cream cake from the International Association of Ice Cream Manufacturers.

Before she married James Madison, Dolley Payne Todd served as the hostess for many of Thomas Jefferson's gatherings at the White

House and became as famous for her lavish fêtes as she did for her elaborately molded ice creams. The pink tower of strawberry ice cream that she served on a silver platter at her husband's second inaugural ball in 1812 captured the public imagination and ice cream became de rigueur at fashionable parties. In one account Augustus Jackson prepared the pink tower using cream from Madison's dairy in Montpelier and strawberries from Dolley's garden at the White House.

Strawberry Buttermilk Sherbet

CHAPEL HILL, NORTH CAROLINA

The richest old-fashioned ice cream was generally made with a custard, but modern versions tend to be heavier on the fruit, lighter on the dairy, almost like sherbet, said Bill Smith, the chef at Crooks Corner. This recipe from his friend Donna Florio is a perfect example: The buttermilk gives a clean, bright flavor to the ripest fruit to create an intense strawberry flavor and deep pink color.

2 cups ripe strawberries, rinsed and hulled, or one 16-ounce package frozen strawberries

2 cups sugar

2 cups buttermilk

½ vanilla bean, scraped or 1 teaspoon high quality vanilla extract

1. Place ½ cup of the strawberries in a food processor and pulse until smooth. Strain through a fine-mesh strainer and set aside. Discard the solids and place the fruit in a bowl with the sugar, buttermilk, and vanilla; stir. Roughly chop the remaining strawberries and add to the mixture. Cover and refrigerate for 1 hour.

2. Pour the strawberry mixture into the freezer container of a 1½-quart electric ice-cream maker, and freeze according to the manufacturer's instructions. (Instructions and times may vary.) Garnish, if desired.

———

MAKES 1 QUART

Help in the Harvest

ICE
is needed to Save Food
for the Starving people
of the World

UNITED STATES
FOOD ADMINISTRATION

NATIONAL ASSOCIATION
OF ICE INDUSTRIES

Children making ice cream for a church benefit.

T he cost of ice and the labor required to freeze cream
    flawlessly ensured that only the wealthy could indulge
in the stuff. It took three servants to freeze the cream—two
turned the freezing canister in its ice bath
and another scraped the cream from the
sides of the canister as it froze.

Technology

   "It is the practice with some indolent cooks, to set the
freezer, containing the cream, in a tub with ice and salt, and put it in the ice-house; it will certainly freeze
there, but not until the watery particles have subsided, and by the separation destroyed the cream,"
wrote Mary Randolph in *The Virginia Housewife*. But in the early 1840s, Nancy M. Johnson mounted a
one-woman revolution in ice cream. She attached a crank and a handle to the side of a metal canister,
placed the canister in a wooden bucket of ice, and turned icing cream into a one-person job.

   Opinion is divided as to where this bit of practical magic occurred—New Jersey, Washington, D.C., or
Philadelphia. Lacking the funds to manufacture her invention, Mrs. Johnson
sold her patent two years later. Some say it fetched $200, others $2,000,
but there is no disputing that the device patented in 1843 is still in use
today. It was also built to giant scale to be powered by horses, and turned
ice cream from a homemade treat into a manufacturing industry.

   Today American consumers spend $8.1 billion a year on home
purchases of ice cream, but $13.3 billion on ice cream eaten away from
home—at restaurants diners, snack bars, ice cream stands, the ballpark,
and the beach.

*Owen E. Williams, who discovered how to preserve sweet cream
indefinitely with sodium chloride,* HARRIS & EWING, 1939.

Early Prohibitionists were concerned by how easily soda water could conceal the addition of booze and by its similarity to champagne. By the 1880s a number of municipalities had banned the sale of the suspicious substance on Sunday. This wreaked havoc on the ice cream soda business. Some enterprising soda fountain owner hit on the idea of offering a soda-free ice cream soda—ice cream with chocolate sauce and whipped cream—on Sunday. The first ice cream Sunday may have been served in Evanston, Illinois, in 1890, or the next year in Two Rivers, Wisconsin, or in 1893 at Platt & Cole's drugstore in Ithaca, New York. Most likely, gilding the ice cream lily was a food concept with multiple points of entry— another example of how good things get better (or at least bigger and richer) in the United States. George Giffy, a soda fountain owner in Manitowoc, Wisconsin, changed the name to the ice cream sundae.

Sunday, Sundae

Janet Cheechuck's Hot Fudge Sauce

GORDONSVILLE, VIRGINIA

For the past thirty years, Janet Cheerchuck and her husband, Steve Shifflett, have raised orchids, a flower nearly as fussy and almost as satisfying as a perfect hot fudge sundae. A baker and a cook, Ms. Cheerchuck gathers recipes from the chefs in Washington, D.C., while delivering orchids to their restaurant. This perfect fudge sauce is an amalgam of several chefs' recipes and the result of years of striving to make the best sundae in the world.

12 ounces unsweetened chocolate

12 ounces sweet butter

2 cups boiling water

4 cups sugar

1 cup light corn syrup

½ teaspoon salt

1 teaspoon vanilla

1½ ounces dark rum

½ ounce triple sec

1. Melt chocolate and butter over hot water in a double boiler until the ingredients are fully incorporated and the chocolate looks shiny. Use a spatula to scrape the melted chocolate into a heavy stainless-steel saucepan and add the rest of the ingredients, except the vanilla, rum, and triple sec.

2. Bring to a boil, stirring constantly, then cover and boil without stirring for 8 to 9 minutes, or until the sauce reaches 230°F on a candy thermometer.

3. When the sauce has cooled , add vanilla, rum, and triple sec.

Nancy Silverton's Salted Caramel and Peanut Sundae

LOS ANGELES, CALIFORNIA

Nancy Silverton, the founder of La Brea Bakery and the pastry chef and coowner of Campanile Restaurant, ignited the twentieth-century artisanal bread movement in the United States.

Having introduced dishes such as the panna cotta that she had in Italy to the United States, Ms. Silverton has a sixth sense for inventing sweets that make Americans swoon. Sundaes are a "no-brainer, everybody loves a sundae," she says, but "there are going to be lots of very firm opinions about any dish that is so universally loved." This combination of two of her favorite things, caramel and peanuts, is Cracker Jack for connoisseurs—salty and sweet, warm and cold, crunchy and smooth, and deeply connected to memories of American childhood.

CARAMEL ICE CREAM

1 vanilla bean, cut in halve lengthwise

2¼ cups sugar

4 cups milk

3 cups heavy whipping cream

20 egg yolks

1 cup crème fraîche

1. Scrape vanilla bean seeds into a large pot and add pod halves. Add the sugar and melt, stirring gently and constantly, over medium-high heat until the sugar liquefies and turns dark caramel. Slowly add the milk and the whipping cream, stirring constantly. Bring the mixture to a boil, remove from the heat, and let stand for 30 minutes.

2. Place the yolks in a bowl and whisk. Return the caramel mixture to a boil. Whisking constantly, ladle a little of the hot cream mixture over the eggs and continue adding and whisking until the two mixtures are combined. Whisk in the crème fraîche. Strain through a fine-mesh strainer into a separate bowl and continue whisking until cool. Chill for 1 hour in the refrigerator and freeze in the ice cream maker according to the manufacturer's instructions. Serve with salty peanut caramel sauce (see recipe below).

———

MAKES ½ GALLON

SALTY PEANUT CARAMEL SAUCE

2¾ cups unsalted, unroasted, peeled peanuts, ideally Virginia nuts (1 pound)

2 tablespoons peanut oil

2 tablespoons plus 1 teaspoon salt

1 large plump or 2 thin vanilla beans, split lengthwise

1¾ cups heavy whipping cream

½ cup (1 stick) butter

½ cup corn syrup

1½ cups sugar

1. Preheat the oven to 325°F. Toss together peanuts, peanut oil, and salt in a small bowl. Spread the peanuts on a baking sheet and discard any excess salt. Toast at 325°F until lightly colored, about 10 minutes. Remove from oven and set aside.

2. Scrape the vanilla bean seeds into a small saucepan, then add pod halves. Add the cream and butter and heat over medium heat until butter melts. Remove from heat and set aside.

3. Heat the corn syrup in a 2-quart saucepan over medium-high heat until it begins to bubble. Begin stirring syrup slowly and continuously and sprinkle in sugar in about 4 batches, waiting until each batch of sugar is incorporated into syrup before adding more. (Don't stir too fast or sugar won't color.) Continue cooking and stirring slowly until mixture is thin, bubbly, and straw-colored. (Don't let sauce get brown at this point.)

4. Remove the syrup from the heat and slowly add half of cream-butter mixture. The caramel will boil up; allow it to settle, then stir to incorporate ingredients. Repeat with remaining cream-butter mixture.

5. Return the caramel to medium-high heat and boil until sauce has thickened and darkened slightly, about 2 minutes. Stir in peanuts, but not any clumps of salt that may have fallen onto baking sheet. Boil slightly longer if color is not dark enough; sauce should be pale brown, not medium or dark brown. Remove vanilla bean pods and serve over ice cream.

———

MAKES 1 QUART

THE CREAM OF LOVE.

"You, icy sweetness of strawberry, chocolate or vanilla, melting, stickily into your inverted dunce cap, ravisher of appetites, leading the younger generation from the straight and narrow paths of spinach, pilferer of the pennies that might go to make a fortune; destroyer of the peace of homes, instrument of bribery and reward of virtue."

—H. L. Mencken, *Baltimore Evening Sun*, 1928

We All Scream

Nearly every Great American Ice Cream Empire sprang from a small ice cream shop, pushcart, or truck. Sold in England prior to 1904, the edible, grab-gobble-and-go cone was introduced to Americans at the St. Louis World's Fair that year. Historians believe that more than fifty vendors sold ice cream cones at the fair.

1920 Prohibition reduced legal alcohol consumption and raised the amount of ice cream eaten in the country by 100 million gallons. Harry Burt, who

Profiles in Ice Cream

owned an ice cream store in Youngstown, Ohio, invented the Good Humor Ice Cream Sucker with its chocolate coating, and wooden stick. The motorized trucks made him the first nationwide ice cream baron.

1925 When Howard Deering Johnson found that the soda fountain was the most profitable section of his drugstore, he offered three flavors—vanilla, chocolate, and strawberry—using his mother's ice cream recipe, which was higher in butterfat than most. By 1950, Howard Johnson's offered 28 flavors and had 400 locations across the country.

AUGUST 4, 1938 John Fremont "Grandpa" McCullough and his son, Alex McCullough, talked their friend Herb Noble into selling all-you-can-eat bowls of their invention—soft-serve ice cream—at his ice-cream store. Two years later, the three men opened the first Dairy Queen in Joliet, Illinois. The first food business to offer independent franchises, the company has 5,900 stores around the world today.

1953 Burt Baskin and Irvine Robbins opened an ice cream parlor in Glendale, California. At the suggestion of their Madison Avenue advertising agency, the partners offered 31 flavors—a new flavor for each day of the month and more flavors than Howard Johnson's—with the slogan "Count the Flavors. Where Flavor Counts." Today there are 5,800 Baskin-Robbins outlets around the world.

1960 Reuben Mattus founded Häagen-Dazs, a high-butterfat ice cream made with all natural ingredients. The nonsensical name was meant to evoke old world quality, but the ice cream was made at a small factory in the Bronx and shipped via Greyhound buses to college students across the country. Mattus and his widowed mother had immigrated to the United States in the early 1920s and sold frozen ices from a horse-drawn cart in the Bronx. In 1983 the company was sold to General Mills for $70 million.

1978 After completing a correspondence course in ice cream making, Ben Cohen and Jerry Greenfield, opened an ice cream

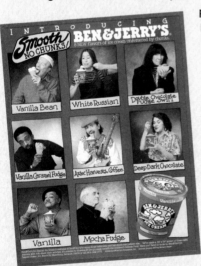

parlor in a former gas station in Burlington, Vermont. Like Häagen-Daz, Ben & Jerry's ice cream was high butterfat, but instead of old world tradition, the owners created tie-died improvisations such as Chubby Hubby and Rain Forest Crunch by mixing candy and even cookie dough into the ice cream and then marketed the flavors with a leftie social conscience. To sell their ice cream they used campaigns such as an annual free cone day and drove a truck painted like a cow—the cow mobile—across the country. They got it placed on the space shuttle and used it to build the world's largest baked Alaska in Washington to protest global warming. Through their foundation they pushed corporate giving and good works to new levels. In 2000 the company was acquired by Unilever for $326 million.

Adria Shimada's Raspberry Sorbet

SEATTLE, WASHINGTON

Although she trained to be a pastry chef, Adria Shimada wanted to make ice cream. "Every time I eat ice cream I feel like a child again," said the founder and owner of Parfait, one of the nation's only all-organic, all-local ice cream trucks. "I love my business because my business is about making people happy. There is a general, cultural love of ice cream and the ice cream truck in the United States, and if you add ice cream made from the very best ingredients, you are basically serving little bowls of sunshine. I just love to watch how happy it makes people. As long as you find really ripe, high quality ingredients, the sorbet itself is easy to make." And this one has a particularly fetching texture.

1 pound (about 2 cups) fresh, ripe raspberries (I get mine from the Alm Hill organic farm)

½ cup water

¾ cup cane sugar

Juice of 1 lemon, preferably Meyer lemon

1. Wash the raspberries. In a heavy-bottomed nonreactive pot, combine the raspberries and water over medium-high heat and cook until the berries have broken apart—5 to 7 minutes—stirring occasionally. The mixture can bubble up a little, but don't overcook. Remove from the heat and stir in sugar and lemon juice. Cool for 30 minutes and then refrigerate at least 4 hours or overnight.

2. Freeze in an ice cream machine according to the manufacturer's instructions. If the ice cream machine has variable speeds, churn at higher speed to create a smoother, less icy texture. Transfer the sorbet to a separate container and put in the regular freezer overnight.

MAKES 1 QUART

People's Pops: Peach, Chamomile, and Honey Pops

NEW YORK, NEW YORK

Nathalie Jordi, Joel Horowitz, and David Carrell, food lovers and farmers' market devotees, are not the sort to suffer a steamy day in the city. Suspecting that they were not alone, the high school pals began to fashion Popsicles from local ingredients and sell them at a flea market in Brooklyn several years ago. Today they field requests for interviews from business school professors and other would-be entrepreneurs. "It's not like we had a plan," said Ms. Jordi, "we just wanted something delicious and cold." Their grown-up combinations—anise-spiced rhubarb, blackberry and lemon verbena, plum and tarragon, raspberry and cream, and this recipe for peach, honey, and chamomile—are better than the frosty pops of childhood. Way, way better.

4 tree-ripened yellow peaches

2 white peaches (slightly soft)

¼ cup fresh honey

Juice of ½ small lemon

Pinch of kosher salt

1 bouquet fresh chamomile flowers

1. Rinse, halve, and pit two-thirds of the peaches, and puree them with the skin on until the mixture is almost smooth. Add the honey, lemon juice, salt, and three finely minced chamomile flowers into the pureed peaches.

2. Coarsely chop remaining one-third of peaches and combine with puree. Add honey to taste. Make the pops a tad sweeter than you want them to be, because they lose a little sweetness after freezing. Pour into 3-ounce Dixie cups or Popsicle molds, add wooden Popsicle sticks, and freeze for at least 2 hours.

———

MAKES 10 POPS

Roy's Chocolate Ice Cream with Chocolate "Rags"

NEW YORK, NEW YORK

⅓ cup sugar

⅓ cup cocoa powder (preferably Valrhona)

1 cup milk

2 cups heavy cream

6 large egg yolks

⅓ cup honey

½ teaspoon kosher salt

½ teaspoon pure vanilla extract

2 ounces bittersweet chocolate, chopped

Sanitary Ice Cream Cone Company, Lewis Hine, 1917.

"My advice is not to inquire why or whither, but just enjoy your ice cream while its on your plate."
—Thornton Wilder

1. Fill a large bowl with ice and water and set a smaller bowl into it. Put the sugar and cocoa in a large saucepan. Add the milk gradually, stirring until the cocoa is dissolved. Stir in the cream and bring to a boil over medium-high heat.

2. While the cream mixture is heating, combine the yolks, honey, and salt in a large bowl. Whisk until the yolks are light and tripled in volume.

3. When the cream mixture is at a full rolling boil, pour it into the lightened yolks and whisk for 1 minute. Strain into the bowl set over ice and cool completely, stirring when you remember to. Stir in the vanilla. If you've planned ahead, chill in the refrigerator overnight. Otherwise, when the ice-cream base is cool, freeze in an ice-cream maker according to the manufacturer's directions.

4. Melt the bittersweet chocolate in a bowl over barely simmering water or in the microwave with 30-second blasts. Transfer to a small zipper-top plastic bag. When the ice cream is nearly done, snip a corner off the bag and slowly pipe the chocolate into the ice cream as it churns. Transfer the ice cream to a plastic container, cover, and put in the freezer for at least 2 hours before serving.

MAKES ABOUT 1 QUART

Jeni's Awesome Dirt Road Ice Cream

COLUMBUS, OHIO

When she was studying art at Ohio State University, Jeni Britton Bauer began to work in the kitchen of Le Chatelaine, a French pastry store and bistro in Columbus, and a strange thing happened. "I stopped painting, I stopped making art. All I could think about was ice cream. I started to look at food as potential ice cream. The mint in the backyard, corn from the farmstand, pumpkins, lavender. Basically ice cream became my art, and we were too young to know any better, so a friend and I opened a little stand in the old covered market." It took about ten years of learning the hard way before Ms. Britton learned to hit the sweet spot between art and commerce. Her salty caramel ice cream changed the way Columbus thought about sundaes and cones, and her Dirt Road Ice Cream—dark milk chocolate ice cream with a swirl of smoked almonds—has remained the bestseller as she and her partner and husband, Charly Bauer, have expanded to seven small stores in central Ohio. The growth of her business pleases residents of the small organic dairy Ms. Bauer has partnered with. The best cream in the heartland, after all, deserves nothing less than some of the best ice cream in America.

1 cup whole milk

1 tablespoon plus 1 teaspoon cornstarch

2 ounces bittersweet chocolate

1 cup evaporated milk

¼ cup heavy cream

⅔ cup sugar

2 tablespoons light corn syrup

⅓ cup unsweetened cocoa powder

¼ teaspoon fine sea salt

8 ounces smoked almonds, chopped coarsely

1. Mix about 2 tablespoons of milk with the cornstarch in a small bowl to make a smooth slurry. Chop the chocolate and place in a medium bowl. Fill a large bowl with ice and water.

2. Combine the remaining milk, evaporated milk, heavy cream, sugar, and corn syrup in a 4-quart saucepan and bring to a rolling boil over medium-high heat. Add the cocoa, whisking until it is incorporated, and continue boiling for 4 minutes. Remove from the heat. Gradually whisk the hot milk mixture into the chocolate. Add salt and stir until melted and incorporated. Pour the mixture into a bowl that can fit an ice bath and stir until completely cold.

3. Pour the mixture into ice cream freezer and freeze according to the manufacturer's instructions. When the ice cream is frozen, layer it into a storage container with thin layers of smoked almonds between each layer. Reserve some of the smoked almonds to garnish individual serves.

MAKES 1 QUART

CHAPTER 10

THE SWEET LIFE

AMERICAN PIE

MIDDLEBURY, VERMONT

When Don McLean sang good-bye to Miss American Pie, he may have bid adieu to the age of innocence in America but he did not dislodge pie as an icon of our national identity. Whether your crust is tender or flaky, your edges crimped or fluted, your filling cherry or peach or patriotic apple, when you bake a pie, any kind of pie, you pledge allegiance to a simple, more optimistic way of life.

The Pie Day Committee of St. Stephen's Episcopal Church in Middlebury, Vermont, gets together the first Friday of every July to organize the annual event that sells pies to finance good works. And for one day, the ladies of St. Stephen's put aside their personal preferences for lard crusts, hot-oil crusts, or all-butter crusts. On Pie Day, all crusts are created equal—they are made from Crisco because, says Ruth Eichner, one of the St. Stephen's bakers, it makes the easiest and most reliable crust. And the

crust that she and the ladies at St. Stephen's bake is invariably tender-flaky.

A tender crust requires a different process from a flaky one. According to Shirley Corriher, a biochemist and the author of *Cookwise*, for a tender crust, you need to grease the proteins in the flour before you add the liquid so the pastry doesn't get mushy. The more completely you work the fat into the flour, the more tender the crust. Corriher says that a hot-oil crust, so popular in the 1930s, is probably the tenderest.

To create a flaky crust, on the other hand, you must combine chunks of cold fat with flour very rapidly, but not incorporate the fat completely. Since the warmth of your hand can melt the fat too soon, you must work quickly. You want the fat to melt as the crust bakes, leaving tiny air gaps for flakiness. But both tender and flaky crusts have drawbacks. Tender crusts tend to crumble, and flaky butter crusts can shrink as they bake. Jim Dodge, author of *The American Baker*, gets around the problem of having the butter melt too soon by freezing the butter and flattening the dough with a rolling-and-folding sequence similar to one used for puff pastry. But this technique is not for beginners, and it doesn't solve the problems of shrinkage or crumbling.

So it is no accident that Crisco is the fat of choice for Pie Day. Solid vegetable shortening is a great equalizer, and the flaky-tender crust that results does not discriminate between novice and master baker. But not even the technological cure-all of solid hydrogenated shortening can supply the expertise about crusts and fillings that distinguishes a serviceable baker from the apron-clad ideal of our imagination.

Take Marion Munford, who says that her sixty-five years of baking have taught her never to get mad at the dough, and always to treat it tenderly. Once you understand it with your hands, she says, the dough will tell you everything you need to know.

Most of St. Stephen's bakers would agree. Experience has taught them that an initial blast of heat will result in a nice brown crust, that Jean Bergesen is Middlebury's best roller, and that a dusting of graham-cracker crumbs or rolled oats on the bottom of the crust will keep it from getting soggy.

But once the crust is in the pan, they know the importance of largesse. What's the point of putting together a pie, Ms. Eichner asks, if you're going to skimp on the fruit?

Pie Day Committee's Crust

MIDDLEBURY, VERMONT

Each pie that makes it to the table for St. Stephen's annual Pie Day sale may be unique, but the crust in each one is the same. Made with Crisco, the dough is easy to handle and always reliable. Vegetable shortening allows it to maintain the same texture over a wide range of temperatures. And best of all, it creates a crust that's both as tender as a good sugar cookie and flaky as pie crust should be.

2½ cups all-purpose flour, plus
    more for rolling

1 teaspoon kosher salt

¾ cup vegetable shortening
    (preferably Crisco)

6 to 7 tablespoons cold water

1. Combine the flour and salt. Place the shortening in the bottom of a large bowl and, using a fork or handheld pastry blender, gently work the dry ingredients into the shortening.

2. When the mixture resembles cornmeal, make a well in the center and add 6 tablespoons water. Blend, adding the additional tablespoon of water if necessary, until the dough comes together in a ball.

3. Divide into two balls, pat each into a thick, flat disk, wrap with waxed paper, and refrigerate for 1 hour before rolling out.

MAKES ENOUGH FOR ONE 9-INCH DOUBLE-
CRUST PIE OR TWO 9-INCH SINGLE-CRUST PIES

Anne LaFiandra's Lard Crust

MIDDLEBURY, VERMONT

Crisco may be the official shortening of choice for Pie Day, but when she's baking for herself, Ms. LaFiandra prefers that old standby, lard. It usually requires knowing a pig farmer, but those who can get hold of pure lard insist that it makes the flakiest, strongest crust. Lard crusts are best suited to heavier tree fruit than they are to delicate ingredients such as berries, and to savory fillings such as mincemeat.

2 cups all-purpose flour, plus more for rolling

¼ teaspoon kosher salt

6 tablespoons frozen lard, cut into 6 pieces

7 tablespoons cold water

1. Combine the flour and salt in a food processor. Add the lard and pulse until clumpy.

2. Add the water by tablespoons, pulsing until the dough comes together in a ball.

3. Divide into two flat disks, wrap each in plastic, and refrigerate for 15 minutes to 1 hour before rolling out.

MAKES ENOUGH FOR ONE 9-INCH LATTICE-TOPPED PIE OR TWO 9-INCH SINGLE-CRUST PIES

One Big Table

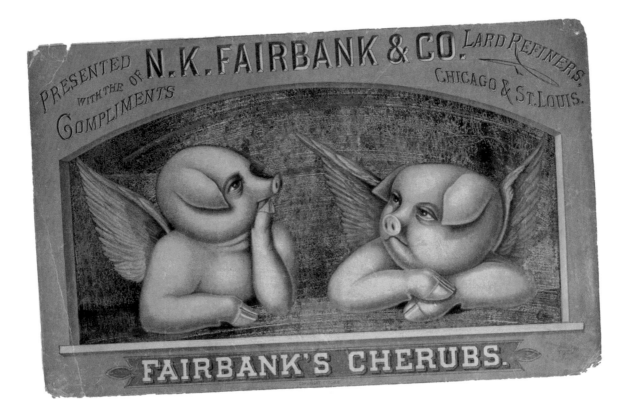

Brenda Harmon's Vinegar and Butter Crust

Getting a pie crust right used to be a gamble for Brenda Harmon. They cracked. They tore. They resisted any attempt at mending. Mrs. Harmon, a stay-at-home mother of two, was undeterred. She tried butter-and-egg doughs, lard, and vegetable shortening. Each variation had its risk, but risk-taking is the air in Show Low. The town took its name from an epic card battle between two nineteenth-century ranchers who thought the settlement wasn't big enough for both of them. The stakes were a 100,000-acre homestead for whoever showed the lowest card. The winner drew the two of clubs.

After years of experimenting, Mrs. Harmon's "two of clubs" is this vinegar and butter crust. "It's rich and tender, but very easy to work with, especially if you are making top crusts or lattices," she says. "I make four crusts at a time and freeze the extra to use later."

4 cups all-purpose flour, plus more for rolling

½ teaspoon kosher salt

1 tablespoon sugar

¾ pound (3 sticks) unsalted butter, cut into small pieces and chilled

1 tablespoon distilled white vinegar

1 extra-large egg

½ cup ice water

1. Combine the flour, salt, and sugar in a large bowl. Using a handheld pastry blender, two forks, or your fingers, cut the butter into the flour until it resembles coarse meal. Create a well in the center of the mixture.

2. Whisk together the vinegar, egg, and water and pour into the well. Using your fingers and working quickly, mix the wet and dry ingredients just until combined.

3. On a clean, lightly floured work surface press the dough together, and divide into 4 equal parts. Shape each into a ball, flatten slightly to form a disk, wrap in plastic, and chill for at least 1 hour.

4. To use: Roll out a disk on a lightly floured work surface to ⅛ inch thick. Transfer to a 9-inch pie pan and fill with fruit. Roll out a second disk and place on top of the fruit. Crimp the edges together. Bake at 375°F for 50 minutes.

MAKES ENOUGH FOR TWO 9-INCH DOUBLE-CRUST PIES OR FOUR 9-INCH SINGLE-CRUST PIES

MICHAEL MULLIGAN'S ALL-BUTTER PIE CRUST

OCALA, FLORIDA

Pie crust was one of the first things Michael Mulligan tackled when he started cooking. Disappointed with shortening-based crusts, he preferred butter crusts for their superior flavor and texture. After countless experiments, he had a breakthrough. "After my hands knew what the dough was supposed to feel like, I could adjust the amount of liquid when I needed to," Mr. Mulligan explains. The result is a dough made with frozen cubes of butter—a technique that helps the fat distribute more evenly, forming little air pockets that produce optimum flakiness.

12 tablespoons (1½ sticks) unsalted butter, cut into ½-inch cubes

2 cups all-purpose flour, plus more for rolling

1 teaspoon kosher salt

1 teaspoon sugar

3 to 7 tablespoons ice water

1. Put the butter into the freezer for at least 15 minutes. An hour is preferable.

2. Combine the flour, salt, and sugar in a food processor. Add the butter and pulse just a few times to get a crumbly, coarse mixture.

3. Add the ice water 1 tablespoon at a time, pulsing briefly after each tablespoon. Pinch the dough. If it holds together, it's ready. If not, add more water and repeat. (You don't want to overwater the dough or it will become mushy. It should hold together just enough for you to work with, but not be so elastic that you could throw it in the air and make a pizza.)

4. Divide the dough into two pieces. Pat each piece lightly into a ball and wrap in waxed paper. Refrigerate for at least 30 minutes.

5. Lightly flour the work surface, dough, and rolling pin. Roll out the dough nice and thin (about ⅛ inch). Gently roll it around the rolling pin and transfer to the pie pan. Trim any ragged edges and finish by fluting, crimping, or marking with a fork; fill and bake according to your pie recipe.

MAKES ENOUGH FOR ONE 9-INCH DOUBLE-CRUST PIE OR TWO 9-INCH SINGLE-CRUST PIES

CLAUDIA'S BETTER THAN STORE-BOUGHT
GRAHAM CRACKER CRUST

One of the nation's most versatile back-of-the-box recipes, the graham cracker crust—crushed graham crackers, sugar, and melted butter—has been used in refrigerator pies, cheesecakes, and custard pies since the early twentieth century. These applications may not have been what Sylvester Graham, the Presbyterian minister, temperance crusader, and dietary reformer had in mind when he preached the benefits of whole-grain bread and crackers in the mid-nineteenth century. Likewise, prefab graham crackers are not what pastry chef Claudia Fleming had in mind for her pies. She and her husband, Chef Gerry Hayden, own the North Fork Table and Inn on Long Island. She minted this "from scratch" version, whose deep flavor can elevate any pie.

2 cups all-purpose flour, plus more for rolling

½ cup whole-wheat flour

1 teaspoon kosher salt

½ teaspoon ground cinnamon

½ pound (2 sticks) unsalted butter, softened

¼ cup packed dark brown sugar

¼ cup granulated sugar

¼ cup honey

1. Combine both flours, the salt, and cinnamon in a large bowl.

2. Cream the butter in the bowl of an electric stand mixer. Add both sugars and blend well. Mix in the honey.

3. Add half of the dry ingredients and mix until fully combined. Add the remainder and mix, scraping down the sides of the bowl as needed.

4. Divide the dough in half and transfer each piece to a sheet of plastic wrap. Pat each into a disk. (The dough will be tacky.) Wrap and refrigerate for 1 hour, until firm. The dough can be wrapped in foil or placed in a zipper-top plastic bag and frozen for up to 3 months.

5. Unwrap one disk but leave the dough on top of the plastic wrap. Lightly dust the surface with flour and put another piece of plastic wrap on top. Roll out the dough between the plastic layers as thinly as possible, about ⅛ inch.

6. Remove the top layer of plastic wrap. Put a 9-inch pie pan upside down on the rolled-out dough and with a sharp knife, cut out a circle in the dough about 1 inch wider than the widest part of the pan. Move the dough scraps out of the way.

7. Slide your hand under the plastic wrap under the dough and carefully flip the circle of dough and the pan right side up. Peel off the plastic and gently fit the dough into the pan. Trim off any excess dough and refrigerate for about 5 minutes before baking.

8. To bake: Preheat the oven to 325°F.

9. Prick the crust all over with a fork to prevent it from bubbling and bursting in the oven. Bake for about 18 minutes, until cooked through and lightly browned. Cool to room temperature on a wire rack and proceed with the recipe for filling.

MAKES ENOUGH FOR TWO 9-INCH
SINGLE-CRUST PIES

Cynthia Godby McGuiness's Crumbly Top Crust for Pies or Cobblers

WINSTON-SALEM, NORTH CAROLINA

Cynthia Godby McGuiness began making this nutty crumb top crust when her children were young and time was at a premium. It makes a wonderful crust for fruit pies. Walnuts are her favorite for fall fruit pies, and almonds create a lighter texture for summer berry pies. Ms. McGuiness also sprinkles this topping over pans of sliced fruit or berries, in place of a pie crust or to create fruit cobblers.

⅔ cup all-purpose flour

½ cup packed light brown sugar

½ teaspoon ground cinnamon

5 tablespoons plus 1 teaspoon (⅔ stick) unsalted butter, cut in small pieces and chilled

½ cup coarsely chopped walnuts, pecans, or almonds

1. Preheat oven to 425°F. Combine the flour, sugar, and cinnamon in a small bowl. Using a pastry blender or two forks, cut in the butter until the crumble starts to clump. Stir in the chopped nuts.

2. To use in place of a pastry top crust on a fruit pie: Partially bake the pricked empty bottom crust for 10 minutes. Remove from the oven and lower the heat to 375°F. Place the filling in the crust, mound the crumble on top, and bake for 40 to 50 minutes, until the filling is bubbling and the crumble is golden. Cover the pie loosely with foil for the last 15 to 20 minutes of baking to prevent overbrowning.

———

MAKES ENOUGH TOPPING FOR ONE 8- TO 10-INCH PIE OR ONE 8 X 8-INCH COBBLER

ANNE LaFIANDRA'S BLUEBERRY PIE

MIDDLEBURY, VERMONT

Anne LaFiandra, who has served as the chair of the St. Stephen's Pie Day Committee, has seen all manner of pie come through the church doors, but this is her standby. A tablespoon of oatmeal acts as a gentle barrier between dough and filling to keep the bottom crust crisp. Packed with fresh Green Mountain blueberries and crowned with an intricate lattice top, it's pie perfection.

1 recipe Anne LaFiandra's Lard Crust (page 694)

1 tablespoon old-fashioned rolled oats

5 cups blueberries

1 teaspoon grated lemon zest

2 teaspoons fresh lemon juice

½ to ¾ cup sugar, plus 1 tablespoon sugar (optional)

Pinch of salt

1¼ cups all-purpose flour

2 tablespoons (¼ stick) unsalted butter, cut into small pieces and chilled

1 large egg, lightly beaten

2 tablespoons heavy cream

1. Preheat the oven to 450°F. Roll out one dough disk between two sheets of lightly floured waxed paper and fit it into a 9-inch pie pan. Sprinkle with the oats and chill.

2. Combine the blueberries, lemon zest, lemon juice, sugar (more or less depending on the tartness of the berries and your taste), and salt. Let sit for 10 minutes.

3. Stir in the flour. Pour the filling into the prepared crust. Dot the top with the butter.

4. Roll out the other disk of dough between waxed paper. Cut into strips and lay over the filling to make a lattice, crimping the edges together firmly. Lightly combine the egg with the cream. Brush the top crust with the egg wash and sprinkle with 1 tablespoon sugar, if desired.

5. Bake for 10 minutes. Lower the heat to 400°F and bake for 30 to 40 minutes more, until the crust is brown and the berries are bubbling.

MAKES ONE 9-INCH PIE

Ruth Eichner's Frozen Raspberry Pie

MIDDLEBURY, VERMONT

Ruth Eichner's house is surrounded by some of Vermont's best berry farms. She picks them, she buys them, she has been known to freeze and hoard raspberries. After being frozen, the berries will weep. Instead of flour or cornstarch to absorb the juices and thicken her pie filling, she uses instant tapioca. "It makes a lighter pie, and allows the berries' natural flavor to shine through."

1 recipe Pie Day Committee's Crust
    (page 693)

3 tablespoons all-purpose flour

1 cup sugar, plus 1 tablespoon for sprinkling

1 rounded tablespoon instant tapioca

5 cups frozen raspberries, barely thawed

1 tablespoon heavy cream

1. Preheat the oven to 450°F. Roll out one of the dough disks between 2 sheets of lightly floured waxed paper and line a 9-inch pie pan with it. Prick the bottom and sides with a fork, trim the sides to a ½-inch overhang, and chill for 30 minutes.

2. Combine the flour, 1 cup sugar, and the tapioca and mix with the raspberries, leaving as many frozen clumps as possible. Pour into the pie shell. Roll out the other disk between sheets of waxed paper, cut a decorative vent in it, and lay it over the fruit. Crimp the edges together firmly and flute.

3. Brush the top of the pie with the cream and sprinkle with the remaining tablespoon of sugar. Bake for 10 minutes. Lower the heat to 400°F and bake for 30 to 35 minutes more, until the berries in the middle are bubbling.

MAKES ONE 9-INCH PIE

EDNA LEWIS'S RHUBARB PIE

Known as the Grand Dame of Southern cuisine, Edna Lewis spent the better part of her 89 years showing the world the nuances of country cooking. At the age of 16, she left home to find work to help support her family. She eventually landed in New York City, where she was the chef at Café Nicholson and at the famous Gage and Tollner. When a broken leg forced her to take a break from the kitchen, Miss Lewis began writing down her recipes. Before her death in 2006, she completed four cookbooks, including *The Taste of Country Cooking*, which became a classic. One day after she had retired, she was foraging around for the fruit for this recipe. Looking at the freshly picked, gangly rhubarb, she said to a reporter, "I just want to treat that food kindly."

FOR THE CRUST

1½ cups plus 2 teaspoons sifted all-purpose flour, plus more for rolling

1 teaspoon kosher salt

¼ cup chilled lard, cut into small chunks

¼ cup cold water

FOR THE FILLING

⅔ cup sugar

¼ teaspoon freshly grated nutmeg

2 teaspoons cornstarch

4 cups chopped fresh rhubarb

1. To make the crust, put 1½ cups of the flour in a bowl with the salt and lard and blend together quickly with your fingertips.

2. Stir in the water; the dough will be sticky. Add the remaining flour, form into a ball, and put in the refrigerator for 15 minutes.

3. Lightly flour a work surface. Roll out half of the dough to fit the bottom and sides of a 9-inch pie pan. Flour the surface again and roll out the remaining dough. Using a pastry wheel or a sharp knife, cut the dough into ¾-inch strips and put on waxed paper.

4. Preheat the oven to 450°F.

5. To make the filling, combine the sugar, nutmeg, and cornstarch in a bowl. Sprinkle 3 tablespoons of this mixture on the pastry in the pie pan.

6. Combine the remaining sugar mixture with the rhubarb and fill the pie. Moisten the rim of the pastry with water and make a latticework top over the pie with the dough strips. Crimp the edges well.

7. Bake the pie for 40 minutes or until the filling bubbles and crust is golden brown.

MAKES ONE 9-INCH PIE

Dean McCord's Strawberry Shortcake

Dean McCord is a lawyer, husband, father of four, and the cook of the family. He's a connoisseur of all types of barbecue and has hosted many pig pickin's, but his interests extend beyond the predictable man-meets-barbecue. There is just about nothing Mr. McCord doesn't cook and have an opinion about. This is his favorite recipe for strawberry season. It creates a single, show stopping strawberry shortcake with minimal time and effort.

FOR THE SHORTCAKE

2 cups self-rising flour, plus more for kneading

¼ teaspoon baking soda

¼ teaspoon kosher salt

3 tablespoons sugar

6 tablespoons (¾ stick) unsalted butter, cut into small chunks and chilled

¾ cup plus 2 tablespoons buttermilk

FOR THE STRAWBERRIES AND CREAM

About 1 quart strawberries

¼ cup plus 3 tablespoons sugar

Splash of orange-flavored liqueur (optional)

2 cups heavy cream

1 teaspoon pure vanilla extract

1. To make the shortcake: Preheat the oven to 450°F. Lightly flour the work surface and line a baking sheet with parchment paper. Combine the flour, baking soda, salt, and sugar in a medium bowl. Using a pastry blender or two forks, cut the butter into the flour until the mixture resembles coarse crumbs. Add the buttermilk all at once, stir together gently, and turn the dough out onto the work surface.

2. Knead gently 2 to 4 times by folding the dough over itself, pressing gently, and turning each time. It will still be somewhat coarse and fairly wet. Drop the dough onto the baking sheet and allow it to spread out into one giant biscuit. Bake about 14 minutes, until golden brown. Remove from the oven and let cool.

3. While the biscuit is baking, hull and slice about 1 quart of strawberries. Add ¼ cup sugar and a splash of orange-flavored liqueur, if desired, and toss to combine. Whip the cream to soft peaks with 3 tablespoons sugar and 1 teaspoon vanilla.

4. Transfer the warm shortcake to a serving platter. Cut it in half horizontally with a long serrated knife. Gently remove top. Spoon ¾ of the juicy strawberries onto the bottom half of the shortcake, followed by ¾ of the whipped cream. Replace the top, then add remaining berries and whipped cream. Cut into wedges and serve.

SERVES 6

Shirley Creacy's Chuckwagon Peach Cobbler

S hirley Creacy of Wild Cow Ranch in the Texas Panhandle firmly believes you can make anything in a Dutch oven over a chuckwagon campfire that you can prepare on a kitchen stove. And from beef tips to biscuits, she's got the cooking prizes to prove it. With their vintage 1912 John Deere wagon, she and her husband, Don, have competed in chuckwagon cookoffs from Texas to Kansas to Wyoming since 1996. Although the chuckwagon's heyday lasted for only about twenty years following the Civil War, it is firmly entrenched in the American imagination thanks to cowboy movies. In 1866, rancher Charles Goodnight retrofitted an army surplus wagon as the first mobile trail kitchen. Today, people who restore old wagons and participate in competitions are passionate about honoring and preserving the cooking skills that were developed on the trail. For her prizewinning peach cobbler, Mrs. Creacy adapted her mother-in-law, Benton Creacy's, pie crust. She prefers using dried peaches because that's what was available to trail cooks, but fresh or canned peaches can be substituted. This recipe is designed to be cooked in Dutch ovens over coals, but it can also be prepared on the stovetop or in the oven.

FOR THE FILLING

4½ pounds dried peaches (or 1 gallon canned)

About 1 quart boiling water for soaking the dried peaches

3 cups granulated sugar

1 cup packed light brown sugar

½ pound (2 sticks) unsalted butter

¼ teaspoon grated nutmeg

1 teaspoon ground cinnamon

1 teaspoon pure almond extract

1 cup all-purpose flour

1 cup water, plus more if needed

FOR THE CRUST

6 cups all-purpose flour, plus more for rolling

2 tablespoons granulated sugar

1 tablespoon kosher salt

2⅔ cups vegetable shortening

2 large eggs

1 cup water

1½ tablespoons distilled white vinegar

Vegetable oil, for greasing the Dutch ovens

½ cup granulated sugar and 1 tablespoon ground cinnamon, mixed together

1. To make the filling: If using dried peaches, put them in a large pot, barely cover with boiling water, and soak until tender, about 20 minutes. If using canned or fresh peaches, place them in the pot, and crush lightly with a potato masher.

2. Stir in the granulated and brown sugars, butter, nutmeg, cinnamon, and almond extract and bring to a simmer.

3. Whisk the flour and water together in a small bowl, adding more water if needed to create a thick slurry. Pour into the simmering peaches and stir until the mixture has thickened, 5 to 10 minutes.

4. To make the crust: Prepare a large charcoal or wood fire in a fire pit or preheat the oven to 375°F. Combine the flour, sugar, salt, and shortening in a large bowl. In a separate bowl, whisk together the eggs, water, and vinegar. Add to the flour mixture and mix with a fork until just combined. Do not overwork the dough.

5. Divide the dough in half and roll one half out on a floured work surface to about ⅛ inch thick. Cut the pastry into 1-inch-wide strips.

6. Lightly oil the bottoms of two 12-inch and one 8-inch round Dutch ovens. Carefully lay the strips across the bottoms of the pots to form a crust and trim to fit. The strips should be touching; they will contract as they cook. Place the pots over the prepared coals (or in the oven) and bake about 10 minutes, until crust is stiff but not brown. Remove from the heat. (If using the oven, increase the heat to 425°F.)

7. Roll out the remaining dough to ⅛ inch thick and cut into 1-inch strips. Divide the peach mixture between the Dutch ovens and create a lattice top crust with the strips. Sprinkle with the cinnamon-sugar mixture.

8. Cover the Dutch ovens and return them to the coals (or the oven). If cooking over coals, put some coals on the Dutch oven lid to cook the top crust. Bake about 20 minutes or until top crust is browned and crisp. Remove the covers. (If baking in the oven, you may need to brown the top crust under the broiler.) Serve warm.

SERVES APPROXIMATELY 40

Charlotte Bero's Cherry Pie

Situated on the narrow Door Peninsula in northern Lake Michigan, Door County has weathered harsh winters and withstood the assault of industrialization. The county is known to many as the Cape Cod of the Midwest, where fish boils take the place of clambakes, and the famed Montmorency cherries eclipse all summer berries. Belgians and Scandinavians settled and farmed the land, fished its waters, and continue to preside over its church suppers. The simple solidity of their cooking is a tribute to the fresh, pure ingredients, as well as a symbol of midwestern resolve. Charlotte Bero spent five decades perfecting her Montmorency cherry pie and now believes there is none better.

FOR THE CRUST

1½ cups all-purpose flour, plus more for rolling

¼ teaspoon baking powder

½ teaspoon kosher salt

⅓ cup lard

3 tablespoons (⅜ stick) unsalted butter

2 tablespoons vegetable shortening

2 tablespoons ice water

1 teaspoons distilled white vinegar

2 large eggs

FOR THE FILLING

5 cups pitted fresh or thawed unsweetened frozen Montmorency cherries

5 tablespoons all-purpose flour

2 tablespoons fresh lemon juice

¼ teaspoon grated lemon zest

1 teaspoon pure almond extract

¾ to 1 cup sugar (depending on sweetness of cherries; the pie should be tart)

Scant ⅛ teaspoon ground nutmeg

1 teaspoon Kirsch or other cherry brandy

1½ teaspoons unsalted butter, cut in pieces

1. To make the crust: Combine the flour, baking powder, and salt in a medium bowl. Add the lard, butter, and shortening and incorporate with your fingers or a pastry blender until mixture forms coarse crumbs. Whisk together the ice water, vinegar, and 1 of the eggs. Add to the flour mixture and mix with a fork until just combined; do not overwork dough. Refrigerate for 30 minutes. While the pastry is chilling, preheat the oven to 350°F.

2. To make the filling: Combine the cherries, flour, lemon juice and zest, almond extract, sugar, nutmeg, and Kirsch in a large bowl.

3. Roll out two-thirds of the dough on a lightly floured surface. Line a 9-inch pie plate with the dough and trim the edges. Pour the filling into the pie shell and dot with butter.

4. Roll the remaining dough out into a 9-inch circle and cut into strips about ⅓ inch wide. Whisk the remaining egg with 2 teaspoons water. Brush some of the egg wash onto the dough at the rim of the pie plate.

5. Make a lattice top, loosely weaving the strips like a basket, and crimping the ends together. Brush the lattice with the egg wash.

6. Place the pie on a baking sheet and bake until the crust is golden brown, 1 to 1½ hours. Cool on a wire rack. Serve.

MAKES ONE 9-INCH PIE

Michigan's National Cherry Festival Queen with a 30-pound cherry pie baked for President Roosevelt, 1939.

Elizabeth Miller's
Mascarpone-Plum Tart with Oat Crust

Elizabeth Miller has honed her cooking skills in communal living situations since college. She cooks intuitively, relying on her senses and her love of flavor rather than rigid rules and measurements. She especially loves making tarts because of their good "fancy-to-easy ratio"—they're really pretty but don't actually require much difficult work, she says.

Ms. Miller's plum tart evolved from her experience baking for vegetarians with food sensitivities. It's gluten-free because she goes to many potlucks and wants as many people as possible to enjoy her food.

The recipe for the tart shell calls for gluten-free oats, but if you are baking for people who have an oat as well as a gluten intolerance, you can make the crust with 1 cup almond meal, ½ cup gluten-free flour, and ½ teaspoon xanthan gum (available at most natural food markets). Ms. Miller usually grinds the oats pretty coarsely, but it is a matter of taste.

2 cups gluten-free oats

5 tablespoons plus 1 teaspoon (⅔ stick) unsalted butter, at room temperature

¼ cup packed light brown sugar

8 ounces cream cheese (whipped or light is fine)

8 ounces mascarpone

1½ teaspoons vanilla paste or pure vanilla extract

⅔ cup confectioners' sugar

⅔ pound plums or other stone fruit

3 tablespoons granulated sugar

¼ cup water

2 small lemon slices, with peel

1. Preheat the oven to 375°F. Grind the oats in a coffee grinder or food processor until there aren't any whole oats left.

2. Mix the oats, butter, and brown sugar until crumbly, and press into an 8-inch square tart pan with a removable bottom. Poke holes in the crust with a fork and bake for 15 to 18 minutes, until brown. Remove the pan from the oven and turn the oven to broil, with the rack about 6 inches from the heat source.

3. Beat together the cream cheese, mascarpone, vanilla, and confectioners' sugar.

4. Line a baking sheet with parchment paper and lightly grease the paper. Cut the plums into ¼-inch slices and place in a single layer on the baking sheet. Broil for 6 to 8 minutes, until browned on top.

5. Combine the granulated sugar, water, and lemon slices in a small saucepan over medium-high heat. Stir intermittently for 7 minutes or until rapidly boiling. Remove from the heat and cool. Discard lemon slices.

6. To assemble the tart, pour the mascarpone mixture into the tart shell. Arrange the fruit on top of the mascarpone, and drizzle syrup over the tart. Chill for at least 1 hour.

MAKES 9 SERVINGS

Coletta Boan's Peach Pie

WINSTON-SALEM, NORTH CAROLINA

Coletta Boan grew up in Statesboro, Georgia, part of the "very traditional South," where the cycles of life were marked by barbecues, fish fries, sugarcane grindings, and peanut boils. She lives in North Carolina where she works in corporate marketing and teaches cotillion class and etiquette. Describing this "fast traditional pie," she confesses, "I'm almost embarrassed how easy it is, but it's one of those that never fail, so what [more] can I say?" adding, "Oh, you can certainly throw in blueberries."

5 cups fresh peaches, peeled and sliced

1 unbaked 9-inch pastry shell (pages 693, 694, 695, 696, or 697)

5 tablespoons plus 1 teaspoon (⅔ stick) unsalted butter, melted

1 cup sugar

⅓ cup all-purpose flour

1 large egg

Real whipped cream or vanilla ice cream, for serving

1. Preheat the oven to 350°F.

2. Place the peaches in the pastry shell. Stir together the butter, sugar, flour, and egg until smooth and pour over the peaches. Do not stir into peaches.

3. Bake for 1 hour and 10 minutes. Cool on a rack.

4. Serve with whipped cream or vanilla ice cream.

MAKE ONE 9-INCH PIE

Dori Sanders's Cobbler

Dori Sanders lives where she has always lived: on a 150-acre farm along Route 321, where her father, a school principal and the grandson of a slave, began farming in 1915. She has written a number of books, but Ms. Sanders says, "I'm just an old peach farmer who loves to cook." In the rural South, people tell their life stories through food. "They talk about how they did it then, how they do it now. The way they talk tells you who they are," she says. Her peach cobbler, a simple symphony of sugar, flour, butter, and ripe fruit echoes the way she describes herself. "If you grow peaches and really love peaches you don't want to do anything to distract from peaches," she says, "you just want peaches to be peaches."

½ cup unsalted butter, melted

1 cup flour

1 cup granulated sugar

3 teaspoons baking powder

¼ teaspoon salt

1 cup milk

4 cups peaches, pitted and quartered (6 medium-sized peaches)

1 cup brown sugar

1 tablespoon fresh lemon juice

¼ teaspoon ground nutmeg

1. Preheat the oven to 375°F. Pour the melted butter into a 13 × 9 × 2-inch baking dish. In a medium bowl, combine the flour, granulated sugar, baking powder, and salt and mix well. Stir in the milk, mixing until just combined. Pour this batter over the butter. Do not stir them together.

2. Combine the peaches, brown sugar, and lemon juice in a bowl and toss. Allow to sit for 10 minutes, then pour the peaches over the batter. Again, do not stir them together. Bake in the preheated oven for 40 to 45 minutes, or until the top is golden brown. Serve warm or cold, with whipped cream or vanilla ice cream or alone.

SERVES 4 TO 6

Dean McCord's Four-Berry Cobbler

RALEIGH, NORTH CAROLINA

"I think I've made this dish at least a hundred times over the years, and there hasn't been a time when I thought it was a dud," says Dean McCord. "And that's because the dessert is all about the fruit. Blackberries, strawberries, blueberries, and raspberries. A little sugar and cinnamon. Topped with some sweet biscuits, this baked dish is summertime nirvana." You can use other fruits, such as peaches and plums with the berries. Mr. McCord has made it with gooseberries, figs, currants, and cherries, but he says the key is to use several different kinds of fruit. "It's the combination of those flavors that create the incredible taste explosion."

This recipe was adapted by the late Bill Neal, chef-owner of the legendary Crook's Corner in Chapel Hill, North Carolina, and author of *Bill Neal's Southern Cooking* (1985). "Neal didn't invent this dish," Mr. McCord says, "but he's the one who introduced it to me, and my dinner guests and I still thank him."

FOR THE FRUIT

Unsalted butter, for greasing the baking dish

8 cups mixed berries (blackberries, blueberries, raspberries, sliced strawberries)

1 cup sugar

¼ cup all-purpose flour

¼ teaspoon ground cinnamon

FOR THE BISCUITS

All-purpose flour, for rolling and cutting the biscuits

2 cups self-rising flour

½ teaspoon kosher salt

2 tablespoons sugar, plus more for sprinkling

6 tablespoons (¾ stick) unsalted butter, cut into small pieces and chilled

½ cup heavy cream

¼ cup milk

Whipped cream or vanilla ice cream (optional)

1. Preheat the oven to 425°F.

2. To make the fruit: Butter a baking dish large enough to hold the fruit. Combine the berries, sugar, flour, and cinnamon in a large bowl and gently toss to mix well. Pour into the baking dish.

3. To make the biscuits: Lightly flour the work surface. In a medium bowl, whisk together the self-rising flour, salt, and sugar. Using a handheld pastry blender or two forks, cut the cold butter into the flour until it resembles coarse crumbs. Combine the cream and milk and add all at once. Stir together gently and turn out onto the work surface.

4. Knead the dough gently 2 to 4 times. It will still be somewhat coarse. Scrape up the dough and dust the surface again with flour. Roll out—or pat out—gently until about ¾ inch thick. Cut out biscuits with a round 2- to 3-inch biscuit cutter. You'll need to dip the cutter in flour after every other biscuit. Gather up the dough scraps and reroll to maximize your yield.

5. Place the biscuits onto the fruit and sprinkle with sugar. Bake about 30 minutes, or until biscuits are browned. Serve warm with whipped cream, vanilla ice cream, or "naked." Moan at will.

SERVES 8

Fay Peterson's Blue Ribbon Apple Pie

Fay Peterson has been entering her baked goods in the Minnesota State Fair for more than thirty years and she probably has "four hundred blue ribbons in a box somewhere." Her secret, she says, is practice and patience, both of which she has in abundance. Ms. Peterson grew up in Braham, Minnesota, where her mother's father homesteaded in the early 1900s, choosing the area because the climate and terrain were similar to his native Sweden. She inherited her kitchen know-how from her mother, who helped run the family's small dairy farm and worked for the local baker. As a youngster Ms. Peterson entered and won baking competitions through her 4-H group, when the county fair was the highlight of her summer. Now in her seventies, she has clocked in countless hours mixing, chilling, waiting, rolling, and just listening to her pie dough and perfecting her fruit fillings.

In 2007 this apple pie won the prize for the single best pie at the Minnesota State Fair, beating out hundreds of entries and a dozen other blue ribbon winners. Ms. Peterson made it with a combination of Harrelson and Granny Smith apples. The following year, the apple pie and her entries in the peach pie, raisin bread, dinner rolls, coffee cake, sweet rolls, and cake with shortening categories all placed.

711

The Sweet Life

FOR THE CRUST

3 cups all-purpose flour, plus more for rolling

1 teaspoon kosher salt

1¼ cups vegetable shortening, chilled

1 large egg, beaten and chilled

6 tablespoons cold water

1 tablespoon distilled white vinegar or fresh lemon juice

FOR THE APPLE FILLING

¾ cup granulated sugar, plus 1 to 2 teaspoons for sprinkling

¼ cup packed light brown sugar

1 teaspoon ground cinnamon

Pinch of ground nutmeg

1 heaping tablespoon all-purpose flour

Pinch of salt

½ teaspoon pure vanilla extract

6 cups peeled, quartered, cored, thinly sliced apples

2 tablespoons (¼ stick) unsalted butter, softened

1. Preheat the oven to 375°F. Lightly flour the work surface.

2. To make the crust: Combine the flour and salt in a large bowl. Using a pastry blender, cut in the shortening until the mixture is crumbly. In a 1-cup liquid measure, combine the egg, water, and vinegar and beat well. Add all at once to the flour mixture, blending with a fork from the outside in, until all the flour is moistened.

3. Divide the dough into three pieces. Pat out one piece on the work surface and using a lightly floured rolling pill, roll to an 11-inch circle. Carefully fold the dough in quarters to transfer to an 8-inch pie plate and unfold without stretching, letting it drop into the pan. Trim the edges. Roll out a second piece of dough and reserve it for the top crust. (The remaining piece of dough can be wrapped in plastic and refrigerated for up to 2 weeks or frozen.)

4. To make the filling: In a large bowl, combine the sugar, brown sugar, cinnamon, nutmeg, flour, salt, and vanilla. Add the apples and toss to combine. Spoon into the bottom crust and dot with the butter.

5. Fold the dough for the top crust in quarters and place on top of the filling, with the point in the center. Unfold gently and trim the crust to a 1-inch overhang. Roll the overhang under the bottom crust, seal, and crimp the edges. Cut steam vents into top crust and sprinkle with granulated sugar.

6. Bake for 15 minutes, then lower heat to 350°F and bake for 45 minutes more, checking occasionally to make sure that the edge of the crust is not browning too fast. If it begins to brown, cover with a ring of foil or a metal pie ring. The pie is done when crust is golden and the filling juices bubble up through the vents. Cool on a wire rack.

MAKES 1 DOUBLE-CRUST 8-INCH PIE

Winner, Butler County Fair, Ohio.

Elma Smucker's Schnitz Pie

Most American Smuckers are descendants of the original family who settled in Lancaster County seeking freedom from religious persecution in their native Alsace-Lorraine. Though most still have a hand in the land, over the decades family members have became merchants and proprietors. The most notable Smucker businessman, Jerome Monroe Smucker, began selling canned applesauce and jams from the back of his horse-drawn cart in Orville, Ohio, in 1900, ultimately building the empire that became Smucker's Jam.

Like most Amish Mennonite families in Lancaster County, the Smuckers have made a life from the mantra "waste not, want not." John Smucker remembers how, as a child, he helped his grandmother and mother maintain a large vegetable garden and can and freeze its bounty in the fall. Apples from their orchard were canned as applesauce, and baked into cakes, bars, and pies. The orchards' surplus bounty would be turned into schnitz, or dried apple slices, which could be stored longer and enjoyed over winter. Elma Smucker and her mother-in-law, Anna Mary "Grussy" Smucker, dried countless bushels of apples after every harvest.

For schnitz pie, the dried apple slices are mixed with applesauce, apple butter, and brown sugar, giving it a texture and flavor distinct from a traditional fresh apple pie. John Smucker grew up eating this pie from his mother's recipe, and he says he cannot have a piece without spreading some butter on the top crust.

1 cup apple schnitz (dried apple slices)

Hot water or apple juice, as needed

5 tablespoons homemade applesauce

¾ cup apple butter

2½ teaspoons granulated sugar

1 tablespoon packed light brown sugar

¾ teaspoon ground cinnamon

⅛ teaspoon grated nutmeg

Pinch of salt

¼ teaspoon fresh lemon juice

1¾ teaspoons instant tapioca

1 recipe Pie Day Committee's Crust (page 693)

All-purpose flour, for rolling

1. Place the slices in a medium saucepan, cover with hot water or apple juice, and simmer until tender and mushy, 20 to 30 minutes. Remove the pot from the heat, add the applesauce, apple butter, granulated and brown sugars, cinnamon, nutmeg, salt, lemon juice, and tapioca, and mix until smooth. Cool to room temperature.

2. While the filling is cooling, preheat the oven to 350°F. Lightly flour the work surface.

3. Roll out half the dough and gently fit it into a 9-inch pie plate. Pour the cooled filling into the shell. Roll out the top crust and drape it over the filling. Cut to fit and crimp the edges. Cut several vents in the top.

4. Bake for 50 minutes or until the crust is brown. Serve hot.

MAKES ONE 9-INCH PIE

Thelma Levenberg's Apple Strudel

Thelma Levenberg left her home in Budapest, Hungary, as a toddler and the family eventually moved from Chicago to Gary, Indiana, where her father bought a grocery store. Mrs. Levenberg's mother, Bertha, loved to bake. "My mother used to make the dough for strudel on the dining-room table. She'd make a dough and would pull it all across the dining-room table, thin as tissue paper—you have to know how to do that, it wasn't easy—and she was an expert, not like me with the premade phyllo. My job was to go all around the dough and even the edges." When Thelma's granddaughter Mandy Levenberg called her recently, the nonagenarian was hosting six people for Shabbat (sabbath) dinner. On the menu were split pea soup, chicken paprikash, homemade applesauce—and, of course, this apple strudel. With frozen phyllo dough.

6 sheets phyllo dough, thawed if frozen

8 tablespoons (1 stick) unsalted butter, melted

Unseasoned dry bread crumbs

⅔ cup sugar mixed with ½ teaspoon ground cinnamon

3 or 4 Granny Smith apples, peeled, cored, and sliced very thin

Confectioners' sugar

1. Place the oven racks in the bottom and top positions and preheat the oven to 400°F. Lightly grease a rimmed baking sheet.

2. Take a single sheet of phyllo dough and spread it out with the longer edge in front of you on top of a clean kitchen towel (which you will use to help roll everything up). Use a spoon to dribble butter over the dough. Add a second sheet, dribble with more butter, then the third sheet and dribble with butter.

3. Lightly sprinkle a thin layer of bread crumbs along the near edge of the top phyllo sheet, covering an area approximately 3 inches in from the edge. Sprinkle 5 to 6 tablespoons of the sugar-cinnamon mixture evenly over the entire sheet. Spread half of the apple slices along the near edge (where you spread the bread crumbs), piling them a few inches high. Sprinkle them with a tablespoon of cinnamon sugar.

4. Roll the apples up into the phyllo sheets by taking the edge nearest to you and rolling it around the apples and away from you, gently but tightly. You can use the towel to get everything started but be sure to remove it as you continue. When you have completed a roll, seal up the ends with water, and transfer it to the baking sheet. Cut the roll into 6 pieces. Poke several holes into the top of each piece with a fork and brush the tops generously with the melted butter.

5. Repeat the process above to make another roll. Leave a little butter to use later.

6. Place the baking sheet on the lower rack. Bake the strudel for 20 to 25 minutes. Remove from the oven and brush more butter on top of the rolls. Return the baking sheet to the oven on the higher rack and bake until lightly browned, about 10 minutes more. Cool on a rack. Just before serving, sprinkle the confectioners' sugar on top. Serve the day it is made.

SERVES 12

Aunt Kajal's Baaghlava

Originally baaghlava was made on special occasions, particularly the Persian New Year, celebrated on March 21, the spring equinox. Shala Nosrat still marks the holiday with her aunt's recipe, as it's a rare chance for her extended family to gather. Back in Iran, large families were a part of everyday life, providing an important support system. "Here, we make do with less—less family, less support, less chance to make time-consuming desserts. Perhaps that is why I wouldn't dream of missing the chance to bake on the holidays."

FOR THE DOUGH

½ cup whole milk

2 tablespoons vegetable oil

2 large egg yolks

1¼ to 1⅔ cups all-purpose flour

½ teaspoon baking powder

Or about 15 sheets of prepared dough

FOR THE FILLING

2 pounds blanched raw almonds, chopped very finely

2 cups confectioners' sugar

1 tablespoon ground cardamom

FOR THE SYRUP

1⅔ cups sugar

1½ cups water

1 tablespoon rose water

FOR THE GARNISH

½ cup finely chopped pistachios

Additional rose water and vegetable oil to brush the top of the baaghlava

1. To make the dough, combine the milk, oil, and egg yolks. Add the flour and baking powder slowly, mixing constantly until the dough doesn't stick to you hands. Lightly flour a board and knead the dough for several minutes to combine well. Place in a bowl, cover with a damp cloth, and put in a warm place for 2 to 3 hours.

2. To make the filling, combine the almonds, confectioners' sugar, and cardamom and set aside. To make the syrup, combine the sugar and water in a medium saucepan and bring to a boil over medium-high heat, until the sugar is completely dissolved, about 2 minutes. Add the rose water and allow to boil for 2–3 minutes more until the syrup is thick enough to stick to a pastry brush. Remove from the heat and set aside.

3. Preheat the oven to 300°F. Sprinkle a work surface lightly with flour. Remove a piece of dough about the size of a golf ball and roll it out until you have the thinnest possible sheet. Cut a piece about ¼ inch larger than a 9 x 13-inch baking pan. Brush the bottom of the pan with oil or butter and fit the sheet of dough in the pan and repeat with the 2 additional layers of dough, oiling or buttering each.

4. Press a layer of the almond mixture that is about 1 inch thick on top of the dough. Sprinkle or spray lightly with additional rose water. Repeat sequence with 3 additional layers of dough, again, lightly oiling or buttering each. Cut the layers into diamond shapes that are about 1½ inches high.

5. Lightly brush the top of the dough with oil, place the baking dish on a baking sheet, and put on the lower rack of the oven. Bake for 15 to 20 minutes, then move to the upper level and bake until golden, about 15 additional minutes. Remove from the oven, cool on racks, and when it is completely cool, brush with the syrup. Wait several minutes for the syrup to be absorbed and then brush on 1 or 2 more coats. Sprinkle with chopped pistachios, cut and serve, with the remaining syrup on the side.

SERVES 12

ALYCE BIRCHENOUGH'S PEAR CROSTADA WITH BLUE CHEESE STREUSEL

ELBERTA, ALABAMA

The region around Elberta, Alabama, is rich coastal farmland with a semi-tropical climate that allows for three growing seasons. It is not the sort of place where cheese is made. But Alyce Birchenough and Doug Wolbert have changed that. Part of the 1970s back-to-the-land movement, the couple was given a Jersey cow as a wedding present and instantly had five gallons of incredibly rich fresh milk every day. They taught themselves to make butter and cheese, found the sixty-acre spread that is now Sweet Home Farm, and have been making cheese for more than thirty years. Ms. Birchenough makes this streusel with Sweet Home Farm Bayside Blue Cheese and the region's sweet-tart sand pears and serves it to "people who can't decide between having dessert or a go at the cheese plate after dinner."

FOR THE PASTRY DOUGH

1¼ cups all-purpose flour, plus more for rolling

¼ cup granulated sugar

⅛ teaspoon kosher salt

8 tablespoons (1 stick) unsalted butter, softened

1 large egg, beaten

FOR THE BLUE CHEESE STREUSEL

¼ cup plus 2 tablespoons all-purpose flour

¼ cup plus 2 tablespoons packed light brown sugar, plus more for sprinkling (optional)

½ cup sliced almonds

1¼ cups crumbled blue cheese (about 5 ounces, preferably Sweet Home Farm Bayside Blue)

FOR THE FILLING

1½ pounds ripe pears (about 4 medium to large), peeled, cored, and cut into ½-inch-thick slices

1 tablespoon fresh lemon juice

Pinch of freshly ground black pepper

2 tablespoons (¼ stick) unsalted butter, softened

1. To make the pastry dough: Lightly flour a sheet of parchment paper. Combine the flour, sugar, and salt in a large bowl. Form a well in the center and into it add the butter and egg. Using a handheld pastry blender or your fingers, mix the ingredients into a soft, pliable dough. Form it into a 4-inch disk and place it on the parchment. Roll the dough into a 10-inch circle. Place the dough, still on the parchment, on a baking sheet, cover with plastic wrap, and chill for at least 10 minutes. Meanwhile, preheat the oven to 350°F.

2. To make the streusel: In a medium bowl, combine the flour, ¼ cup brown sugar, and the almonds. Using a pastry blender or your fingers, work in ¾ cup of the blue cheese until the mixture resembles coarse meal.

3. To make the filling: In a large bowl, combine the pears, lemon juice, the remaining blue cheese, the black pepper, butter, and the remaining 2 tablespoons brown sugar. Toss to coat.

4. Sprinkle the dough with two-thirds of the streusel mixture, leaving a 2-inch-wide border around the edge. Top with the pear filling, followed by the remaining streusel. Fold the border up and around the filling. Sprinkle the folded crust with a little brown sugar, if desired.

5. Bake until the pears are tender and the crust is golden brown, 45 to 50 minutes. Serve warm or at room temperature.

SERVES 6

Vivian Richardson's Fig and Port Tart with Rose Glaze

MARIN COUNTY, CALIFORNIA

Vivian Richardson says of Marin County: "Our hills-and-valley microclimates are hospitable to almost anything we want to grow. From olives, to citrus, to loquats, to persimmons, to your average garden fare, all find a home within our borders." When her neighbor's fig tree is groaning with lush, velvety Black Mission figs, Ms. Richardson feasts on the fruit for weeks. "As I scamper back to my kitchen with my figgy loot," she says, "I am a-brim with plans. There will be fig jam. There will be small birds stuffed with figs and tarragon. There will be fig breads. There will be figs sliced and slathered with warmed Gorgonzola and topped with prosciutto." But among her favorites is this fig tart.

2½ cups good ruby port, or ¼ cup boysenberry or blackberry jam

½ recipe Michael Mulligan's All-Butter Pie Crust (page 696)

½ cup sugar

1 tablespoon all-purpose flour

Generous pinch of salt

4½ cups firm ripe figs (about 30), washed, stemmed, and cut into quarters

1 tablespoon unsalted butter, cut into small cubes and chilled

1 large egg yolk, beaten

½ cup rose jam, melted (see Note)

Vanilla ice cream or crème fraîche, for serving

1. Preheat the oven to 375°F. Place the port into a saucepan over medium-high heat, bring the port up to a simmer and reduce until it is syrupy. This is easily done, but be careful toward the end because it can go from syrup to a burned mess in an instant. When the syrup begins to foam up, you are there. Take it off the heat and set aside to cool.

2. While the port is reducing, roll out the crust and place it in a 9-inch tart pan by folding it into quarters and placing the point in the center of the pan. Unfold and gently press the dough into the pan. Trim the crust to 1 inch above the rim of the pan, then fold back in and press firmly to reinforce the edge. Chill.

3. Whisk together the sugar, flour, and salt in a large bowl. Add the figs and toss until well coated. Add the port syrup (or the jam) and toss until thoroughly distributed.

4. Pour the fig filling into the crust. Dot with the butter. Brush the crust with the beaten egg yolk. Place into the oven and bake for 30 to 35 minutes, brushing the crust once more with egg partway through, until figs are collapsed and bubbly and the pastry is brown and crisp.

5. Remove the tart from the oven and while still warm, brush with the rose jam until it glistens.

6. Serve at room temperature with vanilla ice cream or crème fraîche.

SERVES 8

NOTE: Rose jam is available in most Middle Eastern markets; it can be replaced by boysenberry or blackberry jam. The rose jam gives it a heavenly note; blackberry or boysenberry are also lovely.

Mame's Dried Fruit and Almond Tart

Mariska Eberly "Mame" Loudon, a biochemist, recently completed her doctorate in public health and says that her weekend cooking bonanzas are the counterpoint to her week life analyzing virus patterns in a laboratory. "In my line of work, I can't create big messes and throw things out when they don't suit me. But that is exactly what my boyfriend and I do on the weekends. We garden and put food by. We had a prune and Armagnac pie in the south of France and I thought we'd try to create a similar dessert using some of the fruit we dry on our weekend ranchette. I used recipes from Paula Wolfert and Patricia Wells, made a lot of mistakes, and finally got it right."

FOR THE FRUIT

½ cup pitted prunes (dried plums), quartered

¼ cup dried apricots, halved

¼ cup dried cherries

½ cup dried Calimyrna figs, quartered

¾ cup Armagnac

FOR THE CRUST

1½ cups all-purpose flour

¼ cup sugar

1 teaspoon kosher salt

½ teaspoon ground cinnamon

8 tablespoons (1 stick) unsalted butter, cut into pieces and chilled

1 large egg yolk whisked with 1 tablespoon water

FOR THE FILLING

6 tablespoons (¾ stick) unsalted butter, softened

⅔ cup confectioners' sugar, sifted

2 large eggs

1 teaspoon pure vanilla extract

3 tablespoons all-purpose flour

½ teaspoon kosher salt

1⅓ cups blanched almonds, toasted and finely ground

1. To make the fruit: Combine the prunes, apricots, cherries, and figs in a small bowl and cover with the Armagnac. Let stand for 3 hours, turning the fruit from time to time.

2. To make the crust: Pulse the flour, sugar, salt, and cinnamon in a food processor just to combine. Add the butter and pulse until the mixture resembles coarse meal. With the machine running, pour in the egg mixture. Process just until dough begins to come together. Gently press the dough together with your hands, flatten into a disk, and cover with plastic wrap. Refrigerate for 30 minutes.

3. Preheat the oven to 350°F. Roll out the dough between two large sheets of plastic wrap, then fit it into a 10-inch tart pan with a removable bottom or a 10-inch quiche dish.

4. To make the filling: Cream the butter and confectioners' sugar with an electric mixer. Beat in the eggs one at a time. Mix in the vanilla, flour, salt, and almonds.

5. Drain the fruit, discard the Armagnac and spread evenly over the bottom of the tart shell. Spoon the filling over the fruit. Bake until the filling is set and the crust is browned, about 40 minutes. Place on a rack to cool. Cut into wedges and serve.

SERVES 8

ALICE PERSONS'S BOURBON PECAN PIE

This recipe comes from Alice Persons's mother, Christine Smith Persons, of Montgomery, Alabama. "My mom was an army wife for more than thirty years," Ms. Persons says, "moving frequently and traveling many places with my dad, a career officer, and us three kids. But no matter how far she traveled from Montgomery, she never lost her accent or her ability to feed us all delicious food or throw a party on a budget. She's an old-fashioned steel magnolia with a sharp mind, a fabulous sense of humor, and nonstop glamour. She's now in her eighties and still going to dance class every week, playing bridge, turning out accomplished paintings, doing volunteer work, traveling, and entertaining. To Mom, a day without bourbon is like a day without sunshine. She enjoys her Maker's Mark with a little water. She enjoys her pecan pie with a little Maker's Mark." (Another hint from Mom: A little bourbon improves a sweet potato pie remarkably, too.)

720

One Big Table

6 tablespoons (¾ stick) unsalted butter, softened

1 cup packed dark brown sugar

3 large eggs

¾ cup dark corn syrup

2 teaspoons pure vanilla extract

1 tablespoon Maker's Mark or other good bourbon

½ recipe Pie Day Committee's Crust (page 693)

2 cups pecan halves or pieces

1. Preheat the oven to 350°F. Beat the butter and brown sugar with an electric mixer until light and creamy. Add the eggs one at a time, beating after each one. Beat in corn syrup, vanilla, and bourbon.

2. Roll out the pastry and fit into a 9-inch pie plate. Arrange 1 cup of the pecans on the bottom of the crust. Pour the filling over pecans, then sprinkle the rest of the pecans on top.

3. Bake 55 minutes to 1 hour. Serve warm or at room temperature with whipped cream or ice cream.

MAKES ONE 9-INCH PIE

CAROL WALLACE'S SHOO-FLY PIE

Carol Wallace keeps a sign on her kitchen door that says, "Never trust a skinny cook." Her ancestors were German and Swiss religious dissidents—Mennonites, Huguenots—who settled in Pennsylvania in the 1750s. When Ms. Wallace moved to Portland in the 1970s, she ran a production bakery for food co-ops, and she still caters when she's not working her day job at Portland State University. Her version of shoofly pie reflects her Pennsylvania heritage.

FOR THE CRUMBS

¾ cup all-purpose flour

⅛ teaspoon grated nutmeg

⅛ teaspoon ground ginger

⅛ teaspoon ground cloves

½ teaspoon ground cinnamon

⅛ teaspoon kosher salt

½ cup packed light brown sugar

2 tablespoons vegetable shortening or lard

FOR THE FILLING

½ teaspoon baking soda

¾ cup boiling water

½ cup unsulfured molasses

1 large egg yolk, well beaten

Dough for a 9-inch single-crust pie (pages 693, 694, 695, 696, or 697)

1. Preheat the oven to 400°F.

2. To make the crumbs: Whisk together the flour, nutmeg, ginger, cloves, cinnamon, salt, and sugar. Using a pastry blender or two knives, cut in the shortening until the mixture has a crumbly texture.

3. To make the filling: Dissolve the baking soda in the boiling water in a small bowl. Mix the molasses and egg yolk.

4. Line a 9-inch pie plate with the unbaked crust. Fill with alternating layers of crumbs and filling, ending with crumbs on top.

5. Bake for 10 minutes, or until the pie crust edges begin to brown. Reduce the temperature to 350°F and bake about 20 minutes more, until the filling is firm. Cool and serve at room temperature, with whipped cream if you like.

MAKES ONE 9-INCH PIE

Old-fashioned pies are the stock in trade at Four and Twenty Blackbirds, Brooklyn, New York.

MASON COUNTY TRANSPARENT PIE

MAYSVILLE, KENTUCKY

Transparent pie is a singular specialty known only to a small swath of northern Kentucky surrounding Maysville, the county seat of Mason County. Made of basic pantry staples, transparent pie was a revelation when supplies of nuts and berries were long exhausted. The result is somewhat akin to a pecan pie without the pecans. The following recipe is more than a hundred years old, and was first published in a Mason County Homemakers cookbook called *Bicentennial Favorites*. It came to Debra Coterill from her mother's friend Sarah Jefferson, who lived well into her nineties. Both Ms. Coterill and her mother love this recipe because it's "not typical of the bakery pies, but is more like the old, traditional version with a thin layer of filling."

½ recipe Pie Day Committee's Crust (page 693)

8 tablespoons (1 stick) unsalted butter

1 cup sugar

2 tablespoons light corn syrup

1 teaspoon pure vanilla extract

2 large eggs

1. Preheat the oven to 350°F. Roll pie crust very thin and place in a 9-inch pie pan.

2. Melt the butter and sugar in a double boiler over simmering water, stirring frequently. Remove from the heat and thoroughly whisk in the corn syrup and vanilla.

3. Beat the eggs, then add them slowly to the syrup mixture. Pour into the prepared crust and bake for 25 to 30 minutes, until the filling is set. Serve slightly warm or at room temperature.

MAKES ONE 9-INCH PIE

Pie eating contest, 1923.

AMERICAN FRIED

IT IS IMPOSSIBLE TO OVERSTATE THE AMERICAN appetite for either fried food or sweet food, and when the two come together as fried sweet food, the national response defies logic, health concerns, and often good taste. The uninitiated shake their heads. As early as the first decade of the nineteenth century, Washington

oast
d in

ted

y the question of who put the hole in the doughnut. d one innovator in a story that ran under the headline scovery Was Made and Stomach of Earth Saved." d that he was 16 years old and working on a ship e up with the idea that later revolutionized the nut industry and allowed the balls of dough to cook venly and to avoid raw doughy centers. "No more indigestion, no more greasy sinkers, just well-done fried-through doughnuts," said the inventor, adding "I never took out a patent on it; I don't suppose anyone can patent anything he discovers; I don't suppose Peary could patent the North Pole or Columbus patent America."

Fried dough—funnel cake, zeppoli and fritters, beaver tail, elephant ears and whale tales—was a ation on a similar theme and are still the reigning e of county fairs and carnivals throughout the country, South, fried pies feed the sweet-and-fried habit.

Condition: Used - Good
Entered By: Katie Powell
Entered Date: 10/12/2012
Tracking Code: STORE 38

E-037-01795

THE BRACK FAMILY SHOEBOX APPLE TARTS

GLENWOOD, GEORGIA

"My great-grandmother Dollie Hightower Brack started the shoebox pie tradition," said Vicki Adams Blizzard. "Her parents died when she was ten, and from then until she married at thirteen, she lived with her aunt and uncle on their dairy farm and worked in the kitchen. She was MeMaw and her daughter, Marie Brack Selph, was MawMaw and they were both very talented cooks. They made these little fried pies that were never greasy like other turnovers I've tasted. They always had them in the cupboard. They kept them on the 'silver platters,' which is what they called aluminum pie plates. One Christmas when we were visiting, my brother Frank was about seven and he said that he hated apple pie. Poor MeMaw's face was so downcast. She went to her cupboard and got one just to make sure. Frank said, 'Oh, that apple pie? I love that apple pie!' and she right away put towels in the bottom of a shoebox and filled them up for Frank. That was the start of a Christmas tradition. Frank always got a box of pies. He'd bring them home, put them under his bed, and not share at all. When we get together, this is what we make. They are unlike any turnover I've had, so small you can eat a couple without thinking about it, but big enough to contain all that love. Probably the secret to making them is making them at our home in Georgia. But if you follow these directions, you will come close."

FOR THE APPLE FILLING

24 Granny Smith apples, peeled, cored and sliced in ⅓-inch slices

3 cups sugar

FOR THE DOUGH

4 cups White Lily self-rising flour, plus more if needed

½ teaspoon salt

2 cups Crisco

2 cups buttermilk

Vegetable oil, for deep frying

Confectioners' sugar, for dusting

1. To make the filling, place the apples in a 4- to 6-quart pot over medium-low heat. Add the sugar, and, with a rubber spatula, coat the apples with the sugar. Cover the pot and simmer until the apples are tender, about 10 minutes. Drain in a colander and allow the apples to cool. (Apples can be made ahead to this point, cooled and frozen for up to 6 months.)

2. To make the dough, combine the flour and salt in a large bowl, make a well in the center, and add the Crisco. Using a pastry cutter or forks, combine until the mixture resembles coarse cornmeal. Add the buttermilk. Turn out onto a lightly floured board and knead, adding more flour as necessary until the dough is smooth and shiny, about 3 minutes. Divide the dough into 4 pieces and refrigerate for 15 minutes.

3. Roll out each piece to about ⅛ inch thick. Using a small saucer or biscuit cutter, cut circles 5 inches or so in diameter. Reroll the scraps if necessary to make 12 circles from each of the 4 pieces.

4. Place a tablespoon of apple filling on half a circle, moisten the edges with water, fold over, crimp, and seal with a fork. Prick holes in the top of the crust with a fork. Continue until all the pastry and filling are used.

5. Set a rack over a rimmed baking sheet, or line a baking sheet with several layers of paper towels or brown paper. Fill an electric frying pan with enough cooking oil to almost cover the tart. Warm the oil until it reaches 350 to 375°F on a deep-frying thermometer. Add several tarts and fry on each side until golden brown, about 2 minutes, carefully turning with two forks. Using a slotted spatula, carefully transfer them to a rack or baking sheet to drain briefly. Dust with confectioners' sugar. Serve warm or at room temperature.

MAKES 48 PIES

Tammy Sharp's Fried Chocolate Pies

Tammy Sharp is a veterinarian and Web site designer in central Oklahoma. She lives with a small menagerie that includes seven dogs, four cats, and occasionally assorted pigs, cows, and horses. She likes this recipe because it uses common ingredients you can find in your pantry or freezer, including packaged pie dough. For a particularly decadent version, she drizzles melted chocolate over the pies.

Dough for a 9-inch double-crust pie (pages 693, 694, 695, 696, or 697, or store-bought), thawed if frozen

2 heaping tablespoons all-purpose flour

2 heaping tablespoons unsweetened cocoa powder

6 tablespoons sugar

½ cup milk, plus more as needed to make a thick paste, and to brush pastry (optional)

2 to 4 tablespoons vegetable oil, for frying

Confectioners' sugar, unsweetened cocoa powder, or 2 ounces melted milk chocolate, for garnish

1. Roll out the dough to about ⅛ inch thick. Cut out 5- to 6-inch circles, rerolling and recutting until all the dough has been used.

2. To make the filling, combine the flour, cocoa, and sugar in a medium bowl. Add ½ cup milk and stir to combine. Add more milk, a little at a time, until a thick paste forms.

3. Place about 1 tablespoon of filling in the center bottom half of each crust. Brush the edge of crust with milk or water, fold in half, and pinch closed. Use a fork to crimp the rounded edge.

4. Line a baking sheet with paper towels. Heat the oil until it shimmers in a large skillet over medium-high heat. Fry 3 or 4 pies at a time until light brown on both sides, about 2 minutes a side. Using a slotted spatula, carefully transfer the pies to the paper towels to drain.

5. Sift the confectioners' sugar or cocoa on the pies while they're still warm, or drizzle melted chocolate on them when they've cooled a bit. Serve warm or at room temperature.

MAKES ABOUT 12 PIES

One Big Table

ROSE McGEE'S SWEET POTATO PIE

For four decades, Rose McGee has traveled the pathways of the African-American diaspora in pursuit of sweet potato pie. "It's the sacred dessert of our culture," she says, "and it's got a power that I don't understand, even after all these years." Most people believe that there will never be a sweet potato pie as good as their mama's, but Ms. McGee has developed something close to a universal recipe. She starts with fresh, high quality ingredients, a legacy of her childhood in rural Jackson, Tennessee, where the butter was homemade and the eggs came straight from the hen coop. Inspired by South Florida pies, she adds a hint of lemon, and from Louisiana, a dash of nutmeg. Under the company name Deep Roots Desserts, she sells her pies and preaches the sweet potato gospel in markets around Minneapolis.

3 medium to large well-scrubbed sweet potatoes

8 tablespoons (1 stick) unsalted butter, melted

2½ cups sugar

3 large eggs, beaten

2 teaspoons ground cinnamon

1 teaspoon grated nutmeg

¼ teaspoon ground ginger

½ teaspoon kosher salt (optional)

1 tablespoon pure vanilla extract

1 teaspoon pure lemon extract

One 14-ounce can sweetened condensed milk

1 recipe Pie Day Committee's Crust (page 693)

1. Bring a large pot of water to a boil, add the potatoes, and boil until tender, about 1 hour. (Alternatively, bake the whole sweet potatoes at 350°F for 1 hour.)

2. Drain and run under cold water until cool enough to handle. Peel and remove any dark spots and tough straw-like areas. In a large bowl, mash the sweet potatoes with a potato masher or an electric mixer until only the tiniest lumps remain.

3. Preheat the oven to 350°F.

4. In a medium bowl, blend the melted butter, sugar, eggs, cinnamon, nutmeg, ginger, salt, if using, and vanilla and lemon extracts with an electric mixer on low speed. Add to the sweet potatoes and blend with a mixer on medium speed. Add the condensed milk and mix thoroughly.

5. Divide the dough into two pieces, roll out each, and line two 9-inch pie plates. Crimp the edges.

6. Pour the batter into the crusts and place in the oven. Bake the pies about 1 hour and 20 minutes, until they are golden brown and a toothpick emerges clean. Let sit at room temperature for 1 hour before serving.

MAKES TWO 9-INCH PIES

DEB SUNDSTROM'S LAYERED PUMPKIN PIE

Rather than using sweetened, commercially canned pumpkin for her pie, Deb Sundstrom and her husband, Randy, grow their own. She roasts them in their shells and scrapes out and purees the pulp. Butternut squash combined with the pumpkin gives this pie a deeper, richer flavor.

Flour, for rolling the crust

½ recipe Pie Day Committee's Crust (page 693)

One 8-ounce package cream cheese, softened

¾ cup sugar

½ teaspoon pure vanilla extract

4 large eggs

¼ cup sweetened flaked coconut (optional)

1¼ cups mashed cooked pumpkin (see Note)

1¼ cups mashed cooked butternut squash (see Note)

½ cup sugar

½ teaspoon ground cinnamon

¼ teaspoon grated nutmeg

¼ teaspoon ground allspice

¼ teaspoon ground cloves

1 cup light cream

1. Preheat the oven to 350°F. Lightly flour a work surface, roll out the crust, and gently fit it into a 9-inch pie plate.

2. Beat together the cream cheese, ¼ cup of the sugar, and the vanilla. Stir in 1 egg and the coconut, if using. Spread in the bottom of the pie shell.

3. Combine the pumpkin, squash, the remaining ½ cup sugar, the cinnamon, nutmeg, allspice, cloves, cream, and the remaining 3 eggs and mix well. Carefully pour over the cream cheese mixture.

4. Bake about 1 hour and 5 minutes, until set or until a toothpick comes out clean. Cool on a rack.

MAKES ONE 9-INCH PIE

NOTE: To roast pumpkin and butternut squash, preheat the oven to 350°F. Cut in half and scoop out the seeds. Place cut side down on a baking sheet and roast until tender, about 1 hour.

KAREN'S MAMA'S BUTTERSCOTCH PIE

Because her father worked for the State Department, Karen Cathey spent the first six years of her life in India, Burma, and Hong Kong. But she considers herself a true Southerner at heart. When her family first moved back to the States, they lived in North Carolina, not far from her mother's family and her father's kin in South Carolina. Her true comfort food is Southern, including this pie. Her grandmother was famous for it, and she learned from her mother, Ella Lee, remembered by all simply as Mama. Mama always kept freshly made tea cakes and pies in the old "Baby Blue" woodstove that was the center of her country kitchen.

1½ cups packed light brown sugar

⅛ teaspoon salt

¼ cup cornstarch

2 large eggs, separated

1½ cups milk

2 tablespoons (¼ stick) unsalted butter

1 teaspoon pure vanilla extract

2 tablespoons sugar

½ recipe Pie Day Committee's Crust (page 693), baked in 9" pan

1. Preheat the oven to 350°F. Thoroughly mix the sugar, salt, and cornstarch in a bowl.

2. Beat the egg yolks in a medium saucepan; add the milk and butter and cook over medium heat, stirring constantly, until it comes to a boil. Add the sugar, salt, and cornstarch and cook over medium-low heat, stirring constantly, until thick. Add the vanilla and pour into pie shell.

3. Combine egg whites and sugar and beat into stiff peaks. Spread over the filling and bake until meringue is browned slightly, about 10 minutes.

MAKES ONE 9-INCH PIE

Helen Myhre's Coconut Cream Pie

MIDDLETON, WISCONSIN

Cristie Hurd is a longtime fan of the Norske Nook Diner in Osseo, Wisconsin. She bought the restaurant's cookbook fifteen years ago and it has been her baking bible ever since. The diner's founder, Helen Myhre, is her personal hero. "Helen is a farm-woman-turned-restaurant-owner . . . [who turned] . . . a one-lane town into a tourist attraction," Ms. Hurd explains. The diner is known for Ms. Myhre's homemade cooking and her "from scratch, each crust rolled by hand" pies, which have won thirteen blue ribbons at the National Pie Championship.

Though Ms. Myhre has retired, her recipes—which are re-created regularly by acolytes like Ms. Hurd—live on, as do the pies at the Norske Nook, now in three locations.

½ recipe Pie Day Committee's Crust (page 693) or ½ recipe Claudia's Better Than Store-Bought Graham Cracker Crust (page 697)

1½ cups sugar

¼ cup all-purpose flour

3 tablespoons cornstarch

3 large egg yolks

3 cups milk

1 cup sweetened flaked coconut

1 tablespoon unsalted butter

1 teaspoon pure vanilla extract

FOR THE WHIPPED CREAM (OPTIONAL)

1 cup heavy cream

¼ cup sugar

⅛ teaspoon pure vanilla extract

FOR THE MERINGUE (OPTIONAL)

12 medium egg whites

¼ heaping teaspoon cream of tartar

2 cups confectioners' sugar

1. Roll out the crust to fit a 10-inch pie pan. Bake according to the instructions and cool to room temperature.

2. Whisk together 1½ cups sugar, the flour, and cornstarch in a heavy saucepan. Add the egg yolks but do not mix. Gradually add the milk, and whisk all together thoroughly.

3. Place over medium heat and cook until thick and smooth, stirring constantly. Stir in the coconut and cook for 1 minute. Remove from the heat.

4. Add the butter and 1 teaspoon vanilla and stir well. Cool the pudding to lukewarm and pour into prepared pie crust. Refrigerate before topping with whipped cream or meringue.

5. For the whipped cream: Pour the cream into a large bowl and beat with an electric mixer on high speed just until thickened. Reduce mixer to low speed, and gradually stir in the remaining ¼ cup sugar and ⅛ teaspoon vanilla. Beat until the cream stands in soft peaks. Do not overbeat. Once the pie is cooled, top with whipped cream and serve.

6. For the meringue: Preheat the oven to 400°F. Put egg whites in a large, clean bowl. Add the cream of tartar and beat until soft peaks form, using an electric mixer on high speed. Gradually add the confectioners' sugar and beat until stiff peaks form. With a rubber spatula, spread a layer of meringue onto the pie. Spread to the edge of the crust to keep the meringue from shrinking. Repeat with rest of meringue, then gently swirl the top. Bake for 15 to 20 minutes, until golden brown. Cool on a rack.

MAKES ONE 10-INCH PIE

David Hodges's Fresh Coconut Cream Pie

San Jose, California

David Hodges, a musician, singer, songwriter, composer, actor, painter, and former chef, is a mad scientist in the kitchen. For years he wanted to create a real coconut cream pie from scratch, and in 2008, he dedicated a week to the project, sometimes making three versions a day. Along the way, he "discovered the rich, wonderfully nutty flavor derived from slow-roasted whole coconut, and a syrup made from the coconut fruit, simmered in its own juice." This is a labor-intensive pie, but worth every hour it takes.

FOR THE COCONUT

1 large coconut

⅔ cup sugar

¼ teaspoon kosher salt

FOR THE BUTTER CRUST

1⅓ cups all-purpose flour

1 teaspoon confectioners' sugar

Pinch of salt

7 tablespoons (⅞ stick) salted butter, chilled, grated, and kept cold

¾ teaspoon coconut-flavored rum

¼ teaspoon pure vanilla extract

2 tablespoons ice water

3 egg whites, lightly beaten (save the yolks for the cream filling)

FOR THE COCONUT GARNISH

2 teaspoons confectioners' sugar

Pinch of salt

FOR THE CREAM FILLING

About 2½ cups heavy cream

½ cup cornstarch

3 large egg yolks

4 tablespoons (½ stick) unsalted butter

1 teaspoon distilled white vinegar

1 tablespoon coconut-flavored rum

1 teaspoon pure vanilla extract

FOR THE WHIPPED CREAM TOPPING

1½ cups heavy cream

¼ cup confectioners' sugar

¼ teaspoon pure vanilla extract

¾ teaspoon coconut-flavored rum

1. To prepare the coconut: Place oven racks in the upper and lower thirds and preheat the oven to 350°F. Puncture the soft eyes of the coconut with a screwdriver and hammer. Shake out all the coconut water into a medium bowl. Place coconut on the lower rack in oven and bake for 30 minutes. Remove from the oven and drain any remaining water into the bowl. Strain the water through a sieve into a medium saucepan.

2. Wrap the coconut in a kitchen towel and place on a hard surface and break apart the shell with a hammer. Pry out the meat in large pieces with a table knife or wide-blade screwdriver. Remove the brown skin with a vegetable peeler. Rinse the meat and place in a glass baking dish and bake on the upper rack for 40 minutes. Turn the pieces over using tongs and bake for 40 minutes more. Remove from the oven and raise the heat to 375°F.

3. Add the sugar and salt to the coconut water. Bring to a boil, then reduce heat to low. Add the baked coconut and cover. Simmer for 35 to 45 minutes, until the syrup has turned a rich golden color. Remove from the heat and let cool completely. Chill in the refrigerator.

4. When cold, remove the coconut pieces with tongs, shaking off the syrup. Using a fine-shred grater, grate the coconut until you have 1 cup and set aside. Reserve the rest of the coconut for another use.

5. To make the butter crust: While the coconut is simmering and chilling, combine the flour, sugar, and salt in a food processor; process about 5 seconds. Add the butter and process about 10 seconds. Mix the rum and vanilla with the ice water and pour evenly over the mixture. Process for 10 to 15 seconds.

6. Form the dough into a disk and roll into a circle, 10 to 11 inches in diameter and ⅛ inch thick or less. Between two large sheets of waxed paper, fit the dough evenly into a 9-inch pan. Trim the pastry edge slightly larger than the pan and flute the edge. If the dough becomes too soft, place in the freezer for 2 minutes until firm enough to handle.

Herdcine Williams, Vicksburg, Mississippi, with her famous coconut pie.

7. Prick the finished pie shell with a fork and place in the freezer for 10 minutes. Line the shell with parchment or waxed paper and fill with pie weights or a small ovenproof plate. Bake for 15 minutes. Remove the paper and weights. Brush with a thin layer of the egg whites (you may not need all) to ensure even browning, and bake another 5 to 10 minutes. Remove from the oven and cool on a rack. Reduce the oven temperature to 300°F.

8. To make the coconut garnish: Toss ½ cup of the grated coconut with the confectioners' sugar and salt. Spread in a baking dish and toast on the upper rack about 20 minutes, stirring often to avoid scorching. The coconut should be an even golden brown. Set aside to cool.

9. To make the cream filling: Measure the coconut syrup and add enough cream to make 3 cups. Return to the saucepan. Whisk in the cornstarch, then the egg yolks, until well blended. Bring to a slow boil, whisking constantly. Add the butter, the remaining ½ cup grated coconut, the vinegar, rum, and vanilla. Reduce the heat to low and cook, stirring constantly, until the mixture is smooth and heavily coats a spoon (about the consistency of creamy pudding). Pour into a cooled pie shell. Cover and refrigerate about 2 hours.

10. To make the whipped cream topping: Place the cream in the bowl of an electric stand mixer and whip on high speed, adding the confectioners' sugar gradually, until the cream begins to thicken. Add the vanilla and rum and continue whipping until cream forms soft peaks. Using a spatula, spread the cream over the filling, leaving the crust untouched. Decorate in swirls and sprinkle with the toasted coconut.

MAKES ONE 9-INCH PIE

Barbara J. Duke's Buttermilk Pie with Blackberry Sauce

Nearly thirty years ago, Barbara Duke and her friend Shirley Sandy began creating parties and serving dinners at Rose Hill, a historic plantation, and quickly turned the place into a mecca for traditional Southern cooking. This recipe had been handed down from the family of Mose Smith, who once lived on the estate. "When the settlers came, they didn't have a lot of ingredients," Ms. Duke says, "but many had a cow, which meant they always had buttermilk—the liquid left over after churning butter." The only significant change they made was serving the dessert with a blackberry sauce, which gives a sweet, peppery hint to this deliciously tart pie.

FOR THE PIE

½ recipe Anne LaFiandra's Lard Crust (page 694)

3 large eggs

1 cup sugar

2 tablespoons all-purpose flour

8 tablespoons (1 stick) unsalted butter, melted and slightly cooled

1 cup buttermilk

2 teaspoons pure vanilla extract

FOR THE SAUCE

½ cup highest-quality seedless blackberry preserves

1 tablespoon Chambord liqueur

1. To make the pie: Preheat the oven to 325°F. Roll out and fit the crust into a 9-inch pie pan. Beat the eggs slightly in a large bowl. Combine the sugar and flour, add to the eggs, and continue beating until creamy, about 3 minutes. Add the butter and mix well. Add the buttermilk and vanilla and beat well to combine. Pour into the pie shell and bake for 45 minutes to 1 hour, until the custard is set. Cool on a rack.

2. While the pie is baking, make the sauce: Put the preserves in a saucepan and warm on medium heat, stirring constantly with a whisk until smooth. Remove from the heat and stir in the Chambord.

3. Cool to lukewarm and serve over the pie.

SERVES 6

David's Pinup Cheesecake

MONTCLAIR, NEW JERSEY

David Sterry, a writer, husband, father, and cheesecake freak, uses gingersnaps rather than traditional graham crackers to make his crust. The result, he says, is "light as a feather, yet valuable in hand-to-hand combat. This angelish devil of a cake is so gorgeous you'll want to blow up a picture of it and stick it on your wall. The key to making this work is to whip, stir, and blend as much air as possible into this baby. In the words of the great Devo, 'Whip, whip it good.'"

FOR THE CRUST

One 1-pound box gingersnaps

½ teaspoon freshly grated nutmeg

1 teaspoon ground cinnamon

½ teaspoon ground allspice

1 tablespoon finely chopped candied ginger

6 tablespoons (¾ stick) unsalted butter, melted

FOR THE BATTER

6 large eggs, separated

1 tablespoon finely grated lemon zest

¼ cup fresh lemon juice

1½ teaspoon pure vanilla extract

1¼ cups sugar

1½ pounds cream cheese, softened

½ cup all-purpose flour

1 cup heavy cream

FOR THE SOUR CREAM TOPPING

2 cups sour cream

1 teaspoon pure vanilla extract

3 pinches of salt

1½ tablespoons sugar

1. To make the crust: Preheat the oven to 350°F. Place the cookies in the bowl of a food processor and pulse briefly to create crumbs. Add the nutmeg, cinnamon, and allspice, pulse to combine, and pour into a bowl. Stir in the ginger. Add the melted butter and combine. Press the mixture into a 9-inch springform pan, creating a crust about 1½ inches thick.

2. To make the batter: Using an electric mixer, beat together the egg yolks, lemon zest and juice, the vanilla, and sugar. Beat in the cream cheese in small chunks. When the mixture is liquid, add the flour a little at a time. Set the mixer on its highest setting and continue to mix vigorously for 10 to 15 minutes. Meanwhile, beat the egg whites in a large bowl until they form soft peaks. In a small bowl, whip the cream to soft peaks.

3. With a rubber spatula, alternately fold in a third of the egg whites and a third of the whipped cream, continuing until both are incorporated. Place the springform pan on a baking sheet and carefully pour the batter into the pan. Bake for 50 to 60 minutes until the cake is set but still slightly soft. Remove the cheesecake to a rack to cool and raise the oven temperature to 425°F.

4. To make the sour cream topping, stir together the sour cream, vanilla, salt, and sugar. When the cheesecake is at room temperature, apply the topping evenly. Return to the oven and bake for 5 minutes. Cool at room temperature, then refrigerate for at least 4 and up to 24 hours before serving.

SERVES 12

SHAKER LEMON PIE

PLEASANT HILL, KENTUCKY

"The Shakers were a pastoral people with simple tastes, but they ate well. They brought with them from the East a style of cooking that favored hearty, rich, filling foods, and over the decades of their presence in Kentucky they added regional and local touches that their forebears in New England probably would have considered strange, but altogether satisfying numerous varieties of cornbread, vegetables seasoned with cured pork, country ham, pecan and chess and pecan pies. Shaker lemon pie and sugar pie were among the desserts the missionaries brought with them to Kentucky, and they continue to delight visitors at Pleasant Hill."

—John Egerton, *Southern Food: At Home, on the Road, in History*

2 large lemons

2 cups sugar

2 tablespoons all-purpose flour, plus more for rolling

1 recipe Michael Mulligan's All-Butter Pie Crust (page 696)

4 large eggs, well beaten

3 tablespoons (³⁄₈ stick) unsalted butter, melted

¼ teaspoon kosher salt

1. The day before you plan to serve the pie, slice the lemons as thin as paper, rind and all, pick out the seeds, and place in a shallow bowl. Add the sugar and mix well. Let stand 2 hours, or preferably overnight, stirring occasionally.

2. Preheat the oven to 450°F. Lightly flour a work surface. Roll out half of the dough and gently mold it into a deep-dish 9-inch pie pan. Roll the remaining dough and set aside to use for the top crust.

3. Add the eggs to the lemon mixture and mix well. Add the melted butter, 2 tablespoons flour, and salt and mix well. Turn the mixture into the pie shell, arranging lemon slices evenly. Use a pastry wheel to cut the remaining dough in strips, and use them to weave a lattice top crust. Crimp the edges, place on a baking sheet, and bake for 15 minutes.

4. Reduce the oven temperature to 350°F and bake for 20 to 30 minutes more, until the filling is set and the top crust has begun to turn gold. Serve at room temperature.

MAKES ONE 9-INCH DEEP-DISH PIE

Nora Ephron's Chocolate Cream Pie

NEW YORK, NEW YORK

Nora Ephron was famous for her chocolate cream pie long before she wrote and directed the film *Julie & Julia*. Delving into the life of the country's most beloved French chef did not dilute the director's appreciation of simple American pleasures. "This is an amazingly easy pie," she said, "just as easy as making chocolate pudding from a package. My variation, which is brilliant, if I do say so myself, is putting pulverized English toffee on top of the crust before pouring in the filling. It gives you sort of a Heath Bar crunch chocolate cream pie."

½ recipe Claudia's Better than Store-Bought Graham Cracker Crust (page 697)

¾ cup granulated sugar

3 tablespoons cornstarch

¼ teaspoon kosher salt

3 cups milk

4 ounces best-quality unsweetened chocolate, broken into small pieces

4 large egg yolks, slightly beaten

1 tablespoon pure vanilla extract, plus ¼ teaspoon more for the whipped cream

2 tablespoons (¼ stick) unsalted butter, softened

½ cup pulverized English toffee or Heath Bars

1 cup heavy cream

2 tablespoons confectioners' sugar

Shaved chocolate, for garnish

1. Line a 9-inch pie plate with the graham cracker crust. Bake according to the directions in the recipe. In a small bowl, combine the granulated sugar, cornstarch, and salt.

2. Bring the milk to a boil in a medium saucepan over medium-high heat. Reduce the heat to medium, stir in the chocolate, and let melt. Whisk in the sugar mixture and cook over medium heat, stirring constantly with a wooden spoon, until it starts to thicken.

3. Remove from the heat. So the yolks don't curdle, add a spoonful of the hot melted chocolate mixture to them and whisk, then another spoonful and whisk. Then pour all the yolks into the pan and whisk furiously. Return to the heat and stir for 30 to 60 seconds, until the mixture thickens. Remove from the heat and continue stirring for a minute to dissipate the heat.

4. Stir in the vanilla and butter. Cover with waxed paper and cool to room temperature.

5. When the filling has cooled, cover the bottom of the cooled pie shell with the pulverized toffee, add the filling, and chill for at least 1 hour.

6. Just before serving, whip the heavy cream, ¼ teaspoon vanilla, and confectioners' sugar to soft peaks. Cover the pie with the cream, sprinkle the shaved chocolate atop, and serve.

MAKES ONE 9-INCH PIE

HALEY SCOTT'S BANANAS FOSTER TART

PASADENA, CALIFORNIA

"I went to school in New Orleans and got obsessed with Bananas Foster," said Haley Scott, a documentary film maker. "This tart was my attempt to combine that idea with my favorite dessert, tarte tartin. Use barely ripe bananas for best results—you can often find organic ones in a farmers' market—and turbinado sugar really does make a difference."

FOR THE CRUST

4 tablespoons (½ stick) cold unsalted butter

1½ cups flour, plus more if needed

½ cup ground nuts, preferably macadamia

¼ teaspoon salt

1 egg yolk

FOR THE BANANAS

4 tablespoons butter

¾ cup turbinado sugar

6 barely ripe bananas, peeled and cut in half widthwise

1. To make the crust, cut the butter into small chunks and use fingertips or a wire pastry cutter to combine the flour with the butter until it resembles coarse meal; add the ground nuts and salt. Beat the yolk with a teaspoon of water and add to the mixture; then work briefly on a floured board until it comes together in a ball. Cover and refrigerate for 30 minutes.

2. Preheat oven to 350°F. To make the bananas, melt the butter in an 8- to 10-inch cast-iron skillet. Reduce heat to medium low, add the sugar, and cook, stirring constantly, until dark honey colored, about 4 minutes. Immediately add the bananas and toss. Cook for 1 minute, jiggling the pan to avoid burning and remove from heat.

3. Roll out the crust on a floured board. Tuck around the bananas and bake until the crust is golden and the caramel is bubbling and dark, 40 to 45 minutes. Invert on a plate and serve with ice cream or whipped cream.

SERVES 6 TO 8

Ann Shaffer's Broiled Bananas with Black Ginger Sauce

BLOOMINGTON, INDIANA

"This is a surprisingly elegant and yet simple dessert," Ann Shaffer says, and it's one of her favorite things to do with overripe bananas when she gets tired of banana bread. To get the right soft, custardy flavor, the bananas must be fully ripened—underripe bananas won't produce the same result.

This dish must be served while still warm, but it takes so little time to prepare that as long as the broiler's hot, it can be thrown together for a dinner party while the after-dinner coffee brews. Ms. Shaffer makes one serving of one full banana (two halves), but you can offer half a banana per person for a lighter serving. This recipe can easily be reduced or increased—she often makes herself a single serving with the last banana of the bunch.

4 large bananas, very ripe or slightly overripe

8 tablespoons (1 stick) unsalted butter

¼ cup blackberry preserves (preferably seedless)

¼ cup ginger preserves (preferably Dundee)

Vanilla ice cream, for serving

1. Set an oven rack 6 to 7 inches from the heat and preheat the broiler.

2. Cut off the ends of the unpeeled bananas, then slice each in half lengthwise. (Make sure to remove any labels from the peels.)

3. Place the banana halves peel down in a broiling pan or flameproof baking dish. Broil until tender and starting to brown, 10 to 12 minutes.

4. While the bananas broil, melt the butter and blackberry and ginger preserves in a small saucepan over medium heat, stirring often.

5. Pour the sauce over the bananas and return to the broiler until the sauce bubbles, 2 to 4 minutes more. Remove from the broiler.

6. Gently lift the bananas out of their peels with a spoon, and place one or two halves on each dessert plate or shallow bowl. Spoon up sauce from the broiling pan and drizzle over the bananas. Top each serving with 1 or 2 scoops of vanilla ice cream.

SERVES 4 TO 8

THIERRY'S SAUTÉED FRUIT IN GINGER-CARAMEL SAUCE

WAIKIKI, HAWAII

"My great-grandparents were Japanese, my grandmother was Polynesian-French, and sautéed fruit was something we had for dessert pretty regularly," said Thierry Kawena. "My mother used a simple caramel, sometimes adding honey to it. I added ginger because I like the bite. Exotic fruit like pineapple, mango, and banana work best for this recipe, but I've also used plums and nectarines and peaches. We usually serve it with ice cream." For best results, infuse the sugar with a split vanilla bean one week prior to making this recipe.

1 cup unsalted butter

1 cup sugar infused with 1 vanilla bean

1 tablespoon honey

One 1-inch gingerroot, peeled and grated

2 cups fresh ripe pineapple, peeled and cut into 2-inch wedges

2 barely ripe mangoes, peeled and cut into 1-inch slices

2 bananas, cut into quarters

Melt the butter in a skillet over medium heat. Add the sugar, honey, and half the ginger, reduce heat to low, and cook, stirring frequently, until the sugar is the color of dark honey. Quickly add the fruit and the remaining ginger, toss, cook for 2 minutes, and serve, with ice cream if desired.

SERVES 4 TO 6

Willa Davidsohn's Delectable Jellied Guava

INDIALANTIC, FLORIDA

To Willa Davidsohn, nothing is sweeter—no cake, no pie, not even candy—than a dessert with exotic fruit. For as long as she can remember, she's been a member of the Brevard Rare Fruit Council in her hometown of Indialantic and has tended the council's park, a job that has its perks, including a small plot of land of her own, on which she cultivates as many as thirty trees. She grows black sapote, a dark fruit with soft pulp that can be eaten like chocolate pudding. Roselle makes an excellent tea, and she sneaks carambola into pies and upside-down cakes. She also grows jaboticaba, whose grape-like fruits make a lovely liqueur. Considering all this, guava seems as humdrum as bananas. But she loves it, especially in this refreshing gelatin.

One ¼-ounce packet (1 tablespoon) unflavored gelatin

¼ cup cold water

¼ cup boiling water

¾ cup plus 2 tablespoons sugar, less if fruit is quite sweet

3 tablespoon fresh lemon juice

1 cup guava puree

1 teaspoon grated lemon zest (optional)

4 large egg whites (see Note)

1. Soak the gelatin in the cold water in a shallow baking dish for a few minutes to soften. Stir in the boiling water to dissolve it. Stir in the sugar until dissolved. Stir in the lemon juice, guava puree, and lemon zest, if using. Place the dish in a larger pan of cold water and refrigerate until chilled to a syrupy consistency.

2. Whip the gelatin mixture with an eggbeater or electric mixer until frothy. Clean the beater and whip the egg whites until stiff. Fold the egg whites into the gelatin mixture a little at a time.

3. Taste the mixture when two-thirds to three-quarters of the whites have been added and decide if the dessert is frothy enough for your taste. Cover and refrigerate for 4 hours before serving.

SERVES 4 TO 6

NOTE: If you have any concerns about egg-born bacteria or do not have access to healthy, organic, farm-fresh eggs, reconstituted powdered egg whites or refrigerated pasteurized ones are safer to use in this recipe.

ED BEHR'S BAKED MAPLE CUSTARD

PEACHAM, VERMONT

The northeast kingdom of Vermont changes as slowly and imperceptibly as the Green Mountains that surround it. This portion of the world is less touched than most by modern trends. After summer's relentless bloom and fall's blaze of foliage, the bare-limbed trees might sparkle with a little frost. Ed Behr, the 46-year-old editor of *The Art of Eating*, says that his cooking is resolutely simple and invariably seasonal, less about a particular philosophy or aesthetic than it is about his twenty-five-year residency here. As the subscribers to his quarterly newsletter know, Behr is a man obsessed with geography, agriculture, and language. Having grown up in Washington, D.C., he was drawn to Vermont by the price of real estate, the back-to-the-land movement, and the chance of a simpler life. Too many options, too many things to cook, and too many ways to cook it were "more distracting than exhilarating to me," he said. To be simple in a complicated world—to combine, for instance, local milk and eggs with the first of the year's maple syrup— is, he says, a risky proposition. "We are living in an era in which the challenge tends to be making the least from the most. I sort of like the challenge of making the most from the least."

2½ cups whole milk

4 large eggs

¾ cup maple syrup

1 teaspoon high-quality vanilla extract

1. Preheat the oven to 325 degrees. In a medium saucepan, heat the milk over medium heat until very hot but not boiling. Meanwhile, in a large bowl, gently whisk the eggs with a fork, incorporating as little air as possible. Gradually whisk in the hot milk, then the maple syrup and vanilla. Strain the custard mixture through a fine-mesh sieve and skim off the foam.

2. Place six ⅔-cup ceramic ramekins or custard cups in a shallow roasting pan and pour in boiling water to reach halfway up their sides. Carefully ladle in the custard and bake until just set, about 40 minutes. Serve warm.

SERVES 6

Making maple syrup, 1906.

Adrian Miller's Banana Pudding

Adrian Miller didn't grow up in the geographic South. Raised in Denver by a father from Arkansas and a mother from Tennessee, Mr. Miller, an attorney who was a special assistant to President Clinton and the deputy director of the president's Initiative One America, is a child of the Southern diaspora. Which means he eats and cooks more Southern than many who've never ventured north of the Mason-Dixon. "There were mustard and turnip greens, candied yams, black-eyed peas, cornbread, and chitterlings, the stuff people call 'soul food,' but of course it's not soul, it's southern po-folks, a constant reminder," he said. "No kid can come home to the smell of chitlins and not have questions, so the stories of these foods were shared. We had three desserts: banana pudding, sweet potato pie, and lemon icebox pie. Those desserts weren't reserved for special occasions. My mother, Johnetta, is a revered cook in the church and the community. I'm telling you this as a connoisseur, not just as a sloppy, sentimental mother-loving son: No one makes a better banana pudding. No one. She doesn't measure, but I've watched enough and this version is about as close to hers as I can get."

FOR THE CUSTARD MIXTURE

1 cup sugar

½ cup flour

½ teaspoon salt

4 cups whole milk

4 egg yolks

2 teaspoons vanilla extract

1 box vanilla wafers

8 bananas, not too ripe, sliced crosswise in ½-inch slices

Butter, for greasing the pan

FOR THE MERINGUE

4 egg whites

½ teaspoon cream of tartar

½ cup white sugar

1. A half hour prior to preparing the pudding, place the eggbeaters in the freezer; this helps make a stiffer meringue. Preheat the oven to 350°F. Place water in a double boiler over medium-high heat and bring to a boil.

2. To make the custard, combine the sugar, flour, and salt in the pot and reduce the heat to medium. Add the milk and stir and cook for 15 minutes, stirring constantly to prevent lumps. If lumps do appear, whisk them out.

3. Beat yolks together, add several spoons of the hot milk, whisk to combine, and then slowly pour the egg yolk mixture into the milk, stirring constantly. Cook for 2 minutes. Turn off the heat and add the vanilla and set aside.

4. Lightly butter a 9½ × 13-inch glass baking dish. To make the meringue, beat the egg whites with the cream of tartar at high speed with an electric mixer, gradually adding the sugar until the whites form stiff peaks.

5. Cover the dish with a layer of vanilla wafers and then a layer of bananas. Pour some of the custard mixture over the layers. Continue alternating until all the ingredients are used up. Finish with the custard mixture. Spread the meringue over the top of the custard. Bake in the oven at 350°F for 15 minutes, cool to room temperature, and then cool in the refrigerator. Serve cold.

SERVES 6

The Wisconsin Bakers Association State Fair Cream Puff

WEST ALLIS, WISCONSIN

Cream puffs have been synonymous with the Wisconsin State Fair since the Dairy Bakery began producing and selling them there in 1924. By 1936, the bakery sold more than 27,000 to fairgoers; by 1954, after a wartime hiatus that seemed to increase residents' craving, the number topped 92,000. In 2009, more than 345,000 cream puffs were sold. The bakery had to open two satellite locations and offer six-packs of the dairy bombs to go to ease the long lines at the Cream Puff Pavilion.

1 cup water

4 tablespoons (½ stick) unsalted butter

¼ teaspoon table salt

1 cup all-purpose flour, sifted

4 large eggs

1 large egg yolk, lightly beaten

2 tablespoons milk

2 cups heavy cream, whipped with pure vanilla extract and sugar to taste

Sifted confectioners' sugar

1. Preheat the oven to 375°F. Butter and flour one very large or two small baking sheets, or line with parchment paper.

2. Pour the water into a large heavy saucepan. Cut the butter into small pieces and add to the water. Add the salt. Place the saucepan over medium-low heat so the butter melts before the water boils. Bring just to a boil.

3. Remove the pan from the heat and add the flour all at once, stirring vigorously with a wooden spoon. Return the pan to the heat and continue stirring vigorously until the dough forms into a smooth ball and there is a film on the bottom of the pan. Remove from the heat and let the dough rest for 5 minutes.

4. Add the whole eggs, beating in one at a time. The dough should be stiff but smooth.

5. Immediately drop ¼ cupfuls of dough 3 inches apart on the baking sheet. You should have 12 puffs. (For a neater appearance, use a pastry bag with a ¾-inch plain tip and pipe the dough onto the baking sheet.)

6. Combine the egg yolk and milk in a small bowl. Brush each puff with this glaze, taking care not to let any drip onto the baking sheet.

7. Bake for 35 minutes until puffed and golden brown.

8. Transfer the puffs to wire racks to cool, pricking each with a cake tester or toothpick to allow steam to escape, or leave them in the turned-off oven with the door propped open for about 1 hour, until firm. (If the baked pastry is filled before cool and firm, it will be soggy and may collapse.) Baked puffs should have hollow, moist interiors and crisp, lightly browned outer shells.

9. Cut off the tops and fill with whipped cream, using a pastry bag with a star tip or a large spoon. Replace the tops of the puffs and sprinkle with confectioners' sugar.

MAKES 12 CREAM PUFFS

TYPICAL COWS

HOLSTEIN
AYRSHIRE

JERSEY
SHORT-HORN.

Jeanne Hodesh's Rice Pudding

CASTINE, MAINE

"My father was a chef at the old Gloucester House in New York City when I was very young. The restaurant was owned by Mr. Lillies, and his family's Greek rice pudding was always on the menu," says Jeanne Hodesh, a 27-year-old cook, writer, and local food advocate. "When I was six, my parents moved to Maine and bought a restaurant. My grandmother, who is from France, came to help my father, and along with a local Maine woman, they worked on perfecting Mr. Lillies's rice pudding recipe. It is so delicious that you think it must be complicated. But it's not. In the end, it was not possible to improve on Mr. Lillies's recipe. I started making it when I was thirteen years old. It is important to rinse all the excess starch from the rice and to remove the pudding from the heat before it has thickened. It takes nerve, but you have to remove it before it looks done, that is crucial to a creamy pudding. The rice will continue to release starch and thicken the pudding even after the sugar and butter have been added. You have to trust the future." This recipe is a crowd-pleaser that serves thirty-two people. It can be successfully quartered to serve 6 to 8—but leftovers are not a bad thing.

1 pound (about 2½ cups) white long-grain rice (not Texmati or Basmati)

16 cups milk

2 cinnamon sticks

Zest from 2 lemons

½ teaspoon salt

1 cup sugar

2 tablespoons butter

1 cup raisins

1½ teaspoons high quality real vanilla

1. Place the rice in a sieve under running water and stir grains around with your fingers. Continue rinsing and stirring until the water runs clear.

2. In a 2-gallon pot over high heat, scald the milk with the cinnamon sticks, lemon zest, and salt. Reduce the heat, add the rice, and stir. Simmer slowly, stirring occasionally, until rice is tender, about 30 to 35 minutes. Be careful not to overcook the rice as this will create gooey pudding. Remove from the heat. The pudding will not, at this point, have thickened very much. Add the sugar, butter, and raisins, and allow the pudding to cool nearly to room temperature. Stir in the vanilla. Remove the cinnamon sticks and serve.

SERVES 32

Commander's Palace
Bread Pudding Soufflé

"Our bread pudding is the single most popular dish at our restaurant," said Miss Ella Brennan, whose family has run Commander's Palace for nearly half a century. Originally built in 1880 by Emile Commander in New Orleans's Garden District, the restaurant has long been a bastion for both classic and innovative New Cajun and Creole cooking. But not even luminaries like Paul Prudhomme and Emeril Lagasse, both of whom served as the restaurant's chef, tried to change the lofty bread pudding with strong whiskey sauce. The Commander, said Miss Ella, "always said, 'If it ain't broke, don't fix it.'" It is best to make the pudding and the sauce the day before serving.

FOR THE BREAD PUDDING

¾ cup sugar

1 teaspoon ground cinnamon

⅛ teaspoon nutmeg, freshly grated

3 medium eggs

1 cup heavy cream

1 teaspoon high quality, pure vanilla extract (do not use imitation)

5 cups day-old French bread, cut into 1-inch cubes

⅓ cup raisins

FOR THE WHISKEY SAUCE

1½ cups heavy cream

2 teaspoons cornstarch

2 tablespoons cold water

⅓ cup sugar

⅓ cup bourbon

FOR THE MERINGUE

9 medium egg whites, at room temperature

¼ teaspoon cream of tartar

¾ cup sugar

1. To make the bread pudding, preheat the oven to 350°F and use butter to grease an 8-inch-square baking pan. In a large bowl, combine the sugar, cinnamon, and nutmeg. Beat in the eggs one by one until smooth, then beat in the cream and vanilla. Fold in the bread cubes and set aside for 10 minutes, stirring occasionally to allow the bread to soak up the custard.

2. Scatter the raisins in the baking pan and pour in the egg mixture. Bake until the pudding is golden and firm to the touch, 25 to 30 minutes. The pudding should be moist, not runny or dry. Let cool to room temperature.

3. While the pudding is baking, make the sauce. Bring the cream to a boil over medium heat. Whisk together the cornstarch and water. Remove the cream from the heat and, stirring constantly, add the cornstarch mixture. Return the pan to the heat, bring to a boil, reduce the heat to low and cook, stirring constantly, for 30 seconds. Stir in the sugar and the bourbon, remove from the heat, and cool to room temperature. (The recipe can be done ahead to this point and the pudding and sauce stored, well covered, in the refrigerator, until an hour before serving.)

4. An hour before serving, bring the egg whites, bread pudding, and sauce to room temperature. Preheat the oven to 350°F, butter six 6-ounce ceramic ramekins, and set aside. Thirty minutes before serving, make the meringue: Whisk the egg whites in a clean bowl until frothy. Add the cream of tartar and gradually whisk in the sugar. Continue whipping until the whites are thick and white and stand in soft peaks.

5. In a large bowl, break half the bread pudding into ½- to 1-inch pieces. Gently fold in a quarter of the meringue. Divide the mixture among the 6 ramekins. Break the remaining bread pudding into pieces in a bowl and fold in the remaining meringue. Top off the soufflés with this mixture, mounding it 1½ inches over the top edge of the ramekin. Use a spoon to smooth and shape the tops into a dome. Bake for 20 minutes until golden brown. Remove from the oven, prick holes in the top of each soufflé with a fork, spoon over the whiskey sauce, and serve immediately.

SERVES 6

New Orleans Supper Scene, 1912.

Margaret Hathaway's Sticky Toffee Pudding

Margaret Hathaway grew up in Wichita, Kansas, studied English and anthropology at Wellesley, and after spending a year in Tunisia on a Fulbright scholarship, moved to New York, where she became the manager of the Magnolia Bakery. But city life was not for her, so in 2002, she and her husband, the photographer Karl Schatz, spent a year traveling the United States in search of the perfect goat cheese—and the perfect goat. Today, the couple raises goats—and two toddlers—in Maine. Inspired by a recipe by Marie Simmons, Ms. Hathaway added a few touches garnered from her travels to create this delicious variation of the old British classic.

FOR THE PUDDING CAKE

1 cup plus 1 tablespoon all-purpose flour

1 teaspoon baking powder

¾ cup pitted dates, roughly chopped

1¼ cups boiling water

1 teaspoons baking soda

¼ cup unsalted butter, softened

¾ cup granulated sugar

1 large egg, lightly beaten

1 teaspoon pure vanilla extract

FOR THE TOFFEE SAUCE

½ cup unsalted butter

1½ cups heavy cream

1 cup packed light brown sugar

1. To make the cake, preheat the oven to 350°F and butter a 10-inch-round or square baking dish. Sift the flour and baking powder together and set aside. Chop the dates fine, place in a small bowl, add the boiling water and baking soda and set aside.

2. In a bowl of an electric mixer, beat the butter and sugar until light and fluffy. Beat in the egg and vanilla. Gradually incorporate the flour mixture. Fold in the date mixture with a rubber spatula. Pour into the prepared baking dish. Bake until pudding is set and firm on top, about 35 minutes. Remove from the oven to a wire rack.

3. To make the toffee sauce, combine the butter, heavy cream, and brown sugar in a small heavy saucepan; heat to boiling, stirring constantly. Boil gently over medium-low heat until the mixture is thickened, about 8 minutes. Preheat the broiler. Spread about ⅓ cup of the sauce evenly over the pudding. Place the pudding under the broiler until the topping is bubbly, about 1 minute. Serve immediately. Drizzle each serving with toffee sauce and top with a spoonful of whipped cream.

SERVES 6

Suze Grégoire's Crème Chaud

Josiane Grégoire was born in Haiti, but when she was young, she and her family fled the Duvalier dictatorship. She grew up in New York City, but her upbringing remained very Haitian thanks to her grandmother, Thérèse Bourjolly Théronier. Known as Granny Thé Thé, she ran a formal household with Caribbean warmth—setting her tables with white linen, fine silver, and traditional Haitian dishes.

Sweets were Granny Thé Thé's specialty. As the eldest daughter, she was responsible for making desserts for her father, who had an especially sweet tooth. This warm, fluffy pudding is spicy and made from dark Haitian chocolate.

When Granny Thé Thé got older, she passed the baking torch to her daughters Suze Grégoire (Josiane's mother), Josèphe Théronier, and Enine Kaiembe.

3 large eggs, separated

¼ teaspoon freshly grated nutmeg

Zest of 1 lime

1 tablespoon Maizena cornstarch or flour

¼ cup water

4 cups whole milk

2 ounces rich dark unsweetened chocolate

4 to 5 cinnamon sticks

4 star anise pods

Pinch of salt

¾ cup sugar

1 teaspoon pure vanilla extract

1. Measure and set aside all the ingredients since the preparation steps move quickly. Separate the egg whites and yolks into two bowls. With a whisk, slowly beat the yolks. Grate the nutmeg into the yolks. Set aside.

2. Whisk or beat the egg whites until stiff peaks form then fold in the lime zest. Set aside. Dissolve the cornstarch in the water. Set aside.

3. In a medium pot, bring the milk, chocolate, cinnamon sticks, star anise, and salt to a boil. As the mixture comes to a boil, stir in the sugar, remove from the heat, and keep stirring.

4. Slowly add the yolk mixture, and stir vigorously for 5 minutes until yolks are fully incorporated. Put the pan back on medium heat and keep stirring vigorously for about 5 minutes more.

5. When the mixture starts to boil again, add the cornstarch and water mixture and continue stirring. Remove from the heat.

6. Slightly beat the egg whites until the peaks are stiff again and fold into the cooling pudding.

7. Stir in the vanilla.

8. Serve in glasses with handles (because it's hot).

SERVES 6 TO 8

ABUELA'S MEXICAN FLAN
Crème Caramel

Her given name was Palmyra Cueva, but her grandchildren simply called her Abuela ("grandmother" in Spanish), and they spent most of their visits with her in the kitchen. Mrs. Cueva was from Oviedo in northern Spain. Most of her specialties were simple peasant dishes made with fresh, often homegrown, ingredients. She made her own chorizo and had a smokehouse, and her husband made wine from grapes shipped to West Virginia from California. Among her most spectacular desserts was her flan—which she presented in one massive dish, spooning a generous portion onto each plate and topping it with a dazzling drizzle of caramel. Her grandchildren count this recipe as their most cherished inheritance.

¾ cup plus 6 tablespoons sugar

3 large eggs

3 large egg yolks

¼ teaspoon grated lemon zest

2½ cups whole milk

½ teaspoon pure vanilla extract

1. Preheat the oven to 350°F. Melt ¾ cup of the sugar in a heavy saucepan over medium-high heat, swirling but not stirring, until the sugar is golden brown. Remove from the heat immediately and pour into a 2-quart baking dish. Swirl the caramel around to coat the bottom of the dish.

2. Lightly beat the eggs and egg yolks. Add the lemon zest, the remaining 6 tablespoons sugar, the milk, and vanilla. Pour through a strainer into the caramel-coated baking dish. Place the dish in a larger pan, such as a roasting pan, and carefully pour in warm water about halfway up the sides of the baking dish.

3. Place the pan in the oven and bake for 60 to 75 minutes, until the custard is set; it will still be a little jiggly. A knife inserted in the center should come out clean. Chill before serving.

SERVES 6

JOE CASTIGLIONE'S SHORTBREAD

One beastly hot weekend in the summer of 2008, thousands of people organized bake sales across the country to raise money for their presidential candidate. Dozens of reporters and researchers expected to find a banquet of brownies and chocolate chip cookies stretching from sea to shining sea. Instead, they found as many cellophane bags of store-bought cookies as there were plates of familiar homemade goodies. One recipe appeared on every one of the hundred-some dessert tables visited: Rice Krispies Treats.

Among the few one-of-a-kind recipes that bred envy and gluttony was Joe Castiglione's shortbread. Mr. Castiglione, a parcel deliveryman, has sifted through hundreds of iterations to find a shortbread that was buttery, sandy, and tender enough to make people stop and think.

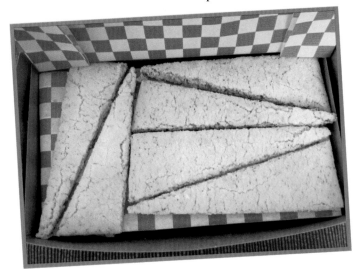

1 pound (4 sticks) unsalted butter, softened

1 cup packed light brown sugar

4 cups all-purpose flour

¼ teaspoon kosher salt

1. Place an oven rack in the center position and preheat the oven to 325°F.

2. In a large bowl, mix the butter and sugar. Blend in the flour, 1 cup at a time. Knead in the last cup of flour and the salt with your hands.

3. Roll out the dough on a lightly floured surface to ½ inch thick. Cut into 3 × 1-inch strips. Prick with a fork and place on two ungreased baking sheets.

4. Bake one sheet at a time for 20 minutes, until lightly browned. Transfer to a wire rack to cool.

MAKES 48 COOKIES

Tom O'Connor's Turtle Cookies

REDMOND, WASHINGTON

Like many family recipes, Tom O'Connor's turtle cookies never changed for a long time. The recipe that his grandmother brought with her from Ireland was a straightforward directive that used unsweetened chocolate, flour, and butter. Mr. O'Connor, a video programmer, loved the cookies. After his girlfriend coached him on the fine art of not scorching the chocolate, he began experimenting and loved the results even more. Using less flour, he developed a shorter, crisper cookie. He began to substitute chocolate with higher butterfat to get a silkier, more nuanced taste. He suffered no guilt for introducing these changes—or for working with someone outside the O'Connor clan to make them. "I wouldn't have gotten better at making these cookies if I'd bought into the whole 'secret-recipe' thing," he says.

FOR THE COOKIES

1 pound (4 sticks) unsalted butter, melted and cooled

⅓ cup packed light brown sugar

1 whole large egg

1 large egg, separated

¼ teaspoon pure maple syrup

½ teaspoon pure vanilla extract

1½ cups all-purpose flour

¼ teaspoon baking soda

1 cup chopped pecans

FOR THE FROSTING

2 tablespoons (¼ stick) unsalted butter

2 ounces unsweetened chocolate, finely chopped

1 tablespoon milk

1 to 2 cups confectioners' sugar

1. To make the cookies, preheat the oven to 350°F. Line two baking sheets with parchment.

2. In a large bowl, combine the butter, sugar, whole egg, egg yolk, maple syrup, and vanilla. Whisk together the flour and baking soda and stir into the wet ingredients.

3. Lightly stir the egg white in a shallow dish. Roll the dough into 48 balls, dip the bottom of each one into the egg white, then press down in the pecan pieces, flattening the bottom. Place on baking sheets and bake for 12 to 14 minutes until light brown.

4. Transfer the cookies to a wire rack and cool to room temperature.

5. To make the frosting, in the top of a double boiler, melt the butter and chocolate in the milk. Remove from the heat and mix in the confectioners' sugar until thick. Spread on the cookies or dip the tops of the cookies in the frosting.

MAKES 48 COOKIES

AMY FITZGIBBONS'S PEANUT BUTTER COOKIES

Amy Fitzgibbons, an executive with American Express, has tried to put her mother's peanut butter cookies on a diet. To appeal to her friends, all of them health-conscious urbanites, she's tried nonhydrogenated vegetable shortenings, reduced-fat peanut butter, and fruit puree for part of the fat. The results were less than pleasant. It turns out you can take a cookie out of the Midwest, but it's more difficult (and far less rewarding) to take the Midwest out of the cookie. This is her mother's unabridged version.

2 large eggs

1 cup packed light brown sugar

1 cup vegetable shortening

1 cup chunky peanut butter

1 teaspoon pure vanilla extract

2 cups all-purpose flour

1 teaspoon baking soda

1 teaspoon baking powder

½ teaspoon kosher salt

1. In a large bowl, combine the eggs, sugar, shortening, peanut butter, and vanilla and beat until smooth. Sift together the flour, baking soda, baking powder, and salt and incorporate into the batter. Refrigerate the dough for 1 hour.

2. Place an oven rack in the center position and preheat the oven to 375°F.

3. Roll the dough into 24 little balls, place on the baking sheet about 1 inch apart, press down slightly, and crosshatch with a fork. Bake for 10 minutes. Transfer to a wire rack to cool.

MAKES 24 COOKIES

THE SERENDIPITOUS CHOCOLATE CHIP

THE NOTION OF BAKING BITS OF CHOCOLATE INTO COOKIE DOUGH IS SO SIMPLE, SO quintessentially American—like mowing the lawn or throwing around a baseball—it's hard to fathom that someone had to *invent* it. But chocolate chip cookies sprang into existence as the Toll House Inn Cookie and later, as the Toll House cookie. Like many great things, they were a serendipitous accident. One day Ruth Wakefield, who owned the Toll House Inn outside Whitman, Massachusetts, with her husband, Kenneth, was about to bake Butter Drop Do cookies—a simple favorite consisting of butter, sugar, flour, and eggs. She thought she'd give them a chocolaty twist by cutting up a Nestlé Semi-Sweet Chocolate bar into small bits and adding them to the dough. Instead of melting, the bits softened but held their shape. Ta-da! Toll House Cookies.

The press loved the story. Nestlé wanted to put the recipe on its packaging. Mrs. Wakefield leveraged a deal that stipulated—presumably among other things—a lifetime supply of chocolate bars. It didn't take long before bakers began to personalize their iterations, using preferred brands of chocolate, tossing in other elements, all giving rise to the more inclusive category, "chocolate chip cookie."

Pricey or cheap, crunchy or chewy, big or small—a chocolate chip cookie will always be America's favorite. The ability to bake a mean batch has long been a badge of honor. In 1992, despite her notorious "stay home and bake cookies" comment, Hillary Clinton offered her family recipe for Oatmeal Chocolate Chips in a *Family Circle* magazine competition with Barbara Bush. (Mrs. Clinton defeated Mrs. Bush's Classic Chocolate Chip—and in 2004, Laura Bush's Oatmeal Chocolate Chunks beat out Teresa Heinz Kerry's Pumpkin Spice.)

With the entrepreneurial spirit and appreciation for good food demonstrated by the Wakefields, amateur and professional bakers alike continue to put their personal mark on the cookie. The 1970s saw more than its share of the gussied-up variety. New York chef David Liederman tempted busy Manhattanites into his store with the aroma of cookies baked with Swiss Chocolate chunks and whole nuts; Palo Alto mother Debbi Fields transformed her humble shop—featuring cookies with milk chocolate, white chocolate, and other twists on the original—into a global empire; and Wally Amos, a talent agent who managed the likes of Marvin Gaye and Dionne Warwick, paid homage to his Aunt Della's cookies with his Famous Amos brand before moving to Hawaii and launching his store, Chip & Cookie, in Waikiki and Kailua.

Holly Lane's Best Cookie

"I originally got this recipe from a friend when we lived in Massachusetts. The recipe originally was called Cohasset Chip Cookies, but I've changed it and made it my own over the years," said Holly Lane, a baker, wife, mother, and baseball fan. "They are so crisp and fabulous, people fall in love with them. We are big baseball fans and I used to bake them when I went to games and send them to the players in the clubhouse. The Yankees loved them most, Derek Jeter used to ask for them. I keep the dough in the refrigerator or freezer and bake them right before serving. I like to make them large, café size. The secret is baking them on a stone, not a tray. That's the only way they come out perfectly."

1 cup unsalted butter, melted

1 cup brown sugar

1 cup granulated sugar

2 eggs

1 teaspoon vanilla extract

1 cup rolled oats

1 cup crushed cornflakes

1⅞ cups flour

1 teaspoon baking powder

1 teaspoon baking soda

½ teaspoon salt

1 cup chocolate chips

2 cups (1 bag) crushed Heath bar chips

½ cup coconut

½ cup raisins

¼ cup dried cherries

1. Preheat the oven to 350°F. Combine the butter, brown sugar, and sugar. Beat in the eggs one at a time. Add the vanilla and stir.

2. In another bowl, combine the oats, cornflakes, flour, baking powder, baking soda, and salt. Fold the dry ingredients into the wet ones. Add the chocolate chips, Heath bar chips, coconut, raisins, and dried cherries and stir to combine.

3. Form into 2-inch balls and bake directly on a baking stone for 12 to 15 minutes, until crisp.

MAKES 32 LARGE COOKIES

Pat McCorkle's Chocolate Chip Cookies

Locals flock to the great Spring Green Literary Festival every September in Southwestern Wisconsin to hear great authors read from great books. But it's fair to say that some arrive to get their fix of the cookies baked by the festival's founder, Pat McCorkle. Raised on a farm in rural Pennsylvania, Ms. McCorkle makes her celebrated cookies with fresh organic ingredients. Her favorite tip for making sure that multiple large batches come out just right: "I make sure the pans aren't still warm when I put the second round of cookies on. In summer, I run cold water over the underside of the pan. In the winter, I plunk the empty hot pan on the deck to cool."

½ pound (2 sticks) unsalted butter

¾ cup granulated sugar

¼ cup packed light brown sugar

1 teaspoon pure vanilla extract

1 teaspoon water

2 large eggs

1½ cups whole-wheat flour

1 teaspoon baking soda

1 teaspoon kosher salt

2¼ cups old-fashioned rolled oats

1 cup chocolate chips

1. Place an oven rack in the center position and preheat the oven to 325°F. Grease two large baking sheets.

2. Beat the butter and sugars until light and fluffy. Add the vanilla, water, and eggs. Beat hard. Add the flour, baking soda, and salt. Mix well, then gently stir in the oatmeal and chocolate chips until just incorporated.

3. Spoon scant 1-teaspoon portions of dough onto the prepared baking sheets. Bake the cookies, one sheet at a time, for 22 to 25 minutes, until quite brown. Transfer to a wire rack to cool.

MAKES 8 DOZEN BITE-SIZE COOKIES

Mariel Chua's Milk Chocolate and Marshmallow Cornflake Cookies

DENVER, COLORADO

Mariel Chua moved from the Philippines to the United States ten years ago to become a beauty writer and editor for a woman's magazine. It took some time, but homesickness eventually caught up with her. She says: "Everything went so fast, like the elevators in the Hearst Tower where I worked, the fastest elevators in the fastest city in the world. My life was like that, moving so fast, everything was a dazzling blur. And then suddenly, I missed the Philippines. I remembered, of all things, the Choco Flakes from the sweet shop in Baguio City. People who vacation in Baguio usually bring canisters of these chocolate flakes back to Manila. I always did. They're quite addictive. At Christmas, people use them to make cornflake cookies. The more I missed home, the more I missed those cookies. One day, a friend who had also relocated to the United States told me about the cornflake chocolate chip marshmallow cookies at Momofuku Milk Bar in New York City. Delicious! After moving to Colorado, I spent time creating a recipe that is a nod to my heritage as well as my first home in my new country. This version essentially combines the two."

8 tablespoons (1 stick) unsalted butter

½ cup granulated sugar

½ cup packed light brown sugar

1 large egg

1 teaspoon pure vanilla extract

1½ cups all-purpose flour

½ teaspoon baking soda

½ teaspoon kosher salt

½ cup cornflakes, plus more for topping

¼ cup miniature marshmallows, plus more for topping

⅔ cup large semisweet chocolate morsels or coarsely chopped semisweet chocolate (preferably Nestlé Tollhouse Chocolate Chunks but the bigger, the better), plus more for topping

½ cup white chocolate morsels, plus more for topping

1. Preheat the oven to 375°F. Lightly grease 2 baking sheets.

2. In a large bowl, cream the butter and sugars with an electric mixer until fluffy. Add the egg and vanilla and mix well.

3. In a separate bowl, combine the flour, baking soda, salt, cornflakes, and marshmallows. Using a rubber spatula, fold the flour mixture into the butter and egg mixture. Then gently fold in the chocolates. Do not overmix.

4. Drop in rounded tablespoons onto the baking sheet. Top each cookie with a chocolate chunk, a white chocolate morsel, and two cornflakes "ears."

5. Bake for 6 to 8 minutes, until lightly browned. Transfer to a wire rack. While the cookies are still hot, top each with a marshmallow. Cool completely before storing.

MAKES ABOUT 36 COOKIES

SANDRA DAMSCHRODER'S SUGAR COOKIES

This recipe had been lost for many years until Sandy Damschroder found it in the handwritten pages of a family recipe book. It calls for lard because the family kept pigs, and lard was cheaper than butter. Today, when Ms. Damschroder mixes the same ingredients that her foremothers did more than a century ago and bakes them in her wood-fired stove, she feels as if Great-Great-Grandma Augusta could walk though the kitchen door any moment.

3 cups all-purpose flour

2 teaspoons baking powder

1 teaspoon baking soda

¼ teaspoon ground cinnamon or freshly grated nutmeg

2 cups sugar

1 cup lard

2 large eggs

1 cup buttermilk

1. Place an oven rack in the center position and preheat the oven to 350°F. Grease two large baking sheets.

2. In a medium bowl, whisk together the flour, baking powder, baking soda, and cinnamon. In a large bowl, cream the sugar and lard, then beat in the eggs until fluffy. Add the buttermilk, alternating with the dry ingredients.

3. Spoon heaping tablespoons of the dough onto the prepared baking sheets. Bake for 8 to 10 minutes, until lightly golden brown and no longer doughy. Transfer to a wire rack to cool.

MAKES ABOUT 36 COOKIES

757

The Sweet Life

LELA MARVIN'S BUTTERSCOTCH COOKIES

MONTPELIER, OHIO

These butterscotch cookies have been made for at least four generations of Mrs. Marvin's descendants. The use of baking soda and cream of tartar indicates that the recipe was written down before baking powder was available in rural markets.

With a layer of butter pecan ice cream, the cookies make a delicious ice-cream sandwich.

1 cup lard or ½ pound (2 sticks) unsalted butter

4 cups packed light brown sugar

4 large eggs

1 tablespoon cream of tartar

1 tablespoon baking soda dissolved in ¼ cup hot water

7 cups all-purpose flour, sifted

1 teaspoon pure vanilla extract

1. In a large bowl, cream the lard and sugar. Add the eggs one at a time and beat until fluffy. Add the cream of tartar, baking soda mixture, flour, and vanilla and mix until just incorporated.

2. Form the dough into 4 loaves, roll in parchment paper, and refrigerate for 8 to 24 hours.

3. Place an oven rack in the center position and preheat the oven to 350°F. Lightly grease 2 baking sheets.

4. Cut 2 of the loaves into slices each. Lay the slices flat on baking sheets, about 1 inch apart, and bake for 8 to 10 minutes, until lightly golden. Transfer to a wire rack to cool. Let the baking sheets cool and repeat with the remaining dough.

MAKES 48 COOKIES

First Lady Grace Coolidge sampling Girl Scout cookies, 1923.

Margit Schott's Swedish Shortbread with Jam

When Margit Schott left Sweden to marry her fiancé in Minneapolis, she packed her most treasured possessions. Few, however, have proven more meaningful than this recipe for shortbread, which she learned to bake in school. What makes this shortbread Swedish? Unlike their plainer counterparts from Scotland, these are made with jam—and so they come out of the oven like glistening edible works of art. Mrs. Schott likes to say, "The only secret to baking good Swedish shortbread is to bake Swedish shortbread for sixty-five years." Her five grandchildren have already started practicing.

½ pound (2 sticks) unsalted butter, softened

½ cup plus 2 tablespoons granulated sugar

¼ teaspoon kosher salt

2¼ cups all-purpose flour

One 8- to 10-ounce jar high quality seedless raspberry jam

1 cup confectioners' sugar

2 teaspoons pure almond extract

1 tablespoon water

1. In a bowl, beat the butter, granulated sugar, and salt until light and fluffy. Sprinkle about one-third of the flour over the butter mixture. Using a rubber spatula, fold the flour into the butter with a few quick strokes. Repeat until all the flour is used. Cover with plastic wrap and refrigerate for at least 1 hour.

2. Preheat the oven to 350°F. Remove the jam jar's lid and place the jar in a small saucepan. Add the water halfway up the outside of the jar and place over low heat until the jam is warm and slightly melted.

3. Divide the dough into two pieces. Roll each out into about 4 × 15 inches, then cut in half lengthwise. Transfer the strips to a baking sheet.

4. Use the tip of a wooden spoon handle to press a narrow canal down the center of each strip. Carefully spoon the jam into this hollow: Don't fill the indentation completely or it will overflow. Bake until dry and just browned on the bottom, about 10 minutes.

5. While the cookies are baking, stir together the confectioners' sugar, almond extract, and water in a small bowl until smooth. As soon the cookies come out of the oven, drizzle them with the glaze. While still warm, cut the strips diagonally into slender bars. Transfer to a rack to cool.

MAKES ABOUT 60 COOKIES

EVA LANCELLO'S SWEDISH DREAMS

Eva Lancello's baking training began in her grandmother's kitchen in her native Sweden, and it is only through her willingness to experiment (and decades of trial and error) that Mrs. Lancello has become the baking maven she is today. She has one piece of advice for would-be Cookie Queens: "Don't be afraid to fail every once in a while." She is known for her airy Swedish Dreams and now passes her tricks along to her grandchildren in Minnesota.

To achieve this cookie's famously delicate crunch, use a light touch. And use the secret ingredient, baker's ammonia, a leavening agent common in many Scandinavian cookies and pastries. Mrs. Lancello also swears by margarine, but butter produces equally ethereal results.

8 tablespoons (1 stick) unsalted butter, softened

1¼ cups sugar

1 teaspoon pure vanilla extract

⅓ cup vegetable oil

1 teaspoon baker's ammonia or 2 teaspoons baking powder

1⅓ cups all-purpose flour

¼ cup slivered blanched almonds (optional)

1. Preheat the oven to 300°F. Use 1 tablespoon of the butter to grease three baking sheets.

2. In a large bowl, beat the remaining 7 tablespoons butter, the sugar, and the vanilla until light and fluffy. Continue beating while adding the oil in a slow, steady stream.

3. Combine the baker's ammonia with 1 tablespoon of the flour and fold into the mixture. Sprinkle half of the remaining flour over the batter and use your hands to quickly knead it in to make a dough. Knead in the remaining flour.

4. Take a piece of dough about half the size of a walnut (about 1 tablespoon), roll into a small ball, and press gently onto a baking sheet. The cookie should look rounded, not flat. Press a slivered almond (if using) into the center. Continue until all the dough is used, leaving about 1 inch between cookies. Bake until firm, 15 to 20 minutes. Transfer to a wire rack to cool. Serve.

MAKES ABOUT 50 COOKIES

Virginia's French Almond Cookies

Virginia O'Neill began making Christmas cookies the day after Thanksgiving and continued making a batch a day until the twentieth of December. "I'd grown up as a single child, raised by a wealthy aunt and uncle who were older and quiet. They had cooks and servants and everything was always perfect. I distinguished myself by preparing dinner on the cook's night off and by baking cookies and pies. I started collecting Christmas cookie recipes in grade school, and even after I married into a different life—my husband was a dashing workingman and I had six children—my aunt and uncle expected me to bake. I used to love doing it. Hundreds of intricate, delicate cookies. It was a way of reconciling where I'd come from and what I'd become, I guess. Always use a little less butter than is called for, that is the secret. The French Almond Cookies last for a month, if you store them in a tin, with wax paper between the layers."

761

The Sweet Life

½ pound (2 sticks) lightly salted butter, cut into chunks

1¼ cups packed light brown sugar

1¼ cups granulated sugar

1 tablespoon honey

2 large eggs, well beaten

2 cups ground almonds

3 cups all-purpose flour

1 teaspoon baking soda

½ cup slivered almonds

1. Preheat the oven to 350°F. Line a baking sheet with parchment paper. Cream the butter and sugars until smooth. Stir in the honey, eggs, and ground almonds. Combine the flour and baking soda, then add to the butter mixture. Mix well.

2. Pinch off a piece of dough the size of a walnut (about 2 tablespoons). Roll it between your palms to form a cigar shape. Place on the baking sheet. Repeat, placing the cookies 2 inches apart. Push a slivered almond into the center of each cookie.

3. Bake until golden brown, about 10 minutes. Immediately transfer to a wire rack to cool. Let the baking sheet cool and reline with parchment before shaping and baking more cookies.

MAKES ABOUT 11 DOZEN COOKIES

DOLLY'S BUTTERBALLS

Melanie Fay is known in Birmingham for her fabulous parties—and she has her mom, Lurene Hall, to thank. Known as Dolly, Mrs. Hall was a local fashion model and avid home cook. "You need to create your own signature," Mrs. Hall always told her daughter—hers was marking her two tiny rows on biscuits with the tines of a fork. These butterballs—what the rest of the country calls Russian Tea Cakes or Mexican Wedding Cookies—were first published in the *Woman's Home Companion Cook Book* in 1943. But when Ms. Fay serves them every Christmas she makes that recipe her own.

½ pound (2 sticks) unsalted butter, softened

¼ cup confectioners' sugar, plus more for rolling

1 teaspoon pure vanilla extract

2 cups all-purpose flour, sifted

1 cup finely chopped pecans or walnuts

1. Preheat the oven to 350°F. Cream the butter. Add the sugar and beat until light and fluffy, then add the vanilla. Add the flour and mix well. Fold in the nuts.

2. Roll into small balls, about the size of walnuts (2 tablespoons). Place on an ungreased baking sheet. Bake for 15 to 18 minutes, until lightly browned on the bottom. Roll in confectioners' sugar while still hot.

3. Transfer to brown paper bags or wire racks to cool.

MAKES ABOUT 36 COOKIES

One Big Table

Palmyra Cueva's
Barcelona Lemon Cookies

CHARLESTON, WEST VIRGINIA

Palmyra Cueva grew up in Spain where the ingredients were homegrown and the cooking was done from the heart. Her recipes have migrated to such far-flung places as Charleston, West Virginia, where her granddaughter lives.

FOR THE COOKIES

3¼ cups all-purpose flour, sifted

1¼ tablespoons baking powder

Pinch of kosher salt

½ pound (2 sticks) unsalted butter, plus more for greasing cookie trays

1 cup sugar

3 large eggs, lightly beaten

1 teaspoon pure vanilla extract

1½ tablespoons pure lemon extract

FOR THE ICING

2 cups confectioners' sugar

1 teaspoon pure lemon extract

½ to ¾ cup evaporated milk

1. To make the cookies: Combine the flour, baking powder, and salt in a large bowl. In a separate bowl, beat the butter and sugar until creamy; add the eggs, vanilla, and lemon extract. Mix in the flour mixture a little at a time until the dough is loose and not dry. (You may not need all of the flour mixture.) Refrigerate the dough for about 2 hours, until chilled.

2. Preheat the oven to 350°F and lightly grease the cookie trays.

3. Roll the dough by hand into ropes about ½ inch wide. Cut the ropes into 2- to 2½-inch-long pieces and place on the baking sheet about an inch apart. Bake for 10 minutes. Transfer to a wire rack to cool.

4. To make the icing: Beat together the confectioners' sugar, lemon extract, and milk until it is the consistency of lightly whipped cream. (Add the milk slowly so the icing doesn't get too thin.) Glaze the cookies with the icing and serve.

MAKES 48 COOKIES

Anne Friend Thacher's Pixie Tangerine Cookies

Anne Friend Thacher is a third-generation citrus farmer. In 1869, when her grandmother was a toddler, her family moved from Devonshire, England, to California. Fifteen years later they began growing citrus in Ojai, and today the family grows fifteen different kinds of tangerines and mandarins, plus several varieties of lemons, oranges, and grapefruit. Mrs. Thacher adapted this cookie recipe to highlight the Pixie tangerine, which is among the last to ripen every season; you can often find them as late as June. The macadamia nuts are a respectful nod to her father-in-law, who once grew them. They're a hard nut to crack (literally, you need a hammer), but they're what makes this recipe so special to her.

8 tablespoons (1 stick) unsalted butter

¾ cup sugar

2 teaspoons grated tangerine zest (preferably Ojai Pixie tangerine)

1 tablespoon fresh tangerine juice (preferably Ojai Pixie tangerine)

1 large egg

1¼ cups all-purpose flour

¼ teaspoon baking powder

½ cup coarsely chopped macadamia nuts (optional)

1. Place an oven rack in the center position and preheat the oven to 350°F. Lightly grease a baking sheet.

2. In a large bowl, cream the butter and sugar. Add the tangerine zest and juice and the egg and mix until incorporated. Stir in the flour, baking powder, and nuts, if using.

3. Dollop by the teaspoonful onto a baking sheet. Bake for about 10 minutes, until lightly golden. Transfer to a wire rack to cool.

MAKES 24 COOKIES

Sandra Scalise Juneau's Cuccidatta
Fig Cookies

To Sandra Scalise Juneau, these fig cookies represent who she is, what she believes in, and where she came from. Keeping alive a tradition that her grandmother and others brought to New Orleans from Sicily, Ms. Juneau bakes the pastries for friends and for her church's altar guild every year on March 19, the feast of St. Joseph. Her grandmother Angellina Caronna Accardo, who lived in Poggioreale, Sicily, also taught her to make fig cakes, which she decorated by carving the outline of the sacred heart of Mary and displayed on the church altar. "I was fascinated by the whole process," says Ms. Juneau of her grandmother's baking ritual. "It was a spiritual exercise. It was a prayer."

FOR THE FILLING

2 pounds dried Greek figs, stemmed

1 tablespoon ground cinnamon

¼ cup honey

2 tablespoons grated orange zest

⅛ teaspoon freshly ground black pepper

FOR THE DOUGH

¾ cup vegetable shortening

5 cups all-purpose flour

1 to 2 cups warm water

¾ cup granulated sugar

FOR THE ICING

2 drops pure almond extract

1 tablespoon milk

2 cups confectioners' sugar

Colored nonpareils or sprinkles (jimmies)

1. To make the filling: Rinse the figs thoroughly in warm water to soften. Drain off any excess water.

2. In a large bowl, toss the figs with the cinnamon, honey, orange zest, and pepper, blending thoroughly. Using a hand-cranked or electric meat grinder (not a food processor), grind the mixture to a fine texture. The filling will keep in the refrigerator for several weeks, or it may be frozen for up to 6 months.

3. To make the dough: Place an oven rack in the center position and preheat the oven to 350°F. Combine the shortening and flour and blend to a cornmeal texture. This can be done by hand in a large bowl or in a food processor.

4. Add 1 cup warm water to the granulated sugar and stir to dissolve. Gradually add the sugar-water to the flour mixture. Mix until the dough forms a ball. If the dough seems too dry and doesn't come together, gradually add more water as needed to form a dough ball. Cover and let the dough rest for 10 minutes.

5. Separate the dough into balls about 3 inches across. Knead each ball until smooth and return to the bowl. Cover again and let the dough rest for several minutes more.

6. Pinch off a small piece of dough (about a 2-inch ball). Roll into a rectangle the thickness of pie dough, about ⅛ inch. Cut the rectangle of dough into strips approximately 4 inches wide by 12 inches long. For each strip, shape some of the filling into a roll that is ½ inch wide and about 12 inches long. Place the filling on the center of the dough. Fold the sides of the pastry over the filling, overlapping the dough slightly. Turn over, seam side down, and pat lightly to flatten.

7. Cut on an angle into 1-inch-long bars. Place on baking sheets, about 1½ inches apart. Cut slits in the sides and on top so the bars cook through.

8. Bake for 20 to 30 minutes. The cookies should be slightly browned on the bottom only. Transfer to a wire rack to cool before icing.

9. To make the icing: Add the almond extract to the milk and gradually blend into the confectioners' sugar until it's a smooth paste.

10. Working over a small bowl, spoon the icing onto each cooled cookie, allowing any excess to drip into the bowl.

11. Allow the icing to dry slightly before sprinkling with nonpareils. Before packaging the cookies, allow them to dry completely (if they last that long!).

MAKES 48 COOKIES

Salwa Atassi's Mamoul
Date-Filled Pastries

When Salwa Atassi and her husband left their home in Damascus and headed to the Arab enclave in Troy, Michigan, she took with her a pile of handwritten cards with her favorite recipes. She inherited the recipe for these rich pastries from her Turkish mother, and it remains her favorite. Her oldest daughter, Maha, makes them often—as the first-born granddaughter, she inherited her grandmother's mamoul molds.

FOR THE DOUGH

½ teaspoon active dry yeast

2 tablespoons sugar

½ cup warm water

3 cups farina (such as Cream of Wheat)

½ pound (2 sticks) unsalted butter, melted

½ cup all-purpose flour, sifted

¼ cup vegetable oil

¼ tablespoon ground mahlab

Pinch of kosher salt

⅓ cup water

⅓ cup milk

FOR THE FILLING

1 pound date paste

1 tablespoon unsalted butter

1. Place an oven rack in the center position and preheat the oven to 350°F.

2. To make the dough: Combine the yeast and 1 teaspoon of the sugar with the warm water.

3. In a large bowl, combine the remaining 5 teaspoons sugar, the farina, melted butter, flour, oil, mahlab, salt, water, and milk. Make a well in the center, add the yeast mixture, and work together until a dough forms.

4. To make the filling, in a medium bowl, combine the date paste and butter.

5. Roll walnut-size balls of dough with your hands. Open a hole in each ball with your forefinger and fill with about 1 teaspoon of the date filling (or press the dough into a wooden mold, tap out of the mold, and fill the same way).

6. Place on ungreased baking sheets about 1 inch apart and bake one sheet at a time for 45 minutes to 1 hour, until golden. Transfer to a wire rack to cool.

MAKES 36 COOKIES

Peggy McClanathan's Melomakarona
Greek Walnut Cookies

When Peggy McClanathan's family arrived from Greece, her parents each worked as many as four jobs. Her mother's mother minded the children, taught them to cook—and kept a sharp eye on them. This walnut cookie is a family heirloom, and Peggy bakes it (along with seventeen other Greek cookies) during the holidays. Her son, Michael, watches, helps, and counts the seconds until the cookies emerge from the oven. Mrs. McClanathan loves the smell of baking cookies and the childhood memories the aroma evokes.

768

One Big Table

FOR THE SYRUP

2 cups sugar

3 cups water

½ cup honey

1 cinnamon stick

1 teaspoon grated orange zest

FOR THE COOKIES

6–8 cups all-purpose flour

2 cups sugar

2 cups chopped walnuts

4 teaspoons baking powder

2 teaspoons ground cloves

2 teaspoons ground cinnamon

3 cups vegetable oil

1½ cups fresh orange juice

1 teaspoon pure vanilla extract

1. To make the syrup: In a saucepan, combine the sugar, water, and honey. Bring to a boil, reduce the heat, and add the cinnamon stick and orange zest. Simmer for 15 minutes. Remove from the heat and set aside to cool.

2. To make the cookies: Preheat the oven to 350°F. Grease two baking sheets.

3. Stir 6 cups of the flour together with the sugar, walnuts, baking powder, cloves, and cinnamon in a large bowl. Add the oil, orange juice, and vanilla and gradually work in additional flour as needed to make a dough. Let the dough rest for 10 to 15 minutes.

4. Roll the dough into walnut-sized balls and press into 2-inch oblongs. Arrange on the baking sheets and bake until lightly golden, about 30 minutes. Transfer to a wire rack to cool. When the cookies reach room temperature, dip into the syrup and serve.

MAKES 48 COOKIES

STEVE COREN'S LACED SANDWICH COOKIES

"I had this lifelong fantasy of making baking better than Pepperidge Farm," says Steve Coren. "It wasn't easy, but if you use intensely fabulous ingredients and are careful not to overhandle the dough, these lacy sandwich cookies could beat the prototype in a blind tasting. I use butter from a small dairy that I get at a farmers' market in my neighborhood and I actually drain it in cheesecloth overnight in the refrigerator to remove as much of the liquid as possible. That is my secret. Now it is out."

FOR THE COOKIES

½ pound (2 sticks) unsalted butter

1 cup granulated sugar

1 cup packed light brown sugar

2 large eggs, at room temperature

½ teaspoon pure almond extract

½ teaspoon pure vanilla extract

2½ cups old-fashioned or quick-cooking rolled oats

1 cup finely chopped pecans

1 teaspoon baking powder

½ teaspoon kosher salt

FOR THE FILLING

12 ounces semisweet chocolate, chopped

4 tablespoons (½ stick) unsalted butter

2 tablespoons orange liqueur

1. To make the cookies: Place an oven rack in the center position and preheat the oven to 350°F. Line several baking sheets with parchment paper or aluminum foil.

2. In a large bowl, beat the butter and sugars until light and fluffy. Add the eggs and extracts and mix until just combined. Mix in the oats, pecans, baking powder, and salt until combined.

3. Drop the batter by rounded teaspoonfuls onto the baking sheets, spacing them 3 inches apart. Bake one sheet at a time until the edges are browned and the center is lighter brown, about 12 minutes. Cool on the baking sheets.

4. To make the filling: Melt the chocolate and butter together in the microwave on high power, checking after 60 seconds. Stir until melted completely and smooth. Stir in the orange liqueur.

5. Choose two cookies of the same size. Spread a teaspoon or so of filling on one cookie top with the other to form a sandwich and press lightly. Repeat with the remaining cookies and filling.

MAKES 36 SANDWICH COOKIES

BECKY HERMAN'S POTATO CHIP COOKIES

MACHIPONGO, VIRGINIA

"I found a recipe for potato chip pecan cookies in *Fine Cooking Magazine* and was fascinated by it," said designer, folk art collector, and cookie baker Rebecca Herman. "The chips give the cookies a crispness and lightness I've never gotten any other way. I've varied the original recipe, using hazelnuts, more vanilla, and for an extra kick, black pepper potato chips. Have you ever tasted a better cookie?"

½ pound unsalted butter, softened, more for shaping cookies

½ cup sugar, more for shaping cookies˙

1¼ teaspoon vanilla extract

1⅞ cups flour, more if necessary

½ cup finely chopped hazelnuts

½ cup black pepper potato chips, crushed

1. Preheat oven to 350°F and lightly grease cookie sheets. Using a stand mixer with a paddle attachment, beat ½ pound of soft butter with ½ cup sugar for about 4 minutes. Add the vanilla and beat to combine. Add the flour, hazelnuts, and potato chips and stir just to combine. Do not overbeat.

2. Take a heaping teaspoon of the dough, shape into a ball, and place on the cookie sheet. Put a few spoonfuls of sugar in a shallow dish. Lightly butter the bottom of a small juice glass or measuring cup and place it in the sugar. Use the glass to flatten each ball to a ¼-inch thickness. Bake until golden, about 10 minutes. Cool for 5 minutes, remove to a rack, and cool completely.

MAKES 30 COOKIES

Theresa Delphin Morgan's "Creole Gold" Praline Pecans

NATCHITOCHES, LOUISIANA

Theresa Delphin Morgan grew up in a Creole community along the Cane River, where her family had thirty pecan trees. She says, "Your pecan has got to be the number one nut. It has its own pie and about one million cookies and candies made from it. I spent my youth picking pecans from our trees. I still like them straight from the shell. I'm a purist. Though I will make an exception for my Creole Gold. It's got a nice flavor."

1 large egg white, lightly beaten

2 tablespoons bourbon or pure vanilla extract

1 cup packed light brown sugar

1 cup granulated sugar

4 cups pecan halves

2 tablespoons all-purpose flour

1½ teaspoons kosher salt

1. Place an oven rack in the center position and preheat the oven to 350°F. Grease two large baking sheets.

2. In a small bowl, combine the egg white and bourbon. In a large bowl, combine the sugars. Add the egg white mixture to the sugars and mix well. Stir in the pecans to coat thoroughly. Spread the pecans evenly on the two pans.

3. Combine the flour and salt, then sift over the pecans. Bake one sheet at a time for about 12 minutes, until aromatic. Cool completely, then break into pieces.

SERVES 8 TO 10

The Sweet Life

MAMA FOLSE'S PECAN PRALINES

Since 1976, chef John Folse has been a one-man Cajun cheerleading society, researching and preserving the foodways along the bayous in southern Louisiana, profiling its cooks and teaching the cooking style at a local college as well as through his books and television. Like his mother's praline recipes, he says, the best recipe of most iconic dishes is always the simplest. A candy thermometer is the key to creating translucent pralines with an irresistible sheen.

1½ cups chopped pecans

1½ cups granulated sugar

¾ cup packed light brown sugar

½ cup milk

6 tablespoons (¾ stick) unsalted butter

1 teaspoon pure vanilla extract

1. Line several baking sheets with aluminum foil and lightly butter the foil, or line with parchment paper.

2. Combine all of the ingredients in a large saucepan and cook, stirring constantly, until the mixture reaches soft-ball stage and registers 240°F on a candy thermometer.

3. Remove from the heat and, working quickly, stir vigorously with a wooden spoon until the mixture becomes creamy and cloudy, slightly thickened, and the pecans remain in suspension.

4. Quickly drop spoonfuls of the mixture onto the prepared sheets. Let sit for about 1 hour, until set.

MAKES 50 PRALINES

BROWNIE SCHRUMPF DID NOT INVENT BROWNIES

BROWNIES ARE THE AMERICAN DREAM. EVERYONE HAS A BROWNIE IN THEIR PAST, AND no other single food is as pervasive, as varied, or as widely adored. A bake sale without brownies is doomed. And the same is true of a bakery lacking a signature version, a restaurant without an upscale variation, or a grocery store deficient in packaged brownies, ingredients for brownies, and a wide array of brownie mixes.

An American who has never eaten brownies is about as likely as one who has never downed a glass of milk. Brownies are easy to make and even easier to eat. In fact, brownies embody many things that Americans hold dear. They are portable, chewy, sweet, nearly indestructible, and—most important—they beg for an individual stamp.

The origin of brownies is unclear, though the most popular myths—that they were the happy result of a mistake—all echo one of America's favorite themes. We love to "make the best of it."

In one story, a cook at the Hotel Touraine in Boston during the 1920s was simultaneously melting chocolate for pudding and making a batch of butter cookies. A fire broke out. In the confusion, the cook combined his melted chocolate and his butter cookie dough. Being a frugal New Englander, the cook couldn't countenance throwing the mistake away so he baked it and cut the flat results into bars. "Boston Brown Bars" were born.

In another, a librarian in Bangor, Maine, affectionately known as "Brownie" Schrumpf intended to bake a cake, forgot to add the baking powder, and ended up with a flat, fudgy mass. Undaunted and thrifty, she cut the cake into squares and served them. The rest is history—though food history often contains as much fancy as it does fact.

The word "brownie" was used to describe sweets as early as 1896. The original *Boston Cooking-School Cook Book* contained recipes for "brownies," a molasses-sweetened cake baked in individual molds, possibly the proto-brownie: a moist bar cookie, simple to make, nearly impossible to destroy. It would be very American to further sweeten and enrich the basic concept of a bar cookie.

As early as 1897, the Sears, Roebuck catalog offered "brownies," though they were not bar cookies, but candies. According to food historian Meryle Evans, Sears named these candies after the silly Lilliputian cartoon characters created by J. Palmer Cox that were popular at the turn of the century.

The 1906 edition of *The Boston Cooking-School Cook Book* contained a recipe for chocolate brownies, and in 1907, *Lowney's Cook Book*, written by Maria Willet Howard, contained two brownie recipes. Lowney's was a manufacturer of chocolate and cocoa, based in Boston.

Brownies may be a paean to homespun Yankee ingenuity or a testament to the central role that food manufacturers have played in the development of American cuisine. Most of the nation's food icons have received support from the food industry, and brownies are probably no exception.

In *Brownies: Over 100 Scrumptious Recipes for More Kinds of Brownies Than You Ever Dreamed Of,* Linda Burum wrote that Dutch farm wives introduced bar cookies to America and that their ease of preparation accounted for their quick rise in popularity. Certainly, the initial rise of brownies in the 1920s dovetails with the demise of widespread household help in America and the beginnings of the era of "convenience." At first, people may have loved brownies just because they were easy.

In fact, the more "easy" became a domestic buzzword—first for the understaffed and overburdened housewife, then in the latter half of the twentieth century as more and more women worked outside the home—the more popular brownies became. Unlike complex layered cakes, tarts, molded desserts, or even delicate cookies, brownies are, wrote Burum, "so easy to whip up that a child could make them." And many have. The widespread use of brownies as a teaching tool in the kitchen helped ensure the devotion of successive generations.

But brownies are not just easy. They travel well. In a national brownie survey conducted by the General Mills Company in 1995, one respondent said that she doted on brownies for two reasons: "I can make them in thirty minutes and eat them on the go." Their durable nature makes them the first choice for care packages from home to camp or college, and a reliable choice for transporting to potlucks or bake sales.

And brownies are wildly adaptable. Little appeals to Americans more than an opportunity to create something in their own image. What mirrors brownies have been! The basic brownie recipe—a mixture of butter, sugar, eggs, chocolate, and flour—can be modified endlessly. Bakers can add mint, caramel, coffee, toffee, white or dark chocolate, mashed fruit such as bananas, crumbled cookies, crackers, or oats; vary the shortening; use sugar or egg substitutes to accommodate their dietary concerns—and still have the satisfaction of eating what America loves best.

Throughout the history of brownies in America, different eras have produced brownies that epitomize their times. In 1971, William Powell provided a recipe for hash brownies in *The Anarchist Cookbook*. Variations were more buttoned down by 1983, when Maida Heatter made brownies for President Reagan's economic summit in Williamsburg.

The General Mills Company estimates that Americans eat about 4 million brownies a year. Lined up and tucked together, as if yet to be removed from a pan, this number of brownies, cut in two-inch squares, would cover a football field, including both end zones, to a depth of 160 feet.

MaMa Nola's Fudgy Brownies

Nola Primeaux's granddaughter, Aimee Primeaux, lucked out with these brownies. It was one of the few recipes her MaMa Nola wrote down. Actually, it was just a list of ingredients, but that was enough for the younger Ms. Primeaux to play with the methodology until the kitchen smelled just like it did when she was a little girl watching MaMa Nola bake. It's tough to resist eating the batch straight out of the oven, but try to wait to the next day, and you'll be rewarded with the perfectly chewy-but-not-too-gooey brownie.

½ pound (2 sticks) unsalted butter, melted

2 cups sugar

½ cup unsweetened cocoa powder

2 large eggs

½ teaspoon pure vanilla extract

1 cup all-purpose flour

1. Place an oven rack in the center position and preheat the oven to 375°F. Grease an 8-inch square pan or line it with parchment paper.

2. In a large bowl, combine the melted butter, sugar, and cocoa. Beat in the eggs and vanilla. Stir in the flour. Pour into the prepared pan. Bake for 30 to 40 minutes, until a toothpick comes out relatively clean (there will be a moist bit of crumb on the toothpick, but it won't look like batter).

3. Cool in the pan and let sit overnight. Cut the next day and enjoy.

MAKES 12 BROWNIES

Joyce Strickland's Cake Brownies

Whenever Joyce Strickland bakes these brownies, she thinks of growing up in Cleveland, where her late mother would bake brownies with walnuts. Now Ms. Strickland, a schoolteacher living in Fort Lauderdale, uses pecans, almonds, or even hazelnuts to make one of the best cakey brownies tasted in two hundred thousand miles.

8 tablespoons (1 stick) unsalted butter or margarine

2 ounces bittersweet chocolate, chopped

2 large eggs

¾ cup sugar

½ cup all-purpose flour

½ teaspoon baking powder

1 teaspoon pure vanilla extract

½ cup chopped pecans or other nuts

1. Place an oven rack in the center position and preheat the oven to 350°F. Grease an 8-inch square pan or line it with parchment paper.

2. Melt the butter and chocolate together in a large bowl in the microwave. Set aside to cool slightly, then stir in the eggs and sugar and beat well. Stir in the flour, baking powder, vanilla, and nuts. Spread the batter into the prepared pan.

3. Bake for 25 to 30 minutes, until a cake tester comes out clean (a few crumbs are okay). Cool in the pan, then cut into squares.

MAKES 9 BROWNIES

Hertha Gall's Chocolate Mint Bar Brownies

Back in the day, this recipe was exotic. People just didn't mix chocolate with mint, out there "in the middle of nowhere," says Darcie Boschee. But when Darcie was growing up, Hertha Gall lived across the street. And after her own children had grown up, Mrs. Gall would cheerfully invite Darcie and her brothers over for snacks after school. Before Ms. Boschee left for college, Mrs. Gall typed up the recipe on a card for her. Since then, wherever Ms. Boschee has settled—Missouri, West Virginia, Minnesota—that card has traveled with her.

FOR THE BROWNIE BATTER

1 cup sugar

8 tablespoons (1 stick) unsalted butter

4 large eggs

1 cup all-purpose flour

½ teaspoon kosher salt

1 teaspoon pure vanilla extract

One 16-ounce can chocolate syrup

½ cup chopped walnuts

FOR THE MINT FILLING

2 cups confectioners' sugar

2 tablespoons milk

8 tablespoons (1 stick) unsalted butter, softened

½ teaspoon pure peppermint extract

Green food coloring (optional)

FOR THE GLAZE

1 cup semisweet chocolate chips

6 tablespoons (¾ stick) unsalted butter

1. Preheat the oven to 350°F. Grease an 8½ x 13-inch baking pan.

2. To make the brownie batter: Cream the sugar and butter. Add the eggs and mix well. Combine the flour and salt and stir in. Fold in the vanilla, syrup, and walnuts. Pour into the pan and spread evenly.

3. Bake for 20 minutes, until a cake tester comes out clean. Cool to room temperature in the pan.

4. To make the mint filling: Combine the confectioners' sugar, milk, butter, peppermint extract, and food coloring, if using. Spread over the cooled brownies. Let set.

5. To make the glaze: Melt the chocolate chips and butter in a small saucepan over low heat and mix well. Pour over the mint layer. Let set. Cut in small squares to serve.

MAKES 24 BROWNIES

ANN SHAFFER'S SPICY CHOCOLATE BROWNIES

BLOOMINGTON, INDIANA

One day when Ann Shaffer was planning to bake her usual brownies for a party, she happened to have a hot chocolate spiked with chiles. Inspiration struck. She decided to add a dash of cayenne to the brownie batter. People loved it. The brown butter offers a warm, rich base and allows the spiciness to "bloom," she says. And using just under two teaspoons of cayenne results in a "slow burn" that emerges in the finish. For adventurous eaters who like an extra kick, she suggests using a good-quality spiced dark chocolate bar or a spiced drinking chocolate in place of the bittersweet.

12 tablespoons (1½ sticks) unsalted butter

1¾ teaspoons cayenne pepper

1½ teaspoons ground cinnamon

¾ teaspoon ground cardamom

5 ounces unsweetened chocolate, chopped

1 cup packed light brown sugar

¾ cup granulated sugar

4 large eggs, at room temperature

2 teaspoons pure vanilla extract

¼ cup strong brewed coffee, at room temperature

1 cup all-purpose flour

½ teaspoon kosher salt

4 ounces bittersweet chocolate, chopped, or heaping ½ cup semisweet chocolate chips

Cinnamon sugar (optional)

1. Place an oven rack in the center position and preheat the oven to 350°F. Grease a 9 × 13-inch baking pan.

2. Melt the butter in a small skillet over medium heat. Cook, stirring often, for 5 to 10 minutes, until the butter turns light golden brown and has a nutty fragrance.

3. Add the cayenne, cinnamon, and cardamom to the butter; turn the heat to low and cook, stirring constantly, about 1 minute. Remove from the heat.

4. Put the unsweetened chocolate in a microwave-safe bowl, and heat in 30-second increments until the chocolate is softened but not melted. Add the chocolate to the butter-spice mixture and stir until the chocolate is completely melted. Cool to room temperature.

5. Combine the sugars and eggs in a large bowl. Beat until well blended and slightly pale. Beat in the vanilla, coffee, and cooled chocolate-butter mixture. Beat for another minute after fully combined.

6. Whisk the flour and salt together in a small bowl. Add to the wet ingredients, stirring until just combined. Fold in the chopped chocolate.

7. Spread the batter into the prepared pan. Sprinkle liberally with cinnamon sugar, if using. Bake for 20 to 30 minutes, until a knife or toothpick inserted into the batter comes out clean.

8. Cool for 10 minutes, then cut into squares and serve.

MAKES 24 BROWNIES

RICE KRISPIES TREATS: HOW SNAP! CRACKLE! POP! BECAME A STICKY SITUATION

AS EARLY AS THE MID-1800S, AMERICAN MOMS HAVE BRAVED A STICKY MESS OF PUFFED grains and molasses and shaped it into treats for their families. A recipe for puffed rice brittle is found in a "domestic science" notebook for New York City schoolkids as early as 1916. In 1938, Lucy Mary Maltby published instructions for puffed wheat squares in *It's Fun to Cook*.

All these homemade concoctions are, of course, the precursors of the iconic bake-sale staple, Rice Krispies Treat. But none of them stood a chance for snack-world greatness until puffed rice—and the treat itself—received the tremendous brand-marketing boost that began in 1927 when Eugene McKay, from the Kellogg company, cooked, dried, and toasted some rice grains and poured milk over them. The resulting "Snap! Crackle! Pop!" is heard loud and clear at breakfast tables around the world. In Spanish, it's "Pim! Pum! Pam!" In German, "Knisper! Knasper! Knusper!" In Swahili, "Click! Click! Nagunga!"

In 1939, when another Kellogg employee, Mildred Day, mixed this noisy cereal into a crisp, sweet, sticky treat, the invention was a hit. The snack was initially prepared for a Campfire Girls' fund-raiser, but word spread and soon Rice Krispies weren't just for breakfast anymore. By 1940, Ms. Day's recipe appeared on Rice Krispies boxes. And when busy lives gave way to less baking and more shopping, the company applied for a patent on a prepackaged version.

The Sweet Life

Ella's Lemon Glazed Tea Cakes

Sixteen-year-old Ella Carlyle describes herself as "an aspiring chef." "My grandmother, who is from Arkansas, makes these at Christmastime," she says. "They are so much better than brownies, so much more Florida, because of the orange and lemon flavors. My grandmother makes them in a pan like brownies and cuts them into bars, but the crust is crumbly so I have been experimenting with making them in nonstick, round, petite four tins with removable bottoms. The baking time is slightly less, you just have to watch them closely and you need to cool them halfway in the tin, then remove them and cool them completely on a wire rack before glazing them. It takes more time, but they look cuter and the crust and filling get a little more caramelized."

10 tablespoons (1¼ sticks) lightly salted butter, softened

1 cup plus 2 tablespoons all-purpose flour

2 large eggs, well beaten

⅛ teaspoon kosher salt

1 teaspoon pure vanilla extract

1½ cups packed light brown sugar

½ cup sweetened shredded coconut

¾ cup chopped pecans

1½ cups confectioners' sugar, sifted

2 tablespoons fresh orange juice

2 teaspoons fresh lemon juice

1. Place an oven rack in the center position and preheat the oven to 350°F. Grease an 8½ x 12-inch rimmed baking sheet or two 12-cup nonstick mini-muffin or petite four tins with removable bottoms.

2. In a bowl, combine 8 tablespoons of the butter with 1 cup of the flour until the mixture comes together to form a ball. Press the dough evenly into the pan. Bake for 15 minutes if using the baking pan, 10 to 12 if using the small cake tins. Remove from oven. Lower the temperature to 300°F.

3. Combine the remaining 2 tablespoons flour, the eggs, salt, vanilla, brown sugar, coconut, and pecans. Spread filling over the crust. Bake until lightly browned, about 20 minutes for the baking pan, 15 to 17 for the tins. Remove from the oven and cool in the baking pan or in the molds.

4. Melt the remaining 2 tablespoons butter. Whisk in the confectioners' sugar and the orange and lemon juices. If using the baking pan, spread the glaze over the cookies, allow to set and then cut into squares. If using the molds, remove each when cool enough to handle and cool them completely on wire racks before glazing.

MAKES 24 BARS OR 24 1-INCH CAKES

LaVerne's Black Raspberry Bars

LaVerne Yost has always been an obsessed home cook, but since retiring, she has had more time to cook, talk about cooking, and eat other people's cooking. She figures that she has traveled about fifty thousand miles in pursuit of fabulous food in the past decade and, sounding a little like Dorothy in Oz, she said that she has yet to find a sweet that can compete with these simple bars that her sister taught her to make "many, many years ago." They are delicious by themselves, or served warm with vanilla ice cream, Greek-style strained yogurt, whipped cream, or custard.

12 tablespoons (1½ sticks) unsalted butter, softened

1 cup packed light brown sugar

1¾ cups all-purpose flour

1 teaspoon baking soda

1 teaspoon kosher salt

1½ cups old-fashioned rolled oats (not instant)

One 12-ounce jar seedless black raspberry preserves

1. Preheat the oven to 400°F. Grease a 9 × 13-inch baking pan.

2. In a large bowl, cream the butter and sugar with a fork. Combine the flour, baking soda, and salt and add to the butter mixture. Stir in the rolled oats.

3. Press half the batter into the prepared pan. Spread the preserves on top. Crumble the other half of the flour-and-butter mixture over the preserves and bake for 25 minutes.

4. Allow to cool slightly, then cut into bars.

———

MAKES ABOUT 24 BARS

Kate Thomas's Raspberry-Filled White Chocolate Bars

NEW ALBANY, OHIO

A real estate broker and the president of her local gourmet club, Kate Thomas got this recipe from her sister. Neither remembers its provenance, and they freely acknowledge that their loss of recall could be sugar burnout from all the bars that they've consumed over the years. "I seem to remember that white chocolate got big back in the 1980s," says Mrs. Thomas, "it's a fuzzy sort of memory, though."

½ pound (2 sticks) unsalted butter

4 cups white chocolate chips (two 12-ounce packages)

4 eggs

1 cup sugar

2 cups all-purpose flour

1 teaspoon kosher salt

2 teaspoons pure almond extract

1 cup seedless raspberry preserves or jam

½ cup sliced almonds

1. Preheat the oven to 325°F. Grease and flour a 9 × 13-inch baking pan.

2. Melt butter in a small saucepan over low heat. Remove from the heat, add 2 cups of the chips and allow to stand. Do not stir.

3. In a large bowl, beat the eggs with an electric mixer until foamy. Gradually add the sugar, beating on high speed until lemon-colored. Stir in the melted chip mixture. Add the flour, salt, and almond extract and mix on low speed until just combined.

4. Spread half of the batter into the prepared pan. Bake for 15 to 20 minutes, until golden brown. Remove from the oven.

5. Melt the raspberry preserves in a saucepan and spread evenly over the baked batter. Stir the remaining 2 cups of chips into the remaining batter. Gently spoon the batter over the preserves. (Some fruit may show through.) Sprinkle with almonds. Return the pan to the oven for 30 to 35 minutes more, until the top is firm. Cool completely and cut into squares.

MAKES ABOUT 48 BARS

A SOCIAL HISTORY OF CHOCOLATE CAKE

AMERICANS' EARLIEST CAKES RESEMBLED YEAST BREADS OR BRITISH- style steamed puddings, dense with dried fruit, nuts, and spices, and often a wallop of booze. Domestically produced, moderately priced chocolate and the invention of baking powder made the majority of yeast-risen cakes history.

In 1765 James Baker and his partner, John Hanna, opened Baker's Chocolate Company in Dorchester, Massachusetts, a mill for grinding cacao beans. The first chocolate mill in the United States, Baker's company produced bars to make drinking chocolate, a beverage colonists had brought with them from Europe. Baker's sons Edmund and Walter expanded the company, and in the mid-1800s, Baker's bars of chocolate were labeled "the essential chocolate-cake-making ingredient." During the California gold rush, the company shipped its chocolate in tin boxes that miners then used to pan for gold.

Today, chocolate cake—fudgy flourless chocolate cake, chocolate layer cake, oil-based "mud cake," and hundreds of other iterations—is the apple pie of cakes. More chocolate cake mixes are purchased in America than any other flavor, and, according to the consumer market research firm Mintel, adult consumers often eat the same brand they ate as children. Whether it's a Ho-Ho, Duncan Hines, or something your mother (or favorite pastry chef) baked from scratch, chocolate cake is a preference that is shaped early and varies little throughout a lifetime. It's nostalgic. It's rich. It's caffeinated. It's impossible to resist.

Initially, chocolate cake was the exclusive province of the wealthy, but as Baker's bars became ubiquitous and the prices dropped, it became a populist sweet. Chocolate cake at first meant a plain cake with chocolate topping. But as more bakers could afford to load up the cake batter with chocolate, the cake became the deliciously dark treat we know today.

Varieties of chocolate cake have multiplied along with varieties of baking chocolate. There's regular chocolate cake and there's devil's food—which, as the 1923 Fannie Farmer cookbook indicates, can contain twice as much chocolate as the usual chocolate cake and is so-called either because it's naughtily indulgent, or as a contrast to the white angel food cake. There is German chocolate cake—an American invention—created by a Texas woman in 1857 using a new chocolate product invented by Sam German, a Baker's employee. Red velvet is devil's food with red dye in it; in earlier days, Southern home bakers would use beets for coloring, as the Waldorf-Astoria Hotel still does today.

In the 1920s, the first cake mixes appeared, joining package mixes for gelatin, pancakes, and biscuits. They were not an overnight sensation. As Susan Marks reported in *Finding Betty Crocker: The Secret Life of America's First Lady of Food,* business psychologists at the time suggested that the lack of appeal was due to the powdered eggs in the mix. Allowing bakers to crack their own fresh eggs made all the difference. Today, more often than not, "baking a cake" means doctoring a cake mix. Entire books are dedicated to that art.

RAMIN GANESHRAM'S TRINIDADIAN BLACK CAKE

Ramin Ganeshram's parents were from Trinidad, and they taught her the family's black cake recipe, a version so renowned that it has run in three magazines, two cookbooks, and has become the gold standard of the New York City Trinidadian expatriate community.

Now a writer, chef, and trend forecaster, Ms. Ganeshram always wondered why Trinidad's Traditional Black Cake, which relies heavily on butter, was so popular in the West Indies, where butter is rare. She got her answer when she accompanied her husband to Ireland to trace his roots. There she came across the Irish Christmas Cake, which is black cake without the "blackening" of burnt sugar syrup. Upon further investigation, she found that Jamaica and Trinidad—the two islands best known for black cake—also had the largest populations of indentured Irish during the colonial period. Perhaps, she says, this explains the popularity of the recipe in the West Indies. She happens to be married to an Irish American, and it certainly explains why, at Christmas, her kitchen becomes a black cake bakery for dozens of lucky recipients.

2¾ cups cherry brandy

2¾ cups dark rum

1½ cups dried currants

1½ cups seedless raisins

1¼ cups pitted prunes

1 cup candied cherries

¼ cup chopped mixed candied citrus peel

1 small cinnamon stick

1 star anise pod

Seeds scraped from a 2-inch piece vanilla bean

½ pound (2 sticks) plus 1 tablespoon unsalted butter, softened

2 cups all-purpose flour

2 teaspoons baking powder

1 teaspoon ground cinnamon

¼ teaspoon freshly grated nutmeg

⅛ teaspoon ground allspice

1 cup packed dark brown sugar

6 eggs

½ teaspoon mixed essence

½ teaspoon pure vanilla extract

1 tablespoon burnt sugar syrup

6 tablespoon sherry

1. Combine 2 cups of the brandy, 2 cups of the rum, the currants, raisins, prunes, cherries, citrus peel, cinnamon stick, star anise, and vanilla seeds in a large saucepan and bring to a gentle boil. Remove from heat, cover, and let steep for 2 hours.

2. Preheat the oven to 350°F. Grease two 8-inch round cake pans with 1 tablespoon of the butter and set aside. Sift the flour, baking powder, cinnamon, nutmeg, and allspice together into a large bowl. Set the flour mixture aside. Using an electric mixer, cream the remaining 1 cup butter and brown sugar in a large bowl until fluffy. Add the eggs one at a time, beating well after each addition. Add the mixed essence and vanilla and beat until just combined. Set this mixture aside.

3. Drain the steeped fruit, discard the cinnamon stick, transfer to a food processor, and pulse until it resembles a coarse paste. Add to the butter mixture and beat well. Add the flour mixture in 4 batches, beating after each addition. Add the burnt sugar syrup and beat until just combined. Divide batter between the prepared cake pans and bake for 40 minutes. Lower the heat to 250°F and bake until a toothpick inserted in the middle comes out clean, about 25 minutes more. Let cakes cool on a rack for 20 minutes.

4. Meanwhile, mix the remaining ¾ cup brandy, ¾ cup rum, and the sherry in a small bowl. Generously brush the cakes with the brandy mixture (save what remains) and let cool completely. Remove cakes from pans. Wrap them tightly in plastic wrap and then foil and seal in an airtight container. Store in a cool, dry place for at least 3 days before eating. Cut into wedges, and serve.

(You may store cakes for up to 3 months. If doing so, use the remaining brandy mixture to rebaste the cakes generously every 7 days. Make another batch of brandy mixture, if necessary.)

MAKES 1 CAKE, SERVES 12 TO 20

ANNE BUTLER'S WHISKEY CAKE

ST. FRANCISVILLE, LOUISIANA

During the reign of King Cotton in Louisiana, West Feliciana Parish was one of the wealthiest areas in the South. Anne Butler is the seventh generation of the original family of owners to live at Butler Greenwood Plantation, which was built by her ancestors in the late 1700s.

"My grandmother didn't actually cook much," Ms. Butler says. "She had a cook, Celie, who lived on the place and did all the cooking in the outside kitchen over a woodstove. [Celie] probably couldn't really read or write—certainly the generation before her could not—and so there were no written recipes, or not many. The older generation is dead now, so the closest we've come is a whiskey cake recipe, created by a cook my cousin hired a few years ago. The cake was made weeks before Christmas and set on a mahogany sideboard, which happened to contain the liquor cabinet. Anybody who passed poured a little bourbon on the cake.

"It was positively reeking by Christmas and it was always accompanied by plum pudding, with hard sauce spiked with plenty of bourbon, and other 'spirited' desserts, plus eggnog filled with even more bourbon. This was English Louisiana. We loved our spirits!"

1 pound raisins

½ pound (2 sticks) unsalted butter

2¼ cups sugar

6 large eggs

4 cups all-purpose flour

1 teaspoon baking powder

1 cup whiskey, plus more for soaking

1 pound pecan halves

8 ounces candied cherries, chopped

1 teaspoon freshly grated nutmeg

1 pound dates, pitted and chopped (optional)

1. Cover raisins with water and let sit overnight.

2. Preheat the oven to 300°F. Grease and flour a 10-inch tube pan.

3. In a large mixing bowl, cream the butter and sugar. Add the eggs one at a time and mix well.

4. In a separate bowl, combine the flour and baking powder. Add to the creamed ingredients, alternating with the whiskey and blending thoroughly.

5. Drain the raisins and add to the batter along with the pecans, cherries, nutmeg, and dates, if using. Pour and scrape the batter into the prepared pan.

6. Bake for 4 hours. Cool slightly in the pan, then turn out onto a wire rack to cool completely.

7. Transfer to a rimmed cake stand and cover lightly with cheesecloth. Each time you pass by the cake, or at least once a day for a few weeks, give it a shot of whiskey.

SERVES 12

GAYNELLE TILLET'S FIG CAKE

Ocracoke, one of North Carolina's barrier islands, is home to a profusion of fig trees, which fill backyards, front yards, and the narrow roadsides in the densely packed residential section. Fig cake has been serious business there for as long as anyone can remember. Most people agree that Gaynelle Tillet's version is the best around. In June and July when the figs are ripe, her son picks them and she makes the jam that, along with buttermilk, is the secret of her sweet and tangy cake. Store-bought fig jam also makes a credible cake.

Fig cake freezes well but should not be frosted until thawed.

787

The Sweet Life

FOR THE CAKE

Butter, for greasing the pan

2 cups all-purpose flour, plus more for dusting the pan

3 large eggs

1½ cups sugar

1 cup vegetable oil

1 teaspoon ground nutmeg

1 teaspoon ground allspice

1 teaspoon ground cinnamon

1 teaspoon kosher salt

½ cup buttermilk

1½ teaspoons baking soda

2 tablespoons hot water

1 teaspoon pure vanilla extract

1 cup Gaynelle Tillet's Fine Fig Jam (recipe follows) or store-bought fig preserves

1 cup chopped walnuts

FOR THE FROSTING

1 cup sugar

4 tablespoons (½ stick) unsalted butter

1 teaspoon baking soda

1 teaspoon cornstarch

½ cup buttermilk

1 teaspoon pure vanilla extract

1. To make the cake: Preheat the oven to 350°F. Grease and lightly flour a 10-inch tube pan.

2. In a large bowl, beat the eggs until light yellow and frothy. Continue beating while adding the sugar a little bit at a time. Beat until thick, and continue beating while slowly adding the vegetable oil.

3. In a small bowl, combine the 2 cups flour with the nutmeg, allspice, cinnamon, and salt. With a rubber spatula fold half the flour mixture into the egg mixture. Add the buttermilk and mix well.

4. Dissolve the baking soda in the hot water. Add the remaining flour mixture to the batter and mix well, then the dissolved baking soda and the vanilla. Gently stir in the fig jam and the nuts, just until they are distributed evenly throughout the batter. Pour the batter into the prepared tube pan.

5. Bake for 40 to 50 minutes, until the cake is brown and a toothpick inserted in the center comes out clean.

6. While the cake is baking, make the frosting: Combine the sugar and butter in a medium saucepan over medium heat and stir as the butter melts. Whisk the baking soda and cornstarch into the buttermilk and add to the butter and sugar. Slowly bring to a boil, then remove from the heat. Beat well, add the vanilla, and cool.

7. When the cake is done, cool it in the pan on a rack for about 15 minutes. Use a knife to loosen the cake, and turn out onto a serving plate. Allow to cool completely. Spoon the buttermilk frosting over the cake and serve.

SERVES 8 TO 10

Gaynelle Tillet's Fine Fig Jam

OCRACOKE, NORTH CAROLINA

Gaynelle Tillet uses less sugar than most in her fig jam. And this, along with the addition of lemon juice and peel, makes for a deep fig flavor with a clean finish. The jam can be used to make her fig cake. It can also be served with yogurt, or pound cake, inside a crepe, or with toast.

4 cups sugar

2 quarts fresh figs (about 5 pounds)

3 cups water

2 tablespoons (¼ stick) unsalted butter

2 tablespoons fresh lemon juice

Peel from 1 lemon (yellow part only), cut into 8 pieces

1. Place the sugar in a flat pan in a warm place or in a 200°F oven.

2. Cover the figs with boiling water for 10 minutes. Drain and cool. Use a sharp knife to remove the stems and tails from the figs and to chop them.

3. Combine the chopped figs, the warmed sugar, and the water in a large saucepan. Slowly bring to a boil, stirring frequently until the sugar dissolves. Raise the temperature to high and boil until thick and syrupy, about 45 minutes. Remove from the heat. Stir in the butter and lemon juice. Cool slightly and beat into the batter.

4. Pour into 8 half-pint sterilized Mason jars, leaving a half-inch head space. Add a piece of lemon peel to each. Adjust the caps and process for 15 minutes in a boiling water bath. Cool completely.

5. Store in a cool place for up to 1 year.

MAKES 8 HALF-PINT JARS

California Fig Ball, 1938.

ANN TINDELL'S SEVENTEENTH BIRTHDAY CAKE WITH CHOCOLATE, BEETS, AND RASPBERRY GLAZE

Ann Tindell grew up on a family farm in Sequatchie, Tennessee, and each season's crops inspired new ways to improvise. She has tossed zucchini into bread and muffins, and mingled tomatoes with cinnamon and nutmeg in a spice cake. When she was 16 she mixed beets and chocolate into cake batter. The result was a sweet, earthy cake, and topped with her grandmother's homemade jam (made from raspberries picked from her patch), it was the perfect way to mark the big one-seven.

4 ounces unsweetened chocolate (preferably Scharffen Berger), chopped into pieces

8 tablespoons (½ stick) unsalted butter, cut into pieces

1 cup boiling water

2 cups sugar

2 large eggs, separated

1 teaspoon baking soda

½ cup plain yogurt, buttermilk, or sour cream

2 cups all-purpose flour

1 teaspoon baking powder

1 cup grated beets (peel only if skins are very thick)

Homemade raspberry jam, or 1 cup raspberries (preferably fresh, but frozen is okay, too), sweetened with sugar to taste

1. Preheat the oven to 350°F. Grease and flour a 10-inch Bundt pan.

2. Place the chocolate and butter into a large bowl and pour boiling water over them. Stir until melted.

3. Add the sugar. Beat in the egg yolks, one at a time.

4. Mix the baking soda and yogurt and fold into the chocolate mixture.

5. Add flour and baking powder and mix.

6. Fold in the beets.

7. Beat egg whites until stiff. Stir in a third of them into the batter, then very gently fold in the remaining whites. (The first addition will help keep the air in the second; it is good to do this every time you add egg whites to batter.)

8. Pour into the pan and bake about 40 minutes or until the edges have just pulled away from the side of the pan and the whole house smells like cake.

9. Let sit in the pan about 10 minutes before turning out onto a cooling rack.

10. Meanwhile, heat the jam or raspberries (with a touch of water) in a saucepan. Cook for a few minutes, stirring frequently, until broken down but still chunky.

11. Pour the raspberries all over the warm cake set on a serving plate.

MAKES ONE 10-INCH CAKE

CARSIE LODTER'S CHOCOLATE POUND CAKE

JOHNSON CITY, TENNESSEE

Carsie Lodter taught textiles and clothing at Milligan College for decades until she retired in 1982. She's an excellent seamstress, but her friends and colleagues loved her baking, especially this pound cake that she would bring to the office. "Everyone seems to have liked it right good," she says.

½ pound (2 sticks) unsalted butter

8 tablespoons (1 stick) unsalted margarine

3 cups sugar

5 large eggs

3 cups all-purpose flour

5 tablespoons unsweetened Dutch-process cocoa powder

½ teaspoon baking powder

½ teaspoon kosher salt

1 cup milk

1 tablespoon pure vanilla extract

1. Preheat the oven to 325°F. Grease and flour a 10-inch tube pan.

2. Cream the butter, margarine, and sugar until fluffy.

3. Add the eggs one at a time, beating well after each addition, then beat it a long time until well mixed and airy.

4. Sift the flour, cocoa, baking powder, and salt together three times. Add to the butter mixture, alternating with the milk. Stir in the vanilla.

5. Pour into the prepared pan and bake for 1 hour and 20 minutes, until a cake tester comes out clean (a few crumbs are okay).

6. Cool in the pan for 10 minutes, then turn out on a rack to cool completely.

SERVES 16 TO 24 (A QUARTER OF A CAKE MAKES A NICE GIFT FOR THOSE WHO JUST CAN'T FINISH A WHOLE ONE)

PATRICIA TSAI'S TORTA DE CHOCOLATE
Intense Mexican Chocolate Cake

Patricia Tsai, a self-confessed chocolate freak, painstakingly imports and processes cocoa beans to make the intense varietal chocolate that she sells at the farmers' market in Venice, California. This cake, she said, "I learned initially in a cooking class, and it struck me as a great use for the spiced Mexican chocolate that I make. The flavor is so full and rich that you need just a taste, but of course you can't stop eating it any more than I can stop tasting chocolate." (Spiced chocolate is available in specialty markets or through Ms. Tsai's website.)

FOR THE CAKE

¾ cup plus 3 tablespoons all-purpose flour

1 teaspoon baking powder

½ teaspoon baking soda

1 teaspoon ground cinnamon (Mexican canela preferred)

¼ teaspoon salt

4 ounces ChocoVivo chocolate (use the Mayan Tradition or one of the plain chocolates), chopped into pieces

¾ cup sugar

⅓ cup boiling water

3 large eggs

½ stick unsalted butter (4 tablespoons), softened

½ cup sour cream

1 teaspoon pure vanilla extract

FOR THE SAUCE

3 ounces spiced chocolate

2 tablespoons heavy cream

1. Preheat oven to 350°F. Grease bottom of a 9-inch round cake pan. Line bottom of the pan with a round of parchment or waxed paper. Grease the paper and sides of the pan.

2. In a small bowl, mix flour, baking powder, baking soda, cinnamon, and salt. Reserve.

3. Put the chocolate pieces and sugar in a food processor. Process until finely chopped. With machine on, pour boiling water through feed tube, processing until chocolate is melted. Add the eggs. Process for 20 seconds. Scrape down sides of bowl. Add butter, sour cream, and vanilla. Process 20 seconds. Add the reserved flour mixture. Pulse 6 to 8 times, or just until mixed. Transfer batter to prepared cake pan.

4. Bake 30 to 35 minutes, or until a cake tester inserted in the center comes out clean. When cake is done, cool cake in the pan on a rack 5 minutes. Then invert onto the rack and remove the liner. Invert cake again right side up onto a plate. Let sit 15 to 20 minutes and serve warm, in wedges, topped with whipped cream and any sort of fruit from mangoes or berries. Drizzle with chocolate sauce, if desired. Cake will keep, covered, at room temperature for 3 days, or freeze for about 1 month.

5. Ten minutes prior to serving, melt the chocolate with the cream over low heat. Drizzle over each serving of cake and serve.

MAKES 1 (9-INCH) ROUND CAKE,
8 TO 10 SERVINGS

BIG MAMA'S WHIPPING CREAM POUND CAKE

Lillian Cadenhead's pound cake doesn't abide by the conventional pound cake rules of using a pound of sugar, a pound of flour, a pound of butter, and a pound of eggs. But because it steers clear of leavening, it's still very much old school, and a sweet tradition of the Cadenhead family. Big Mama, the name Ms. Cadenhead's grandchildren call her, serves it in the summer with sliced peaches or strawberries, and in winter she toasts, butters, and tops it with homemade fig preserves when the occasion calls for a special breakfast. This recipe starts out in a cold oven to ensure that a crust doesn't form before the cake has fully risen. The gradual rise in temperature makes for a very fine crumb.

½ pound (2 sticks) unsalted butter, softened

3 cups sugar

6 large eggs, at room temperature

3 cups cake flour

1 cup heavy cream

2 teaspoons pure vanilla extract

Pinch of sea salt

1. Butter and flour a 10-inch tube pan. Fit a ring of parchment paper into the bottom.

2. With an electric mixer, cream the butter and sugar in a large bowl until light and fluffy, about 10 minutes.

3. Add the eggs one at a time and beat well after each one.

4. Add the cake flour and cream, alternating, beginning and ending with flour. Add the vanilla and salt. Mix until just combined.

5. Pour the batter into the prepared pan. Place in a cold oven and set the temperature at 325°F. Bake for 1½ hours or until a wooden pick inserted in the center comes out clean.

6. Cool in the pan for 1 hour. Turn the cake out onto a wire rack and cool completely before serving.

MAKES 1 CAKE, SERVES 12

DAVID BURD'S BLACK SAPOTE POUND CAKE

NAPLES, FLORIDA

Every Saturday, David Burd and his wife set up shop at the Third Avenue Farm Market. He sells fresh tropical fruits from the trees he cultivates and she sells the dried fruit leathers and candies that she makes from the fruits. Their inventory is like a trek around the globe. Visit their stall often enough and you'll eventually count seventy varieties of mangoes, mamey, canistel, carambola, papaya, and black sapote, a Central American persimmon that Mr. Burd uses for this pound cake.

1 pound (4 sticks) unsalted butter, softened

8 large eggs, separated

1 pound (about 2¼ cups) sugar

1 pound (about 4 cups) all-purpose flour

1½ teaspoons baking powder

1 large black sapote, pureed

1. Preheat the oven to 325°F. Grease and flour a 10-inch tube pan.

2. Beat the butter with the egg yolks, sugar, and half the flour until smooth.

3. In a separate bowl, beat the egg whites just until they form soft peaks. Fold the egg whites into the yolk-sugar-flour mix.

4. Stir in the rest of the flour, baking powder, and sapote puree.

5. Pour into the pan and bake for 1 hour and 15 minutes, or until golden brown and a cake tester comes out clean.

MAKES ONE 10-INCH CAKE

MRS. VALA'S POPPY SEED TORTE

GRETNA, NEBRASKA

Lois Vala was part Irish, part Swedish, but when she married Ernie Vala, she became an honorary Czech, at least in the kitchen. He described the meals he missed from the homeland, and she read cookbooks like novels and paid close attention to the foods and flavors at the local Czech festivals. Mr. Vala acknowledges that "her cooking got to be far better than that of the native Czechs." One of her best-loved creations is this impressive poppy seed torte. Lois Vala's daughter-in-law bakes it for her husband and his father. The secret to a perfect torte, she discovered, lies in soaking the poppy seeds in milk before adding them to the batter. And adding Kahlúa to the ganache-like frosting is divine. The cake is a perfect ending to a Czech-style dinner of sauerkraut and dumplings.

FOR THE CAKE

¾ cup poppy seeds

1 cup milk

2 cups all-purpose flour

¼ teaspoon table salt

2 teaspoons baking powder

10 tablespoons plus 2 teaspoons (1⅓ sticks) unsalted butter

1½ cups sugar

1 teaspoon pure vanilla extract

4 large egg whites, beaten stiff (reserve yolks for filling)

FOR THE WALNUT FILLING

½ cup sugar

1 tablespoon cornstarch

1½ cups milk

4 large egg yolks

¾ cup chopped walnuts

FOR THE FROSTING

1½ cups sugar

6 tablespoons milk

6 tablespoons (¾ stick) unsalted butter

3 tablespoons coffee liqueur (preferably Kahlúa)

½ cup chopped semisweet chocolate

1. To make the cake: Soak the poppy seeds in the milk for 2 hours.

2. Line three 9-inch round cake pans with waxed paper or parchment paper. Preheat the oven to 375°F.

3. Sift together the flour, salt, and baking powder.

4. Cream the butter and sugar. Alternately add the poppy seeds and milk and the sifted flour mixture. Stir in the vanilla. Fold in the egg whites.

5. Pour the batter into the prepared pans. Bake for 20 to 25 minutes, until a toothpick inserted in the middle of the cake comes out clean. Cool layers on a rack and peel off the paper.

6. Make the filling: Combine sugar, cornstarch, and milk in a medium saucepan. Cook over medium heat for 10 minutes, stirring frequently.

7. Stir the egg yolks together in a small bowl. Add a little of the hot mixture to the yolks, then add all the yolks to the saucepan. Cook 2 minutes longer, until thickened.

8. Transfer to a bowl to cool completely. Stir in the walnuts. Cover and chill until you're ready to assemble the cake.

One Big Table

9. To make the frosting: Combine the sugar, milk, and butter in a medium saucepan and bring to a boil for 30 seconds. Remove from the heat and add the Kahlúa and chocolate. Beat with an electric mixer until thick. (The mixture will thicken more as it cools.)

10. To assemble, spread half of the walnut filling on the bottom of one upside-down layer. Top with the next layer, also upside-down, and spread with the remaining filling. Top with the third layer, right side up. Spread the frosting over the top and sides of the cake. Store the cake in the refrigerator.

MAKES ONE 9-INCH LAYER CAKE

Cakes for sky riders.

CAROLYN MARGOLIS'S THOUSAND-LAYER CAKE

There may not actually be a thousand layers in this cake, but chances are, no one is counting. With marshmallow crème between the layers, the cake is an instant crowd pleaser and has won bids at local wine and food auctions. It's the grand finale at the Margolises at just about every Thanksgiving. The original recipe, from Ms. Margolis's grandmother, who included it in a handwritten cookbook she gave each of her three daughters, required eight 8-inch cake pans. Ms. Margolis bakes four layers and slices them in half. "It's faster," she says. There is, however, one original ingredient that's crucial to the cake—and a surprising one, since Grandmother Margolis was born in 1886: Marshmallow Fluff.

FOR THE CAKE

6 large eggs, separated

1 cup sugar

1 cup all-purpose flour

1 teaspoon pure vanilla extract

FOR THE FILLING

½ pound (2 sticks) unsalted butter, softened

One 16-ounce jar marshmallow crème (preferably Marshmallow Fluff)

½ cup unsweetened cocoa powder

FOR THE ICING

4 ounces unsweetened chocolate

½ cup confectioners' sugar, or more as needed

½ cup heavy cream, or more as needed

1. Preheat the oven to 350°F. Grease four 8-inch round cake pans.

2. To make the cake: Beat the egg whites until stiff, slowly adding the sugar. Add the yolks one at a time, beating after each addition. Stir in the flour and vanilla.

3. Divide the batter among the prepared pans. Bake for about 20 minutes, until the cakes pull away from the sides of the pans. Check the layers with a cake tester, which should come out clean.

4. Cool in the pans for 5 minutes, then turn out and cool completely on wire racks.

5. To make the filling: In a medium bowl, thoroughly mix the butter, marshmallow crème, and cocoa powder.

6. To make the icing: Melt the chocolate in the top of a double boiler. Remove from the heat and beat in ½ cup confectioners' sugar and ½ cup cream. The consistency should resemble mayonnaise; add confectioners' sugar and cream as needed.

7. Cut each layer in half horizontally. Spread the filling over each of seven layers. Stack them and top with the eighth layer. Frost the top and sides of the cake with the icing.

8. The cake is best when fresh, but can be refrigerated.

MAKES ONE 8-INCH CAKE, SERVES 6 TO 12

Mary Ada Marshall's Smith Island Cake

TYLERTON, MARYLAND

Every state has an official flower, bird, and nickname. Why not a cake? That's what the Maryland legislature decided in January 2008, and right then and there, the Smith Island Cake became the state's own. As with all things in politics, there were intense lobbying efforts—450 slices of cake were delivered to state lawmakers to "sweeten the deal"—and truth be told, elevating the cake to official state status wasn't so much a matter of culinary devotion, as marketing for the state's tourism industry. Rather than being packed in a boatman's lunch pail (as was tradition, when the English first brought over this torte-like cake), it's now tucked into the shopping bags of tourists. Still, the cake—which comes in a slew of flavors, including coconut, banana, and yellow—is a local favorite.

Mary Ada Marshall, one of the islanders who lobbied for the cake, bakes the ten- to twelve-layer treats for her son's grocery store, and also ships them to curious cake lovers all over the world.

2 sticks butter, softened

3 cups sugar

5 eggs

3 cups flour

1 teaspoon baking powder

¼ teaspoon salt

1 cup milk

1 cup water

1 teaspoon vanilla, or to taste

1. Preheat the oven to 350°F. Grease 8 to 10 pans (Ada likes 10-inch pans best), or as many pans as you have and bake in batches.

2. In the bowl of an electric mixer, cream together the butter and sugar. Add the eggs, one at a time until smooth.

3. Meanwhile, sift the flour, baking powder, and salt together. Add to the creamed mixture on low speed, then add the milk, water, and vanilla and beat just until smooth.

4. Divide evenly among 10 to 12 cake pans. Bake at 350°F for 6 to 7 minutes. Layers will be very thin, like a torte. Cool slightly and begin assembly on a large plate.

5. Assemble with chocolate frosting. Flavor variations include cream cheese, butter cream, peanut butter, and coconut frosting.

———

SERVES 12 TO 20

JILL SAUCEMAN'S APPLE STACK CAKE

JOHNSON CITY, TENNESSEE

Jill Sauceman's grandmother used a less spicy filling when she made this old-fashioned cake during the Depression because spices were hard to come by. Two generations later this recipe, a classic from Appalachia, has a much bigger kick. "In the mountains of southern Appalachia—parts of Virginia and West Virginia, Kentucky and Tennessee, North Carolina, and Georgia—dried apple stack cake is among the oldest and most favored of desserts. Dried apples are a mountain staple, preserved in great quantities from the summer and fall crops, and the cake has long been a natural consequence of their availability," writes John Egerton in *Southern Food*. The recipe that Jill Sauceman inherited from her grandmother was less spicy than the version she has developed. "I reduced a bit of the sugar and increased the spice for a bigger kick," says Mrs. Sauceman, whose stack cake is accorded something seldom given to a dish that everyone thinks that their Mama Makes Best: respect.

FOR THE DRIED APPLE FILLING

18 ounces dried apple slices

6 cups water

1 cup packed light brown sugar

1 teaspoon ground ginger

1 teaspoon ground cinnamon

½ teaspoon ground allspice

½ teaspoon ground nutmeg

FOR THE CAKE

⅓ cup vegetable shortening

½ cup plus 2½ teaspoons sugar

1 large egg

4 cups all-purpose flour, plus extra for pressing the dough

1 teaspoon baking powder

1 teaspoon baking soda

½ teaspoon kosher salt

½ cup buttermilk

½ cup molasses

1. To make the apple filling: Combine the apples and water in a large saucepan or Dutch oven. Bring to a boil; reduce the heat and simmer for 30 minutes or until tender.

2. Stir in the sugar, ginger, cinnamon, allspice, and nutmeg. Return to a boil. Reduce the heat and simmer, stirring occasionally, for 10 to 15 minutes or until most of the liquid has evaporated. Transfer to a bowl and cool completely.

3. While the filling is cooling, make the cake layers: Place an oven rack in the center position and preheat the oven to 400°F. Grease and flour five 9-inch-round cake pans or cast-iron skillets. (If you don't have that many, you can bake the layers in shifts.)

4. In a large bowl, beat the shortening with an electric mixer at medium speed for 2 minutes or until creamy. Gradually add ½ cup sugar and beat for 5 to 7 minutes, until very fluffy. Add the egg and beat until the yellow disappears.

5. Combine the flour, baking powder, baking soda, and salt. In a large measuring cup, combine the buttermilk and molasses. Gradually add the flour to shortening, alternating with buttermilk, beginning and ending with flour. Beat until blended.

6. Divide the dough into five equal portions. With lightly floured fingers, press one portion evenly into each pan. Prick the dough several times with a fork. Sprinkle each layer evenly with ½ teaspoon sugar.

7. Put the pans on middle rack of oven and bake 10 minutes or until golden brown. (Only bake layers on one rack at a time. Do not crowd.) Repeat as needed for the number of pans and space in the oven, cooling the pans between uses. Remove the layers from the pans and cool completely on wire racks.

8. To assemble the cake, set aside the prettiest cake layer for the top. Spread one-quarter of the filling (about 1½ cups) on each of the other four layers to within ½ inch of edge. Stack the layers and top with the reserved layer. Loosely cover cake and let stand 2 days at room temperature.

MAKES 12 TO 16 SERVINGS

IF YOU VOTE, I'LL BAKE YOU A CAKE

IN THE MID- TO LATE EIGHTEENTH CENTURY, ELECTION
Cake was an annual ritual. According to the *Colonial Records of Connecticut* from May 1771, one Ezekial Williams, Esq., billed the cost of making the cake to the Connecticut General Assembly. It was a reasonable expense at the time. Town representatives from all over the state would gather in Hartford, the state capital, on Election Day. It was a long day: Vote tallying often took well into the night, so local housewives provided food that kept well, like Election Cake (also called Hartford Cake). More like a sweet, yeasty coffee cake, it was a loaf chock full of dried fruit and spices.

Birthday cake for Women's Suffrage, 1996.

Historians have identified it as a New World derivation of English loaf cake (or "rich cake" or "fruit cake"). All versions require yeast (frugal cooks used the dregs from ale), flour, butter, sugar, and eggs. It is the sweet equivalent of the vat of beef stew served today at local fairs for a couple of dollars, except that these cakes were offered free to the legislators who had traveled long distances in the name of democracy. The ritual faded in the second half of the nineteenth century, but Election Cake still found its way into period cookbooks.

Beyond the basic ingredients, housewives—who couldn't vote—chose from a wide range of extras— whatever was available or captured their fancy. An 1844 recipe from *The Improved Housewife* called for "two and a half pounds of raisins soaked for several hours in a gill of brandy." A recipe from *Miss Beecher's Domestic Receipt-Book,* published in the same year, recommends "half an ounce of nutmeg" and two pounds of unspecified "fruit." The recipe below is thought to be the earliest. It appears in its original wording, as printed in Amelia Simmons's *American Cookery.*

ELECTION CAKE

30 quarts of flour, 10 pound butter, 14 pound sugar, 12 pound raisins [note the word "raisin" and "plumb" were used interchangeably], 3 dozen eggs, 1 pint wine, 1 quart brandy, 4 ounces cinnamon, 4 ounces fine coriander seed, 3 ounces ground allspice; wet flour with milk to the consistency of bread over night, adding one quart yeast; the next morning work the butter and sugar together for half an hour, which will render the cake much lighter and whiter; when it has rise light. Work in every other ingredient except the plumbs, which will work in when going in the oven.

Maria Arsenault's Boston Cream Pie

JOHNSTON, RHODE ISLAND

Maria Arsenault, is a classical mandolin player and violinist with the Rhode Island College Chamber Orchestra. Her forays into baking had focused on her myriad versions for biscotti, but a few years ago, the passion her brother, Michael Magnelli, had for Boston cream pie inspired her to expand her horizons. She started baking it for his birthday and, delighted with the results, he pressed her to compete in the Boston cream pie contest of the Great American Bake Sale in Boston, which raises funds for hunger relief. Having lived on Cape Cod for thirty years, Mrs. Arsenault was well versed in the iterations of the dessert that had been created at the Parker House Hotel in the mid-nineteenth century. She experimented, searching for a lighter cake and a more balanced filling, and used her brother along with her husband, mother, and aunt as tasters. Always up for a little healthy competition with his wife, Mr. Arsenault decided to enter the contest as well. Mrs. Arsenault placed first (secret ingredient: a dash of Amaretto). Mr. Arsenault took second.

Boston cream pie put her on the map, she says. "Whenever I go to an event or a function, folks just expect me to bring Boston cream pie."

FOR THE CAKE

2 large whole eggs, separated, plus 1 extra white

¾ cup sugar

2¼ cups sifted cake flour

1 tablespoon baking powder

1 teaspoon kosher salt

⅓ cup extra-light olive oil

1 scant cup whole milk

1 tablespoon Amaretto liqueur

1½ teaspoons pure vanilla extract

FOR THE CUSTARD

2 cups whole milk

2 large eggs

⅓ cup sugar

⅓ cup all-purpose flour

1 scant teaspoon cornstarch

1 teaspoon Amaretto liqueur

FOR THE GLAZE AND GARNISH

½ cup mini semisweet chocolate chips

6 tablespoons heavy cream

1 tablespoon dark corn syrup

1 teaspoon Amaretto liqueur

1 cup sliced blanched almonds, lightly toasted

2 tablespoons shaved white chocolate

1 maraschino cherry

1. Preheat the oven to 325°F. Grease and flour two 9-inch round cake pans.

2. To make the cake: With an electric stand mixer, beat the egg whites until they form soft peaks. Gradually add ¼ cup of the sugar. Beat until very stiff peaks form. Transfer to another bowl (unless you have a second mixer bowl).

3. Sift the remaining ½ cup sugar, the flour, baking powder, and salt together into the bowl of an electric stand mixer. Make a well in the center. Add the oil, egg yolks, milk, Amaretto, and vanilla. Beat on medium speed just until smooth.

4. Pour the yolk mixture gradually over the whites, gently folding them together with a spatula, just until blended. Pour the batter into the prepared pans. Bake for 30 to 40 minutes, until a toothpick inserted into the cake comes away clean. Take care not to overbake.

5. Cool in the pans for 15 minutes, then turn the layers out onto wire racks and cool completely.

6. While the cakes are baking, make the custard: In a blender, combine the milk, eggs, sugar, flour, and cornstarch. Blend until smooth.

7. Pour the mixture into a medium saucepan and cook over medium heat, stirring constantly, for 5 to 7 minutes, until smooth. When the custard thickens, bring it to a gentle simmer. Cook, stirring constantly, for 1 minute, then remove it from the heat. Stir in the Amaretto. The consistency should be like a pudding; it will thicken as it cools.

8. Transfer the custard to a bowl. Cool to room temperature, then cover and refrigerate until cold.

9. To make the glaze and garnish: Place the chocolate in a medium bowl. Combine the cream and corn syrup in a small saucepan. Cook over medium heat, stirring, until the mixture comes to a gentle boil. Pour the cream over the chocolate and let it stand for 30 seconds. Whisk gently until smooth. Stir in the Amaretto.

10. Place one layer upside down on a cake platter. Reserve ¾ cup of custard. Spread the remaining custard on top of the cake. Gently place the second layer on top right side up. Spread the reserved custard on the sides of the cake in a thin layer. Press the almonds onto the sides.

11. Spread the chocolate glaze over the top of the cake.

12. Refrigerate the cake to set the glaze. Sprinkle the top with the white chocolate and place the cherry in the center.

SERVES 8

REAL DOWNEAST WHOOPIE PIE

CUMBERLAND, MAINE

Y ou can find whoopie pie—a New England and Amish invention—in just about any convenience store in Maine. But you have to go to the Cranberry Island Kitchen to find the best pies in the state. The shop's owners, Karen Haase and Carol Ford, who began baking together about twenty years ago, describe most modern whoopee pies as "dry cake and Crisco-based filling." Their red velvet recipe is based on Ms. Haase's mother's recipe. "I'm not sure if we brought it back to its roots, or gourmet-ed it," says Ms. Ford.

FOR THE CAKES

1 cup buttermilk

1½ teaspoons baking soda

1 tablespoon distilled white vinegar

3 tablespoons red food coloring

½ cup unsweetened cocoa powder (20-24% fat content)

6 tablespoons boiling water

8 tablespoons (1 stick) unsalted butter

1½ cups sugar

¼ teaspoon table salt

2 large eggs

1½ teaspoons pure vanilla extract

2 cups all-purpose flour

FOR THE BUTTERCREAM FILLING

12 tablespoons (1½ sticks) unsalted butter, softened

3½ cups confectioners' sugar

2 tablespoons heavy cream

¼ teaspoon pure vanilla extract

1. Preheat the oven to 325°F. Butter 24 muffin top tins (available at specialty cookware stores). If you don't have enough tins, you can bake the cakes in shifts.

2. To make the cakes: Combine the buttermilk, baking soda, vinegar, and food coloring. In a separate bowl, mix the cocoa and boiling water until smooth.

3. Using an electric mixer, cream the butter and sugar. Add the salt, eggs, and vanilla, and beat until light and fluffy. Add a little of the flour and combine, then a bit of the cocoa mixture and combine. Continue alternating, mixing well between each addition. Make sure you add the last of the flour after the last of the cocoa.

4. Fill the tins and bake for 15 to 20 minutes, until a toothpick comes out clean. Cool the cakes in the tins briefly, then turn out onto a wire rack to cool completely. If you need to bake in shifts, cool and rebutter the tins before refilling with batter.

5. While the cakes are baking and cooling, make the filling: Cream the butter with an electric mixer for about 30 seconds on medium speed. On low speed, gradually beat in the confectioners' sugar. Add the cream and vanilla, and beat on medium speed for about 3 minutes, until the frosting is light and fluffy.

6. When the cakes have cooled, spread the bottom halves with the filling. Make sandwiches with the remaining cakes, so that both rounded tops are outside. Serve immediately.

———

MAKES 10 TO 12 ASSEMBLED PIES

VARIATION: You can add other flavorings to the buttercream filling, such as grated orange zest with ½ teaspoon of orange liqueur or orange juice in place of the vanilla extract. Or you could add crushed peppermint candy.

Colorful beads and moon pies—chocolate-covered cookies sandwiching marshmallows—are thrown to revelers during Mardi Gras, Mobile, Alabama.

MARY HILL'S MISSISSIPPI MUD CAKE

WINNEMUCCA, NEVADA

After Charlie Hill left his hometown of Sunflower, Mississippi, to work on the Southern Pacific Railroad, he built a life in Nevada and he and his wife, Mary Hill, raised seven children. But he couldn't shake his Southern roots and the family made frequent pilgrimages back to Mississippi. On one of these visits, back in the 1960s, Mr. Hill's sister Mignon Black pressed this recipe into his hand. Mrs. Hill perfected it over the years, and Mississippi Mud Cake became a standard family treat, served straight from the pan. Presentation isn't crucial, according to the Hills, since everyone grabs a hunk as soon as the pan lands on the table. Says Season Kilgore, Mr. Hill's granddaughter, "Recently, one of my aunts had a meltdown when she got back from bird watching, and she found that we had eaten her piece of cake while she was gone."

The Sweet Life

FOR THE CAKE

½ pound (2 sticks) unsalted butter or margarine

½ cup unsweetened cocoa powder

2 cups sugar

4 large eggs, slightly beaten

1½ cups all-purpose flour

Pinch of salt

1½ cups chopped walnuts

1 teaspoon pure vanilla extract

One 16-ounce package mini marshmallows

FOR THE FROSTING

4 tablespoons (½ stick) unsalted butter or margarine

⅓ cup unsweetened cocoa powder

½ cup milk

1 teaspoon pure vanilla extract

Pinch of salt

One 16-ounce package confectioners' sugar, plus more as needed

½ cup chopped walnuts (optional)

1. Preheat the oven to 350°F. Grease a 13 x 9-inch baking dish.

2. To make the cake: Melt the butter in large saucepan over low heat. Remove from the heat. Add the cocoa and mix well. Add the sugar, eggs, flour, salt, nuts, and vanilla and mix well.

3. Pour into the prepared pan and bake for 30 to 35 minutes, until a cake tester comes out clean (a few crumbs are okay).

4. While cake is baking, make the frosting so it's ready as soon as the cake comes out of the oven: Place the butter, cocoa, and milk in a small saucepan and bring to a boil, stirring frequently. Remove from the heat and stir in the vanilla, salt, and confectioners' sugar. You may have to add more confectioners' sugar, as the frosting should be thick. Keep warm.

5. When cake is done, sprinkle the marshmallows over the top while it is still warm. Spread the frosting over the marshmallows. If desired, sprinkle with the chopped walnuts.

6. Cool in the pan and serve at room temperature.

SERVES 12 TO 15

TAYARI JONES'S RED VELVET CAKE

Author Tayari Jones grew up in Atlanta and adores red velvet cake. The cake features prominently in her book *The Untelling*. And she serves it at her readings and book signings. "To me, it's a truly Southern dessert," she says. "It's the equivalent of wearing crinolines under your skirt. It's a symbol of what it means to be a Southern woman. But it is also a great equalizer—white Southerners and black Southerners have equal claim to it. Yes, there's red dye in it, but so what? One of my friends complained about the amount in my mama's recipe—it calls for one and a half ounces. That's about a bottle and a half. To make the cake taste right (let alone look right), you're going to have to use the coloring. If you remove that much liquid from your cake, it's going to be dry. And it's going to look stupid. If you're afraid of red food color, make another cake."

FOR THE CAKE

2½ cups sifted all-purpose flour

1 teaspoon baking soda

1 teaspoon kosher salt

1 teaspoon unsweetened cocoa powder

10 tablespoons plus 2 teaspoons (1⅓ sticks) unsalted butter or margarine, softened

⅔ cup vegetable oil

1½ cups sugar

2 large eggs

1 teaspoon distilled white vinegar

1 teaspoon pure vanilla extract

1½ ounces (3 tablespoons) red food coloring

1 cup buttermilk

FOR THE CREAM CHEESE FROSTING

10 tablespoons plus 2 teaspoons (1⅓ sticks) unsalted butter, softened

8 ounces cream cheese, softened

¾ teaspoon pure vanilla extract

2⅔ cups confectioners' sugar

⅔ cup chopped pecans

1. Preheat the oven to 350°F. Line the bottom of three 8-inch round baking pans with waxed or parchment paper. Grease the sides of the pans.

2. To make the cake: Sift together the flour, baking soda, salt, and cocoa.

3. Combine the butter or margarine and vegetable oil using an electric mixer. Add the sugar and cream until fluffy. Beat in the eggs one at a time. Add the vinegar and vanilla and mix until fluffy. Stir in the food coloring.

4. Fold in the flour mixture, alternating with the buttermilk.

5. Divide the batter evenly among the three pans. Bake for about 25 minutes, until a cake tester comes out clean (a few crumbs are okay).

6. Cool briefly in the pans, then turn out onto wire racks to cool to room temperature.

7. To make the frosting: Cream the butter and cream cheese, using an electric mixer, until light and fluffy. Add the vanilla and mix well, then stir in the confectioners' sugar on low speed. Mix until creamy and smooth.

8. Assemble cake with frosting between the layers and on the sides and top. Sprinkle the top with chopped pecans.

MAKES 1 CAKE, SERVES 8 TO 12

BUNDT, THE AMERICAN KUGELHOPF

BUNDT CAKE IS A SYMBOL OF AMERICAN GUMPTION AND THE powerful pull that native foods exert on the hearts, minds—and pot racks—of American cooks. According to an article in the fall 2005 issue of *Generations*, the newsletter of the Jewish Historical Society of the Upper Midwest, Fannie Schanfield remembers a Hadassah luncheon In Minneapolis in 1950 at which she and her friend Rose Joshua bemoaned the fact that fluffy, American-style cakes lacked the density of rich European cakes. What they needed were special pans, like the ceramic one her mother used to bake kugelhopf.

Mrs. Schanfield's husband arranged for the women to meet with the founder of the Nordic Ware Aluminum Bakeware Company and, soon after she described the pan she remembered, she received a prototype in aluminum. The fluted edges were new, but the all-important center hole remained so heat could easily circulate inside the cake and result in faster, more even baking. Nordic Ware trademarked the name Bundt—from the German *bundkuchen*.

In 1966, a Bundt cake (cleverly named the Tunnel of Fudge Cake) won the Pillsbury Bake-Off. In 1972, a Bundt again took the top prize, and eleven other winners in the years since have also been Bundts. Two women chatting in Minneapolis planted the seed for a new style of American cake—and tens of millions of Americans of all heritages were soon flocking to their nearest department store for the deep cake pan with the odd fluted sides and the hole in the middle.

Jesse Rosenberg's
Flourless Chocolate Cake

SAN CARLOS, CALIFORNIA

One Big Table

Growing up in Paris, Jesse Rosenberg came to appreciate how the French valued quality over quantity. She learned her greatest lessons from a woman who hired her as a babysitter. "She was very intense and organized," says Ms. Rosenberg. "She taught me everything"—including how to bake this very rich but simple flourless chocolate cake.

½ pound (2 sticks) butter

1 cup sugar, plus extra for the pan

14 ounces dark chocolate, chopped

8 large eggs

1. Preheat the oven to 300°F. Grease a 9-inch-round cake pan with 2 teaspoons of the butter. Then sprinkle with sugar and rotate to lightly coat the inside.

2. Combine the chocolate and butter in a heavy medium saucepan and melt over low heat, stirring constantly. Transfer to a large bowl to cool slightly.

3. Using an electric mixer, beat the eggs until light. Add the sugar gradually and beat until pale and fluffy, about 8 minutes. Fold into the melted chocolate-butter.

4. Pour into the prepared pan. Bake for 1 hour, testing after 45 minutes; the top should have formed a crust and feel solid, though still slightly soft. Cool in the pan for 5 minutes, then turn out onto a cake plate. Cool to room temperature.

SERVES 8

ALLYSON LAW KISSELL'S
STEAMED CHOCOLATE PUDDING

Allyson Law Kissell recalls the curious path of her family's Christmas recipe: "My grandmother Helen Beveridge Law wrote the recipes for me many years ago. I am not certain, but I believe she got the recipes from her own grandfather, Samuel Bullock, who was born in Worcester, England, in 1827. He reportedly had a lovely voice and sang at Queen Victoria's coronation when he was eleven years old.

"He was apprenticed as a baker, and in 1848, when he was twenty-one, he emigrated to Utica, New York, and learned house and sign painting from his uncle George Bullock. After marrying Eliza Dudley, he moved to Fremont, Nebraska. He owned a paper hanging, painting, and interior-decorating business there until 1875. The family moved to San Jose [California] and then in 1879, they moved to Portland, Oregon.

"My grandmother spoke often of how her grandfather would bake loaves and loaves of breads to give as gifts for the holidays and how the kitchen always smelled of fresh baking. She took after [him] in that respect; whenever we would come to her home for Christmas, there would be the wonderful smell of baking bread. Then, after Christmas dinner, was the anticipated Steamed Chocolate Pudding. I didn't like the hard sauce until I was much older, but as a child, I looked forward to that pudding that was, of course, like a very moist cake, not a pudding at all."

FOR THE PUDDING

4 tablespoons (½ stick) unsalted butter, softened, plus more for the steaming mold

½ cup sugar

1 large egg, beaten

2¼ cups all-purpose flour

1½ tablespoons baking powder

¼ teaspoon table salt

1 cup whole milk

2 ounces unsweetened chocolate, melted

FOR THE HARD SAUCE

8 tablespoons (1 stick) unsalted butter, softened

1½ cups confectioners' sugar

1 tablespoon fine bourbon

1. To make the pudding: Cream the butter and sugar. Stir in the egg.

2. Sift together the flour, baking powder, and salt. Add to the butter mixture, alternating with the milk. Add the chocolate and beat everything until will blended. The batter will be very thick.

3. Butter a 2-quart pudding mold or a deep heatproof bowl (Pyrex works well). Pour in the batter. Cover the mold or cover the bowl tightly with parchment and aluminum foil secured with kitchen twine or a rubber band. Place on a rack in a large saucepan or stockpot. Fill with hot water one-third up the mold. Cover the pot, bring to a boil, and steam for 2 hours, replenishing the boiling water as needed to maintain the level.

4. Meanwhile, make the hard sauce: Cream the butter and confectioners' sugar. Stir in the bourbon.

5. The pudding is done when a knife inserted in the center comes out clean. Carefully remove the mold from the pot and remove the cover. Cool on a rack for 15 minutes. Place a serving plate upside down on top of the mold and carefully turn out the pudding. Serve warm with a dollop of sauce on each slice.

SERVES 8 TO 10

Julie Shafer's
German Chocolate Layer Cake

After Julie Shafer's grandparents moved from San Francisco, where they owned a small Italian bakery, to the Napa Valley they continued to bake every day. "They'd originally been vintners in Asti, making Asti spumante, but there was a baking gene somewhere in the mix. My father inherited it, and so did I. I'd be happy if I could bake all day," she says. "When a few days go by and nothing's come out of the oven, my sons ask me what's wrong." This cake, a riff on the back-of-the-box chocolate cake that was layered with coconut and frosted with chocolate and was called German Chocolate Cake or Swiss Chocolate Cake is the one her family and friends always ask her to bake for their birthdays.

FOR THE CAKE

1²⁄₃ cups unsweetened cocoa powder

1½ cups boiling water

10 tablespoons (1¼ sticks) unsalted butter

2¾ cups packed light brown sugar

3 large eggs

3 cups cake flour

2 tablespoons all-purpose flour

1¼ teaspoons baking powder

1¼ teaspoons baking soda

1¼ cups buttermilk

1½ teaspoons pure vanilla extract

FOR THE FILLING

1 cup heavy cream or evaporated milk

1 cup packed light brown sugar

5 large egg yolks

12 tablespoons (1½ sticks) unsalted butter

Pinch of salt

1 cup unsweetened shredded coconut

1 cup chopped pecans

1 teaspoon pure vanilla extract

FOR THE CHOCOLATE FROSTING

1 cup heavy cream

2 tablespoons sugar

2 tablespoons light corn syrup

1 pound good-quality semisweet chocolate, chopped fine

4 tablespoons (½ stick) unsalted butter

1. To make the cake: Preheat the oven to 350°F. Butter (or grease) and flour three 9-inch round cake pans.

2. In a small bowl, whisk the cocoa and boiling water until smooth. Cool slightly.

3. Using an electric mixer, cream the butter and sugar until fluffy, about 5 minutes. Add the eggs, one at a time, beating well after each addition and scraping down the bowl as necessary.

4. Sift the flours, baking powder, and baking soda together onto waxed paper. With the mixer on low speed, add the flour mixture, alternating with the buttermilk. Gently stir in the cocoa paste and vanilla. Divide the batter evenly into the pans.

5. Bake for 20 to 25 minutes, until a cake tester comes out clean (a few crumbs are okay). Cool briefly in the pans, then turn out onto wire racks to cool completely.

6. While the layers are baking, make the filling: Whisk the cream, brown sugar, and egg yolks together in a small heavy saucepan over medium heat. Add the butter and salt, and cook, stirring constantly, until the butter melts. Cook over low heat, stirring frequently, about 10 minutes. Remove from the heat. Stir in the coconut and pecans. Cool to room temperature. Stir in the vanilla.

7. To make the frosting: Combine the cream, sugar, and corn syrup in a heavy medium saucepan and bring to a low boil over medium heat. Stir until the sugar is completely dissolved. Remove from the heat. Add the chocolate and stir until it is melted and smooth. Add the butter and stir until smooth. Cool to room temperature.

8. To assemble the cake, put the first layer on a serving plate, right side up. Spread the top with one-third of the filling. Place the second layer on upside down, and spread with another third of the filling. Place the final layer right side up, and spread with the remainder of the filling. Frost the sides with the frosting.

MAKES ONE 9-INCH LAYER CAKE, SERVES 12

FLO BRAKER'S SIMPLY PERFECT YELLOW CAKE

PALO ALTO, CALIFORNIA

Flo Braker, the award-winning author of four books on baking and columnist for the *San Francisco Chronicle*, says that it was a chemistry set she owned as a child that sparked her love affair with baking. With the help of the toy's instruction manual, Mrs. Braker learned how to mix chemicals and discovered how important it was to measure accurately and follow directions carefully. She also learned how to experiment and created her own chemical concoctions. Today, she encourages the same precision and creativity when she teaches others to bake. Her Simply Perfect Yellow Cake is a perfect example of this—a foolproof cake base that bakers can make their own by adding different fillings and frostings.

Have all the ingredients at room temperature. To measure the cake flour, lightly spoon it into dry measuring cups until they overflow. Sweep off the excess with a straight knife edge. Do not pack the flour down.

Nonstick spray or butter, for the pans

All-purpose flour, for the pans

½ cup sour cream

½ cup whole milk

1 teaspoon pure vanilla extract

2⅓ cups cake flour

1½ teaspoons baking powder

½ teaspoon baking soda

¼ teaspoon fine sea salt

½ pound (2 sticks) unsalted butter

1½ cups sugar

3 large eggs, lightly beaten

1. Center a rack in the oven and preheat the oven to 350°F. Lightly coat two 9 × 2-inch round cake pans with nonstick spray or butter, then flour them, tapping out the excess. Line the bottoms with parchment paper.

2. In a small bowl, blend the sour cream, milk, and vanilla.

3. Sift the flour, baking powder, baking soda, and salt together onto a large sheet of waxed paper.

4. In the bowl of a stand mixer fitted with the paddle attachment, beat the butter on medium speed until it is lighter in color, clings to the sides of the bowl, and is smooth and creamy, about 45 seconds. Add the sugar in a steady stream, then stop the mixer to scrape down the sides of the bowl. Beat on medium speed until the mixture is very light in color and texture, about 4 minutes, continuing to scrape down the sides of the bowl.

5. With the mixer on medium, add the beaten eggs about 3 tablespoons at a time, beating after each addition until incorporated. The entire process of adding and beating the eggs should take about 3 minutes, at which point the mixture should appear fluffy and increased in volume.

6. On the lowest speed, add the flour mixture in three additions, alternating with the sour cream mixture in two additions, beginning and ending with flour and mixing well after each addition. Stop the mixer often to scrape down the sides of the bowl.

7. Spoon equal amounts of the batter into each pan. With a rubber spatula, spread the batter from the center outward, creating a slightly raised ridge around the outside rim to ensure that the layers bake evenly and level.

8. Bake the cake layers 30 to 35 minutes, until the tops are golden, spring back when lightly touched in the center, and the edges are beginning to pull away from the sides of the pans. Transfer the pans to wire racks and cool about 10 minutes.

9. Tilt and rotate each pan and gently tap it on a work surface to release the cake edges. Remove the parchment liner and cool on a rack.

10. If serving the cake within 24 hours, wrap each layer individually in plastic wrap and store at room temperature. To freeze, cover the plastic-wrapped layers with foil. Label each package with the contents and date, and freeze for up to 2 weeks. To thaw, remove the foil and leave at room temperature for 2 to 3 hours.

MAKES TWO 9-INCH CAKE LAYERS

PUFF THE MAGIC SODA

FOR ALL THE INGREDIENTS THAT HAVE BEEN LOVINGLY mixed into cake batters over the centuries, none has more drastically transformed the art and business of baking than baking powder. This leavening agent—sodium bicarbonate with acids—brought a consistency to previously unknown results. As an 1852 ad for Durkee's Baking Powder promised:

> Housewives . . . will find a cessation of complaints from husbands . . . about sour or heavy bread, biscuits, pastry, &c, and on the contrary, will hear accompanied by smiles "What nice biscuits you've made, my dear."

Invented in 1843 by British chemist Alfred Bird, baking powder causes batters to rise. Before its invention, housewives had to beat and beat and beat eggs to ensure a decently fluffy cake. When baking powder meets wet ingredients, carbon dioxide forms. Add heat: The gas molecules expand and the batter rises. (Baking soda contains only sodium bicarbonate, and while it works fine in recipes with an acidic component, it tastes bitter.) With the invention of baking powder, a world of baking opportunity opened up. Cake mixes became possible. Home cooks experimented. Thanks to baking powder, just about everyone who bakes a cake receives nary a complaint.

James McCourt's Mile High White Cake with Caramel Frosting

WASHINGTON, D.C.

Author James McCourt is the designated cook in his household and the designated cake baker for all special occasions among his friends and colleagues. "Americans," he says, "go ga-ga for dense-moist or high-high cakes. This one caters to the latter preference. It is the birthday cake of dreams."

One Big Table

FOR THE CAKE

2½ sticks unsalted butter

2 tablespoons Greek-style yogurt

2 teaspoons fresh lemon juice

2 cups milk

1½ cups all-purpose flour

4 teaspoons baking powder

2 teaspoons kosher salt

3 cups sugar, sifted

4 large eggs

2 teaspoons pure vanilla extract

FOR THE ICING

½ cup sugar

¼ cup water

½ cup heavy cream

2 teaspoons vanilla extract

3 sticks unsalted butter, cold, cut into 1-inch chunks

1 to 2 teaspoons highest quality sea salt

2 cups powdered sugar

1 cup shaved almonds, lightly toasted

1. Preheat the oven to 350°F. Use two tablespoons of the butter to generously grease two 10-inch springform pans. Cut wax paper liners for the bottoms of the pan, insert and smear with additional butter. Dust the pan with flour and tap out the excess.

2. To make the cake: Combine the yogurt and lemon juice. Warm the milk until it is lukewarm, then add to the yogurt and lemon juice and set aside for 15 minutes to allow it to sour. Sift together the flour, baking powder, and salt. In another bowl, combine the butter and sugar, and beat with an electric mixer until creamy yellow and fluffy. Add the eggs one by one, beating between each addition. Add the vanilla and beat to combine. With the mixer on low speed, alternately add some of the flour mixture and some of the soured milk mixture, beating after each addition. Be careful not to overbeat, which will make the cake tough.

3. Divide the batter between the two prepared pans and bake until the center is firm and a toothpick inserted in the center comes out clean, about 40 minutes. Remove, cool on rack for 30 minutes. Use a knife to loosen the sides of the cakes from the pans, turn out onto a plate, and remove the parchment. Allow to cool completely.

4. To make the frosting, combine the granulated sugar and water in a small saucepan over medium heat. bring to a boil and cook, without stirring until the mixture turns dark. Remove from the heat, allow to cool slightly and then slowly add the cream and the vanilla, stirring constantly. Set aside for 30 minutes to cool completely.

5. Combine the butter and salt in a large bowl or in the bowl of a stand mixer fitted with the paddle attachment. Beat on medium-high speed until the butter is light and fluffy, about 3 minutes. Reduce speed to low, add powdered sugar, and mix until completely incorporated. Turn off the mixer. Scrape the sides of the bowl and add the cooled caramel. Beat on medium-high speed for another 5 to 10 minutes until very fluffy, cover, and refrigerate for about 45 minutes.

6. To assemble the cake, cut each cake in half horizontally to create four layers. Assemble the layers, spreading a layer of frosting between each one. Frost the top and sides of the cake. Press the toasted almonds to the sides of the cake, refrigerate for 10 minutes, or up to one day, and serve.

SERVES 12 TO 20

Mary Jennifer Russell's
Extraordinary Southern Caramel Cake

Mary Jennifer Russell opened her bakery, Sugaree's, because, she says, "I wanted to make sure our homestyle Southern cakes didn't get lost." Lane Cake, Hummingbird Cake, red velvet cake, and caramel cake are some of the layer cakes prized by home cooks south of the Mason-Dixon, part of the pantheon of dishes that include fried chicken, grits, fried green tomatoes, peach ice cream, and pecan pie that most Southerners assume cannot be made anyplace but home—and at Sugaree's.

FOR THE CAKE

2 cups flour, preferably White Lily

1½ teaspoons baking soda

⅓ teaspoon salt

8 tablespoons (1 stick) unsalted butter, at room temperature

½ cup vegetable shortening such as Crisco

¼ cup sugar

5 eggs, cold

1 cup whole buttermilk, cold

1 tablespoon vanilla extract

FOR THE FROSTING

8 tablespoons (1 stick) unsalted butter

1 cup evaporated milk

Pinch of salt

3 cups sugar

1. Preheat oven to 350°F. Grease and flour three 9-inch cake pans.

2. Whisk together flour, soda, and salt. In another bowl, beat the butter, shortening, and sugar together for about 5 minutes until fluffy and light in color. Add the eggs one at a time until fully incorporated. Beat for 2 minutes.

3. Mix in half of the flour mixture just until combined, then half the buttermilk and the vanilla. Add the remaining flour mixture and mix until just combined, then the remaining buttermilk and vanilla. Stir well.

4. Pour batter into the prepared pans. Shake pans gently to level the batter. Bake 18 to 22 minutes until golden and firm to touch. The cake should look moist and should have pulled away from sides of pan.

5. To make the frosting: Melt the butter in a saucepan over medium heat. Add the milk, salt, and 2½ cups of sugar and cook until it reaches a full rolling boil, stirring as necessary to prevent burning. Continue cooking until the mixture is honey colored. Set aside.

6. Place the remaining ½ cup sugar in a cast-iron skillet over medium-high heat and melt, stirring as necessary as the sugar melts and caramelizes. When the sugar is the color of dark honey, carefully add the milk mixture a little at a time. Continue cooking a few minutes longer until the mixture bubbles.

7. Pour into the bowl of a standing mixer and beat until it starts to look creamy.

8. Spread icing between the layers, then scrape mixer down and beat the remainder another minute. Frost the top and sides, working quickly. Go around the cake one more time without lifting the spatula.

MAKES ONE CAKE, SERVING 8 TO 12

DUNCAN HINES, THE MAN, THE MIX, THE MUSEUM, THE FESTIVAL

CORA JANE SPILLER OF OAKLAND, KENTUCKY, CAN ATTEST TO THE FACT that Duncan Hines was a real person—not the figment of a marketer's imagination like Betty Crocker or Aunt Jemima.

Ms. Spiller is Duncan Hines's great-niece. He and her grandfather, Porter Hines, were brothers. There were six children in the Hines family and when their mother died, they were farmed out to various relatives. Porter and Duncan, the two youngest, were sent to "Grandma Duncan's down in the country, where everybody cooked with good butter and eggs," Ms. Spiller says. Duncan became a traveling salesman and his territory covered more than thirty states. As he traveled, his niece says, he kept a journal of his favorite places to dine, which he included in list form with his 1936 Christmas card. He friends and family were so enthusiastic about the list that they encouraged him to publish it as a book. When *Adventures in Good Eating*, a guide to eating establishments along American's back roads was published in 1939, a new spokesman for American cuisine took the stage. Hines's weekly column soon appeared in more than a hundred American newspapers.

When Ms. Spiller went to dinners in restaurants with Uncle Duncan, he would order three or four entrees that everybody would share. He never wrote notes on a restaurant until he got out to the car. He believed in eating local specialties, and was particularly fond of country ham.

One of the restaurants he recommended was the Sanders Café in Corbin, Kentucky. Some think the national recognition so spurred Harland Sanders's business that he soon became the Colonel.

In 1948, Mr. Hines and Roy Park formed Hines-Park Food Corporation to license products with the Duncan Hines name. When Nebraska Consolidated Mills developed a cake mix that called for the home cook to add a whole egg (prior dry mixes included powdered eggs), Hines agreed to put his name on the product.

There were eventually more than two hundred Duncan Hines brand items on grocery shelves, in addition to kitchen tools and appliances. In 1956, the brand was sold to Proctor & Gamble.

Today, Hines's memory and accomplishments are kept alive by an annual festival in Bowling Green, Kentucky, his birthplace. The festival was the brainchild of local tourism official Gary West, who felt it was important to celebrate the town's ties to Hines and to educate people about him as a man, not just a brand. Pinnacle Foods, which now owns the Duncan Hines label, is a sponsor, and the Bowling Green Junior Women's Club distributes the festival's profits back into the community.

A juried art exhibit, a children's pageant, a duck derby, and a street dance are all popular events—but the biggest draw is the recipe contest. According to the rules, the more Duncan Hines products you use, the more points you get. One recent winner, High Five Bars, included two.

The Duncan Hines Festival is held in Bowling Green every August. For dates, visit www.duncanhinesfestival.com.

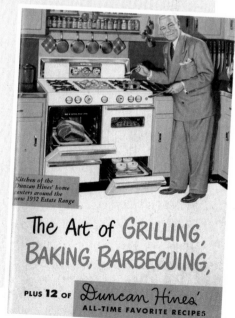

Kitchen of the Duncan Hines' home centers around the new 1952 Estate Range

The Art of GRILLING, BAKING, BARBECUING,

PLUS **12** OF *Duncan Hines'* ALL-TIME FAVORITE RECIPES

Grandma Stevens's Coconut Cake

RALEIGH, NORTH CAROLINA

Hugh Stevens's profession is lawyering, but his passion is Southern food. His mother, who taught him how to cook and bake, left him her square cake pans. After she died, he searched through many pieces of paper before he found this recipe, which she used right up to the year before she died.

Mr. Stevens says: "At our house, the two signs that Christmas was approaching were the arrival of the Sears, Roebuck Christmas catalog and my mother saying, 'I guess they'll expect me to make a coconut cake again this year.' 'They' were her brothers and sisters, with whose families we gathered every Christmas afternoon for a potluck dinner which, despite its description, was as orchestrated as the Radio City Christmas Show.

"My father would come home from Kroger's with a fresh coconut and punch holes in it with a hammer and a ten-penny nail to drain the water. Then he would cut away the husk with his pocketknife and carefully grate the coconut by hand. My mother insisted on fresh coconut. One year, for reasons I don't remember, she resorted to canned coconut; she judged the result so disastrous that she threw the cake out rather than inflict it on her family.

"My mother always baked the layers in two square aluminum pans—that was all she had. In the early days she made them from scratch, but eventually she switched to white cake mix to which she added her own butter. When they were completely cooled she would carefully slice them horizontally into four thin layers, three of which were spread with the mixture that she called the 'filling' and sprinkled with fresh coconut. The fourth, which went on top, was left plain. Each layer tended to be uneven, so she'd secure them to each other with toothpicks at the corners. When all four were in place she would set them in the refrigerator for three or four days.

"A day or so before Christmas, my mother would remove the cake from the refrigerator, cover the top and sides with the icing, and sprinkle coconut on top. She carried it to the family dinner in a large Tupperware cake box. She usually insisted on slicing and serving it herself—not out of pride, but to prevent any toothpick accidents. When we realized we had the cake pans after she died, we knew we had to continue the tradition."

FOR THE FILLING

2 cups sour cream

2 cups sugar

Three 6-ounce packages frozen shredded or grated coconut, thawed

FOR THE CAKE

3 cups cake flour

1 tablespoon baking powder

½ teaspoons salt

1 cup unsalted butter, cut into 1-inch pieces and slightly softened

2 cups sugar

5 large eggs

2 teaspoons vanilla

1¼ cups buttermilk

FOR THE CAKE AND FROSTING

Seven-Minute Icing (recipe follows)

1. Two days before serving, make the filling: In a large bowl, stir together the sour cream, sugar, and most of the coconut. (Save a bit for sprinkling on top at the end.) Cover and refrigerate.

2. The day before serving, make the cake: Preheat the oven to 350°F. Butter two 8 x 2-inch cake pans, line with parchment or wax paper, butter again, and set aside. In a medium bowl, sift the flour, baking powder, and salt together and set aside. Place the butter in another bowl and beat until light and fluffy with an electric mixer, about 2 minutes. Add the sugar a little at a time, beating after each addition. Reduce the mixer speed to low, add the vanilla, then the buttermilk, and beat again at high speed for 10 seconds.

3. Divide the batter between the two pans and tap on the counter to remove air bubbles. Bake until the cake is lightly browned and firm to the touch, about 45 minutes. Remove, cool completely on a rack, then turn out each layer onto plates. Split each one horizontally into two equal layers.

4. Set aside 1 cup of the filling. Use the rest to "build" the four-layer cake. Spread a thin layer of filling underneath the first layer so that the cake doesn't stick to the plate. Then spread a layer of filling on the top of the first layer, and add the second layer. Repeat until four layers have been assembled (this is like stacking bricks with a layer of mortar in-between). Cover the top with only a thin layer of filling, as icing will be added. Lightly cover the unfrosted cake and refrigerate overnight.

5. Just before serving, mix the reserved filling with the Seven-Minute Icing and ice the whole cake. Sprinkle the top with the reserved coconut.

MAKES 1 CAKE, SERVES ABOUT 12

Seven-Minute Icing

2 large egg whites

1½ cups sugar

⅛ teaspoon table salt

¼ cup water

1 tablespoon light corn syrup

1 teaspoon pure vanilla extract

With a handheld mixer, beat together the egg whites, sugar, salt, water, and corn syrup in the top of a double boiler. Place over boiling water and beat until soft peaks form. Remove from the heat and add the vanilla. Continue beating until stiff peaks form and the sides of the double boiler top are cool. (Note: this may take longer than 7 minutes!)

YIELD: 3 CUPS

KRISTIN HORTENBACH'S FAMOUS BLOOD ORANGE YOGURT CAKE

MINNEAPOLIS, MINNESOTA

Kristin Hortenbach was teaching math to middle schoolers when her love affair with cooking and baking began to consume her life—and her substantial capacity for precision. Her blog, PickyCook .com has since garnered serious devotees and her blood orange yogurt cake has all but a cult following. "I had made a grapefruit yogurt cake that came out very well, and like most recipes that work well, I always want to use the same idea with slight variations. I thought that the blood orange would taste amazing—and it's so stinkin' pretty that I can barely resist this variation, though grapefruit and lemon are delicious in this cake as well."

FOR THE CAKE

1½ cups all-purpose flour

2 teaspoons baking powder

½ teaspoon kosher salt

1 cup plain whole-milk yogurt (Greek-style)

1 cup plus 1 tablespoon sugar

3 extra-large eggs

Zest of 3 blood oranges, about 1 tablespoon

½ teaspoon pure vanilla extract

½ cup vegetable oil

⅓ cup freshly squeezed blood orange juice

FOR THE GLAZE

2 tablespoons freshly squeezed blood orange juice (I used a little less—about 1½)

1 cup confectioners' sugar

1. Preheat the oven to 350°F. Grease an 8½ x 4¼ x 2½-inch glass loaf pan, line the bottom with parchment paper. Grease and flour it and set aside.

2. Sift together the flour, baking powder, and salt. In another bowl, whisk together the yogurt, 1 cup sugar, the eggs, blood orange zest, and vanilla. With a rubber spatula fold in the dry ingredients a little at a time, stirring between each addition. Fold in the vegetable oil, making sure it's all incorporated. Pour the batter into the prepared pan. Bake for about 50 minutes, or until a cake tester placed in the center of the loaf comes out clean.

3. Meanwhile, in a small pan over medium heat, cook ⅓ cup blood orange juice and remaining 1 tablespoon sugar until the sugar dissolves and the mixture is clear. Set aside. When the cake is done, allow it to cool in the pan for 10 minutes. Use a knife to loosen the edges and turn out onto a rack. While the cake is still warm, pour the mixture over the cake and allow it to soak in. Let cool.

4. To make the glaze, combine the blood orange juice with the confectioner's sugar and use a spoon to drip this glaze over the cake.

SERVES 8

Sylvie Rowland's
Pineapple Upside-Down Cake

Washington, Virginia

Sylvie Rowland grew up on Reunion Island, a small French département below the equator in the Indian Ocean—France's Hawaii. She ate lots of pineapple desserts, usually tarts. She didn't discover American-style pineapple upside-down cake—at least not one she could love—until she went to college in Philadelphia and stumbled upon a gorgeous picture in a 1996 issue of *Saveur* magazine. Using the recipe as a starting point, she began creating the gold-standard upside-down cake that she serves to the local volunteer fire department and rescue squad (her husband, Keith, is a member). For large groups, she makes the cake in a rectangular pan and uses canned pineapple. She notes that a variation using fresh pineapple caramelized in a cast-iron skillet "is utterly delicious, can be made in advance, and makes a great show piece for dinner parties."

Canola oil, for the pan

¾ pound (3 sticks) unsalted butter, at room temperature

3 cups packed light brown sugar

6 tablespoons pineapple juice

½ fresh pineapple, peeled, cut in half lengthwise, and cored; each half cut into 6 wedges

1 cup whole milk

2 teaspoons pure vanilla extract

1 cup plus 6 tablespoons all-purpose flour

1 teaspoon baking powder

¼ teaspoon kosher salt

1 cup granulated sugar

2 large eggs

1. Preheat the oven to 350°F. While the oven is heating, use a pastry brush to coat a 10-inch cast-iron skillet with the canola oil, making sure to coat the corners and sides well. Roughly chop 2¼ sticks of the butter and scatter across the bottom of the pan, and place over medium heat to melt. Sprinkle the brown sugar evenly into the pan and allow to melt. Add the pineapple juice, stir, cook for 1 minute to combine, and remove from heat. Carefully arrange the pineapple slices over the caramelized sugar and set aside.

2. In a small bowl, combine the milk and vanilla. Sift the flour, baking powder, and salt together into another bowl. In a large bowl, beat the remaining 6 tablespoons of butter and the granulated sugar until light and pale lemon–colored. Beat in the eggs one by one. Add the flour (1 cup at a time), alternating with the milk, beating well after each addition. Pour the batter over the pineapple rings, smoothing it out as necessary.

3. Bake for 35 to 40 minutes until the cake is brown and a toothpick or skewer comes out clean. Remove from oven and let cool for 4 minutes. Run a knife around the edge of the cake and, working quickly and wearing oven mitts, invert the cake onto a plate. Keep the plate and skillet firmly pressed together, tap on the counter and then carefully lift the skillet off the cake. If necessary, scrape up any stuck bits of caramel from the skillet and press them back onto the cake.

SERVES 8

RUTH'S CAKE

MT. VERNON, INDIANA

This was Florence Krietenstein's friend Ruth's favorite cake and Mrs. Krietenstein has baked it once a week for more than eighty years. The recipe, she says, is reminiscent of an old-fashioned Lady Cake but uses lemon and vanilla rather than almond extract and is the sort of light, filled cake from the 1930s that she and her friends enjoyed with coffee when their children were young. Having recently turned 102, she says that none of her old friends is around to share the cake, but she continues her weekly ritual. "It just leaves more for me and my new friends."

FOR THE CAKE

11 large eggs, separated

1 teaspoon cream of tartar

1½ cups granulated sugar, sifted 6 times

1 cup all-purpose flour, sifted 6 times

Pinch of salt

1 teaspoon lemon extract

1 teaspoon pure vanilla extract

FOR THE FILLING

5 egg yolks, beaten well (left from the cake)

1 scant cup sugar

Pinch of salt

1 tablespoon all-purpose flour

2 teaspoons gelatin, softened in ¼ cup cold water

1½ cups milk

1 teaspoon pure vanilla extract

2 cups heavy cream

1. Preheat the oven to 350°F. Grease and flour a 10-inch tube pan.

2. To make the cake: Beat the egg whites in a large mixing bowl until frothy. Add ½ teaspoon of the cream of tartar. Add the sugar very gradually, beating the whites until stiff peaks form. Add the flour, salt, remaining cream of tartar, lemon extract, and vanilla. Mix well. In a separate bowl, beat 6 of the egg yolks (set aside the remaining 5 for the filling). Fold the egg yolks into the batter.

4. Pour into the prepared pan and bake for 1½ hours until golden and firm to the touch. Invert the pan onto a bottle and cool the cake to room temperature.

5. To make the filling: Mix the egg yolks, sugar, salt, flour, and softened gelatin in the top of a double boiler. Whisk in milk and blend thoroughly. Cook in a double boiler until thickened. Stir in vanilla and chill.

6. Whip the heavy cream and fold it into the filling.

7. When the cake is cool, split in half horizontally. Spread the bottom half with some of the filling. Replace the top. Cover top and sides of cake with the rest of the filling. Cover and refrigerate overnight.

SERVES 8 TO 12

GUADALUPE LOZANO'S PASTEL IMPOSSIBLE
Impossible Cake

In the fifteen years since she immigrated to the United States from rural north-central Mexico, Guadalupe Lozano has become a global-minded foodie. A cardiac nurse, she's crazy about Thai takeout and loves sushi for date night with her husband. But when her 4-year-old daughter, Victoria, began to take an interest in baking, Ms. Lozano started her on that great American sweet, the chocolate chip cookie, and then they graduated to English scones.

As mother and daughter sought greater challenges, Ms. Lozano looked to her roots. She returned from a visit to her hometown, Calvillo, Aguascalientes, with a recipe scrawled in her sister's handwriting for pastel impossible ("impossible cake"), so called because it is seemingly undoable (it combines chocolate cake and flan). But mother and daughter persevered and their cake came out perfect.

1 box chocolate cake mix

½ cup cajeta, softened

One 14-ounce can sweetened condensed milk

2 cups whole cow milk or goat milk

4 large eggs

1 teaspoon pure vanilla extract

1. Preheat the oven to temperature indicated on cake mix box. Grease a 9 x 13-inch baking pan and flour it with a bit of the cake mix. (Plain white flour will ruin the final appearance of the cake.)

2. Pour half of the cajeta in a thin layer evenly into the pan.

3. Prepare the cake batter according to the package directions. Pour the batter over the cajeta layer.

4. To prepare the flan, combine the condensed milk, milk, eggs, and vanilla. With an electric mixer on high, beat for 2 to 3 minutes to incorporate air.

5. Pour the flan mixture over the cake batter. Bake according to the cake mix directions but note that the baking time will be longer. The cake is done when a toothpick comes out clean. The flan will have sunk to the bottom of the cake.

6. Cool the cake in the pan for 1 hour. To remove the cake from the pan, place a platter over the pan and flip over. The flan will be on top. Place a second platter over the flan and flip again. Spread the remaining cajeta evenly over the top.

SERVES 12

Lorraine Landis's Funny Cake

Funny cake is a cross between a cake and a pie, like shoofly pie, said Julie Musselman, whose Mennonite ancestors, the Landises, arrived in Pennsylvania from Switzerland in 1703. Mrs. Musselman grew up speaking Pennsylvania Dutch in Sellersville, "right smack in the middle of the Meno Belt. I was the oldest of five, we had a sixty-acre farm, and everybody including grandparents, aunts, and uncles lived under one roof in this massive farmhouse. We took garden goods to the city to sell. When the corn came in, we'd clean about a thousand ears, husk it, blanch it, freeze it. We ate funny cake for breakfast. It is a cake filling surrounded by a pie crust. When I was thirteen I started creating my own clothes out of chicken feed bags. I cut my pigtails off and flushed them down the toilet so I could be like the girls in *Grease*. I consider myself an offbeat Mennonite, an ethnocentric Mennonite. I had to marry a Mennonite to feel fully understood. I wanted to look good and do things in the world, but I wanted to start the day with someone who appreciates a slice of good funny cake after a breakfast of cereal, scrapple, or poached eggs. This is my mother's recipe; it goes back a few generations."

FOR THE PASTRY CRUST

2 cups bleached all-purpose flour (do not use unbleached)

2 teaspoons sugar

1 teaspoon kosher salt

¾ cup vegetable shortening

¼ cup cold water

1 small egg, beaten

1½ teaspoons distilled white vinegar

FOR THE CAKE

¼ cup vegetable shortening

Generous ¾ cup sugar

1 large egg

1 teaspoon baking powder

1 cup bleached all-purpose flour

½ cup milk

½ teaspoon pure vanilla extract

FOR THE SYRUP

½ cup sugar

¼ cup unsweetened cocoa powder

½ cup hot water

¼ teaspoon pure vanilla extract

1. Preheat the oven to 375°F.

2. To make the pastry crust: In a large bowl, combine with flour, sugar, salt and shortening with a fork. Mix until the particles are the size of small peas.

3. In separate bowl, whisk together the cold water, egg, and vinegar. Stir into the flour mixture, using a fork. Gather the dough together and shape into a disk. Divide into two pieces. Roll out one piece and line 9-inch pie pan. Use the other for another pie or wrap well and freeze for later use.

4. To make the cake: Cream the shortening and sugar. Beat in the egg. Sift together the baking powder and flour. Add the milk, alternating with the flour. Stir in the vanilla.

5. To make the syrup: Combine sugar and cocoa. Add the hot water and vanilla and stir until blended.

6. Pour the syrup into the pastry crust and then pour the cake batter over it.

7. Bake for about 40 minutes, until a cake tester comes out clean. Cool on a rack.

MAKES 1 CAKE, SERVES 8

NOTE: The crust is enough for two 9-inch pie crusts, although Funny Cake requires only one.

Charlotte Jorgensen's Angel Food Cake

Charlotte Jorgensen wasn't that fond of angel food cake at first. She thought the egg white–based cake was often dry and tasteless. But this version, which she prefers to make with the egg whites of home-reared chickens, is so moist and tasty, she's seen it turn even the staunchest angel food cake agnostics into true believers. Her rendition is known throughout town, perfect for fund-raisers, church banquets, and holiday fund-raising events. When her neighbors pitched in to help out on her farm while her husband was sick, her angel food cake made a perfectly sweet gift of gratitude.

1 cup cake flour

1½ cups plus 2 tablespoons sugar

12 large egg whites

1½ teaspoons cream of tartar

¼ teaspoon table salt

1½ teaspoons pure vanilla extract

½ teaspoon pure almond extract

Fresh strawberries and whipped cream or whipped cream topping, for serving

1. Preheat the oven to 375°F.

2. Sift together the cake flour and ¾ cup plus 2 tablespoons sugar.

3. Beat the egg whites, cream of tartar, and salt until soft peaks form. Slowly add the remaining ¾ cup sugar, then beat on high until stiff peaks form. Beat in the vanilla and almond extracts.

4. Fold in the flour in two additions.

5. Spoon the batter into an ungreased 10-inch tube pan with a removable bottom. Move a knife through the batter to remove air pockets. Bake 30 to 35 minutes, until top springs back when touched lightly with a finger.

6. Invert the pan onto a funnel or bottle and leave to cool completely.

7. To remove the cake from the pan, run a knife around the rim of the pan. Firmly tap the sides of the pan. Invert onto a serving plate, then gently cut the cake away from the bottom. Give the pan a gentle tap to release the cake onto the plate.

8. Serve with fresh strawberries and whipped cream or whipped cream topping.

MAKES 1 CAKE, SERVES 12

Josie Rea-Tomlinson's Superior Cupcakes

LOS ANGELES, CALIFORNIA

Josie Rea-Tomlinson began baking when she was 7. The 13-year-old has already constructed a wedding cake for 150 and spends as much time reading baking books as she does studying to stay at the top of her class. In an era when the young can be whiplashed by choices, her destiny has always been set. "I'll go to college and everything, but I'm a baker," she says. She says of this recipe, "I wanted a perfect cupcake and tried different recipes almost every day one summer. This recipe borrows the best of at least a dozen versions. Equal parts icing to cake is the style in cupcakes today, but I wanted something closer to a glaze. I am not a big fan of numbing by sugar. Those who prefer icing that will mound can add more powdered sugar and soft butter to the recipe. My friends always think they want more icing, but after they have one of these they change their minds."

2 cups all-purpose flour

1 teaspoon baking soda

½ pound (2 sticks) unsalted butter, softened

1 cup granulated sugar

1 cup firmly packed light brown sugar

4 large eggs, at room temperature

6 ounces bittersweet or semisweet chocolate, melted and cooled until warm, not hot

1 cup buttermilk

1 teaspoon pure vanilla extract

Vanilla Icing (recipe follows)

1. Preheat the oven to 350°F. Line two 12-cup cupcake tins with cupcake papers.

2. Sift the flour and baking soda together into a small bowl.

3. In a large bowl, cream the butter until smooth with an electric mixer on medium speed. Add the granulated and brown sugars and beat until fluffy, about 3 minutes. Add the eggs, one at a time, beating well after each addition. Add the chocolate, mixing until well incorporated. Add the flour mixture in three parts, alternating with the buttermilk and vanilla. With each addition, beat until the ingredients are incorporated, but do not overbeat. Using a rubber spatula, scrape down the batter in the bowl to make sure the ingredients are well blended and the batter is smooth.

4. Carefully spoon the batter into the cupcake tins, filling the cups about three-quarters full. Bake for 20 to 25 minutes, until a cake tester inserted in the center of a cupcake comes out clean.

5. Cool the cupcakes in the tins for 15 minutes. Remove from the tins and cool completely on a wire rack before icing.

MAKES 24 CUPCAKES

Vanilla Icing

½ pound (2 sticks) unsalted butter, softened

6 to 8 cups confectioners' sugar

½ cup milk (preferably nonfat, but any kind will do)

2 teaspoons pure vanilla extract

Food coloring (optional)

Place the butter in a large mixing bowl. Add 4 cups of the sugar a little bit at a time mixing well between each addition, then add the milk and vanilla. With an electric mixer on medium speed, beat until smooth and creamy, 3 to 5 minutes. Gradually beat in two additional cups of sugar. If you prefer a thicker icing, continue to add sugar, beating well between each addition. Use the icing immediately or store at room temperature. (It will set if chilled.) It can be stored in an airtight container for up to 3 days.

MAKES ENOUGH FOR ONE 2-LAYER 9-INCH CAKE OR 2 DOZEN CUPCAKES

Icing cupcakes, Tisbury, Massachusetts.

Scappoose Senior Center's Chocolate-Sauerkraut Cupcakes

SCAPPOOSE, OREGON

Steinfeld's Sauerkraut, the company that brought fame to the town of Scappoose, Oregon, back in the early 1950s, closed more than ten years ago, the 'kraut is now made in Illinois, but the Sauerkraut Festival, inspired by Steinfeld's product, is still going strong. Sauerkraut lovers come from miles around to get any kind of food imaginable in sauerkraut flavor, from vanilla sauerkraut ice cream to sausage-sauerkraut sandwiches. Among the most unconventional offerings are the chocolate-sauerkraut cupcakes, courtesy of the residents of three area senior centers—Scappoose, Saint Helens Senior Center, and Rainier Senior Center. Discovered in an old Steinfeld's cookbook, the recipe for these sweet-and-tart treats consists of chocolate cake batter spiked with sauerkraut and topped with chocolate frosting. "They taste like chocolate. The sauerkraut doesn't really affect the flavor, other than to give it a slight tang," assures Beth Pulito, a festival organizer, "but it does give a texture similar to coconut." The senior bakers accommodate all customers: The cupcakes come in regular, sugar-free, and gluten-free, so there's no excuse not to give them a try.

10 tablespoons plus 2 teaspoons (1⅓ sticks) unsalted margarine or butter

1½ cups sugar

3 large eggs

1 teaspoon pure vanilla extract

½ cup unsweetened cocoa powder

2¼ cups sifted all-purpose flour

1 teaspoon baking powder

1 teaspoon baking soda

¼ teaspoon table salt

1 cup water

1 cup sauerkraut (preferably Steinfeld's), rinsed and drained

Your favorite chocolate frosting

1. Preheat the oven to 350°F. Lightly grease the cups of two standard 12-cup cupcake tins, or line them with paper liners.

2. Cream the margarine with the sugar. Beat in the eggs and vanilla.

3. Sift together the cocoa powder, flour, baking powder, baking soda, and salt. Add cocoa mixture to creamed mixture, alternating with the water. Stir in the sauerkraut.

4. Divide the batter evenly among the cupcake tins. Bake 15 to 20 minutes. Test for doneness by inserting a toothpick in the center of the cakes. The toothpick should come out clean (a few crumbs are okay).

5. Cool for a few minutes in the tin, then remove the cupcakes to a rack and cool completely. Frost with your favorite chocolate frosting.

MAKES 24 CUPCAKES

ACKNOWLEDGMENTS

From the day it began, *One Big Table* has been a group effort. I am indebted to more people and more goodwill than I may ever know, but without the following people this book would never be in your hands.

Long before social networking had become a way of life, Arthur Samuelson understood that cooking and eating together have a powerful ability to turn strangers into friends, to create communities, and to celebrate what makes us human. His vision of building both real and virtual tables across the country guided me for over a decade. I am indebted to his prescience and his brilliance.

To widen the net that I cast across the nation, Arthur also helped forge a partnership with the nation's food-bank network, now called Feeding America, and helped create potluck dinners across the country. The potlucks raised money to fight hunger and introduced me to thousands of home cooks I might not otherwise have met. Robert H. Forney, Alice Archabal, Carol Gifford, and Phil Zepeda provided invaluable support in the charity's national office, and a portion of profits generated by the sale of this book will be donated to Feeding America.

Hundreds of people opened their homes and hearts to these potlucks, and I am especially grateful to Nancy Hechinger, Michael and Jane Hoffman, David Leite, Daisy Martinez, Geoff Drummond, Stephen Peters, Tommy and Karolyn Burkett, Barbara and Robert Blum, Marcy and Bill Ferris, Judge George Chew, Marilyn Yee, and Beth Wareham.

The national cooking contest that grew from these potlucks could not have occurred without the generous support of two great American businesses, Sur La Table and the Viking Range Corporation. I am grateful to both Doralece Dullaghan and Jane Crump for that support as well as for their personal effort, counsel, and goodwill. A number of gourmet clubs and food societies also helped in this effort, and I am grateful to Laverne Yost for her help in organizing Les Dames d'Escoffier in Washington, D.C., as well as several Slow Food chapters that contributed recipes.

I am indebted to the wise and steady support of family, friends and colleagues, especially Ed Breslin, Sam Busselle, Nancy Hechinger, Paul, Nevalee and Virginia O'Neill, Carol Puckett, Eric Rayman, Marie Salerno, and Alice Truax, whose boundless patience, insight, and generosity helped me do the next right thing, over and over again—at least when I took their advice. My agent, Andrew Wylie, remained steadfast even as the project morphed and grew and I required multiple extensions. At the Wylie Agency, Jeffrey Posternak worked far too hard filling every imaginable empty space, and I am more grateful than I can say to him for his help as a reader, a strategist, a cheerleader, an accountant, and a shrink.

Dozens of researchers across the country opened their hearts, minds, and Rolodexes to this project. As I began to grapple with the complexity of America, my friend and colleague Nancy Harmon Jenkins gave me hundreds of the files that she accumulated in over a decade of research into ethnic cooking in America. Sandy Oliver, Andy Smith, and Laura Shapiro could not have been more generous with their knowledge of food history, sharing their own research as well as commenting on the manuscript. I must have done something really good in a past life to be the beneficiary of such brilliant, generous, and stalwart friends.

Or perhaps I just got lucky. I also had the honor of working with some remarkable up-and-coming writers, food historians, reporters, and cooks. In Kentucky, the chef and former librarian Sara Gibbs was indefatigable in finding fabulous cooks. She gathered recipes from Maryland to Indiana, and her determination and ear for the weird helped keep me on my own game. In Michigan, Kim Bayer scoured the community cookbook collection at the William L. Clements Library and enriched both the regional and the ethnic contexts of this book. I am grateful both for this and for her family's United Nations of fine salsas.

In Louisiana, Michaela York, the director of communications for Chef John Folse, helped me go deep into the bayous. I was inspired by the way she combined her own encyclopedic knowledge with grace and charm to pull the best from even the most reticent subjects. In Mississippi, LeAnne Gault was an inexhaustible font of good information and good humor as I pursued catfish and tried to outrun hurricanes. In Texas, Mary Margaret Pack taught me that impeccable historic research can have life, poetry, and humor—particularly when it comes to barbecue, tamales, gumbo, God, and food trucks.

California has become synonymous with the market-to-table approach pioneered by Alice Waters at Chez Panisse—so much so that it was difficult to scratch beneath the surface. Four dogged researchers—Valerie D'Ippolito Rodgers, Faith Kramer, Dianne Jacob, and Leticia Landa of La Cocina street vendor project—helped me find some of the home cooks whose daily efforts combine a sensitivity to seasoning and ingredients with family tradition and cultural history to create durable and of course delicious songs of place.

In New York, I am indebted to the pastry chef and researcher Judy Chen and her sister, the writer and editor Joanne Chen. Combining their vast knowledge of all things sweet, the Chens were indispensible in winnowing several thousand dessert recipes into the hundred or so that comprise that chapter of this book. Hail, Sugar.

And hats off to the people who raise the heritage breeds of plants and animals whose DNA holds the history of American meals. Sarah Obraitis of Heritage Foods USA, a fine writer with an uncanny eye for detail, scoured her files for growers who also cooked and enriched this book with their stories from the land. In West Miller's Cove, Tennessee John Coykendall, an artist and seed saver and the master gardener at Blackberry Farm, taught me what how hard times and good times can all be tasted in a bean.

Rachel Kelsey in Cambridge, Massachusetts, brought a working chef's perseverance and grit, a detective's eye, and a poet's sensitivity to the idiosyncratic tastes and methods of other people's cooking as she edited the recipes in this book. Underpaid and pregnant with her first child, she showed me a new level of the art of recipe testing and editing, and my gratitude is as large as the talent and determination she brought to this task.

I am also grateful to the deeply annoying and nitpicking copy editor, Suzanne Fass. Knowing that she was merrily ripping apart each line of this book allowed me to sleep at night. My blissful rest was further abetted by the cantankerous Roy Finamore, cook, editor, and all-around food savant, whose close reading of the edited manuscript ferreted out even more imperfections. Nora Sherman and Kate Sonders spent months chasing leads and organizing information, and Dana Silverstein, keeper of all lists, files, budgets, whereabouts, and formats, found my memory when I lost it—thank you all for your patience, efficiency, good humor, and goodwill.

Sydny Miner and David Rosenthal originally brought this project to Simon & Schuster and I remain grateful for their vision and support. Against all odds and a loudly ticking clock, Ruth Fecych and Michelle Rorke shepherded the outsize, complicated manuscript into type. No one should have to inherit such a project, and few would do so with such determination to do it well—thank you.

Even as she juggled hundreds of moving parts with unflagging courtesy and optimism, Nancy Singer, Simon & Schuster's director of interior design, allowed the photo editor, Rebecca Busselle, and me to work with the wonderful designers, Joel Avirom and Jason Snyder, to find the book's visual voice over frustrating months of iterations. Jackie Seow was equally stalwart in managing my visual obsessions while creating a cover that expressed the spirit of this book. Through it all, as editors changed and the landscape of publishing shifted, Nancy Inglis, the wise and unflappable director of copyediting at Simon & Schuster, maintained both the admirable can-do-ism and the drawer full of sugary snacks that helped in creating a book even more substantial, generous, and quirky than I'd hoped.

I'm also indebted to Ramin Ganeshram, cook, reporter, writer, and eternal spring of pithy worst-case scenarios, whose insight, resourcefulness, generosity, and love for this project helped move this book through its gawky adolescent stage, enriching both its pages and my life. Working with Ramin was like working with a younger (and much improved) version of myself, and I am as grateful for the mirror she held up as I am for the wonderful gifts she gave to this book.

About halfway through this project I was introduced to Rebecca Busselle, a writer, photographer, cook, and editor who is the great-grandniece of Irma Rombauer, the author of *The Joy of Cooking*. After listening to what I was doing, Rebecca put aside the book she was writing and began traveling with me, taking photographs, researching, editing, driving, reading maps, sharing rooms, and carrying this book—and me—to the finish line. For Rebecca, *One Big Table* was a new chapter in a family story; for me, Rebecca was a saving grace. I love her more than bacon.

Speaking of bacon, I will never be sure whether the cooking in the American South is more real, more vivid, more regional than in other parts of the country, or if my friends at Southern Foodways just make it seem that way. In either case, I am grateful to the entire organization and especially to John T. Edge and Amy Evans for their deep roots, boundless enthusiasm and unwavering commitment to pig. Up with Lard.

Vincent Virga, the legendary photo editor, shared his decades of experience at the Library of Congress and was unwavering in his support for this project. We would have been sunk without the finely honed technical abilities of the photographer Damaso Reyes, who presided over our image archives. Paula Kupfer, a photographer with a quirky eye and a steady hand, was dogged in tracking down vintage and contemporary images and irrepressible in finding—and taking—pictures for this book. Thank you.

I am also indebted to Peter Workman and Suzanne Rafer of Workman Publishing, whose patience and guidance as I wrote the *New York Cookbook* taught me how to translate joy and excitement into recipes and stories. I am also grateful to the ever-raunchy Ms. Beth Wareham, whose lessons in all forms of Twittering have been most invaluable, and to my friend Mary Bissbee-Beek, whose marketing acumen is matched only by her belief in the American people, American cooking, and this project. Thank you.

I am also grateful to those whose love of place changed the way that I saw the world. Experiencing New Mexico through the eyes of Phyllis Montgomery, Pat West Barker, and Ronni Lundy was the start of what I hope will be a long-term affair with chiles, corn, and the mystical beauty of the high desert. Getting to know the salmon fisheries from the Pacific Northwest to the most remote corner of the Alaskan Yukon with Jon Rowley was a rare and glorious introduction to the spirit and pathos of that corner of earth. These adventures were perhaps all the more epic because I shared them with my stepdaughter, Ariana Samuelson, who is game for just about anything and lives for the subtle connections and unexpected synchronicities that give meaning and magic to daily life.

Exploring the Eastern Shore of Virginia under the tutelage of Bernie Herman, who has documented the region's foodways and folkways for nearly thirty years, changed the way I thought about soft-shell crabs, sweet potatoes, and unschooled art. Through his introduction, I was able to ravel the back roads of the South from Atlanta to Gee's Bend, Alabama, with the legendary art collector Bill Arnett and his son Matt Arnett. Those trips and the artists we met—particularly Thornton Dial, Lonnie Holley, and Mary Lee Bendoph—remind me every day of why I do what I do.

For all its imperfection, the United States remains a place where an individual can be what he or she was born to be—fully human, full of imperfection, and one of a kind. Making art, music, poems, gardens—or dinner—is an ode to this opportunity. Not many have the courage to seize that opportunity. I am in awe of those of do, and finally, my greatest thanks goes to those who risked being exactly who they are as they stood facing their stoves.

Thank you all for making me better than I am.

INDEX

RECIPE INDEX

Recipe Index

CREDITS AND ACKNOWLEDGMENTS

Text

The author is grateful to a number of publications and organizations for permission to reprint several essays and recipes whose creators also contributed to this volume.

Portions of the essays "Chowder Tales" and "American Pie," as well as recipes for lobster chowder, pine-cured salmon, Fenway Chowder, Spring Beach Soup, Pollo Criollo, Old-Fashioned Meatloaf, Arturo Zampaglione's Polenta, Chester Aaron's Very Garlic Pasta, Pie Committee Pie Crust, Ruth Eichner's Frozen Raspberry Pie, Edna Lewis's Rhubarb Pie, and Ed Behr's Baked Maple Custard originally appeared in *The New York Times* and appear here with permission.

A portion of the essay "The Patron Saint of Poultry" originally appeared in *Saveur* magazine and appears here with permission.

The recipe for Nancy Silverton's Salted Caramel and Peanut Sundae originally appeared in the *Los Angeles Times* and appears here with permission.

The recipe for James Beard's Chicken with 40 Cloves of Garlic originally appeared in *Delights & Prejudices: A Memoir with Recipes* (Atheneum, 1964) and appears here with permission from the James Beard Society, New York City.

The recipe for Flo Braker's Simply Perfect Yellow Cake originally appeared in *The Simple Art of Perfect Baking* (Houghton Mifflin, 1992) and appears here with permission.

The recipe for John Fleer's Blackberry Farm Tea-brined, Batter-Fried Picnic Chicken originally appeared in *Fried Chicken: An American Story* (Putnam) by John T. Edge and appears here with permission.

The recipes for Elisabetta Lecce Baiamonte's Devilish Eggs and Dorothy Steen's Award-Winning Pimento Cheese Dip were originally published by Southern Foodways Alliance and appear here with permission

The recipe for Thomas Jefferson's Vanilla Ice Cream is in the collection of Library of Congress. The museum at Monticello has logged mentions of the recipe and created a modern interpretation of the recipe.

Portions of the essay accompanying "Kate's Compost Social Soup" and "Catching Fire" originally appeared in *The New Yorker* and appear here with the permission of the magazine.

For an up-to-date listing of websites, bloggers, and other organizations whose recipes appear in this book, please see www.OneBigTable.com.

Photographs

Courtesy of Albany Institute of History & Art Library Photo Collection: 302, 304: bottom left

©Gary Allen: 772

Courtesy of the Arnett Collection: 133; 219; 514: bottom

Courtesy Gabrielle Arnold: 648

Courtesy Attic Gallery, Vicksburg, MS: 462: top left; 627

©Charles Baum: 652

Courtesy Martha Bayer: 85: top right, bottom left, bottom right

©Nicolas Beckman: 681

Courtesy Bloodroot Restaurant, photo by Todd Bryant: 170

©Jon Bonjour/Jon Bonjour Photography: 803

Courtesy the Brack Family: 724

Courtesy Browne Family: 14

Courtesy Grace Brucato: 553

Courtesy Josef Bruchac, ©Michael Greenlar: 106

Courtesy of Angela Warnick Buchdahl: 427

©Tessa Burpee: 145

©Chris Burrill: 193

©Rebecca Busselle: iv: top left, top center, top right, center, bottom left; xi: top left circle, center right circle; 5: bottom left; 7; 10; 11; 12; 16; 21; 23; 25: top, bottom; 29, ; 30; 35; 39: bottom left; 50; 56; 65: bottom right; 67; 69; 76; 78: left, right; 79; 82; 84; 89; 91; 95; 110; 112; 113: top, bottom; 116; 126; 128; 138; 139; 141: top; 147; 154: top right, bottom; 155: center left, bottom right; 156; 157: top; 160: bottom; 161; 162; 165; 166; 170: bottom; 175; 178; 186; 188; 197; 198; 204; 205; 210; 212; 213; 214; 216; 220; 222; 225; 226; 227: top left, top right, bottom right; 229: top right, bottom left; 240; 244; 245; 247; 261; 264; 272; 281; 292; 296; 301; 307: bottom right; 309; 310; 311; 314: center right, bottom left; 317; 319; 322; 327: bottom left, bottom center; 335; 343; 345; 350; 371; 372; 377; 383; 390; 393; 394; 399: bottom; 401; 402; 403; 404: top left; 409; 417; 419; 420: center right, bottom; 421: top left, center; 422; 424; 425; 436; 449; 457: top right; 462: center right; 465; 468; 481; 490; 491; 503; 504; 505: bottom left, bottom right; 506; 513; 518; 519; 529; 536; 537; 538; 541; 546; 547; 552; 561; 570; 573: top right, center left, bottom right; 580; 586; 587; 595; 598; 599; 600; 603: bottom left; 607; 613: top left; 615; 616; 619; 626; 633; 634; 636; 639; 643; 649; 651; 655; 667; 673; 675: center left, center right, bottom right; 682: top left; 682 top right, bottom center; 686; 687; 699; 701; 702; 708; 709; 712; 715; 723; 728; 729; 732; 734; 738; 749; 753: top left, bottom right; 757; 762; 763; 764; 766; 771; 774; 775; 781; 782; 783; 786; 791; 805; 807: top left, top right; 808; 811; 825; 827; 828

Courtesy Frances Butler: 392

Courtesy Isabel Caudillo: 131

Courtesy George Chew: 507

Courtesy Mariel Chua: 756

Courtesy Laurie Constantino: 318

Courtesy Henrietta Cosentino: 527

©Henrietta Cosentino: 159, 160: top

©Tiziana Costamagna: 167

Courtesy David Densmore: 279

Courtesy Katherine Dieckmann: 196

Courtesy Lawrence Diggs: 173

Courtesy Ila Douglas: 62

Courtesy Doug DuCap: 40

©Joe Dunlap: 430: top left, bottom right

Courtesy Clay Dunn and Zach Patton: 342

©Chris Epting: 366

©Amy Evans: iv: center left, bottom center, bottom right inset; xi: center right, bottom right, center left circle, bottom right circle; 13; 28; 75: center left; 104; 201;241; 258: top right; 269; 276: bottom left; 407; 412; 493; 496; 497; 499; 539; 551; 637; 658; 747; 815

Courtesy The Fort restaurant, Morrison, CO: 466

©Owen Franken: 248

Courtesy Fresh Water Fishing Hall of Fame, Hayward, WI: 268

Courtesy Fresina Family: 664

Courtesy Javier H. Freyre: 32

Courtesy Bianca Garcia: 502: top

Courtesy Mika Garnett: 328

©LeAnne Gault: 276

©Alyssa Glimm: 49

©Bernadette Grosjean: 171

©Rowena Halper: 508

Courtesy Rosalie Harpole: 107

©Laura Norton Harris: 750; 752; 779; 783: bottom right; 803; 807: bottom right

Courtesy Bernard L. Herman, 380

©Bernard L. Herman: 18: top right, bottom left; 253; 254; 257; 258: center left; 515; 727; 770

Courtesy Bernard L. Herman: 380

Courtesy Adria Herndon: 333

Courtesy Jeanne Hodesh: 744

Courtesy Dan Huntley: 200

Courtesy Cheryl Jamison: 458

©Aashish Jethra: 365

Courtesy J.H. Fentress Antique Popcorn Museum: 65: top right, center left

©Andrea Johnson: 588: bottom left, bottom right

©Pableaux Johnson: 414; 745

©Deborah Jones: 659

Courtesy Ourania Kallas: 54

Courtesy Deseree Anne Kazda: 576

Courtesy Knight Communications: 334

Courtesy Karl Koster: 1; 2: top left, bottom right; 3.

©Paula Kupfer: 39: top left; 67; 190; 560; 693; 698; 711; 720; 721; 826

Courtesy Holly Lane: 754

Courtesy Mary Lasater: 437

©Jim Landry: 590

Courtesy Library of Congress, Prints and Photographs Division:
vii: LC-DIG-npcc-23695; vii-ix: LC-DIG-ppmsca-09303; x: LC-USF35-268; xi: top right: LC-USZ62-69577; 1: LC-USZ62-58784; 3 bottom left: LC-USZC2-5283, bottom right: LC-USZ62-66423; 5 bottom right: LC-D401-19577; 15: LC-F9-04-5709-012-17; 33: LC-USZC2-5427; 55 top right: LC-DIG-nclc-03339; 64: LC-USZ62-136122; 68: LC-DIG-ppmsca-12757; 74: LC-DIG-ppmsca-12757; 75 bottom: LC-DIG-nclc-04385; 88: LC-USE6-D-010090; 93: LC-USW3-003390-D; 99: LC-DIG-ggbain-00189; 101: LC-DIG-ppmsca-19052; 102: LC-USZ62-99940; 131: LC-USF34-010650-D; 136: LC-USZ62-92861; 142: LC-USZC4-9056; 143 center right: LC-USZC4-1064; 144 top left: LC-USF34-034215-D, bottom right: LC-USZC4-10124; 146: LC-USZ62-46947; 147 bottom: LC-USZ62-71470; 148 bottom left: LC-DIG-ppmsca-09480, bottom right: LC-USZC2-253; 149 top: LC-DIG-nclc-05178, bottom right: LC-USZC4-9732; 150 top: LC-USZ62-63966, bottom: LC-DIG-ggbain-18309; 151 bottom center: LC-USW3-054178-D, bottom right: LC-DIG-ppmsca-4a09005; 152 top: LC-USW3-016933-C, bottom: LC-DIG-hec-04037; 153 top: LC-USF34-070046-D; 157 bottom: LC-DIG-fsa-8e10761; 158: LC-DIG-hec-27690; 168: LC-DIG-matpc-14960; 172 bottom: LC-USZC4-13962; 174: LC-DIG-ppmsca-20732; 176: LC-USZ62-113398; 180-181: PAN US GEOG - Utah no. 7 (F size) [P&P]; 191: LC-DIG-highsm-04944; 194: LC-USF34-028855-D; 199: LC-DIG-hec-11199; 208: LC-DIG-npcc-32487; 217 top: LC-DIG-nclc-00968, bottom: LC-USF34-070310-D; 224: LC-DIG-ppmsca-12779; 230: LC-DIG-ppmsc-01691; 236: LC-USW38-002077-C; 239: LC-USZC4-13225; 242: LC-DIG-ppprs-00545; 246: LC-DIG-ppprs-00545; 249 bottom left: LC-USZ62-88721, bottom center: LC-USZ62-55842, bottom right: LC-USZ62-73863; 250: LC-DIG-ggbain-10143; 251: LC-DIG-ggbain-18896; 252: LC-USZ62-47049; 255: LC-USZ62-90615; 258 bottom: LC-DIG-hec-24528; 260: LC-DIG-nclc-00983; 267: LC-DIG-pga-03695; 268 top left: LC-D4-4744, bottom left: LC-DIG-pga-00596; 275: LC-DIG-fsac-1a34367; 277: PAN SUBJECT - Groups no. 256 (E size) [P&P]; 280: LC-DIG-hec-24177; 285: LC-USW38-002016-C; 289: LC-DIG-ppmsca-12771; 290 top: LC-DIG-highsm-04372, bottom: LC-USZ62-46996; 303 bottom right: LC-DIG-pga-04045; 304 bottom right: LC-USZ62-107527; 305: LC-DIG-ggbain-24341; 306 top left: LC-DIG-ppmsca-04798, top right: LC-USZ62-42001; 308: LC-DIG-hec-23725; 321: LC-DIG-fsa-8a40071; 325: LC-DIG-ppmsca-12730; 326: LC-DIG-fsa-8a40088; 338: LC-DIG-nclc-04444; 340: LC-HS503-530; 347: LC-DIG-pga-02398; 348: LC-DIG-highsm-04652; 352: LC-USZ62-113114; 362: LC-DIG-hec-14526; 368: LC-DIG-pga-04174; 370: LC-USF34-056072-D; 375: LC-USZ62-33178; 378: LC-DIG-highsm-04905; 385: LC-DIG-hec-28297; 386 top: LC-USZC4-1206; 388: LC-DIG-npcc-18179; 397: LC-USZ62-70874; 398: LC-DIG-cwpbh-03312; 399 bottom left: LC-DIG-ggbain-33702, bottom right: LC-DIG-fsac-1a34300(picnic); 400: PAN SUBJECT - Events no. 143 (E size) [P&P]; 404 bottom: LC-DIG-npcc-24740; 405: LC-USZC4-8919; 410 top: LC-USF34-033320-D, bottom: LC-DIG-cwpb-01678; 411 top left: LC-USF34-004700-D, center: LC-DIG-fsa-8a26301, bottom: LC-DIG-fsa-8a26301; 413: LC-DIG-stereo-1s02052; 418: LC-DIG-ggbain-01452; 423: LC-USZC2-1316; 428: LC-DIG-ppmsca-05587; 432: LC-DIG-highsm-04591; 433: LC-DIG-fsa-8c52231; 434: LC-DIG-pga-00876; 438-439: PAN US GEOG - Missouri no. 1 (F size) [P&P]; 440: LC-DIG-highsm-05765; 442: LC-DIG-fsa-8b29793; 443: LC-USZC2-5162; 448: LC-DIG-hec-24942; 453: LC-USZ62-51782; 454: LC-USW3-013445-D; 457 top left: LC-DIG-fsa-8c33476, bottom left: LC-DIG-highsm-04940, bottom center: LC-USF33-012002-M2; 459 bottom: LC-DIG-highsm-04821; 462 bottom: LC-USZC4-2740; 475: LC-DIG-nclc-04426; 476: LC-USZ62-63331; 478: LC-USZ62-11417; 482: LC-DIG-pga-03724; 483: LC-DIG-pga-03169; 484: LC-DIG-hec-29232; 486: LC-DIG-highsm-04388; 488: LC-USZ62-57953; 489: LC-DIG-npcc-15219; 494: LC-DIG-fsa-8e11050; 500: LC-USF345-007835-ZA; 502 bottom: LC-USZ62-135948; 509: LC-DIG-nclc-04434; 511: LC-DIG-pga-02857; 512: LC-USZ62-69917; 515 left:

LC-USZ62-50164; 524: LC-DIG-fsac-1a34435; 531: LC-USF33-012092-M1; 533: LC-DIG-npcc-18533; 535: LC-DIG-highsm-04488; 542 top right: LC-USZC4-10321, center left: LC-USZC4-5561, bottom left: LC-USZC4-6465; 545: LC-USW3-003660-E; 555 bottom: LC-DIG-prokc-20084; 556: LC-USZ62-75878; 557 top: LC-DIG-fsac-1a34323, bottom right: LC-DIG-highsm-04562; 558: LC-USF34-028244-D; 565: LC-DIG-highsm-04815; 568: LC-DIG-npcc-01307; 577: LC-DIG-fsac-1a34117; 597: LC-DIG-fsac-1a33844; 603 bottom right: LC-USF34-100265-D; 609: LC-USZ62-77883; 610: LC-USZ62-83970; 612 top right: LC-USZC4-7910, bottom left: LC-USZ62-46950; 613 bottom: LC-DIG-highsm-04563; 617: LC-USF34-026384-D; 621: LC-DIG-fsac-1a34131; 624-625: LC-USZ62-51001, LC-USZ62-51002; 629: LC-USF33-011732-M5; 644: LC-USZ62-127236; 657: LC-DIG-pga-00504; 662: LC-DIG-ppmsca-12648; 665: LC-D4-16347; 666: LC-B2-80-2; 669: LC-USE6-D-006203; 674: LC-USF347-016109-M3-A-Q; 676: American Treasures of the Library of Congress; 677: LC-DIG-hec-22589; 678: LC-DIG-highsm-05281; 726: LC-USZ6-921; 733: LC-DIG-fsa-8b09770; 739: LC-DIG-highsm-04483; 741: LC-D4-19213; 743: LC-DIG-pga-02277; 746: LC-USZ62-58962; 748: LC-USZC4-11169; 758: C-DIG-npcc-09719; 776: LC-USZ62-92565; 784: LC-DIG-ggbain-37876; 788: LC-DIG-hec-24554; 790: LC-USZC2-2265; 793: LC-USZ62-55135; 795: LC-DIG-hec-25128; 800 top: LC-DIG-hec-07052, bottom: LC-DIG-hec-20476; 804: LC-DIG-highsm-05374; 807 bottom left: LC-DIG-hec-24935; 813: LC-USZC4-2469; 823: LC-DIG-hec-26437

©David Liittschwager: 184

Courtesy Mike Longhofer: 469: bottom left, bottom right

Courtesy Doris Lum: 329

©Amanda Marsalis: 661

Courtesy Toni Martin: 202

©Preston Merchant photo: 34

©Elena Moiseeva/FOTOLIA: 584

Courtesy Debbie Morse: 164

©Aleksey Moryakov, Exit Zero Publishing: 334

Courtesy Homa Movafaghi: 98

©Clyde Mueller/The New Mexican: 406

©Catherine Nakajima: 124

Courtesy New Mexico Tourism Department: 459

Courtesy Okuno family: 463

Courtesy Virginia O'Neill: 761

Courtesy Valeria Ponte: 134

Private collection: iv: top left inset; xii; 31; 55: center left; 75: top right; 121; 122; 129; 234; 151: top right, center left; 163; 172: top right; 182; 306: center left; 307: center right; 324; 360; 399: center right; 415; 447; 479; 514: top; 516; 517; 523; 585; 680 top left; 684 top left, bottom center, bottom right; 685 center right, bottom left; 705; 735; 737: bottom left, bottom center; 817: top left, bottom right

Project Gutenberg: 148

Courtesy Clay Quinn and Zach Patton, 342

Courtesy Didi Rea: 656; 826: top right

©Kay Rentschler: 611

Courtesy Laurent Roffe: 487

Courtesy Jonathan Rosenberg

©Jon Rowley: 19; 20: top right, bottom left; 294; 299; 323; 400: bottom right

Courtesy Ron Rozman: 575

Courtesy Cecylia Roznowska: 593

©Ariana Samuelson: 6; 143: bottom

Courtesy Jam Sanitchat: 63

Courtesy Scavenger's, New York: 70; 141: bottom left; 386: bottom left; 391; 684: center right

©Fred Sauceman: 799

©Victor Schrager: 48; 117; 207; 363; 467; 530; 563

©Ed Semmelroth: 304: top left, center right; 306: bottom right; 307: top right

Courtesy Shaheen Family: 59

Courtesy Chau Tran Smith: 223

©Larry Smith, ETSU photo lab: 331

©Larry Smith: 798

Courtesy Maggi Hall Smith: 4

Courtesy of Society for the Preservation of Poultry Antiquities: 310

Courtesy Kurt Spiridakis: 543

Courtesy Thad Starr: 578

Courtesy Aron Streit, Inc.: 108

Courtesy Mitra Stricklen: 548

Courtesy Superdawgs, Chicago: 39

Courtesy Susmita Sharma: 37

© Alida Thorpe: 379

Courtesy El Tonayense, San Francisco, CA: 83

©Jean Paul Vellotti: 43; 235

Courtesy Viking Range Company: 303

Courtesy Alex Vlack: 195

©Karen Walker: 431

Courtesy Sue Wespy: 22

Courtesy Pat West-Barker: 77

©Marilyn Yee: 564